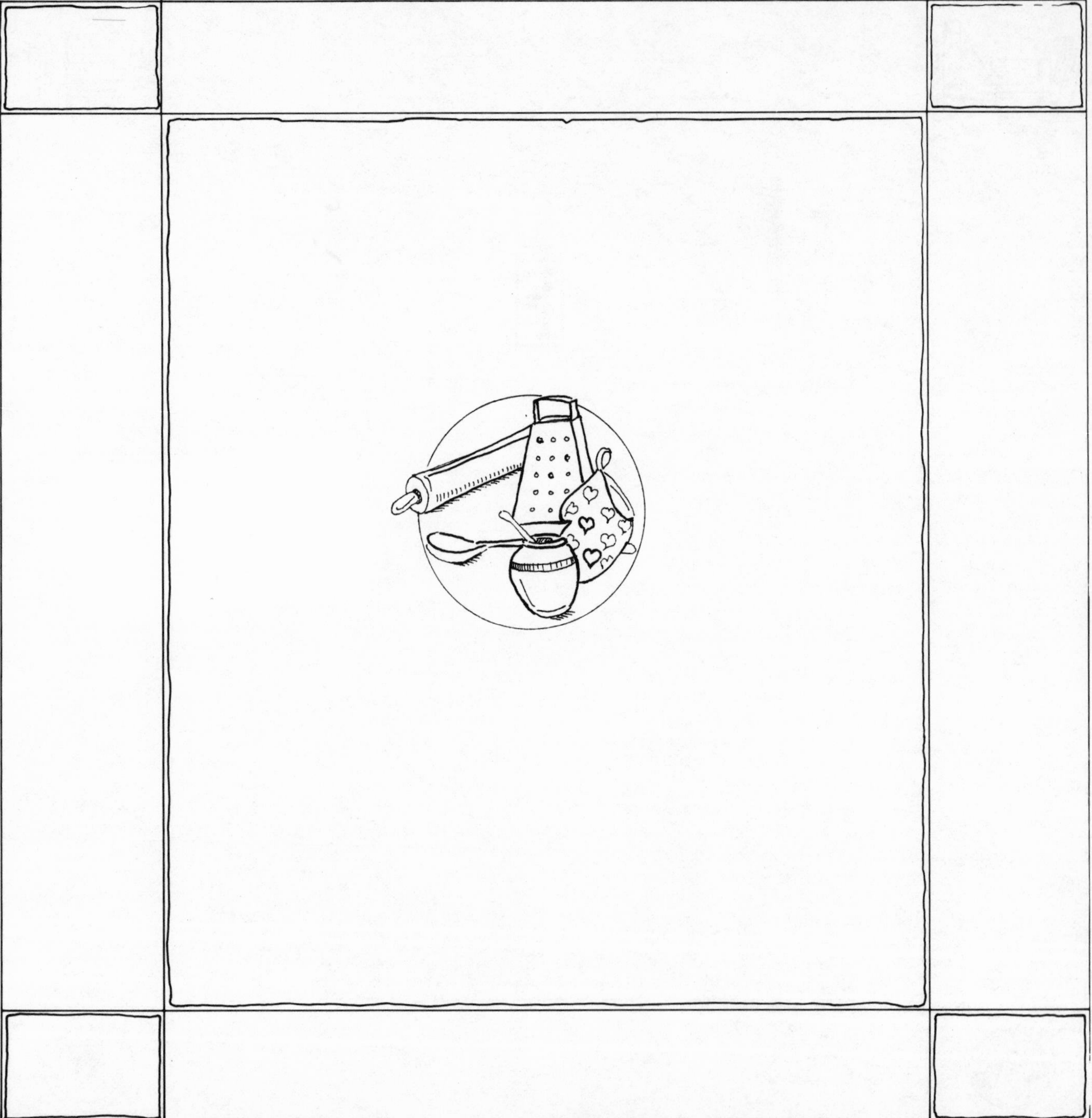

RECIPEX

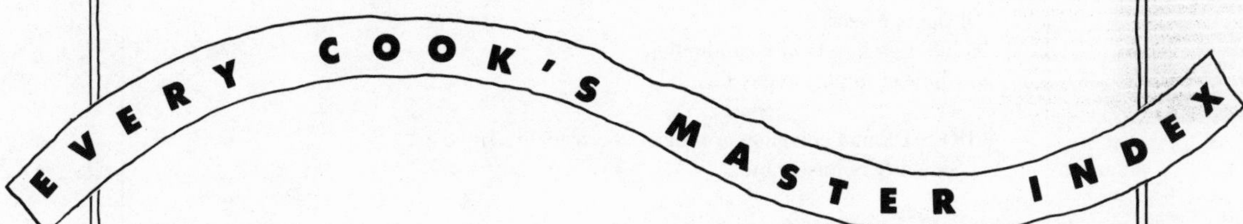

ANNIE GILBAR

A FIRESIDE BOOK PUBLISHED BY SIMON & SCHUSTER INC. NEW YORK, LONDON, TORONTO, SYDNEY, TOKYO

Fireside
Simon & Schuster Building
Rockefeller Center
1230 Avenue of the Americas
New York, New York 10020

Designed by Bonni Leon
Manufactured in the United States of America

10 9 8 7 6 5 4 3 2 1

Library of Congress Cataloging in Publication Data
Gilbar, Annie.
Recipex: every cook's master index/Annie Gilbar.
p. cm.
"A Fireside book."
1. Cookery—Indexes. I. Title. II. Title: Every cook's master index.
Z5776.G2G53 1990
[TX651]
016.6415—dc20 90-17162
CIP

ISBN 0-671-66827-7

TO ARTHUR ZUCKERMAN,

my patient and brilliant computer mentor and friend, who immediately knew how to make it work, who gave me the tools without which this book would not have seen the light of day, who shares my amazement at the miracles these machines create, even though I know he really knows what all those little symbols mean.

TO GARY H. GILBAR,

without question the better half of this duo, whose ideas are behind everything I do.

A C K N O W L E D G M E N T S

THANK YOU, THANK YOU, THANK YOU, TO:

KATHY ROBBINS, for knowing we would be perfect for each other, for loving to read the manuscripts at least as much as making the deals, but especially for always getting it the first time;

CARA FAMILIAN, who, even when Harvard bound, channeled her tireless energy, quick intelligence, and infectious enthusiasm to enter these 35,000-plus recipes effortlessly and happily;

RONNA (alias Ronny) Feldman Gordon, who knew in violin class all those many years ago that we would be bound forever, and that's why she volunteered to spend her extra hours coding thousands of recipes;

SUE KRITZ, whose knowledge about food and cooking and generosity in giving her time led her to actually ask to spend weeks coding recipes;

SYLVIA GILBAR, coder par excellence, who was happy when the project was over lest she be tempted to try yet another recipe;

NACHEM WAXMAN, owner and soul behind Kitchen Arts and Letters, the best cookbook store I have ever been to, for his incomparable advice, his eagerness to share his vast knowledge about cookbooks, and his generous guidance;

 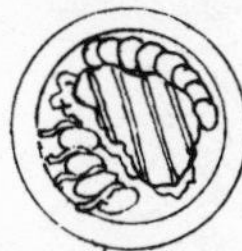 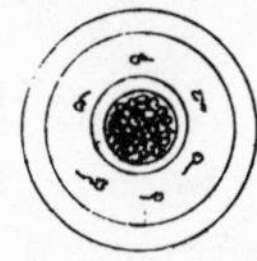 

KERRI CONAN, the ultimate editorial assistant and best friend to us authors, whose inevitable good humor, perfect common sense, enviable intelligence, and never-ending hard work always make my work easier and more fun;

THE PEOPLE AT RAPIDFILE: It works! It actually works! It did everything I needed and never failed me. And every time this amazing program alphabetized or re-categorized 35,000 entries, I just know there was actually a troop of little munchkins in there, smiling at me, saying, "We know you think it's just too much for us this time, but we won't let you down!";

SAUL ASH, who first introduced me to the wonder of computers, who encouraged me to explore their uses, and who warned me that whatever I learned today would probably be obsolete tomorrow;

AND CAROLE LALLI, friend and editor, in that order, for those many years of friendship, for her inimitable wit, for always seeing the possibilities, for sharing her extraordinary knowledge (especially about food and cooking), and for invaluable and unwavering editorial support.

CONTENTS

  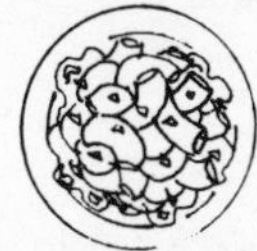 

INTRODUCTION

It all started when the kids asked me to make them a chocolate cake, ("Please, Mom, not a flourless chocolate cake, not a double chocolatty chocolate cake, not a chocolate brownie surprise with walnuts or a chocolate cream pie—just a plain, old-fashioned, chocolate cake!"). It seemed like such a simple request. All I needed was a recipe for a plain, old-fashioned, chocolate cake. I was certain there would be a dozen of them at my fingertips. I went to my kitchen library of over one hundred books (I like to cook, but I *love* to collect and read cookbooks!), certain that finding this would be a breeze.

Twenty minutes later, I had still not come across a recipe for a plain, old-fashioned chocolate cake. One book had Double Chocolate Pie; another had chocolate nut loaf cake; a third had chocolate soufflé cake, and so on. It was the thirteenth cookbook that had what I was looking for.

How many times has that happened to you? How many books did you have to read when you wanted to find a recipe for Veal Scallopine with Wild Mushrooms? How many books did you have to leaf through before you found a Coq Au Vin or an explanation of how to clarify butter? I thought so.

It happens to all of us. It doesn't matter if you own ten cookbooks or two hundred—every time you want to find a specific recipe for a dish, a definition of a cooking term, or an idea for what to do with a certain food, you have to make your way through your cookbooks, and maybe, just maybe, you will eventually find it. As I thought back, I realized that this frustrating search for specific recipes had become a somewhat common occurrence. I also suspected that it was this constant frustration and wasted time that accounted for those many cookbooks sitting on my bookshelves unused. It had become too much trouble to look through them all—so the number of books I actually used began to dwindle, and the recipes I followed became more and more mundane. In our busy world, spending time and energy searching for recipes makes the process of cooking aggravating rather than enjoyable. It seemed to me that there had to be a proverbial "better way."

At first I began to make a list of my own favorite recipes—a list of recipe titles and the cookbooks that contained them. But that didn't answer the problem of finding recipes I didn't already know—which, after all, was the point.

And then, one day, suddenly, it seemed simple. As a matter of fact, it seemed *so* simple that I thought I must be nuts—why hadn't anyone thought of it before? A master index! Of course! If I could combine the indexes of my favorite books, I would have a master index that would enable me to find *any* recipe I wanted.

And so *Recipex—Every Cook's Master Index*—was born. The first step was to compile a list of cookbooks you are most likely to have in your kitchen. We wanted to assemble the most complete and serviceable list possible, so we asked all kinds of cooks (those who cook occasionally, those who cook daily, those whose cookbook libraries contain six books, and those who have amassed collections of over one hundred cookbooks), plus cookbook authors, restaurant owners, cooking teachers, and cookbook store owners. We then did a survey of bookstores, *Publisher's Weekly*, and book editors and publishers to find out which books had sold the most, and which books had been reprinted again and again over the years.

Not so surprisingly, the lists coincided. Those best-selling cookbooks found on the lists from stores, magazines, and publishers were the same as those on your shelves. So, if you have six cookbooks in your kitchen, chances are they will be in *Recipex*. Likewise, if you have fifty, most of *them* are likely to be in *Recipex*.

As the list was compiled, something my husband calls the "While we're at it, why don't we . . ." principle took over. Why not be able to get more information while you are looking up a recipe in the index? For example, wouldn't it be valuable to know how long it would take to make a dish? And how about knowing before choosing a recipe how many people it will serve? With this added information at your fingertips, you could differentiate among recipes when there are more than one for a specific dish. Thus, when you look up Sweet Potato Pudding with Apples, you will not only find out which book has such a recipe and what page it is on, but you will also know how many people it serves and how long it takes to make.

While we're at it, why don't we include techniques of cooking—boning a chicken, butterflying shrimp, cooking a lobster, clarifying that butter? And charts? I love charts! I can't count the times I've needed to get an equivalent measurement or a calorie count or an understanding of what kind of cut is a porterhouse steak—and couldn't find them.

Now, *Recipex* gives you all this information, easily and clearly. From fifty-two books (including those major best-sellers that are sure to be in your kitchen, and a few gems that should), a list of over 35,000 recipes emerged. Methodically, book by book, page by page, we noted every recipe and the page it was on. We read through each recipe and coded it for preparation time, degree of difficulty, and number of servings it made. We listed every technique, definition, chart, and drawing we thought would be valuable for any cook.

And it works! If you are looking for a recipe, you will find it listed in *Recipex*. And you'll probably find it listed more than once. Let me explain. Unlike most indexes, *Recipex* is a *specific* index. Our criterion was: What would be useful for a reader to look for? Thus, if you just want to make a soup—any soup—you really can look in any cookbook index and find a listing of "soups." Some will be lengthy—others will have just one or two. You can also look under soup in *Recipex*. But the beauty of *Recipex* is that the soups found in our fifty-two cookbooks are listed under the *specific* soup in one place. Twenty Carrot Soups. Sixteen Cauliflower Soups and seven Cauliflower and Potato Soups. A variety of Leek Soups. Tomato and Rice Soups. Cream of Tomato Soups. Vegetable Soups. Pasta Soups. Etc.

And chances are there will be a dozen Pasta Soups—with variations. Pasta Soup with Vegetables. Pasta Soup with Veal Bones. Pasta Soup with Beans. Or how about Onion Soup? Onion Soup, Creamy? Onion Soup with Six Onions? Onion Soup Les Halles? Onion Soup you can make in under an hour—or one you can simmer all day? It's all at your fingertips.

Here's another clever way to find a recipe in *Recipex*. For example, Gingered Shrimp with Brussels Sprouts—one of my favorites. You can obviously find it under "Gingered Shrimp with Brussels Sprouts" and under "Shrimp, Gingered, with Brussels Sprouts." But suppose you had Brussels sprouts in the house and wanted to know what to do with them? With *Recipex*, you can also look under "Brussels Sprouts" and find an entry that reads, "Brussels Sprouts, Gingered Shrimp with."

The same goes for doughnuts. If you just want to make doughnuts, you can look under doughnuts. But if you want a "Sugar Doughnut" or a "Potato Doughnut" or a "Chocolate Doughnut" —that's what you'll find under "Chocolate Doughnut" and under "Doughnut, Chocolate." *Specifics!*

Have some extra basil in the refrigerator or in the garden and want to know what to do with it? Look under Basil. You'll find "Basil and Zucchini Soup" (in *The Complete Book of Soups and Stews*, page 370, it will take more than an hour to make and will feed four to eight people); "Basil Dressing" for your favorite salad (in *Betty Crocker's Cookbook*, page 284, made quick as a whistle); or how about "Basil Breakfast Strada" (in *The Silver Palate Good Times Cookbook*, page 123, will serve eight but will take some time to bake).

While we're in the "B's," let's look under "Borscht." There's "Iced Borscht," "Russian Cabbage Borscht" (enough for dinner for eight), "Winter Borscht" (that will serve an army!), chilled "Buttermilk Beet Borscht" (it will take longer to make, so leave some time), or plain old "Easy Borscht" you can make in minutes.

Recipex is easy to use—in the following pages, you will find charts explaining the codes, the abbreviations for each book—and that's it! All you have to do is turn to *Recipex* every time you want to look up a recipe.

Recipex is also fun. And informative. Just look through the pages—you'll learn so much about cooking and foods, about combinations of foods, about creativity in recipes and unusual use of ingredients and techniques you've never heard of—and those you have always heard of but have never tried.

Recipex presents you, within easy reach, information you need about more than 35,000 recipes. You will never again spend precious time searching for recipes you cannot find. You will be able to use cookbooks you have set aside. You will be able to find and prepare any dish you desire. You will be able to choose a specific recipe that fits your needs—the time you have, the number of people you want to serve, and the ingredients you have on hand.

And you will wonder how you ever managed without it!

Below is the list of books used in *Recipex*. There are fifty-two books in all, with over 35,000 recipes listed.

The books chosen to be included filled the following criteria:

- books that are considered by cookbook critics, cooks, restaurant owners and other cooking devotees to be classics that should be part of any kitchen library, no matter how small;
- "Bestsellers": books that sold over 50,000 copies (and are, therefore, more likely to be on your kitchen shelves);
- books that have been reprinted more than once;
- books that are still selling years after the original printing;
- books that have a devoted following and are special additions to your kitchen library.

A WORD ABOUT EACH

JAMES BEARD'S AMERICAN COOKERY
BY JAMES BEARD, LITTLE BROWN AND COMPANY, BOSTON, PAPERBACK, 1972

Among the master's two or three best books, this is the one to turn to for traditional American cookery. It has combinations of foods I'll bet you never thought of, plus wonderful stories of how certain dishes originated. It is not only great to cook from but entertaining to read.

BARBECUE WITH BEARD
BY JAMES BEARD, GOLDEN PRESS, NEW YORK, PAPERBACK, 1975

As usual, Beard makes it sound simple, and explains the why behind all his tips and suggestions.

THE BEST OF BON APPETIT
THE KNAPP PRESS, PUBLISHERS, LOS ANGELES, 1979

Recipes collected over the years from the magazine of the same name. It has sold over 700,000 copies to date.

BETTY CROCKER'S COOKBOOK
GOLDEN PRESS, NEW YORK, RINGBOUND, 1986

A collection of simple, basic recipes including old favorites. It continues to sell over 350,000 a year in this ringbound edition (plus an additional 100,000 in the trade paperback edition).

BETTER HOMES AND GARDENS, NEW COOK BOOK
RINGBOUND, 1981

A steady standby compendium of simple recipes for all occasions; contains basic, everyday dishes that are a staple of your kitchen. This book has sold millions of copies.

BETTER THAN STORE BOUGHT
BY HELEN WITTY AND ELIZABETH SCHNEIDER COLCHIE, PERENNIAL LIBRARY, HARPER & ROW, PUBLISHERS, NEW YORK, PAPERBACK, 1979

Using fresh and ingenious ingredients is the philosophy behind this gem. The hints are plentiful.

BERNARD CLAYTON'S NEW COMPLETE BOOK OF BREADS
BY BERNARD CLAYTON, SIMON & SCHUSTER, NEW YORK, HARDCOVER, 1973, 1987

Bread-making made understandable. It truly is a complete guide to baking breads.

THE COMPLETE BOOK OF SOUPS AND STEWS
BY BERNARD CLAYTON, JR., SIMON & SCHUSTER, NEW YORK, HARDCOVER, 1984

Everything you ever wanted to know about these cold weather favorites, plus explanations of basic soup-making techniques.

CITY FOOD

BY LEE BAILEY, CLARKSON N. POTTER, INC., PUBLISHERS, HARDCOVER, 1984

You'll find many more hearty dishes that weren't included in the first book, *Country Weekends*.

THE CLASSIC ITALIAN COOKBOOK

BY MARCELLA HAZAN, ALFRED A. KNOPF, NEW YORK, HARDCOVER, 1977

Everything you ever wanted to know about Italian cooking made understandable and easy. You'll find popular recipes next to more inventive Italian treats.

THE CHEZ PANISSE MENU COOKBOOK

BY ALICE WATERS, RANDOM HOUSE, NEW YORK, HARDCOVER, 1982

From the master chef at the famous Berkeley restaurant come superb recipes using only fresh ingredients.

CHEZ PANISSE PASTA, PIZZA & CALZONE

BY ALICE WATERS, PATRICIA CURTAN AND MARTINE LABRO, RANDOM HOUSE, NEW YORK, HARDCOVER, 1984

After Alice Waters opened her restaurant, Chez Panisse, to rave reviews, she opened the cafe that specializes in pizzas and other Italian dishes. These recipes are from the cafe and include other Italian treats from Alice's kitchen.

COOKING WITH FIRE AND SMOKE

BY PHILLIP STEPHEN SCHULZ, SIMON & SCHUSTER, NEW YORK, HARDCOVER, 1986

A must for lovers of grilling and barbecuing.

COUNTRY WEEKENDS

BY LEE BAILEY, CLARKSON N. POTTER, INC., PUBLISHERS, HARDCOVER, 1983

Lee Bailey was a successful entrepreneur, selling tableware and kitchen accessories to wide acclaim. But the books brought him a far wider audience. The recipes are easy to make, inventively created, and the book is absolutely gorgeous! Even though some of the dishes may sound like strictly picnic fare, in fact they are perfect any time.

ELEGANT BUT EASY COOKBOOK

BY MARIAN BURROS AND LOIS LEVINE, COLLIER BOOKS, MACMILLAN PUBLISHING COMPANY, NEW YORK, PAPERBACK, 1967

Entertaining made easy. Easy to read, the book is arranged in step-by-step explanations.

THE FINE ART OF ITALIAN COOKING

BY GIULIANO BUGIALLI, TIMES BOOKS, HARDCOVER, 1977

Another master chef at work. These recipes are creative versions of those favorites. It is a truly valuable collection of Italian classics.

THE FANNIE FARMER BAKING BOOK
BY MARION CUNNINGHAM, ALFRED A. KNOPF, NEW YORK, HARDCOVER, 1984

For the baker in all of us, from the simplest muffins to the most complicated desserts, this is a must.

THE FANNIE FARMER COOKBOOK
REVISED BY MARION CUNNINGHAM WITH JERI LABER, ALFRED A. KNOPF, NEW YORK, HARDCOVER, 1984

Another everything-you-ever-wanted-to-know-about-cooking compendium. The recipes are detailed and well explained. Fannie Farmer cookbooks have sold over 1 million copies over the years.

THE FRUGAL GOURMET
BY JEFF SMITH, WILLIAM MORROW AND COMPANY, INC., NEW YORK, HARDCOVER, 1984

A bestseller from its first printing, it contains not only good money-saving tips but good, solid recipes as well.

THE FRUGAL GOURMET COOKS WITH WINE
BY JEFF SMITH, WILLIAM MORROW AND COMPANY, INC., NEW YORK, HARDCOVER, 1984

All of the above, plus wine.

GLORIOUS FOOD
BY CHRISTOPHER IDONE, STEWART, TABORI & CHANG, INC., PUBLISHERS, NEW YORK, HARDCOVER, 1982

Fabulous, glamorous recipes by a famous caterer. It is a beautiful book containing glorious photographs.

GREENE ON GREENS

BY BERT GREENE, WORKMAN PUBLISHING, NEW YORK, PAPERBACK, 1984

You don't have to love vegetables to appreciate Greene's expertise. And, conversely, even if you don't love vegetables you will be pleasantly surprised at these superb recipes.

THE GOOD HOUSEKEEPING ALL-AMERICAN COOKBOOK

HEARST BOOKS, NEW YORK, HARDCOVER, 1987

A terrific collection of recipes from all over the country, including standards you thought you'd never see again.

GRILL BOOK

BY KELLY MCCUNE, PERENNIAL LIBRARY, HARPER & ROW, PUBLISHERS, NEW YORK, PAPERBACK, 1949, 1977

Another grilling must—this book has been a huge success because it is simple and beautiful.

THE JAMES BEARD COOKBOOK

BY JAMES BEARD, SECOND REVISED EDITION, A DELL TRADE PAPERBACK, 1959, 1987

Another Beard classic. A must.

JANE BRODY'S GOOD FOOD BOOK

BY JANE BRODY, BANTAM BOOKS, NEW YORK, PAPERBACK, 1985

The newest bible—it has recipes and is chock-full of information about nutrition. A must for your kitchen library.

JOY OF COOKING

BY IRMA S. ROMBAUER AND MARION ROMBAUER BECKER, THE BOBBS-MERRILL COMPANY, INC., HARDCOVER, 1971

A must in every kitchen. A complete collection of recipes and cooking techniques that includes both basics and more sophisticated recipes. It is the "encyclopedia" of cooking that has been reprinted more than 25 times since 1931. It has sold over 10 million copies.

KEEP IT SIMPLE

BY MARIAN BURROS, POCKET BOOKS, NEW YORK, PAPERBACK, 1982

Just like it says—a great book for simple and delicious cooking.

LA METHOD

BY JACQUES PEPIN, A WALLABY BOOK, PUBLISHED BY POCKET BOOKS, NEW YORK, PAPERBACK, 1979

Besides methods, this volume includes recipes. The photographs are essential to learning how to cook and to the understanding of how to cook well.

LA TECHNIQUE

BY JACQUES PEPIN, POCKET BOOKS, NEW YORK, PAPERBACK, 1976

A self-explanatory book—it will teach you everything about cooking techniques you need, and includes photographs illustrating every step of the way.

MASTERING THE ART OF FRENCH COOKING
VOLUME ONE, BY JULIA CHILD, LOUISETTE BERTHOLLE, AND SIMONE BECK, ALFRED A. KNOPF, HARDCOVER, 1973

Published twenty-five years ago, it continues to be the bible of French cooking and the watershed book in the American experience with French cooking. Others have come along, French cooking has changed, but this still remains a must to learn the basics.

MOOSEWOOD COOKBOOK
BY MOLLIE KATZEN, TEN SPEED PRESS, PAPERBACK, 1977

Recipes from the Moosewood Restaurant in Ithaca, New York, have become favorites. The hand lettered book, complete with illustrations (and hints on techniques) is a nice addition to a kitchen library.

MORE CLASSIC ITALIAN COOKING
BY MARCELLA HAZAN, ALFRED A. KNOPF, NEW YORK, HARDCOVER, 1978

More gems from the Hazan kitchen.

WOLFGANG PUCK'S MODERN FRENCH COOKING FOR THE AMERICAN KITCHEN
BY WOLFGANG PUCK, HOUGHTON MIFFLIN COMPANY, BOSTON, HARDCOVER, 1981

Formerly a chef at Los Angeles' famous Ma Maison restaurant, Puck went on to his own Spago and Chinois On Main and proceeded to make his style and cooking famous worldwide. This is his collection of signature dishes that help define the Nouvelle Cuisine style.

MASTERING THE ART OF FRENCH COOKING
VOLUME TWO, BY JULIA CHILD AND SIMONE BECK, ALFRED A. KNOPF, HARDCOVER, 1973

A continuation of Volume I.

MAIDA HEATTER'S NEW BOOK OF GREAT DESSERTS
BY MAIDA HEATTER, ALFRED A. KNOPF, NEW YORK, HARDCOVER, 1982

The master of dessert making at her best. The book is detailed with recipe information and explanations and stories that help make cooking fun. It will make you feel like an expert.

MAKE IT EASY IN YOUR KITCHEN
BY LAURIE BURROWS GRAD, J. P. TARCHER, INC., LOS ANGELES, HARDCOVER, 1982

Easy-to-repeat recipes by a wonderful cook whom you may remember from the television show *Hour Magazine*. The recipes are both imaginative and simple.

ENTERTAINING
BY MARTHA STEWART, CLARKSON N. POTTER, INC., PUBLISHERS, NEW YORK, HARDCOVER, 1982

From the catering expertise of Martha Stewart comes this book, containing both simple and slightly more complicated recipes for parties of all sizes. It contains beautiful photographs that make you want to begin cooking immediately. It has sold more than 250,000 copies.

MARTHA STEWART'S QUICK COOK
BY MARTHA STEWART, CLARKSON N. POTTER, INC., PUBLISHERS, NEW YORK, HARDCOVER, 1983

A must for those of us in a hurry—this book has simple recipes that can be made quickly.

DESSERTS BY NANCY SILVERTON
BY NANCY SILVERTON, HARPER & ROW, PUBLISHERS, NEW YORK, HARDCOVER, 1986

This is a beautiful book with those hard-to-find dessert recipes that are a treasure.

THE NEW YORK TIMES COOKBOOK
BY CRAIG CLAIBORNE, HARPER & ROW, PUBLISHERS, NEW YORK, HARDCOVER, 1961

I can't imagine having a kitchen library without this perfect, all-around cookbook. It may not have every recipe you've ever searched for, but each recipe Claiborne includes is for delicious dishes that are failsafe. This classic continues to be a best-seller every year.

THE NEW YORK TIMES INTERNATIONAL COOKBOOK
BY CRAIG CLAIBORNE, HARPER & ROW, PUBLISHERS, NEW YORK, HARDCOVER, 1971

Although not an in-depth book of international recipes (for more complete ethnic recipes, you really have to go to books that are covered by country or region), this is, nevertheless, the perfect depository for a wide sampling of popular international dishes.

OUTDOOR COOKING

BY THE EDITORS OF TIME-LIFE BOOKS, VIRGINIA, HARDCOVER, 1983

All you need and want to know about grilling, barbecuing, smoking and other outdoor cooking techniques.

CHEF PAUL PRUDHOMME'S LOUISIANA KITCHEN

BY PAUL PRUDHOMME, WILLIAM MORROW AND COMPANY, INC., NEW YORK, HARDCOVER, 1984

Prudhomme is responsible for taking Creole cooking nationwide. This book contains all his favorite recipes. It has sold over 300,000 copies in the hardcover edition.

THE SETTLEMENT COOKBOOK

THIRD EDITION, SIMON & SCHUSTER, NEW YORK, HARDCOVER, 1976

Years after the first edition came out, this classic continues to be an enormous bestseller. It is well written, easy to understand and follow, and full of old-fashioned advice that holds up today.

THE NEW YORK TIMES 60 MINUTE GOURMET

BY PIERRE FRANEY, TIMES BOOKS, HARDCOVER, 1980

For dishes that are fast and simple, yet sophisticated in look and taste, Franey's book is an important addition to a complete kitchen library.

THE SILVER PALATE COOKBOOK

BY JULEE ROSSO & SHEILA LUKINS, WORKMAN PUBLISHING, NEW YORK, PAPERBACK, 1982

This is a best-seller that contains new versions of delicious standard recipes plus many new and inventive dishes. The authors began the trend for including many tips and tidbits in the sidebars, which is an additional informative treat. It has sold over 750,000 copies in its hardcover edition, with the paperback running close behind.

THE SILVER PALATE GOOD TIMES COOKBOOK
BY JULEE ROSSO & SHEILA LUKINS,
WORKMAN PUBLISHING, NEW YORK, PAPERBACK, 1985

Another success for Rosso and Lukins, this version contains more of the above plus many party recipes.

THE VEGETARIAN EPICURE
BY ANNA THOMAS, ALFRED A. KNOPF, NEW YORK,
HARDCOVER, 1980

Whether or not you are a vegetarian, these recipes have become favorites for all cooks. A small book when first published, it continues to sell well years later, and has become a standard in many cooks' collections.

THE VICTORY GARDEN COOKBOOK
BY MARIAN MORASH, ALFRED A. KNOPF, NEW YORK,
PAPERBACK, 1982

Chock-full of recipes, this collection contains many recipes made with fresh vegetables. At over 200,000 copies sold, it continues to be a favorite for both new and more experienced cooks.

WOK COOKERY

BY CEIL DYER, HP BOOKS, PAPERBACK, 1983

A simple, readable, and easy-to-reproduce cookbook about using a wok. There must be a lot of us wok lovers out there—the book has sold over 1 million copies in paperback.

YOU'VE GOT IT MADE

BY MARIAN BURROS, WILLIAM MORROW AND COMPANY, INC., NEW YORK, HARDCOVER, 1984

Superb, simple and delicious recipes from the food critic of *The New York Times*. A standard standby for the kitchen.

CODES FOR DEGREE OF DIFFICULTY AND PREPARATION TIME (TD)

The recipes in *Recipex* have been coded to make it easier for you to differentiate between the choices. Below is an explanation of how the recipes were coded. After using the index a few times you will be able to quickly familiarize yourself with the categories. You will then find that recognizing the various guidelines (e.g., soaking beans overnight gets a "3," using canned beans makes the recipe a "1"; making homemade pasta gives it a "2" or "3," using store-bought pasta makes it a "1") will be simple to remember. I encourage you to refer to this chart when you first start using *Recipex*, and guarantee that you will remember the categories in no time.

1 Easiest and shortest time to make; a recipe with this code takes an hour or less preparation time. It requires no special cooking skills or technique, no extraordinary equipment, and a small number of ingredients that you probably will have on hand. Sometimes, however, you will find an unusual dish coded with a "1." For example, venison may not be your every night choice, and it may not be available everywhere. But it is often simple to cook, so it gets a "1."

2 Will take more than one hour and up to several hours (but not overnight) to prepare; may require you to buy some additional ingredients you wouldn't normally have on hand; you may need a simple knowledge of some cooking technique; you may need a gadget or piece of equipment that is not ordinarily found in a kitchen (e.g., a pasta-making machine, fish steamer,

etc.). An example: A pasta dish that calls for homemade pasta would be a "2"; a chicken dish that needs to be marinated for two hours would be a "2"; chilling a dessert until set would be a "2" (if it called for freezing overnight, it would be a "3"); a dish that requires knowing how to bone a chicken or fillet a fish would also be a "2."

3 This category requires at least overnight preparation, a knowledge of more advanced cooking or preparing techniques, and/or ingredients that are more exotic and more difficult to obtain. Usually, it doesn't mean you won't have the ability to make this recipe—it will just take longer. You will find a mixture of recipes in this category. The beauty of *Recipex* is that, with very few exceptions, you will find several recipes for the same dish, with different codings for preparation time. Thus, if you are in a hurry to prepare a dish, don't choose a recipe coded with a "3." If you want to make a Coq Au Vin and one recipe has a "3," choose the one that is coded "1" or "2" instead. But if you are anxious to try a new recipe and you have the time, *don't be intimidated* by a code of "3." This recipe may not be difficult, just *more* difficult or *more* time-consuming than some others. Any recipe that requires overnight freezing, marinating, soaking or preserving will naturally have a code of "3" even though it may not be difficult.

 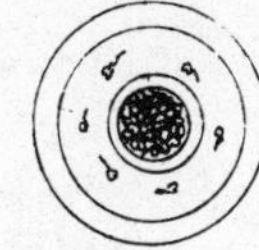  

CODES FOR NUMBER OF SERVINGS (S)

A UP TO 3 SERVINGS
B 4 TO 8 SERVINGS
C OVER 9 SERVINGS

IF THERE IS NO CODE FOR THE NUMBER OF SERVINGS FOR A PARTICULAR RECIPE, IT MEANS YOU CAN ADAPT IT TO YOUR NEEDS.

BOOK ABBREVIATIONS

AC	James Beard's American Cookery
BB	Barbecue with Beard
BBA	The Best of Bon Appetit
BCC	Betty Crocker's Cookbook
BHGN	Better Homes and Gardens, New Cook Book
BTSB	Better Than Store Bought
CBB	Bernard Clayton's New Complete Book of Breads
CBSS	The Complete Book of Soups and Stews
CF	City Food
CIC	The Classic Italian Cookbook
CPMC	The Chez Panisse Menu Cookbook
CPPC	Chez Panisse Pasta, Pizza & Calzone
CFS	Cooking with Fire and Smoke
CW	Country Weekends
EBE	Elegant but Easy Cookbook
FAIC	The Fine Art of Italian Cooking
FFBB	The Fannie Farmer Baking Book
FFCB	The Fannie Farmer Cookbook
FG	The Frugal Gourmet
FGCW	The Frugal Gourmet Cooks with Wine
GF	Glorious Food
GG	Greene on Greens
GHAC	The Good Housekeeping All-American Cookbook
GRIL	Grill Book
JBC	The James Beard Cookbook
JBGF	Jane Brody's Good Food Book

JOC	Joy of Cooking
KIS	Keep It Simple
LM	La Method
LT	La Technique
MAFC	Mastering the Art of French Cooking I
MC	Moosewood Cookbook
MCIC	More Classic Italian Cooking
MFC	Wolfgang Puck's Modern French Cooking for the American Kitchen
MFC2	Mastering the Art of French Cooking II
MHGD	Maida Heatter's New Book of Great Desserts
MIE	Make It Easy in Your Kitchen
MSE	Martha Stewart's Entertaining
MSQC	Martha Stewart's Quick Cook
NSD	Desserts by Nancy Silverton
NYT	The New York Times Cookbook
NYTI	The New York Times International Cookbook
OC	Outdoor Cooking
PPLK	Chef Paul Prudhomme's Louisiana Kitchen
SC	The Settlement Cookbook
SMG	The New York Times 60 Minute Gourmet
SP	The Silver Palate Cookbook
SPGT	The Silver Palate Good Times Cookbook
VE	The Vegetarian Epicure
VGCB	The Victory Garden Cookbook
WC	Wok Cookery
YGM	You've Got It Made

  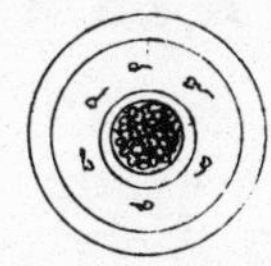 

RECIPEX

A

RECIPE	BOOK	PAGE	TD	S
A la king sauce, quick	JOC	333	1	B
Abalone, all about	JOC	371		
Abalone chowder	CBSS	140	3	B
Abalone, pan fried	FFCB	127	1	A
Abalone, sauteed	JOC	371	1	A
Acid liquid to tenderize	OC	10		
Acorn cookies	BCC	108	2	C
Acorn squash (see squash, acorn)				
Adas bi haamud (lentil soup)	AC	96	2	
Age of innocence cup	NYT	652	1	C
Agresto sauce (grape sauce)	FAIC	59	1	B
Aigo bouido (garlic soup)	MAFC	46	1	B
Aioli (garlic mayonnaise)	FFCB	272	1	B
◆	GRIL	39	1	B
◆	MC	71	1	B
◆	GF	218	2	C
◆	JOC	314	1	B
◆	GG	324	1	B
◆	VGCB	180	1	B
Bourride (garlic fish soup)	GF	218	2	C
w Chick peas	NYTI	135	3	B
Green beans, beets, warm w	CPMC	219	1	B
Grilled vegetables, mixed w	GRIL	72	2	B
Platters, vegetables, fish & beef, for	SP	40	2	C
Potatoes, for	NYTI	135	1	B
Sauce	MAFC	92	2	B
◆	FG	278	1	B
◆	NYTI	134	1	
◆	SP	40	1	C
Sauce, chicken bouillabaisse	MFC2	263	2	
Sauce, horseradish	BBA	88	1	B
Snails for	NYTI	135	1	B
Tartar sauce	GRIL	39	1	B
& Tomatoes	NYTI	135	1	B
Aji sauce (herb sauce)	BBA	30	1	B
Ajiaco (chicken soup w corn)	BBA	30	3	B
Akee pureed	JOC	110	2	A
Alaskan ice cream ball	GHAC	303		
Albacore, Hawaiian sesame	OC	141	2	B
Albert's favorite (orange & walnut torte)	FFBB	376	1	C
Albondigas (meatballs)	FGCW	90	1	
Albufera rice (Spanish rice)	NYTI	222	1	B
Alcohol desserts	NSD	16		
Alcohol, to substitute other liquids for	NSD	16		
Alexander (drink w creme de cacao)	JOC	37	1	
Alexander cocktail	SC	60	1	A
Alexander pie (w creme de cacao & brandy)	BCC	94	2	B
Alkermes di Firenze red liqueur: zuppe inglese	FAIC	453		
All purpose sauce, almost	KIS	329	1	A
All Souls' Day cookies, almonds, pine nuts	MCIC	438	1	C

RECIPE	BOOK	PAGE	TD	S
Allemande sauce (cream sauce for chicken & vegetables)	BCC	328	1	B
Allemande sauce	JOC	324	1	B
Allemande sauce	NYTI	265	1	B
Alligator pear filling	SC	382	1	
Almond				
Apricot bread	MC	196	1	B
Apricot bread	FFBB	555	1	B
Apricot wedding cake	SPGT	116	3	C
Baked apples w	SC	260	1	
Bark fudge	BCC	116	2	C
Bavarian cream	NYT	591	2	C
Bavarian cream	MAFC	599	3	C
Black cherry aspic	JOC	101	2	B
Blanched	MAFC	582		
Blanching	NYTI	485		
Blanching	MAFC	582		
Blancmange	AC	726	1	
Bran bread	JOC	576	1	B
Bread slices	SC	158	1	
Bread slices, cocoa	SC	158	1	
Brickle cookies	BCC	97	1	C
Brittle	LM	364	3	
Brittle	BTSB	267	2	B
Brittle	SC	174	1	
Broccoli hollandaise, chicken w	WC	63	1	B
Brownies	BCC	101	1	C
Bundt kuchen	SC	117	1	B
Burnt	JOC	737	2	B
Burnt	SC	174	1	
Butter	JOC	338	1	A
Butter	BTSB	292	1	A
Butter crunch	BCC	117	2	C
Butter crunch	BTSB	268	2	C
Cafe	BHGN	53	1	A
Cake	SC	111	1	B
Cake	MCIC	425	1	B
Cake	FFCB	529	1	B
After Lisbon's Tavares Restaurant	BBA	186	2	C
Chocolate	MAFC	677	3	B
Chocolate	BBA	188	3	C
Meringue, individual (bresiliens)	MFC2	504	3	
Mocha	YGM	220	2	C
Puff paste	LM	273	2	
Candy, caramelized	CIC	450	1	B
Caramel pudding, steamed	SC	189	1	
Caramelized	MAFC	583	1	A
& Cauliflower	AC	506	1	
& Cauliflower, buttered	JBC	303	1	B
Charlotte, burnt	FFCB	624	2	B
Cheese slices	EBE	32	2	C
& Cherry flan	MAFC	655	1	B
Chestnuts	LM	351	2	C
Chicken	NYT	196	1	B
◆	NYTI	486	3	C
◆	EBE	80	1	B
◆	SC	311	2	
Chicken supreme	FFCB	256	1	B
Chili flavored	BTSB	288	1	C
Coffee cake	SC	117	1	B
Cookies	BHGN	163	1	C
Cookies	MSE	125	1	C
Belgian	MHGD	326	2	C
Bitter	FAIC	464	1	C
Bitter	FAIC	464	1	C
Chinese	FFBB	247	1	B
Chinese	AC	709	1	
Chocolate	SC	152	1	
Little	FAIC	462	1	C

RECIPE	BOOK	PAGE	TD	S
Almond (*cont.*)				
Cream	MFC	146	1	B
Cream	JOC	737	2	B
Baked French puff pastry	MFC2	468	3	B
Chocolate	MAFC	607	2	C
Crepes	MAFC	652	2	B
w Fresh strawberries	MAFC	605	2	C
Jellied	NYT	590	2	B
Molded	MFC2	446	2	C
Pie, toasted	FFBB	114	2	B
Puff paste, French	MFC2	468	3	B
Raspberries	MAFC	607	2	C
Strawberries	JBC	114	1	
Creme brulee	NYTI	295	2	B
Crepes	VE	189	1	B
Crescents	SC	159	1	
Crescents	YGM	176	2	C
Crescents	FFBB	246	1	C
Croquettes, chicken	FFCB	258	2	B
Crust	NYT	521	1	B
Curd	NYTI	93	2	C
Curls	JOC	667	2	C
Curried	BTSB	288	1	C
Curry sauce	GHAC	206	1	B
Custard, chocolate	MAFC	608	2	C
Custard filling	SC	147	1	
Custard filling	MAFC	591	2	B
Custard filling	SC	147	1	
Deviled	SC	41	1	
Divinity	NYT	636	2	C
Dumplings	SC	407	1	
Enchiladas, eggplant w	MC	156	2	B
Filling	JOC	647	1	B
Filling	BCC	33	1	B
Filling, custard	JOC	648	1	B
Frangipani pie	AC	629	1	
Garnish	JOC	343	1	A
& Green beans	AC	476	1	
& Green beans	FFCB	362	1	B
Ice cream, burnt	FFCB	630	3	C
Ice cream, chocolate	BHGN	182	3	C
Ice cream, chocolate burnt	MFC2	421	3	B
Icebox cake	SC	135	3	B
Icebox cookies	SC	159	1	
Lace rolls	GHAC	350	1	C
Macaroons	FFCB	556	2	C
◆	NYT	577	1	C
◆	FFBB	218	1	C
◆	SC	163	1	
Meal, making	NSD	16		
Meringue rings	JOC	670	1	C
Milk	JOC	487	2	
Mousse & chicken	FFCB	449	2	B
Muffins, bran	CBB	573	1	C
Nougatine	NSD	352	2	B
Nut bread	FFBB	451	2	B
Orange cookies, Greek	FFBB	269	2	C
Paste	JOC	729	2	B
Paste	FFCB	688	2	B
Paste	BTSB	265	2	B
Blender	FFCB	688	1	B
Filling for coffee cake	SC	83	1	
Filling for Danish pastries	NYT	535	1	
Flowers	LM	368	3	
Homemade	FFBB	219	1	B
Pea pods	BHGN	398	2	A
Peaches, stuffed	FAIC	493	2	B
Pear flan	MAFC	658	1	B
Pie, chocolate ricotta	JBGF	627	2	C
Plum tart, Viennese	BBA	205	2	B
Pound cake	BCC	69	1	C

RECIPE	BOOK	PAGE	TD	S
Pretzels	AC	708	1	
Pretzels	SC	157	1	
Pretzels	JOC	663	2	C
Pudding, chocolate	SC	190	2	
Pulverized	MAFC	582		
& Raisin braid	GHAC	359	2	B
Rice & bacon salad	BBA	146	2	B
Rice, raisins &	SMG	51	1	B
Rice, steamed	JBC	116	1	B
Rusks	FFBB	227	1	C
Salad, chicken	BCC	264	2	B
Salted & roasted	BTSB	288	1	C
Sauce	BHGN	355	1	B
Sauce	BCC	328	1	B
Sauce, burnt	SC	216	1	
Sheet cake	NSD	271	2	B
Sheet cake, chocolate	NSD	267	2	B
Shells, chocolate	JOC	664	3	C
Souffle	MAFC	618	3	B
Souffle, caramel unmolded	MAFC	622	3	B
Soup	VE	78	2	B
Soup	SC	400	1	
Soup, cream of	FFCB	86	1	B
Soup, onion	CBSS	313	2	B
Spice cookies	FFCB	550	1	C
Sponge cake, orange	MAFC	676	3	B
Sponge roll	JOC	642	1	B
Spread, blue cheese	EBE	30	1	B
Spread, curry	EBE	36	2	B
Steak, an old recipe for	AC	316	1	
Sticks	SC	151	1	
Strudel	SC	354	2	
Studded potatoes	AC	572	1	
Sugar coated	SC	174	1	
Sugar cookies	MHGD	328	1	C
Sugared	JOC	737	2	B

RECIPE	BOOK	PAGE	TD	S
Taffy	BCC	119	2	B
Tart	SP	305	2	C
Lemon	MHGD	214	2	C
Lemon	MAFC	646	2	B
Lindsey's	CPMC	21	2	B
Peach	MHGD	212	2	C
Pear	MSE	246	2	B
Pear	MHGD	206	2	C
Pear	MAFC	642	2	B
Purple plum	MHGD	210	2	C
Tartes	YGM	191	2	C
Tiles	MFC	217	3	C
Toast	BTSB	238	1	C
Toasted	FGCW	89	1	
Toasted or grilled	MAFC	582		
Toffee	SC	171	1	
Topping	BCC	79	1	B
Torte	EBE	147	1	B
◆	MSE	259	3	B
◆	SC	124	1	B
◆	FFCB	520	1	B
Chez Panisse	FFBB	176	2	B
Cockaigne	JOC	637	1	B
Jellied filled	SC	124	1	B
Matzo meal	SC	130	1	B
Or Mandel torte	AC	688	1	
Truffles	BCC	116	3	C
Tuiles	NSD	48	2	C
Tuiles	SPGT	108	1	C
Wafers, lacy curved	MFC2	475	1	C
Walnut puffs	MFC2	473	1	C
Zucchini, cheese	MFC2	374	1	B
Aloo Dham (Indian) (fried potatoes w yogurt & spices)	NYTI	360	1	C
Altitude, cooking at high	BHGN	438		
Amalgamation cake	FFBB	316	1	C
Amandine garnish	JOC	343	1	A

ANCHOVY
43

RECIPE	BOOK	PAGE	TD	S
Gratin, onions, potato &	MAFC	154	1	B
Grilled fresh	OC	142	1	B
Hamburger & egg	SMG	246	1	B
Hollandaise	AC	460	1	
Lemon butter, salmon steaks w	WC	73	1	B
Marinara sauce	JBC	214	1	
Mayonnaise	MSE	70	1	C
Mayonnaise	AC	77		
Mayonnaise, cauliflower &	CPMC	107	1	
Mozzarella beef patties with	CIC	245	1	B
Mushrooms, stuffed	NYTI	373	1	B
Oil	CIC	36	1	B
Olive butter, squab spit roasted w	CPMC	25	3	B
Onion rings	NYT	40	2	B
Onion tart, black olives &	MAFC	151	2	B
Pappardelle, whole wheat, tomatoes	CPPC	100	2	B
Pasta w onion	FGCW	147	1	B
Pastries	FAIC	89	2	B
Peppers	CIC	37	2	B
Pesto	JOC	539	1	
Pizza w garlic & red onions	CPPC	160	3	B
Pizza, mozzarella	MCIC	66	3	B
Pizza, onion confit, walnuts &	CPPC	153	3	B
Potatoes	NYT	270	1	B
Potatoes, pan roasted	MCIC	401	1	B
Potatoes, scalloped w tomatoes, onions &	MAFC	525	1	B

RECIPE	BOOK	PAGE	TD	S
Rolls	JOC	73	1	
Roquefort dressing, blender	JOC	312	1	B
Salad, potatoes &	NYTI	258	1	B
Sandwich	AC	811	1	
Sauce (see also bagna cauda)				
◆	MAFC	66	1	B
◆	FAIC	64	1	B
◆	NYT	340	1	B
◆	SC	387	1	
Beef casserole w garlic &	MAFC	324	1	B
Cauliflower	FAIC	411	1	B
Cold	GG	12	1	B
For fish	JOC	324	1	B
For pasta	GHAC	265		
Green	NYT	340	1	
Halibut w white wine	MCIC	212	1	B
Pasta, broccoli &	CIC	174	1	B
Spaghetti &	FAIC	159	1	B
Veal chops &	MCIC	272	1	B
Spaghetti	BCC	62	1	B
Clam sauce &	NYTI	420	2	B
Garlic, parsley &	CPPC	145	1	B
Thin, tomato sauce &	CIC	97	1	B
Spread, chive	EBE	33	1	A
Steak sauce	BB	145	1	
Sticks	LT	422	2	
Stuffed eggs	FFCB	308	1	A
Stuffed tomatoes, baked	NYT	405	1	B
Swordfish steaks	OC	152	1	A
Tomato sauce, shrimp & spaghetti	SMG	297	1	B
Tomatoes, stuffed	SC	361	1	

RECIPE	BOOK	PAGE	TD	S
Anchovy (*cont.*)				
Tomatoes, stuffed w bread crumbs	JOC	308	1	B
Veal chops	NYTI	395	1	B
Veal patties, tuna &	MAFC	375	1	B
Veal rolls	NYT	165	1	B
Andalouse sauce	JOC	315	1	B
Andouille smoked sausage				
Dressing	PPLK	226	2	B
Filling	PPLK	130	2	C
Gumbo, chicken &	PPLK	202	1	B
Sauce	PPLK	250	2	B
Seafood gumbo, Cajun &	PPLK	208	2	C
Angel almond cake	JOC	621	1	B
Angel balls	JOC	633	1	C
Angel cake	JOC	620	1	B
Angel cake	BHGN	100	1	C
Angel cake	NYT	544	1	C
Apricot	EBE	148	3	C
Chocolate	SC	122	1	B
Chocolate, high altitude	JOC	649	1	B
Cocoa	JOC	620	1	B
Flavored	JOC	621	1	B
Fruit	SC	122	1	B
High altitude	JOC	648	1	B
Indians	SC	122	1	B
Marble	SC	122	1	B
Marble	JOC	621	1	B
Roll	JOC	643	2	B
Spice, high altitude	JOC	649	1	B
Angel Charlotte russe	SC	136	2	B
Angel cream	FFBB	417	1	C
Chocolate	FFBB	417	1	C
Citrus	FFBB	417	1	C
Coconut	FFBB	417	1	C
Angel cupcakes	JOC	633	1	C

RECIPE	BOOK	PAGE	TD	S
Angel food cake	GHAC	327	2	C
◆	FFCB	520	1	C
◆	AC	684	1	
◆	BCC	75	1	C
◆	JBC	35	2	B
◆	SC	121	1	B
Basics	BCC	75		
Chocolate	FFBB	294	1	C
Chocolate	BCC	75	1	C
Chocolate or cocoa	AC	686	1	
Custard	AC	686	1	
Easy	SC	121	1	B
Grand finale	FFBB	296	2	C
Imperial	SC	121	1	B
Mocha	AC	686	1	
Praline	AC	686	1	
White mountain frosting	FFBB	286	2	B
Whole wheat	FFBB	295	2	C
Angel food custard cake	FFBB	294	1	C
Angel food surprise	SC	137	2	B
Angel hair	LT	454	2	
Angel hair, broccoli &	MSQC	20	1	B
Angel hair pasta, broccoli, three cheese &	FG	123	1	B
Angel hair pasta, feta w	GHAC	260	1	B
Angel hair pasta, ricotta, custard &	CF	109	2	B
Angel parfait	SC	213	2	
Angel parfait	FFCB	626	3	B
Angel pie	FFCB	594	2	B
◆	JOC	613	2	B
◆	EBE	160	1	B
◆	AC	631	1	
Berry or cranberry	AC	632	1	
Coffee	BHGN	287	2	B
Lime	AC	632	1	
Orange	MHGD	171	2	B

RECIPE	BOOK	PAGE	TD	S
Orange	AC	632	1	
Slices	JOC	666	1	C
Angel toffee dessert	BCC	151	2	C
Angel Torte	SC	125	1	B
Angelica parfait	JOC	721	2	C
Angels on horseback	JOC	62	1	
Angels on horseback	KIS	306	1	C
Angels on horseback	GHAC	125	1	A
Anguilles quo vadis (eels in a green herb sauce)	NYT	18	2	B
Animal crackers	NSD	59	1	C
Anise				
Caps	AC	709	1	
Cookies	SC	160	1	
Cookies	AC	703	1	
Drop cookies	JOC	656	1	C
Kuchen	CBB	336	2	C
Rice	KIS	161	1	A
Seed cookies	MHGD	314	1	C
Sponge fingers, toasted	BTSB	240	1	C
Toast, crunchy	BTSB	239	2	C
Antipasti	FAIC	83		
Antipasto	MSE	137	14	1
Antipasto	SC	359	3	
Celery	VGCB	78	2	B
Italian	MC	60	2	B
Plate	FG	61		
Vegetable mixed	VGCB	336	1	B
Ants climbing up a tree (Chinese)	FGCW	320	3	B
Apfeltorte (apple cake)	NYT	568	1	B
Apple				
& Amaretto	KIS	318	1	B
Aspic, rum-flavored, unmolded	MAFC	627	2	B
& Avocado salad	BCC	297	1	B
& Bacon, sauteed	JOC	111	1	B

RECIPE	BOOK	PAGE	TD	S
Baked	MSE	115	1	A
◆	BCC	124	1	
◆	SC	260	1	
◆	JBC	95	1	
◆	BHGN	179	1	B
◆	SMG	283	1	B
◆	JOC	111	1	B
◆	BBA	208	1	B
Almonds &	SC	260	1	
Brown sugar &	JBC	95	1	
Cortland maple yogurt	MSQC	213	1	A
Creme fraiche &	NSD	124	1	B
Filled w sausage meat	JOC	112	1	B
Flamed	JBC	95	1	
Ginger honey	MHGD	413	1	B
Glazed	FFCB	652	1	B
Grenadine	BCC	124	1	
Honey	BCC	124	1	
w Macaroons	MCIC	441	1	B
Maple sugar	JBC	95	1	
Mincemeat	BCC	124	1	
Sherry	JBC	95	1	
Spiced	JBC	95	1	
& Variations	AC	746	1	
Bananas & caramel sauce	GHAC	292	1	B
Barley, pilaf &	YGM	224	1	C
Bars, caramel	BCC	105	1	C
& Beets, puree	SP	196	2	B
Beets, sweet sour	JOC	264	2	B
Betty, Connecticut	MHGD	419	1	B
Bluefish, baked, mustard	SP	114	2	B
Braised w butter & orange sauce	MAFC	628	1	B
Brandy sauce	SP	270	1	B
Bratwurst w phyllo	YGM	166	3	C

RECIPE	BOOK	PAGE	TD	S
Apple (*cont.*)				
Bread	NYT	483	2	B
Chopped	CBB	469	2	C
Fresh	MHGD	271	1	B
Or cake, raw	AC	673	1	
Brown Betty	FFCB	651	1	B
Brown Betty	AC	723	1	
Brown Betty	GHAC	287	2	B
Butter	JOC	777	2	C
◆	BHGN	128	2	B
◆	SC	442	1	
◆	MSE	133	1	C
◆	NYT	509	1	B
◆	FFCB	707	2	C
Butter, baked	JOC	777	2	C
Cabbage	SC	415	2	
Cabbage, red	BBA	134	2	B
Cake (apfeltorte)	NYT	568	1	B
Cake	BCC	72	1	C
Cake	FAIC	475	1	B
Chunky	GHAC	323	2	C
Cockaigne	JOC	606	2	B
Cockaigne w sour cream	JOC	691	2	B
Dutch	FFCB	523	2	B
Dutch	SC	197	1	
French	JOC	607	1	B
Fresh	FFBB	343	1	B
German	BBA	186	2	B
Or cupcakes, double	AC	672	1	
'Cake,' flourless	JBGF	614	2	B
Calvados tarts, individual	NSD	114	3	B
Candied	JOC	741	1	
Candy	GHAC	354	2	B
Candy	BTSB	264	1	C
Canning	BHGN	128		
Caramel	BHGN	113	1	C
◆	SC	177	1	
◆	BCC	121	1	B
◆	NYT	617	1	B
Caramelized, baked	GF	207	1	C
Casserole, onion &	JOC	286	1	B
Celery & nut salad, molded	SC	369	2	
Charlotte	AC	723	1	
Charlotte	LT	432	2	C
Charlotte, unmolded	MAFC	623	1	B
Chart	SP	264		
Cheddar strudel	MC	211	1	B
Cheese	MSQC	161	1	
Cheese, coleslaw	BCC	282	1	B
Cheese pancakes	MC	147	1	B
Cheesecake	NSD	138	3	B
Cherry salad	BCC	291	2	B
Chicken, ginger	YGM	45	1	B
Chocolate & caramel	BCC	121	1	B
Chunks, sauteed	MSQC	169	1	B
Chutney	JOC	786	3	C
◆	FFCB	716	2	C
◆	AC	827	1	
◆	BBA	167	1	C
Chutney, ginger	FFCB	716	2	C
Cider	SC	436	2	
Cider glaze	SP	272	1	C
Cider sherbet	CPMC	97	2	B
Cinnamon	FFCB	652	1	B
Cinnamon	JOC	111	2	B
Cinnamon & funnel cakes	GHAC	369	1	B
Cinnamon tart	BCC	84	2	B
Cinnamony baked	SP	266	2	B
Cobbler	BHGN	180	2	B
Cobbler	FFBB	96	2	B
Cobbler	FFCB	524	2	B
Coffee cake filling	JOC	573	1	C
Compote	FFCB	651	1	B

RECIPE	BOOK	PAGE	TD	S
Compote	AC	746	1	
Conserve, pear	SC	444	1	
Cookies, fresh	AC	710	1	
Cranberry raisin pie	FFCB	584	2	B
Cranberry sauce	SC	262	1	
Cream pie, Marlborough pie	AC	625	1	
Crepes, mound of	MAFC	653	2	B
Crisp	VE	280	1	B
◆	NYT	618	1	B
◆	BCC	124	1	B
◆	JBGF	620	1	B
◆	FFCB	650	1	B
Crisp, cranberry	JBGF	622	1	B
Crumble	MIE	318	1	B
Crumble pie	BHGN	276	1	B
Curry sauce, pork	BHGN	249	2	C
Custard pie	GHAC	311	2	B
Custard tart, Swiss	FFBB	170	1	B
Cutting up	BHGN	424		
Deep dish pie	BCC	83	1	C
Dressing	JOC	458	1	C
Onion	JOC	458	1	C
Prune	JOC	458	1	C
Sage	BBA	83	1	B
Sweet potato	JOC	458	1	C
Dumplings	AC	723	1	
◆	BHGN	180	2	B
◆	FFBB	157	2	B
◆	BCC	84	2	B
Dumplings, baked	SC	196	1	
Dumplings, making	GHAC	311		
Endive salad w grapefruit dressing	YGM	233	1	C
Filling	FFBB	538	2	C
Flan	MAFC	657	1	B
Freezing	BHGN	128		
Fritter rings	BHGN	83	1	C
Fritters	SC	101	1	
Fritters	CIC	435	1	B
Fritters	BBA	208	2	B
Fritters, English	CF	83	1	B
Fritters, Sadie Heatter's	MHGD	411	2	B
Game hens w smoked apricot glaze	GF	195	2	C
Ginger upside down cake	NSD	136	2	B
Glazed	NYT	617	1	B
Beef brisket w	GHAC	217	2	C
Broiled	SC	260	1	
Franks, cabbage &	GHAC	212	1	B
Pork tenderloin &	GHAC	191	2	B
Gratin of sauteed, (cold)	MAFC	626	3	B
& Green tomato pie w cream	CW	137	2	B
Griddle cakes	FFCB	496	1	B
Grill, pork &	GHAC	193	1	B
Herb stuffing	GHAC	170	1	B
Honey	JOC	111	1	
Honey custard pie	MC	194	1	B
Jelly	NYT	513	3	
◆	JOC	775	2	
◆	FFCB	702	2	C
◆	BHGN	149	2	B
◆	SC	446	1	
Blueberry	FFCB	702	2	C
Cinnamon	BHGN	149	2	B
Mint	NYT	513	3	
Mint	BHGN	149	2	B
Peeling	NYT	513	3	
Rose geranium	NYT	513	3	
Rose geranium, quick	NYT	513	1	C
Spiced	FFCB	702	2	C
Thorn	SC	446	1	

RECIPE	BOOK	PAGE	TD	S
Apple (*cont.*)				
Juice	BHGN	129	1	B
Krisp	MC	186	1	B
Leather	BTSB	263	2	B
Leather	AC	832	2	
Lemon filling	SC	149	1	
Marshmallow dessert	SC	192	1	
Meringue pie	SC	345	1	
Mint jelly	NYT	513	3	
Molasses muffins	GHAC	368	1	C
Molasses pudding, steamed	JOC	704	2	C
Mousse w apple brandy sauce	SP	269	2	C
Mousse Bretonne	BBA	208	2	B
Muffins	BCC	31	1	C
Muffins	SC	90	1	
Muffins, raisin	BHGN	87	1	C
Muffins, whole wheat	FFBB	567	1	C
New England baked	GHAC	287	2	B
& Noodles	SC	336	1	
Nut filling	BCC	33	1	B
Oatmeal cookies	BHGN	160	1	C
Omelet	FG	95	1	A
Omelet, Roquefort	VE	169	1	A
Onions	SC	423	1	
Or pear tart, baked w French puff pastry	MFC2	457	2	B
Pan dowdy	AC	724	1	
Pancake	BBA	208	2	B
Pancake, puffed	JBGF	623	1	B
Pancakes w broiled apple cider ice cream	NSD	110	2	B
Pandowdy	FFCB	524	2	B
◆	FFBB	96	2	B
◆	GHAC	287	1	C
◆	SC	191	1	

RECIPE	BOOK	PAGE	TD	S
Parsnip sauce	GG	259	1	B
Peanut, caramel	BHGN	113	1	C
Peanuts, curried turkey w	GHAC	163	1	B
Pear salad	BCC	297	2	B
Pectin, homemade	SC	446	2	
Peeling jelly	NYT	513	3	
Pheasant &	BHGN	302	2	B
Pickled	SC	458	3	
Pie	AC	613	1	
◆	FFCB	579	2	B
◆	JBC	38	2	B
◆	JOC	600	3	A
◆	SC	345	1	
◆	BHGN	276	1	B
◆	BCC	83	1	B
Caramelized	SC	345	1	
Deep dish	BHGN	276	1	C
◆	FFBB	93	2	C
◆	GHAC	312	2	C
◆	AC	613	1	
◆	NSD	128	3	C
◆	FFCB	582	2	B
Dutch	BCC	83	1	B
Easy	BCC	83	1	B
French	BCC	83	1	B
Juiced	NYTI	564	2	B
Mock	FFBB	100	2	B
Mock cracker pie	AC	614	2	
Mom's	MHGD	138	2	B
Old fashion, deep fried	WC	142	2	C
Old fashioned w bottom crust	MSQC	125	2	B
Old fashioned w double crust	MSE	247	2	B
Open face	GHAC	311	2	B
Pear, old fashioned	GHAC	312	2	C
Purely	FFBB	80	2	B

RECIPE	BOOK	PAGE	TD	S
Sour cream	SP	272	3	B
Spiced sherry	FFBB	80	2	B
Sugar frosted	GHAC	309	2	C
Sweet potato &	AC	627	1	
Pink	SC	261	1	
Pizza pie, Helen's	FFBB	175	2	C
Poached	SC	261	1	
Pork chops				
Dappled	CFS	146	2	B
& Ginger prunes	YGM	138	1	B
Outdoor roasted	OC	122	2	B
Sauteed	BBA	59	2	B
Pork grill	GHAC	193	1	B
Pork loin of	CFS	154	2	B
Pork patties, spicy	BHGN	251	1	B
Pork, skewered	OC	126	2	B
Praline cream	BBA	209	3	B
Preserves, ginger	SC	439	3	
Pudding	VE	268	2	B
Pudding	BCC	142	1	B
Pudding, brandy	WC	145	2	B
Pudding, Cape Cod	FFCB	650	1	B
Puff	SC	191	1	
Puff pastry or pear tart, baked in	MFC2	457	2	B
Raisin cake w	MHGD	98	1	C
Raspberry crumble	MSQC	129	1	B
Red cabbage, braised	FFCB	370	1	B
Ricotta pie	JBGF	625	1	B
Rings	JOC	111	1	
Caramel	AC	747	1	
Fried	FFCB	282	1	B
◆	AC	747	1	
◆	SC	260	1	
◆	JBC	95	1	
Glazed	BCC	124	1	B
Glazed	JBC	95	1	
Spiced	SC	260	1	
Spiced, making	GHAC	290		

RECIPE	BOOK	PAGE	TD	S
Spiced, roast wild duck w	GHAC	167	2	B
Roast goose w chestnut stuffing & sausage &	GHAC	167	3	B
Roly poly	SC	196	2	
Rose geranium jelly	NYT	513	3	
Rose geranium jelly, quick	NYT	513	1	C
Salad	JBGF	533	1	B
Salad, celeriac	VGCB	72	1	B
Sauce	SC	260	1	
Baked	SC	260	1	
& Cake	JOC	629	1	B
Cookies &	AC	710	1	
Homemade	CFS	147	1	B
Johnny	SP	266	2	B
Parsnip &	GG	259	1	B
Sausage, baked	JOC	231	1	B
Sausage, stuffed	FFCB	212	1	B
Sauteed	GF	196	1	C
Sauteed, Calvados	SP	267	2	B
Scallop w sweet potato	FFCB	405	1	B
Scalloped	SC	192	1	
Sherry honey, poached	BBA	209	1	B
Sliced, baked w rum, raisins, egg & cream	MFC2	434	2	C
Slices				
Crystallized	SC	176	3	
Geraldine's	OC	97	1	B
Grilled	GRIL	90	1	B
Pate &	MSE	45	2	C
Snow	AC	746	1	
Snow	FFCB	651	1	B
Snow	GHAC	288	2	B
Snowballs	SC	200	1	

RECIPE	BOOK	PAGE	TD	S
Apple (*cont.*)				
Souffle	SC	191	1	
Souffles, individual in apples	MFC2	437	2	B
Soup, Hungarian	NYTI	341	1	B
Soup Polonais	CBSS	157	2	B
Sour cream pie	BCC	83	1	B
Spiced	NYT	507	1	B
Squares	BCC	84	2	C
Steam, baked	WC	136	1	B
Steamed	SC	261	1	
Streusel	AC	751	1	
Streusel	SC	192	1	
Strudel	NSD	194	2	B
Strudel	SC	354	2	
Strudel, filling	NYT	541	1	
Strudel, making (photographs)	NYT	542		
Stuffed w sauerkraut	JOC	111	1	B
Stuffed w sausage	FFCB	212	1	B
Stuffed, sausage patties &	BHGN	260	1	B
Stuffing	FFCB	279	1	B
Stuffing, duck roast sausage w	MAFC	275	2	B
Stuffing, prune	FFCB	279	1	B
Swan, making (photographs)	LM	62		
& Sweet potatoes	KIS	298	1	A
& Sweet potatoes	JBGF	530	2	B
& Sweet potatoes	JOC	299	1	B
Tapioca	SC	198	1	
Tart	MFC	224	3	B
◆	LT	384	2	
◆	MAFC	635	2	B
◆	JOC	601	1	B
Custard	MAFC	637	2	B
Ellen's	SP	268	3	C
French	MHGD	194	2	B
Medieval	SP	265	3	B
Normande	MSE	106	2	B
Paper thin	MSQC	65	2	B
Puff pastry, free form	FFBB	179	2	B
Suet	NYTI	30	1	B
Upside down	MAFC	638	2	B
Upside down	LT	387	2	
Tartin, tomato	GG	379	2	B
Tomato marmalade	NYT	512	1	B
Topping for carrot souffle	VGCB	59	1	B
Torte, matzo meal	SC	131	2	B
Torte, Viennese	NYTI	15	2	B
Turnovers	AC	615	1	
Upside down cake, spiced	BCC	71	2	B
Varieties, best ways to use	GHAC	288		
Walnut cake, chunky	SP	271	1	C
Walnut salad, autumn	SP	219	1	B
Walnut salad w chutney yogurt dressing	YGM	87	1	B
Wine turnovers	FFBB	156	2	B
Applesauce	JOC	112	1	
◆	BCC	124	1	B
◆	AC	745	1	
◆	BHGN	128	1	B
◆	MSE	133	1	C
◆	JBC	94	1	B
◆	BHGN	186	1	C
◆	FFCB	650	1	B
Amaretto	YGM	237	1	B
Baked	BBA	128	1	B
Bundt cake	WC	134	2	C
Cake	AC	672	1	
◆	BCC	72	1	C

RECIPE	BOOK	PAGE	TD	S
Applesauce (*cont.*)				
◆	SC	111	1	B
◆	EBE	148	1	C
◆	FFCB	514	1	B
Cake, hot	FFBB	344	1	C
Caramel mold, warm or cold	MAFC	624	1	B
Carrot cake	JBGF	615	2	C
Carrot cake	JBGF	615	2	C
Chocolate torte	SC	125	1	B
Chunky	BHGN	186	1	C
Chunky	GHAC	379	1	B
Coffee cake	BHGN	81	1	B
Cookies	BCC	100	1	C
Cookies	FFCB	552	1	C
Cranberry	JOC	112	1	
Danish	BBA	128	1	B
Horseradish	AC	746	1	
Horseradish	AC	464		
Lemon	JBC	94	1	B
Lemon rum	GG	389	1	A
Loaf	MHGD	260	1	B
Muffins	JBGF	595	1	C
Muffins, rye	FFBB	566	2	C
Oat bread	JBGF	584	1	B
Orange or lemon flavored	AC	746	1	
Potato boats, chunky	BBA	128	2	B
Quick	MSQC	200	1	B
Raisin cake	SP	270	1	C
Raw	BBA	128	1	B
Relish	SC	391	1	
Souffle, sweet potato	JOC	205	1	B
Spice cake	BHGN	95	1	C
Spice cake	MSE	189	2	C
Spice cake	CW	84	1	C
Spiced	JBC	94	1	B
& Squash	BHGN	405	1	A
Strained	JBC	94	1	B
Torte	FFBB	374	1	B
Appliances	FFBB	30		
Appliances for your kitchen	FFCB	37		
Apricot	AC	747		
A la cognac	NYT	618	3	B
Almond bread	FFCB	486	2	B
Almond bread	MC	196	1	B
Almond bread	FFBB	555	1	B
Almond wedding cake	SPGT	116	3	C
Angel cake	EBE	148	3	C
Angel dessert	BHGN	177	2	C
Aperitif	BCC	23	1	C
& Apples	MIE	324	1	B
Baked	MSQC	121	1	B
Baked w vanilla sugar	MSE	88	1	B
Balls	SC	176	1	C
Banana cream	BCC	125	1	B
Bars, oatmeal	BHGN	155	1	C
Bavarian cream	FFCB	653	3	B
Betty	JOC	701	2	B
Blueberry compote	NSD	140	1	B
Bread, quick	JOC	575	2	B
Broiled	FFCB	283	1	B
Brown Betty	FFCB	651	1	B
Butter	JOC	777	2	C
Butter	GHAC	379	1	B
Cake, chocolate	JOC	628	1	B
Cake, pineapple	BCC	73	1	C
Canning	BHGN	129		
Carrots, steamed	CF	31	1	B
Cherry upside down cake	BBA	186	2	C
Chicken	BHGN	301	1	B
Chicken, barbecued	GHAC	221	1	B
Chicken, currant	SPGT	104	1	B
Cobbler	FFBB	96	2	B

RECIPE	BOOK	PAGE	TD	S
Apricot (*cont.*)				
Coconut upside down cake	FFBB	329	1	B
Cookie filling	AC	716	1	
Cream	JBC	96	1	
Cream pie	NYT	523	1	B
Creme	JBGF	633	1	B
Crisp	BCC	124	1	B
Custard filling	JOC	647	1	B
Custard w golden raisins	MSQC	205	1	B
Dreams	EBE	178	1	C
Dressing	JOC	458	1	C
Dried	JOC	112	1	C
Dumplings	SC	104	1	
Filling	FFBB	538	2	C
For coffee cake rolls	JOC	573	1	B
Or sauce using canned apricots	MCF2	507	1	
Walnut cake w, glazed w fondant	MFC2	492	1	
Freezing	BHGN	129		
Glaze	GF	249	1	B
◆	FFCB	542	1	
◆	SC	83	1	
◆	BBA	202	1	
Almonds or glaceed fruits w	MAFC	670	1	
Chicken	FG	241	1	B
For ham	AC	441		
Pears	BCC	131	1	B
Ham, glazed, baked	SP	99	2	C
Ham patties	BHGN	256	1	B
Honey glazed, duck	JOC	473	2	A
Horns	SC	352	1	
Ice	SC	211	2	
Ice	JOC	722	2	C
Ice cream	JOC	717	2	C
Ice cream	SC	205	2	
Ice cream	JBC	97	1	B
Ice cream, flamed	JBC	97	1	B
Ice cream w raspberry syrup	JBC	97	1	B
Icing	JOC	680	1	B
Imperatrice	WC	132	3	B
Jam	MSE	133	1	C
Jam	SC	442	3	
Brandied	BTSB	167	2	C
Dried	SC	442	2	
Pineapple	FFCB	703	2	B
Pineapple, quick	JOC	777	2	
Jelly roll	GHAC	328	2	C
Kuchen	SC	353	1	
Lamb chops, broiled	YGM	132	1	A
Layer loaf	EBE	187	2	B
Leather	JOC	740	1	B
Leather	AC	832	2	
Leather	BTSB	262	2	B
Liqueur	JBC	96	1	
Maple glazed ham	GHAC	202	2	B
Marmalade, pineapple	SC	443	3	
Meringue strips	GHAC	349	1	C
Meringue torte	SC	125	1	B
Mold, fruited	EBE	137	2	B
Mold, spiced	BCC	292	2	B
Mousse	VE	283	2	C
Chantilly	MFC2	417	3	B
Evaporated milk	JOC	720	2	B
Frozen	NYT	632	2	B
Frozen	FFCB	625	3	B
Molded sherbet or ice cream	MFC2	417	3	C
Nectar	BTSB	214	2	C
Nectar	BHGN	129	1	B
Nut bread	SC	85	1	
Nut bread	CBB	487	2	C

RECIPE	BOOK	PAGE	TD	S
Omelet souffle	JOC	692	1	B
Orange balls	JOC	740	1	B
Orange bread	BHGN	78	1	B
Other fruits	JBC	96	1	
Peaches, pickled	GHAC	379	3	C
Pie	BCC	87	1	B
◆	EBE	161	2	B
◆	FFBB	84	2	B
◆	BHGN	277	1	B
◆	JOC	604	1	B
◆	FFCB	580	2	B
Deep dish	AC	614	1	
Peach	BCC	87	1	B
Two crust	AC	614	1	
Pineapple conserve	AC	820	1	
Pineapple jam	FFCB	703	2	B
Pineapple jam, quick	JOC	777	2	
Pineapple pie, deep dish	FFBB	94	2	C
Pineapple preserve	AC	749	1	
Poached	JBC	96	1	B
Poached	AC	748	1	
Dried	AC	748	1	
Flamed	JBC	96	1	B
Liqueur	JBC	96	1	B
w Pear puree	CF	103	1	B
Whole	AC	748	1	
Pork tenderloin	SC	294	2	
Preserves	AC	748	1	
Preserves	JOC	778	2	C
Prune upside down cake	BCC	71	2	B
Raisin bread	SP	251	1	B
& Raisins, baked	SC	261	2	
Rice	MIE	197	1	B
Rum cake	BCC	71	3	B
Rum dip	KIS	329	1	B
Salad, molded	BCC	291	2	B
Sauce	BBA	192	1	A
◆	NSD	331	1	C
◆	GF	250	1	
◆	MHGD	417	1	B
◆	NYT	611	1	B
Sauce, cookies w	AC	710	1	
Sherbet	NSD	230	1	B
Sherbet	MFC2	415	3	B
Sherbet	SC	212	2	
Souffle	JOC	690	2	B
Souffle	SC	195	1	
Cold	FFCB	624	3	B
Frozen	FFCB	627	3	B
Salad	BHGN	339	2	B
Stewed brandy	MHGD	405	1	B
Stewed, okra w (bamiya)	GG	227	1	B
Sticks	EBE	173	2	C
Strudel, prune	SC	355	2	
Swizzle	BHGN	49	1	B
Tart	MAFC	639	2	B
Tart	MHGD	186	2	B
Tipsy	AC	748	1	
Truffles	BCC	116	3	C
Turnovers	FFBB	156	2	B
Whip	FFCB	653	1	B
Whip	JOC	690	2	B
Wine jelly	FFCB	621	2	B
Apulia pasta, homemade	CIC	173		
Aquavit salmon tartare	SPGT	16	2	C
Arancini fried rice balls	FGCW	163	2	C
Armagnac ice cream, prune	NSD	220	1	B
Arni psito (roast leg of lamb, Greek style)	NYT	121		B
Arroz con gandules (rice w pigeon peas)	NYTI	503	1	B

RECIPE	BOOK	PAGE	TD	S
Arroz con pollo (rice w chicken)	NYT	195	1	B
◆	BB	95	1	B
◆	JBGF	430	2	B
◆	BHGN	304	1	B
Artichoke	SC	412	1	
Artichoke	MAFC	423		
Artichoke	JOC	256		
A l'orange	NYTI	490	2	B
A la Grecque	NYT	419	1	A
A la Grecque	MFC	46	3	B
A la Grecque	MAFC	538	1	
As an hors d'oeuvre	JBC	286	1	
Baked, herbed	BCC	333	1	B
Baked, stuffed	AC	468	1	
& Beet, stuffed	NYT	349	2	B
Benedict	GF	116	2	A
Boiled	FAIC	397	1	
Boiled, whole, hot or cold	MAFC	424	1	B
Bottoms				
Canned, uses for	AC	558		
Carrot puree in	MIE	214	1	B
Eggs poached w	MAFC	118	2	B
Filled w spinach	BBA	129	2	B
Fonds	AC	469	1	
Fried	AC	469	1	
w Mushroom sauce	NYT	350	1	B
Preparing	GHAC	228		
Shrimp &	NYT	23	2	B
Stuffed w mushroom puree	MFC2	412	1	B
Braised				
Carrots, onions, turnips w	MAFC	427	1	B
Leeks &	CIC	348	1	B
Mortadella stuffing	CIC	343	2	B
Peas &	GG	16	1	B
Peas &	CIC	347	1	B
Potatoes &	CIC	349	1	B
w Wine, garlic & herbs	MAFC	426	1	B
Butter sauce	BHGN	388	1	A
Butter sauce for cooked	BBA	131	1	B
Capers, shrimp &	NYTI	99	1	C
Casserole, crab &	BBA	100	2	C
Casserole, shrimp, mushroom &	SC	256	2	
Casserole, spinach &	FG	193	1	C
Celery root & potato salad	BBA	129	3	B
Chicken cutlets &	GHAC	158	1	B
Cleaning (photographs)	FAIC	394		
& Cold meat salad	GG	13	1	B
Cold, poached eggs &	GG	21	2	B
Cold, stuffed	AC	468		
Cooking	AC	467		
Cored	JOC	256		
Crisp, fried, whole	CIC	344	1	B
Croisette	GG	21	2	B
Curried egg &	FG	57	1	B
& Eggs, cold, poached	GG	21	2	B
Fava beans, peas, Palermo style	MCIC	360	1	B
Filet mignon &	SC	271	1	
For aioli	NYTI	134	1	B
For roast lamb	NYTI	332	1	C
French fried	BBA	129	2	C
Fried	FAIC	398	1	B
Fried, baby	GG	16	1	B
Fritters, baby	SPGT	21	2	C
& Grapefruit salad	CPMC	146	2	B
Gratin of	MCIC	357	1	B

ARTICHOKE
55

RECIPE	BOOK	PAGE	TD	S
Greek stewed	VE	125	2	B
Grilled	OC	92	1	B
Grilled, pancetta, thyme, tagliatelle &	CPPC	23	2	B
Hearts	JOC	257	1	
Baked	MIE	37	1	B
Buttered w diced vegetables	MAFC	432	1	B
Buttered, quartered	MAFC	431	1	B
Buttered, whole	MAFC	431	1	B
Carrots, braised mushrooms &	MAFC	478	1	B
w Chicken	MIE	106	1	B
w Chipped beef	NYT	118	1	B
Cooked	MAFC	430	1	B
Creamed	MAFC	432	1	B
Creamed	SC	412	1	
Frozen	MAFC	434	1	B
w Gratineed cheese sauce	MAFC	433	1	B
w Herbs, deep fried	CPMC	205	2	B
Marinated	BTSB	140	2	C
w Melted goat cheese	CPMC	201	2	B
Or bottoms, preparing	MAFC	428		
Pasta, asparagus &	CPPC	22	2	B
& Peas (Jerusalem artichoke)	FFCB	433	1	B
Pizza, pancetta, stewed in garlic	CPPC	154	3	B
Preparing (photographs)	LT	173		
Prosciutto, fettuccine &	CPPC	105	2	B
Sauteed	FFCB	359	1	B

RECIPE	BOOK	PAGE	TD	S
Scallops, zucchini &, skewered	GRIL	71	2	B
Steak filet &	MAFC	298	2	B
Stuffed	JBC	11	1	
Stuffed au gratin	MAFC	433	1	B
Vinaigrette	WC	20	1	B
& Zucchini, fried	GHAC	88	1	B
Zucchini, oven fried &	GHAC	88	1	B
w Hollandaise sauce	PPLK	309	1	B
Hot, stuffed	AC	468		
Italian appetizer	BHGN	16	2	A
Italian omelet, crab &	GG	20	1	B
Jerusalem (see Jerusalem artichoke)				
Lamb chops & endive	SP	121	1	B
Lamb riblets, breast of, grilled &	OC	110	3	B
Lasagne	MCIC	184	3	B
Leaves, shrimp &	SC	47	1	
Leaves, stuffed or dipped	AC	470	1	
Lemon butter	MSQC	68	1	B
Monterey, stuffed	GHAC	229	1	B
Moussaka	BBA	100	3	C
Mousse	MFC	168	2	B
Mousse, pigeon puff pastry &	MFC	96	3	B
Mustard sauce	GHAC	229	1	B
Nibbles	BBA	130	2	B
Oil	NYTI	371	1	B
Omelet, Italian crab &	GG	20	1	B
One step	SP	140	1	B
Parsley, stuffed	NYT	349	1	B
Pasta	GG	17	2	B

RECIPE	BOOK	PAGE	TD	S
Artichoke (*cont.*)				
Pasta & broken garlic	CPPC	104	2	B
Pie w a flaky crust	MCIC	335	3	B
Pie & rice, Dolores Tottino's	BBA	99	2	B
Pizza, pancetta, thyme &	CPPC	162	3	B
Poached	GG	12	1	B
Potato casserole	GG	15	1	B
Potatoes, gratin of	MCIC	358	1	B
Preparing	CIC	339		
Preparing	GG	12		
Preparing (photographs)	LT	171		
For cooking	MAFC	423		
For stuffing or baking	NYTI	3		
French	BCC	333		
Step by step	BBA	128		
Provencal baby	SPGT	162	2	B
Prudhomme	PPLK	288	2	B
Puree, Alice B. Toklas'	GG	14	1	B
Puree of	MFC	167	1	B
Puree, ramequins	VE	179	2	B
Quiche, no crust	GHAC	114	1	B
Ramaki (wrapped in bacon)	EBE	11	1	B
Raw celery, fennel, & pinimonio	FAIC	83		
Rice	BBA	99	2	B
Rice	BCC	56	1	B
Risotto	FAIC	216	1	A
Risotto	GG	17	2	B
Risotto, spring lamb kidneys &	CPMC	198	2	B
Risotto w	FAIC	216	1	A
Roman	AC	470	1	
Roman style	NYTI	431	1	B
Roman style	CIC	337	1	B
Salad	BCC	290	1	B
Salad	SC	359	1	
Shrimp &	SP	225	1	B
Shrimp &	FFCB	439	2	B
Stuffed	JOC	84	2	
Sauces for cold	MAFC	426		
Sauces for hot or warm	MAFC	426		
Sausage, carciofi ripieni &	GG	16	1	B
Saute	BBA	130	1	B
Seafood &	BBA	130	2	B
Shrimp & mushroom salad	BBA	140	2	B
Shrimp stuffed	NYT	350	1	B
Shrimp stuffed	AC	54	1	
Smothered w tomatoes & herbs	MSE	174	2	A
Souffle	GG	20	2	B
Soup	BBA	30	1	B
Cream of	CBSS	225	3	B
Creamed	VE	70	1	A
Creamy, California	GHAC	98	2	B
Squid	MCIC	99	2	B
Spinach, Cajun	GG	14	1	B
Steamed	NYT	347	1	B
Stuffed	AC	469	1	
Stuffed	JBC	285	2	
Stuffed	FAIC	398	1	B
Armenian style	NYTI	3	2	B
Baked	JOC	257	1	
Cold	JBC	286	2	
Fontecchio	SP	141	2	B
Sausage &	GG	19	2	B
Sicilian style	WC	30	1	B
Stuffing	NYT	347		
Sunflower	BBA	130	2	B

RECIPE	BOOK	PAGE	TD	S
Tarragon, rabbit stuffed w	FAIC	327	2	B
Tart	CPMC	158	3	B
Tart, hearty	GG	18	2	B
Velvet	BHGN	388	1	B
Vinaigrette	SC	47	1	
Vinaigrette	VE	124	1	
Vinaigrette	BBA	130	2	B
Wedges, fried	CIC	346	1	B
Arugula				
Boston lettuce, julienne red pepper salad	CW	49	1	B
Chicken stuffed w	SPGT	92	2	B
Garden lettuce salad	CF	31	1	B
Limestone & red leaf lettuce salad	GRIL	72	1	B
Pasta w basil, pesto, &	SPGT	63	2	B
Potato soup	MCIC	105	1	B
Salad w cherry tomatoes	MSQC	121	1	B
Salad	VGCB	247	1	B
Salad	SP	211	1	
Soup	VGCB	251	1	B
& Sweet red pepper salad	SP	210	1	B
Veal stew, asparagus &	SPGT	35	2	B
What to do w	SP	210		
Asopao (Puerto Rican casserole w chicken & ham)	WC	55	2	B
Asparagus	YGM	153	1	A
◆	MAFC	434		
◆	JOC	257	1	
◆	NYT	351		
A Chinese way of cooking	AC	561		

RECIPE	BOOK	PAGE	TD	S
A la Holstein, Margi Smith's	GG	29	1	B
A la Parmagiana	GG	29	1	B
All about	VGCB	3		
Ambush	AC	473	1	
Ambush, a modern version	AC	474	1	
w Artichoke heart, pasta &	CPPC	22	2	B
Au gratin	NYT	353	1	B
Baked	BCC	334	1	B
Baked	MIE	211	1	B
Baked w cheese	NYT	352	1	B
Bedded	GG	30	1	B
Beef &	FG	310	1	B
w Beurre blanc	MSE	171	1	B
Blanched or boiled	VGCB	5	1	A
Boiled	JBC	287	1	
Boiled, hot or cold	MAFC	435	1	B
Braised, California celery w	GHAC	230	1	B
Buttered	SMG	243	1	B
California w braised celery	GHAC	230	1	B
Canapes, rolled	JOC	59	1	
Canned, uses for	AC	558		
Canning	BHGN	135		
& Cashews, stir fry	SPGT	31	1	B
Cherry tomatoes &	GHAC	230	1	B
Chicken				
Breasts &	SMG	26	1	B
Grilled w	OC	132	2	B
On toast w	VGCB	8	1	B
Stacks w	BHGN	306	1	B
Cockaigne eggs creamed w	JOC	202	2	B
Cold, lemon	GRIL	71	1	B
Cold, mustard cream	GG	25	1	B
Cold, plain	JBC	288	1	

RECIPE	BOOK	PAGE	TD	S
Asparagus (*cont.*)				
Consomme w dill	SP	150	2	B
Cooked Italian asparagus cooker	CIC	355		
Cooked without asparagus cooker	CIC	355		
Cooking	AC	471		
Corn, timbales, ham	WC	38	1	A
Crab soup	CBSS	227	3	B
Creamed	AC	473	1	
Creamed w eggs	NYT	353	1	B
Crepes	VGCB	8	1	A
Crepes w carrots	FG	100	1	B
Crisp, fresh	MIE	210	1	B
& Dried beef	AC	473	1	
& Dried beef sticks	SC	41	1	
Dutch fashion	AC	473	1	
Egg	AC	473	1	
Egg	VGCB	8	1	A
Egg & bacon w	AC	106	1	
Egg salad	JOC	84	1	B
Egg salad	AC	46	1	
En croute	SP	151	2	B
Florentine style	FAIC	288	1	B
Flounder fillets	VGCB	8	1	A
Freezing	BHGN	135		
French fried	GG	28	1	B
French style	JBC	288	1	
Fresh pasta w	FGCW	143	1	B
Fresh tomato sauce w	NYT	351		
Fried	CIC	358	1	B
Fried egg, lemon &	GG	29	1	B
Frozen	MAFC	439	1	B
Green	SC	412	1	
Green sauce for	SPGT	29	1	B
Grilled & herbed	CFS	236	1	B
Ham &	AC	473	1	
Ham toast rolls &	JOC	246	1	B
Helen Evans Brown	JBC	288	1	

RECIPE	BOOK	PAGE	TD	S
Hollandaise	PPLK	262	2	B
Hot mayonnaise w	SC	412	1	
Hot sauces to serve w	MAFC	437		
Italian style	JBC	288	1	
Lemon buttered	GHAC	177	1	C
Macaroni, cream, ham &	MCIC	142	1	B
Marinated	FG	59	2	C
Meringue	GG	32	1	B
w Mint cream	GG	30	1	B
Minute	AC	474	1	
Mold	MAFC	440	2	B
Mold, chicken lemon &	FFCB	449	2	B
Mousse, chicken &	BBA	68	2	B
Mushroom sauce &	MC	67	1	B
& Mushrooms sauteed	MCIC	366	1	B
Nutmeg butter	SMG	81	1	B
Omelet	MSE	88	1	C
Omelet	SC	225	1	B
Omelet, bacon &	BHGN	197	1	A
Omelet, cheese &	SC	225	1	B
Pan, steamed	CF	139	1	B
w Parmesan cheese	CIC	356	1	B
w Parmesan cheese	AC	473	1	
w Parmesan cheese, fried eggs &	CIC	357	1	B
Parmesan souffle	SP	150	3	B
Pasta	FGCW	143	1	B
Pasta	VGCB	7	1	B
Pasta, lobster &	CPMC	207	3	B
Pastry	VE	126	2	
& Pecans	YGM	167	1	C
Pepper salad	SC	359	1	
Poached, fried eggs w	GF	169	1	A
Polonaise	NYT	353	1	B

ASPARAGUS

RECIPE	BOOK	PAGE	TD	S
Pork, skewered	OC	92	1	B
Preparing	MAFC	435		
◆	GG	24		
◆	BCC	334		
◆	LT	175		
◆	CIC	354		
Prosciutto &	SP	148	1	B
Prosciutto bundles &	MCIC	328	1	B
Puff	VGCB	7	1	B
Puff pastry	BCC	334	2	B
Puff pastry	MFC	42	3	B
Quiche	JBGF	486	2	B
Quiche	GHAC	114	1	B
Quiche	FG	103	1	B
Raw, lettuce salad w mustard vinaigrette	CF	59	1	B
Rice	NYT	325	1	B
Ring	SC	412	1	
Risotto	GG	28	1	B
Risotto	CIC	189	2	B
Roll ups	SPGT	115	2	C
Rolled sticks	SC	42	3	
Salad	JOC	84	1	
◆	AC	46	1	
◆	BCC	281	2	B
◆	SC	359	1	
◆	CIC	411	1	B
Salad, nutty	JBGF	534	1	B
Salad w spicy dressing, Chinese	MIE	264	1	B
Sandwich & ham w cheese sauce, hot	SC	384	1	
Sandwiches, rolled	JOC	59	1	
Sauce	SP	146	1	B
Sauce	MFC	109	2	A
Sauteed	VGCB	6	1	B

RECIPE	BOOK	PAGE	TD	S
w Sauteed sesame seeds	SMG	37	1	B
& Seedless grape, aspic	JOC	99	2	C
Sesame	BHGN	389	1	B
& Shrimp pie	GG	32	2	B
& Shrimp salad	GG	27	1	B
Souffle	VE	173	1	B
Soup	VE	71	2	B
Soup	VGCB	6	1	B
Cold	MFC2	6	1	B
Cream of	JOC	157	1	B
◆	MC	3	1	B
◆	FFCB	84	1	A
◆	SP	149	2	C
◆	SC	400	1	
Cream of, fresh	MFC2	5	1	B
Cream of, quick	JOC	166	1	B
Cream of, stock base	SC	401	1	
Rich	SPGT	28	2	B
& Sour cream casserole	NYT	351		
Spanish	NYT	354	1	B
Spears, garnished	JOC	68	1	
Spears & ham sliced w egg sauce	NYT	151	1	B
Spears, pickled	BBA	166	1	B
Steamed	KIS	157	1	A
◆	YGM	174	1	C
◆	KIS	110	1	A
◆	MSQC	16	1	A
Steamed w orange butter	MSQC	40	1	B
Stew	LM	120	1	B
Stir fried	FFCB	361	1	A
Stir fried	BCC	334	1	B
Stir fried w beef	VGCB	6	1	B
Stir fry	WC	32	1	B

RECIPE	BOOK	PAGE	TD	S
Asparagus (*cont.*)				
Straight talk about	SP	145		
Strudel	SP	148	3	C
Stuffed flounder w	JBGF	452	1	B
Ties	GG	33	1	B
Timbales	JOC	208	2	B
Tip salad	JOC	84	1	
Tips	MAFC	438		
Buttered	MAFC	438	1	B
Ham rolls	AC	451	1	
Prosciutto	NYT	354	1	B
Tomato, stir fry	BHGN	389	1	B
Tomatoes, stuffed	SC	361	1	
Toss	BHGN	331	1	B
Veal stew, arugula &	SPGT	35	2	B
Vinaigrette	NYT	351		
◆	FFCB	360	1	B
◆	MFC	191	1	
◆	SMG	85	1	B
Classic cold	GG	26	1	B
Cold	JBC	288	1	
Salad	NYTI	256	1	B
White	SC	412	1	
& Whipped cream Alice B. Toklas'	GG	31	1	B
Wild	AC	474	1	
Yellowtail fillets w	SPGT	32	2	B
w Yogurt sauce, chilled	JBGF	512	2	B
Aspic	LT	88		
Aspic	LM	162	3	C
Aspic	MAFC	544		
A fine court bouillon for fish	AC	135	1	
All about	JOC	95		
All about	FFCB	442		
Almond black cherry	JOC	101	2	B
Asparagus & seedless grapes	JOC	99	2	C
Avocado	EBE	134	2	B
Avocado ring	NYT	431	2	B
Avocado salad	JBC	253	2	
Beef, boiled, cold	JBC	253	2	
Beef, braised, cold	MAFC	556	3	C
Beef, vegetables, cold	FFCB	448	3	B
Caviar eggs in	NYTI	111	2	C
Chicken	MFC2	255	2	
Chicken	JOC	97	2	B
Cold	JBC	227	2	
Livers	MAFC	548	2	B
& Tarragon	MAFC	549	3	B
Clear	NYTI	264	2	B
Crab	MAFC	549	2	B
Cucumber	FFCB	443	2	B
Duck & orange	FFCB	447	3	B
Eggs (see eggs, in aspic)				
Eggs & tongue	AC	321	3	
For coating salmon steaks	BBA	87	1	A
For salads, basic	JBC	252	1	
For salads, quick	JBC	252	1	
Garnishing (photographs)	LT	89		
Gelatina	FAIC	107	2	
Glaze	JOC	341	1	
Goose liver pate	LM	162	3	C
Ham	MFC2	310	3	C
Ham	LT	291	3	
Ham, parsleyed	FFCB	448	2	B
Ham salad	JBC	253	2	
Jelly	SC	367	2	
Lobster	MAFC	549	2	B
Pea	LM	168	2	
Preparing	MAFC	544		
Quick	NYTI	264	2	B
Quick	NYT	431	2	B

RECIPE	BOOK	PAGE	TD	S
Rum flavored, apple, unmolded	MAFC	627	2	B
Salad	JBC	252	2	
Avocado	JBC	253	2	
Basic	JOC	96	2	B
Ham	JBC	253	2	
Luncheon	JOC	96	2	B
Poached egg	JBC	253	2	
Stuffed egg	JBC	253	2	
Vegetables, meat	JBC	253	2	
Salmon				
Molded	LT	143	3	
Mousse	NYT	435	3	B
Mousse, making	NYT	434		
Sardine & tomato	SC	46	2	
Seafood	SC	372	2	
Seafood	FFCB	447	2	B
Shrimp	MAFC	549	2	B
Shrimp	AC	55	1	
Shrimp, glazed	JOC	73	2	
Stuffed whole fish in	FAIC	264	3	B
Tomato	JOC	100	2	B
◆	BHGN	337	2	C
◆	LM	167		
◆	FFCB	445	2	B
◆	SC	367	2	
Fresh	FFCB	446	2	B
Quick	SC	367	2	
Seafood	JBGF	406	2	B
Vegetables	FFCB	445	2	B
Tongue	NYT	174	2	B
Tongue	JOC	447	2	B
Tongue, eggs in	AC	321	3	
Trout, cold	NYT	260	2	B
Unmolding	JBC	253		
Variations	MAFC	112	3	C
Veal shoulder, braised	JBC	168	2	B

RECIPE	BOOK	PAGE	TD	S
Vegetable juice, canned	JOC	101	2	B
Atjar (Indonesian pickles)	NYTI	367	1	B
Atjar ketimun (cucumbers in tumeric)	NYT	376	2	C
Au gratin	JOC	342	1	
Aubergines (eggplant)	MFC2	344		
Aubergines a la Boston (eggplant in Gruyere cheese sauce)	NYT	377	2	B
Auflauf (apple souffle)	SC	191	1	
Auflauf macaroon souffle	SC	192	1	
Aurore sauce (tomato cream)	JOC	324	1	B
Aurore sauce	VE	86	1	
Avgolemono sauce (golden lemon)	NYTI	321	1	B
Celeriac	VGCB	73	1	B
Grape leaves stuffed w	NYTI	321	2	C
Kohlrabi w	GG	215	2	B
Avgolemono soup	CBSS	99	1	B
Avgolemono soup	NYT	66	1	B
Avgolemono soup, hot	MIE	75	1	B
Avocado				
Apple salad	BCC	297	1	B
Aspic	EBE	134	2	B
Aspic ring	NYT	431	2	B
Aspic salad	JBC	253	2	
Bacon sandwiches	GF	45	1	C
Baked & stuffed, creamed	JOC	112	1	
Balls, piquant	AC	32	1	
& Blue cheese dip	EBE	29	1	A

RECIPE	BOOK	PAGE	TD	S
Avocado (*cont.*)				
& Broccoli salad	SMG	73	1	B
Butter	GHAC	151		
Chicken				
Creamed	SC	317	1	
Curried	GG	42	2	B
Mousse	FGCW	293	2	B
& Potato salad, papaya	GHAC	280	2	B
Stuffing	FFCB	437	2	B
Chutney	JOC	68	1	
& Cocktail shrimp	SC	46	1	
Consomme	JBC	275	2	
Crab Louis	SMG	319	1	B
Cream, Brazilian	GG	43	1	B
Cream, chicken &	SMG	30	1	B
Cream soup	CBSS	230	1	B
Curried chicken &	GG	423	2	B
Dessert, whipped	BCC	125	1	A
Dip	SP	21	1	B
Dressing	JOC	311	1	A
Dressing	BHGN	351	1	B
Filling	SC	382	1	
Filling, crabmeat	BBA	14	1	A
Fruit cocktail	SC	43	1	
Fruit salad	JOC	93	1	
Gazpacho	GG	39	1	B
Grapefruit & honey yogurt	GHAC	283	1	B
Grapefruit salad	JBC	241	1	
Gratinee	GG	38	1	A
Halves & vinaigrette, variations	JBC	240	1	
Ham salad	SP	201	1	B
Heart of palm salad	FFCB	432	1	B
Jody Gillis' sweet & sour	GG	38	1	B
Mayonnaise	GG	40	1	B
Mayonnaise	FFCB	455	1	B
Mayonnaise, cold poached fish w	GG	40	1	B
Mousse, chicken &	FGCW	293	2	B
& Mushroom sprouts salad	KIS	107	1	A
& Onion salad	JBC	241	1	
& Onion salad	KIS	180	1	A
& Orange salad	JBC	241	1	
Orange salad	BCC	298	1	B
Papaya, chicken, potato salad w	GHAC	280	2	B
& Pear grand duc	NYT	419	1	A
Pineapple salad	SC	364	1	
Pizza, tomato &	GHAC	374	1	B
Raspberry vinaigrette	SPGT	95	2	B
Ring	SC	370	2	
Salad	SC	364	1	
Salad	JBGF	534	1	B
Salad	KIS	208	1	B
Cup, variations	JOC	93	1	
First course	GHAC	91	1	B
Hot	GG	39	1	A
Molded	JOC	101	2	A
Orange, grapefruit &	SC	365	1	
Salmon	BBA	14	1	A
Shallot &	VGCB	180	1	B
Spinach &	NYT	417	1	B
Stuffed	SC	361	1	
Salsa	BCC	363	1	
Sandwiches, chicken &	BCC	322	1	B
Sauce	OC	165	1	A
Sauce	BCC	161	1	
Seafood stuffing	FFCB	437	2	B
Seasoned	GHAC	111		
Senegalese soup	BBA	44	2	B
w Shrimp, stuffed	AC	54	1	
Shrimp velvet	GG	41	1	B

RECIPE	BOOK	PAGE	TD	S
Slices	JOC	92	1	
Souffle	BBA	123	2	B
Soup	NYT	80	1	B
Acapulco	CBSS	229	2	B
Chilled	AC	97	2	
Cold	MFC	75	2	B
◆	CBSS	231	1	B
◆	NYT	80	2	B
◆	FFCB	90	1	B
Cream of, quick, chilled	JOC	166	1	B
Cucumber, cold	MIE	80	2	B
Gerald	NYT	80	1	B
& Spinach	GG	41	1	B
Spread	JOC	60	1	
Tomato buffet salad, lobster &	AC	62	1	
& Tomato pizza	GHAC	374	1	B
Veal chops w	GHAC	209	1	B
Vinaigrette New Orleans style	GG	37	1	B
Watercress ring	NYT	432	2	B
Awendaw bread (South Carolina pepper bread)	GG	282	2	B

B

RECIPE	BOOK	PAGE	TD	S
Baba	MAFC	658	3	C
Baba au rhum (rum cake)	WC	128	3	B
◆	MSE	254	3	B
◆	JOC	640	3	
◆	FFBB	338	2	C
◆	NYT	545	2	B
◆	MAFC	661	3	C
Baba cakes	FFCB	526	3	B
Baba ghanouj (eggplant appetizer w garlic)	NYTI	541	1	B
Baba ghanoush (eggplant, tahini spread)	JBGF	293	1	B
Baba paste	MAFC	658	3	C
Babas aux fruits	MAFC	661	3	C
Babas savarin yeast cake	LM	270	2	C
Babka (yeast raised coffeecake)	CBB	606	3	C
Babka	MSE	229	3	C
Babka	MHGD	234	2	C
Baby back pork ribs barbecued in honey, tamari & oranges	GRIL	98	2	B
Baby beets & beet greens	VGCB	23	1	B
Baby leeks, grilled	GRIL	90	2	B
Bacardi	SC	60	1	A
Baccala cream sauce, dried cod w	FGCW	347	2	B
Bacon	SC	298	1	
Bacon	JBC	58	1	
Almond rice salad	BBA	146	2	B
Avocado sandwiches	GF	45	1	C
Batter bread	CBB	602	2	C
Bean rolls	OC	92	1	B
Biscuits	NYT	478	1	C
Bit cornbread	FFBB	569	1	B
Bites, crab	BHGN	44	1	C
Bits, cauliflower	JBC	303	1	B
Blanket				
Chicken livers &	SC	42	1	
Cracker	SC	42	1	
w Deviled olives	SC	42	1	

RECIPE	BOOK	PAGE	TD	S
Bacon Blanket (*cont.*)				
Shad roe &	SC	42	1	
Shrimp &	SC	42	1	
Blue cheese soup w	SP	61	2	B
Broiled	JOC	411	1	
Brussels sprouts &	VGCB	38	1	B
Brussels sprouts &	AC	490	1	
Brussels sprouts &	JBC	297	1	
Buns, Lithuanian	CBB	551	3	C
Cabbage savoy	BCC	341	1	B
& Calf's liver, sauteed	AC	353	1	
Canadian	JOC	412	2	B
Canadian	JBC	59	1	
Baked	JBC	59	1	B
Baked	AC	453	1	
Peach glazed	GHAC	203	1	B
Style	SC	298	1	
Style, cooking	BHGN	257		
& Cheese canapes	EBE	12	1	C
& Cheese canapes	JOC	59	1	
& Cheese pastries	BCC	233	1	B
& Cheese sandwich	JOC	247	1	B
Cheeseburger, the classic	GHAC	187	1	
& Chicken, fried	AC	193	1	
& Chicken livers	BCC	244	1	B
& Chicken livers, onion, apple	GHAC	168	1	B
& Clams, olive oil, linguine &	CPPC	94	2	A
Cooked	AC	453	1	
Cooked	BCC	233		
Cooking	BHGN	257		
Cooking	BCC	233		
Corn bread	GHAC	366	1	C
& Crabmeat, chunks or legs	AC	25		
Crackers	AC	24		

RECIPE	BOOK	PAGE	TD	S
Crepes, Swiss cheese	FG	99	1	B
& Dandelion salad	FFCB	431	1	B
Dressing	FFCB	456	1	B
Dressing, hot	SC	376	1	
& Egg salad, horseradish	SPGT	81	1	C
& Eggs (see also eggs & bacon)				
& Eggs	SC	223	1	
& Eggs, smoked	CFS	278	2	B
Fat, using in cookies	AC	699		
Filet mignon &	SC	270	1	
Filling turnover, cocktail	WC	22	1	C
Flat bread, Bolognese	MCIC	58	3	B
& Frankfurter, wrapped	BHGN	33	1	B
Fried brown rice	GHAC	266	1	B
& Fried chicken	AC	193	1	
Golden rice &	GHAC	268	1	B
Herb bread &	SC	70	2	C
Lettuce & tomato sandwich	FFCB	290	1	A
& Lima beans	AC	483	1	
& Lima beans, boiled	JBC	292	1	A
& Lima beans, onions & mushrooms	AC	483	1	
& Liver appetizers	NYT	15	2	C
& Liver, barbecued	OC	129	1	B
Muffins	NYT	481	1	C
Muffins	FFCB	489	1	C
& Mushrooms, sauteed	AC	525	1	
& Mussels	NYT	18	2	B
Olives in	AC	24		
Omelet	BCC	160	1	A
Omelet, asparagus &	BHGN	197	1	A
Onion & white beans	JBC	341	2	B

RECIPE	BOOK	PAGE	TD	S
Onions & apple, chicken livers w	GHAC	168	1	B
& Onions, pan fried liver w	GHAC	211	1	B
& Orange, glazed, Canadian	BHGN	257	1	B
Oysters &	FFCB	71	1	B
Pasta shells, peas, ricotta &	MCIC	150	1	B
Pasta, three meats, peas &	FGCW	146	1	C
& Pea salad	FG	85	1	B
& Peanut butter sandwiches, hot	SC	384	1	
& Peas	AC	539	1	
Peas	AC	539	1	
Pie, Canadian	BHGN	257	2	B
& Pineapple glazed, Canadian	BHGN	257	1	B
& Potato salad	AC	42	1	
Potatoes baked &	JBC	327	1	
Quiche, cheese &	FFCB	301	2	B
& Rice custard	JOC	181	2	B
Rice & okra	GG	225	1	B
Rice, steamed w onion &	JBC	116	1	B
& Rice stuffing	GHAC	164	1	
Rolls	AC	805	1	
Rolls, liver	NYT	170	1	B
Salad, chicken	BCC	263	2	B
Salad, chicken	GHAC	280	1	B
Salad, chicken &	GHAC	280	1	B
Sandwich	AC	25		
Sandwich, broiled cheese &	SC	231	1	
Sandwich, peanut butter	JOC	248	1	B
Sauce, spaghetti w spicy tomato &	CF	123	2	B

RECIPE	BOOK	PAGE	TD	S
Sausages in	AC	25		
Sauteed	JOC	412	1	
& Shad roe sauteed	SPGT	38	2	B
& Shrimp	EBE	25	1	C
& Shrimp	AC	25		
Shrimp in	AC	25		
w Sour cream sauce	BHGN	209	1	
& Spoon bread	CBB	185	1	B
Tidbits	JOC	71	1	
& Tomato sandwich	AC	805	1	
& Tomato soup	CBSS	358	1	B
Waffles	JBC	23	1	
Waffles, cornmeal	JOC	217	1	B
Wrapped, broiled tomatoes	GHAC	247	1	B
Wrapped, chicken mushroom kabobs	GHAC	222	1	B
Wrapped hors d'oeuvre	AC	24		
Bagel	FFBB	502	3	C
◆	SC	74	2	
◆	BHGN	73	2	C
◆	BTSB	93	3	C
Bites, cheesy	BCC	8	1	C
Egg	BCC	42	3	C
Herb	BHGN	73	2	C
Jo Goldenberg's	CBB	556	2	C
Light rye	BHGN	73	2	C
Onion	FFBB	503	3	C
Onion	BHGN	73	2	C
Poppy seed	BHGN	73	2	C
Pumpernickel	BTSB	95	3	C
Sesame, salted	CBB	531	3	C
Sesame seed	BHGN	73	2	C
Whole wheat	FFBB	503	3	C
Bagel burger, the big apple	GHAC	186	1	

RECIPE	BOOK	PAGE	TD	S
Bagna cauda (anchovy sauce)	NYT	340	1	
◆	VGCB	334	1	A
◆	MSE	71	1	C
◆	BBA	19	1	B
◆	FG	279	1	B
Bagno caldo, celery	NYTI	372	1	B
Bagno caldo, peppers	NYTI	372	1	B
Bagno Maria, double boiler technique	FAIC	27		
Baguettes	MSE	107		
Baguettes, baking (photographs)	LM	249	3	
Bain-Marie	SP	27		
Baked Alaska	FFBB	329	2	B
◆	FFCB	628	3	C
◆	JOC	692	2	C
◆	GHAC	300	3	C
◆	SC	209	3	
◆	AC	740	2	
◆	BHGN	184	3	B
Chocolate	BCC	151	3	C
Flambee French	MFC2	432	3	B
For children	FFBB	330	2	B
Orange	AC	740	2	
Pumpkin	BBA	213	3	C
Baked apples sliced w rum, raisins, eggs & cream	MFC2	434	2	C
Baked apples variations	AC	746	1	
Baked bean soup	SC	399	1	
Baked beans (see beans, baked)				
Baked potatoes, all about	JOC	292		
Baked potatoes, crusty	FFCB	397	1	A
Baker's clay	CBB	723	1	
Baking, high altitude	JOC	648		

RECIPE	BOOK	PAGE	TD	S
Baking powder				
All about	JOC	504		
Biscuits (see biscuits, baking powder)				
Coffee cake	SC	116	2	B
Dumplings	SC	103	1	
Baking soda, all about	JOC	504		
Baking soda, to activate	NSD	17		
Balsamic vinegar dressing	MSQC	56	1	B
Balsamic vinegar, leg of lamb in	FGCW	225	3	B
Balsamic vinegar, what is it	SP	211		
Bamboo shoots	JOC	258	1	
Bamiya okra apricots	GG	227	1	B
Banana				
A Brasileira	NYTI	25	1	B
& Apples in caramel sauce	GHAC	292	1	B
Apricot cream	BCC	125	1	B
Au rhum	NYTI	339		
Baked	JOC	113	1	A
◆	JBC	97	1	B
◆	SC	261	1	
◆	FFCB	654	1	B
◆	AC	749	1	
& Glazed	SC	261	1	
In flambeed rum	FFCB	654	1	B
In their jackets	AC	749	1	
& Rum butter	MSQC	53	1	B
Blankets	JOC	113	1	
Bourbon cake w bourbon creme Anglaise	SPGT	99	2	C
Bran bread	NYT	484	1	B
Brazilian style	NYTI	25	1	B
Bread	SP	248	1	B
◆	SC	85	1	

RECIPE	BOOK	PAGE	TD	S
Banana (*cont.*)				
◆	PPLK	38	1	C
◆	GHAC	366	1	B
◆	JBGF	585	1	B
◆	MSE	299	2	B
◆	BCC	37	2	B
◆	MC	189	1	B
Barley	CBB	175	1	B
Coconut	CBB	473	1	B
Cuban	MHGD	263	1	C
Kona Inn	FFBB	551	2	C
Quick	JOC	575	1	B
Rum raisin	FFBB	551	2	C
Whole wheat	MHGD	262	1	B
Broiled	JBC	97	1	B
Broiled	AC	749	1	
Cake	BHGN	93	1	C
◆	JOC	630	1	B
◆	FFBB	342	1	C
◆	SP	299	2	C
◆	SC	112	1	B
◆	FFCB	516	1	B
Caribbean	BCC	125	1	B
Caribbean	NYT	618	1	B
Caribbean	JOC	113	1	
Chicken wings	MSE	154	2	C
Chiffon cake	SC	122	1	B
Clafouti	CF	139	1	B
Coconut Betty	GHAC	287	2	B
Cookies, soft	FFBB	208	1	C
Cranberry bread	GHAC	366	1	B
Cream				
Filling	FFCB	542	1	B
Filling	FFBB	414	1	C
Freeze	JBC	98	1	B
Peach	BCC	125	1	B
Pie	SC	346	1	
◆	GHAC	320	2	C
◆	FFCB	592	2	B

RECIPE	BOOK	PAGE	TD	S
◆	AC	625	1	
◆	FFBB	111	2	B
◆	BCC	90	2	B
◆	BHGN	281	2	B
Crepes filled w papaya	GF	113	2	C
Crisp cookies	FFBB	207	1	C
Crisp w rhubarb	JBGF	621	1	B
Cupcakes	FFBB	382	1	C
Custard ice cream	SC	208	2	
Custard pie	FFCB	590	2	B
Date bread	GHAC	366	1	B
Drop cookies	BHGN	160	1	C
Flambe	WC	133	1	B
Flambe	EBE	182	1	A
Flambe, grilled	BB	158	1	
Flamed	LT	446	1	
Flamed w rum	JBC	97	1	B
Flaming & glazed	NYT	619	1	B
Fritters	MHGD	412	2	B
Frosting, butter	BHGN	160	1	
Gem pie	EBE	161	1	B
Gratin of	NSD	120	3	B
Green, boiled	NYTI	449	1	B
Grilled	BB	158	1	
Halves, broiled	NYTI	363	1	C
Honey ice cream	NSD	217	1	B
Hot chocolate	KIS	319	1	
Ice cream	NYTI	307	3	B
Ice cream	SC	205	2	
Ice cream w rum	MCIC	452	2	B
Icing	JOC	680	1	B
In their skins	OC	98	1	B
Jam, peach &	BHGN	149	2	
& Muenster cheese	KIS	318	1	
Muffins	PPLK	38	1	C
Muffins, nut &	BHGN	87	1	C
Nut bread	MIE	302	2	B
◆	GHAC	366	1	B

RECIPE	BOOK	PAGE	TD	S
Banana (*cont.*)				
◆	BHGN	79	1	B
◆	FFCB	488	1	B
Nut cake	BCC	73	1	B
Nut loaf, Hana	CBB	466	1	B
Nut salad	JOC	93	1	
Pecan layer cake	NSD	288	3	B
Pie, chocolate	BCC	90	1	B
Pie, sour cream	MC	203	2	B
Pineapple sherbet	JOC	724	2	B
Poached	CW	161	1	B
Raita (bananas w yogurt & spice)	VE	260	1	B
Salad	SC	365	1	
Sauteed	FFCB	654	1	B
Shortcake	NYT	565	1	C
Souffles	NYT	605	2	B
Spiced	BBA	166	1	B
Split	SC	208	2	
Split, Brooklyn	GHAC	302		
Squash, giant, stuffed for a crowd	VGCB	289	2	C
Squash, puree	MIE	228	2	B
Tea bread	NYT	483	2	B
Wheat germ bread, quick	JOC	575	1	B
Banbury tarts (tarts w nuts & raisins)	SC	351	1	
Banbury tarts	FFCB	596	2	C
Banbury tarts	JOC	604	2	B
Banon baked	SP	240	2	B
Bar de luc	SC	448	1	
Bar le duc	JOC	708	1	B
Bar le duc jam (currant jam w honey)	JOC	776	2	
Bar, stocking, $100–$200	BBA	26		
Bar, the ideal home	MSE	33		

RECIPE	BOOK	PAGE	TD	S
Barbecue (see also barbecue sauce, beef, capon, chicken, clams, corn on the cob, duck, eggplant, flank steak, frankfurters, ham, lamb, liver, lobster, spareribs, squid, steak, trout, tuna, turkey, veal)				
Barbecuing	SP	342		
Basting sauce	NYT	445	1	B
Desserts, quick	GHAC	226		
Grilling chart	BHGN	22		
Hamburger	CFS	74	1	B
Making one out of a garbage can	FG	271		
Marinade, kinds of	GHAC	223		
Marinade, soy basting sauce	AC	463		
Mayonnaise marinade	CFS	298	1	B
Pot roast, Al Cribari's	FGCW	207	2	B
Sauce	FFCB	276	1	B
◆	BCC	329	1	B
◆	OC	160	1	B
◆	JBC	265	1	
◆	AC	463	1	
◆	PPLK	247	2	B
◆	SP	14	1	B
◆	JOC	332	1	B
◆	GHAC	226	1	C
A classic	OC	12		
All American	CFS	299	1	B
Basic	BB	146	1	
Basic	SC	390	1	
Brown sugar	JBC	265	1	
California	BB	148	1	
Chicken	FFCB	277	1	B
Chili	JBC	265	1	
Chinese	BB	150	1	
Coca cola	CFS	301	1	B
Cranberry honey	GHAC	226	1	C
Dinah's	CFS	306	1	B

RECIPE	BOOK	PAGE	TD	S
Dynamite	GG	280	1	B
Easy	BHGN	358	1	B
Ferocious	OC	160	1	A
Ferocious	JOC	332	1	
For baked chicken	JBGF	639	1	B
For fowl	JOC	332	1	B
For spareribs	AC	417		
Freetown	CFS	305	1	B
Garlic	JBC	265	1	
Ginger peanut	GHAC	226	1	C
Green pepper	JBC	265	1	
Hawaiian style	SC	327	2	
Hottish	OC	160	1	B
Italian	OC	159	1	B
Italian	BB	147	1	
Jiffy	BBA	152	1	B
LBJ	CFS	303	1	B
Light	FFCB	277	1	B
Lime	NYT	199	1	
Low salt low fat	FG	274	1	B
Mail order	CFS	308		
Mean, meaner, meanest	SPGT	136	2	C
Mexican	BB	147	1	
Mexican I	BB	149	1	
Mexican II	BB	150	2	
New American spicy	GRIL	38	2	C
Oregano	JBC	265	1	
Pungent	BB	148	1	
Quick	BBA	152	1	B
Snappy	BHGN	358	1	B
Southern	FG	272	2	B
Spicy	OC	161	1	B
Spicy	BCC	329	1	A
Tabasco	BB	147	1	
Thyme	JBC	265	1	
Tomato	OC	163	1	B

RECIPE	BOOK	PAGE	TD	S
Traditional	GRIL	38	2	C
Uncooked	BB	147	1	
Zesty	KIS	369	1	A
Southern style, facts (drawings)	FG	270		
Barbecuing, aids to	BB	10		
Barbecuing steaks & chops	SC	328		
Barches (raisin bread)	SC	68	2	B
Barley	SC	179	2	
Bake chicken	JBGF	420	1	B
Bake, toasted	BHGN	326	1	B
Baked	NYT	327	2	B
Banana bread	CBB	175	1	B
Bean soup	GG	340	2	B
Beef soup	BHGN	368	2	B
Beef vegetable soup	GHAC	102	2	C
Bread, Finnish flat	CBB	176	1	B
Broccoli soup, homemade	MCIC	106	2	B
Broth	FFCB	311	1	B
Buttermilk bread	FFBB	449	2	C
Casserole	FFCB	312	1	B
Casserole	AC	584	1	
Casserole	MIE	203	2	B
Baked	FG	120	2	B
Mushroom	BB	137	1	B
Variations	JBC	119	1	B
Curried	FFCB	311	1	B
Garnish	SC	410	1	
Herbed	YGM	75	1	A
Mushrooms	BCC	57	2	B
Orange bread	CBB	177	1	B
Prosciutto soup	CBSS	175	1	B
Rice	FFCB	311	1	B
Ring	SC	179	1	
Salad, crunchy	JBGF	535	2	B
Skillet	BHGN	326	1	B

RECIPE	BOOK	PAGE	TD	S
Barley (*cont.*)				
Soup	JOC	150	1	C
Bean &	GG	343	2	B
Italian	FG	41	2	B
Leek &	VGCB	159	1	B
Mushroom &	MC	25	2	B
Mushrooms, chicken &	CBSS	183	2	B
Variations	FFCB	311	1	B
Vegetable beef soup	BCC	306	1	B
Walnut salad	GHAC	275	2	B
Walnuts	FFCB	311	1	B
Barm bread (Irish tea bread)	CBB	322	2	C
Barolo pappardelle w duck gizzard sauce	CPPC	132	3	B
Barszcz (clear borscht)	VE	55	1	B
Basil (see also pesto)				
Breakfast strata	SPGT	123	3	B
Butter	BBA	152	1	A
Chicken & potatoes	YGM	206	1	C
Cream, baked cucumbers in	GG	151	1	B
Dressing	BCC	284	1	
Dressing, garlic &	BCC	270	1	
Eggplant a la Grecque	MFC2	351	1	B
Eggplant salad	SP	166	1	B
Eggplant sauteed	MFC2	351	1	B
Everything you wanted to know about	SP	166		
Frittata	FAIC	98	1	B
Garlic pizza bread	FFBB	472	1	B
Jelly, sweet	BTSB	172	2	C
Leaves, braised celery in	GG	119	1	B
Macaroni	MFC	173	1	B
Mayonnaise	OC	165	1	B
Mustard butter	SP	116		1
Pesto	JOC	539	1	
Phyllo, seafood	YGM	193	3	C
Pizza w extra cheese	GHAC	374	2	B
Pork chops	NYT	133	2	B
Ratatouille, lemon &	SPGT	165	2	B
Salad, spinach, warm	SPGT	68	1	B
Sauce	FAIC	77	1	C
For linguine, creamy	YGM	95	1	A
Salmon in	MFC	124	2	B
Trenette, pasta in	FAIC	153	2	B
Sliced potatoes in cream	MFC2	388	1	B
Soup, watercress, potato &	SPGT	143	2	B
String beans & tomatoes	FAIC	405	1	B
& Tomato salad	FGCW	377	1	B
Tomato soup, minced	CBSS	354	1	B
& Zucchini soup	CBSS	370	2	B
Zucchini, tomatoes & garlic	MFC2	368	1	B
Basket cake	NYT	560	3	
Basque rice & pepper soup	SP	62	2	B
Basque salad	SP	217	2	B
Bass (see also striped bass)				
Black barbecue, steamed	OC	143	1	B
Coulibiac	MSE	148	3	C
w Fennel, baked striped	SP	116	2	C
Fillets, w grilled mushroom stuffing	GHAC	224	1	B

RECIPE	BOOK	PAGE	TD	S
Or sea trout in puff paste	LM	105	3	C
Oven, steamed, sea	GHAC	134	1	B
Poached in green sauce	GF	73	2	C
Puff paste	LM	105	3	C
Puff pastry	MFC	125	3	B
Salmon, avocado &	MFC	37	1	B
Striped, grilled whole (photographs)	OC	66		
Stuffed, baked, sea	GHAC	134	2	C
Basting sauce for fresh ham	BB	69	1	B
Batter				
A tender for frying	AC	133	1	
Beer	AC	555		
Bread	KIS	351	1	B
Bread, whole wheat w sesame & millet	FFBB	469	2	B
Buttermilk	AC	555		
Crisp, for frying	AC	133	1	
Lemon for frying	AC	132	1	
Tempura	AC	133	1	
Bauernbrot	CBB	204	3	C
Bavarian				
Berry cream	JOC	694	3	B
Butterscotch	SC	203	2	
Charlotte russe	SC	203	2	
Chocolate	JOC	693	3	B
Coffee	JOC	693	3	B
Cream	SC	202	2	
Cream	FFCB	622	2	B
Cream	NYTI	292	2	C
Almond	NYT	591	2	C
Almond	MAFC	599	3	C
Apricot	FFCB	653	3	B
Caramel	JOC	694	3	B
Chocolate	MAFC	599	3	C

RECIPE	BOOK	PAGE	TD	S
Chocolate	NYTI	292	2	B
Coconut	NYT	591	2	B
Coffee	NYT	591	2	B
Eggless	JOC	694	3	B
Hazelnut	JOC	694	3	B
Liqueur	EBE	188	2	B
Maple	JOC	694	3	B
Orange	MAFC	596	3	C
Peppermint candy	AC	736	2	
Raspberry	MHGD	367	1	B
Raspberry	MAFC	600	3	C
Rice & fruits, cold	MAFC	601	3	C
Strawberry	MAFC	600	3	C
Strawberry	NYT	592	2	B
Vanilla	NYT	592	2	C
De Luxe	JOC	693	3	C
Orange	BCC	147	2	B
Orange pineapple	GHAC	294	2	C
Pie pineapple	EBE	169	2	B
Pineapple orange	GHAC	294	2	C
Bavarois a l'orange	NYTI	293	2	B
Bay scallops, fondu bourguignonne w	JOC	370	1	
Bean	AC	592		
All about	JOC	259		
All about	VGCB	9		
Bacon rolls	OC	92	1	B
Baked	SC	183	3	
Baked	BB	100	2	B
Baked	JOC	261	3	B
A la charente	VE	127	3	B
Boston	AC	593	3	
◆	GHAC	232	2	C
◆	FG	285	3	B
◆	JBC	342	2	B
◆	BCC	170	2	B
◆	FFCB	324	3	B
Boston, baked & spareribs	JBC	342	2	B

RECIPE	BOOK	PAGE	TD	S
Bean, Baked (*cont.*)				
Chutney	VE	129	2	B
French	MAFC	399		
Italian	BHGN	391	1	B
Jamaican	NYT	357	3	B
Lamb shanks, &	GHAC	207	2	B
Mutton, shoulder of	MAFC	401	3	C
New York	AC	594	3	
Pennsylvania	AC	594	3	
Pinto	BCC	171	2	B
Pork loin	MAFC	401	3	C
Quick	SC	183	1	
Refried	BCC	174	1	B
Southern	AC	594	3	
Spinach, Santa Fe	GG	316	2	B
Tuscan	FAIC	403	3	B
Without pork	AC	595	2	
Barley	SC	183	3	
Barley soup	GG	343	2	B
Black (see also black bean)				
Black Caribbean	AC	611	3	
Black Cuban	NYTI	68	2	C
Black eyed Hoppin John	GHAC	232	1	B
Black w rice	GHAC	232	1	
Black, tipsy	AC	611	3	
Blanched	VGCB	11	1	A
Boiled	JOC	261	2	B
Boiled	AC	595	2	
Boiled, dried	SC	183	3	
Boiled, Tuscan	FAIC	400	3	
Bretonne	FFCB	325	3	B
Bretonne & ham	NYTI	392	2	C
Brettone	AC	596		
Broad, garlicked	AC	481	1	
Broad, raw	AC	481	1	
Buttered, boiled	AC	596		
Campfire	JOC	261	2	B
Canned, baked & bacon or frankfurters	JOC	261	1	B
Canned, baked fruit	JOC	261	2	B
Canned, uses for	AC	558		
Cannellini, pureed pumpkin & parsnips	VGCB	230	1	C
Canning	BHGN	135		
Casserole	SC	184	1	
Baked	VE	131	3	B
Chili, pungent	JBC	343	3	B
w Ham	JBC	341	2	B
Onion & tomato, pungent	JBC	343	3	B
Pungent	JBC	343	3	B
Three	BCC	173	1	B
Cheese	MC	154	2	B
Chili	FFCB	324	2	B
Chili & dumplings	BCC	173	1	B
Chili, southwestern	AC	605	2	
Chowder, Shaker	CBSS	242	2	B
Cognac, California	AC	606	3	
Cooked w a flask, Tuscan	FAIC	400	3	B
Cooking	JBGF	102		
Cuban, black	CF	47	1	B
Curd	BTSB	283	3	B
Broccoli, pork &	YGM	145	2	A
Hot meat sauce	FG	302	1	B
Oyster sauce Chinese	FG	311	2	B
Soup, stuffed	CBSS	233	2	B
Sukiyaki	SC	414	1	
Different kinds of	SP	152		
Dill	SC	453	3	
Dilly	BBA	166	1	B
Dinner, one dish	JOC	260	2	B

RECIPE	BOOK	PAGE	TD	S
Dip, chilled	JBGF	292	1	B
Dried, cooking	CIC	78		
Dried, cooking chart	FFCB	323		
Dry, soaking	BHGN	375		
Duck	NYT	218	2	B
Easy, baked	BHGN	392	2	B
Eggs, zesty Mexican	GHAC	109	1	B
Egyptian	NYT	41	3	B
Finishing touches for	VGCB	11	1	A
Flageolets, red runner	MSQC	17	1	B
Frankfurters &	AC	599	2	
Freezing	BHGN	135		
Fried, Mexican	BB	108	2	C
Fritter	SC	407	1	
Green, filbert salad	FGCW	138	1	B
Green (see green bean)				
Greene's, out of season	GG	347	1	B
Haricot mutton lamb	AC	393	2	
Hole beans	AC	595	3	
Hot wax, chef's salad w	GG	345	2	B
In sour cream	BCC	336	1	B
In tomato sauce	AC	594	3	
In tomato sauce, baked pork &	AC	594	3	
In tomato sauce, Greek style	FG	114	1	B
Italian, cold	AC	597	1	
Italian style	BCC	335	1	B
& Kale soup	FAIC	124	2	B
Katie's pioneer	AC	595	3	
Kidney (see kidney bean)				
Lemon strings	GG	348	1	B
Lima (see lima bean)				

RECIPE	BOOK	PAGE	TD	S
Loaf	SC	183	1	
Macaroni	NYTI	414	2	B
Marinated	JOC	68	2	
Molasses	AC	594	3	
New England, baked	BHGN	392	2	B
Norman, eggs &	GG	353	1	B
Onion	KIS	219	1	A
Pasta soup	CIC	80	1	B
Pasta soup	CBSS	243	2	B
Pasta soup	FAIC	127	3	B
Pasta soup (see also pasta e fagioli)				
Paste miso, chicken &	FGCW	358	3	B
Paste soup	FGCW	356	2	B
Patties, dried	JOC	260	2	B
Pepper salad	GHAC	274	2	C
Pickled	SC	453	3	
Dilly	VGCB	19	1	B
Green sweet	GG	350	1	B
Sweet	SC	453	3	
Pinto or bolitas frijoles, boiled	AC	605	3	
Puree	AC	596	1	
Pureed, dried	SC	183	1	
Quintet, baked	BHGN	392	2	C
Ranch style	GHAC	233	2	B
Red	PPLK	304	3	B
Red rice	GHAC	232	2	B
Red, stew	AC	604	2	
Refried	SC	183	3	
Refried, cheese	FFCB	325	3	B
Refried, frijoles refritos	AC	605	3	
Rice	AC	606	3	
Rice, Italian style	NYT	319	2	B
Rice, Jamaican	NYTI	448	2	C
Roman green & fontina cheese	GG	345	1	B

RECIPE	BOOK	PAGE	TD	S
Bean (*cont.*)				
Salad	VGCB	12	1	A
Chinese	JBGF	536	2	B
Dilly	JBGF	537	1	B
Dried	JOC	84	1	B
Dried	NYT	427	1	B
Green	AC	46	1	
Green, old fashioned, hot	AC	477	1	
Hot	JBC	291	1	B
Hot five	BHGN	336	1	C
Marinated	VE	115	3	B
Marinated, three	BHGN	336	2	B
Multi	MC	52	2	B
Quick, three	BHGN	336	2	B
Technicolor	SP	220	3	C
Three	BCC	281	2	B
Three	VGCB	18	1	B
Vaguely Chinese string	GG	344	2	B
White	JBC	342	1	
White	AC	596	2	
Salted	SC	455	3	
& Sauerkraut soup	CIC	75	2	B
& Sausage, baked	MAFC	401	3	C
& Sausage, Tuscan	FAIC	354	1	B
Sauteed string & bay scallops	GG	352	1	B
Savory, baked	BCC	171	2	B
Scarlet, runner, cooking	AC	482	1	
Shell				
& Bacon	AC	480	1	
Butter & onions	AC	480	1	
Cooking	AC	480	1	
Hot, finishing touches for	VGCB	13		
Skillet	BCC	174	1	B
Snap (see snap bean)				
Soaking, quick method	NYT	64		
Soup				
Baked	FFCB	92	1	B
◆	NYTI	452	1	
◆	FFCB	92	1	B
◆	SC	399	1	
Black (see black bean soup)				
Chunky, lamb	GHAC	101	2	C
Cream of Sunday	CBSS	252	3	B
Dried	SC	396	3	
Dried	JOC	152	2	B
For the Lombards	FAIC	129	1	B
Frankfurter, quick	BHGN	370	1	B
Hearty	VGCB	16	1	B
Lamb, chunky	GHAC	101	2	C
Lima, hearty	FGCW	110	2	C
Navy	BCC	313	2	B
Navy	AC	94	1	
Parsley, garlic &	CIC	79	2	B
Pistou	VGCB	16	2	B
& Sauerkraut	CIC	75	2	B
Sausage, peppers &	SP	159	3	B
Seven	CBSS	239	3	C
Tomato & fennel	VGCB	124	1	B
Tuscan, pureed	FAIC	119	3	B
U.S. Senate	CBSS	241	2	B
Vegetable	JOC	152	3	C
White pasta	CPPC	147	2	B
White puree, eggplant & tomato	MFC2	22	2	B
Sprout	SC	413	3	
Casserole	SC	413	1	
Cooked	JOC	259	1	B
Salad	MIE	265	1	B
Salad, mung	JBGF	538	1	B

RECIPE	BOOK	PAGE	TD	S
Salad, Oriental	JOC	80	1	B
& Scallions	KIS	268	1	A
Soup	CBSS	235	1	B
Wheat berries & tomato & avocado salad	FFCB	431	1	B
Steamed	VGCB	11	1	A
String (see string bean)				
Sweet & sour	SC	413	1	
Sweet & sour	JOC	259	1	B
Tacos, prairie	GHAC	233	1	B
& Tortilla soup	JBGF	333	1	B
& Tripe	MCIC	309	1	B
Turkish string & lamb cakes	GG	351	2	B
Tuscan w sausages	FAIC	354	1	B
Tuscan, tuna & fresh onions	FAIC	102	3	B
& Vegetable soup	FFCB	94	1	C
& Vegetable soup w ham	BHGN	375	2	C
Vermont pork &	GHAC	193	2	C
Vinaigrette	AC	597	1	
Wax (see wax bean)				
Western style	BCC	173	1	B
White, lamb w	WC	93	1	B
White, sausage w	NYTI	403	2	B
White (see white bean)				
Zesty, Mexican eggs &	GHAC	109	1	B
Bear	AC	246		
Bear, all about	JOC	454		
Bear claws	FFBB	535	3	C
Bear steak	BB	51	2	
Bearnaise				
Mayonnaise	SPGT	155	1	B
Meat glaze	MAFC	85	2	B

RECIPE	BOOK	PAGE	TD	S
Sauce	SC	389	1	
◆	PPLK	306	1	B
◆	FG	225	1	B
◆	SP	340	2	B
◆	BB	154	2	
◆	NYTI	266	1	B
◆	MAFC	84	1	B
◆	JBC	263	1	
◆	AC	460	1	
◆	FFCB	272		
◆	OC	166	2	A
◆	MFC	104	1	B
◆	NYT	446	1	B
◆	BCC	327	1	A
Beef fillet in puff pastry	MFC	149	3	B
Blender	BBA	152	1	B
Blender	BB	154	2	
Cabernet sauce & steak chopped	MFC	152	2	B
Classic	BHGN	356	2	A
For steak	MSQC	172	1	A
New Orleans	PPLK	261	1	B
Quick	NYT	446	1	A
Salmon steaks grilled w	OC	148	2	B
Steak broiled w	MSQC	172	1	A
Steak filet, artichoke hearts &	MAFC	298	2	B
Steak pan broiled &	MAFC	295	2	B
Tomato	CFS	312	1	B
Tomato, flavored	MAFC	85	2	B
Tomato, herbs	BBA	162	1	B
Beaver	JOC	454	2	
Beaver tail	JOC	454	2	
Bechamel (butter sauce)	FGCW	287	1	B

RECIPE	BOOK	PAGE	TD	S
Bechamel	FAIC	52	1	B
Beets	AC	485	1	
Parmigiano cheese	FAIC	76	1	B
Potatoes, mashed & herbed	GF	226	1	C
Sauce	NYT	443	1	B
◆	MFC	108	1	B
◆	MAFC	57	1	B
◆	FFCB	265	1	B
◆	VE	84	1	
◆	NYTI	267	1	B
◆	AC	457	1	
◆	SP	341	2	B
◆	CIC	28	1	B
◆	JBC	261	1	
◆	MCIC	20	1	
◆	FG	224	1	B
Enriched	BBA	90	1	A
For pastitso	FG	343	1	B
Making (photographs)	LT	42		
Stuffed mushrooms w	CIC	46	1	B
& Variations	JOC	322	1	B
Beef (see also hamburger, steak, liver)				
A la flamande, carbonnades of	NYTI	21	2	B
A la Lindstrom	FFCB	170	1	B
A la Lindstrom	NYTI	528	2	B
A la mode	SC	272	2	
A la mode	FFCB	159	2	C
Al Cribari's, barbecued pot roast	FGCW	207	2	B
All about	JBC	122		
& Asparagus	FG	310	1	B
Aspic, braised, cold	MAFC	556	3	C
Au jus	BHGN	234	1	
Au Madere	NYTI	160	1	B
Baguette, slices of	BCC	316	1	B
Balls, cumin	YGM	178	1	C
Balls, Oriental	NYT	108	1	B
Barbecued	NYTI	459	1	B
& Barley soup	MIE	69	2	C
& Barley soup	BHGN	368	2	B
& Barley vegetable soup	GHAC	102	2	C
Beer	GHAC	180	2	B
Birds	BBA	52	3	B
Birds	AC	299	2	
Birds	SC	275	2	
Black bean sauce, stir fried	MIE	171	1	B
& Bleu cheese	FGCW	205	1	B
Boeuf a la Bourguignonne	AC	297	2	
Boeuf en daube glace (casserole served cold)	AC	292	2	
Boiled	JOC	413	2	B
◆	JBC	153	2	B
◆	NYT	94	1	B
◆	FAIC	268		
◆	SC	276	1	
& Accompaniments	NYTI	165	2	B
Basic dinner	AC	301	2	
Cold	JBC	153	2	B
Leftover w leeks	FAIC	272	2	B
Viennese	NYT	95	2	B
Bones, deviled	BB	22	1	
◆	JBC	138	1	
◆	AC	283	1	
◆	BBA	50	1	B
◆	MIE	124	1	B

RECIPE	BOOK	PAGE	TD	S
Bouillion	FFCB	80	3	C
Canned	MAFC	67	1	B
& Marrow balls	FFCB	80	3	C
& Noodles	FFCB	80	3	C
Bouquetiere, fillet of	AC	282	1	
Bourgeois, emince of	NYT	93	1	B
Bourguignonne	BHGN	367	2	C
Braciole, stuffed Sicilian style	MCIC	247	1	B
Braised	JBC	144	2	B
A la mode	JBC	143	2	B
A la mode cold	JBC	143	2	B
Aspic	LT	278	3	
& Beer	JBC	144	2	B
Bordeaux fashion	JBC	142	2	B
w Celery & onions	MCIC	255	1	B
Cold	MAFC	312	3	C
Fillet of	WC	89	2	B
w Ham stuffing	MFC2	386	1	B
Hungarian style	JBC	144	2	B
In red wine	JBC	144	2	B
In red wine	MAFC	309	3	C
In red wine sauce	CIC	242	2	B
Italian style	JBC	140		B
Larded	NYT	99	3	B
w Onions	MCIC	253	1	B
Pot roast Provencal	MFC2	161	3	C
Pot roast, stuffed	MFC2	166	3	C
Stuffing ham	MFC2	386	1	B
Texas barbecued	WC	86	1	B
Brandy broth	BBA	30	2	B
Brew	BBA	96	2	C
Brisket (see also brisket, beef)				
Apple glazed	GHAC	217	2	C
Barbecue	BCC	198	2	C
& Beans	SC	276	2	
& Cabbage	SC	277	1	
Carving a	BCC	199		
& Green sauce boiled	FG	154	2	
& Sauerkraut	SC	276	2	
& Sauerkraut	JOC	415	2	B
Smoked barbecue	FG	272	2	C
Spicy	GHAC	178	2	C
Broccoli w curried rice	WC	86	1	B
Broiled w sauteed onions	CIC	244	1	B
Broth	WC	125	2	B
Broth	BCC	306	2	B
Broth, molded (brawn or head cheese)	AC	419		
Brown rice fet casserole	FFCB	172	1	B
Bulgur	KIS	243	1	B
Bulgur salad	BCC	272	2	B
Burgers	OC	106	2	B
Burgundy	FG	329	3	B
Burgundy	FFCB	164	2	B
Burgundy popovers	BCC	205	2	B
& Cabbage leaves	JOC	431	2	B
Cannelon of	FFCB	170	1	B
Carbonnade	SP	126	2	B
Carbonnade of	EBE	51	2	C
Carving	JOC	388		
Casserole				
& Garlic anchovy sauce	MAFC	324	1	B
Oriental	SC	279	2	
& Red wine	SC	274	2	
Stew	SC	274	2	
w Wine & vegetables, hot or cold	MAFC	322	1	B
Celery soup	GG	120	2	B
Chart	SC	267		
Chart (photographs)	BHGN	228		

RECIPE	BOOK	PAGE	TD	S
Beef (*cont.*)				
Chicken soup	SC	396	3	
Chinese	EBE	52	1	B
Chipped				
& Creamed baked potatoes	AC	307	1	
& Creamed mushrooms	AC	307	1	
& Macaroni, baked	SC	339	1	
w Scrambled eggs	AC	307	1	
Chops				
& Bread crumbs	OC	114	1	B
Classic	CFS	174	2	A
Groundhog	CFS	176	2	A
Minted	CFS	175	2	A
Pan broiled	FFCB	186	1	B
Super	CFS	177	2	A
Churrasco roaste	EBE	53	3	C
Coated & skewered	OC	103	2	B
Cold boiled in aspic	JBC	253	2	
Cold, roast	AC	283		
& Corn casserole	FFCB	169	1	B
& Corn, stir fry, Mexican style	WC	82	2	B
Corned (see corned beef)				
Corned	SC	277	3	
Corned w cabbage & horseradish cream	GG	81	2	B
Corned, glazed	SP	98	2	B
Cornucopias, chipped	JOC	71	2	
Creamed dried	JBC	61	1	
Creamed dried	BHGN	241	1	A
Creamed dried	FFCB	163	1	B
Cubes, marinated & peppered	BB	86	1	
Cubes, piquant	BB	86	2	
Cubes, shaking	YGM	173	3	C

RECIPE	BOOK	PAGE	TD	S
Cubes, tenderized	BB	85	1	
Curry	SC	275	1	
Curry	NYTI	31	2	B
Curry Vindaloo	NYTI	353	1	B
Cutlets or veal, deep fried	FAIC	281	2	B
Cuts of, chart	JOC	390		
Cuts of, chart	CFS	70		
Daube de boeuf en gelee	NYTI	164	3	C
Daube de boeuf Provencale	EBE	54	3	B
& Deviled beans	WC	100	2	A
& Deviled noodles	WC	100	1	B
Diable w ground fried noodles	WC	85	1	B
Dried, asparagus w	AC	473	1	
Dried & eggs	SC	224	1	
Eggplant casserole	NYT	109	1	B
Eggplant salad	BCC	272	2	B
En casserole	NYT	96	2	B
Enchiladas	GHAC	181	2	B
Esterhazy	NYTI	6	1	B
Etouffee (roast beef w vegetables)	AC	291	2	
Extract	BTSB	34	3	C
Filet	SP	97	1	C
Fillet	JOC	399	1	
Braised, w stuffed foie gras	MAFC	303	3	B
Flambe	AC	281	1	
w Madeira sauce	NYTI	160	1	C
Pan fried	MSQC	164	1	A
Puff pastry w sauce bearnaise	MFC	149	3	B
w Red wine	MCIC	249	1	B
Rosemary on French bread	MSE	50	2	C
w Truffle sauce	LM	39	3	B

RECIPE	BOOK	PAGE	TD	S
Filling for enchilladas	FFCB	303	1	C
Filling for tacos	FFCB	303	1	C
Filling, smoked	SC	381	1	
Filling, turnover cocktail	WC	22	1	C
Fondue	BHGN	238	1	B
Goulash	JOC	417	1	B
Budapest I	NYT	105	2	B
Hungarian I	NYTI	343	2	B
Hungarian II	NYTI	343	2	B
Stew, quick	BHGN	368	1	B
Gratin of	FFCB	172	1	B
Green beans, ground	JBGF	466	1	B
Grilled, fillet of, w black peppercorns	MSQC	188	1	B
Grilled, leftover, boiled	MCIC	257	1	B
Grilled, whole fillet of	CPMC	63	2	B
Ground				
Hungarian goulash	WC	92	1	B
On toast	SC	282	1	
Onions & herbs	MAFC	301	1	B
Stew country style	WC	88	2	B
Stir fry Hawaiian style	WC	77	1	B
Stroganoff	WC	104	1	B
Gumbo	JOC	152	2	C
Hash (see also corned beef hash)				
Braised	WC	79	1	B
Roast	GHAC	176	1	C
Roast	AC	283	1	
Heart, broiled	AC	319	1	
Heart hamburgers	AC	319	1	
Heart, stuffed	AC	319	2	
Herb, wrapped filet of	SPGT	131	2	C
Hibachi	BB	94	2	B
In wine on skewers	FGCW	210	2	B
Kebabs	JOC	402	1	B
Chicken	OC	133	2	B
Curried	CFS	95	2	B
Fiesta	BHGN	27	3	B
Grilled Caribbean style	CFS	96	2	B
Molded	OC	107	2	B
Kidney pie, English	NYT	117	2	B
Kidney stew	JBC	161	2	B
Kidney stew	AC	318	1	
Kidney stew	NYT	169	2	A
Leeks & peppers, Chinese	FG	312	1	B
Liver				
A la bourguignonne	AC	318	1	
Creole	JOC	440	1	B
En brochette	AC	317		
Roast	AC	317		
w Sage	MSQC	216	1	A
Steak	AC	317		
Lo mein	JBGF	466	2	B
Loaf	SC	277	1	
Loaf	AC	309	1	
Loaf, Chinese, ground	MIE	148	1	B
Loaf w tomato	AC	310	2	
Lucien, tendret filet of	CPMC	102	2	B
Marinade	PPLK	269	2	B
Marinade of, fillet	MAFC	306	3	B
Marinated, fillet of	AC	281	2	
Marinated, on skewers	OC	104	2	B
Mushroom loaf	SC	278	1	
Mustard sauce	BCC	200	1	B
Noodle, Boston style	WC	79	1	B
Noodle casserole	FFCB	331	2	B
Noodle, Chinese	KIS	227	1	A

RECIPE	BOOK	PAGE	TD	S
Beef (*cont.*)				
Olive	NYT	104	2	B
On skewers	JOC	402	1	B
Onion	FGCW	236	2	A
Braised in beer	MAFC	317	1	B
Chinese	EBE	47	1	B
Deviled	WC	78	1	B
Or lamb vinaigrette & variations	AC	71	1	
Orange, flavored	YGM	200	2	C
Oyster, Ming's	FG	161	1	B
Oyster pie	GHAC	181	2	B
Oyster, sauce for	PPLK	246	2	B
Paprika stew	KIS	215	1	B
Patties w anchovies & mozzarella	CIC	245	1	B
Paupiettes de boeuf	MAFC	318	2	B
& Peanuts	WC	87	1	B
Peas & onions	FFCB	172	1	B
& Pepper salad, marinated, Oriental	MIE	284	2	B
Perigourdine	NYTI	102	2	C
Peter Hyun's barbecued Korean	OC	101	2	B
Picadillo	NYTI	25	1	B
Pickled	SC	277	3	
Pie	AC	324	2	
w Biscuit crust	AC	326		
Corn &	YGM	182	2	C
Herbs &	NYT	116	2	B
Leftover	AC	326	1	
Potatoes & variations	AC	325		
Pork				
Chicken, sausage & vegetables, boiled	MAFC	306	3	C

RECIPE	BOOK	PAGE	TD	S
& Liver terrine	FG	177	3	C
Meat loaf	SC	278	2	
Sweet potatoes Madras style	GG	361	1	B
Terrine, ham &	FG	178	3	C
Pot pie	JOC	225	2	
Pot pie	FFCB	173	1	B
Pot roast (see also pot roast of beef)				
Pot roast	BHGN	235	2	B
Pot roast	JOC	414	2	B
Basic	AC	286	2	
Braised, Provencal	MFC2	161	3	C
Braised, stuffed	MFC2	166	3	C
Florentine style	FAIC	340	2	B
w Port & mushrooms	FGCW	202	2	B
Pumpkin	GG	330	2	B
w Sour cream wine	JOC	414	1	
Potato & pickled herring salad	CF	74	1	B
& Potato salad, cold	MAFC	543	2	B
& Potato shells	BCC	210	1	B
Potted, Italian style	NYT	102	2	B
Pressed, cold	AC	301		
& Pumpkin pot roasted	GG	330	2	B
Quick saute of	SMG	252	1	B
& Radish sticks	FGCW	327	1	B
Ragout of	BCC	238	2	B
Ragout of	NYTI	171	2	B
Ragout of	NYT	97	2	B
Red, cooked Chinese style	WC	78	1	B
Red w wine broth	SP	61	2	B
Red w wine mushrooms	FGCW	203	2	C
Rib steaks, Gypsy style	OC	101	2	B

RECIPE	BOOK	PAGE	TD	S
Ribs, Chinese style	BHGN	239	3	B
& Rice casserole, western	NYT	109	1	B
Ring, hidden	BCC	213	1	B
Roast				
Fillet of	SC	269	1	
Fillet of, tenderloin roast	AC	280		
Fillet of w vegetables	SC	269	1	
French style	BCC	197	2	B
Leftover	JBC	137	1	
Tuscan	CFS	99	1	B
Roasting chart	SC	268		
Roll	JOC	418	1	
w Anchovies & red wine	AC	300	2	
Braised & stuffed	MAFC	318	2	B
Chipped	FFCB	57	1	C
Cuban	CF	94	2	C
Deviled	BHGN	241	1	B
Dried	FFCB	57	1	C
w Egg filling	SMG	254	2	B
Italian	NYTI	388	2	B
Piquant	JBC	147	2	B
Stuffed	BB	85	1	
Stuffed	GHAC	176	2	C
Stuffed, giant	MFC2	156	3	B
Stuffed w peppers, onions & mustard bread	MFC2	159	1	B
Roulades	EBE	48	3	B
Saffron	NYTI	522	2	B
Salad	AC	70	1	
Salad	JBC	154	1	
Cold	MSE	287	3	C
Filling	BCC	321	1	B
Marinated	SP	203	2	B
Marinated using prepared beef	SP	203	1	B
Salade vinaigrette	NYTI	174	1	B
Sandwich, cold boiled or pressed	AC	805	1	
Sauce, spaghetti	BCC	209	1	B
Sausages Provencale, left over	MFC2	306	3	C
Saute w cream mushroom sauce	MAFC	325	1	B
Saute of, Hungarian style	NYTI	343	1	B
Saute w red wine mushrooms, bacon & onion	MAFC	326	1	B
Saute w tomato sauce, olives & herbs	MAFC	327	1	B
Scallions	YGM	152	1	A
Scallions w mushroom sauce	FFCB	173	1	B
Seamen's (ground beef w potato patties)	SC	280	1	
Sesame	BCC	206	1	B
Shanks, braised	BCC	216	2	B
Shanks w summer squash	OC	98	2	B
Short ribs (see also short ribs, beef)				
Short ribs, savory	BCC	206	1	B
Shreds, hot	FG	159	1	B
Shreds, Korean	NYTI	461	1	B
Sirloin rolled & stuffed	FAIC	337	1	B
Skewered	OC	106	1	B
Skillet, Texas	BHGN	245	1	B
Slices, deviled	JBC	138	1	
Smoked & eggs	SC	1		

RECIPE	BOOK	PAGE	TD	S
Beef (*cont.*)				
Smoked, filling	SC	381	1	
Snacks, dried	SC	41	1	
Soup & meatballs	FG	43	2	B
& Sour cream	NYT	106	2	B
& Soy sauce, spiced	NYTI	48	1	B
Spaghetti, quick	JOC	185	1	B
Spiced	JOC	416	3	B
Steak	SC	328	1	
Broiling	BHGN	238		
Broiling timetable for	BCC	199		
Panbroiling	BHGN	238		
Provencale	BCC	201	2	B
Stew	BHGN	367	1	B
Stew	SC	275	2	
Stew	BCC	205	2	B
American	AC	295	2	
Belgian	JOC	418	2	B
Brown	AC	294	2	
Carbonada criolla	VG	232	2	B
Chianti Florentine style	FAIC	342	2	B
Cicely's (Pennsylvania beefstew)	AC	296	2	
w Cuminseed	SP	125	2	B
Easy	SC	276	1	
Florentine Chianti	FAIC	342	2	B
w Garlic & anchovy finish	MFC2	152	2	B
w Garnish of peppers & tomatoes	MFC2	152	2	B
Gaston (stew w sherry or white wine)	JOC	414	2	B
w Ginger, capers & herbs	MFC2	154	2	B

RECIPE	BOOK	PAGE	TD	S
Greek	CBSS	64	2	B
Hearty Creole	WC	80	1	B
Herb, cheese & garlic finish	MFC2	152	2	B
In a pumpkin shell	BBA	96	3	B
Marsala	FG	356	1	B
Old fashioned	FFCB	163	2	B
Olives, potatoes &	MFC2	153	2	B
Onions & red wine	MFC2	149	2	B
Peasant style	FGCW	206	3	B
Peppery	FAIC	323	2	B
Peruvian (bistee a la caserola)	NYTI	495	2	B
Pressure cooked	GHAC	180	2	B
Provencale	BBA	97	3	B
Provencale	BCC	201	2	B
Pumpkin in a pumpkin shell, carbonada	VGCB	232	2	B
Quinces	NYTI	329	2	B
Red wine, bacon, onions & mushrooms	MAFC	315	2	B
Red wine, Burgundy style	CBSS	78	3	B
Red wine & peas	MCIC	251	1	B
Rice, onions & tomatoes	MAFC	321	1	B
Rosemary, Italian	NYTI	389	2	B
w Rum & olives	CF	118	2	C
Sour cream	CBSS	76	3	B
Southwestern	AC	295	1	
w Turnips	GG	393	2	B
Variations	JBC	151	2	B
w Wine	JOC	415	2	B
w Wines & herbs	NYT	100	2	B
Stir fried	BCC	204	2	B
Stir fried w cauliflower	VGCB	68	1	A

RECIPE	BOOK	PAGE	TD	S
Stock (see also stock, brown)				
◆	SP	341	2	C
◆	BHGN	366	3	C
◆	FFCB	79	3	C
◆	GG	409	2	B
◆	NYTI	115	2	B
◆	JBGF	309	2	B
Or bouillon	NYT	57	2	C
Ordinary	AC	86	2	
Strips w paprika cream sauce	SMG	250	1	B
Strips, smoky	FG	323	1	B
Strips, soy	BB	86	1	
Stroganoff	NYTI	511	1	B
◆	FFCB	160	1	B
◆	JOC	401	2	B
◆	BHGN	237	1	B
◆	BCC	202	1	B
◆	SP	128	2	B
◆	NYT	90	2	B
◆	SMG	248	1	B
◆	JBC	152	1	B
◆	SC	271	2	
Stroganoff, fillet of	AC	273	1	
Stuffed, Cuban	NYTI	67	3	C
Stuffed, eggplant	WC	101	2	A
Stuffed, fillet of	AC	281	2	
Stuffed, peppers	SC	425	1	
Stuffing for cabbage leaves	NYT	369	2	B
Sukiyaki (see also sukiyaki, beef)				
Sukiyaki	NYT	89	2	B
Sweet & sour, boiled	SC	277	2	
Tangy, barbecued	OC	98	2	B
Tartare	FFCB	63	1	B
Tea	JOC	147	1	A

RECIPE	BOOK	PAGE	TD	S
Tenderloin (see also tenderloin, beef)				
Tenderloin	JOC	399	1	
Teriyaki (see also teriyaki, beef)				
◆	WC	87	2	B
◆	KIS	211	1	A
◆	SC	272	2	
◆	BHGN	26	1	B
◆	BCC	200	2	B
Barbecued	BB	91	2	
I	NYTI	454	1	B
II	NYTI	454	2	C
Thai barbecue	OC	101	2	B
Tofu loaf	JBGF	461	2	B
Tomato sauce	JBGF	364	1	B
& Tomatoes, stir fried	KIS	235	1	A
Tongue (see also tongue, beef)				
Tongue, glazed	BCC	218	2	B
Tongue, smoked	JBC	161	2	B
Turnip stew	GG	393	2	B
Veal, cold fillet of, mustard sauce	GF	26	2	C
Vegetable				
Aspic of cold	FFCB	448	3	B
& Fettucine salad	JBGF	411	2	B
Kabobs in peanut sauce	GHAC	220	2	B
Oriental	SC	272	1	
Soup, southern style	SC	397	2	C
Stew, Columbian	NYTI	65	2	B
Stir fry	BHGN	239	1	B
Venetian style, quick fried	FGCW	208	1	B
Wellington	BHGN	233	3	B

RECIPE	BOOK	PAGE	TD	S
Beet (*cont.*)				
In mustard sauce	GG	51	1	B
In sour cream	NYT	364	1	B
In sour cream	JBC	244	2	B
In sour cream	AC	484	1	
In sour cream, cold	JBC	294	1	A
Khuta chicken	NYTI	356	2	B
Leaves, young	JOC	264	1	B
Madrilene	BBA	44	2	B
Mint, tangy	GG	50	1	B
& Onion	JBC	294	1	A
Onion & endive salad	CF	15	1	B
& Onion salad	JBC	244	1	B
& Onion salad	NYTI	257	1	C
Onions & herbs	AC	485	1	
& Orange	BCC	337	1	B
& Orange	NYT	365	1	B
Glazed	BHGN	392	1	B
Scented	GG	52	1	B
Vinaigrette	CPMC	106	1	
Oven steamed	GG	49	1	
Panned	SC	414	1	
Pasta & spinach greens	CPMC	223	2	B
Persian	GG	48	1	B
Pickled	BCC	285	3	B
◆	FFCB	365	1	B
◆	GHAC	378	3	C
◆	FFCB	711	2	C
◆	AC	485	1	
◆	NYT	498	3	B
◆	VGCB	24	2	B
◆	NYTI	83	2	B
◆	AC	485	1	
◆	SC	453	3	
◆	BHGN	362	3	B
◆	MSE	188	2	B
Cold	SC	414	1	
Hot	JBC	294	1	A

RECIPE	BOOK	PAGE	TD	S
Irma Wehausen's	GG	52	2	B
Salad w red onions, wilted	CW	100	2	B
Sweet	SC	453	3	
& Pineapple	BHGN	393	1	B
& Potato salad	JBC	244	1	B
& Potato salad, Russian	VGCB	25	1	B
Preparing	GG	46		
Preparing	BCC	337		
Preserves	SC	440	2	
Preserves	NYT	503	1	B
Puree of	MSQC	161	1	A
Relish	SC	456	3	
Relish	VGCB	27	1	B
Relish	FFCB	283	1	B
Roquefort salad, walnuts	SP	218	2	B
Salad	LM	154	1	B
Celery &	NYT	421	1	B
Cold	MSE	105	1	C
Herring &	SC	363	3	
& Horseradish dressing	JBGF	540	2	B
Jeweled	GHAC	277	2	C
Molded	SC	369	2	
Mustardy	JBGF	539	2	B
Pickled	JOC	85	2	B
Potato &	MAFC	543	3	C
Rice &	MAFC	543	3	C
Scandinavian	VGCB	25	1	B
Yellow tomato &	SC	360	1	
Scallion appetizer	NYT	41	2	B
Shredded	FFCB	366	1	B
Sorbet	GF	136	2	B
Sorbet, sour cream yogurt sauce for	GF	136	1	B
Souffle	GG	53	2	B

RECIPE	BOOK	PAGE	TD	S
Soup (see also borscht)				
◆	NYT	67	1	B
◆	SC	394	3	
◆	JOC	151	1	B
Cabbage &	FFCB	85	1	B
Meatless	SC	399	1	
Vegetable &	GHAC	102	1	C
Zucchini &	MSQC	104	1	B
Steamed	VGCB	22	1	A
Stuffed	NYT	420	2	B
Stuffed, herring &	BBA	18	1	B
Stuffed, peas &	SC	359	1	
Sugared	FFCB	365	1	B
Sweet & sour	JOC	264	1	B
Sweet & sour, apple &	JOC	264	2	B
Tangy & minted	GG	50	1	B
Tartar	VGCB	24	1	A
Tops, salad, red	MCIC	418	1	B
& Vegetable soup	GHAC	102	1	C
Vinaigrette	VGCB	24	1	B
Vinaigrette, cold	JBC	294	2	A
Vinaigrette, cold	CF	39	1	B
Vinegar	SC	437	3	
Walnut & orange vinaigrette	CPMC	201	1	B
Beetroot salad, chicory	JOC	80	1	B
Beignets (New Orleans style doughnuts)	JOC	706	2	B
A la New Orleans	WC	148	2	C
Au fromage	NYT	47	2	C
New Orleans	GHAC	369	1	C
Souffles	NYT	533	2	
Souffles dessert	BBA	194	3	B
Belgian waffles	AC	798	1	
Bellinis a la Venezia	CF	134	1	B

RECIPE	BOOK	PAGE	TD	S
Benedictine	JOC	39	1	
Benne				
Pastries	FFCB	67	1	C
Seed biscuits	CBB	533	1	B
Seed cookies	YGM	244	1	C
Seed wafers	FFBB	211	1	C
Wafers	JOC	669	1	C
Wafers, Charleston	FFCB	558	1	C
Bercy sauce	FFCB	266	1	A
Bercy sauce	JOC	331	2	A
Berliner kranser (butter cookies)	BHGN	165	1	C
Berliner pfannkuchen (filled doughnuts)	SC	100	1	
Bermuda salad	MC	59	2	B
Berry				
Brandy	KIS	324	1	B
Canning	BHGN	130		
Cobbler	FFCB	524	2	B
Cream	JOC	113	1	
Cream cheese pie, glazed	AC	620	1	
Cream pie, glazed	AC	620	1	
Dessert pancakes	NSD	112	3	B
Freezing	BHGN	130		
Fresh w creme fraiche	NSD	123	1	B
Jam tarts	CW	61	2	B
Jelly, pectin	SC	447	1	
Jelly, waterless	JOC	775	2	
& Melon	AC	759	1	A
Milk sherbet	SC	210	2	
Muffins	FFBB	563	1	B
Or cranberry angel pie	AC	632	1	
Pastry, three	GHAC	316	2	C
Pie	FFBB	86	2	B
Pie	SC	345	1	

RECIPE	BOOK	PAGE	TD	S
Berry (*cont.*)				
Pie	AC	618	1	
Cooked, fruit &	JOC	602	2	B
Deep dish	AC	614	1	
Deep dish	FFBB	94	2	C
Fresh fruit	JOC	601	2	B
Frozen fruit &	JOC	602	2	B
Gelatine glazed	AC	619	1	
Glazed	AC	619	1	
Glazed, frozen	AC	620	2	
Rhubarb	SC	263	2	
Soup, cold	NYT	84	2	B
Soup, fresh	MC	37	1	B
Sour cream pie, glazed	AC	620	1	
Sparkler	SPGT	125		A
Sundae cake	SC	209	2	
Tart	FFCB	595	2	B
Brown butter	NSD	88	1	B
Maple creme brulee, individual	NSD	166	3	B
Pastry cream	FFBB	168	2	B
Vanilla creme brulee, individual	NSD	166	3	B
Walnut salad	BBA	140	1	B
Wine salad	BCC	291	2	B
Besetti sauce (mustard sauce for seafood)	SC	45	1	
Best sauce (creamy chocolate dessert sauce)	BCC	135	1	
Beurre blanc	LM	46	1	
Beurre blanc	FGCW	286	1	B
Beurre blanc	MFC	106	1	B
Beurre Montpellier	MAFC	90	1	B
Beurre noisette	MAFC	270	1	
Biafran stew	FG	299	2	B
Bialys	BTSB	96	3	C
Bialys	CBB	534	3	C
Bibb lettuce w buttermilk dressing	KIS	197	1	A
Bibb lettuce salad	CF	51	1	B
Bibb mushroom salad	AC	38	1	
Bible or Scripture cake	AC	669	2	
Bigos	NYTI	498	2	B
Bigos traditional hunter's stew	FG	375	2	C
Billi Bi	MSE	219	2	B
Billi Bi	NYTI	124	1	B
Billi Bi	NYT	77	1	B
Billi Bi fish soup	CBSS	205	2	B
Billy goats (cookies w dates & nuts)	FFBB	204	1	C
Bimini w chocolate sauce	MHGD	177	1	B
Bing cherries, iced cookies w	MSQC	97	1	A
Bird				
Cutting up a drawn	JOC	461		
Disjointing a (photographs)	OC	54		
In a grove	AC	245		
Marinated, wild	JOC	477	2	A
Mock veal cutlets	AC	343	1	B
Mounting on a spit	BHGN	32		
Roasting, domestic, (chart)	BHGN	312		
Skewered, small	JOC	481	1	
Stuffing & trussing	JOC	463		
Tongue, stuffed	AC	300	2	
Trussing & stuffing	JOC	463		
Wild, preparing	JOC	475		
Birthday cake	FFCB	512	1	B
Birthday candlesticks	SC	138	1	

RECIPE	BOOK	PAGE	TD	S
Biscotti, Pat's (cookies)	CPMC	190	2	B
Biscuit	BTSB	124	1	B
Biscuit	BHGN	83	1	C
Biscuit	FFCB	474	2	B
Angel	BCC	41	2	C
Angel	CBB	561	3	C
Bacon	NYT	478	1	C
Baked, fillings, hot	JOC	245	2	C
Baking powder	NYT	478	1	C
◆	FFBB	572	1	C
◆	SC	86	1	C
◆	AC	793	1	
◆	BCC	29	1	B
◆	FFCB	490	1	C
Baking powder, crusty	FFCB	490	1	C
Beaten	GHAC	364	1	C
◆	CW	28	1	
◆	JOC	585	1	C
◆	CBB	549	2	C
Benne, seed	CBB	533	1	B
Blue cheese	BCC	29	1	B
Buttermilk	JOC	584	1	C
◆	BCC	29	1	B
◆	FFBB	573	1	C
◆	AC	794	1	
◆	MSE	132	2	C
◆	BHGN	84	1	C
◆	GHAC	363	1	C
◆	NYT	478	1	C
◆	FFCB	490	1	C
Camembert	MAFC	198	1	C
Cheese	JBC	19	1	
◆	EBE	32	2	C
◆	SC	86	1	
◆	NYT	478	1	C
◆	FFCB	490	1	C
Cinnamon, rolled	FFBB	576	2	C
Corn	CBB	199	1	C

RECIPE	BOOK	PAGE	TD	S
Cornmeal	BHGN	84	1	C
Cornmeal	BCC	29	1	B
Cornmeal	FFBB	573	1	C
Cottage oat, quick	JBGF	582	2	C
Crackling	FFBB	575	2	C
Cream	AC	793	1	
Cream	FFBB	574	1	C
Dog	CBB	716	2	C
Dog bone	FFBB	598	2	C
Dough, basic	JBC	19	1	B
Dough, for shortcake	SC	196	1	
Drop	FFBB	573	1	C
◆	BCC	29	1	B
◆	FFCB	490	1	C
◆	NYT	478	1	C
◆	SC	86	1	
Drop, buttermilk	CW	41	1	C
Drop, quick	JOC	583	1	B
Easter bunnies	JOC	585	1	
Feta	CBB	589	1	B
Flaky w parsley butter	CW	108	1	C
Fluffy	JBC	19	1	
Fluffy	JOC	584	1	C
Foie gras	JBC	4	1	
Foil, baked	BB	117	2	B
For teething baby	FFBB	597	2	C
Fruited, drop	GHAC	363		
Garden	BHGN	84	1	C
Ginger	FFBB	573	1	C
Grandmother's southern	CBB	546	1	B
Griddle	JOC	585	1	C
Ham	NYT	478	1	C
Ham	JBC	5	1	
Ham, small	FFCB	68	1	C
Herb	BCC	29	1	B
Herbed	NYT	478	1	C
Hors d'oeuvres	EBE	12	1	C

RECIPE	BOOK	PAGE	TD	S
Biscuit (*cont.*)				
Hot, all about	JOC	582		
Kentucky ham	GHAC	363	1	C
Little salted	CBB	529	2	C
Marmalade	JBC	19	1	
Mix	BTSB	123	1	C
Mix, homemade	BHGN	83	1	C
Montpelier, cheese	FFCB	67	1	
Mother's	CBB	540	1	B
Muffins, southern	PPLK	38	1	C
Or buns, sourdough	AC	789	2	
Orange	FFBB	573	1	C
Parsley	AC	793	1	
Parsley	JBC	19	1	
Pineapple	JOC	584	1	C
Pinwheel	FFCB	474	2	B
Pinwheel	JOC	584	1	B
Plain	GHAC	363		
Potato	SC	87	1	
Potato	FFCB	477	3	C
Pungent	JBC	19	1	
Rich	JBC	19	1	
Rolled	JOC	583	2	C
Rolls	NYT	474	2	
Roquefort	MAFC	197	1	C
Round	JBC	19	1	
Sandwich	SC	86	1	
Sausage	JBC	5	1	
Ship's	JOC	585	1	C
Shortcake	SC	88	1	
Soda	SC	88	1	
Sour cream	BHGN	84	1	C
Sour cream	GHAC	363	1	C
Sour milk	SC	88	1	
Square	JBC	19	1	
Sticks	JOC	584	1	C
Supreme	BHGN	84	1	C
Sweet potato	SC	88	1	
Sweet potato	JOC	585	1	C
Tea, New England	SC	86	1	
Thumbprint cocktail	BBA	173	3	C
Tortoni	SC	214	2	
◆	JOC	718	2	B
◆	NYTI	446	2	C
◆	FFCB	628	3	B
Vermont	GHAC	363	1	B
Water	FFBB	596	2	C
Watercress	NYT	478	1	C
Wheat, easy	JBGF	581	2	C
Whipped cream	JOC	584	1	C
Whole wheat	FFBB	573	1	C
Bishop's bread	SC	164	1	
Bishop's cake	SP	295	2	C
Bismarcks	BHGN	70	3	C
Bismarcks	SP	318	1	A
Bisque				
Curried winter squash	GG	334	2	B
Elysian carrots	GG	91	2	B
Scallop	SP	52	2	B
Tomato fish	GG	370	1	B
Bistee a la caserola (Peruvian beef stew)	NYTI	495	2	B
Bittersweet chocolate sauce	SPGT	99	1	B
Black bass barbecue, steamed	OC	143	1	B
Black bean				
Baked	BCC	171	2	B
Caribbean	AC	611	3	
Casserole	BB	109	3	C
Cuban	FG	112	2	B
Cuban	NYTI	68	2	C
Haitian	JBGF	513	2	B
Marinade, Asian	CFS	294	1	A

RECIPE	BOOK	PAGE	TD	S
Rum &	NYT	357	2	B
Sauce, shrimp	NYTI	43	1	B
Shrimp bisque	CBSS	248	1	B
Soup	GHAC	100	1	C
◆	SC	399	1	
◆	JOC	152	2	C
◆	CBSS	245	3	B
◆	BCC	313	2	B
◆	AC	94	3	
◆	FFCB	93	1	C
◆	SP	156	2	C
Brazilian	CBSS	249	2	B
Brazilian	MC	26	2	B
Cuban	FG	52	3	C
Cuban	FGCW	108	2	B
Cumin	JBGF	313	1	B
I	NYTI	66	3	B
II	NYTI	66	2	B
w Lemon & egg	FFCB	93	1	C
Rice &	FFCB	93	1	C
Sherry	FFCB	93	1	C
Split pea &	JBC	278	2	
& Spareribs, Chinese	NYTI	50	2	B
Tipsy	AC	611	3	
Black bottom pie	MSE	247	2	B
◆	FFCB	593	2	B
◆	AC	630	2	
◆	BHGN	287	2	B
◆	GHAC	321	2	C
◆	FFBB	129	2	B
◆	EBE	162	2	B
Black bread	CBB	241	2	B
Black bread	VE	41	2	B
Pheasant	CBB	151	3	C
Russian	BBA	173	2	B
Russian	CBB	144	2	C
Russian	FFBB	474	2	C
Black cherry almond aspic	JOC	101	2	B

RECIPE	BOOK	PAGE	TD	S
Black currant				
Jam	FFCB	704	2	B
Jelly	SC	448	1	
Sauce for wine poached pears	MSQC	193	1	B
Sauce, Napoleon	MSE	182	3	C
Black eyed beans Hoppin John	GHAC	232	2	B
Black eyed Susan salad	JOC	94	1	
Black eyed Susan salad	SC	366	1	
Black forest crepe torte	SP	319	2	B
Black forest cake	BHGN	98	2	C
Black grape ice cream	MCIC	453	2	B
Black olive soup, chilled	CBSS	167	3	B
Black pudding	NYTI	20	2	C
Black pudding	LM	208	3	C
Black pudding	JOC	438	2	
Black raspberry currant jelly	SC	449	1	
Black sangria	SP	329	1	B
Black satin pie	GHAC	319	3	C
Black truffle ice cream	NSD	222	3	B
Black walnut				
Bread	CBB	654	3	C
Caramel loaf cake	FFBB	324	1	C
Cookies	FFBB	202	2	C
Cookies	SP	258	2	C
Fudge frosting	NYT	575	1	B
Black & white bread	FFBB	449	2	C
Black & white layer cake	MHGD	69	3	C
Black & white soda	GHAC	302	1	A
Blackberry	AC	750		
Cobbler	CW	149	1	B
Cobbler	MIE	320	1	B
Cordial	SC	438	1	
Cream freeze	JBC	99	1	
Custard tart	NSD	104	2	B

RECIPE	BOOK	PAGE	TD	S
Blackberry (*cont.*)				
Flan	MAFC	657	1	B
Fool	MSQC	17	1	A
Ice	SP	281	2	B
Ice cream	JBC	98	1	
Jam	JOC	776	2	
Jam	FFCB	703	2	B
Jelly	FFCB	703	2	C
Jelly	SC	449	1	
Mousse	SP	282	1	C
& Other fruits	JBC	98	1	
Pie	AC	618	1	
◆	GHAC	314	1	C
◆	BCC	85	1	B
◆	BHGN	279	1	B
Pie, rhubarb &	BCC	89	1	B
Roll	SC	196	1	
Rolypoly	FFCB	655	2	B
Sauce	NSD	329	1	C
Stewed	JBC	98	1	
Stewed w custard sauce	JBC	99	1	
Stewed, ice cream w	JBC	99	1	
Stewed, other fruit	JBC	99	1	
Wine	SC	438	3	
Blackened redfish, making (photographs)	PPLK	32		
Blackstone salad dressing	SC	376	1	
Blaetter teig (puff pastry)	SC	343	3	
Blanc mange (cornstarch pudding)	SC	197	1	
Blanching	JOC	132		
Almonds, how to	MAFC	582		
Eggplant, sauteeing	MFC2	355	1	B
Vegetable chart	FFCB	733		
Vegetables chart	JOC	763		
Vegetables for crudites	MSE	68		
Blancmange	JOC	696	2	B
Blancmange	JOC	688	2	B
Almond	AC	726	1	
Chocolate	AC	726	1	
Chocolate pudding	FFCB	610	1	B
Foamy	AC	726	1	
Lemon	AC	726	1	
Old fashioned	AC	726	1	
Orange	AC	726	1	
Rose	AC	726	1	
Vanilla pudding	FFCB	610	1	B
Blanquette de veau (veal stew)	MFC	145	2	B
◆	NYTI	195	2	C
◆	MAFC	359	2	
◆	EBE	49	2	B
◆	JOC	419	2	B
◆	AC	339	2	
Blanquette de veau, dilled	SP	134	2	B
Blender cress dressing (watercress dressing)	JOC	312	1	
Blender mayonnaise (see mayonnaise, blender)				
Bleu broccoli & walnuts (w bleu cheese)	GG	61	1	B
Bleu cheese (see also blue cheese)				
Bleu cheese, beef &	FGCW	205	1	B
Bleu cheese dressing, pan fried, ravioli &	FGCW	152	2	B

RECIPE	BOOK	PAGE	TD	S
Blini	VE	186	2	B
A la russe	CPMC	86	2	B
Buckwheat	NYT	487	2	C
For caviar	NYTI	505	1	C
Quick	JBGF	501	1	B
Red caviar & sour cream	MSE	46	2	C
Russian, raised pancakes w	JOC	214	2	C
White flour	NYT	487	2	C
Blintz	JOC	213	2	B
◆	EBE	12	1	B
◆	FG	351	2	C
◆	SC	94	1	
Blueberry	BBA	111	2	C
Casserole	SC	94	1	
Cheese	VE	208	2	B
Cheese, filling for	SC	94	1	
Cherry	BCC	139	2	B
Potato, filling for	SC	94	1	
Strawberry	GHAC	371	2	C
Blitz kuchen (crumb cake)	AC	653	1	
Blitz kuchen	SC	116	1	B
Blitz torte	SC	132	2	B
Bloaters, baked (kippers)	JOC	357	1	
Bloaters, grilled	JOC	357	1	
Bloc de foie gras, about	SPGT	249		
Blond brownies	AC	712	1	
Blondies	GHAC	345	1	C
Blood oranges, sugared	CF	63	1	B
Bloody Mary	BB	164	1	A
◆	SC	63	1	
◆	BHGN	48	2	C
◆	BBA	26	1	A
◆	JOC	40	1	
◆	NYT	648	1	
Bloody Mary, good, spicy	SP	328	1	B
Bloody Mary marinade	CFS	291	1	B
Blossoms egg-glazed	JOC	741	2	B
Blowfish, all about	JOC	359		
Blue cheese				
Almond spread	EBE	30	1	B
Anchovy dressing	FG	81	1	B
Avocado dip	EBE	29	1	A
Biscuits	BCC	29	1	B
Burgers	GHAC	185	1	B
Butter	FFBC	57	1	B
Dip	JBC	3	1	
Dressing	BCC	301	2	B
Dressing	JBGF	549	1	B
Dressing	MC	46	1	B
Chunky	BHGN	351	1	B
Creamy	GHAC	284	1	A
Garlic yogurt	FFCB	454	1	B
Fan's sandwich	MC	89	1	B
Filling, nut	SC	380	1	
French dressing	JOC	312	1	A
Hamburgers	BHGN	28	1	B
Noodles	FG	125	1	B
Nut filling	SC	380	1	
Onion dip	BHGN	18	1	B
Salad dressing	PPLK	275	1	B
Sauce	BHGN	355	1	B
Sauce, green wax beans w	GHAC	231	1	B
Sauce, whole green wax beans w	GHAC	231	1	B
Soup, bacon &	SP	61	2	B
Sourdough rolls	YGM	99	1	B
Spread	GHAC	92	1	B
Spread	BB	123		
Spread, dip or ball	AC	14	1	
Tossed salad	SC	357	1	
Yogurt dressing	BCC	302	1	A

RECIPE	BOOK	PAGE	TD	S
Blueberry	AC	750		
Apple jelly	FFCB	702	2	C
Apricot compote	NSD	140	1	B
Blintzes	BBA	111	2	C
Bread pudding	FFCB	656	3	B
Buckle	NSD	142	2	C
Buckle	BHGN	81	1	B
Cake w bourbon cream	AC	663	1	
Casserole, peach &	MHGD	406	1	B
Chicken, glazed	SP	90	2	A
Cobbler	JBGF	620	1	B
Cobbler, fresh	BCC	125	1	B
Coffee cake	GGBB	578	1	B
Crabapple jam	SC	442	1	
Custard sauce	JBC	99	1	
Dried, frozen	AC	751	1	
Flan	MAFC	657	1	B
Ginger	KIS	331	1	
Grenadine pie	BCC	85	1	B
Griddle cakes	FFCB	496	1	B
Grunt	AC	724	1	
Ice cream	MHGD	436	1	C
Jam	JOC	776	2	
Jam	GHAC	381	3	C
Kuchen	SC	353	1	
Lemon mold	EBE	134	2	C
Lemon tart	SP	281	2	B
Mayonnaise	SP	118	1	B
Melba parfaits	BHGN	181	2	B
Meringue torte	SC	125	1	B
Mold, red, white &	GHAC	293	2	C
Mousse, Eleanor's	EBE	194	3	B
Muffins (see muffins, blueberry)				
Nut loaf cake	MHGD	106	1	C
Orange bread	MIE	304	1	B
& Other fruits	JBC	99	1	
Pancakes	BCC	30	1	B

RECIPE	BOOK	PAGE	TD	S
& Peaches ice cream	JBC	99	1	
& Peaches in mint sauce	JBGF	612	1	B
Pecan loaf	CBB	468	1	B
Pie	BHGN	279	1	B
◆	BCC	85	1	B
◆	JBC	39	2	B
◆	FFCB	580	2	B
◆	AC	618	1	
I	MHGD	146	1	B
II	MHGD	148	2	B
Bran crust, open faced	JBGF	626	1	B
Cobbler crust	GHAC	314	2	C
Deep dish	FFCB	582	2	B
Easy	BCC	85	1	B
Open	FFCB	581	2	B
Poached	AC	751	1	
Pudding	SC	192	1	
Pudding	MIE	319	1	B
Sauce	NYT	612	1	B
Shortcake	BHGN	179	2	B
Soup	SP	58	2	B
Soup, bluenose	CBSS	160	2	B
Sour cream cake	FFBB	347	1	B
Sour cream tart	FFBB	167	2	B
Streusel	AC	751	1	
Tart	JOC	603	2	B
Tart, strawberry	MHGD	204	2	B
Vinegar, chicken livers sauteed w	SP	320	2	B
Waffles	BCC	30	1	A
& Whipped cream	AC	751	1	
Bluefish				
Baked	NYT	232	1	B
A piperade garnish	VGCB	208	1	B
w Apples & mustard	SP	114	2	B

RECIPE	BOOK	PAGE	TD	S
Aromatic vegetables	FFCB	110	1	B
Fennel &	VGCB	124	1	B
w Potatoes Genoese style	MCIC	208	1	B
Rosemary	NYTI	133	1	B
Broiled	FFCB	110	1	A
Filleting for grilling (photographs)	OC	68		
Fillets w mustard	CFS	209	1	A
Horseradish	CFS	210	1	A
Oven baked	GHAC	134	2	B
Steak, hint of ginger	CFS	215	2	B
w White wine, cold	JBGF	447	1	B
Blushing bunny	AC	118	1	
Bnashed neeps (mashed rutabagas potatoes)	GG	389	1	B
Boar wild	JOC	454	2	
Bobotie (lamb pie)	CF	30	2	B
Boeuf				
A la mode	JOC	415	1	
A la mode en gelee	NYTI	103	2	C
Bouilli (broiled beef brisket)	JOC	413	2	B
Bourguignonne	AC	297	2	
◆	MAFC	315	2	B
◆	JOC	415	2	B
◆	EBE	50	2	B
Fondu	JOC	401	2	B
I	NYT	98	2	B
II	NYT	98	2	C
En daube Provencale	NYTI	172	2	C
Miroton (beef w onion sauce)	JOC	228	1	
Boiled beef, definition	AC	300		
Boiled dinner				
Corned pork, New England	JBC	155	2	B
Grand mixed	FAIC	271		
New England	SC	277	2	
◆	BHGN	235	2	B
◆	JBC	155	2	B
◆	NYT	96	2	C
◆	FFCB	160	2	B
w Salt pork, New England	JBC	155	2	B
Spanish	NYTI	521	3	B
w Tongue, New England	JBC	155	2	B
Boiled dressing	SC	375	1	
Boiled dressing	FFCB	451	1	B
Boiled dressing, oil	SC	376	1	
Boiled eggs (see eggs, boiled)				
Boiled frosting	AC	693	1	
Boiled salad dressing	JBC	258	1	
Boiled salad dressing	JOC	316	1	B
Boiled water soup	CBSS	278	1	B
Boiling	BHGN	429		
Bok choy au gratin	BCC	339	1	B
Bok choy, preparing	BCC	338		
Bok choy stir fry	BCC	338	1	B
Bok sui ngui (poached sea bass Chinese style)	NYTI	39	2	A
Bolitas frijoles or boiled pinto beans	AC	605	3	
Bollito misto (Italian chicken & beef casserole)	NYT	95	2	C
Bollito misto	GF	211	3	C
Bologna cornucopias	JOC	71	2	
Bologna salad macaroni	BCC	266	2	B
Bologna sandwich	AC	809	1	
Bolognese sauce	JOC	335	2	B
Bombay toast	AC	109	1	
Bombe al zabaglione	NYTI	446	2	B

RECIPE	BOOK	PAGE	TD	S
Bouchees	MFC2	123		
Bouchees, making	MFC2	123		
Bouchees petites	AC	639	1	
Boudin blanc	FGCW	244	2	B
Boudin blood sausage	AC	434		
Boudin noir	JOC	438	2	
Bouillabaisse	JOC	163	2	B
◆	NYT	265	1	B
◆	SP	48	2	C
◆	MAFC	52	2	B
◆	FG	327	2	B
◆	BHGN	372	1	B
◆	MSE	179	2	C
Catalan	NYT	265	2	B
Chez Panisse	CPMC	176	3	C
Crabmeat	NYT	278	1	B
I	NYTI	118	2	C
II	NYTI	119	2	B
Native American	GG	324	1	B
Of chicken aioli sauce	MFC2	263	2	
Of scallops	MFC2	37	1	B
Provencale	CBSS	221	3	B
Bouillon	NYT	57	2	C
Bouillon	SC	394	3	
Chicken tomato	AC	87	1	
Clarified	NYT	58	2	
Court	BBA	86	1	A
Court	NYT	229	1	B
Court	FFCB	83	2	B
Court, a simple	AC	135	1	
Court, simplified	BBA	88	2	B
Cubes	BTSB	39	2	C
Egg	JOC	146	1	A
Jellied	SC	398	1	
Louisiana, court	AC	181	1	
Potatoes	AC	573	1	
Boula boula	JOC	154	1	B
Boula boula soup	AC	93	1	
Boules sur chocolat	NYT	598	1	C

RECIPE	BOOK	PAGE	TD	S
Bouquet garni (herbs tied together for flavoring)	BCC	247	1	
Bouquet garni, making a	SP	110		
Bouquet garni, making a	GHAC	208		
Bouquets garnis	JOC	541	1	
Bourbon				
Balls	BCC	120	3	C
◆	MSE	200	3	C
◆	SC	178	1	
◆	AC	711	1	
◆	JOC	737	1	A
Bread	MSE	200	2	B
Cake, sweet potato	VGCB	301	1	B
Cream blueberry cake	AC	663	1	
Filling	FFBB	414	2	C
Ham baked w peaches &	JBC	207		
Marinade	OC	159	1	B
& Onion slices, braised	AC	532	1	
Pie, pecan	BBA	204	3	B
Sauce	CW	133	1	B
Steaks	CFS	217	2	B
Bourguignonne fondue	NYTI	174	1	B
Bourride	CPMC	131	3	B
Bourride aioli (garlic based fish soup)	GF	218	2	C
Bourride Mediterranean	VGCB	223	1	
Boursault, romaine leaves w	GF	61	1	C
Boursin, salmon smoked, cucumber cups	BBA	17	3	C
Bovril cheese loaf	CBB	388	2	B
Bow ties	FFBB	263	2	C
Bowknots	FFCB	474	2	B

RECIPE	BOOK	PAGE	TD	S
Brandied cherries	FFCB	708	2	B
Brandied cherries	BTSB	157	2	C
Brandied cherry sauce	GHAC	302		
Brandied foamy sauce	NYT	615	2	B
Brandied peaches	AC	764	1	
Brandied peaches (see peaches brandied)				
Brandied strawberry sauce for ice cream	GHAC	306	1	C
Brandy				
Alexander bars	BCC	101	1	C
Alexander pie	NYTI	563	2	
Balls	AC	711	1	
Balls	BCC	120	3	C
Berries	KIS	324	1	B
Broth, beef in	BBA	30	2	B
Butter sauce	SC	218	1	
Butter sauce	FFBB	420	2	C
Cream	BCC	24	2	B
Cream sauce	SC	218	1	
Cup	JOC	49	2	
Frosting	SC	144	1	
Hard sauce	GHAC	315	2	A
◆	FFCB	641	1	B
◆	BHGN	278	1	
◆	BHGN	186	1	C
Or rum loaf cake	AC	649	1	
Peach	SC	438	3	
Peaches, hot	KIS	321	1	A
Peaches, stewed	MHGD	405	1	B
Pecan pie	BCC	92	2	B
Prunes	MHGD	426	1	B
Pumpkin soup	BBA	41	2	C
Rye bread torte	SC	133	1	B
Sauce	JBC	268	1	
Sauce	AC	742	1	
Brown sugar	JBC	267	1	
Foamy	SC	218	1	
For pepper steak	MAFC	296	1	B
Golden	SC	218	1	
Peaches baked in	SC	263	1	
Quick	SC	217	1	
Whipped	SC	218	1	
Shrimp & apple	KIS	127	1	A
Snaps	FFBB	240	1	C
Snaps	JOC	668	1	C
Snaps	NYT	578	1	C
Strawberries w cream	MHGD	395	1	B
& Veal kidneys, flamed, cream mushrooms w	MAFC	418	1	B
Brasciole all'oreste cianci (beef w grated cheese)	NYTI	389	2	B
Bratwurst	FG	182	1	B
Bratwurst	KIS	277	1	A
Apple phyllo	YGM	166	3	C
Broiled or sauteed	AC	433	1	
Creamed	BHGN	263	1	B
Brawn (see head cheese) (molded beef broth)				
Brawn or head cheese	AC	419		
Brazil nut bars	BCC	103	1	C
Brazil nut clam spread	NYT	52	1	B
Brazil nut crust	NYT	521	1	B

Bread (see also almond, anadama, apple, apricot, awendaw, bacon, banana, barley, basil, batter, bishop, black, blueberry, Boston, Bourbon, bran, brandy, broccoli, brown & white, bruschetta, buckwheat, buttermilk, caraway, carrot, challah, cheese, cherry pecan, chili, chocolate, Christmas, cinnamon, citrus, clabber, coconut, coffee, corn, country, cranberry, Cuban, currant, dark, date nut, egg,

RECIPE	BOOK	PAGE	TD	S
Bread (*cont.*) fennel, fig, flat, French, fruit, garlic, ginger, graham, herb, honey, jalapeno, maple, molasses, nut, oatmeal, olive, onion, orange, peanut butter, peasant, pecan, pepper, pita, pizza, pocket, poppy, potato, prosciutto, prune, pumpernickel, pumpkin, raisin, rhubarb, rye, sausage, shortbread, soda, sourdough, spoon, squash, sweet potato, walnut, wheat, white, whole wheat, zucchini)				
A simple recipe for	AC	777	2	
Almond raisin, toasted	FFBB	461	2	C
Amish, old order	NYT	462	2	C
Anadama	BHGN	62	2	B
Applesauce, oat	JBGF	584	1	B
Apricot almond	FFCB	486	2	B
Awendaw	GG	282	2	B
Baking for beginners	JBGF	554		
Basic white I	AC	778	2	
Basic white II	AC	779	2	
Basic white w cheese	AC	779	2	
Baskets, making (photographs)	LT	60		
Black pumpernickel	BTSB	108	3	C
Blocks, puffed	JOC	174	1	C
Boat, Italian	SC	385	1	
Boston brown	BTSB	118	2	C
Braiding	BHGN	66		
Butter custard	NYTI	295	1	B
& Butter pickles (see pickles, bread & butter)				
& Butter pudding	FFCB	613	1	B
& Butter pudding	NYT	586	2	C
& Butter pudding, French	NYTI	299	1	B
& Butter pudding, the Coach House	AC	726	1	
& Butter sandwiches	SC	382	1	
Cakes, corn, cold water	CF	135	1	B
Carrot (see carrot bread)				
Cases	JOC	223	1	
Cases, toasted	MAFC	200	1	
Cheese, scallion &	YGM	103	1	B
Cinnamon raisin	BTSB	89	3	C
Corn (see corn bread)				
Country	LM	245	2	C
Cracked wheat	BTSB	84	3	C
Crumb crust	JOC	593	1	B
Crumb griddle cakes	SC	91	1	B
Crumb sauce	FAIC	82	1	B
Crumbs	JBC	25	1	
Crumbs, homemade	FAIC	45	1	
Crumbs, toasted, pasta &	SPGT	66	1	B
Cuban style	JBC	16	2	B
Cubes, butter	JOC	174	1	
Cubes, cheese	JOC	174	1	
Curry, honey	SPGT	86	3	B
Date nut	BTSB	120	1	B
Dressing, oyster	JOC	457	1	B
Dressing, sherry	JOC	456	1	B
Dumplings	SC	103	1	
Everything but the kitchen sink	JBGF	568	2	C
Fingers cream	FFCB	478	2	B
Five grain	BTSB	87	3	C
Flat (see flat bread)				
French pan toasted	MSQC	29	1	A
Garlic (see garlic bread)				
High protein three grain	JBGF	569	2	C

RECIPE	BOOK	PAGE	TD	S
Hints about	VE	25		
Honey	MFC2	481	2	
Honey bran	BTSB	82	2	C
Honey pineapple	CBB	482	1	B
Honey (see honey bread)				
Horse, birthday (shaped)	JOC	587	3	
Hungarian fennel	GG	181	2	B
Irish tea (barm)	CBB	322	2	C
Jewish corn	BTSB	106	3	C
Loaf, toasted	SC	72	1	
Loaf, toasted, buttered	JOC	586	1	
Making bread, general rules for	SC	66		
Making variables in	MCIC	46		
& Meat dumplings	SC	407	1	C
& Milk	LM	252	2	C
Nut almond	FFBB	451	2	B
Olives	FAIC	40	2	B
Omelet	SC	226	1	A
Onion & prosciutto	GG	242	2	C
Orange (see orange bread)				
Pan baked	BB	118	1	B
Pepper cheese	VE	42	2	B
Pepper spice	CBB	432	3	C
Pretzels	JOC	562	1	B
Procedures for making	BTSB	79		
Pudding	GF	163	1	B
◆	SC	186	1	
◆	SP	306	2	C
◆	NSD	144	2	B
◆	BCC	142	1	B
◆	BHGN	172	1	B
Baked in a pumpkin shell	VGCB	234	1	C

RECIPE	BOOK	PAGE	TD	S
Blueberry	FFCB	656	3	B
Butter	JBC	47	1	B
Butter, the Coach House	AC	726	1	
Cheese	FFCB	353	1	B
Chocolate	MFC	230	2	C
Chocolate	FFCB	612	1	B
Lemon sauce Chantilly cream	PPLK	312	2	B
Maple	GHAC	298	2	B
Meringue	SC	187	1	
Meringue	JOC	700	2	B
New England	NYT	587	2	B
Old fashioned	MC	205	1	B
Orange	NYT	587	2	B
Orange vanilla sauce, molded	BBA	211	2	C
Peach sauce &	CW	132	1	B
Puffs	SC	186	1	
Steamed	SC	189	2	
Pullman	LM	255	2	B
Pumpernickel light	BTSB	102	2	B
& Pumpkin soup, Haitian	NYTI	339		
Quick	FFCB	484		
Raisin (see raisin bread)				
Red pepper & cheese	GG	281	2	C
Richard's best (sweet)	JBGF	572	2	C
Rounds, plain	MAFC	199	1	
Rounds, sauteed	MAFC	199	1	
Rye (see rye bread)				
Salad	FAIC	92	2	B
Salt rising (Abigail's)	CBB	299	3	C
Salt rising	CBB	301	3	B
Salt rising	FFBB	467	2	C
Sauce	AC	242	1	
Sauce	JOC	325	1	C

RECIPE	BOOK	PAGE	TD	S
Bread (*cont.*)				
Sauce for poultry	NYTI	91	1	A
Sausage	FAIC	39	2	B
Sausage	CBB	595	3	C
Shaping (photographs)	BCC	43		
Shrimp	LM	75	1	B
Slices, fried French	CW	60	1	B
Socle, making (photographs)	LT	62		
Soup	FAIC	230	2	B
Sour, rye caraway seeds	BTSB	105	3	C
Spice	MFC2	481	2	
Squares for soup, fried	CIC	88	1	B
Starters	CBB	273		
Sticks	SC	74	2	
◆	JOC	558	3	B
◆	FFCB	477	3	C
◆	FFBB	495	1	C
◆	BTSB	101	3	C
◆	BHGN	73	2	C
Barbecue	BHGN	73	2	C
Caraway	NYT	49	2	C
Parmesan	BHGN	73	2	C
Rye	JOC	570	1	C
Soft	BCC	41	2	C
South of the border	SPGT	138	3	C
White	JOC	570	1	C
Whole grain	JOC	570	1	C
Storing & freezing	CBB	707		
Stuffing	BCC	257	1	B
Stuffing, basic forcemeat variations	AC	232	1	
Stuffing, moist	GHAC	170	1	C
Swedish (julbrod)	NYT	464	2	C
Sweet, for All Saints' Day	FAIC	471	2	B
The big	SP	326	3	B
Three flours	CBB	237	2	C
Torte	JOC	638	2	B
Torte or brottorte	AC	687	2	
Twice baked	JOC	587	1	
& Vegetable salad, anchovies &	CIC	410	1	B
Westphalian pumpernickel	BTSB	114	3	B
What went wrong & how to make it right	CBB	709		
Wheat sprouted	BTSB	86	3	C
Whole wheat Italian herb butter	MSQC	157	1	B
Zaartar	FG	365	2	C
Breadfruit	JOC	264		
Breadfruit seeds	JOC	264		
Breading foods	JOC	501		
Breading seasoned	JOC	502	3	
Breakfast colada	SPGT	126		
Breakfast, instant	KIS	366	1	A
Breakfast puffs	FFBB	531	3	B
Breakfast sausage	AC	434		
Breakfast shake	JBGF	511	1	A
Bresaola (cured beef filet)	CIC	47		
Bresiliens (individual meringue almond cakes)	MFC2	504	3	
Bretonne beans	AC	596		
Briarpatch herb bread	CBB	444	2	C
Brick oven, improvising	FAIC	32		
Bride's cake or white loaf cake	AC	658	2	
Brie				
Almonds, hot	FG	334	1	B
Brioche dough	LM	268	2	C
Fried	KIS	308	1	B
Omelet & parsley	MSE	88	1	A

RECIPE	BOOK	PAGE	TD	S
Pinwheel	SP	238	2	C
Romaine	GG	189	1	B
Rye bread	CBB	395	3	C
& Smoked salmon tortilla triangles	GHAC	86	1	C
Souffle	SP	239	1	B
Soup	CBSS	151	2	B
Soup, cream of	FGCW	111	1	B
Soup, oyster &	PPLK	198	2	B
Wrapped phyllo	SP	239	2	C
Brill, stuffed	LM	100	3	B
Brine bath	NYT	13		
Brine, spices & salt to create a	OC	10		
Brining vegetables	JOC	787		
Brioche (yeast raised French bread)	JBC	17	2	B
◆	BCC	44	2	C
◆	SP	244	3	B
◆	BHGN	74	3	C
◆	CPMC	234	3	B
◆	GF	248	2	C
◆	JOC	566	3	C
◆	MFC	206	3	C
A tete	CBB	669	3	C
All about	CBB	657		
American	NYT	470	2	C
Apricot jam sandwiches	GF	46	2	B
Au chocolat	JOC	567	3	C
Batter bread, buttered	FFBB	523	2	B
Bread	FFBB	522	2	C
Bread	AC	787	2	
Bread	FFCB	469	3	B
Camembert	CBB	671	3	B
Cheese raisins	CBB	668	3	C
Classic	FFBB	520	2	C
Croissant	CBB	674	3	C
Dough	NYTI	510	2	
◆	MFC2	85	3	C
◆	LT	402	2	
◆	NSD	148	2	C
Chicken liver sausage	MFC2	296	1	B
Freezing	MFC2	96		
Pork liver pate	MFC2	322	3	C
Processor	CBB	666	3	B
Sausage	MFC2	299	3	
Starter	CBB	663	3	C
Without starter	CBB	665	3	C
French	NYT	471	3	C
Individual	MFC2	92		
Large ball shaped head	MFC2	90	3	B
Le Havre Parisienne Nanterre	CBB	667	3	C
Loaf cockaigne	JOC	557	2	B
Making a (photographs)	NYT	472		
Mousseline	CBB	675	3	C
Prune filling	CBB	672	3	C
Raisins	MFC2	93	3	C
Ring	JBC	18	2	B
Ring shaped	MFC2	92		
Rolls	FFCB	469	3	B
Rum soaked strawberry shortcake	MFC2	448	2	B
Savoy, sausage in	LM	196	3	B
Vendeenne	CBB	629	3	C
Brisket (see also beef brisket)				
& Baked prunes	SC	273	3	
Beef, apple glazed	GHAC	217	2	C
Carbonnade	BHGN	235	2	C
& Carrot stew	SC	273	2	
Like my mother makes	MIE	119	2	B
Of beef, boiled	CW	148	1	B

RECIPE	BOOK	PAGE	TD	S
Brisket (*cont.*)				
Of beef, braised & potted	CW	124	1	B
Of beef, carrots Bordelaise	AC	290	1	
Pot roast, a simple braised	AC	289	1	
Smoked, fancy country fair	CFS	272	3	B
Smoked, rarified	OC	99	2	B
Sweet & sour	MIE	120	2	B
Brittle				
Almond	LM	364	3	
Almond	BTSB	267	2	B
Almond	SC	174	1	
Butterscotch nut	FFCB	685	2	B
Nuts	SC	174		
Peanut (see peanut brittle)				
Preparing	NSD	226		
Broa (Portuguese corn bread)	CBB	183	2	B
Broad beans, garlicked	AC	481	1	
Broad beans, cooking	AC	480	1	
Broad beans, raw	AC	481	1	
Broccoli	JOC	264	1	B
Broccoli	NYT	365		
Broccoli	SC	414	1	
All about	VGCB	28		
Amandine	NYT	366	1	B
Anchovy sauce for pasta	CIC	174	1	B
& Avocado salad	SMG	73	1	B
Bake, chicken &	SC	316	1	
Bean curd & pork	YGM	145	2	A
& Black olives	NYT	366	1	B
Blanched	VGCB	29	1	B
Blanched plain, boiled, variations	MFC2	337		

RECIPE	BOOK	PAGE	TD	S
& Bleu walnuts	GG	61	1	B
Boiled	JBC	295	1	B
Boiled cold	MFC2	339		
Braised	JOC	266	2	B
Braised & butter	MFC2	340	1	
Butter almond sauce	GHAC	234	1	B
Buttered gratineed cheese	MFC2	341	1	
w Capers	NYT	366	1	A
& Carrot, stir fry	JBGF	517	1	B
Casserole, chicken &	SC	312	1	
& Cauliflower in lemon butter	LM	130	2	C
& Cauliflower, Mandarin style	WC	31	1	B
Cheese &	BCC	340	1	B
& Cheese custard	FFCB	367	1	B
Chevre'd	GG	62	1	B
& Chicken salad	FG	83	1	B
Chinoise	JBGF	296	1	C
Chokes, stir fry	VGCB	138	1	B
Chopped gratineed, w cheese sauce	MFC2	342	1	
Chopped, sauteed w butter	MFC2	341	1	
Chopped & simmered in cream	MFC2	342	1	
Cooking	AC	487		
& Crab bisque	JBGF	335	2	B
& Crabmeat crepes	VGCB	33	2	B
Creamed, quick	JOC	264	1	B
Crepes, salmon &	BHGN	222	2	B
Custard	VGCB	32	1	B
De rabe penne	VGCB	134	1	B
De rabe soup, cream of	VGCB	131	1	B
De rabe, spaghetti &	VGCB	134	1	B
Deep fried	JOC	266	1	

RECIPE	BOOK	PAGE	TD	S
Dip, hot	BHGN	17	1	B
En rouille	CFS	237	1	B
Finishing touches for blanched or steamed	VGCB	30	1	
Finishing touches for sauteed & chopped	VGCB	31	1	
Flammifero	GG	58	2	B
Florets, fried	MCIC	370	1	B
Florets, vinaigrette	MIE	266	2	B
Freezing	BHGN	136		
French fried	BCC	340	1	B
w Fresh tomato sauce	JBGF	640	1	B
Frittata, Parma style	GG	63	1	B
Frittata potatoes	JBGF	483	1	B
Golden crumb	BHGN	393	1	B
Grilled Parma style	CFS	238	1	B
& Ham, stir fry	WC	112	1	B
Homemade barley soup &	MCIC	106	2	B
Hot pot	GG	58	1	B
Italian style	JBC	295	1	B
Lemon, stir fried	KIS	131	1	A
Mold, cauliflower marbelized	VGCB	65	2	B
Molds	MFC2	343	1	
Mornay, chicken &	VGCB	33	2	B
Morsels	VGCB	31	1	B
Mousseline	GG	63	1	B
Mousseline, mushroom sauce &	MFC	47	3	B
Mousses, individual	VGCB	31	1	B
& Mushroom noodle casserole	MC	107	1	B
Omelet, oven	BCC	161	1	B
& Onion casserole	BHGN	393	1	B
& Onions savory	YGM	141	1	B

RECIPE	BOOK	PAGE	TD	S
Oriental	BHGN	393	1	B
Oriental	KIS	236	1	A
Pan fried	FGCW	263	2	B
Pasta	MIE	187	1	B
Pasta	VGCB	32	1	B
Pasta timbale	GG	64	2	B
Pesto	GG	65	1	C
Pickled, tarragon	BBA	166	3	B
Pie	BCC	165	1	B
Pie	BCC	339	1	B
Pizza, deep dish	VGCB	33	2	B
Poached eggs &	MFC2	339	1	
Pork chops &	VGCB	134	1	B
Preparing	BCC	339		
Preparing for cooking	MFC2	336		
Puree	AC	488	1	
Puree	JBC	296	1	
w Cream	JBC	296	1	
w Creme fraiche	SP	197	1	B
w Onion	JBC	296	1	
Quiche, Swiss cheese &	FG	104	2	B
Quiche, whole wheat crust	GHAC	114	1	B
Rabe, sauteed	FFCB	368	1	A
& Red pepper salad	MSE	104	1	C
& Red wine smothered	MCIC	372	1	B
Refrigerator, pickled	CW	60	2	B
Ring	SC	414	1	
Ring mold	JOC	209	2	B
Salad	AC	47	1	
Salad, sardine &	JBGF	406	1	A
Sauces, to serve w	MFC2	339		
Sauteed				
Bread crumbs, egg &	MFC2	338	1	
Butter, cheese &	CIC	364	1	B
Chopped	VGCB	31	1	

RECIPE	BOOK	PAGE	TD	S
Broccoli, Sauteed (*cont.*)				
Garlic	CIC	363	1	B
Onions, bacon & bread crumbs	MFC2	339	1	
Sesame	YGM	49	1	A
Sicilian	NYTI	432	1	B
Souffle	JBC	271	1	B
◆	BCC	350	2	B
◆	AC	556	2	B
◆	BHGN	394	2	B
Souffle, ricotta	JBGF	488	1	B
Souffle, salmon	BBA	124	3	B
Soup	MSQC	152	1	B
Soup	VGCB	32	1	B
Cream of	FG	48	1	B
◆	MC	11	1	B
◆	CBSS	257	1	B
◆	NYT	68	1	B
Creamy	BCC	311	1	B
Curried, cream of	JBGF	314	1	B
w Sour cream sauce	GHAC	234	1	
& Spinach pie	FG	340	3	B
Stalks, julienned	VGCB	31	1	B
Steamed	FFCB	367	1	A
Steamed	VGCB	29	1	B
Steamed	KIS	100	1	A
Steamed, di rape	SMG	39	1	B
Stir fried	AC	561	1	
Stir fry	WC	34	1	B
Stir sauteed	FAIC	406	1	B
Stuffed mushroom caps	EBE	110	1	B
Timbales	JOC	207	2	B
Tomato	GG	60	1	B
Tuna shells	KIS	149	1	A
Turkey bake	SC	316	1	
Valencienne	GG	59	1	B
Vichyssoise	GG	59	2	C
Vinaigrette, cold	JBC	296	1	
Vinaigrette, potato, hot	YGM	98	1	B
w Yogurt ginger dressing, cold	YGM	213	1	C
Brod torte (rye bread torte)	SC	132	2	B
Broiler, stuffed	JOC	466	1	
Broilers, braised	JOC	467	2	
Bronx (gin, vermouth, orange juice)	JOC	37	1	
Bronx	SC	60	1	A
Brook trout meuniere	NYT	261	1	B
Brook trout pan fried	FFCB	125	1	B
Broth (see also beef broth, chicken broth)				
Broth	MCIC	21	2	B
Basic chicken	AC	87	2	
Facts about	CIC	10		
Oriental noodles pork saimin	CBSS	215	2	B
Scotch (see Scotch broth)				
Veal	AC	86	2	
Brottorte (bread torte)	JOC	638	2	B
Brottorte	AC	687	2	
Brown beauty frosting	SC	146	1	
Brown Betty	JOC	700	2	B
Brown Betty	SC	192	1	
Brown bread	AC	792	2	
Baked	CBB	231	1	B
Baked	JOC	576	1	C
Boston (see also Boston brown bread)				
Boston	CBB	232	1	B
Boston, steamed	JOC	577	3	C
Ice cream	FFCB	633	3	C

RECIPE	BOOK	PAGE	TD	S
Brown butter brandy frosting	SC	144	1	
Brown butter frosting	SC	144	1	
Brown chicken sauce	NYTI	216	1	
Brown deglazing sauce w wine	MAFC	271	1	B
Brown egg sauce	SC	388	1	
Brown loaf, royal Hibernian	CBB	131	1	B
Brown nut bread	SC	85	1	
Brown onion sauce	JOC	327	1	B
Brown pudding, steamed	JOC	703	2	C
Brown rice soup, zucchini &	VGCB	278	1	B
Brown sauce	BBA	50	2	B
◆	GF	247	2	B
◆	JOC	326	3	C
◆	BHGN	357	1	B
◆	SC	387	1	
◆	BCC	327	1	B
◆	NYT	445	2	B
◆	NYTI	268	2	B
◆	FFCB	269	1	A
Brown roux	AC	456	1	
Basic	FGCW	283	2	B
Basic	JBC	262	1	
Flour based	MAFC	67	1	C
For egg foo young	BCC	162	1	
For game	MAFC	70	1	C
For venison	MAFC	70	1	C
Giblets, flour based	MAFC	69	1	C
Peppery	MAFC	71	1	B
Pickles, capers &	MAFC	72	1	B
Quick	AC	456	1	
Quick	JOC	326	1	B
Spicy	BCC	327	1	B
Starch, thickened	MAFC	70	1	B
Sweet & sour	SC	388	1	

RECIPE	BOOK	PAGE	TD	S
Brown soup stock	AC	85		
◆	JOC	490	2	B
◆	NYTI	163	2	
◆	MAFC	110	2	C
Basic	FGCW	100	3	B
Basic	FG	40	2	B
Classic, half glaze	LM	34	3	
Fast	LM	37	2	
Reduced	FGCW	284	2	B
Brown sugar				
Brandy sauce	JBC	267	1	
Butter sauce	JOC	712	1	A
Chocolate chip cookies, Alexis's	MSE	93	1	C
Cookies	PPLK	336	1	C
Cookies, criss cross	SC	156	1	
Cream sauce	JOC	713	1	B
Custard sauce	NYT	614	1	B
Filling	BCC	33	1	B
Fudge	AC	833	1	
Glaze for ham	BCC	228	1	
Hard sauce	JOC	714	1	B
Hard sauce	SC	98	1	
Icing, marshmallow	JOC	677	1	B
Icing, quick	JOC	679	1	A
Kisses	AC	711	1	
Kisses	FFBB	223	1	C
Loaf cake	SC	112	1	B
Macaroons	SC	164	1	
Marshmallow frosting	SC	145	1	
Orange sauce	JOC	713	1	B
Pound cake, Willard Scott's	YGM	186	2	C
Rhubarb pie	BHGN	283	2	B
Sauce, hot	JOC	712	1	B
Spice cake	JOC	629	1	B
Brown trout, broiled	FFCB	125	1	B
Brown & white braided bread	FFBB	462	2	C

RECIPE	BOOK	PAGE	TD	S
Browned crumb sauce (garnish for vegetables)	JOC	340	1	B
Brownie				
◆	JBC	36	1	
◆	SP	260	1	C
◆	SC	165	1	
◆	NYT	578	1	C
◆	GF	50	1	C
◆	FFCB	563	1	C
◆	AC	711	1	
Almond	BCC	101	1	C
Barbara's	EBE	174	1	C
Bittersweet	BBA	189	2	C
Black & white	NYT	578	1	C
Blond	AC	712	1	
Blonde	BHGN	155	1	C
Butterscotch	FFBB	226	1	C
◆	GHAC	345	1	C
◆	BCC	103	1	C
◆	FFCB	564	1	C
◆	AC	712	1	
◆	JOC	653	1	C
Cake like	FFBB	225	1	C
Chewy	SC	165	1	
Chewy fudge	FFBB	224	1	C
Chocolate	CF	71	1	B
Cake	BHGN	154	1	C
Chip	MSQC	201	1	B
Chunk	GHAC	345	1	C
Cream cheese	BHGN	154	1	C
Mint	GHAC	345	1	C
Moist	FFBB	224	1	C
Syrup	BHGN	154	1	C
Christmas	MHGD	291	1	C
Cockaigne	JOC	653	1	C
Cocoa	BCC	101	1	C
Coconut butterscotch	BCC	103	1	C
Coffee blond	SPGT	141	2	C
Deluxe	BCC	101	1	C
Denver	MHGD	293	2	C
Frosted	AC	712	1	
Fudge	BHGN	154	1	C
Iced	MSE	106	1	B
Marble	GHAC	345	1	C
Mix	KIS	340	1	C
Peanut	AC	712	1	
Peanut butter	FFBB	225	1	C
Peanut butter	FFCB	564	1	C
Pie, chocolate	BCC	92	2	B
Polka dot	AC	712	1	
Pudding	BHGN	174	1	B
Wholesome	JBGF	604	1	C
World's tastiest	MIE	330	1	C
Brownstone front cake	AC	667	1	
Brownstone front cake	FFBB	323	1	C
Brownstone soup	GG	120	2	B
Brulee crusts	JOC	686	2	
Brummagems spinach rolls	GG	308	1	C
Brunswick stew	BB	103	3	C
◆	SC	313	2	
◆	FFCB	246	2	B
◆	JOC	470	2	B
◆	NYT	199	2	B
◆	GHAC	154	2	C
Brunswick stew, variations (made w squirrel or chicken)	AC	248	1	
Bruschetta garlic bread, Roman	CIC	49	1	B
Bruschetta garlic toast	FGCW	341	1	
Brussels sprout				
◆	SC	414	1	
◆	NYT	366		
◆	SMG	263	1	B

RECIPE	BOOK	PAGE	TD	S
Brussels sprout (*cont.*)				
◆	MAFC	449		
◆	JOC	266	1	B
A California recipe for	AC	490	1	
A la brecque	GG	69	1	B
All about	VGCB	34		
& Anchovies	WC	20	1	B
Bacon &	JBC	297	1	
Bacon &	AC	490	1	
Bacon &	VGCB	38	1	B
Blanched	MAFC	450	1	B
Blanched	VGCB	37	1	
Boiled	JBC	296	1	
Braised	YGM	131	1	B
Braised	JBC	297	1	
w Braised butter	MAFC	451	1	B
Braised, chestnuts &	MAFC	452	2	B
Brown butter	NYT	367	1	B
Browned cheese	MAFC	453	1	B
Butter, steamed	AC	490	1	
Caraway	BBA	131	1	B
Caraway seeds	NYT	366	1	B
Chestnut soup	VGCB	39	1	B
Chestnuts &	FFCB	368	1	B
◆	VGCB	38	1	B
◆	AC	489	1	
◆	SC	414	1	
Chestnuts & brown sauce	SC	414	1	
& Chestnuts, baked	JOC	266	1	B
Chopped in simmered cream	MAFC	453	1	B
Classic, creamed	GG	70	1	B
Cream	MSQC	145	1	B
Creamed	MAFC	452	1	B
Dilled	BBA	166	3	B
Finishing touches for steamed or blanched	VGCB	37	1	
Frozen	MAFC	454	1	B
Gingered shrimp w	GG	72	1	B
Glazed	KIS	137	1	A
Gratineed cheese sauce	MAFC	453	1	B
Green onions &	JBC	297	1	
Halves, tossed w butter	VGCB	38	1	B
In lemon mustard sauce	JBGF	514	1	B
In tomato sauce tangy	KIS	93	1	A
Leaves, steamed	VGCB	37	1	
Mold	MAFC	454	2	B
& Mushrooms	JBC	297	1	
Oven braised parsnips &	MSE	188	2	B
Parmesan	BCC	340	1	B
& Pecan butter	GG	69	1	B
Polonaise	VGCB	38	1	B
Polonaise	FGCW	264	1	
Preparing	BCC	340		
Preparing	GG	68		
Puree of	BBA	131	1	C
Salad, cold	FGCW	133	1	B
Salad, cold caraway	FGCW	133	1	
Saucy	BHGN	394	1	B
Sauteed	JBC	297	1	
Sauteed	SMG	267	1	B
Shrimp &	VGCB	39	1	B
Souffle	GG	71	1	B
Souffle	BHGN	394	2	B
Steamed	VGCB	37	1	
Stuffed	JOC	69	1	
Whole, braised	MSE	168	1	B
Bryani (curry)	VE	262	1	B
Bubble & squeak (sausage & cabbage)	FFCB	211	1	B

RECIPE	BOOK	PAGE	TD	S
Burgundy (*cont.*)				
Sauce	JOC	331	1	B
Sauce	SC	279	1	
Burgur beef salad	BCC	272	2	B
Burnt almond ice cream	FFCB	630	3	C
Burnt almond sauce	SC	216	1	
Burnt leather cake	AC	667	1	
Burnt sugar cake	JOC	629	2	B
Burnt sugar icing	FFBB	404	1	C
Burritos chicken	GHAC	157	2	B
Burritos sausage	BCC	320	1	B
Burro rosso (red butter peppers)	GG	277	1	B
Busy day cake	BHGN	92	1	C
Butter				
Adding to sauces	MFC	8		
All about	JOC	509		
All about	LT	41		
Almond	BTSB	292	1	A
Almond	JOC	338	1	A
Anchovy	SC	379	1	
◆	BBA	152	1	A
◆	MAFC	101	1	A
◆	BB	62	1	B
◆	JOC	339	1	B
◆	GRIL	39	1	B
◆	FFCB	57	1	B
◆	JBC	266	1	
◆	NYT	457	1	
◆	SP	116	1	
Anchovy & tomato	NYT	457	1	
Apple	NYT	509	1	B
◆	FFCB	707	2	C
◆	SC	442	1	
◆	JOC	777	2	C
◆	MSE	133	1	C
◆	BHGN	128	2	B
Apple, baked	JOC	777	2	C
Apricot	GHAC	379	1	B
Apricot	JOC	777	2	C
Avocado	GHAC	151		
Balls	SC	156	1	
Basil	BBA	152	1	A
Beer batter bread	CBB	450	1	B
Bercy	JOC	339	1	B
Black	BCC	332	1	
Black	JOC	338	1	B
Black	JBC	265	1	
Blender, quick	NYT	456	1	A
Blue cheese	FFCB	57	1	B
Bran bread	CBB	96	1	B
Brown	JOC	338	1	B
Brown	JBC	265	1	
Brown	FFCB	268	1	A
Browned	BCC	332	1	
Cake yellow	MFC2	482	1	
Caviar	JOC	339	1	B
Chervil	CPMC	67	2	
Chili	GHAC	243	1	
Chili, grilled fish steaks	GHAC	223	1	B
Chive	GRIL	39	1	B
◆	FFCB	56	1	B
◆	AC	189		
◆	GHAC	243	1	
Chocolate	FFBB	455	2	C
Clarified	VE	254	1	
Clarified	GF	245	1	
Clarified	JOC	338	1	
Clarifying	MFC	8		
◆	NSD	17		
◆	BHGN	423		
◆	NYT	456		
Colbert	NYT	457	1	
Colbert	JOC	339	1	B
Compound	OC	165	1	B
Compound	GRIL	39	1	B
Concord grape	NYT	510	1	B

RECIPE	BOOK	PAGE	TD	S
Cookies	NYT	578	1	C
Cookies	SC	152	1	
Cookies	FFBB	253	2	C
Egg	SC	152	1	
Greek	NYT	580	2	C
Hurry up	SC	166	1	
Norwegian	FFCB	562	1	C
Rich	FFCB	550	1	C
Sweet	NYTI	338	2	C
Coral	GRIL	39	1	B
Coral	FFCB	133	1	A
Cream	SPGT	117	1	B
Cream	NSD	299	2	C
I, powdered sugar	MAFC	681	1	A
II, sugar syrup	MAFC	681	2	B
III, custard base	MAFC	683	2	B
Chocolate	NYT	574	1	B
Chocolate	LT	361		
Dressed, cooked	SC	376	1	
Filling	NYTI	285	1	B
Filling	FFCB	543	1	C
Frosting	GHAC	344		
Frosting	NYTI	11	2	B
Frosting, variations	AC	695	1	
Hazelnut	SP	289	2	B
Icing	MAFC	671	1	
Icing, lemon	MAFC	676	1	C
Icing, orange	MAFC	674	1	C
Mousseline frosting, expresso	NYTI	286	1	B
Reconstituting frozen	NSD	299		
Rich	NYT	573	1	B
Creaming	NSD	17		
Crumb topping for vegetables	BHGN	388	1	
Crunch	SC	175	1	
Crust	BCC	88	1	
Curry	AC	190		
Curry	NYT	456	1	A
Custard filling	SC	148	1	
Damson, plum	JOC	777	2	C
Decoration (photographs)	LT	16		
Deviled, for seafood	JOC	339	1	B
Dill	GHAC	243	1	
Dill	BBA	105	1	A
Drawn	NYT	447	1	B
Drawn	BCC	332	1	
Drawn	JOC	338	1	
Drawn white roux	AC	455	1	
Egg yolk	MAFC	101	1	A
Enrichment	MAFC	58	1	B
Filling for cakes	FFCB	531	1	B
Fish	NYT	457	1	
Flavored	FFCB	56	1	B
Flavored	SP	116		
Fondant	FFCB	687	2	
Frosting				
I	FFCB	539	1	A
II	FFCB	539	1	B
Basic	SC	143	1	
Brown	SC	144	1	
Brown brandy	SC	144	1	
Browned	BCC	77	1	C
Caramel	SC	143	1	
Coffee	SC	143	1	
Fluffy	FFCB	539	1	B
Lemon	SC	144	1	
Mocha	SC	144	1	
Orange	SC	144	1	
Quick	NYT	573	1	B
Fruit	AC	821	1	
Fruit, preparing the fruit	AC	821		
Garlic	BHGN	361	1	A

RECIPE	BOOK	PAGE	TD	S
Butter, Garlic (*cont.*)				
◆	NYT	457	1	A
◆	JOC	339	1	B
◆	EBE	55	1	A
◆	MAFC	101	1	A
◆	BBA	152	1	A
◆	AC	189		
◆	JBC	266	1	
Garlic sauce, browned	PPLK	242	1	B
Green	JOC	339	1	B
Green pepper	SC	379	1	
Herb	FFCB	56	1	B
◆	KIS	365	1	
◆	BHGN	361	1	A
◆	JBC	265	1	
◆	GRIL	39	1	B
◆	SP	116	1	
◆	MSE	92	3	C
For meats	NYT	457	1	A
For vegetables	NYT	457	1	A
For whole wheat Italian bread	MSQC	157	1	B
Mixed	MAFC	102	1	A
Herbed	BHGN	42	1	
Herbed	BB	61	1	A
Honey	BHGN	361	1	A
Honey, spiced	SC	98	1	
Horns	SC	80	2	
Horseradish	FFCB	57	1	B
Horseradish	GRIL	39	1	B
& Lecithin mixture	FG	243	2	
Lemon	JOC	338	1	B
◆	AC	189		
◆	AC	726	1	
◆	JBC	266	1	
◆	SMG	151	1	B
Lettuce watercress salad	GRIL	87	1	B
Lobster	NYTI	269	1	
Lobster	JOC	339	2	A
Maitre d'hotel	NYT	458	1	A
Maitre d'hotel	JOC	339	1	B
Mushroom	NYT	458	1	B
Mushroom, blender	JOC	57	1	
Mustard	NYT	457	1	
Mustard	MAFC	100	1	A
Mustard, steaks w	GHAC	173	1	A
Nasturtium	CFS	312	1	A
Nasturtium	GF	153	1	B
Nut	JOC	57	1	
Olive	SC	379	1	
Olive	CFS	317	1	A
Onion	SC	379	1	
Onion	BHGN	361	1	A
Orange	SP	249	1	
Orange	BHGN	361	1	A
Parsley	CW	108		
◆	BBA	152	1	B
◆	AC	189		
◆	MAFC	102	1	A
◆	AC	189		
◆	BHGN	361	1	A
◆	FFCB	267	1	A
◆	MAFC	102	1	A
◆	JBC	265	1	
Pastry, for two crust pie 9 inch	AC	635	1	
Peach	GHAC	379	1	B
Peach	JOC	777	2	C
Pecan cookies	CW	101	1	C
Ice cream	BBA	229	2	B
Ice cream	JOC	719	2	B
Rolls, Karen's	GG	303	2	C
Pimiento	SC	379	1	
Piquant	NYT	457	1	
Poor man's	AC	463	1	
Ravigote	JOC	339	1	B

RECIPE	BOOK	PAGE	TD	S
Red wine for steak	NYT	458	1	A
Roe	GRIL	39	1	B
Rolls, aberdeen	CBB	571	3	C
Roquefort w walnuts	KIS	313	1	B
Rosemary	AC	189		
Rum glaze	BCC	78	1	C
Sandwiches, bercy (wine & shallot flavored butter)	CF	94	1	C
Sardine	SC	380	1	
Sardine, French	NYTI	278	1	B
Sauce	NYT	447	1	B
Anchovy	SC	391	1	
Anchovy	BB	153	1	B
Bechamel (see bechamel sauce)				
Brown	MAFC	98	1	A
Brown	MAFC	270	1	
Brown sugar	JOC	712	1	A
Drawn	SC	391	1	
For cooked artichoke	BBA	131	1	B
For vegetables	GHAC	256		
Lemon	MAFC	98	2	B
Lobster	SC	391	1	
Maitre d'hotel	SC	391	1	
Mustard	SC	391	1	
Parsley	SC	391	1	
Red	CFS	311	1	A
Shallots, white wine &	SMG	17	1	A
White	LM	46	1	
White	LM	83		
White	MAFC	96	2	B
Seafood	JOC	57	1	
Seasoned	BCC	332		
Shallot red wine	MAFC	103	1	A
Shallot, tarragon	BBA	152	1	A
Shallot white wine	MAFC	103	1	A
Shellfish	MAFC	104	2	A
Shrimp	FFCB	56	1	B
◆	SC	379	1	
◆	AC	12	2	
◆	JOC	339	2	A
Smoked salmon w	SC	379	1	
Snail	NYT	297		
Snail	MAFC	103	1	A
Snail	JOC	339	1	B
Spreads	JOC	57	1	
Stars	FFCB	551	1	C
Strawberry	MSE	298	1	B
Strawberry	SP	249	1	
Sugar creaming	MAFC	581		
Sweet	BTSB	61	2	A
Sweet	JOC	509	2	
Sweet, making	JOC	509		
Sweetened	JOC	713	1	A
Tabasco	AC	189		
Tabasco	BB	153	1	
Tarragon	AC	189		
Tarragon	MAFC	102	1	A
Tarragon	BHGN	361	1	A
Tarragon, meat flavoring for	MAFC	102	1	C
Thins	JOC	661	1	C
Vegetarian nut	SC	380	1	
Wafers, drop	JOC	655	1	C
Watercress	FFCB	57	1	B
Whipped	JBC	266	1	
White	JOC	340	1	B
Butterballs	SP	257	2	C
Buttercups	SC	171	1	
Buttered crumbs	JBC	266	1	
Buttered toast	SC	72	1	
Butterfish, sesame speckled	CFS	224	1	A
Butterflies	SC	75	2	

RECIPE	BOOK	PAGE	TD	S
Butterfly salad	SC	365	1	
Butterfly steak, Albert Stockli	AC	270	1	
Butterhorns, making	BHGN	71		
Butterkloesse (butter-flavored dumplings)	JOC	172	1	A
Buttermilk	JOC	485	2	
1, 2, 3, 4 cake	AC	651	1	
Batter	AC	555		
Biscuits, drop	CW	41	1	C
Biscuits (see biscuits, buttermilk)				
Bread	CBB	55	2	C
Bread, barley	FFBB	449	2	C
Bread, Scottish	CBB	48	1	B
Butter rolls	FFBB	491	1	C
Cake	AC	652	1	
Cake	SC	108	1	B
Cake, chocolate	FFCB	507	2	B
Cake, lemon	MHGD	115	1	C
Cheese bread	CBB	375	2	B
Chicken, fried	BCC	242	1	B
Coffee cake, spicy	BHGN	80	1	B
Corn bread, crackling	JOC	578	1	C
Custard cherry tart	NSD	97	3	B
Dill dressing, low calorie	MIE	253	1	B
Dip	BCC	16	1	B
Doughnuts (see doughnuts, buttermilk)				
Dressing	JBGF	550	1	B
Dressing	BHGN	351	1	B
Dressing	BCC	301	2	B
Dressing, greens	YGM	85	1	A
Graham, quick bread	SC	84	1	
Griddle cakes	FFCB	496	1	B
Griddle cakes	SC	92	1	
Lemon pound cake	FFBB	366	1	C
Loaf cake	MHGD	117	1	C
Muffins	JOC	581	1	C
Muffins bran flake	JBGF	597	1	C
Oat potato bread	JBGF	563	2	C
Oaten cakes	CBB	215	1	B
Pancakes (see pancakes, buttermilk)				
Pecan waffles	GHAC	371		
Pie	FFBB	100	2	B
Potato rolls	JOC	565	3	C
Potato salad	YGM	180	3	C
Quick bread	SC	84	1	
Raisin pie	FFBB	140	1	B
Raisin pie	AC	624	1	
Rolls	JOC	563	3	C
Rolls butter	FFBB	491	1	C
Rolls potato	JOC	565	3	C
Rye whole wheat bread	CBB	160	3	B
Scones currant	FFBB	582	1	C
Sherbet pineapple	JOC	725	2	B
Soup, chilled	MC	35	1	B
Soup peach	CBSS	168	3	B
Spice cake	FFBB	345	1	C
Squash (see squash, buttermilk)				
Thousand Island dressing, low calorie	MIE	256	2	B
Waffles	AC	798	1	
Waffles, plain	GHAC	371		
Whole wheat bread	CBB	103	2	C
Zucchini soup	JBGF	331	2	B
Butterscotch	AC	829	2	
Butterscotch	JOC	733	1	B
Bavarian	SC	203	2	
Brownies	GHAC	345	1	C

RECIPE	BOOK	PAGE	TD	S
Butterscotch Brownies (*cont.*)				
◆	JOC	653	1	C
◆	FFCB	564	1	C
◆	BCC	103	1	C
◆	AC	712	1	
Brownies, coconut	BCC	103	1	C
Chiffon pie	FFBB	122	2	B
Coconut slices	BCC	109	3	C
Cookies Schrafft's	FFBB	200	1	C
Cream pie	SC	347	1	
Cream pie	FFBB	112	2	B
Filling	FFCB	545	1	B
◆	BHGN	70	1	B
◆	FFCB	414	1	C
◆	JOC	646	1	B
Hard	SC	172	1	
Ice cream	FFCB	630	3	C
Icing	JOC	678	1	B
Marble cake	BHGN	102	1	C
Meringue pie	AC	626	1	
Meringue pie	SC	347	1	
Nut brittle	FFCB	685	2	B
Nut cookies	JOC	658	1	C
Nut pie	AC	626	1	
Nut sauce	SC	216	1	
Old fashioned	JOC	733	1	B
Parfait	JOC	721	2	B
Pie	JOC	610	2	B
◆	NYT	523	1	B
◆	AC	626	1	
◆	FFCB	589	2	B
Pie, date	AC	626	1	
Pie, old fashioned	MHGD	178	2	B
Pudding	BCC	141	1	B
Refrigerator cookies	AC	701	2	
Refrigerator cookies	JOC	660	1	C
Sauce	BCC	153		
◆	JBC	267	1	
◆	NYT	612	1	B

RECIPE	BOOK	PAGE	TD	S
◆	JOC	712	1	A
◆	SC	216	1	
◆	FFCB	637	1	B
◆	BTSB	162	1	B
Sauce, clear	SC	216	1	
Sauce, rich	FFCB	638	1	B
Sauce, two ways	AC	741	1	
Soft	SC	172	1	
Spice roll	JOC	642	1	B
Spritz	AC	708	2	
Sundae cake	BCC	133	1	C
Sundae sauce	SC	220	1	
Tapioca	FFCB	612	1	B
Toast	SC	72	1	
Buttery rowies	CBB	571	3	C

C

RECIPE	BOOK	PAGE	TD	S
Cabbage				
A la Bretonne	NYT	367	1	B
A la Russe	NYT	418	1	B
A piquant, crab salad &	AC	59	2	
All about	VGCB	41		
Amish sweet & sour	GG	79	1	B
Apple glazed, franks &	GHAC	212	1	B
& Apples	SC	415	2	
Apples & onions	KIS	278	1	A
Au gratin	SC	415	1	
Baked	JOC	267	1	B
Baked	JBC	300	2	B
Ball shaped stuffed leaves	MFC2	386	1	
Blanched buttered	FFCB	369	1	B

RECIPE	BOOK	PAGE	TD	S
Cabbage (*cont.*)				
Blanched or boiled green	VGCB	42	1	
Boiled	SC	415	1	
Boiled ham &	AC	447		
Boiled red	FG	199	1	B
Braised	JBC	300	1	B
Braised	AC	492	1	
Chinese	FFCB	371	1	B
Choux farcis	LM	139	2	B
Red wine & chestnuts	MAFC	496	2	B
& Stuffed	LM	139	2	B
Broth, braised	VGCB	43	1	B
Butter, braised	VGCB	43	1	B
Buttered	AC	492	1	
Buttered	NYT	367		
& Caraway, braised	JBGF	516	1	B
& Caraway, cream	NYTI	82	1	B
Carrots & corned beef	GHAC	178	2	C
Casserole, potato &	JBGF	379	1	B
& Celery	JOC	272	1	
& Celery	SC	415	1	
& Cheese soup, quick	BHGN	380	1	B
& Chestnuts, red	SC	415	1	
Chicken & carrots	JBGF	424	1	B
Chinese	JOC	272	1	
Chinese or celery preparing	BCC	343		
& Chinese pork	WC	120	2	B
Chinese, stir fry	VGCB	43	1	B
Chopped	SC	415	1	
Cooking	SC	415		
Cooking	AC	491	1	
Corned beef &	BCC	199	2	B
Corned beef &	JOC	412	2	B
Corned beef &	WC	85	1	B
Corned beef & carrots	GHAC	178	2	C
Corned beef & horseradish cream	GG	81	2	B
Corned beef, stir fry	WC	89	1	B
Cornish hens stuffed	JBGF	437	2	B
Country fried	JBC	300	1	B
Crab salad &, a piquant	AC	59	2	
Creamed	JBC	299	1	B
Dilled creamy French chou chou	GG	80	1	B
Filling	BBA	16	1	C
Finishing touches for cooked	VGCB	42	1	
& Franks, apple glazed	GHAC	212	1	
French fried	JOC	267		
Fried	FGCW	262	1	B
Goulash, Transylvanian	YGM	223	3	C
Green savoy red, preparing	BCC	341		
& Ham, dilled	AC	493	1	
Hot pot q pork spicy	GG	76	2	B
Individual stuffed leaves	MSE	150	3	C
Kielbasa	BBA	98	2	B
Ladies	AC	493	1	
Layered Transylvanian	NYTI	349	2	B
Leaves				
Beef in	JOC	431	2	B
Beef stuffing for	NYT	369	2	B
Ham & mushroom stuffing for	NYT	370	2	B
Lobster & roasted peppers	CPMC	202	3	B

RECIPE	BOOK	PAGE	TD	S
Stuffed	VGCB	47	2	B
Stuffed	FFCB	306	3	B
Stuffing (drawings)	FFCB	307		
Loaf	VGCB	44	1	B
Mold, confetti	BCC	289	2	B
Molded celery pepper salad	SC	369	2	
Mornay	NYTI	243	1	B
Mound, stuffed	JOC	69	1	
Pancakes	GG	81	1	B
Partridge	NYTI	28	3	B
Pecans, company	BHGN	394	1	B
Pennsylvania, red	BHGN	394	1	B
& Pheasant, sauteed	AC	241	2	
Pickle, sweet hot	MSE	124	3	C
Pickled	SC	454	3	
Pickled, Korean	NYTI	460	3	A
Pierogi	MSE	226	3	C
& Polish sausage, red	GHAC	213	1	B
& Pork				
Baked cream	FFCB	201	1	B
Chops, apple cumin	KIS	263	1	A
Chops w sherry vinegar sauce	MFC	155	2	A
Eb adobo	WC	113	1	B
Noodles	WC	115	1	B
Soup, old country	CBSS	262	2	C
Potatoes & ham	JOC	267	1	B
Quartered & boiled	JBC	299		B
Red	JOC	268	2	B
Alsatian style	GG	85	3	B
w Apples	BBA	134	2	B
w Apples braised	FFCB	370	1	B
Baked	AC	501	2	
Braised	JBGF	516	1	B
Braised red wine	AC	501	2	
w Chestnuts	JOC	269	2	B
w Chicken fricassee	MCIC	313	1	B
Duck braised in	MAFC	280	2	B
German style	NYT	371	1	B
Sausage &	MCIC	302	1	B
Sausage Polish &	GHAC	213	1	B
Sweet & sour	BCC	341	1	B
& Wine	FGCW	262	1	
Relish, green	VGCB	49	2	B
Relish, marinated red	VGCB	49	2	B
Rice dish	JOC	267	1	B
Rolled	EBE	62	2	B
Rolls, baked & stuffed	SC	282	2	
Rolls, stuffed	BHGN	251	2	B
◆	SC	282	2	
◆	WC	105	2	B
◆	BCC	211	2	B
◆	GHAC	183	2	B
Rolls, stuffed w rice & cheese	JOC	268	2	B
Rose salad	SC	358	1	
Salad	BCC	282	2	B
Caraway seeds	MIE	263	2	B
German	NYTI	316	1	B
Molded red white	SC	369	2	
Raw savoy	MCIC	412	1	B
Red white	GF	137	1	B
Shrimp &	AC	51	1	
Wilted	VGCB	45	1	B
Sausage savoy	NYTI	402	1	B
Sausages	SC	416	1	
Sauteed	GHAC	178	1	
Sauteed	JOC	267	1	B
Sauteed red apples	JBC	300	1	B
Savoy bacon	BCC	341	1	B
Savoy creamed	AC	495		
Savoy stuffed	AC	494	2	
Scalloped	FFCB	370	1	B

RECIPE	BOOK	PAGE	TD	S
Cabbage (*cont.*)				
Scalloped	JOC	268		B
Shredded boiled	JBC	298	1	B
Slaw, sweet & sour	BCC	282	1	B
Slaw, three	MSQC	140	1	B
Smothered	AC	492	1	
Smothered, green Venetian style	MCIC	374	1	B
Smothered, Venetian verze sofegae	GG	80	2	B
Soup (see also borscht)				
◆	CBSS	260	2	B
◆	FGCW	109	2	C
◆	JOC	151	2	B
◆	VGCB	45	1	B
Beet	FFCB	85	1	B
Cold	JBGF	325	2	B
Leek	MSQC	212	1	B
Main course	MAFC	48	2	B
Old fashioned	CBSS	259	1	B
Rice smothered	MCIC	109	1	B
Russian style hearty	VGCB	45	2	B
Sour cream	NYT	367	1	B
Sour cream	BCC	343	1	B
Spiced	NYT	494	3	C
Steamed	CW	25	1	B
Steamed, green	VGCB	42	1	
Steamed, potatoes &	VGCB	44	1	B
Stewed, red Italian sausage &	VGCB	46	1	B
Stir fried	AC	562		
Stir fried	BCC	341	1	A
Stir fry, three	SPGT	172	1	B
Strudel	NYTI	349	2	C
◆	SC	355	2	
◆	JOC	267	2	C
◆	BCC	342	2	B
Strudel, sweet	VGCB	47	3	B

RECIPE	BOOK	PAGE	TD	S
Stuffed	NYT	368	2	
◆	MSE	150	3	C
◆	MC	109	1	B
◆	JOC	430	2	B
◆	NYTI	184	3	C
Chou farci	GG	83	2	B
Corned beef hash &	JOC	268	1	B
Danish	NYTI	82	2	B
Dutch	NYT	370	2	B
Fijian	NYTI	95	2	B
Ham cheese	JOC	268	2	B
Leaves individual servings	MFC2	384	2	B
Pork apple	CW	116	3	B
Sweet & sour	JBGF	468	2	C
Whole	MFC2	379	3	C
Whole	VGCB	48	2	B
Sweet & sour	NYTI	315	2	B
Sweet & sour	SC	416	1	
Sweet & sour, red	VGCB	43	2	B
Timbales, carrot &	VGCB	55	2	B
& Tomato cheese dish	JOC	268	1	B
& Tomato sauce	JOC	268	1	B
Variations	JOC	266		
& White wine, California	AC	493	2	
Wilted	GG	82	1	B
& Wine, red	SC	416	1	
& Zucchini skillet	AC	494	2	
Cabernet sauce & bearnaise sauce, chopped steak &	MFC	152	2	B
Cabernet sauce, duck w	FGCW	184	3	A
Cabinet pudding	JOC	693	3	C
Cabrito asada (oven roasted kid)	NYTI	471	2	C
Cacciucco (fish stew)	NYT	266	2	B
Cacciucco broth risotto	FAIC	221	1	A

RECIPE	BOOK	PAGE	TD	S
Caesar croutons	BHGN	331	1	
Caesar salad	BCC	279	1	B
◆	SPGT	154	2	B
◆	GRIL	75	3	B
◆	VGCB	247	1	B
◆	SC	357	1	
◆	JOC	80	1	B
◆	MIE	259	1	B
◆	GHAC	271	1	B
◆	AC	39	1	
◆	FFCB	428	1	B
◆	NYT	416	1	B
◆	BB	139	1	
Caesar salad, easy	BCC	279	1	B
Caesar salad, original	BHGN	331	1	C
Cafe almond	BHGN	53	1	A
Cafe				
Au lait	SC	50	1	
Au lait	BCC	25	1	B
Au lait	JOC	28	1	
Au lait cream pie	FFBB	115	2	B
Benedictine	BHGN	53	1	A
Brulot	NYT	647	1	C
◆	SC	64	1	B
◆	JOC	28	1	
◆	FFCB	740	1	B
Colombian	BHGN	53	1	A
Diable	JOC	28	1	
Filtre	JOC	27	1	
Israel	BHGN	53	1	A
Pousse	SC	64	1	
Royal	JOC	28	1	
Royal	SC	64	1	
Caffe espresso	SC	50	1	
Cajun				
Artichoke & spinach	GG	14	1	B
Bubble & squeak (sausage & cabbage)	FFCB	211	1	B
Bubble & squeak	FG	216	2	B
Bubble & squeak	PPLK	299	3	B
Chicken morsels	SPGT	25	2	B
Meat loaf	PPLK	112	2	B
Meat pies	PPLK	128	2	B
Popcorn w sherry wine sauce	PPLK	281	2	B
Potatoes, stuffed	PPLK	235	2	B
Prime rib	PPLK	111	1	B
Sauce for beef, very hot	PPLK	251	2	B
Seafood gumbo & andouille & smoked sausage	PPLK	208	2	C
Shepherd's pie	PPLK	119	2	B
Cake				
1, 2, 3, 4	AC	650	1	
All about	FFCB	501		
All about	FFBB	277		
Baking, basic facts about	ACCB	644		
Baking, basic facts about	AC	644		
Baskets	SC	138	1	
Batters, mixing	FFCB	504		
Binding to bake an empty pie shell	NSD	27		
Carrot (see carrot cake)				
Coffee	BTSB	124	1	B
Cutting & serving	FFBB	283		
Decorating	FFBB	395		
Doneness testing for	FFBB	281		
Double fudge chip	MIE	331	1	B
Doughnuts	AC	799	1	
Election Day	MHGD	238	2	C
Equipment for	FFBB	284		
Foam types, hints for success	BCC	75		

RECIPE	BOOK	PAGE	TD	S
Head, preparing	AC	360		
Heart	SC	301	2	
Liver (see also liver, calf)				
Bacon, sauteed	AC	353	1	
Baked	SC	300	2	
Fried & breaded	CIC	298	1	B
Ginger pink peppercorns	MFC	156	2	B
Grilled, Florentine style	FAIC	357	1	B
Herbs & madeira, sauteed	AC	353	1	
Larded, braised, whole	AC	353	1	
& Onion, sauteed	AC	353	1	
& Onions	VGCB	183	1	B
& Onions	SMG	212	1	B
Potted	SC	300	1	
Sauteed	MAFC	405	1	B
Sauteed w herbs	SMG	210	1	B
Sauteed w onions, vegetarian style	CIC	296	1	B
Sauteed piccata style w lemon	MCIC	306	1	B
Sauteed, Tuscan style	FAIC	358	1	B
Vinegar	SMG	214	1	B
Lungs or lights	JOC	449	2	B
Lyonnaise	JOC	439	1	A
Tongue (see also tongue, calf)				
Tongue	SC	301	1	
Braised	SC	301	2	
Braised red wine onions	MFC	157	3	B
Vinegar capers	MFC	158	3	B
Calico salad	JOC	90	1	B
California casserole	BBA	96	2	C

RECIPE	BOOK	PAGE	TD	S
California cream	MHGD	387	1	B
California salad	GHAC	271	1	B
Calorie tally alphabetized by food	BHGN	388		
Calories table of	FFCB	756		
Calvados apples sauteed w	SP	267	2	B
Calvados, tripe w wine &	LM	214	2	C
Calzone (cheese filled Italian pastry)	MC	159	2	B
Chez panisse	CPPC	163	3	B
Ground beef	BCC	319	2	B
Pepperoni	BCC	319	2	B
Stuffed kale	VGCB	146	3	B
Cambridge sauce	FFCB	643	1	B
Camembert				
A la vierge	VE	217	1	
Biscuits	MAFC	198	1	C
Brioche	CBB	671	3	B
Cheese quiche	MAFC	148	2	B
Fried	KIS	308	1	B
Glace	EBE	30	2	C
Roquefort spread	SC	37	1	
Spread	SC	37	1	
Camp fire, building a	SC	334		
Camp stove stew	GHAC	213	1	B
Campari orange ice	SP	309	2	B
Canadian bacon	JOC	412	2	B
Canadian bacon	JBC	59	1	
Canadian bacon	SC	298	1	
Baked	JBC	59	1	B
Cooked	AC	453	1	
Cooking	BHGN	257		
Peach glazed	GHAC	203	1	B
Canapes				
A la simon	NYT	45	1	C
Anchovy butter	SC	38	1	

RECIPE	BOOK	PAGE	TD	S
Canapes (*cont.*)				
Anchovy curry	NYT	45	1	C
Asparagus rolled	JOC	59	1	
Bacon cheese	JOC	59	1	
Bacon cheese	EBE	12	1	C
Black radish	JOC	60	1	
Caviar cucumber	JOC	61	1	
Caviar onion	JOC	60	1	
Cheese baked	NYT	45	1	C
Cheese curried	NYT	43	1	C
Cheese mushroom	EBE	14	1	B
Cheese olive	SC	39	1	
Cheese puff	JOC	58	1	
Chicken liver	SC	39	1	
Chicken liver mushroom	SC	39	1	
Christmas	JOC	54		
Chutney cheese	SC	40	1	
Clam cheese	NYT	43	1	C
Crab & artichoke	NYT	45	1	C
Crab, hot	JOC	62	2	
Crabmeat	EBE	16	2	C
Crabmeat	SC	40	1	
Crabmeat	NYT	46	1	C
Flower	JOC	53		
Glazed	JOC	56		
Harlequin	SC	39	1	
Liver sausage	JOC	61	1	
Lobster	SC	40	1	
Lobster, hot	JOC	62	2	
Making (photographs)	LT	63		
Minced clam	SC	40	1	
Mushroom	JOC	60	1	
Of liver paste & juniper berries	FAIC	91	1	B
Onion parsley	JOC	60	1	
Oyster creamed, hot	JOC	62	2	
Parmesan cheese	NYT	44	1	C
Pickled herring	SC	39	1	
Pickled herring tidbit	SC	39	1	
Pizza small	JOC	61	1	
Rolls sardine	JOC	62	1	
Salmon smoked	JOC	62	1	
Sangroniz (toast w Roquefort cheese & caviar)	NYT	44	1	C
Sardine	SC	39	1	
Sardine	NYT	42	1	C
Sardine anchovy	SC	40	1	
Sardine deviled	NYT	42	1	B
Shrimp a la suede	NYT	43	1	B
Smoked salmon	SC	39	1	
Tartare	SC	39	1	
Tenderloin caviar	JOC	61	1	
Tomato cheese anchovy	SC	40	1	
Tuna cheese	NYT	42	1	C
Tuna hot	JOC	62	2	
Wheel rainbow	SC	39	2	
Candied				
Cherries	BTSB	258	2	B
Citrus peel	FFCB	691	2	B
Citrus peel	BCC	121	2	C
Flowers	NYT	635	2	B
Fruits sugar icing or frosting	MFC2	505	3	
Grapefruit peel	MFC	229	2	C
Grapefruit peel	NSD	77	2	C
Grapefruit peel	BTSB	255	2	C
Grapefruit rind	CW	109		
Leaves & blossoms, making	JOC	741		
Lemon peel	NSD	77	2	C
Lemon peel	BTSB	255	2	C
Orange peel	BTSB	255	2	C
Orange slices	NSD	117		
Oranges, roast stuffed goose &	GHAC	166	3	C

RECIPE	BOOK	PAGE	TD	S
Cantaloupe				
Dessert	BCC	129	1	B
Farmer's style	NYT	430	2	B
Gelato	SPGT	78	3	B
Mint	GF	157	1	B
Port wine sherbet w raspberries	MFC	243	2	B
Potato soup	GG	293	2	B
Preserves	SC	440	2	
Salad tuna	BCC	269	2	B
Salads	BCC	297	1	B
Sorbet	GF	130	2	B
Soup potato	GG	293	2	B
Spiced pickled	NYT	498	2	B
Cantonese chicken	SC	314	1	
Cantonese roast duck	NYTI	60	2	B
Capers				
All about	MCIC	23		
Beef stew w ginger, herbs &	MFC2	154	2	B
Beef stew w ginger	MFC2	154	2	B
Bread, whole wheat	FFBB	456	2	C
Broccoli	NYT	366		
Calf's tongue vinegar	MFC	158	3	B
Carrots	MCIC	375	1	B
Dip	MIE	24	2	B
Dressing dill	FG	82	1	B
Eggplant	VE	136	1	B
Fish en papillote	MIE	154	2	A
Lamb, leg of, w onions & tomato sauce	MAFC	342	1	
Lamb patties w sour cream	SMG	182	1	B
Mayonnaise w anchovies pickles & herbs	MAFC	91	1	B
Mustard sauce	FG	242	1	A
Nasturtium pickled	BBA	167	3	B
Parsley sauce for carpaccio	MSQC	80	1	B
Pickles brown sauce	MAFC	72	1	B
Pizza fontina escarole	CPPC	161	3	B
Sauce	MAFC	65	1	B
◆	JOC	324	1	B
◆	AC	372	1	
◆	FAIC	68	1	B
◆	JBC	262	1	
◆	NYTI	268	1	B
◆	NYT	447	1	B
◆	AC	455		
◆	SC	387	1	
Sauce, lamb leg of boiled	AC	372	1	
Sauce meatballs Danish	FG	187	2	B
Sole black butter	MSQC	128	1	B
Sole sauteed w lemon	SMG	116	1	B
Tomato salad w	FAIC	392	1	B
Tomato sauce	NYTI	437	2	C
Tomatoes	KIS	183	1	A
Tomatoes stuffed w tuna	CIC	38	1	B
Tuna tomatoes stuffed	CIC	38	1	B
Veal	YGM	72	1	A
Vinaigrette herbs onions	MAFC	95	1	A
Capon	BB	76	1	B
Barbecue mayonnaise roasted	CFS	262	2	B
Braised fennel boats	VGCB	125	2	B
Garlic rosemary roasted	GF	234	1	B
Grilled	SC	331		
Roast	AC	211	1	
Roasting, how to	JOC	463		

RECIPE	BOOK	PAGE	TD	S
Stuffed cranberry poached pears	GHAC	147	2	B
Stuffed giblet gravy	GHAC	147		
Caponata (Italian eggplant appetizer)	BTSB	143	2	C
◆	FG	60	2	C
◆	AC	520	1	
◆	VGCB	111	1	B
◆	WC	39	1	C
Cappellacci, butter cheese	CIC	170	3	B
Cappellacci filled sweet potatoes parsley	CIC	168	3	B
Cappellacci meat sauce	CIC	170	3	B
Cappelletti	MCIC	173	3	
Brodo	NYTI	377	3	B
Broth	CIC	158	3	B
Butter, heavy cream	CIC	159	3	B
Creamy	GHAC	262	2	B
Filled w meat & cheese	CIC	155	3	C
Fish stuffing w shrimp sauce	MCIC	180	3	B
Cappon magro	NYTI	376	2	C
Cappon magro sauce	NYTI	376	1	B
Cappuccino	SC	50	1	
Cappuccino coffee	JOC	27	1	
Cappuccino ice	SP	309	2	B
Caramel	NYT	598	1	
◆	NSD	333	2	C
◆	MAFC	583	1	A
◆	BHGN	112	1	B
◆	FFCB	682	2	B
◆	BCC	117	1	C
◆	BTSB	272	2	C
Almond pudding steamed	SC	189	1	

RECIPE	BOOK	PAGE	TD	S
Almond souffle unmolded	MAFC	622	3	B
Apple bars	BCC	105	1	C
Apple rings	AC	747	1	
Apples	BCC	121	1	B
Apples chocolate	BCC	121	1	B
Apples (see apples, caramel)				
Bavarian cream	JOC	694	3	B
Buns	JOC	566	3	C
Butter frosting	SC	143	1	
Cage	LM	363	2	
Cake	AC	667	1	
Cake	AC	652	1	
Cake, hurry up	JOC	635	1	B
Charlotte	FFCB	624	2	B
Chicken parsnips	GG	260	1	B
Chiffon cake	FFBB	304	2	C
Chocolate	BHGN	112	1	B
Chocolate	SC	170	1	
Chocolate caramel apples	BCC	121	1	B
Chocolate cream	JOC	732	1	B
Cookies curled	JOC	668	1	C
Corn	BHGN	115	1	C
Corn	BCC	121	2	C
Corn w caramel nuts	AC	830	1	
Corn w peanuts	BTSB	271	2	C
Cornflake ring	JOC	635	1	B
Covered marshmallows	SC	170	1	
Covered stuffed date rolls	FFBB	243	2	C
Cream	SC	203	2	
Cream divinity	JOC	732	1	B
Cream sauce	JOC	713	1	B
Creme renversee au	EBE	192	3	B
Cupcakes	JOC	633	1	C
Custard	JBC	44	1	B

RECIPE	BOOK	PAGE	TD	S
Caramel Custard (*cont.*)				
◆	JOC	685	2	B
◆	AC	728	1	
◆	SC	199	1	
◆	BCC	140	1	B
◆	FAIC	437	2	B
◆	NYT	594	1	B
◆	FFCB	609	2	B
Cornstarch pudding	JOC	688	1	B
Pie	JOC	610	2	B
Run cake flambee	MFC2	451	3	B
Spanish	NYTI	526	2	B
Unmolded warm or cold	MAFC	610	1	B
Filled	JOC	733	1	B
Filling	SC	148	1	
Flavored custard	SC	199	1	
Fluff	BCC	79	1	C
Fondant	JOC	728	2	B
Frosting (see frosting, caramel)				
Fudge frosting	SC	147	1	
Glaze	YGM	176	1	B
Glaze clear	JOC	683	1	B
Glazed chestnuts	LM	352	1	
Honey nut squares	FFBB	244	2	C
Ice cream	NSD	203	1	B
◆	JOC	716	2	B
◆	FFCB	630	3	C
◆	SC	205	2	
Ice cream, quick	SC	207	2	
Ice cream, walnut	MFC2	423	3	B
Icing	JOC	676	1	B
Lemon souffle	LM	320	1	B
Lined mold	MAFC	584	1	C
Marshmallows covered	SC	170	1	
Mold applesauce warm or cold	MAFC	624	1	B
Mr. B's	FFCB	683	2	B
Nut corn	BCC	121	2	C
Nuts	AC	830	1	
Nuts spiced	JOC	737	2	B
Oat bars	BCC	105	1	C
Parfait	JOC	720	2	C
Pears on puff paste	LM	285	2	B
Pecan rolls	BHGN	68	2	C
Popcorn balls	BCC	121	1	B
Potato cake, chocolate	AC	675	1	
Pudding frozen	SC	214	2	
Pudding, steamed	JOC	704	2	C
Pudding, steamed, w lady fingers	SC	189	2	
Rolled cookies	AC	703	1	
Rolls, Karen's	GG	302	2	C
Rolls, skillet	SC	80	2	
Rolls, tea	SC	81	2	
Sauce	BCC	153		
◆	NSD	334	2	C
◆	AC	741	1	
◆	MFC	248	1	B
◆	JOC	713	1	B
◆	FFCB	638	1	B
◆	GF	250	1	
◆	SC	216	1	
◆	FFBB	419	1	C
Ginger	NYT	612	1	B
Pear tart w	MFC	226	3	B
Skillet rolls	SC	80	2	
Squares	SC	165	1	
Sundae sauce	SC	220	1	
Syrup	SC	142	1	
Syrup	MAFC	584	1	A
Syrup	JOC	738	1	B
Tart	NSD	284	3	B
Upside down cake	SC	115	1	B
Vanilla	SC	170	1	
Walnut ice cream	MFC2	423	3	C

RECIPE	BOOK	PAGE	TD	S
Walnut tart	NSD	154	3	B
Winter squash cream	VGCB	291	2	B
Caramelized cookies, tongue shaped pastry dough	MFC2	477	1	
Caramelized sugar	SC	175	1	
Caramelized sugar cookies, palm leaf pastry dough	MFC2	478	2	
Caramelized sugar for coloring	JOC	508	2	
Caramelized sugar for glazes	JOC	507	2	
Caramelizing a dessert	NSD	339		
Caramelizing a mold	MHGD	354		
Caramelizing fruit	NSD	136		
Caramelizing sugar	BHGN	423		
Caramels coffee cream	SC	170	1	
Caramels vanilla cream	SC	170	1	
Caraway				
Batter bread w cheese	CBB	373	2	B
Bread, German	FFCB	467	2	C
Bread, sticks	NYT	49	2	C
Bread, Swedish	CBB	59		B
Bread, tomato	CBB	414	2	B
Brussels sprouts	BBA	131	1	B
Brussels sprouts salad cold	FGCW	133	1	
Cabbage, braised	JBGF	516	1	B
Cheese spread	NYT	51	1	A
Cheese spread	BHGN	41	1	
Cheese spread	BBA	19	1	B
Coffee cake orange prune	FFBB	580	2	B
Cole slaw	NYT	418	1	B
Cookies	AC	703	1	
& Cream cabbage	NYTI	82	1	B

RECIPE	BOOK	PAGE	TD	S
Dressing, honey	GHAC	284	1	B
Lamb stew	NYT	127	2	A
Liqueur	BTSB	220	2	C
Potato wafers	SC	406	1	
Potatoes, grilled	OC	95	1	A
Quiche onion, crustless	FG	107	1	C
Rolls rye	SC	73	2	C
Rye batter bread	FFBB	470	1	B
Rye roll	SC	73	2	C
Salt	BCC	221	1	
Seed cookies	NSD	53	1	C
Seed rye dough	FFBB	61	2	B
Seed soup dumplings	NYTI	341	1	B
Seeds				
Brussels sprouts &	NYT	366	1	B
& Cabbage salad	MIE	263	2	B
& German white bread	CBB	69	2	B
& Noodles buttered	SMG	217	1	B
& Pasta, whole wheat	KIS	110	1	A
Rump roast &	NYT	101	2	B
Carbonada criolla (beef stew w pumpkin shell)	VGCB	232	2	B
Carbonara pasta	SP	73	2	B
Carbonara sauce, pasta w	BHGN	320	2	C
Carbonnade flamande	BB	97	2	B
Carbonnade flamande	JOC	418	2	B
Carbonnades a la flamande	NYT	97	2	B
Carciofi alla giudea (fried baby artichokes)	GG	16	1	B
Carciofi ripieni artichoke sausage	GG	19	2	B

RECIPE	BOOK	PAGE	TD	S
Cardamom				
Braid	BHGN	66	2	B
Braid Swedish	CBB	460	3	B
Christmas wreath	GHAC	360	2	B
Cookies	SC	152	1	
Cookies orange	NSD	67	2	C
Cardinal sauce	NYTI	268	1	C
Cardoons	JOC	269		
Cardoons, boiled	FAIC	407	1	B
Cardoons, cut form of tripe	FAIC	407	1	B
Cardoons, deep fried	FAIC	408	1	B
Carnabeet cauliflower	GG	104	1	B
Carne asada (Mexican-style steak)	WC	81	1	B
Carne mechada (Cuban stuffed beef)	NYTI	67	3	C
Carnitas	NYT	14	2	
Carob	FFBB	5		
Carob brownies iced	MC	202	1	B
Carob candy squares	BHGN	116	2	C
Carob walnut cake	FFBB	324	1	C
Carp broiled marinated	FFCB	111	1	B
Carp red wine	NYT	233	1	B
Carp sweet sour	AC	138	1	
Carpaccio (thinly sliced raw beef)	FG	156	1	
◆	SP	40		
◆	MIE	33	2	B
◆	GF	129	2	B
Caper parsley sauce	MSQC	80	1	B
On French bread	MSE	44	3	C
Uses for	SPGT	74		
Carpetbag steak	AC	266		
Caribbean sunrise	BBA	26	1	A
Carrot				
All about	VGCB	51		
Appetizer Moroccan	NYTI	481	1	B
Apricots steamed	CF	31	1	B
Au naturel, baked	GG	92	2	B
Baby	MSE	219	1	B
Baked	JOC	270	1	B
Baked	VGCB	54	1	
Baked	FFCB	372	1	B
& Beer dill	FG	190	1	B
& Beets puree	CW	108		
& Beets soup	CF	10	1	B
Blanched	VGCB	54	1	
Boiled	JBC	301	1	B
Boiled	FAIC	409		
Boiled	SC	416	1	
Boiled, chives & parsley &	JBC	301	1	B
Boiled, green onions &	JBC	301	1	B
Boiled, lemon juice &	JBC	301	1	B
Braised	JBC	302	1	B
Braised	VGCB	53	1	
Braised	MSE	168	1	B
Artichoke hearts & mushrooms	MAFC	478	1	B
Broth	VGCB	53	1	
Butter	VGCB	53	1	
Butter	MAFC	477	1	B
Herbs	MAFC	477	1	B
Bread	FFBB	552	2	B
◆	CBB	413	1	C
◆	PPLK	40	1	C
◆	MSE	60	1	B
◆	VGCB	60	1	A
Bread, orange	JBGF	571	2	C
& Broccoli, stir fry	JBGF	517	1	B
Burnished	BBA	134	1	B
Butter, simmered	SC	417	1	
Buttered	NYT	371		
& Cabbage timbales	VGCB	55	2	B

RECIPE	BOOK	PAGE	TD	S
Cake	JBGF	587	2	C
◆	BHGN	94	1	C
◆	BCC	72	1	C
◆	VGCB	59	1	B
◆	MC	188	1	C
◆	EBE	110	1	B
◆	SP	296	2	C
Applesauce	JBGF	615	2	C
California	MHGD	111	1	C
w Cream cheese frosting	GHAC	323	2	C
Dark	FFBB	351	1	B
Fresh	AC	673	1	
Pineapple	VGCB	60	1	B
Rabbit's (baked in two 8″ loaves)	FFBB	351	1	C
Whole wheat bran	FFBB	355	1	C
Candied	FFCB	372	1	B
Canned uses for	AC	558		
Canning	BHGN	137		
& Capers	MCIC	375	1	B
Caramelized	JOC	271		
Casserole	BCC	344	1	B
Casserole chicken parsnip	VGCB	191	1	B
& Cauliflower mold	VGCB	66	2	B
& Celeriac soup, cream of	VGCB	57	1	B
& Celery	SC	417	1	
& Champagne dill	FGCW	265	2	B
Charlotte	VGCB	59	2	B
Cheese &	JOC	67	1	
Cheese &	SC	372	1	
Consomme	JBC	275	2	
Cookies	BCC	99	1	C
Cookies	AC	712	1	
Cookies oatmeal	JBGF	605	1	C
Cooking	AC	502		
Coriander	YGM	212	1	C

RECIPE	BOOK	PAGE	TD	S
Corned beef cabbage &	GHAC	178	2	C
Cranberries	VGCB	55	1	B
Cream	MSQC	69	1	B
Cream sauce	BBA	131	2	C
Creamed	MAFC	478	1	B
Crepes asparagus	FG	100	1	B
Curls or zigzags, making	BHGN	440		
Curry	VE	257	1	B
Custard	CW	28	1	
Dill	AC	504	1	
Drop cookies	JOC	657	1	C
Dumplings, Amish	GG	94	2	B
Elizabethan braised glazed	GG	93	1	B
Finishing touches for, blanched or steamed	VGCB	54	1	
For aioli	NYTI	135	1	B
Freezing	BHGN	137		
Fricassee, chicken &	VGCB	57	2	B
Fritters, cocktail size	VGCB	56	1	C
Fritters, sweet	VGCB	56	1	C
Fruited	GHAC	235	1	C
Ginger, cream of	CBSS	264	2	B
w Ginger & cumin	YGM	184	1	C
& Ginger soup	SPGT	48	1	B
Gingered, candied	SP	162	1	B
Glazed	MAFC	479	1	B
◆	GHAC	234	1	B
◆	AC	504	1	
◆	BCC	343	1	B
◆	BHGN	394	1	B
◆	NYT	371	1	B
◆	JBC	302	1	B
Grapes	GHAC	234	1	B
Grated hot walnut oil vinaigrette	CW	165	1	A

RECIPE	BOOK	PAGE	TD	S
Carrot (*cont.*)				
Grilled	GRIL	84	1	B
Herbs	NYT	372	1	B
Honey	CW	149	1	B
Hunter's style	SP	162	2	B
Huntington	FFCB	373	1	B
Icicle radishes snow peas papaya	GF	209	1	B
Italian	SPGT	74	2	B
Leaf	MFC	169	2	B
Loaf	MFC	169	2	B
Marinated	VGCB	55	2	B
Marinated	JOC	69	2	
Marinated raw shredded	FAIC	387	2	B
Marmalade	SC	443	1	
Mashed	FFCB	372	1	B
Mashed	AC	503	1	
Mashed	JOC	270	1	B
& Mashed potatoes	AC	503	1	
Mint	SMG	271	1	B
Muffins	PPLK	40	1	C
& Mushroom loaf	MC	99	1	B
Oatmeal cookies, honey	MHGD	318	1	C
& Onions	BCC	353	1	B
& Onions, garlic casserole of creamed	MAFC	480	1	B
& Orange				
Baby	GHAC	178	1	
Bars	VGCB	59	1	C
Cardamom	YGM	99	1	B
Glazed	BHGN	395	1	B
Soup	SP	44	2	B
Parmesan cheese	CIC	365	1	B
& Parsnips combined	MIE	212	1	B
& Peanut puree	SPGT	57	1	C
& Peas	JOC	288	1	
◆	AC	503	1	
◆	SC	417	1	
◆	FFCB	372	1	B
& Peas, 80's style	VGCB	196	1	B
Pennsylvania Dutch, barbecued	GG	94	1	B
Pickled	SC	454	3	
Pickled	VGCB	60	2	B
Pickled	NYT	499	1	B
Pie, sausage &	GG	96	2	B
& Pineapple, poached	JBGF	518	1	A
& Pineapple salad	BCC	289	2	B
& Plum, crazed	GG	93	1	B
& Potatoes, mashed	AC	503	1	
& Potatoes, pureed	SMG	259	1	B
& Potatoes, scalloped cream	MAFC	525	1	B
Preparing	GG	90		
Preparing	BCC	343		
Pudding	AC	732	1	
Pudding	SC	417	1	
Pudding, savory	VGCB	53	1	B
Puree	MFC	170	1	B
◆	NYTI	245	1	B
◆	YGM	232	1	C
◆	MSE	175	1	B
◆	LT	178	2	
Artichoke bottoms &	MIE	214	1	B
Sweet potato &	SP	198	2	B
Pureed	VGCB	55	1	B
Pureed	FFCB	372	1	B
& Raisin salad	BCC	285	1	B
& Raspberry, marinated	SP	164	3	B
& Rice bake	BHGN	395	1	B
& Rice pudding	GG	97	1	B
Ring	JOC	270	1	B

RECIPE	BOOK	PAGE	TD	S
Ring	FG	348	1	C
Ring	FFCB	372	1	B
Ring, crabmeat, cucumber &	AC	59	2	
Salad	MSE	104	1	B
Salad	LM	155	1	B
Dressing	VGCB	56	1	
Green papaya &	GRIL	97	2	B
Mandarin orange &	MSQC	213	1	B
Marinated	BCC	285	3	B
Raisins, nuts &	JOC	85	1	B
Shredded	CIC	406	1	B
Sauteed	VGCB	54	1	
Sauteed	AC	504	1	
& Shallot soup, chervil cream	CPMC	169	1	B
Slaw	FFCB	429	1	B
Slaw	VGCB	56	2	B
Slaw, kohlrabi &	GG	214	2	B
Souffle	EBE	189	1	B
Souffle	AC	556	2	
Souffle	SC	417	1	
Souffle, candied w carrot topping	VGCB	58	1	B
Souffle, chilled	VGCB	58	2	B
Soup	MC	28	1	B
Soup	VGCB	56	1	B
Cream of	NYTI	125	1	B
Cream of	NYT	68	1	B
Cream of	FFCB	86	1	B
Orange chilled	BBA	44	2	B
Puree of	CBSS	263	1	B
Puree of	JBGF	316	1	B
Squash, puree	MSE	194	2	C
Steamed	SMG	121	1	B
◆	JBC	302	1	B
◆	VGCB	54	1	
◆	SMG	233	1	B

RECIPE	BOOK	PAGE	TD	S
Sticks	CIC	41	1	B
Sticks, pickled	BBA	167	3	B
& String beans, julienned	MSE	172	2	B
Sweet & sour	SC	417	1	
& Tomato soup	CF	103	1	B
Topping candied for carrot souffle	VGCB	58	1	B
Torte	FFBB	374	1	C
Torte	SC	125	2	B
Torte	FFCB	522	2	B
Turnip cups	AC	504	1	
Vanilla tart	GG	98	2	B
Velvet	GG	95	1	B
Vermouth	FGCW	261	1	B
Vichy	MAFC	479	1	B
Vichy	JOC	270	1	B
Vichy cold	GG	92	1	B
Waterless	JOC	270	1	B
Whole young braised	MSQC	164	1	A
Yeast bread	VGCB	60	1	B
Yogurt salad	MC	53	1	B
Zucchini	FGCW	257	1	B
Zucchini salad	FGCW	134	1	
Carrottes rapees	SP	164	2	B
Carving a standing rib roast	BCC	195		
Carving a turkey or chicken	BCC	257		
Carving a whole fish	BCC	179		
Carving a whole ham	BCC	229		
Carving meats, how to	JOC	388		
Cascadilla (chilled tomato soup)	MC	29	1	B
Casera sauce Mexican (tomato and onion sauce)	BCC	329	2	B

RECIPE	BOOK	PAGE	TD	S
Cashew				
Asparagus stir fry	SPGT	171	1	B
Bake sweet potato	BHGN	403	1	B
Butter	BTSB	292	1	A
Chicken	WC	60	1	B
Chili	GHAC	92	1	B
Clusters	BCC	120	2	C
Ginger sauce	MC	69	1	B
Sticks	SPGT	115	1	C
Triangles	BCC	103	1	C
Truffles	BCC	116	3	C
Casserole dinner	BCC	254	1	B
Casserole pudding	NYTI	503	2	C
Casserole three layer	BBA	97	3	B
Casseroling	JOC	130		
Cassis				
Froth	MIE	311	1	B
Granite pink grapefruit	NSD	235	1	B
Grapefruit	MHGD	402	1	A
Sherbet	NSD	232	2	B
Sorbet	MSQC	185	1	A
Sorbet	MHGD	446	1	B
Syrup, strawberries w	MSQC	61	1	B
Vacherin	NSD	320	3	B
Cassoulet	BHGN	310	2	B
◆	FG	330	3	C
◆	NYT	360	2	C
◆	GF	100	3	C
◆	SP	157	3	C
◆	MAFC	399		
◆	JOC	423	3	C
◆	AC	598	2	
◆	NYTI	242	3	C
◆	VGCB	18	2	B
Cassoulet chez panisse	CPMC	108	3	C
Cassoulet, dietetic, no fat	VGCB	19	2	B
Catahoula chow chow (chopped vegetable relish)	BBA	167	1	C
Catfish				
Chowder	CBSS	124	2	B
Creole	BCC	177	1	B
Fried	GHAC	135	1	B
Fried	AC	133	1	
Fried pan	FFCB	111	1	A
Fried southern	JOC	354	1	
Hushpuppies, fried	PPLK	55	2	B
Cat's tongue	JOC	633	1	C
Cat's tongue	FFBB	259	1	C
Cat's tongue shells	LM	311	2	C
Catsup				
Cream dressing w	SC	377	1	
Prune	BBA	163	1	B
Sauce	SC	386	1	
Spiced tomato	SC	455	2	
Tomato	BTSB	177	2	C
◆	BHGN	141	2	
◆	SC	456	2	
◆	OC	163	2	C
◆	JOC	784	3	C
◆	FFCB	715	2	B
Cau yang roh (Mongolian grilled meat)	NYTI	49	2	B
Caul fat	MFC2	287		
Caul fat, pork liver broiled & wrapped w	CIC	302	1	B
Cauliflower	NYT	372		
◆	LT	180	1	
◆	JOC	271	1	B
◆	MAFC	456		
A la Grecque marinated	VE	111	3	B

CAULIFLOWER

RECIPE	BOOK	PAGE	TD	S
A la Huntington	AC	506	1	
All about	MAFC	456		
All about	VGCB	61		
w Almonds or walnuts	AC	506	1	
w Anchovy butter	NYT	372		
w Anchovy mayonnaise	CPMC	107	1	
w Anchovy sauce	FAIC	411	1	B
Au gratin	SC	417	1	
Au gratin w cheese	MAFC	459	1	B
Austro-Hungarian, green topped	GG	105	1	B
w Bacon bits	JBC	303	1	B
Baked	BCC	344	1	B
Baked	FG	196	1	B
w Bechamel sauce, gratin of	MCIC	379	1	B
Beets, & green bean salad	FFCB	433	1	B
w Black butter	AC	506	1	
Blanched	MAFC	457	1	B
Blanched	VGCB	63	1	
Boiled	JBC	303	1	B
Boiled	FAIC	410		
& Broccoli w lemon butter	LM	130	2	C
& Broccoli, mandarin style	WC	31	1	B
& Broccoli mold, marbleized	VGCB	65	2	B
Buttered	AC	505	1	
Buttered w almonds	JBC	303	1	B
Casserole w rice Venetian	GG	108	1	B
Cheese	BCC	344	1	B
& Cheese casserole	JBC	304	1	
Cheese, frosted	BHGN	395	1	B
Cheese pie	MC	130	1	B

RECIPE	BOOK	PAGE	TD	S
Cheese sauce, baked	GHAC	235	1	B
Cheese soup	MC	20	2	B
Cheese waffles	GG	111	1	B
Cheesed	JBC	303	1	B
Cheesed	AC	505	1	
Cold	JBC	304	1	
Cooking	SC	417		
Cooking	AC	505	1	
Cream, baked	GG	107	1	B
Creamed	SC	417	1	
Creamed, au gratin	FFCB	374	1	B
Crumbed	JBC	303	1	B
Crumbs w shallots	VGCB	66	1	B
Curry	VE	255	1	B
Curry, Satyamma's famous	MC	136	2	B
Custard	VGCB	64	1	B
Finishing touches for	VGCB	63	1	
For aioli	NYTI	135	1	B
Freezing	BHGN	137		
Fried	CIC	367	1	B
Fried	SC	417	1	
Fried deep	JOC	271	1	
Fried deep	FAIC	410		
Fried w parmesan cheese batter	MCIC	377	1	B
Fried, pureed	AC	507	1	
& Garlic oil, penne w	MCIC	149	1	B
& Gingered crumbs, gratin of	GG	106	1	B
Gratineed w butter & cheese	CIC	366	1	B
Gratineed w cheese & tomato	MAFC	459	2	B
& Ham gratin	GG	110	2	B
Headed	GG	108	1	B
Herbed	AC	506	1	
Hollandaise	AC	506	1	
Italian	AC	506	1	

RECIPE	BOOK	PAGE	TD	S
Cauliflower (cont.)				
Marinated	VGCB	67	2	B
Marranca	MC	117	1	B
Mexican style	NYT	372	1	B
Mold	MAFC	461	2	B
Mold w carrots	VGCB	66	2	B
Molded	VGCB	65	2	B
Molding cooked into its shape	MAFC	458		
Mornay	AC	506	1	
& Mushrooms in cheese sauce	JOC	271	1	B
Nicoise	GF	223	1	B
w Olive oil	FAIC	411	1	B
Parma style, fried	GG	109	1	B
Parmesan	GHAC	235	1	B
Parmesan	AC	506	1	
Penne w garlic oil	MCIC	149	1	B
& Peppers	BCC	356	1	B
Pickle	NYT	499	2	B
Pickled	SC	454	3	
Polonaise	NYT	372	1	B
Polonaise	SC	417	1	
Preparing	GG	102		
Preparing	BCC	344		
Puree	VGCB	64	1	B
Puree	YGM	232	1	C
Puree, turnip &	GG	105	1	B
Puree, watercress cream &	MAFC	460	1	B
Pureed	AC	507	1	
& Rice casserole, Venetian	GG	108	1	B
Salad	AC	47	1	
Salad	FGCW	136	1	
Salad	BCC	285	2	B
Salad, broiled	CIC	413	1	B
Salad, Italian style	VGCB	67	1	B
Salad, lobster &	AC	62	1	
Sauces for hot	MAFC	458		
Sauteed	JOC	271	1	B
Sauteed & braised	VGCB	64	1	B
Sephardic carnabeet	GG	104	1	B
Shrimp	AC	507	1	
Shrimp a blanket of mayo	GG	103	1	B
Shrimp dill sauce	NYTI	494	1	B
Shrimp sauce	EBE	111	1	B
Sieved egg parsley	SMG	195	1	B
Souffle	BHGN	394	2	B
Souffle	VGCB	64	2	B
Soup				
Copenhagen style	VGCB	68	1	B
Cream of	CBSS	266	1	B
Cream of	JBGF	316	2	B
Cream of	JOC	157	1	B
Cream of, creme du Barry	GG	100	1	B
Cream of, quick	JOC	167	1	B
Cream of, watercress &	MFC2	13	1	B
Super easy	VGCB	68	1	B
Spicy	VGCB	66	1	B
Steamed	KIS	231	1	A
Steamed	VGCB	63	1	
Stir fried	AC	561		
Stir fried, beef &	VGCB	68	1	A
Stuffed	VGCB	64	1	B
Swordfish steaks w cheese sauce &	WC	71	1	B
Timbales	JOC	207	2	B
Tomato &	MCIC	376	1	B
Turnip puree	GG	105	1	B
Veal chops &	SMG	194	1	B
& Watercress soup, cream of	MFC2	13	1	B
Cauliflowerets, boiled	JBC	304	1	
Caviar	BTSB	45	3	C

RECIPE	BOOK	PAGE	TD	S
Caviar	JBC	8	1	
Black, potatoes, new w	SP	35	1	B
Blini	NYTI	505	2	B
Blini, sour cream & red	MSE	46	2	C
Butter	JOC	339	1	B
Canapes, tenderloin	JOC	61	1	
Classic	BCC	6	1	
Coeurs a la creme	BBA	15	3	B
Cornucopia, smoked salmon &	SC	41	1	
w Creme fraiche & buckwheat noodles	CPPC	142	2	
Cucumber canapes	JOC	61	1	
Dip	JOC	75	1	
Dip	SP	36	1	B
Dip, red	NYTI	492	2	C
Dip, red	FFCB	54	1	B
Dunk	BB	122		
Eclairs	SP	36	3	C
Egg	SC	38	1	
Egg appetizer	SC	44	1	
Eggplant	MSE	71	2	B
Eggplant	FFCB	53	1	B
Eggplant	AC	16	2	
Eggplant, walnuts, cold filling	MFC2	353	1	B
Eggs	AC	17		
Eggs aspic	NYTI	111	2	C
Eggs, scrambled	MFC	59	2	A
Golden, pasta, smoked trout &	CPMC	184	2	A
Hearts, salmon	SPGT	112	2	C
Kinds of	SPGT	347		
Madrilene, red	NYT	81	2	B
Mock	BCC	20	2	C
Mold	FG	55	2	C
Mold	EBE	31	2	B
Mound	FFCB	58	1	B
Mushroom	YGM	170	2	C
Onion canapes	JOC	60	1	
Onions &	SC	38	1	
Oysters &	SP	36	1	B
Oysters, spinach &	SP	37	3	C
Pasta &	GF	96	1	A
Pasta & golden	CF	102	1	B
Peasant	SP	166	2	B
Potato chips &	SC	39	1	
Potatoes &	GF	177	1	C
Red, celery stuffed w	NYT	40	1	B
Red, celery stuffed w	JBC	9	1	
Red, omelet w sour cream &	MSE	91	1	C
Rose, preparing for	JOC	756	3	
Roulade crepe, filling for, herbed	SP	35	1	C
Roulade, herbed	SP	34	1	
Salad, egg, molded	JOC	90	2	
Sauce	JOC	317	1	B
Sauce	BBA	161	1	B
Spread	SC	381	1	
Tartlets & scrambled eggs &	GF	113	2	C
Texas	GHAC	274	2	C
Tomatoes stuffed w crabmeat &	SC	361	1	
Cazuela (Spanish seafood stew)	NYTI	503	2	C
Cazuela	NYTI	521	2	B
Celeri rave remoulade	JOC	85	1	B
Celeri remoulade (mustard-celery appetizer)	NYT	40	1	B
Celeriac (see also celery root)				
◆	SC	418	1	

RECIPE	BOOK	PAGE	TD	S
Celeriac (*cont.*)				
◆	JOC	272	1	B
◆	LT	183		
All about	VGCB	69		
An Avgolemono sauce	VGCB	73	1	B
Apple salad	VGCB	72	1	B
Boiled	VGCB	72	1	B
Boiled	JBC	305	1	B
Braised	MAFC	492	1	B
Brown butter	VGCB	73	1	B
Cake, potato &	VGCB	73	1	B
Cheesed	JBC	305	1	B
Cold	JBC	306	1	
Crumbed	JBC	305	1	B
Finishing touches for, boiled	VGCB	72	1	
Hollandaise	JBC	305	1	B
Mayonnaise sauce, salami &	SMG	305	1	C
Mayonnaise sauce, mussels w	SMG	304	1	C
Meat salad	VGCB	72	1	B
Parsnip stew	VGCB	73	1	B
Potato cheese gratin	VGCB	74	1	B
Potato puree	VGCB	74	1	B
Potato puree of	MSE	182	1	C
Potatoes, scalloped	JBC	305	1	B
Pureed	JBC	305	1	B
Remoulade	JOC	85	1	B
Remoulade dressing, classic	VGCB	71	1	B
Salad	JBC	244	1	
Salad	JOC	85	1	
Salad, raw	JBC	306	1	B
Sauteed	FFCB	375	1	B
Soup, carrot &	VGCB	57	1	B
Steamed butter	JBC	305	1	B
The Basque style	VGCB	74	2	B
& Tomato soup	VGCB	75	1	B
& Tuna sauce	VGCB	71	1	B
Turkey mornay	VGCB	70	1	B
Vinaigrette	SC	47	1	
Vinaigrette dressing	VGCB	72	1	B
Celery	JOC	271	1	B
A la Grecque	MAFC	538	1	
All about	VGCB	75		
& Almonds	JBC	307	1	B
Antipasto	VGCB	78	2	B
& Basil leaves, braised	GG	119	1	B
Beef soup	GG	120	2	B
Beet salad	NYT	421	1	B
Boiled	JBC	307	1	B
Boozy	GG	118	1	B
Braised	SC	418	1	
◆	JOC	271	1	B
◆	FFCB	374	1	A
◆	MAFC	491	1	B
◆	AC	509	1	
◆	JBC	307	1	B
◆	VGCB	79	1	B
Au gratin	FFCB	374	1	A
Consomme	NYT	374	1	B
Gratineed, parmesan cheese w	CIC	368	1	B
w Marrow sauce	NYT	373	2	B
Tomatoes, onions, pancetta &	MCIC	380	1	B
Bread, sage &	CBB	447	2	B
Butter, crumbed	GG	118	1	B
& Cabbage	JOC	272	1	
& Cabbage	SC	415	1	
& Cabbage, pepper salad, molded	SC	369	2	
& Cabbage salad	JOC	85	1	B
California, braised, asparagus &	GHAC	230	1	B

RECIPE	BOOK	PAGE	TD	S
& Carrots	SC	417	1	
Casserole, saucy	BHGN	395	1	B
Chicken &	VGCB	81	1	B
Cod, cream	VGCB	82	2	B
Cold, collected	GG	117	2	B
Consomme	VGCB	81	1	B
Cream, snails &	FGCW	334	1	B
Creamed	NYT	374	1	B
Creamed	JBC	307	1	B
Creamed, amandine	NYT	374	1	B
Curls	JOC	69	1	
Finishing touches for, braised	VGCB	79	1	
Fish & olive salad, molded	SC	371	2	
Glazed	JOC	271	1	B
Halves in broth, braised	VGCB	79	2	B
Herb soup	CBSS	269	1	B
Hollandaise	JBC	307	1	B
Lemon soup, chilled	VGCB	81	2	B
Nut salad, cherry, molded	SC	369	2	
Oyster &	JOC	365	1	B
& Pickles	SC	452	3	
Pieces, blanched, braised, butter	VGCB	80	1	A
Pieces, finishing touches for	VGCB	80	1	
Polynesian	BCC	345	1	B
Potatoes, braised in olive oil w	CIC	369	1	B
Preparing	BCC	345		
Puree of knob	NYT	374	1	B
Raw, fennel, artichoke, pinzimonio	FAIC	83		
w Red caviar stuffing	JBC	9	1	
w Red caviar stuffing	NYT	40	1	B
Relish	NYT	494	1	B
Relish	FFCB	284	1	B
Rice & peas	VGCB	82	1	B
& Rice salad	VGCB	78	1	B
Ring	AC	509	2	
Risotto	MCIC	122	1	B
Salad	AC	47	1	
Salad	JBC	244	1	B
Salad, cooked	JOC	85	1	B
Sauce	FG	285	1	
Sauce	VGCB	83	1	B
Sauteed	AC	509	1	
Scalloped w cheese sauce	NYT	374	1	B
Seed buns	CBB	559	3	C
Seed dressing	JOC	317	1	B
Seed w french dressing	SC	373	1	
Seed rolls	CBB	559	3	C
& Seedless grape ring	JOC	103	2	C
Slaw	VGCB	78	2	B
Slaw	GG	116	2	B
Sliced, w broth braised shallots	VGCB	80	1	B
Souffle	GG	120	2	B
Soup	FG	46	1	B
Cold	MFC2	16	1	B
Cream of	FFCB	88	1	B
◆	CBSS	267	2	B
◆	JOC	157	1	B
◆	SC	401	1	
◆	VGCB	81	1	B
◆	MC	6	1	B
Cream of, quick	SC	401	1	
Potatoes, leeks, rice &	MFC2	15	1	B
Rice &	CIC	62	1	B
Spinach saute	VGCB	262	1	B
Spread, cheese &	BBA	20	1	B

RECIPE	BOOK	PAGE	TD	S
Celery (*cont.*)				
Stalks, stuffed w cheese	SC	41	1	
Stalks, stuffed w crabmeat	SC	41	1	
Steam cooking, & variations	AC	508		
Stew	VGCB	82	1	B
Sticks, stuffed	BCC	8	1	B
Stir fry	VGCB	80	1	B
Stuffed	JOC	69	1	
Stuffed	JBC	11	1	
Stuffing	FFCB	280	1	C
Tarragon	NYT	373	1	B
Victorious	BBA	140	1	A
Vinegar	SC	437	3	
Wine	SC	418	1	
Celery root (see also celeriac)				
◆	JOC	272	1	B
◆	LT	183		
◆	SC	418	1	
Ablush	GG	122	2	B
All about	GG	116		
Braised	FFCB	375	1	B
Braised	MAFC	492	1	B
Cooking	AC	510	1	
Creamed, again	GG	122	1	B
Dressing, chicken, roast w	GG	123	2	B
Dressing, crispy roast chicken w	GG	123	2	B
& Green bean salad	GG	121	1	B
Hollandaise	AC	510	1	
Mashed potatoes w	AC	510	1	
Mushroom hash w	GG	125	1	B
w Mustard sauce	MAFC	540	1	B
Potatoes scalloped w	AC	510	1	
Potatoes scalloped w	FFCB	401	1	B

RECIPE	BOOK	PAGE	TD	S
Preparation	GG	116		
Puree of	BBA	131	2	B
Puree of	MFC	171	1	B
Puree of	NYT	374	1	B
Puree potato	YGM	135	1	B
Remoulade	NYT	40	1	B
Remoulade	NYTI	112	2	C
Remoulade	MIE	34	2	B
Ring	SC	418	1	
Ring mold	JOC	209	2	B
Salad	SC	360	2	
◆	NYT	421	3	B
◆	JOC	85	1	
◆	JBC	244	1	
Salad, red pepper &	YGM	195	3	C
Sauteed	FFCB	375	1	B
Sauteed	AC	510	1	
Scalloped potatoes &	AC	510	1	
& Shrimp salad	BBA	140	2	B
Souffle	SC	418	1	
Soup	BBA	30	2	B
Sour cream &	SC	360	1	
Wild mushroom hash &	GG	125	1	B
Cellophane noodles, lamb shreds w	NYTI	49	1	B
Cenci (deep-fried pastry snacks)	FAIC	457	1	B
Cereal crust	FFBB	69	1	B
Cereal griddle cakes	SC	92	1	B
Cereal pie crust	JOC	593	1	B
Cereals, coarsely milled	JOC	176	1	B
Cereals, finely milled	JOC	175	1	B
Cereals, kinds of	FFCB	310		
Cereals, puffed for cocktails	JOC	66	1	
Cervelas (garlic sausage)	NYTI	245	1	A
Cervelles (brains)	LT	284		

RECIPE	BOOK	PAGE	TD	S
Charleston benne wafers	FFCB	558	1	C
Charleston pudding	AC	724	1	
Charlotte				
Apple	SC	192	1	
Apple	LT	432	2	C
Apple, spiced	NYTI	294	1	B
Apple, unmolded	MAFC	623	1	B
Au chocolat	MSE	257	3	B
Burnt almond	FFCB	624	2	B
Caramel	FFCB	624	2	B
Chocolate	LT	435	3	
Chocolate	FFCB	624	2	B
Chocolate	JOC	644	2	B
Coffee	NYTI	293	2	B
Malakoff	NYT	593	1	C
Maple	JOC	644	2	C
Matzos	SC	194	1	
Matzos & apples	SC	194	1	
Molds	MAFC	162		
Nesselrode	NYT	593	1	B
Orange	FFCB	624	3	C
Royale	LT	438	3	
Russe	GF	35	2	C
Russe	FFCB	623	2	B
Russe	JOC	644	2	B
Angel	SC	136	2	B
Bavarian	SC	203	2	
Cherry	SC	137	2	B
Chocolate	SC	136	2	B
Kirsch	NYT	593	2	C
Orange	SC	137	2	B
Strawberry	SC	137	2	B
Charocis for seder	SC	44	1	
Chartreuse				
Jeffersonian, baked	GG	84	3	C
Sauteed w string beans	GG	348	1	B
Souffle, creme Anglaise	GF	61	2	B

RECIPE	BOOK	PAGE	TD	S
String beans, sauteed w	GG	348	1	B
Chasseur (see also sauce, chasseur)				
Chasseur (chicken cacciatorre)	JOC	469	3	B
Chateaubriand, definition	AC	260		
Chateaubriand, marchand de vin	BB	19	1	
Chateaubriand, sauce for	BB	19	1	B
Chawanmushi (steamed egg custard)	NYTI	456	1	B
Chayote sauteed tomatoes	MIE	215	1	B
Chayotes (Mexican squash)	JOC	272	1	B
Checkerboard cake	FFBB	334	1	C
Checkerboards, constructing	NSD	56		
Cheddar cheese				
Anchovy filling	SC	380	1	
Balls	SC	42	1	
Bread	CBB	390	2	C
Bread	SC	67	2	B
Chowder, corn &	VE	58	1	B
Cream cheese ring	SC	368	2	
& Cumin toast	YGM	222	1	B
Dough	FFBB	66	1	B
Fondue	MSE	71	1	B
Fondue	GHAC	88	1	C
Loaf, lentil &	NYT	360	1	B
Log	AC	15	1	
Macaroni salad	BHGN	334	2	B
Pie, New England	FFCB	354	2	B
Potted	SC	38	1	
Roll	AC	15	1	
Sherry spread	NYT	51	2	B
Soup	BCC	312	1	B

RECIPE	BOOK	PAGE	TD	S
Soup	AC	99	1	
Spread	GHAC	92	1	B
Spread	SC	38	1	
Spread dip or ball	AC	14	1	
Squash puff	BHGN	404	1	C
Sticks	SC	43	1	
Straws	EBE	13	2	C
Vermont sticks	GHAC	93	2	C
Cheese (see also parmesan, Gruyere)				
A word about	VE	195		
All about	JOC	511		
All about	JBC	27		
Almond slices	EBE	32	2	C
Anchovy	JOC	67	2	
Appetizers, fried	FGCW	97	1	
Appetizers, spicy	BB	114	1	B
Appetizers, toasted	BB	114	1	
Bacon sandwich casserole	SC	231	1	
Bake	BHGN	202	1	B
Bake, salsa	BCC	19	1	C
Baked, fennel	GG	174	1	B
Ball	BCC	17	2	C
Ball	FFCB	60	1	B
Ball, chili	BBA	14	2	C
Ball, mystery	EBE	37	1	C
Ball, smoky	BHGN	14	1	C
Balls				
Cheddar	EBE	31	1	C
Florentine	JOC	67	2	
For soup	JOC	173	1	B
Fried	FFCB	351	1	B
Pastry	JOC	68	2	C
Roquefort, cold	MAFC	196	1	B
Batter bread	CBB	392	3	C
Beans	MC	154	2	B
Beer fondue	BHGN	17	1	B
Beer soup	FG	49	1	B
Beer triangles	BHGN	84	1	C
Blintzes (see also blintzes, cheese)				
Blintzes	VE	208	2	B
Boiled	SC	227	1	
Boiled, baking soda	SC	230	1	
Bread	BHGN	62	2	B
◆	KIS	232	1	A
◆	JOC	556	2	
◆	SC	67	2	C
Baltimore	YGM	242	3	C
Buttermilk	CBB	375	2	B
Cheddar	SC	67	2	B
Cheddar	CBB	390	2	C
Corn, Mexican	MC	179	1	B
Double	FFBB	451	2	C
Flowerpot	BBA	175	2	C
Gannat	CBB	383	2	C
Jalapeno	PPLK	46	2	C
Pudding	FFCB	353	1	B
Quick	GHAC	365	1	B
Ring	CBB	381	2	C
Tabasco	CBB	379	2	B
Tomato	CBB	420	1	B
Broccoli &	BCC	340	1	B
Brussels sprouts, browned	MAFC	453	1	B
Buns	NYTI	350	2	B
Cake	FFCB	527	2	B
Canapes (see canapes, cheese)				
Caraway batter bread	CBB	373	2	B
& Carrots	SC	372	1	
& Carrots	JOC	67	1	
Casserole	JOC	243	1	B
Casserole, bread &	BCC	47	3	B
& Cauliflower casserole	JBC	304	1	
Cazuela, kidney bean &	AC	602	1	

RECIPE	BOOK	PAGE	TD	S
Cheese (*cont.*)				
& Celery spread	BBA	20	1	B
Chart	BCC	8		
Chart (photographs)	BHGN	198		
Chili dip	GHAC	94	1	B
Cooking	SPGT	362		
Corn	BCC	348	1	B
Corn bread, onion &	KIS	351	1	C
Cornmeal casserole	AC	584	1	
Crab apples	SC	372	1	
Cracker cheddar	CBB	704	2	C
Cream, French	JOC	708	1	B
Creamy	BBA	111	3	B
Crepes, chicken &	BHGN	304	2	B
Crepes, raising	MFC	234	1	B
Crisps	NYTI	113	1	C
Croquettes	JOC	218	3	C
Croquettes	AC	117	1	
Croquettes, rice &	JOC	219	3	C
Croquettes, rice &	NYT	325	2	B
Cups, ham &	GHAC	86	1	C
Custard pie	JOC	227	2	B
Decorating a whole	GHAC	84		
Descriptive chart of natural	SC	228		
Different kinds of (drawings)	FFCB	349		
Different kinds of Italian	MCIC	23		
Different kinds of	SP	235		
Dip	BHGN	13	1	B
Dip, chili	GHAC	94	1	B
Dip, long-keeping	JOC	74	1	
Dips	JOC	74	1	
Dreams	AC	117	1	
Dreams	JOC	58	1	
Dreams, fried	JOC	67	2	
Dressing, frozen	SC	378	1	
& Egg dip, Mare's	EBE	37	1	B
& Eggplant rolls	FGCW	273	2	B
Enchiladas	VE	212	2	B
Enchiladas	BCC	169	2	B
English	SPGT	232		
Exceptional	MSQC	189	1	
Filled pasta fritters	MCIC	77	3	B
Filling	FFBB	540	2	C
For blintzes	SC	94	1	
For cream horns mille-feuilles	MFC2	137		
For crepes	FFCB	498	2	
For Danish pastries	NYT	535	1	
For pierogi	FG	373	1	
For ravioli	GHAC	263	1	
Turnover, cocktail	WC	22	1	C
Fondue (see also fondue, cheese)				
Fondue	BHGN	204	1	C
Fondue	BCC	169	1	B
Baked	SC	231	1	
Cheese custard	AC	117	1	
Creamy	BHGN	204	1	B
Neufchateloise	VE	201	1	B
For salads, frozen	SC	369	2	
Frankfurters stuffed w	BB	27	1	
Fried	FG	336	2	
Fried, fennel &	GG	175	1	B
Frittata, vegetables &	FFCB	343	1	B
Garlic & parsley bread	KIS	150	1	A
Halibut, baked w	SC	237	1	
& Ham ball	BHGN	14	2	B
& Ham dip	EBE	20	1	B
& Ham spread	AC	12	1	
Head (see head, cheese)				
Head or brawn	AC	419		
Holiday, kinds of	SPGT	348		

RECIPE	BOOK	PAGE	TD	S
Hominy casserole	AC	581	1	
Horseradish ring	SC	368	2	
Hungarian	NYT	48	1	C
Hungarian	NYTI	340	1	B
Italian, kinds of	SPGT	66		
Leek & ham pie	SC	232	1	
Lettuce	SC	41	1	
& Lima beans	JOC	263	1	B
& Lima beans	AC	483	1	
Liptauer	GHAC	92	1	B
◆	JOC	708	2	B
◆	FFCB	59	1	B
◆	NYTI	340	1	B
Liptauer, variation	VE	208	2	B
Loaf	BB	113	1	B
Bovril	CBB	388	2	B
Pepper	CBB	371	2	B
Spinach, tomato &	JOC	301	2	B
Twisted	CBB	369	2	C
Logs, toasted	JOC	59	1	
Making unripened soft	JOC	512		
Milk dessert	JOC	708	1	
Mix, eternal	KIS	361		
Montrachet leaves (photographs)	OC	80		
Muffins	NYT	481	1	C
Muffins	BHGN	87	1	C
Muffins	JOC	582	1	C
Mushrooms on toast, puffed	JOC	247	1	B
Mustard dressing	BCC	280	2	
Napoleons	MFC2	139	3	B
Nut bread	BHGN	79	2	B
Nut bread loaf	JOC	243	1	B
Nut & raisin strudel	SC	355	2	
& Olive canapes	SC	39	1	
& Olive sandwich, broiled	SC	384	1	

RECIPE	BOOK	PAGE	TD	S
& Olives, whole garlic, marinated	CPMC	19	2	B
Omelet (see omelet, cheese)				
On toast, hot	SC	233	1	
Onion pie, savory	VE	210	1	B
Pastries	NYTI	326	2	B
Pie	BCC	165	1	B
Baker's	JOC	611	2	C
Cauliflower	MC	130	1	B
Old fashioned	SC	347	2	
Pumpkin	VGCB	235	1	B
Swiss	SC	232	1	
Three	YGM	210	3	C
Tomato	SC	232	2	
Pimento sauce	NYT	447	1	B
Potato pudding	VE	216	2	B
Potted	JOC	708	1	A
Pudding	JBC	29	1	B
Pudding w actual cheese	AC	727	1	
Pudding, colonial	AC	726	1	
Pudding, Mexican	VE	215	2	B
Puff canapes	JOC	58	1	
Puffs	MAFC	181	1	C
Puffs	FFCB	65	1	C
Puffs	SC	39	1	
Puffs, chutney	SC	40	1	
Quiche, bacon	FFCB	301	2	B
Quiche, beef	SC	232	1	
Quiche, camembert	MAFC	148	2	B
Quick, boiled	SC	230	1	
& Raisin brioche	CBB	668	3	C
Rice &	FFCB	317	1	B
Rice w	AC	577	1	
Rice, chilies and	FGCW	159	1	B
Ring	SC	368	2	
Ring, frozen	SC	368	2	
Ring, noodle	SC	336	1	

RECIPE	BOOK	PAGE	TD	S
Cheese (*cont.*)				
Ring, prune	SC	370	2	
Roll, curried	EBE	35	2	B
Rolls, jalapeno	PPLK	46	2	C
Rolls, refrigerator	EBE	24	2	C
Rolls, toasted	JOC	59	1	
Rounds, melba	JOC	174	1	
Salad, Alsatian	MC	51	2	B
Salad, peach &	JOC	94	1	B
Sandwich				
Broiled	SC	384	1	
Casserole	SC	231	1	B
Grilled	SC	384	1	
Grilled Italian	BB	115	1	
w Mushroom sauce	JOC	247		
& Variations	AC	813	1	
Sandwiches	BCC	12	1	
Sandwiches, hot, rolled	SC	384	1	
Sandwiches, spicy	BB	114	1	B
Sandwiches, toasted	BB	114	1	
Sauce	BHGN	255	1	
◆	JBC	261	1	
◆	BHGN	355	1	B
◆	JOC	326	1	B
◆	BCC	326	1	B
◆	AC	459	1	
◆	FFCB	265	1	B
◆	SC	386	1	
◆	MAFC	61	1	B
Broccoli chopped w	MFC2	342	1	
Brussels sprouts, gratineed	MAFC	453	1	B
Chicken pieces poached w	MFC2	256	1	
Chipped beef w	JOC	232	1	A
Fish fillets, poached w	SC	235	1	

RECIPE	BOOK	PAGE	TD	S
Green beans &	AC	478	1	
Herbed	CBSS	408	2	B
Mix	KIS	344	1	C
Quick	FG	228	1	
Scallops in	FGCW	117	1	B
White, variations	FGCW	288	1	B
Zippy	MC	82	1	B
Savory, hot	FFCB	354	1	B
Scallion quiche	VE	206	1	B
Scones, Hungarian	CBB	566	3	C
Sherry dip	SC	37	1	
Shortbread	CBB	394	1	B
Shorties	EBE	15	1	C
Shrimp nibblings	EBE	25	1	C
Smokey	EBE	42	1	B
Souffle	SC	232	2	B
◆	NYT	309	2	B
◆	BCC	163	2	A
◆	JBC	270	1	B
◆	SMG	86	2	B
◆	AC	115	1	
◆	MAFC	163	2	B
◆	BHGN	201	2	B
◆	VE	175	1	B
◆	FFCB	346	2	B
◆	AC	115	1	
Blender	JOC	204	1	B
Cockaigne	JOC	205	2	B
w Egg white only	MAFC	173	2	B
Fannie Farmer's	AC	116	1	
French	SC	232		B
Ham &	AC	452	2	
Herb	GHAC	116	1	B
Lobster &	NYTI	239	2	B
Low calorie	KIS	204	2	A
Made in advance	JOC	204	2	B
Make it easy	MIE	60	2	B
Parmesan	JBC	270	1	B
Swiss	JBC	270	1	B

RECIPE	BOOK	PAGE	TD	S
Cheese, Swiss (*cont.*)				
◆	AC	116	1	
◆	FGCW	338	1	B
◆	JBC	270	1	B
Soup	BHGN	379	1	B
Soup	FFCB	85	1	A
Soup	SC	401	1	
Cauliflower &	MC	20	2	B
Double Gloucester	CBSS	155	2	B
Quick	JOC	167	1	B
Swiss onion &	MC	13	1	B
& Spinach canapes	MAFC	472	2	B
Spoon bread	BHGN	86	1	B
Spread				
Baked	BCC	19	1	C
Chive &	EBE	33	1	B
For toasted sandwiches	JOC	58	1	
Herbed	FG	251	2	B
Long keeping	JOC	74	1	
New Mexican	YGM	206	1	C
Serving	GHAC	92		
Sherried cheddar	KIS	314	1	B
Sticks				
Cheddar	SC	43	1	
Parmesan	SC	43	1	
Potato	MAFC	198	2	C
Quick	SC	43	1	
Strata	BCC	168	2	B
Strata	BHGN	203	2	B
Straws	FFCB	65	1	C
◆	NYT	49	2	C
◆	YGM	192	3	C
◆	SP	7	2	C
◆	JBC	29	1	B
Straws, refrigerator	JOC	174	1	C
Strudel	SC	354	2	
Strudel, assembling your	MC	161		
Strudel, variations & fillings for	MC	160	3	B
Stuffed bread	GHAC	93	2	C
Stuffed eggs	FFCB	308	1	A
Tangy Sunday night	SC	38	1	
Tart, onion flamiche	GG	250	2	B
Tart, peekaboo of French puff pastry	MFC2	140	3	B
Tart, Swiss	SC	232	1	
Timbales	JOC	208	2	B
Tips	BBA	121		
Toast	JBC	25	1	
Toast	FFCB	351	2	B
Toast, white wine	NYT	318	1	B
Tomato & bacon sandwich, grilled	SC	384	1	
& Tomato fondue, quick	KIS	309	1	B
& Tomato pie	AC	552	1	
& Tomato rarebit	SC	233	1	
Torte	SC	125	1	B
& Tuna sandwich casserole	SC	231	1	
Twists, flaky	BTSB	115	2	C
Varieties of natural, chart	BCC	164		
Wafers	FFCB	66	1	C
Wafers	MAFC	197	1	C
Wafers, refrigerator	JOC	174	1	C
Waffles	SC	97	1	B
Waffles	JOC	217	1	B
Bacon &	BCC	30	1	A
Cauliflower &	GG	111	1	B
Warming the fire (photographs)	OC	80		
Whirls	SC	87	1	
Wine log	BHGN	13	1	B
Yogurt	FG	249	3	A

RECIPE	BOOK	PAGE	TD	S
Cheeseburger	BB	23	1	A
Cheeseburger	AC	314	1	
Cheeseburger	BCC	317	1	B
Cheeseburger, grilled	SC	328	1	
Bacon flecked	CFS	74	1	B
Classic bacon	GHAC	187	1	
Pan broiled	JBC	158	1	
Pie	BCC	211	1	B
Cheesecake	FFBB	340	2	B
Cheesecake	NYTI	562	2	C
Cheesecake	BBA	186	3	C
Apple	NSD	138	3	B
Baker's	JOC	611	2	C
Black & white	YGM	227	2	C
Blender	NYT	548	1	B
Chocolate	BCC	137	2	C
Chocolate semisweet	GHAC	340	2	C
Cookies	FFBB	229	1	C
Cottage cheese, w strawberry glaze	NYT	546	2	C
Cranberry swirl	GHAC	340	2	C
Cream	SC	348	3	
Crust	JOC	592	1	B
Currant	MHGD	39	1	C
De menthe	EBE	149	2	C
Easter	SPGT	60	2	C
Ellen's	EBE	152	2	C
Fruit gelatin	JOC	612	2	B
Gelatin	JOC	612	2	B
Genoise	NYTI	282	3	C
Ginger	YGM	226	2	C
Ginger	VE	272	1	B
Ginger brandy	MC	204	1	B
w glaceed berries	MSE	252	2	B
Italian	FAIC	446	2	B
Lemon	BCC	137	2	C
Lemon	JBGF	616	2	C
Light creamy	GHAC	341	2	C
Lindy's	BCC	136	3	C
Longchamp's	MHGD	41	2	C
Manhattan style	GHAC	341	2	C
Montana's mom's dynamite	MC	187	3	B
New York style	FG	348	2	C
Peanut	BCC	136	2	B
Pumpkin	BCC	137	2	C
Pumpkin, w nut crust	YGM	234	3	C
Refrigerator	SC	347	2	
Ricotta	MCIC	434	2	B
Rum refrigerator	NYT	547	2	C
Semisweet chocolate	GHAC	340	2	C
Sour cream	BHGN	175	1	C
Sour cream	JOC	611	2	C
Sour cream	SC	348	2	
Squares, Lindy's	BCC	136	3	C
Supreme	BHGN	176	3	C
Unbaked	FFBB	341	2	C
w Whipped cream	JOC	611	2	C
w Zwieback crust	SC	347	2	B
Cheesed bread	FFCB	469	3	C
Cheesefurters	BB	27	1	
Cheesy butter spread	BHGN	41	1	
Cheesy French bread, bake	BCC	168	2	B
Cheesy grits	BCC	57	1	B
Cheesy tortilla, bake	GHAC	115	1	B
Cheesy tuna soup, quick	BHGN	380	1	B
Chef's salad	BHGN	346	1	B
◆	SP	202	2	B
◆	FFCB	426	2	B
◆	BCC	272	1	B
◆	SC	362	1	
Deluxed & layered	GHAC	278	1	B
Hot wax bean	GG	345	2	B
w Tuna mayonnaise dressing, layered	SPGT	84	3	B
Chelsea buns, spicy raisins	CBB	584		

RECIPE	BOOK	PAGE	TD	S
Cherries	AC	751		
Bing, iced cookies w	MSQC	97	1	A
Bing, mallard duck w	NYT	179	2	B
Brandied	SC	459	1	
Brandied	FFCB	708	2	B
Brandied	BTSB	157	2	C
Candied	SC	175	1	
Candied	BTSB	258	2	B
Canning	BHGN	130		
Chocolate covered	BHGN	112	2	C
Chocolate dipped	SC	173	1	
& Currant jelly	SC	448	1	
Duck roast w	MAFC	278	2	B
Duckling w	SC	320		
Freezing	BHGN	130		
Fresh	JBC	100	1	
Ginger spiced	SC	261	1	
Ground poached	AC	756	1	
In Barlo wine	BBA	209	1	B
Jubilee	FFCB	656	2	B
◆	BCC	126	2	C
◆	NYT	619	1	B
◆	AC	752	1	
◆	BHGN	185	1	B
◆	EBE	182	1	B
◆	GHAC	302		
◆	NYTI	279	1	B
& Kiwi fruit	BCC	126	1	B
Mold of orange flavored rice &	MFC2	444	1	C
Pickled	SC	458	3	
Pickled	GF	196	1	C
Pickled, Dutch	JOC	785	3	C
Poached	JBC	100	1	B
Poached	AC	752	1	
& Rice yellow loaf cake, rum, raisins	MFC2	485	2	
Sunshine	SC	439	3	
& Wine soup	SC	405	1	

RECIPE	BOOK	PAGE	TD	S
Cherry				
& Apple salad	BCC	291	2	B
Apricot upside down cake	BBA	186	2	C
Black conserve	JOC	780	2	C
Blintzes	BCC	139	2	B
Bounce	SC	438	3	
Cake, chocolate	BCC	68	1	C
Cake, maraschino	SC	114	1	B
Celery nut salad, molded	SC	369	2	
Chiffon pie	EBE	163	2	C
Chocolate cake, maraschino	SC	114	1	B
Cider salad	BHGN	340	2	C
Clafouti	GF	229	1	B
Clafouti, sour	MSQC	89	1	B
Cobbler	BHGN	180	2	B
Cobbler	SC	196	1	
Cobbler	FFCB	524	2	B
Cobbler, fresh	BCC	125	1	B
Compote, red	AC	752	1	
Conserve	SC	444	3	
Conserve, black	JOC	780	2	C
Cordial pie	BCC	94	2	B
Cream cheese cookies	BCC	100	1	C
Cream pie	BCC	87	1	B
Cream torte	SC	126	1	
Crisp	BCC	124	1	B
Crunch, quick	JOC	607	1	B
Currants	SC	441	1	
Drop cookies, chocolate	BCC	99	1	C
Filling for strudel	NYT	543	1	
Filled torte	SC	126	1	B
Filling	BHGN	98	1	
Filling, pineapple &	SC	382	1	
Flan	MAFC	655	1	B
Flan, w almonds	MAFC	658	1	B

RECIPE	BOOK	PAGE	TD	S
Cherry (*cont.*)				
Flan, w liqueur	MAFC	656	1	B
Freeze	BCC	149	2	B
Fritters	SC	102	1	
Frosting, creamy	BCC	77	1	C
Ice cream, peach &	BHGN	182	3	C
Jam, sour	GHAC	381	3	C
Jam, sour	MSE	133	1	C
Jam, sweet	GHAC	381	3	C
Jelly	SC	447	1	
Jubilee sauce	JOC	709	1	B
Juice	SC	436	1	
Kuchen	SC	353	1	
Layer dessert	BCC	148	2	C
Layered salad	BCC	291	2	B
Leaf pickles	SC	452	3	
Lemon ring	BHGN	339	2	B
Liqueur	BTSB	221	2	C
Macaroon crumb pie, canned	FFBB	91	2	B
Macaroons	FFCB	556	2	C
Milk shakes	BCC	24	1	A
Mold, bing	FFCB	444	2	B
Mold, polka dot	EBE	135	3	B
Nut frosting	BCC	77	1	C
Nut ice cream	BHGN	182	3	C
Pecan bread	CBB	497	1	B
Pecan bread	BHGN	78	1	B
Phyllo pie	BCC	86	2	B
Pie	BHGN	277	1	B
Pie	BCC	85	1	B
Pie	FFBB	83	2	B
Canned	SC	345	1	
Canned	FFBB	90	2	B
Canned	AC	620	1	
Cooked fruit	JOC	602	2	B
Deep dish	FFBB	95	2	C
Fresh	SC	345	1	
◆	BCC	85	1	B

RECIPE	BOOK	PAGE	TD	S
◆	BHGN	277	1	B
◆	JOC	602	2	B
Frozen	BCC	85	1	B
Frozen fruit	JOC	602	2	B
German	JOC	602	2	B
Sour	FFCB	581	2	B
Sour cream	JOC	602	2	B
Sweet	FFCB	581	2	B
Tart	AC	620	1	
& Pineapple conserve	SC	444	1	
& Pineapple filling	SC	382	1	
Preserves	JOC	778	2	C
Preserves	SC	440	3	
Preserves, baked	SC	442	2	
Preserves, ground	SC	440	2	
Pudding	SC	193	1	
Ring, bing	SC	370	2	C
Roll, steamed	SC	189	2	
Sauce	BCC	330	1	B
◆	JOC	709	1	B
◆	NYT	613	1	B
◆	BHGN	176	1	
Sauce, brandied	GHAC	302		
Sauce, hot	EBE	193	1	B
Sauce, spicy	BHGN	359	1	B
Shrub	AC	752	1	
Soup	AC	98	2	
Soup, chilled	CBSS	161	2	B
Soup, chilled	NYT	84	2	B
Soup, sweet black	SP	57	2	B
Streusel pie	GHAC	315	2	C
Strudel	SC	355	2	
Strudel filling	NYT	543	1	
Sweet, jam	GHAC	381	3	C
Tart, buttermilk custard	NSD	97	3	B
Tart flambee	MAFC	643	2	B
Tarts, glazed	BCC	86	2	B

RECIPE	BOOK	PAGE	TD	S
Torte	SC	126	1	B
Torte	BHGN	176	3	B
Truffles	BCC	116	3	C
Turnovers	FFBB	156	2	B
Upside down cake	SC	112	1	B
Cherry tomatoes				
Flavored w dill	MIE	232	1	B
w Garlic	SMG	139	1	B
w Garlic & parsley	SMG	117	1	B
Herbed	CFS	249	1	B
Sauteed	KIS	81	1	A
Sauteed	SP	191	1	B
Sauteed	NYTI	166	1	
Sauteed shallots w	SMG	169	1	B
Skillet	BCC	366	1	B
Stuffed	SP	194	1	
Stuffed	FG	56	1	C
Stuffed w bulgur	JBGF	307	1	C
w Vinaigrette, hot	YGM	219	1	C
Cherubs	AC	713	1	
Chervil butter	CPMC	67	2	
Chervil butter, trout mousse, smoked w	CPMC	66	3	B
Chess pie	SC	348	1	
I	FFBB	99	2	B
II	FFBB	99	2	B
Lemon	BHGN	282	2	B
Lemon	NYTI	565	1	B
Or tarts	AC	628	1	
Southern version	AC	629	1	
Chess tarts	JOC	605	2	B
Chestnut	SP	196		
Chestnut	MAFC	517		
All about	MAFC	517		
Baked	JOC	273	1	B
Boiled	JOC	272	1	B
Boiled	SC	418	1	
Boiled & pureed	NYT	375	1	B

RECIPE	BOOK	PAGE	TD	S
Boiled w red wine	MCIC	443	1	B
Braised	FFCB	376	1	B
& Brussels sprouts	FFCB	368	1	B
◆	SC	414	1	
◆	AC	489	1	
◆	VGCB	38	1	B
& Brussels sprouts, baked	JOC	266	1	B
& Brussels sprouts in brown sauce	SC	414	1	
Burned drunken	FAIC	477	1	B
& Cabbage, red	JOC	269	2	B
& Cabbage, red	SC	415	1	
Cake	SP	299	2	C
Cake, flat	FAIC	479	1	B
Caramel glazed	LM	352	1	
Chocolate cake	LM	354	2	C
Cooking in their shells	AC	511		
Cream mousse	GHAC	299	3	C
Croquettes	SC	186	1	
Dessert	SC	200	1	
Dessert, puree	BTSB	248	2	C
Deviled	SC	41	1	
Dressing for game	JOC	457	2	C
Filling, chocolate	NYTI	290	1	
Fingers, finish	BHGN	165	1	C
Flour crepes	FAIC	481	1	C
Glazed	JOC	743	2	
Ice cream	FFCB	630	3	C
Ice cream	SC	206	2	
In English custard	NYTI	295	1	B
Lamb chops ragout	AC	382	2	
Mound	JOC	688	2	B
Mound, pureed chocolate	CIC	440	2	B
Mousse	NYTI	305	2	B
Mousse, cream	GHAC	299	3	C
& Other vegetables	AC	511		

RECIPE	BOOK	PAGE	TD	S
Pate	BCC	19	2	B
Peppers stuffed w tomato, basil &	SPGT	167	1	B
Phyllo kisses	SPGT	116	2	C
Tarts, miniature	SP	6	2	C
Chez Panisse bread	CPMC	230	3	C
Chianti beef stew, Florentine style	FAIC	342	2	B
Chianti wine, peaches in	FAIC	496	2	B
Chianti wine, strawberries in	FAIC	496	2	B
Chick pea (see also chickpea)				
Casserole	NYTI	358	3	C
For aioli	NYTI	135	3	B
Loaf	SC	185	1	
Pasta soup	FAIC	128	3	B
Salad	NYT	427	1	B
Salad, salmon &	SMG	313	1	B
Soup	CIC	85	1	B
Soup	CBSS	274	2	C
Spread	MIE	27	1	B
Stew chicken	FGCW	366	3	B
Peas, Indian	NYT	359	2	B
Peas, lamb cracked wheat w	NYTI	542	1	B
Peas, pasta &	CIC	87	1	B
Peas & rice soup	CIC	86	1	B
Chicken				
A la campagne	JOC	472	2	C
A la Kiev	NYT	186	2	B
A la king	BCC	253	1	B
◆	FFCB	256	2	A
◆	BHGN	304	1	B
◆	SC	310	1	
◆	JOC	235	1	B
◆	GHAC	158	1	B
A la king, cheesy	BHGN	304	1	B
A la king, creamed	AC	202	1	

RECIPE	BOOK	PAGE	TD	S
A la king, scalloped w noodles	SC	311	1	
A la Maryland or Maryland fried chicken	AC	193	1	
A la Providence	FFCB	245	2	B
A modern way to fry	AC	192	1	
A richer creamed	AC	201	1	
Almond croquettes	FFCB	258	2	B
Almond mousse	FFCB	449	2	B
Almond salad	BCC	264	2	B
Almond supreme	FFCB	256	1	B
Almonds	NYTI	486	3	C
◆	SC	311	2	
◆	NYT	196	1	B
◆	EBE	80	1	B
Almonds w broccoli hollandaise	WC	63	1	B
Aloha	WC	52	1	B
Appetizer, spicy	FAIC	302	2	B
Applejack sauce	SMG	44	1	B
w Apples & ginger	YGM	45	1	B
Apricot	BHGN	301	1	B
Apricot & currant	SPGT	104	1	B
w Apricot glaze	FG	241	1	B
& Apricot salad	YGM	183	2	C
w Artichoke hearts	MIE	106	1	B
& Asparagus cream mold, lemon	FFCB	449	2	B
& Asparagus mousse	BBA	68	2	B
& Asparagus on toast	VGCB	8	1	B
& Asparagus stacks	BHGN	306	1	B
Aspic	MFC2	255	2	
Aspic	JOC	97	2	B
Aspic, cold	JBC	227	2	
Autumn roast	BCC	241	2	B
& Avocado cream	SMG	30	1	B
& Avocado, creamed	SC	317	1	
& Avocado mousse	FGCW	293	2	B

RECIPE	BOOK	PAGE	TD	S
Chicken (*cont.*)				
& Avocado sandwiches	BCC	322	1	B
Baby, on the spit	BB	75	1	
& Bacon, fried	AC	193	1	
& Bacon salad	BCC	263	2	B
& Bacon salad	GHAC	280	1	B
Bake, crowd size	BHGN	310	1	C
Baked	SC	308	2	
Chinese style	MIE	99	1	B
Cream	NYT	194	1	B
w Imperial cumberland sauce	EBE	69	1	B
On a soft onion roll	CF	142	1	B
Or oven fried	AC	196	1	
Sour cream	NYT	194	2	B
Balls, curried	EBE	35	1	C
Barbecue, roasted	FFCB	237	1	B
Barbecue, sauce for baked	JBGF	639	1	B
Barbecued	NYTI	560	1	B
◆	JBC	222	1	
◆	JOC	466	1	
◆	MSE	136	3	C
#1	CFS	105	2	A
#2	CFS	106	1	B
Apricot	GHAC	221	1	B
Oven	BCC	243	1	B
Oven	SC	309	1	
w Polynesian sauce	OC	133	2	B
Stove top	JBGF	425	1	B
Whole	SC	331	2	
& Barley bake	JBGF	420	1	B
& Barley & corn soup	JBGF	338	2	B
Basic				
Boiled, poached	AC	198	1	
Broiled	BHGN	307	1	B
Broiled	AC	188	1	

RECIPE	BOOK	PAGE	TD	S
Cutlet Kiev & variations	AC	216	2	
Roast	AC	211	1	
Vertically roasted	MIE	93	2	B
Batter	JOC	467	1	B
Bean paste miso	FGCW	358	3	B
Beef kebabs	OC	133	2	B
& Beef soup	SC	396	3	
& Beets khuta	NYTI	356	2	B
Bengal	NYTI	356	2	B
Big mamou, on pasta	PPLK	156	2	B
Bits, sherried	JOC	71	1	
w Black olives	FAIC	294	1	B
Blanquette of	FFCB	255	1	A
Blanquette of	AC	203	1	
Bobbie's	SPGT	51	2	B
Boiled	SC	308		
Boiled	NYTI	473	1	B
Boiled	NYTI	229	1	
Boiled & oven browned	SC	308		
Bon bon	YGM	222	2	C
Boned	JOC	472	2	
Boned, whole & stuffed	FAIC	307	3	C
Boneless, w oyster dressing gingersnap	PPLK	177	3	B
Boning	MFC2	269		
Boning a	MAFC	570		
Boning a whole	MCIC	317	2	B
Bordeaux	NYT	197	1	B
Bouillabaisse w aioli sauce	MFC2	263	2	
Bouillon, jellied	SC	398	1	
Braised w wine	JOC	468	2	B
Breast				
A l'empereur	NYTI	223	2	B
w A pecan crust	GHAC	156	1	B

CHICKEN

RECIPE	BOOK	PAGE	TD	S
Albufera	NYTI	222	1	B
All' alba	NYT	187	1	B
Alla parmigiana	NYTI	407	1	B
w Asparagus butter	SMG	26	1	B
Baked	FFCB	247	1	B
Baked on a bed of wild mushrooms	SP	89	2	B
Boning	BHGN	294		
Boning	NYT	185		
Boning	MAFC	570		
Boning a whole	MCIC	317	2	B
Brandied	SC	310	1	
Brandied	JOC	470	1	B
Breaded	SMG	28	1	B
Breaded	AC	215	1	
Broth topini, potato	FAIC	111	2	B
Chaud froid	MAFC	551	2	B
Chaud froid, diced	MAFC	552	3	B
w Chicken mousse on chaud-froid	MAFC	552	3	
Cockaigne	JOC	471	1	
w Cream	MAFC	268	1	B
Cured & smoked	CFS	274	2	B
Diced, vegetables & cream	MAFC	269	1	B
Escoffier	CPMC	184	2	A
Filleting	CIC	313		
Fillets sauteed w lemon & parsley	CIC	314	1	B
Florentine style	FAIC	292	1	B
Gismonda	NYTI	406	1	B
w Grapes	SMG	22	1	B
w Green peppercorn sauce, chilled	BBA	69	2	B
Hungarian	NYTI	348	1	B
In port	NYTI	501	1	B
w Leeks	VGCB	160	1	B
w Livers on a skewer	OC	135	1	B
w Many mustards	GRIL	90	2	B
Maryland	EBE	71	2	B
Maryland	WC	57	2	B
Moroccan	MIE	102	1	B
w Mushrooms & cream	MAFC	269	1	B
Mustard, grilled & boneless	MIE	103	1	B
Of a l'archiduc	BBA	68	3	B
w Paprika, onions & cream	MAFC	268	1	B
Piquant	EBE	72	1	B
Poached	NYTI	227	1	A
Poached & stuffed	AC	218	1	
Pudding of veal, prosciutto &	FAIC	375	2	B
Quantity for creaming	JOC	471	2	
Quantity for salad	JOC	471	2	
Ratatouille	YGM	46	1	B
w Red sauce	OC	135	1	A
Rolled in parmesan w bread crumbs	MAFC	271	1	B
Rolled, stuffed w pork	CIC	315	2	B
Sauteed	FFCB	246	1	B
Sauteed w butter	MAFC	270	1	B
Sesame	CW	68	1	B
w Sesame seeds	YGM	55	1	A
Sienna style	NYTI	407	1	B
w Spinach	SMG	24	1	B
Stuffed	JOC	471	2	A
Stuffed	MSE	294	2	C
Stuffed w crab	BHGN	306	2	B
Stuffed w goose liver	MFC	86	3	B

RECIPE	BOOK	PAGE	TD	S
Chicken Breast (*cont.*)				
Stuffed w mushrooms	FFCB	247	1	B
Stuffed w orange & leeks	SPGT	89	3	B
Supremes, preparing	MAFC	267		
w Tarragon	NYT	189	1	B
w Tarragon	KIS	81	1	A
Tomato a la marengo	VGCB	321	2	B
Viennese	NYT	187	2	B
w White wine sauteed & stuffed	AC	218	1	
Breezy, barbecued	EBE	70	3	B
& Broccoli bake	SC	316	1	
& Broccoli casserole	SC	312	1	
& Broccoli mornay	VGCB	33	2	B
& Broccoli salad	FG	83	1	B
Broiled	SC	308	1	A
◆	SMG	16	1	B
◆	GHAC	149	1	B
◆	FFCB	237	1	B
◆	BCC	246		
◆	OC	136	1	B
◆	BB	40	1	
Barbecue	BHGN	307	1	C
w Chili	BCC	246	1	
Country style	BCC	246	1	B
Deviled	AC	190	1	
Lemon	BCC	246	1	
Mustard, herbs, & bread crumbs	MAFC	265	1	B
Oven	FFCB	237	1	B
Paprika	GHAC	149	1	B
Spring	JOC	466	1	
Broiler barbecued	AC	190	1	
Broth	BCC	304	2	B
◆	JOC	146	1	B
◆	JBC	277	2	
◆	WC	53	1	B
◆	SC	394	3	
◆	CBSS	86	2	B
Basic	AC	87	2	
Clam, quick	JOC	168	1	
Double	JBC	277	2	
Egg	JOC	146	1	A
w Brown gravy	BCC	259	1	B
Bubbling tomato	GG	377	2	B
w Bulgur & lemon	JBGF	434	2	B
w Bulgur, Middle Eastern	YGM	218	2	C
Burritos	GHAC	157	2	B
Buttermilk, fried	BCC	242	1	B
Cacciatore	EBE	72	1	B
◆	BHGN	301	2	B
◆	FFCB	240	2	B
◆	GHAC	150	1	B
◆	JOC	469	3	B
◆	BB	96	1	B
Cacciatore w noodles	JBGF	423	1	B
California	AC	207	2	
Californian	WC	51	1	B
Cantonese	SC	314	1	
Canzanese	NYTI	404	2	B
Cappelletti w cucumber	CPPC	40	3	B
w Carrot, fricassee	VGCB	57	2	B
w Carrots & cabbage	JBGF	424	1	B
Carving a	BCC	257		
w Cashews	WC	60	1	B
Casserole	JBC	226	2	
◆	FFCB	240	1	B
◆	SC	316	1	
◆	AC	209	1	
◆	AC	210	1	

RECIPE	BOOK	PAGE	TD	S
Baked	SC	316	1	
w Carrot & parsnip	VGCB	191	1	B
w Onion	FGCW	322	2	B
Poached w wine & tarragon	MFC2	265	3	B
Roasted w bacon, onions & potatoes	MAFC	252	2	B
Roasted w tarragon	MAFC	247	2	B
Serbian	NYTI	553	2	B
w Vegetables	JOC	235	2	B
w Celery	VGCB	81	1	B
w Champagne sauce	NYTI	207	2	C
w Champagne sauce au pavillon	NYTI	206	2	A
Charbroiled, marinated w pepper oil	CIC	307	2	B
Charcoal grilled w garlic puree	CPMC	169	2	B
Chart four kinds of	SP	86		
Chasseur	NYTI	208	2	B
Chaud froid (cold dish)	MFC2	258	2	B
Cheese cache	BBA	68	2	B
& Cheese crepes	BHGN	304	2	B
& Cheese, Greek	JBGF	422	1	B
& Cheese w hot peppers	PPLK	171	2	B
& Chick-pea stew	FGCW	366	3	B
& Chickpeas, ginger	JBGF	435	1	B
& Chickpeas w turnips	VGCB	333	1	B
Chilled, orange	GHAC	156	2	C
Chinese walnut	BBA	81	2	B
Chinoise	EBE	72	1	B
Chop suey for 15	SC	313	1	C
Chow mein	SC	313	1	
Chowder, curried	CBSS	142	2	B

RECIPE	BOOK	PAGE	TD	S
w Cilantro	BCC	252	1	B
w Cinnamon	KIS	105	1	A
City	JOC	420	2	B
City	FFCB	199	1	B
Clay pot, Chinese	BBA	81	2	B
Coating mix (shake it & bake it)	KIS	357	1	
Coffee w paprika	FGCW	383	1	B
Cold				
Deviled	EBE	81	1	B
Glass noodle salad w peanut sauce	FG	305	2	B
Glazed	LM	167	3	
Noodles w spicy sauce	SMG	303	1	B
Stuffed & poached	AC	200	1	
Colombiana	NYTI	65	2	B
Confit	FGCW	200	1	A
Confit of	FGCW	200	1	A
Consomme	CBSS	60	3	C
Contadine	FFCB	241	1	B
w Coriander	YGM	62	1	A
w Coriander, baked	YGM	188	1	C
& Corn				
Casserole	FFCB	260	2	B
Chowder	CBSS	143	1	B
Chowder, cheesy	BHGN	380	1	B
Crisped	AC	197	1	
w Sauce, spicy	VGCB	90	1	B
Soup	NYTI	467	1	B
Soup	NYT	66	2	C
Soup, Pennsylvania Dutch	GHAC	104	2	C
w Cornmeal batter, fried	BHGN	295	1	B
Country, captain	BHGN	303	3	C
Couscous	JBGF	432	2	B
Cousin Bette's	MIE	101	1	B

RECIPE	BOOK	PAGE	TD	S
w Sun dried tomatoes & mozzarella	GHAC	158	1	B
Cutting into eight pieces (drawings)	MFC	10		
Cutting up a	BHGN	294		
Deep-fried batter	FAIC	275	2	B
Defrosting frozen	MAFC	235		
Demi devil	NYTI	208	2	B
Deviled	FFCB	240	1	B
Diavolo, Italian	BBA	70	2	B
Diced w white wine, quenelles, truffles, etc	MFC2	145		
Dijon	BHGN	296	1	B
Dijonnaise	SP	91	2	B
Divan	FFCB	257	1	B
◆	NYT	201	2	B
◆	SC	312	1	
◆	JOC	236	1	B
◆	BHGN	309	1	B
◆	EBE	74	1	B
Done, how to tell	MAFC	239		
Drums tandoori	CFS	118	3	B
Drumsticks, mock	JOC	420	2	B
Drunk	FG	309	2	B
Duck or goose, timetable for roasting	BCC	241		
Dumpling pie, double-crust	CW	96	3	B
Dumplings	BHGN	302	2	C
Dumplings	FFCB	245	2	B
Dumplings	JBC	226	1	
Dumplings, Creole	PPLK	154	2	B
Dumplings, old fashioned	AC	205	2	
w East West sauce	OC	134	2	B
Easy	AC	197	2	
& Egg terrine	FG	138	3	B
& Eggplant	JBGF	427	1	B
El parador	NYTI	472	3	B
En casserole	SC	310	1	
En papillote, breast of	NYT	188	2	B
Enchilada casserole	BHGN	309	2	B
Enchiladas	JBGF	419	1	B
Enchiladas w green sauce	FFCB	303	3	B
& Endive, extra-easy	VGCB	118	1	B
Escabeche of	NYTI	473	3	B
& Escarole soup	GHAC	104	2	C
Espanol	NYTI	523	1	B
Etouffee	PPLK	166	2	B
Extract	BTSB	37	3	C
Far Eastern	YGM	58	1	A
Farce	JOC	458	2	
Farmhouse	GHAC	149	1	B
Fat, rendering	SC	307		
Fat, seasoned cracklings	BTSB	41	1	C
Fat, using cookies	AC	699		
Fenneled	FAIC	300	1	B
Fillets	SC	309	1	
Filling for knishes	SC	95	1	
Filling, nut	SC	382	1	
Filling, turnover cocktail	WC	22	1	C
Flavorings inserted under skin	OC	52		
Florentine	BBA	69	3	B
Florentine	EBE	75	1	B
Florentine, breasts of	NYT	188	2	B
For supper	AC	208	2	
French, casserole	JOC	470	2	B
Fricassee	BCC	247	2	B
◆	BHGN	301	2	B
◆	FFCB	243	2	B

RECIPE	BOOK	PAGE	TD	S
Chicken Fricassee (*cont.*)				
◆	JBGF	418	2	B
◆	SC	309	1	
◆	JBC	225	1	B
◆	JOC	467	2	C
◆	NYTI	219	2	B
I	NYTI	218	2	B
II	NYTI	219	2	B
A country style, white	AC	203	2	
Biscuits	SC	309	1	
Brown	JBC	226	1	B
Brown w mushrooms	JBC	226	1	B
w Dried wild mushrooms	CIC	310	1	B
w Dumplings	SC	309	1	
w Dumplings	GHAC	150	1	B
w Egg lemon sauce	MCIC	315	1	B
Florentine	FAIC	295	1	B
w Green peppers & tomatoes	CIC	309	1	B
w Red cabbage	MCIC	313	1	B
w Tarragon	SMG	60	1	B
w Tarragon	NYTI	220	2	B
Fried	AC	191		
Fried	SC	308	1	A
Fried	BCC	242	1	B
Batter	BCC	243	1	B
Batter	FFCB	238	1	B
Buttermilk	BCC	242	1	B
Campfire	BB	43	1	
Country captain	AC	195	1	
w Crab sauce	BHGN	297	2	B
Creole	AC	194	1	
Old fashioned	JBC	222	1	B
Oven	JOC	466	1	A
◆	BHGN	295	1	B
◆	BHGN	299	1	B
◆	BCC	242	1	B
◆	SC	308	1	A
Oven a la Maryland	SC	308	2	
Oven, crunchy	BCC	242	1	B
Pan	JOC	466	1	
Pan	BHGN	295	1	B
Pan	FFCB	238	2	B
w Rice	BCC	227	1	B
Skillet	BHGN	295	1	B
Southern	AC	191		
Southern	GHAC	149	2	B
Southern	NYTI	560	2	B
Southern, batter	BBA	67	2	B
Southern, country captain	AC	194	1	
Steak	AC	267	1	
Steak w creamy gravy	GHAC	173	1	B
Steak, round	BHGN	237	1	B
Tabasco	AC	193	2	
Fruit sauce w sweet potato	VGCB	298	1	B
Galveston style, Tex-Mex	OC	132	2	B
Garlic, 40 cloves	JBGF	436	2	B
Garlic, garlic, garlic	FGCW	174	2	A
Garlic, roasted	BB	75	1	B
Giblet sandwich	AC	810	1	
Giblet sandwich, chopped	AC	223	1	
Giblets	JOC	451	2	
Giblets w mushrooms	NYT	212	1	B
Ginger	NYT	190	1	B
w Ginger cream	BBA	69	2	B
Gizzard sauce, spaghetti &	FAIC	157	2	B
Gizzards	AC	221	1	
Gizzards, sauce of	FAIC	73	2	B
Gizzards w marsala	FGCW	344	2	B

RECIPE	BOOK	PAGE	TD	S
Glazed & apricot curry	WC	58	1	B
Gloriosa	EBE	76	1	B
Granny Smith	JBGF	426	1	B
& Grapes	EBE	70	1	B
Gravy, pan	JOC	322	1	B
& Green bean casserole	SC	315	1	
w Green mole sauce	BB	107	2	B
w Green noodles, sherried	NYT	203	1	B
w Greens	BBA	66	2	B
w Greens casserole	VGCB	133	2	B
Grilled	OC	132	1	B
w Asparagus	OC	132	2	B
Bloody Mary	CFS	113	2	B
Galveston	CFS	108	3	B
Gold flecked	CFS	112	2	A
w Green chile	CFS	110	2	B
w Horseradish	CFS	109	2	A
Mustard	SMG	56	1	B
Mustard, seeded	CFS	111	2	A
Tangy	CFS	107	2	B
Gumbo	JOC	151	2	C
Gumbo	FFCB	243	1	B
& Andouille & smoked sausage	PPLK	202	3	B
Okra &	NYT	210	2	C
Okra &	CW	48	2	B
Okra & ham &	GG	231	2	B
Oyster &	GHAC	150	1	B
Soup	SC	395	3	
Soup	FFCB	89	1	B
Half boned	MFC2	269		
Half boned, stuffed w fois gras, livers, etc	MFC2	271	2	
Half boned, stuffed w pastry crust	MFC2	276	3	
Halves, grilled w goat cheese	CFS	114	2	B
Halves, grilled w hummus	CFS	115	2	B
Halves, twice-cooked	CFS	116	2	A
& Ham, baked, crammed cucumbers	GG	153	2	A
Ham & okra gumbo	GG	231	2	B
& Ham rolls	FGCW	172	1	B
Hash	AC	205	1	
◆	NYT	209	1	B
◆	SC	315	1	
◆	JOC	235	1	B
◆	FFCB	257	1	B
Havana	GHAC	152	1	B
Hawaiian, broiled	BHGN	307	1	C
Hearts	AC	221	1	
Herb fried	NYT	208	1	B
Herb roasted w baked shallots	MSQC	221	1	B
Herb scented, roasted on the hearth	OC	58		
Herbed & baked	NYT	193	2	B
w Herbs, fricassee of	NYT	206	2	B
Hibachi	BB	94	2	B
Hoisin, w nuts	MIE	170	2	B
Hollandaise	FFCB	257	1	A
w Honey & ginger	YGM	40	1	A
Hoosier	OC	133	2	B
Hungarian	AC	220	1	
Hungarian	NYTI	348	1	B
Hunter	LM	40	3	B
Hunter style	FAIC	297	1	B
Hunter's	JOC	469	3	B
Indian	NYT	191	1	C
w Indian spices	YGM	42	1	B
In pineapple shell	NYT	201	2	B

RECIPE	BOOK	PAGE	TD	S
Chicken (*cont.*)				
In port	FGCW	175	1	B
In potato shells	BCC	210	1	B
In red wine	BCC	247	1	B
In red wine	FGCW	168	2	B
In red wine w onions mushroom & bacon	MAFC	263	2	B
In sherry cream sauce	WC	59	1	B
In walnut sauce	NYTI	553	2	B
Islander	NYT	195	1	B
Italian, low salt & low fat	FG	245	1	B
Italiano	BHGN	299	1	B
Italienne	EBE	77	1	B
Jade	FGCW	358	3	B
w Jalapeno & nachos, creamy	SPGT	135	1	C
Jambalaya	FFCB	241	2	B
◆	BCC	248	2	B
◆	JOC	182	2	B
◆	GHAC	153	2	B
◆	PPLK	217	2	B
◆	GHAC	153	2	B
◆	NYTI	559	1	B
Javanese	BB	88	2	
Jellied	SC	318	1	
Jubilee	SC	312	2	
Kebabs Egyptian style	OC	135	2	B
Kiev	JOC	470	2	B
◆	BHGN	296	2	B
◆	EBE	78	2	B
◆	FFCB	248	3	B
Kiev, oven	BCC	250	2	B
Kiev, oven	BHGN	296	2	B
Kinds of	ACCB	186		
Lake Como	FFCB	247	1	B
Leek & carrot loaf	CW	60	1	B
& Leek soup	BCC	305	1	B
& Leeks in cream	FG	139	2	B
Leg, boning (drawings)	MFC	8		
Legs				
Deviled	SMG	36	1	B
Deviled	GHAC	155	1	B
Mock	SC	275	2	
Oven "fried"	JBGF	421	2	B
Puttanesca	SPGT	73	1	B
w Shrimp, stuffed	GHAC	155	2	B
Steamed & thyme	MFC	85	3	B
Stuffed	AC	219	2	
Stuffed	JOC	471	1	
Stuffed w mushrooms & rice	BBA	67	2	B
& Thighs, baked	AC	220	1	
Tiny	AC	26		
Lemon	SP	93	3	B
◆	FG	245	1	
◆	NYTI	53	2	B
◆	SPGT	104	3	B
◆	NYTI	491	3	B
Broiled	AC	189	1	
w Herbs	SP	123	1	B
Mold	FGCW	295	2	B
Soup	CBSS	100	1	B
Steamed	FG	266	1	B
& Lentil soup	CBSS	287	2	B
Lime	KIS	85	1	A
Lime, basil, slivered	BBA	70	2	C
Lime, broiled	NYT	199	2	B
Liver				
A la king	JOC	441	1	
w Bacon	BCC	244	1	B
w Bacon, onion & apple	GHAC	168	1	B

RECIPE	BOOK	PAGE	TD	S
Chicken Liver (cont.)				
w Bacon & water chestnuts, skewered	FFCB	64	1	C
Batter	JOC	441	1	
Braised	LM	166	3	C
Chopped	JOC	71	1	
w Creole sauce	SMG	68	1	B
Curried	FFCB	249	1	B
Custards	LM	164	2	B
Custards, unmolded	MAFC	174	2	B
Deviled	EBE	82	1	B
& Eggs	WC	47	1	B
En brochette	AC	221	1	
En brochette	FFCB	249	1	B
Filling, turnover cocktail	WC	22	1	C
Grilled	JBC	7	1	
In aspic	MAFC	548	2	B
In bacon blankets	SC	42	1	
Kebabs	OC	137	1	B
Lamb chops stuffed w	AC	381	1	
Lyonnaise	JOC	439	1	A
w Marsala	NYT	211	1	B
Mousse	MAFC	559	1	B
Mousse soup	CBSS	83	2	B
Mushroom ragout	GHAC	168	1	B
& Mushrooms	EBE	79	1	B
& Mushrooms	SC	318	1	
& Mushrooms	FFCB	249	1	B
& Mushrooms w madeira wine sauce	SMG	76	1	B
& Mushrooms, spaghetti &	WC	50	1	B
On skewers	SMG	70	1	B
Onions, apple, bacon &	GHAC	168	1	B
Pasta	FG	127	2	B
Pate	FFCB	61	2	C
Pate	JOC	433	3	C
Pate	BHGN	15	2	B
Pate, antique	FAIC	363	2	B
Pate, French	MIE	30	3	B
Pate w green peppercorns	SP	25	3	C
Pate, quick	NYT	11	1	B
Pilaf w tomato & mushroom sauce	SMG	72	2	B
w Pineapple	NYT	211	1	B
Ragout w mushrooms	GHAC	168	1	B
& Rice	SMG	19	1	B
& Rice, Italian	SC	181	1	
w Rice & mushrooms	SMG	67	1	B
Risotto	NYT	323	1	B
Risotto & mushrooms	NYT	322	2	B
w Sage	SMG	75	1	B
Sauce	FAIC	77	1	B
Sauce crests wattles	FAIC	75	1	B
Sauce w fresh tagliatelle	FAIC	149	2	B
Sauce pappardelle w	CIC	137	3	B
Sauce, potato ricotta ring w	FAIC	361	2	B
Sauce, tagliatelle w	FAIC	149	2	B
Sausage brioche dough	MFC2	296	1	B
Sauteed	SC	318	1	
Sauteed	AC	222	1	

RECIPE	BOOK	PAGE	TD	S
Chicken Liver (*cont.*)				
Sauteed w blueberry vinegar	SP	320	2	B
Sauteed w madeira	FFCB	248	2	B
Sauteed w sage	CIC	303	1	B
Shirred eggs w	FFCB	338	1	A
Skewered	OC	137	2	B
Spaghetti &	NYTI	422	2	B
Spinach salad w	LM	150	2	B
Spread	SC	38	1	
Stroganoff w	BHGN	303	2	B
Terrine	NYT	11	2	C
Timbales	JOC	208	2	B
Timbales	SC	318	1	
Timbales	AC	222	1	
w Tomato sauce	BHGN	303	1	B
Tomatoes stuffed w	SC	433	1	
Topping for pasta dishes	JOC	343	1	
Veal birds &	NYT	166	1	B
& Vegetables, spiced	NYT	210	1	B
Loaf	SC	316	1	
Loaf, cooked	JOC	236	1	B
Loaf, quantity	JOC	236	2	C
w Lots of garlic	VGCB	184	1	B
Louisiana casserole	GHAC	154	1	B
& Macaroni	SC	315	1	
& Macaroni salad	BCC	269	2	B
Made in manner of suckling pig	FAIC	299	1	B
Mahogany, fried	MSQC	204	1	B
Maintenon, broiled	NYT	202	2	B
w Mango chutney	SPGT	91	2	B
Manu	OC	132	2	B
Marbella	SP	86	3	C
Marengo	SP	312	1	
Marengo	FFCB	242	1	B

RECIPE	BOOK	PAGE	TD	S
Marengo, easy	MIE	104	1	B
Marsala	FGCW	170	1	B
Marsala w grapes	KIS	89	1	A
Maryland	JOC	468	2	B
Maryland, fried	FFCB	239	1	B
Maryland, fried	BCC	242	1	B
Mayonnaise of, salad	LM	171	3	
Mexican	NYT	192	1	B
Mexican	FFCB	242	1	B
Mexican	SC	313	1	
Mixed grill	CFS	121	2	B
Mixed grill	SMG	54	1	B
Mole poblano (breaded)	NYTI	472	2	C
Montego	SC	312	2	
Monterey	BBA	70	2	B
Monterey	SP	92	2	A
Monterey, oven fried	BHGN	297	2	B
w Morels	LM	179	2	B
Moroccan, steamed	BBA	71	3	B
Morsels, Cajun	SPGT	25	2	B
Morton Clarke's Shenendoah	AC	194	1	
Mousse	NYT	433	2	B
Mousse	NYTI	230	1	B
Mousse	MAFC	560	1	C
Chicken breasts on chaud froid	MAFC	552	3	
Hot	SC	318	2	
Jellied	SC	318	1	
Jellied	JOC	97	2	C
Mushroom crepes, Florentine	NYTI	228	2	B
Mushroom croquettes	FFCB	259	2	B
Mushroom kabobs, bacon wrapped	GHAC	222	1	B
Mushroom soup	FG	47	1	B

RECIPE	BOOK	PAGE	TD	S
w Mushrooms	SC	310	1	
w Mushrooms in brandy cream	WC	49	2	B
w Mushrooms, gratin of	MAFC	157	1	B
w Mustard wine sauce	FGCW	171	1	A
Napa Valley	GHAC	152	1	B
Newburg	NYT	203	1	B
Noodle	FFCB	255	1	B
Noodle	BHGN	302	2	C
Bake, chilled	BHGN	310	1	B
Casserole	FFCB	331	2	B
w Campari	NYTI	415	1	B
In wine sauce	NYTI	210	1	B
Parisien	NYTI	224	2	B
Ring	AC	203	1	
w Sesame-ginger dressing	YGM	65	2	A
Soup	CBSS	95	2	C
Soup	BCC	304	1	B
Soup	FFCB	81	3	B
Soup w vegetables	AC	88	2	
Normande	BBA	71	2	B
w Nut filling	SC	382	1	
Old West, barbecued	GHAC	221	1	B
w Olives	FGCW	178	1	B
w Olives, black	FAIC	294	1	B
Omelet	JBC	56	1	
Omelet	SC	226	1	B
Omelet, poached	SMG	80	1	B
On a spit	OC	131	2	B
On the bone, deviled	FFCB	254	1	B
On the spit	JBC	224	2	
On the spit w fennel	CFS	261	2	B
& Onion casserole	FGCW	322	2	B
& Onion stew	FFCB	246	1	B
& Onion, stuffed, roast	BB	74	1	
& Onions, Chinese, boiled	FG	312	1	B
& Onions w green peas	FG	263	2	B
Or duck, livers bacon w	AC	25		
Or meat croquettes, deep-fried	FAIC	278	1	B
Or turkey, ham & cheese sandwich	AC	809	1	
Orange	KIS	117	1	A
Orange, chilled	GHAC	156	2	C
Oreganato	KIS	93	1	A
Oriental	BB	41	1	B
Oriental, stewed	JBGF	430	2	B
Oven crisped, orange	BHGN	300	1	B
& Oyster gumbo	GHAC	150	1	B
& Oyster gumbo	GHAC	150	1	B
& Oyster pie	AC	213	2	
& Oysters, creamed	AC	201	1	
& Oysters for a chafing dish	FFCB	259	2	B
Paillard	MSQC	32	1	B
Pancakes	SC	317	2	
Paneed, fettucini &	PPLK	161	2	B
Paper, Chinese	FG	259	3	C
Paprika	SC	309	1	
◆	BCC	249	1	B
◆	FFCB	242	2	B
◆	NYT	207	1	B
◆	JOC	468	2	A
Paprika, coffee	FGCW	383	1	B
Paprikash	NYTI	347	1	B
Paprikash	BHGN	295	2	B
Paprikash	KIS	99	1	A
Parmesan	NYTI	405	1	B
Parmesan	BHGN	299	1	B
Parmesan w cream sauce	NYT	196	1	B

RECIPE	BOOK	PAGE	TD	S
Chicken (*cont.*)				
Parsley, roast	FG	139	2	B
Parsleyed w vegetables	SMG	32	1	B
Parsleyed, roast	SPGT	50	2	B
& Parsnips, caramel	GG	260	1	B
Party, stuffed	GHAC	148	3	B
Pasta Alfredo	MIE	188	1	B
Pasta primavera	BCC	254	1	B
Pasta salad, party	GHAC	281	1	B
Patties	JOC	428	2	C
In patty shells, sweetbread &	JOC	236	3	C
Paysanne	NYTI	211	2	B
& Pea soup, cold	NYT	84	2	B
& Peaches, stir fry	WC	60	1	B
Peas & cream, cloaked	GG	270	1	B
& Peas in wine	FGCW	326	1	B
& Peppers	NYTI	52	1	B
& Peppers	BCC	252	1	B
& Peppers	VGCB	209	1	B
Peruvian	SC	311	2	
Petit Sirah	MFC	84	2	B
Piccata	BBA	71	2	B
Piccata	FG	133	2	B
Piccata	BCC	225	1	B
Pickled	AC	207	2	
Pie	LM	184	2	B
Pie	JBC	225	2	B
Pie	FFCB	254	3	B
A very old fashioned country	AC	214	2	
Deep dish	GHAC	154	2	B
Morels &	MFC	81	3	B
Old fashioned, rich	AC	213	2	
Oyster &	AC	213	2	
Quail, squab, sausage, tortelli &	FAIC	383	3	C
Pieces, lime	FG	136	1	B
Pieces, poached w cheese sauce	MFC2	256	1	
Pieces, poached w white wine & vegetables	MFC2	253	1	B
Pilaf	FFCB	318	1	B
& Pineapple salad	SPGT	149	1	B
Pineapple-glazed	BHGN	31	1	C
Plain, broiled	JBC	221	1	
Plain, broiled w fruit juice	JBC	222	1	
& Plum sauce	BBA	81	2	B
Poached	JBC	228	2	B
Poached	FFCB	244	1	B
Poached	SMG	81	1	B
w Bourbon sauce	SMG	42	1	B
In cream sauce	SMG	41	1	B
w Vegetables	BBA	99	2	B
w White wine, Provencale	MFC2	261	1	B
w White wine, vegetables & egg	MFC2	259	2	B
Young w hollandaise	AC	201	1	
Poaching	AC	197		
Pojarsky (cutlets)	MSE	149	3	C
Pork				
Beef & sausage w vegetables	MAFC	306	3	C
Casserole, Philippine	FGCW	307	2	B
Espanol	NYTI	523	2	B
Pate	FFCB	60	2	C
Shrimp, en adobo	WC	53	1	B

RECIPE	BOOK	PAGE	TD	S
Portuguese	NYT	198	1	B
Pot, Henri Soule's	SMG	49	1	B
Pot pie	SC	314	2	
Pot pie	GF	166	2	B
Pot pie, quick	JOC	225	2	
Pot pies	BHGN	308	2	B
Potato boat, creamed	SC	317	1	
& Potato chip	BHGN	299	1	B
& Potato salad w avocado & papaya	GHAC	280	2	B
Potatoes & basil	YGM	206	1	C
Prairie	JOC	479		B
Preparing for poaching	MFC2	264		
Preparing, ready cut for cooking	MFC2	252		
Preparing to cook (photographs)	LT	225		
Pressed	SC	318	1	
Prosciutto, tomatoes w green fettuccine	GG	378	1	B
Provencal	YGM	51	1	B
w Prunes & hot peppers	CF	58	3	B
Pudding	FG	283	1	B
Puu puu	OC	136	2	C
Quarters & cherry tomatoes, stuffed	GHAC	153	2	B
Quenelles	MAFC	189	2	B
Quenelles	NYTI	227	2	C
Quenelles	FG	185	2	C
Quiche	BCC	166	1	B
Raspberry	SP	87	2	B
Rea	NYTI	544	2	B
w Red wine sauce	SMG	34	1	B
w Red & yellow peppers	SPGT	90	2	B

RECIPE	BOOK	PAGE	TD	S
w Rice	SC	313	1	
w Rice	AC	199		
Casserole	SC	314	1	
Casserole	SMG	47	1	B
Casserole	SC	315	1	
Charleston	WC	55	1	B
Glazed	BHGN	308	1	B
Salad	CIC	423	1	B
Salad, oriental	JBGF	403	1	B
Soup	FFCB	81	3	B
Soup	GHAC	105	1	C
Soup	BCC	304	1	B
w Spinach, stuffed	GG	317	2	A
Supper	BCC	254	1	B
Risotto	JBC	117	1	
Roast	JBC	222	1	
◆	GF	209	1	B
◆	BCC	241		
◆	FFCB	236	2	B
◆	MAFC	240	1	B
◆	JOC	465	1	B
◆	NYT	185	1	B
Basted, cream, herb & giblet stuffing	MAFC	243	2	B
Breast w lemon mustard sauce	GF	68	3	C
Carving (photographs)	LT	316		
w Celery root dressing	GG	123	2	B
Cold	NYTI	218	2	B
w Cream sauce	BB	75	1	B
Lemon	MCIC	311	1	B
Squab &	JBC	224	1	
Steeped in port wine	MAFC	245	2	B
Stuffed	JBC	224	1	
Stuffed w ham	JBC	224	1	

RECIPE	BOOK	PAGE	TD	S
Tarragon	SP	205	2	B
Veal &	BBA	148	2	B
w Salt crust	MFC	82	3	B
Saltimbocca	BHGN	301	2	B
Sandwich	JOC	248		
Sandwich	GF	44	1	C
Chopped	AC	809	1	
Hot	JOC	248		
& Variations	AC	810	1	
Sauce				
Brown	NYTI	216	1	
For spaghetti	BCC	209	1	B
Omelet, baked w	BHGN	201	2	B
Piquant	PPLK	140	3	B
Sausage	MFC2	290	3	C
Sausage	LT	232	3	
Sausage gumbo	CBSS	384	3	B
Sausage patties	CW	128	2	C
Saute				
Au parmesan	NYTI	212	1	B
Chasseur	NYT	199	1	B
Chili	BB	42	1	
Italian	JBC	219	1	B
Of, basic	SMG	14	1	B
Pink	NYT	207	1	B
Rosemary &	SMG	15	1	B
& Variations	JBC	218	1	B
w White wine	BB	42	1	
Sauteed	JOC	466	1	
Sauteed	MAFC	254	1	B
Flambe	JBC	220	1	B
w Herbs, garlic, egg yolk & butter	MAFC	257	1	B
Tomatoes	SMG	18	1	B
w Variations	BB	41	1	
w Vinegar sauce & wild mushrooms	MFC	83	2	B
w Wine & herbs	SMG	52	1	B

RECIPE	BOOK	PAGE	TD	S
& Scallions, kerry	GG	249	1	B
Scallops, enlivened spices (photographs)	OC	56		
Scheherazade	OC	134	2	B
Seafood jambalaya	PPLK	218	2	B
Sesame	FG	350	1	B
Sesame	SP	90	1	A
Sesame & acorn squash	MSQC	124	1	B
Sesame, Chinese style	FG	321	1	B
Sherried	SC	310	2	
Shortbread	JBC	226	1	
Simmered in cream & onions	MAFC	262	1	B
Skewers, peanut	GRIL	97	2	B
w Sliced peaches	EBE	86	1	B
Slices, baked	BCC	324	1	B
Small ballotine of	LM	175	3	B
Smitane, smothered	NYTI	347	1	B
Smoked	BTSB	30	3	C
Smoked, Chinese	NYTI	54	3	B
Smoked & pasta salad	CPPC	41	2	B
Smothered	JOC	468	2	B
Souffle	JOC	206	2	C
Souffle	FFCB	258	2	B
Souffle, leftover	JOC	206	2	B
Souffle, wild rice &	GHAC	116	2	B
Soup	FFCB	81	3	B
Soup	SC	394	3	
Chinese	FG	313	1	B
Clear	CBSS	101	3	B
w Corn (ajaco)	BBA	30	3	B
Cream of	FFCB	81	3	B
◆	BHGN	374	1	B
◆	MFC	67	1	B
◆	JOC	158	1	B

RECIPE	BOOK	PAGE	TD	S
w Peppers	SC	425	1	
& Poached	AC	200	1	
w Potatoes & olives	FG	133	2	B
Quarters & cherry tomatoes	GHAC	153	2	B
w Spinach & cheese	BBA	66	3	B
Supremes of	SC	311	2	
w Tomatoes	BHGN	349	1	B
Under the skin	LM	182	2	B
w Zucchini	GG	405	2	A
Stuffing, avocado	FFCB	437	2	B
Stuffing, tomatoes baked	FFCB	417	2	B
Subs, super	BHGN	306	1	B
Sugar smoked	GHAC	221	3	B
Sukiyaki	BB	93	2	
Summer	SP	88	2	B
Summer w fruit	WC	63	1	B
Supreme en papillote	JOC	471	2	
w Sweet peppers, hoisin	KIS	120	1	A
w Sweet potato & fruit sauce	VGCB	298	1	B
& Sweet potato pot pie	SC	316	2	
Sweet & sour, curried	NYTI	356	2	B
& Sweetbread salad	SC	362	1	
Szechwan	NYTI	54	2	B
Szechwan, hot	FG	319	2	B
Tabasco, fried	AC	193	2	
Tagliatelle w fava beans & pancetta	CPPC	29	2	A
& Tamale pie	NYT	193	2	B
Tamales	WC	62	1	C
Tandoori	NYTI	357	1	B
◆	BCC	252	3	B
◆	CF	86	3	B
◆	OC	134	3	B
Tarragon	AC	199		
Tarragon	SMG	58	1	B
Tarragon	JBC	223	1	
Cold	NYTI	217		C
w Green onions	JBC	223	1	
In aspic	MAFC	549	3	B
Popover	BHGN	309	1	B
Roasted	BB	73	1	A
w Sour cream	NYTI	212	1	B
w Wine	JOC	469	2	B
Tasso jambalaya	PPLK	220	2	B
Tchoupitoulas	PPLK	152	3	B
Teriyaki	FGCW	355	1	B
Teriyaki, barbecued	BB	92	2	B
Teriyaki, broiled	AC	190	2	
Teriyaki kebabs	BHGN	308	1	B
Terrapin	AC	206	1	
Terrine	JOC	435	3	
Tetrazzini	AC	202	1	
◆	NYT	204	2	B
◆	SC	314	1	
◆	JOC	186	2	C
◆	FFCB	256	2	B
◆	EBE	79	2	B
Thighs, baked & crispy	GHAC	155	1	B
Deviled	KIS	96	1	A
& Legs in teriyaki marinade	AC	220	2	
Stuffed	FG	134	2	B
Yaki	FGCW	357	2	A
Thyme roasted	FFCB	237	2	B
Tidbits	JBGF	298	2	C
Timbales	SC	315	1	
Timbales	JOC	208	2	B
Timetable for whole	MAFC	239		

RECIPE	BOOK	PAGE	TD	S
Chicken (*cont.*)				
Tomato	AC	208	1	
Bouillon	AC	87	1	
Bubbling	GG	377	2	B
Crepes &	BBA	71	3	B
Cups, curried	GHAC	280	1	B
Fondue	MFC	87	1	B
& Shallots & vermouth w	FGCW	173	1	A
Stuffed w	BHGN	349	1	B
& Tongue ring, variations	AC	208	2	
Tostadas	GHAC	151	2	B
Tostadas	BCC	253	2	B
Truffled, steamed	NYTI	215	2	B
Trussing	LT	218		
Trussing (drawings)	MFC	12		
Trussing (drawings)	MAFC	237		
Trussing (photographs)	LT	218		
& Turkey baked in foil	JOC	465	1	
Turmeric	NYTI	357	2	B
Under a brick	FGCW	179	2	A
Valle d'auge	NYT	200	1	B
Valle d'auge	NYTI	213	2	B
& Vegetable mousseline w fresh tomato sauce	MFC	26	3	B
Vegetable soup	BCC	304	1	B
& Vegetables	BCC	248	1	B
& Vegetables, curried	BHGN	311	2	B
& Vegetables, Dolly Martin's favorite	BBA	67	2	B
Veloute	NYTI	214	2	B
Veloute sauce	NYTI	214	2	B
Vielle France	NYTI	216	2	B

RECIPE	BOOK	PAGE	TD	S
Viennese	NYTI	7	1	B
w Walnuts	BHGN	299	1	B
White, cut	NYTI	55	2	B
w White wine	SMG	38	1	B
Whole bag	FG	254	2	B
Whole, baked, bread	FAIC	304	2	B
Whole, cooked in a clay pot	MIE	91	2	B
& Wild rice casserole	BHGN	309	1	B
& Wild rice salad	BCC	266	2	B
w Wine vinegar	FGCW	239	2	B
Wings				
Appetizers, baked	GHAC	85	1	C
Baked	FG	147	1	
Bananas &	MSE	154	2	C
Barbecued	FFCB	71	1	B
Buffalo	FG	149	3	B
Buffalo style	GHAC	85	1	C
Bunny's	CFS	117	2	B
Charcoal-grilled w lemon pepper	CPMC	188	2	B
Cocktail	SP	13	2	
w Hot pepper-butter sauce	CW	120	1	B
Looed	FG	150	2	B
Mahogany	BBA	82	3	C
Oven fried	GHAC	85	1	C
Piquant	FG	148	1	B
Saucy	GHAC	85	1	C
w Spaghetti sauce	FG	148	1	
w Spanish rice	NYT	209	2	B
Steamed	FG	147	1	B
Wrapped, herb	BBA	70	1	B
Yakitori	BBA	81	3	B
Yogurt	BCC	249	1	B
Yogurt	KIS	109	1	A
Yucatan	GHAC	151	1	B
& Zucchini soup	GG	398	2	B

RECIPE	BOOK	PAGE	TD	S
Chiffonade salad dressing	AC	79		
Chilaly (vegetable-cheese sauce for toast)	FFCB	352	1	B
Chilaquiles (Mexican casserole)	NYTI	474	2	B
Children's nut chews	FFBB	237	1	C
Chilean seafood casserole, chupe	NYT	296	1	C
Chili/Chile	YGM	93	1	B
Chili/Chile	JOC	540	1	
Chili/Chile	KIS	218	1	A
All about	CBSS	107		
& Bacon rub	CFS	283	1	A
Barbecue sauce, fiery	GHAC	226	1	C
Batter, fried, stuffed	GHAC	240	2	B
Beans	FFCB	324	2	B
Beans, dumplings &	BCC	173	1	B
Beans, southwestern	AC	605	2	
Burger, the Tex-Mex	GHAC	187	1	
Burgers	BCC	317	1	B
Butter	GHAC	243	1	
Butter, grilled fish steaks w	GHAC	223	1	B
Cashews	GHAC	92	1	B
Cheese				
Balls	BBA	14	2	C
Balls	BCC	8	1	C
Corn bread	GHAC	367	1	C
Dip	GHAC	94	1	B
Rice	KIS	106	1	A
Sandwiches	BCC	324	1	B
Chicken, broiled	BCC	246	1	B
Chicken, grilled, green	CFS	110	2	B
Chicken saute w white wine	BB	42	1	
Cincinnati	CBSS	117	1	B

RECIPE	BOOK	PAGE	TD	S
Cincinnati style	BCC	212	1	B
Con carne	FFCB	167	1	B
◆	GHAC	182	2	C
◆	BCC	212	1	B
◆	AC	18	1	
◆	BHGN	368	1	B
◆	NYT	110	2	B
◆	JOC	430	2	B
◆	SC	278	1	
◆	WC	101	1	B
◆	EBE	51	1	B
Easy	BCC	212	1	B
Hernandez	CBSS	110	3	B
Vegetable	JBGF	464	1	B
Wine	SC	279	1	
Con queso	BHGN	18	1	B
Con queso	AC	13	1	
Con queso	KIS	306	1	C
Corn bread	BCC	36	1	C
Corn bread, cheese &	GHAC	367	1	C
Corn bread, cheese &	FFBB	569	1	B
Corn muffins, green	GRIL	98	1	B
Corn souffle	AC	557	1	
Corn soup w poblano chilies	CPMC	48	2	B
Cumin dressing, endive &	KIS	282	1	A
Dip	JBC	4	1	
Dip, cheese &	GHAC	94	1	B
Dip, sour cream	AC	11		
Dip, zippy	BCC	15	1	C
Dogs	SC	327	1	
Dogs	BCC	318	1	B
Dogs	GHAC	373		
For a big party	BB	106	2	C
For a crowd	SP	130	1	C
Frankfurters	BB	27	1	

RECIPE	BOOK	PAGE	TD	S
Green hominy w sour cream	AC	581	1	
Grilled, whole	GRIL	79	1	B
Hamburger	BCC	317	1	B
Hamburger	KIS	363	1	B
Hamburger, the Tex-Mex	GHAC	187	1	
& Lima beans	JOC	263	2	B
Minnie's, mild	CBSS	115	2	B
"Mom" Unser's	CBSS	114	2	B
Omelet, green	BCC	160	1	A
Pedernales River	CBSS	113	1	C
Peppers w rice & cheese	FGCW	159	1	B
Peppers, stuffed	VGCB	210	2	B
Pot pie	JBGF	462	2	B
Pot roast	AC	287	2	
Potatoes, twice baked w cheese	SP	179	2	B
Powder	BTSB	197	1	C
Preparing	GHAC	240		
Preparing, fresh	NYTI	467		
Preserved, sherry	JOC	785	3	C
Prime rib	CFS	258	2	B
Quiche, California	GHAC	114	1	B
Relish	OC	164	1	C
Rellenos con queso	NYTI	475	2	B
Rice & cheese	FGCW	159	1	B
Sauce	SC	456	2	
◆	BTSB	180	2	C
◆	FFCB	284	1	B
◆	AC	827	2	
◆	JOC	784	3	C
Ancho	OC	164	1	A
Ancho (photographs)	OC	15		
Barbecue sauce	JBC	265	1	
Green flounder	GHAC	138	1	B
Pork w	NYTI	470	2	B

RECIPE	BOOK	PAGE	TD	S
Red	NYTI	477	2	B
Spanish	SC	390	1	
Sweet	FFCB	714	2	B
Tomato	NYTI	478	1	B
Tomato	VE	85	1	B
Tomato	KIS	180	1	
Tomato sauce, tortilla stack w	KIS	179	1	A
Vegetable	SC	456	2	
Salve, New Mexico	CFS	284	1	A
Sausage	KIS	238	1	A
Seasoning mix	KIS	348	1	C
Slices, baked	BCC	324	1	B
Stuffed w cheese, fried	NYTI	475	2	B
Texas style	GHAC	182	2	C
Tomato & eggs in bread crumb cups	CW	160	2	B
Tomato sauce, eggs, poached w	CF	135	1	B
Treatment, green	CFS	284	1	A
Vegetable	JBGF	388	2	B
Vegetarian	MC	110	2	B
Venison	AC	239		
Without carne	JBGF	386	2	B
Chili-bobs, New Mexico	CFS	94	2	B
Chimichurri marinade	CFS	291	3	B
China honey pork greens	BBA	31	2	B
Chinese (see also oriental)				
Almond cookies	AC	709	1	
Almond cookies	FFBB	247	1	B
Ants climbing up a tree	FGCW	320	3	B
Beef, oyster, Ming	FG	161	1	B
Buns, steamed	CBB	519	2	B
Cabbage & pork	WC	120	2	B

RECIPE	BOOK	PAGE	TD	S
Chinese (*cont.*)				
Chicken	EBE	72	1	B
Baked	MIE	99	1	B
Soup	FG	313	1	B
w Sweet peppers, hoisin	KIS	120	1	A
Szechwan	NYTI	54	2	B
Szechwan, hot	FG	319	2	B
Chrysanthemum pot	NYTI	47	3	
Cucumber salad	BBA	142	1	B
Drumsticks	FG	147	2	B
Duck, roast	NYTI	60	2	B
Duck, roast	JBC	230	3	B
Duck sauce	MC	70	1	B
Egg drops	SC	409	1	
Fish, baked	MIE	157	1	A
Fish fillets	KIS	156	1	A
Five spice powder	BBA	165	1	A
Five spice powder	BTSB	200	2	C
Ginger ribs	BBA	58	3	B
Hot & sour soup	JBGF	318	2	A
Hunan lamb, marinated	YGM	194	2	C
Hunan onion cake	FG	301	1	B
Hunan spareribs, steamed w black bean sauce	FG	303	1	
Lamb	AC	395	1	
Lion's head	VGCB	46	2	B
Low calorie dressing	JOC	313	1	A
Marinade, basic	FGCW	238	1	
Meatballs	JOC	429	1	B
Mustard, hot	BHGN	358	1	A
Mustard sauce	BBA	164	1	B
Noodle salad, chicken	KIS	102	1	A
Noodle salad, cold	YGM	172	3	C
Noodles	YGM	145	1	A
Noodles	SC	335	1	
Onion cake, Hunan	FG	301	1	B
Pancake sandwiches	FGCW	299		
Pancakes I	SC	226	1	
Pancakes II	SC	227	1	
Pea pods, preparing	BCC	345		
Pearl balls	MSE	41	2	B
Peas	AC	539		
Pepper steak	NYTI	48	1	B
Plum sauce	BTSB	181	3	C
Plum sauce	BBA	164	1	B
Pork	NYT	139	1	B
Chops	WC	111	1	A
Chops, Cantonese	SC	294	1	
Fruited	WC	116	1	B
In plum sauce	WC	14	1	C
Kidney	AC	418	2	
Northern	FG	165	1	B
Roast	NYTI	50	2	B
Sweet & sour	SC	304	1	
Szechwan	NYTI	51	2	B
w Wine sauce, slow cooked	FGCW	320	2	B
Radishes	NYT	423	1	A
Radishes	VGCB	241	1	B
Red sauce	BBA	164	1	B
Rice	SC	180	1	
Rice, fried	BHGN	324	1	B
Rice, fried	SC	182	1	
Rice, fried	JOC	179	1	B
Sauce for vegetables	JOC	331	1	B
Sea bass, poached	NYTI	39	2	A
Seafood salad	MIE	286	2	B
Sesame seed cookies	NYT	583	2	C
Shrimp	MSQC	108	1	B
Shrimp balls	SC	40	1	
Shrimp egg foo young	JOC	199	1	
Shrimp foo young soy w ginger sauce	KIS	160	1	A

RECIPE	BOOK	PAGE	TD	S
Shrimp w hoisin sauce	NYTI	43	2	B
Shrimp toast	NYT	36	1	B
Spareribs	AC	417	2	
Barbecued	OC	123	2	B
Barbecued	NYT	15	2	C
Barbecued, Cantonese style	OC	123	2	B
w Black beans	NYTI	50	2	B
Hunan, steamed w black bean sauce	FG	303	1	B
Roast	BB	72	2	A
Spinach	BHGN	404	1	B
Squid	FG	324	2	B
Steak, grilled	SC	328	1	
Style saute	MC	149	2	B
Sweet & sour sauce	BB	151	1	C
Sweet & sour sauce	JOC	330	1	B
Swiss chard soup	VGCB	306	1	B
Szechwan sauce for dumplings	NYTI	64	1	A
Vegetables, chowed	FG	314	1	B
Vermicelli	KIS	121	1	A
Vermicelli	YGM	41	1	A
Walnut chicken	BBA	81	2	B
Watercress salad	JBC	247	1	B
Chip dip ABC (almonds, bacon & cheese dip)	EBE	29	1	B
Chipped beef				
& Artichoke hearts	NYT	118	1	B
& Corned beef (canned soup)	JOC	232	1	B
& Creamed mushrooms	AC	307	1	
Creamed	JOC	232	1	B
Creamed w baked potatoes	AC	307	1	
w Creole sauce	JOC	232	1	A
In cheese sauce	JOC	232	1	A
Dried (definition)	AC	306		
w Scrambled eggs	AC	307	1	
& Sweet potato casserole	JOC	232	1	B
White or brown sauce, dried	SC	277	1	
Chips & corn	BTSB	117	1	C
Chitlins or chitterlings	AC	417		
Chitterling sausages	LM	211	3	C
Chitterlings	JOC	450	3	B
Chitterlings, sauteed	JOC	450	3	B
Chive				
& Anchovy spread	EBE	33	1	A
Butter	FFCB	56	1	B
◆	GRIL	39	1	B
◆	AC	189		
◆	GHAC	243	1	
Salmon steaks w	GRIL	76	2	B
Sauce, pike steamed w	MFC	122	3	B
w Carrots, boiled, parsley &	JBC	301	1	B
Cheese filling, sardine &	BBA	14	1	A
Cheese spread	EBE	33	1	B
Hollandaise sauce	NYTI	272	1	B
Omelet	BCC	160	1	A
Potatoes				
Baked	JBC	326	1	
Boiled, w parsley	JBC	325	1	B
& Lemon	GHAC	243	1	B
& Lime	BCC	357	1	B
Mashed w	JBC	325	1	B
Scalloped, parsley &	JBC	327	1	B
Red snapper w wild mushrooms &	MFC	128	3	B
Sauce, lemon	BHGN	355	1	B

RECIPE	BOOK	PAGE	TD	S
Chive (*cont.*)				
Sauce, steak w	SMG	230	1	B
Scallops, red peppers, sauteed	GF	236	1	B
Souffle, corn &	VGCB	88	1	B
Choco coffee toffee squares	BHGN	177	3	C
Choco mint velvet	BHGN	184	3	C
Choco Scotch crunchies	BHGN	116	2	C
Choco velvet ice cream	BHGN	184	3	C
Chocolat Charlotte	MSE	257	3	B
Chocolate	JOC	31	1	B
Chocolate	SC	51	1	B
Almond				
Cake	MAFC	677	3	B
Cake	BBA	188	3	C
Cookies	SC	152	1	
Figs	BBA	216	2	B
Ice cream	BHGN	182	3	C
Pudding	SC	190	2	
Ricotta pie	JBGF	627	2	C
Sheet cake	NSD	267	2	B
Shells	JOC	664	3	C
Angel				
Cake	SC	122	1	B
Cake, high altitude	JOC	649	1	B
Food cake	BCC	75	1	C
Pie	BCC	93	2	B
Apricot cake	JOC	628	1	B
Baked Alaska	BCC	151	3	C
Balls	SC	177	1	
Banana pie	BCC	90	1	B
Band, making a	NSD	350	2	B
Bark	LM	336	1	
Bars, cockaigne, Christmas	JOC	653	1	C
Bavarian	JOC	693	3	B
Bavarian cream	MAFC	599	3	C
Bavarian cream	NYTI	292	2	B
Blancmange	AC	726	1	
Blancmange pudding	FFCB	610	1	B
Bombe	JOC	719	2	C
Bonbons	FFCB	687		
Box	LM	339	2	
Bran cake	FFBB	355	1	B
Brandy frosting	SC	146	1	
Brazilian	JOC	31	1	B
Bread	FFBB	454	2	B
Bread pudding	FFCB	612	1	B
Bread, quick	CBB	619	1	B
Brownie pie	BCC	92	2	B
Brownies (see brownies, chocolate)				
Burnt almond ice cream	MFC2	421	3	B
Butter	FFBB	455	2	C
Cream	LT	361		
Cream	NYT	574	1	B
Cream w orange frosting	AC	695	1	
Frosting	SC	143	1	
Icing	MAFC	684	1	B
Cake	JOC	627	2	B
◆	FFCB	507	2	B
◆	MFC	221	2	B
◆	SC	110	1	B
◆	LT	370	2	
A very rich, very light	MFC2	495	1	C
Bittersweet	SP	291	2	C
Buttermilk	FFCB	507	2	B
Chestnut	LM	354	2	C
w Chocolate glaze, French	BBA	187	3	B
Coach House	NYTI	9	3	C
Decadent	SP	290	2	C

RECIPE	BOOK	PAGE	TD	S
Double	BCC	68	1	C
Gayle Wilson's	FFBB	334	1	C
Huntington	FFCB	507	2	B
Little light	FFBB	379	1	C
w Mayonnaise	FFBB	336	2	C
Mix the pan	FFBB	352	1	B
w Mocha icing	PPLK	328	2	C
Moist	NSD	255	2	B
One bowl	NYT	549	1	C
One of a kind	FFBB	337	1	B
Peerless	FFBB	331	2	C
Quick	SC	110	1	B
Roll	BHGN	101	2	C
Sour cream	BHGN	98	1	C
Sour cream	BCC	66	1	C
Sweet	NYT	549	1	C
Sweet	AC	676	1	
Trifles, individual	MSQC	29	1	B
Triple layer	BBA	187	2	B
Candies form of truffles	MFC2	472	2	C
Caramel	SC	170	1	
◆	BCC	117	1	C
◆	JOC	732	1	B
◆	BHGN	112	1	B
Apples	BCC	121	1	B
Frosting	SC	146	1	
Sauce	JOC	712	1	B
Cases, semisweet	JOC	644	1	B
Chantilly	MFC	146	1	B
Charlotte (see also Charlotte, chocolate)				
◆	JOC	644	2	B
◆	FFCB	624	2	B
◆	LT	435	3	
Mousse	NSD	249	2	C
Russe	SC	136	2	B
Cheesecake	BCC	137	2	C
Cheesecake, semisweet	GHAC	340	2	C
Cherries, covered	BHGN	112	2	C
Cherries, dipped	SC	173	1	
Cherry cake	BCC	68	1	C
Cherry drop cookies	BCC	99	1	C
Chiffon cake	AC	691	1	
Chiffon cake	FFBB	304	2	C
Chiffon cake, seven layer	GHAC	330	3	C
Chiffon pie	FFCB	592	2	B
◆	NYT	524	1	B
◆	SC	350	1	
◆	BHGN	284	2	B
◆	FFBB	124	2	B
Chip				
Bars	BCC	97	1	C
Cake	FFCB	523	1	B
Cake	BHGN	92	1	C
Cake date	BCC	72	1	C
Cookie mix	KIS	349	1	C
Cookies	BCC	97	1	C
◆	FFCB	553	1	C
◆	FFBB	197	2	C
◆	AC	713	1	
◆	GHAC	346	1	C
◆	BHGN	159	1	C
◆	SP	262	1	C
Cookies, Big Sur	MHGD	299	1	C
Cookies w brown sugar	MSE	93	1	C
Cookies, crisp	BCC	97	1	C
Cookies, jumbo	BCC	97	1	C
Drop cookies	JOC	655	1	C
Glaze	BCC	79	1	C
Ice cream	FFCB	630	3	C
Ice cream	BHGN	182	3	C
Lace cookies	NSD	44	1	C
Mousse	SC	212	2	

RECIPE	BOOK	PAGE	TD	S
Chocolate Chip (*cont.*)				
Oatmeal cookies	FFCB	553	1	C
Squares, children's	FFBB	239	1	C
Topping	BCC	72	1	C
Chippers, Lori Taylor's	PPLK	338	1	C
Chips, homemade	NSD	244	2	B
Chocolate chip brownies	MSQC	201	1	B
Chocolate pie	YGM	169	2	C
Chunk bars, meringue topped	FFBB	226	1	C
Chunk brownies	GHAC	345	1	C
Chunk cookies	AC	713	1	
Chunk cookies	YGM	209	1	C
Chunk cookies	FFBB	205	2	C
Cigarette rolls & curls	BBA	188	3	C
Cigarettes	LT	452	1	
Clusters	JOC	738	1	A
Coating	BBA	209	1	C
Coating	JOC	730	1	B
Coating over boiled white icing	JOC	676	1	B
Cocoa, all about	JOC	522		
Coconut				
Cookies	FFCB	552	1	C
Crust	FFCB	578	1	B
Drop kisses	SC	163	1	
Macaroons	EBE	175	1	C
Macaroons	JOC	659	1	C
Mousse	EBE	189	3	B
Coffee, Russian	SC	51	1	
Cognac mousse cake	NSD	260	3	B
Cookie ice cream	SC	208	2	
Cookies	FFCB	563	1	C
Cookies	SC	152	1	
Chewy	FFBB	206	2	C
Delicate	SC	160	1	
Hurry up	SC	166	1	
Marjorie Kinnan Rawling's	MHGD	295	1	C
Thin crisp	FFBB	205	1	C
Cornflake macaroons	SC	164	1	
Cornstarch pudding	SC	197	1	
Cornstarch pudding	JOC	688	1	B
Cracker kisses	JOC	659	1	C
Crackletops	GHAC	346	1	C
Cream				
Cake or sour cream cake	AC	656	1	
Caramels	JOC	732	1	B
Dip	SC	173	1	
Filling	GHAC	344	2	B
Filling	FFCB	542	1	B
Frosting	NYT	574	1	B
Frozen	BCC	151	3	C
Pie	AC	625	1	
◆	GHAC	320	2	C
◆	JOC	610	2	B
◆	FFBB	111	2	B
◆	FFCB	592	2	B
◆	BCC	90	2	B
Pie, dark	BHGN	281	2	B
Pie, light	BHGN	281	2	B
Pie, meringue topped	GHAC	320	2	C
Pie, Parker House	FFBB	299	2	B
Puffs	BCC	138	1	C
Roll	JOC	643	2	B
Creme patissiere	BBA	202	1	B
Crepes	JBC	48	1	
Crepes, frozen	BBA	216	2	C
Crinkles	BCC	106	2	C
Crinkles	AC	714	1	
Cupcakes	GHAC	331	1	
Cupcakes	SC	140	1	C
Cupcakes	JOC	633	1	C

RECIPE	BOOK	PAGE	TD	S
Cupcakes, enough	FFBB	378	1	C
Cups, Linda's	CPMC	26	3	C
Curls, making	BHGN	440		
Curls, ruffles & cigarettes, making	NSD	344		
Custard	VE	266	2	B
◆	FFCB	609	1	B
◆	NYT	599	1	
◆	AC	676	1	
◆	JOC	687	2	B
Filling	SC	148	1	
Ice cream	SC	208	2	
Pie	SC	348	1	
Pie	CW	117	2	B
Pie, topped	JOC	609	2	B
Rennet	SC	200	1	
Sauce	JOC	712	1	B
Soft	SC	199	1	
Date	SC	173	1	
Date torte	JOC	639	1	B
Designs, pulled	NSD	343		
Dessert or layer cake from leftovers	MFC2	493	1	C
Dessert sauce, bittersweet	GHAC	290		
Dessert sauce, creamy ("best" sauce)	BCC	135	1	
Different kinds of	FFBB	5		
Dip	SC	173	1	
Dipping	BHGN	112		
Dough nutty	FFBB	63	1	B
Doughnuts	FFCB	499	3	C
Doughnuts cake	BHGN	82	2	C
Doughnuts yeast	BHGN	69	2	C
Dragonflies	BBA	216	3	C
Drop cookies	BCC	99	1	C
Drops double	BCC	99	1	C
Drops double	BHGN	161	1	C
Eclairs	JOC	598	3	
Eclairs	SC	140	1	
Egg malted milk	SC	51	1	
Feather pudding	JOC	702	2	B
Figs	SC	173	1	
Filled roll	JOC	643	2	B
Filling	SC	148	1	
Filling	BHGN	70	1	B
Butter cream	FFBB	412	1	C
Butter cream, cooked	FFBB	413	1	C
Butter cream frosting	FFBB	312	1	B
Chestnut	NYTI	290	1	
Cream	GHAC	344	2	B
Cream	FFBB	414	1	C
Custard	SC	148	1	
Dobos	SC	128	3	
For cakes	FFCB	531	1	B
For sponge cake	EBE	156	2	B
Walnut	GHAC	344	1	B
Flower	LM	342	3	
Foam, cold	CIC	443	1	B
Fondue	NYT	595	2	B
Fondue	BHGN	181	1	B
Frango	BCC	151	2	B
Frangoa frosting filling	FFBB	117	2	B
Frangoa mousse	FFBB	117	2	B
Frangoa pie	FFBB	117	2	B
Frosting (see frosting, chocolate)				
Fruit cake	FFCB	509	2	B
Fruit cake	GHAC	342	3	C
Fruits	SP	291		
Fudge	NSD	70	2	B
◆	SC	168	1	
◆	FFCB	679	2	B

RECIPE	BOOK	PAGE	TD	S
Chocolate Fudge (*cont.*)				
◆	AC	833	1	
◆	BCC	115	2	C
◆	GHAC	354	1	C
Frosting	AC	694	1	
Marshmallow	FFCB	679	2	B
Sauce	SP	293	1	B
Sauce, milk	SC	219	1	
Sour cream	FFCB	679	2	B
Triple	BBA	225	1	C
Fudgeswirl ice cream	GHAC	304	3	C
Garnishes, making	GHAC	330		
Gelatin chiffon pie	JOC	614	2	B
Genoise	AC	681	2	
Glaze	FFBB	409	1	C
◆	SC	143	1	
◆	BHGN	82	1	
◆	SP	292	1	B
◆	BBA	187	1	A
◆	FFCB	542	1	
Glaze, bitter	NSD	348	2	B
Glaze, speedy	FFBB	410	1	C
Glazed Easter bunnies	MSE	229	3	B
Glazed Easter lambs	MSE	229	3	B
Glazed Easter turkeys	MSE	229	3	B
Glazed pears	SP	291	2	B
Graham icebox cake	SC	136	3	B
Grapes, dipped	SC	173	1	
Grating	BHGN	440		
Hazelnut cake	NSD	172	2	C
Hazelnut cake	SPGT	75	2	C
Hazelnut cake	SP	288	2	B
Hazelnut torte	FFBB	371	2	C
Hermits	MHGD	297	1	C
Hot	BCC	24	1	B
Hot	BHGN	50	1	B
Hot	JOC	31	1	A

RECIPE	BOOK	PAGE	TD	S
Hot, banana	KIS	319	1	
Ice cream	BTSB	74	2	B
◆	BCC	152	2	B
◆	BBA	228	2	B
◆	AC	738	3	
◆	FFCB	631	3	C
◆	JOC	716	2	B
Burnt almond	MFC2	421	3	B
Evaporated milk	JOC	718	2	B
Jack Daniels	NSD	210	1	B
Made in the freezer	AC	739	3	
Old fashioned	FFCB	631	3	B
Old fashioned	SC	206	2	
Quick	SC	208	2	
Rich	SC	206	2	
Roll	BCC	76	2	C
Icebox cake	SC	134	1	B
Icebox cake, graham	SC	136	3	B
Icebox cake, sweet	SC	134	1	B
Icebox dessert, marshmallow	SC	136	2	B
Iced	JOC	31	1	B
Iced, egg	SC	51	1	
Icing	GHAC	344	1	B
◆	SC	143	1	
◆	MAFC	671	1	
◆	BHGN	106	1	B
◆	SP	289	1	B
Butter	JOC	678	1	B
Cream cheese	JOC	679	1	B
Easy	JOC	679	1	B
European	JOC	679	1	A
Fudge	JOC	677	1	B
Marshmallow	JOC	677	1	B
Quick	JOC	679	1	B
Sour cream	FFBB	401	1	C
Intemperance	BBA	187	2	C
Jelly	SC	202	2	
Kisses	AC	720	1	

RECIPE	BOOK	PAGE	TD	S
Kisses	SC	162	1	
Layer cake, sour cream	SC	118	1	B
Le marquise au (chocolate mousse cake)	MSE	240	3	C
Leaves	LM	337	1	
Lemon cookies	SC	155	1	
Loaf cake, French	MHGD	27	2	C
Lovers, only for	MFC	223	2	C
Macaroons	SC	164	1	
Macaroons	BBA	189	2	B
Macaroons	SC	164	1	
Malt shake syrup	JOC	31	1	C
Malts	BCC	24	1	A
Mandarine ice cream	NSD	211	1	B
Marble cake	BHGN	101	1	C
Marbled cake	FFBB	318	1	C
Marshmallow				
Balls	SC	177	1	
Bars	BCC	122	1	C
Fudge	GHAC	354	1	C
Fudge	FFCB	679	2	B
Ice cream	SC	207	2	
Icebox dessert	SC	136	2	B
Sauce	SC	219	1	
Sauce for ice cream	GHAC	306	1	B
Matzo meal torte	SC	130	1	B
Melting	NSD	19		
Melting	BHGN	423		
Melting	MAFC	582		
Meringue	FFBB	222	1	C
Meringue	FFCB	560	2	B
Meringue	MFC	232	3	B
Frosting	SC	145	1	
Nut cake	LT	347	2	C
Pie	MIE	333	2	C
Mexican hot	BCC	24	1	B
Milk shake	BHGN	51	1	A
Milk shake	BCC	24	1	A
Mint				
Brownies	GHAC	345	1	C
Cookies	NSD	46	3	C
Cookies	BCC	98	1	C
Ice cream	NSD	212	1	B
Sandwich cookies	SPGT	110	2	C
Sauce	JOC	712	1	B
Sauce	NYT	613	1	B
Mocha cake, quick	FFCB	528	1	B
Molasses frosting	SC	146	1	
Mousse	PPLK	333	1	B
◆	JBC	45	1	B
◆	MSE	93	1	C
◆	MFC	231	3	B
◆	MAFC	604	2	B
◆	EBE	199	1	B
◆	SP	287	2	B
◆	BCC	148	2	B
Brandy	BCC	148	2	B
Cake	BCC	66	2	C
Cake	NSD	253	3	B
Cake (le marquise au)	MSE	240	3	C
Cake (chocolate Charlotte)	MFC	222	2	C
French	JOC	687	2	B
French	FFCB	610	2	B
Frozen	FFCB	625	3	B
Frozen in molded meringues	MFC2	425	3	C
I	NYT	596	2	B
II	NYT	597	2	B
Marbled	GHAC	299	2	C
Minted	MSQC	113	2	B
Quick	MIE	325	3	B
Quick	SC	212	2	

RECIPE	BOOK	PAGE	TD	S
Chocolate Mousse (*cont.*)				
Quick & easy	BBA	225	1	B
Rum	JOC	687	2	C
Tart, Jane's	MSQC	165	2	B
Muffins	SC	90	1	
Nut				
Balls	BHGN	115	2	C
Bread	FFBB	550	2	C
Brittle sauce	JOC	712	1	B
Butter balls	FFBB	271	1	C
Cake, sweet potato	VGCB	300	1	B
Frosting	SC	146	1	
Logs	BCC	108	2	C
Slices	BCC	109	3	C
Oil cake, quick	JOC	635	1	B
Or chocolate caramel potato cake	AC	675	1	
Or cocoa angel food cake	AC	686	1	
Parfait, hazelnut orange	NSD	312	3	B
Pastry cream	FAIC	432	1	B
Pastry shell	NYT	530	1	B
Pave au	NYT	599	2	B
Peanut bars, children's crispy	FFBB	239	1	C
Peanut butter bars, crispy	BHGN	157	2	C
Peanut butter bites	SP	294	1	C
Peanut butter pie	GHAC	324	2	C
Peanut butter prunes	BBA	225	2	C
Peanut cookies	BHGN	159	1	C
Pecan grapefruit tartes	YGM	235	3	C
Pecan kisses	SC	163	1	
Pecan pie	BCC	92	2	B
Pecan pralines	PPLK	326	2	C
Pecan tartlets	MSE	197	2	B
Peel, dipped & candied	SC	175	1	

RECIPE	BOOK	PAGE	TD	S
Pepper pretzels	MHGD	300	1	C
Pie	JOC	610	2	B
Pie	SC	348	1	
Pie, double	EBE	164	1	B
Pie, German sweet	NYT	524	2	B
Popcorn balls	BCC	121	1	B
Poppy seed torte	SC	132	2	B
Pot de cream	NYT	600	2	B
Potato cake, Lynn's	VGCB	227	1	B
Potato drop cakes	SC	139	1	
Potato torte	SC	126	1	B
Pots de creme	BHGN	173	2	B
Pots de creme	BCC	141	1	B
Pretzels	SC	158	1	
Prune cake, spiced	JOC	628	1	B
Pudding (see also pudding, chocolate)				
Pudding, macaroon	SC	204	2	
Pudding mix	BTSB	250	1	C
Pureed chestnut mound	CIC	440	2	B
Raspberry mousse cake	NSD	258	3	B
Refrigerator cookies	FFBB	217	1	C
Refrigerator cookies	AC	701	2	
Refrigerator cookies	JOC	660	1	C
Rennet custard	SC	200	1	
Revel bars	BHGN	156	1	C
Revel frosting	BCC	77	1	C
Rice pudding	SC	201	2	
Rice pudding	FFCB	611	2	B
Roll	AC	681	2	
◆	JBC	36	2	B
◆	FFCB	523	2	C
◆	BBA	225	3	B
◆	FFBB	306	2	C
◆	SC	123	1	B
◆	EBE	150	3	B

RECIPE	BOOK	PAGE	TD	S
Roll (roulage leontine)	AC	678	2	
Rolled cookies	AC	703	1	
Rolls, small	LM	264	2	B
Roulade	MSE	260	3	C
Russian	SC	51	1	B
Rye bread torte	SC	133	1	B
Sable cookies, hazelnut	NSD	64	2	C
Sandwich cookie ice cream	BCC	152	2	B
Sauce	FFBB	419	1	C
◆	NYTI	17	1	B
◆	JBC	267	1	
◆	SC	216	1	
◆	JOC	711	1	B
◆	FFCB	638	1	B
◆	AC	741	1	
◆	JBC	48	1	
Bimini	MHGD	177	1	B
Bitter	NYT	614	1	B
Blender	JOC	711	1	B
Cockaigne	JOC	711	1	B
Creamy	FFCB	639	1	B
Crunchy	BCC	153	1	B
Dark	BTSB	160	1	C
Easy	SC	216	1	
Fluffy	SC	219	1	
Mint	BTSB	160	1	C
Nuts &	JBC	267	1	
Orange	BTSB	160	1	C
Pears &	FFCB	667	1	B
Pears, spiced	GHAC	291	2	B
Rich & thick	BBA	201	1	A
Rum	JBC	267	1	
Sausage	SC	177	1	
Shake syrup	JOC	31	1	C
Soda	BHGN	51	1	A
Soda, double	BHGN	51	1	A
Souffle	MSQC	209	1	B
◆	FFCB	619	3	B
◆	JBGF	638	2	B
◆	BHGN	175	2	B
◆	JOC	690	2	B
◆	SC	195	1	
◆	CF	31	2	B
◆	MAFC	619	3	B
◆	NYT	603	1	B
◆	NYTI	302	1	B
◆	JBC	271	1	B
◆	AC	679	1	
Baked	BCC	135	2	B
Cake	MHGD	36	2	C
Cold	NYTI	303	2	B
w Rum sauce	LM	322	1	B
Sweet	SC	195	1	
Vanilla	LM	324	1	
Soup	CBSS	162	3	B
Sour cream				
Frosting	GHAC	331	1	
Frosting	BCC	78	1	C
Fudge	FFCB	679	2	B
Sauce	NYT	613	1	B
Torte	GHAC	331	2	C
Spice cake	BCC	68	1	C
Spice cake, citron, old world	JOC	628	1	B
Spicy	BHGN	50	1	B
Sponge	NYT	603	2	B
Sponge	SC	190	2	
Sponge cake	FFCB	518	1	B
Sponge cake	MAFC	679	3	B
Sponge cake	JOC	622	1	B
Sponge cake butter	FFBB	301	2	C
Sponge roll	SC	123	1	B
Spritz	AC	708	2	
Spritz	BCC	114	1	C
Sticks	SC	153	1	
Storing	NSD	19		
Sundae sauce	SC	219	1	

RECIPE	BOOK	PAGE	TD	S
Chocolate (*cont.*)				
Sweet pudding, frozen	SC	214	2	
Swirl coffee cake	BHGN	67	3	B
Syrup cake	EBE	151	1	B
Syrup for drinks	SC	51	1	C
Tart, chestnut	NYTI	290	1	B
Tart, strawberry	SP	278	2	B
Terrine w wild strawberries	NSD	250	3	C
Thumbprints	GHAC	346	1	C
Toffee bars	SC	165	1	
Torte	SC	126	1	B
Torte, applesauce	SC	125	1	B
Torte, ventana	YGM	197	1	C
Torte, white, strawberry	NSD	264	3	B
Tortoni	BBA	226	2	B
Truffle cake	LM	328	3	C
Truffle cake	NSD	278	3	C
Truffle ice cream	NSD	214	1	B
Truffles (see truffles, chocolate)				
Upside down cake	AC	678	1	
Vanilla souffle	LM	324	1	
Velvet	NYT	631	2	C
Victoria tartlets	MSE	93	2	C
Wafer crumb crust	GHAC	321	1	B
Wafer crust	BHGN	290	1	B
Wafer shells	SC	344	2	
Waffles	JOC	218	1	B
Waffles	SC	97	1	B
Walnut				
Cake	BCC	68	1	C
Clusters	FFBB	203	2	C
Filling	GHAC	344	1	B
Torte	JOC	639	2	B
Torte	SC	127	1	B
Wafers	FFCB	554	1	C
Whipped cream filling	FFCB	546	1	B
White macadamia nut glaze	FFBB	411	2	C
Yeast cake	SC	79	2	
Yogurt	FG	251	3	
Zabaglione dessert	NYTI	445	2	B
Zucchini cake	FFBB	346	1	C
Zwieback torte	SC	134	1	B
Cholla I	SC	67	2	C
Cholla II	SC	67	2	C
Chongos (Mexican custard)	NYTI	479	2	C
Chop Scotch (pork chops)	CFS	149	2	B
Chop suey	JOC	229	2	B
Chop suey	GHAC	192	1	B
Chop suey shrimp	WC	72	1	B
Chop suey shrimp	GHAC	192	1	
Chopping	BHGN	429		
Chopping (drawings)	MFC	14		
Chops a l'orange	CFS	147	2	B
Chops w bread crumbs	OC	114	1	B
Choreki (braided Greek sweet bread)	BBA	179	3	B
Choreki Grecian sweet braid	CBB	331	3	C
Chorizo	FG	183	1	B
Chorizo	FGCW	250	2	B
Chorizo	NYT	147	1	B
Chorizo potato cubes, skewered	CFS	202	1	B
Choron sauce	PPLK	261	1	B
Chou chou French, dilled creamy cabbage	GG	80	1	B
Chou farci (stuffed cabbage)	NYTI	186	3	C

RECIPE	BOOK	PAGE	TD	S
Chou farci	GG	83	2	B
Chou farcis (braised cabbage)	LM	139	2	B
Chou pastry, basic	BBA	191	3	C
Choucroute	BCC	231	2	B
A l'alsacienne (sauerkraut w meats)	NYT	141	2	B
Braised pheasant	GF	206	3	C
Garni	BHGN	263	2	C
Garnie	SP	133	3	B
Garnie	JBC	196	2	B
Garnie	NYTI	244	2	C
Choux paste fritters, unsweetened	JOC	221	2	
Choux paste garnish	JOC	171	2	B
Choux paste swan	JOC	597	3	
Choux stuffed	JOC	55	2	B
Chow chow (mustard pickles)	JOC	783	3	C
◆	FFCB	713	2	B
◆	SC	454	3	
◆	AC	826	3	
Chow mein	JOC	229	2	B
Chow mein	SC	335	1	
Chow mein shrimp	BHGN	219	2	B
Chowder				
Clam (see clam chowder)				
Mixed turnip	GG	387	1	B
New England	BCC	307	1	B
Potted pepper	GG	278	1	B
Christmas				
Bread				
Bohemian	CBB	310	3	C
Greek	CBB	338	3	C
Hungarian	CBB	342	2	B
Mother's	CBB	305	3	C
Swiss	CBB	353	3	C

RECIPE	BOOK	PAGE	TD	S
Brownies	MHGD	291	1	C
Canapes	JOC	54		
Chocolate bars cockaigne	JOC	653	1	C
Cookies	FFBB	271	1	C
Cookies, all about	FFBB	265		
Cookies (pfeffernusse)	BTSB	233	2	C
Fruit loaf, Danish	CBB	307	3	B
Ham, Swedish	NYTI	532	3	C
Loaf	JOC	571	2	C
Log cake (buche de Noel)	AC	682	2	
Log chocolate bark	LM	332	2	C
Pudding	NSD	192	2	C
Salad	JOC	87	1	B
Spice cookies	SC	153	1	
Stollen (Christmas fruitcake)	NYTI	317	3	B
Stollen	FFCB	480	3	B
Stollen (stolle de Noel)	CBB	331	3	C
Tree cookies	GHAC	352	2	C
Wreath	JOC	701	2	B
Wreath cardamom	GHAC	360	2	B
Yule log	LT	360	2	
Christopsomo Greek Christmas bread	CBB	338	3	C
Chrysanthemum bowl, Chinese	BBA	31	2	B
Chrysanthemum pot, Chinese	NYTI	47	3	
Chuck, boneless, Indonesian style	CFS	84	2	B
Chuck roast, barbecued	CFS	273	3	B
Chuck roast foil	JOC	416	2	C
Chuck roast, lemon-marinated	BHGN	28	3	B
Chuck steak, ballpark	CFS	84	2	A

RECIPE	BOOK	PAGE	TD	S
Chuck steak, definition	AC	262		
Chuck steak, marinated	AC	293	3	
Chuletas (Mexican meat patties)	AC	314	1	
Chupe Chilean seafood casserole	NYT	296	1	C
Churrasco (Mexican beefsteak)	BB	15	1	B
Churrasco roast	EBE	53	3	C
Churrasco sauce	BB	16	1	B
Chutney	MC	73	2	B
Chutney	AC	827	1	
American heirloom	GHAC	383	1	C
Apple	BBA	167	1	C
◆	JOC	786	3	C
◆	FFCB	716	2	C
◆	AC	827	1	
Avocado	JOC	68	1	
Baked beans w	VE	129	2	B
Beets	VGCB	27	1	B
Cheese canapes	SC	40	1	
Chicken mango	SPGT	91	2	B
Cream cheese	MSE	191	3	C
Cream cheese, gingersnaps w	MSE	191	3	C
Curry-butter	SP	116	1	
Date lemon	BBA	167	1	B
Dressing	JOC	313	1	B
Dressing	BCC	278	1	
Dressing, mango, for duck & pear salad	SP	206	2	B
Eggplant, smoked	NYTI	360	2	B
English	SC	456	2	
Ginger apple	FFCB	716	2	C
Green tomato	JOC	786	3	C
Mango	JOC	785	3	C
Mango	BTSB	149	2	C
Mango	WC	114	2	C

RECIPE	BOOK	PAGE	TD	S
Nectarine	BTSB	148	2	C
Peach	AC	827	1	
◆	BTSB	148	2	C
◆	BBA	167	2	C
◆	JOC	785	3	C
◆	FFCB	715	2	C
Pear	BBA	168	1	B
Pear	AC	827	1	
Sauce for ham	NYT	448	1	B
Steamed pudding, gooseberry	CF	43	2	B
Tomato-apple	BBA	168	2	B
Tomato, green	JOC	786	3	C
Tomato, green	AC	827	1	
Worthy's	BBA	168	2	B
Cibreo sauce tagliatelle	FAIC	148	2	B
Cider				
Apple	SC	436	2	
Apple, glaze	SP	272	1	C
Ham baked in	JBC	207		
Ham baked in	AC	443	3	
& Ham, beer-glazed	GF	226	2	C
Ham braised	NYTI	187	3	C
Hot	JOC	33	1	
Hot mulled	BHGN	52	1	B
Mulled	MSE	217	1	C
Mulled	JOC	33	1	
Mulled	SC	56	1	B
Mulled, nonalcoholic	JBGF	287	1	C
Orange, hot	BCC	21	1	C
Pork, leg of, cream &	AC	406		
Pork steak & sauerkraut casserole	JBC	202	1	
Punch	FFCB	743	1	C
Salad, cherry	BHGN	340	2	C
Sauce	JOC	711	1	B
Stew	BHGN	367	2	B

RECIPE	BOOK	PAGE	TD	S
Vinegar	SC	437	3	
Waldorf mold	BHGN	341	2	B
Cigarette, chocolate, rolls & curls	BBA	188	3	C
Cigarettes, chocolate	LT	452	1	
Cilantro chicken	BCC	252	1	B
Cinnamon				
Apple rings	BHGN	362	1	C
Apple tart	BCC	84	2	B
Apples	JOC	111	2	B
Apples	FFCB	652	1	B
Balls	SC	171	1	
Biscuits, rolled	FFBB	576	2	C
Bread	AC	781	1	
Broth, Renaissance	FAIC	112	1	B
Buns	NYT	474	2	
Buns	FFBB	517	2	C
Buns	JOC	565	3	B
Buns, pecan	GHAC	362	2	C
Buns, walnut	GHAC	362	2	C
Buns, whole wheat	NYT	475	2	C
Chicken	KIS	105	1	A
Chiffon cake w golden raisins	FFBB	304	2	C
Cookies, hurry up	SC	166	1	
Crisps	BHGN	68	3	C
Custard, old fashioned	FAIC	436	2	B
Frosting	AC	693	1	
Glazed toast	SC	72	1	
Jelly apple	BHGN	149	2	B
Loaf	JOC	586	1	
Meringue	BCC	145	2	B
Mousse	SC	213	2	
Nutmeg cookies, whole wheat	MHGD	320	1	C
Oatmeal bread	CBB	220	2	C
Oranges	BCC	128	1	B
Pears	JOC	111	2	B
Pecan buns	GHAC	362	2	C
Raisin bread	BTSB	89	3	C
Raspberry cookies	NSD	68	3	C
Refrigerator cookies	FFCB	562	1	C
Rolls	BCC	51	2	C
◆	BHGN	68	2	C
◆	SC	80	2	
◆	JBC	16	2	B
◆	FFCB	479	3	C
Rolls, quick	SC	87	1	
Snails	JOC	565	3	B
Sourdough rolls, orange	BHGN	76	2	C
Stars	JOC	670	1	C
Stars	SC	153	1	
Sticks	JOC	586	1	
Sugar	JOC	508	1	
Swirl bread	BHGN	64	2	B
Swirl bread, orange	CBB	462	2	C
Toast	SC	72	1	
◆	FFCB	491	1	B
◆	SC	72	1	
◆	JBC	25	1	
◆	JOC	586	1	
Walnut buns	GHAC	362	2	C
Walnut cookies	NSD	55	1	C
Cioppino	BHGN	373	1	B
Cioppino	FFCB	103	2	B
Fish stew	AC	181	1	
Quick & easy	MIE	161	1	B
Seafood stew	CBSS	197	3	B
Citrus				
Bread	FFBB	553	2	B
Cartwheels & twists	BHGN	440		
Filling, butter cream	FFBB	412	1	C
Filling, butter cream, cooked	FFBB	413	1	C
Fruit flavored sugars	JOC	508	1	
Fruit juice melody	JOC	33	1	B

RECIPE	BOOK	PAGE	TD	S
Citrus (*cont.*)				
Marmalade	SC	443	3	
Peel, candied	BCC	121	2	C
Peel, candied	FFCB	691	2	B
Peel, candied	JOC	742	2	
Rum punch	BHGN	47	1	C
Salad	BCC	292	2	B
Salad, spinach	JBGF	548	1	B
Sauce	BCC	128	1	
Clabber bread, Gannat	CBB	385	3	C
Clam				
A la St. Louis	SC	247	1	
All about	JOC	367		
Au beurre blanc	NYTI	96	2	B
Aux blinis	NYT	21	2	B
Bacon & olive oil, linguine &	CPPC	94	2	A
Baked	JBC	74	1	B
Baked	FFCB	128	1	B
Barbecued	MSE	156	2	C
Bisque	NYTI	122	2	C
Bisque, mushroom &	JOC	162	1	A
Bordelaise	FG	332	1	B
Broiled	FFCB	128	1	B
Broiled on the half shell	JOC	369	1	
Broth	FFCB	84	2	A
Broth	JOC	161	2	B
Broth from steamed hard shell clams	JOC	369	2	
Cakes	JOC	240	2	B
Casino	EBE	16	2	C
Cheese canapes	NYT	43	1	C
Chicken broth, quick	JOC	168	1	
Chowder	JBC	281	2	
◆	AC	173	1	
◆	SC	404	1	
◆	AC	176	1	
For a big party	BB	105	2	C
Long Island	NYTI	556	2	C
Manhattan	BCC	307	1	B
◆	GHAC	106	1	C
◆	CBSS	131	2	B
◆	SP	51	2	B
◆	BHGN	372	1	B
◆	FFCB	102	2	B
◆	JOC	164	2	B
My favorite	AC	176	1	
New England	JOC	164	2	B
◆	FFCB	102	2	C
◆	NYTI	556	1	B
◆	BHGN	372	1	B
◆	GHAC	106	1	C
◆	CBSS	127	2	B
◆	GHAC	106	1	C
New England, Boston style	NYT	73	2	C
Nora Bennett's	CBSS	132	2	C
Old western	AC	174	1	
Quick	SC	404	1	
Southern, New England	CBSS	129	2	B
Standard, New England	AC	175	1	
Very rich	FGCW	104	1	B
Cocktail	SC	45	1	
Cocktails, oyster, individual	AC	26		
Corn chowder	FGCW	106	1	B
Corn chowder	GG	131	1	B
Cream cheese spread	SC	380	1	
Cream filling	MAFC	202	1	C
Creamed chicken w	AC	201	1	
Dip	JOC	75	1	
◆	FFCB	54	1	B
◆	KIS	312	1	B
◆	EBE	34	1	B

RECIPE	BOOK	PAGE	TD	S
Dip, crab &	EBE	35	1	B
Dip, hot	FFCB	55	1	B
Dow see	FG	315	2	A
Egg pie	AC	172	1	
Filling	BBA	15	1	A
Fish soup, French	SMG	100	1	B
Florentine, stuffed	NYTI	97	3	C
Fra diavolo, mussels &	GHAC	126	1	B
Fricassee of	FFCB	129	1	B
Fried	BHGN	217	1	B
Fried	JOC	369	1	
Fritters	FFCB	65	1	C
Fritters	GHAC	119	1	B
Green sauce, hot	SMG	148	1	B
Gremolata, linguine w	CPPC	96	3	B
Grilled	GRIL	101	2	B
Haddock, stuffed	NYT	237	1	B
Hard shell, steamed	JOC	372	1	
Hash	JBC	75	1	B
Hash	AC	166	1	
Juice	JOC	32	1	B
Juice	MAFC	115	1	B
Juice ring, jellied	JOC	97	2	B
Linguine or spaghetti w	AC	590	1	
Littleneck, on the half shell	MSQC	120	1	
Little necks, steamed in cream & thyme	GF	152	1	B
Mirepoix vegetables, linguine &	CPPC	97	3	A
On the grill	SC	333	1	
On the half shell	AC	166	1	
On the half shell	JBC	73	1	
broiled mussels &	CIC	34	1	B

RECIPE	BOOK	PAGE	TD	S
On toast	NYT	273	1	B
Opening (photographs)	LT	106		
& Oysters, barbecued	BB	89	2	
& Oysters, pan fried	JBC	9	1	
& Oysters, scalloped	SC	247	1	
Pan fried	JBC	75	1	
Parsley smoked	FG	57	1	C
Pasta sauce	BBA	102	1	B
Pasta w vegetable sauce	FG	122	1	B
Pie	AC	171	1	
Pie a la Springs	NYTI	558	2	B
& Pork Portuguese	YGM	211	3	C
Puffs	JOC	61	1	
Quiche	AC	172	1	
Razor	JBC	75	1	
Rhode Island	AC	175	1	
Risotto	CIC	192	2	B
Sauce	JBC	216	2	B
Linguine &	SMG	294	1	B
Linguine & red	NYTI	412	1	B
Linguine & white	GHAC	260	1	
Linguine & white	SP	75	2	B
Quick	JBC	216	1	
Red	NYT	343	2	C
Red	JBGF	366	1	B
Red, thin spaghetti w	CIC	100	1	B
Shrimp &, for pasta, quick	JOC	336	1	B
Spaghetti squash w	JBGF	448	1	B
White	NYT	343	1	C
White	JBGF	365	1	B
White fettuccine w	CIC	135	3	B
White, for vegetable spaghetti	VGCB	286	1	

RECIPE	BOOK	PAGE	TD	S
Coconut Cream pie (*cont.*)				
◆	BHGN	281	2	B
◆	FFCB	592	2	B
◆	AC	625	1	
◆	BCC	90	2	B
◆	MHGD	179	2	B
◆	NYT	524	1	B
◆	MSE	245	3	B
Cream pie, toasted	BBA	201	3	B
Crust	BHGN	289	1	B
Crust, chocolate	FFCB	578	1	B
Crust, toasted	FFBB	70	1	B
Cupcakes	JOC	634	1	C
Curls, pineapple &	MSQC	41	1	B
Custard	FFCB	609	1	B
◆	MHGD	352	2	B
◆	SC	199	1	
◆	AC	729	1	
Pie	SC	349	1	
Pie	FFCB	591	2	B
Pie, slipped	GHAC	319	2	C
Divinity	NYT	636	2	C
Drop kisses	SC	163	1	
Drops	SC	160	1	
Drops, pineapple	BHGN	159	1	C
Dulcie	JOC	713	1	C
Extravaganza	JOC	47	1	A
Filling, raisin	FFBB	405	1	C
Flan	CF	35	2	B
Frosting	SC	145	1	
Frosting	FFCB	540	1	B
Frosting	FFBB	406	1	C
Broiled	SC	144	1	
Pecan	BHGN	105	1	B
Pecan	NYT	576	1	B
Raisin	FFBB	405	1	C
Fudge	JOC	731	1	B
Graham cracker cake	SC	113	1	B
Icing	JOC	673	1	B

RECIPE	BOOK	PAGE	TD	S
Jumbles	CF	79	1	C
Kisses	SC	162	1	
Kisses	AC	720	1	
Kisses or macaroons	AC	720	1	
Layer cake	SC	109	1	B
Layer cake	JOC	626	1	B
Loaf	JOC	626	1	B
Macadamia bars	BCC	100	1	C
Macadamia cookies	BCC	100	1	C
Macaroons	BCC	100	1	C
◆	GHAC	351	1	C
◆	FFBB	220	1	C
◆	JOC	658	1	C
◆	SP	256	1	B
◆	BHGN	161	1	C
Chocolate	JOC	659	1	C
Chocolate	EBE	175	1	C
Cornflake	SC	164	1	
Marshmallow bars	BCC	122	1	C
Meringue cookies	JOC	658	1	C
Milk	BBA	161	1	B
Milk	NYT	139	1	
Cake	JOC	624	2	C
Made in a blender	NYTI	34	2	B
Pudding, chilled	NYTI	504	2	C
Moruga, spinach &	GG	313	1	B
Nougatine	NSD	352	2	B
Nougatine ice cream	NSD	221	2	B
Oatmeal cookies	MHGD	318	1	C
Orange mold	EBE	136	2	C
Peanut butter candy	SC	178	1	
Pecan frosting	BCC	67	1	
Pecan frosting	NYT	576	1	B
Pecan topping	BCC	137	1	
Pecan upside down cake, quick	FFBB	353	2	B
Pineapple tapioca	GHAC	295	1	B
Pound cake, Cuban	MHGD	93	1	C
Pound cake, orange	BCC	69	1	C

RECIPE	BOOK	PAGE	TD	S
Coconut (*cont.*)				
Pudding	SC	188	2	
Pudding, milk, chilled	NYTI	504	2	C
Pumpkin chiffon pie	BBA	205	2	B
Raisin cherry strudel	SC	355	2	
Refrigerator cookies	FFCB	562	1	C
Shredded	BTSB	289	1	C
Side dish	NYTI	180	2	
Slices, oatmeal	BCC	109	3	C
Snowballs	BCC	152		
Snowballs	SC	139	1	
Squares	FFCB	564	1	C
Topping, broiled	BHGN	105	1	B
Tuiles	NSD	48	2	C
Cocotte potatoes, cutting	LT	199	1	
Cod				
A la Portugaise	JOC	354	1	B
Baked, oyster stuffing	NYTI	233	1	B
Boulangere	JOC	355	1	B
Curried	NYT	233	1	B
Dried, in cream sauce	FGCW	347	2	B
Dried, salted, Florentine style	FAIC	254	3	B
Fillets, grilled	OC	143	2	B
For aioli	NYTI	134	3	B
& Grapefruit, baked	GHAC	136	1	B
In celery cream	VGCB	82	2	B
In cream sauce, baked	NYTI	94	1	B
Provencale	NYT	234	1	B
Salt, bouillabaisse w	CPMC	36	3	B
Scalloped	JOC	354	1	B
Steaks, broiled	AC	125	1	B
Steaks, foil-steamed	FFCB	112	1	B
Steaks, Montauk, broiled	GHAC	136	1	B
Tomato crowned	JBGF	449	1	B
Vegetable bake	BCC	179	1	B
Coddled eggs	AC	101	1	
Codfish				
w Ackee, Jamaican	NYTI	447	1	B
Balls	JOC	354	2	B
◆	AC	27	1	
◆	SC	245	3	
◆	GHAC	137	1	
Cakes	FFCB	148	1	C
◆	AC	142	1	
◆	JOC	354	2	B
◆	NYT	235	1	B
Creamed	SC	245	3	
Creamed	FFCB	149	1	B
Creole	SC	245	2	
Hash, salt w tomatoes & garlic	FFCB	149	1	B
Loaf	NYT	234	1	B
Salad	AC	65	1	
Coeur a la creme (dessert)	NYT	606	3	B
◆	FFCB	615	3	B
◆	FG	335	1	B
◆	JOC	708	1	B
Coeur a la creme, caviar	BBA	15	3	B
Coeur a la creme sauce	NYTI	298	2	B
Coffee	BB	162		
Coffee	FAIC	499		
Coffee	SC	49		
All about	SC	49		
Angel pie	BHGN	287	2	B
Bavarian	JOC	693	3	B
Bavarian cream	NYT	591	2	B
Blender, frozen	JOC	29	1	
Boiled	SC	50	1	
Brandy, iced	CW	37	1	C

RECIPE	BOOK	PAGE	TD	S
Bread, Cincinnati	FFCB	473	2	B
Bread, date & apple	BHGN	77	1	B
Buns, Bohemian	SC	81	2	
Butter cream	LT	364	1	
Butter frosting	SC	143	1	
Cake	BTSB	124	1	B
Almond	SC	117	1	B
Angie's	SP	322	3	C
Any fruit	BHGN	80	1	B
Applesauce	BHGN	81	1	B
Baking powder	SC	116	2	B
Blueberry	FFBB	578	1	B
California	EBE	149	1	C
Cardamom	MC	207	1	C
Coconut	JBGF	617	1	C
Easy	SC	117	1	B
Filling, (see filling)				
French	SC	79	2	
Fruit topped yeast	JOC	571	2	C
German	CBB	651	3	C
Honey bran	FFBB	580	1	B
Honey twist	BCC	51	2	B
Kneaded for filled braid rings	JOC	570	3	C
No knead yeast	JOC	570	2	C
Orange & date	BHGN	80	1	B
Orange, prune & caraway	FFBB	580	2	B
Pecan crumb	GHAC	329	2	C
Proust's small	LM	272	1	C
Quick (snickerdoodle or snipdoodle)	AC	648	1	
◆	JOC	577	1	B
◆	SC	117	1	B
◆	JBC	23	1	
◆	FFCB	495	1	B
Quick, rich & moist	JOC	577	1	B

RECIPE	BOOK	PAGE	TD	S
Raisin	CBB	510	3	C
Raisin spice	BCC	33	1	B
Ring	SC	77	2	
Ring, "blooming"	FFBB	515	2	C
Ruth's	FFCB	481	3	B
Scandinavian	JOC	572	3	B
Short cut	SC	77	2	
Sour cream	FFBB	579	1	B
◆	BCC	33	2	B
◆	SC	118	1	B
◆	GHAC	329	2	C
◆	SP	321	2	C
◆	MHGD	104	1	C
Sour cream, quick	JOC	577	1	B
Spice, quick w oil	JOC	578	1	B
Spicy buttermilk	BHGN	80	1	B
Streusel	BHGN	81	1	B
Streusel	BCC	33	1	B
Streusel, quick	AC	659	1	
Sunday	FFBB	577	1	C
Yeast raised (babka)	CBB	606	3	C
Charlotte	NYTI	293	2	B
Chart, serving large quantities	BCC	25		
Chicken paprika	FGCW	383	1	B
Chiffon pie	FFCB	592	2	B
Chocolate	BHGN	50	1	B
Chocolate custard	JOC	685	1	B
Clearing boiled	SC	50		
Cognac cream pie	MHGD	181	2	B
Concentrate	SC	50	3	
Cookies	PPLK	337	1	C
Cordial pie	BCC	94	2	B
Cream	SC	203	2	
Cream milk shake	BHGN	51	1	A
Cream torte	SC	127	1	B
Cream whipped	FFCB	644	1	B
Creme	SC	127	1	B

RECIPE	BOOK	PAGE	TD	S
Coffee (*cont.*)				
Creme patissiere	BBA	202	1	B
Crunch	FFBB	417	1	C
Custard	FFCB	609	1	B
Custard	SC	199	1	
Custard filling	SC	148	1	
Custard sauce	FFCB	640	1	B
Custards, baked	GHAC	296	2	B
Dessert	BHGN	53	1	A
Doughnut holes	SPGT	128	3	C
Drip	JOC	27	1	
Drops	JOC	733	1	B
Filling				
Butter cream	FFBB	412	1	C
Butter cream, cooked	FFBB	413	1	C
Custard	SC	148	1	
For cakes	FFCB	531	1	B
French	FFCB	546	1	C
Fondue	BHGN	181	1	B
For 40 people	SC	50	1	
Frosting	BCC	77	1	C
Frosting	FFBB	406	1	C
Frosting	FFCB	540	1	B
Frosting, butter	SC	143	1	
Fudge	JOC	731	1	B
Ice	FGCW	385	3	
Ice cream	BHGN	182	3	C
◆	BTSB	72	2	B
◆	JOC	716	2	C
◆	FFCB	630	3	C
◆	SC	206	2	
Ice cream, rich	FFCB	633	3	C
Ice cream, Sambuca &	FGCW	385	1	
Ice w whipped cream	CIC	449	1	B
Iced	SC	50	1	
Iced	JOC	28	1	
Icing	JOC	679	1	B

RECIPE	BOOK	PAGE	TD	S
Icing	SC	143	1	
Instant	JOC	27	1	
Irish	BHGN	53	1	A
◆	BCC	25	1	B
◆	SC	64	1	
◆	JOC	28	1	A
Jelly	FFCB	621	2	B
Jelly	SC	202	2	
Jelly w praline cream	AC	735	2	
Liqueur	SC	64	3	
Liqueur Kahlua style	FGCW	384	3	
Making	FFCB	737		
Making	BHGN	53		
Making, European & variations	SP	332		
Making, w the Moka machine	FAIC	500		
Mallow	EBE	190	1	B
Marshmallow cream	JOC	698	2	B
Marshmallow ice cream	SC	208	2	
Meringue layers	NSD	317	3	B
Meringue peach	BCC	145	2	B
Mousse caramel	MFC	237	3	B
Mousse frozen	FFCB	625	3	B
Nuts, candied	SC	174	1	
Parfait	JOC	720	2	B
Parfait	SC	213	2	
Parfait	NSD	318	3	B
Percolated	JOC	27	1	
Pie	JOC	610	2	B
Pudding, frozen	SC	215	2	
Quantity	JOC	27	1	
Ring	FFBB	537	3	C
Rum chiffon pie	FFBB	120	2	B
Sauce	SC	218	2	
Sauce	JOC	713	2	B
Sauce	NSD	335	2	C
Schaum torte	SC	131	1	B

RECIPE	BOOK	PAGE	TD	S
Souffle	MAFC	617	3	B
Souffle	FFCB	618	3	B
Spiced	BTSB	218	1	B
Sponge	FFCB	622	2	B
Sponge cake	SC	119	1	B
Sponge cake, cream	MHGD	73	2	B
Squares, toffee, chocolate	BHGN	177	3	C
Steeped	JOC	27	1	
Tarts	JOC	610	2	B
Toffee pie, Blum's	FFBB	148	2	B
Torte, hazelnut	SC	128	1	B
Turkish	JOC	28	1	
Vacuum method	JOC	27	1	
Velvet	NYT	631	2	C
Viennese	SC	50	1	
Viennoise iced	JOC	29	1	A
Walnut roll	EBE	151	3	B
Coffolate iced	SC	52	1	B
Cognac				
California beans w	AC	606	3	
Coffee mousseline	MHGD	370	2	B
Cream pie, coffee &	MHGD	181	2	B
Fish soup	NYTI	117	1	B
Mousse cake, chocolate	NSD	260	3	B
Peaches	BB	159	1	B
Peaches, sliced, w brown sugar	MSQC	157	1	B
Pears, baked	JBC	108	1	B
Pears, poached	JBC	108	1	B
Roquefort	NYT	51	1	C
Sauce	AC	742	1	
Sauce	JBC	268	1	
Sauce w mayonnaise, for shrimp	NYT	451	1	A
Steak w green peppercorns & raisins	BBA	49	1	B

RECIPE	BOOK	PAGE	TD	S
Strawberries	BB	160	1	
Tomato soup, creamed	VE	72	1	B
Cointreau pears	FFCB	667	2	B
Cola, ham baked in	AC	443		
Colbert butter	NYT	457	1	
Colbert butter	JOC	339	1	B
Colcannon (mashed potato & kale)	VGCB	145	1	B
Colcannon potato cabbage casserole	JBGF	379	1	B
Cold cut slices	EBE	34	1	B
Coldslaw	AC	495		
Coleslaw (Kohlslau)	AC	495	1	
◆	CW	113	1	B
◆	JBC	247		
◆	VGCB	44	1	B
◆	JOC	80	2	B
◆	BB	140	1	B
◆	SC	358	1	
◆	FFCB	428	1	B
◆	BCC	282	1	B
A favorite	AC	496	1	
Apple-cheese	BCC	282	1	B
Billy's	AC	498	2	
Boiled dressing	AC	497	1	
Caraway	NYT	418	1	B
Chinese cabbage w watercress	FFCB	429	1	B
Creamy	BHGN	335	2	B
Creamy	SP	219	2	B
Curried	JBGF	542	2	B
Deluxe	JOC	81	1	B
Deluxe	GHAC	272	1	B
Diet, Mrs. Peretsman's	VGCB	45	1	B
For barbecue	JOC	81	1	B
Mayonnaise dressing	BB	140	1	B

RECIPE	BOOK	PAGE	TD	S
Coleslaw (*cont.*)				
Mrs. Crowen's	AC	495	1	
Mustard ring w	AC	497	2	
Old fashioned	JBC	248	2	B
Pineapple marshmallow	BCC	282	1	B
Pungent	JBC	248	2	B
Roquefort	JOC	81	1	B
Shortcut	JBC	248	2	B
Sour cream	JBC	249	2	B
Tangy	BB	140	1	B
Vinaigrette	BHGN	335	1	B
Colettes (frozen chocolate dessert)	EBE	191	2	C
Colettes	KIS	361	1	C
Collard				
Braised	FFCB	376	1	A
Cooking	AC	521		
For a feijoada	NYT	363	1	B
Green custard (green timbale)	GG	192	2	B
Greens, ham hocks &	GHAC	203	2	B
Greens, sauteed	JBGF	518	1	A
& Rice	JBGF	528	1	B
& Rice	VGCB	131	1	B
Soup, lentil &	VGCB	132	1	B
Collins	SC	62	1	
Collops (stewed, spiced beef)	NYT	101	1	B
Colonial bread	FFCB	470	2	C
Colonial cheese pudding	AC	726	1	
Colorful cookies	BCC	108	1	C
Combination bread	SC	69	2	C
Composed salad	FAIC	387	1	
Composed salad, serving a	GHAC	332		

RECIPE	BOOK	PAGE	TD	S
Compote	MC	209	1	B
Cherry red	AC	752	1	
Cranberry orange	AC	464	1	
Cranberry strawberry	AC	464	1	
Conch chowder	JOC	165	2	B
Conchiglie w sausage & cream sauce	CIC	109	1	B
Cone, making a paper (decorating)	MFC2	509		
Cone, paper, making (photographs)	LT	73		
Coney Islands	BHGN	261	1	B
Confectioners' icing	NYT	576	1	B
Confetti rice mold	GHAC	282	2	C
Confetti sauce	BHGN	355	1	B
Confit				
D'oie (potted goose)	JOC	474	3	
D'oie	SC	321	3	
Of chicken	FGCW	200	1	A
Of duck	FGCW	198	2	B
Of goose	FGCW	197	3	B
Of goose, marsala pasta w	FGCW	200	1	B
Of pork	FGCW	199	1	B
Of turkey	FGCW	199	1	B
Onion, pasta, winter greens	CPPC	123	2	B
Onion, w walnuts & anchovies (for pizza)	CPPC	153	3	B
Connecticut pie	EBE	164	1	B
Conserve				
Black cherry	JOC	780	2	C
Blue plum	JOC	780	2	C
Cherry	SC	444	3	
Cherry pineapple	SC	444	1	
Cranberry	SC	444	1	
Cranberry fruit	NYT	506	1	B
Four fruit	SC	444	1	

RECIPE	BOOK	PAGE	TD	S
Gooseberry	SC	444	1	
Grape	SC	444	1	
Grape	NYT	506	1	B
Peach pineapple	SC	444	1	
Pear	SC	444	3	
Pear apple	SC	444	1	
Plum	SC	445	1	
Plum rum	BTSB	166	2	C
Quince	SC	445	1	
Rhubarb	SC	445	1	
Rhubarb	FFCB	705	2	C
Rhubarb spiced	JOC	780	2	C
Consomme	JOC	146	2	
◆	FAIC	106	1	B
◆	CBSS	58	3	C
◆	FFCB	82	3	C
◆	JBC	274	2	
◆	LT	86	2	
◆	SC	394	3	
A la Madrilene	NYT	58	2	B
Argenteuil	NYT	59	2	
w Asparagus & dill	SP	150	2	B
Aux cheveux d'ange	NYT	59	2	
Avocado	JBC	275	2	
Brunoise	JOC	146	1	A
Canned, quick & variations	JOC	165	1	
w Carrots	JBC	275	2	
w Celery	VGCB	79	2	B
Celery braised in	NYT	374	1	B
Garnishing	NYT	59		
Indienne	BBA	31	1	B
Jellied	CBSS	60	3	C
Lucette	NYT	59	2	
Madrilene	JOC	146	1	B
Madrilene	CBSS	60	3	C
Madrilene, jellied	SC	398	1	
Marrow	NYTI	116	3	B
w Mushrooms	JBC	275	2	

RECIPE	BOOK	PAGE	TD	S
w Noodles	JBC	275	2	
Oxtail	AC	86	2	
w Peas	JBC	275	2	
Quick, tropical	JOC	165	1	B
w Rice	JBC	275	2	
Royale	NYT	59	2	
Consum (unleavened dough), cooking on soapstone	MCIC	75		
Convenience foods, list of	KIS	335		
Coo-koo codfish sauce	NYTI	18	3	B
Cooked dressing	BHGN	352	1	B
Cookie				
All about	FFBB	183		
Almond, bitter (Amaretti)	FAIC	464	1	C
Carrot oatmeal	JBGF	605	1	C
Chalets	GHAC	353	2	C
Chinese almond	BTSB	231	1	C
Crumb shells	SC	344	2	
Crusts	JOC	592	2	
w Dates & nuts (billy goats)	FFBB	204	1	C
Dough for open pies	SC	342	1	
Filling pans w dough	FFCB	547		
Freezing, dough	AC	698		
From pastry dough, caramelized palm leaf	MFC2	478	2	
General rules for baking	AC	698		
German, Christmas (pfeffernusse)	BTSB	233	2	C
Glaze	BCC	112	1	C
Granola	BTSB	232	2	C
Houses	JOC	654	3	
Jumbles (sour cream)	AC	718	1	
Les petites	MHGD	330	2	C

RECIPE	BOOK	PAGE	TD	S
Cookie (*cont.*)				
Little almond	FAIC	462	1	C
Making	BCC	96		
Making	BHGN	153		
Mix, basic	KIS	346	1	C
Press	JOC	664	2	C
Press cookies	FFBB	253	2	C
Press cookies	AC	707	2	
Serving cups for ices, fruits, creams	MFC2	419	3	B
Sheet, coating a (photographs)	LT	90		
Sour cream (Jumbles)	AC	718	1	
Tongue-shaped, caramelized from pastry	MFC2	477	1	
Using chicken fat or bacon fat in	AC	699		
Cooking procedures	FFCB	42		
Cooking terms	JBC	xvi		
◆	BHGN	430		
◆	FG	13		
◆	FFCB	42		
Cooking terms you should know	BCC	371		
Coq au vin (chicken in wine)	FGCW	168	2	B
◆	FFCB	239	2	B
◆	MAFC	263	2	B
◆	NYT	197	2	B
◆	JOC	468	2	B
◆	BHGN	300	2	C
Coquilles Saint Jacques	JBC	88	2	
◆	FFCB	140	1	B
◆	SC	254	1	
◆	NYTI	98	2	B
◆	GF	24	2	C
◆	FGCW	117	1	B

RECIPE	BOOK	PAGE	TD	S
A la creme	MFC	135	2	B
A la Parisienne	MAFC	216	3	B
A la Provencale	MAFC	218	2	B
Monteil	AC	168	1	
Provencale	NYTI	98	1	B
Coquina broth	JOC	161	2	
Cordials frappes	SC	64	1	
Cordon bleu oven	BCC	250	2	B
Coriander bread, North African	CBB	453	2	C
Corn				
All about	VGCB	84		
Baked	SC	419	1	
Dried	VGCB	91	1	B
Fresh	NYT	376	1	B
Layered tomatoes	VGCB	87	1	
Swiss cheese &	VGCB	87	1	
& Basil	BCC	346	1	B
& Beef casserole	FFCB	169	1	B
& Beef pie	YGM	182	2	C
Biscuits	CBB	199	1	C
Boiled	JBC	308	1	
Boiled	BB	131	1	
Bread	FFCB	493	1	C
◆	MSE	188	2	B
◆	VE	47	1	B
◆	BBA	174	1	B
◆	BHGN	86	1	C
◆	JOC	578	1	C
◆	BCC	36	1	C
◆	AC	792	1	
◆	PPLK	41	1	C
Bacon &	GHAC	366	1	C
Bacon bit	FFBB	569	1	B
Batter	CBB	191	2	C
Buttermilk crackling	JOC	578	1	C
Cheese & onion	KIS	351	1	C
Chili	BCC	36	1	C

RECIPE	BOOK	PAGE	TD	S
Chili cheese	GHAC	367	1	C
Crackling	SP	247	1	B
Custardy	MIE	301	1	B
Delicious	MC	178	1	B
Double	VGCB	91	1	C
Dressing	PPLK	227	3	B
Dressing, crawfish w	PPLK	228	3	B
Dressing, herbed	MSE	187	2	B
Duck stuffed w wild mushrooms &	CPMC	75	3	A
Golden	GHAC	367		
Green chili cheese	FFBB	569	1	B
Ham, deviled	GHAC	367		
Jalapeno	CBB	193	1	C
Jalapeno	CW	153	1	B
Jewish	BTSB	106	3	C
Mexican	BBA	174	1	B
Mexican	JBGF	588	1	C
Mix	BTSB	126	1	C
Mix	KIS	350	1	C
Onion-cheese	BCC	36	1	C
Pizza	KIS	352	1	B
Portuguese	CBB	183	2	B
Quail, roasted, stuffed w crawfish	PPLK	144	3	B
Quick	SC	84	1	
Rich	CBB	187	1	B
Rich	CBSS	404	1	C
Ring	GHAC	367	1	B
Sausage	BHGN	260	2	B
Shortcake	GHAC	367	1	C
Skillet	JOC	578	1	B
Sour cream	CW	57	1	B
Sour milk	CBB	181	1	B
Southern	CBB	182	1	B
Spider	AC	583	1	

RECIPE	BOOK	PAGE	TD	S
Steamed	CBB	200	2	C
Stuffing (see also stuffing, corn bread)				
Stuffing, bacon &	BHGN	316	1	B
Stuffing, sausage &	GHAC	169	1	B
Tamale pie	JOC	225	3	B
White	FFBB	569	1	B
Yankee	CBB	180	1	B
Yellow	FFBB	568	1	B
Bubble bread	CBB	194	2	C
Cake	CBB	202	1	B
Crackling	NYT	482	1	C
Littleton spider	FFCB	494	1	C
Rich	FFCB	493	1	C
White	FFCB	493	1	C
Campfire roast	OC	93	1	B
Canned, uses for	AC	558		
Caramel nut	BCC	121	2	C
Casserole	BB	136	1	B
Chicken &	FFCB	260	2	B
Fresh	BBA	108	1	B
Rice, cheese &	JBGF	375	1	B
& Cheddar cheese chowder	VE	58	1	B
& Cheese	BCC	348	1	B
& Cheese bread, Mexican	MC	179	1	B
& Cheese casserole, kasha &	YGM	86	1	B
Chicken on rice &	VGCB	90	1	B
& Chicken soup, Pennsylvania Dutch	GHAC	104	2	C
Chicken & squash	NYTI	474	2	B
& Chili souffle	AC	557	1	
Chips	BTSB	117	1	C
& Chive souffle	VGCB	88	1	B
Chowder	CBSS	145	2	B

RECIPE	BOOK	PAGE	TD	S
Corn (*cont.*)				
Rye bread	SC	69	2	C
Rye, deli	BBA	174	2	C
Salad	CF	75	1	B
Salad	VGCB	247	1	B
Amagansett	GG	132	1	B
Daufuskie quilt	GG	132	1	B
Festive	GHAC	275	1	B
Salted	SC	455	3	
Sauce, chicken, w spicy	VGCB	90	1	B
Sauteed	BB	131	1	B
Sauteed	JBC	308	1	
Cream	JBC	309	1	
Green onion &	JBC	309	1	
Green pepper	JBC	309	1	
& Variations	AC	513		
& Vegetables	GG	136	1	B
Scalloped	BCC	346	1	B
◆	FFCB	380	1	B
◆	BHGN	396	1	B
◆	JOC	274	1	B
Scalloped w cheese	BCC	346	1	B
Scoring	SC	419		
& Shrimp, marinated	CW	64	1	B
Skillet	BCC	348	1	B
Skillet	GHAC	236	1	B
Skillet, baked	CW	129	2	B
Souffle	AC	556	2	
Souffle	FFCB	380	2	B
Souffle	GF	221	2	B
Souffle, chili	AC	557	1	
Souffle filling	GG	139	1	C
Soup				
Chicken &	NYTI	467	1	B
Chicken &	NYT	66	2	C
Cream of	JOC	158	1	B
Cream of	SC	401	1	
Cream of	JBC	280	2	
De maiz	BBA	42	2	B
Fresh	SC	402	1	
Mexican	NYTI	468	1	B
Roasted poblano chiles w	CPMC	48	2	B
w Sour cream	EBE	111	1	B
Sour, creamed	GG	135	1	B
Southwestern, baked	AC	515	1	
Spoon bread	JOC	580	1	B
Sticks	CBB	186	1	C
◆	BCC	36	1	C
◆	BHGN	86	1	C
◆	JOC	578	1	C
Sticks, golden	GHAC	367	1	C
Sticks, quick	SC	84	1	
Stuffed peppers	SC	425	1	
Succotash	JOC	274	1	B
w Sweet herb butter	GHAC	236	1	C
Syrup frosting	SC	146	1	
Tart, New Mexico	GG	139	1	B
Timbales	VGCB	88	1	B
Timbales	SC	420	2	
Timbales, egg & cheese	JOC	208	2	B
Timbales, ham & asparagus	WC	38	1	A
Tomato & hot pepper trio	VGCB	87	1	B
Tomatoes, fried onions & olives	AC	551	1	
Tomatoes & okra	AC	530	1	
Tomatoes & okra, sauteed	CW	140	2	B
Tomatoes stuffed w	NYT	424	1	B
Tomatoes stuffed w	JOC	307	1	B
Whole kernel, canning	BHGN	138		

RECIPE	BOOK	PAGE	TD	S
Cottage pudding (*cont.*)				
◆	VE	274	2	B
◆	AC	727	1	
◆	JOC	701	1	B
Cottage pudding cake	FFCB	523	1	B
Cottage sauce, creamy	JBGF	640	1	B
Coucou (cornmeal cake w okra)	NYTI	547	1	C
Coulibiac (brioche filled w salmon & vegetables)	NYTI	510	3	C
Coulibiac, pike & crayfish	MFC	123	3	B
Coulis, reduced puree or sauce	SP	191	2	C
Country bread	LM	245	2	C
Country bread honfleur	CBB	246	3	C
Country brunch pancakes	GHAC	370	1	B
Country cake w fresh pears	MCIC	432	1	B
Country captain	NYT	198	1	B
Country captain	AC	196	1	
Country captain, chicken	GHAC	152	1	B
Country captain, Southern fried chicken	AC	194	1	
Country fair bread	AC	787	2	
Country pate, Joan Hackett's	BBA	20	3	C
Country style potatoes	FAIC	417	1	B
Country terrine	FFCB	62	2	C
Country turkey hash	GHAC	163	1	B
Coupe (ice cream w fruit)	NYT	629	1	
Jacques	NYT	629	1	
Eugenie	NYT	629	1	
Melba	NYT	629	1	
Romanoff	NYT	629	1	
Couques (puff pastry caramel cookies)	MFC2	477	1	
Court bouillon	JBC	69	1	
◆	MFC	66	1	B
◆	GF	246	1	B
◆	MAFC	536	1	C
About	JOC	493		
Blanc	JOC	493	1	
For fish	JOC	493	1	
Garlic	JBC	69	1	
Vermouth	JBC	69	1	
Couscous	JOC	423	3	B
◆	CF	47	1	B
◆	MIE	206	1	B
◆	BCC	237	1	
◆	FG	299	2	B
I	NYTI	487	2	C
II	NYTI	488	3	B
III	NYTI	489	3	C
Chicken	JBGF	432	2	B
Lamb	BCC	237	2	B
Pudding	JBGF	634	2	C
Tomatoes, baked, stuffed	SPGT	161	2	B
Cozze alla marinara (mussels marinara w linguine)	NYTI	384	2	B
Crab	MFC2	29		
All about	JOC	371		
& Artichoke canapes	NYT	45	1	C
& Artichoke casserole, luxurious	BBA	100	2	C
& Asparagus soup	CBSS	227	3	B
Aspic	MAFC	549	2	B
Au gratin, deviled	SC	248	1	
& Bacon bites	BHGN	44	1	C
Bisque	MFC2	36	3	B
Bisque	FFCB	99	2	B

RECIPE	BOOK	PAGE	TD	S
Boiled	BHGN	217	1	A
Boiled	FFCB	129	2	B
Boiled dungeness	BCC	189	1	B
& Broccoli bisque	JBGF	335	2	B
Cakes	JOC	240	2	B
Cakes	GHAC	121	1	B
Cakes, Maryland	CF	62	1	B
Canapes, hot	JOC	62	2	
Casserole, company	BCC	190	1	B
Casserole, piquant	EBE	96	1	B
Chaud froid (or lobster)	MAFC	553	3	B
Chervil & fennel, linguine w	CPPC	30	2	B
Chicken breasts stuffed w	BHGN	306	2	B
& Chicken pie	AC	170	1	
& Clam dip	EBE	35	1	B
Claws w cocktail sauce	MSE	50	2	C
Claws, spicy	SP	18	2	B
Claws, spicy w red pepper dip	GHAC	89	1	C
Cleaning & cutting up	MFC2	29		
Cocktail	BHGN	15	1	B
Corn ring	SC	419	1	
Cracked w mayonnaise	AC	149		
Cracked w mayonnaise	JBC	76	1	
Creamed	FFCB	131	1	B
Creamed	SC	249	1	
Creamed, prosciutto on toast w	SMG	144	1	B
Croissants, lobster w	MFC	39	3	B
Deviled	GHAC	121	1	B
◆	NYT	276	1	B
◆	JBC	79	1	B
◆	JOC	239	1	B
Deviled, a very Southern recipe for	AC	151	1	
Dip, hot	MIE	26	1	B
Dressing, cobbled	GG	13	1	B
Dressing w tomato mayonnaise	SMG	309	1	B
Dungeness	MSE	156	2	A
Filled tartlets	MSE	275	2	C
Flounder stuffed w	SMG	146	1	B
Fresh cooked	GHAC	120	2	B
Fritter w ginger sauce	BBA	91	2	C
Hard shell	SC	248	1	
Hard shell, boiled	BCC	189	1	B
Hard shell, cleaning	JBC	76		
Imperial	GHAC	121	1	B
Ipswich, deviled	FFCB	131	1	B
Italian omelet, artichoke &	GG	20	1	B
Legs, king, broiled	BB	55	1	
Legs, king, grilled & frozen	SC	333	1	
Legs, palace court	AC	58	1	
Louis	JOC	90	1	B
◆	FFCB	439	1	B
◆	AC	57	1	
◆	SMG	319	1	B
◆	BHGN	348	1	B
◆	GHAC	279	1	B
◆	NYT	430	1	B
Louis dressing	AC	58	1	
Martiniquais (bacon)	JBC	78	1	B
Meat	SC	40	1	
Avery	PPLK	286	2	B
Bachelor	EBE	89	1	B
Bisque	SC	403	1	
Bouillabaisse	NYT	278	1	B
& Broccoli crepes	VGCB	33	2	B
Canapes	EBE	16	2	C
Canapes	NYT	46	1	C

RECIPE	BOOK	PAGE	TD	S
Crab Meat (*cont.*)				
Casanova	AC	150	1	
Casserole	FFCB	132	1	B
Casserole	NYT	278	1	B
Celery stalks, stuffed	SC	41	1	
& Cheese	SC	248	1	
& Cheese on toasted rolls	JOC	249	1	B
Chunks or legs in bacon	AC	25		
Cocktail	SC	46	1	
Crepes	EBE	17	3	C
& Cucumber, carrot ring w	AC	59	2	
Curried	JBC	78	1	
w Curry & almonds, sauteed	AC	150	1	
Custard	JOC	238	1	B
Deviled	SC	248	1	
Dip	JOC	75	1	
Egg foo yung	WC	67	1	B
Filling	SC	381	1	
Filling, avocado &	BBA	14	1	A
French	SC	248	1	
Gumbo	NYT	277	2	B
Herbed	NYT	275	1	B
Herbed, saute of	AC	151	1	
Indienne	FFCB	132	1	B
Madeira, shrimp &	BBA	92	2	A
Mandarin	EBE	92	1	B
Mold, Cajun	BCC	20	2	C
Mongole, quick	JOC	238	1	B
Mornay	JBC	77	1	B
Mornay, creamed mushrooms	JBC	77	1	
Mornay in curry sauce	JBC	77	1	
Mornay in madeira sauce	JBC	77	1	

RECIPE	BOOK	PAGE	TD	S
Mousse	SPGT	20	3	C
Mousse, cold	NYT	434	2	B
Omelet, cold	SMG	308	1	B
Orientale	AC	61	1	
& Pine nuts saute	AC	150	1	
& Potato casserole	SC	249	1	
Quiche	EBE	18	2	B
Quiche	NYT	27	1	C
Remick	NYT	19	1	B
Remoulade	AC	60	1	
Ring, carrot, cucumber &	AC	59	2	
Salad	JOC	90	1	
Salad	SC	363	1	
Salad	AC	59	1	
Salad w hazel dressing	PPLK	294	1	B
Sandwiches, lobster, shrimp &	AC	812	1	
Sauce, pine nuts w	AC	150	1	
Sauteed	JBC	77	1	B
Sauteed w almonds	NYT	276	1	B
Sauteed w almonds & cream	JBC	77	1	
Sauteed, herbed	JBC	77	1	
Sauteed, mushrooms &	JBC	77	1	
Sauteed w wine	JBC	77	1	
Scrambled eggs &	NYT	278	1	A
Sea bass stuffed w	NYT	231	1	B
Shrimp or lobster sandwiches	AC	812	1	
Special on English muffins	FFCB	295	1	B
Stew	NYT	277	1	B
Terrapin style	FFCB	131	1	B
Tetrazzini	SC	248	1	

RECIPE	BOOK	PAGE	TD	S
Crab apple (*cont.*)				
Jelly	SC	446	1	
Jelly	FFCB	702	2	C
Jelly	JOC	775	2	
Pickled	FFCB	717	2	B
Pickled	SC	458	3	
Plum jelly	SC	447	1	
Preserves, baked	SC	441	2	
& Rosemary jelly	MSE	199	2	B
Spiced	FFCB	281	1	C
Spiced	GHAC	379	3	C
Sweet pickled	NYT	508	1	B
Cracked wheat bread	FFCB	465	2	C
Cracked wheat bread	JOC	559	2	B
Cracked wheat salad	SP	215	1	B
Cracker				
All about	CBB	694		
All about	FFBB	583		
in Bacon	AC	24		
Bacon blankets	SC	42	1	
Balls	SC	407	1	
Black pepper	MHGD	342	2	B
Bread	CBB	681	3	C
Cheddar cheese	CBB	704	2	C
Cornmeal	NYT	50	1	C
Cream	FFBB	595	2	C
Crisped	SC	406	1	
Dumplings	SC	103	1	
Ice water	CBB	706	1	B
Ice water, toasted	CW	121	1	B
Mexican	FFBB	592	1	C
Nut fruit	FFBB	591	1	C
Oatmeal	FFBB	591	1	C
Oatmeal Swedish	CBB	701	1	C
Onion	CBB	697	2	C
Parsley dumplings	SC	407	1	
Pie (mock apple pie)	AC	614	2	
Plain soda	CBB	695	3	C
Puffed	SC	406	1	
Rich	CBB	702	1	C
Sesame	CBB	699	2	C
Short aniseed	FFBB	592	1	C
Shredded wheat, olive oil	FFBB	597	2	C
Soda	FFBB	594	3	C
Walnut	FFBB	593	1	C
Whole wheat, peanut butter	FFBB	596	2	C
Crackling bread	CBB	610	3	C
Cracklings	MFC2	317		
Cran raspberry mold	BCC	292	2	B
Cranapple jelly	GHAC	380	3	C
Cranapple stuffing, pork crown roast w	GHAC	188	3	C
Cranapple walnut cake	MC	206	1	B
Cranapple wine sauce	GHAC	206	1	B
Cranberry				
Angel pie	AC	632	1	
Apple crisp	JBGF	622	1	B
Apple relish	GHAC	383	1	B
Apple salad, molded	JOC	102	2	C
Applesauce	JOC	112	1	
Baked	SC	262	1	
Baked	AC	464	1	
Baked cherry	SC	262	1	
Banana bread	GHAC	366	1	B
Barbecue sauce, honey	GHAC	226	1	C
Beans & endive salad	MCIC	415	1	B
Beans savory, fettuccine &	CPPC	80	2	B
Bread	SP	250	3	B
Bread	FFBB	554	2	C
Bread brody	JBGF	589	2	B
Bread, quick	JOC	575	2	B
Candied	JOC	743	3	
Candied	SC	262	1	

RECIPE	BOOK	PAGE	TD	S
Carrots	VGCB	55	1	B
Cherry	SC	262	1	
Chiffon pie	GHAC	323	2	B
Citrus mold	BHGN	340	2	C
Cocktail	MSE	158	1	A
Cocktail, frosted	BHGN	52	1	B
Compote	SC	262	1	
Compote, orange	AC	464	1	
Compote, strawberry	AC	464	1	
Conserve	FFCB	706	3	C
Conserve	SC	444	1	
Cookies, pumpkin	VGCB	236	1	C
Cordial	MSE	201	3	B
Cumberland sauce	VE	89	1	
Currant walnut sauce	MSE	188	1	C
Filling	FFBB	407	2	C
Frappe	SC	210	2	
Frost salad	BHGN	342	2	C
Frosting	FFBB	407	2	C
Fruit conserve	NYT	506	1	B
Ginger conserve	FFCB	706	3	C
Glaze, curried	BHGN	254	1	B
Glaze for fowl	JOC	341	1	
Honey barbecue sauce	GHAC	226	1	C
Ice	BCC	149	2	B
Ice cream	MHGD	437	1	C
Jelly (see also jelly, cranberry)				
Jelly, crabapple	SC	447	1	
Juice	JOC	33	1	B
Juice	BTSB	212	1	C
Juice cocktail	SC	44	1	
Kuchen	MSQC	145	1	B
Kuchen batter	MSQC	145	1	B
Kuchen topping	MSQC	145	1	B
Loaf, Kathy's	MHGD	100	1	C
Muffins (see muffins, cranberry)				
Mustard, turkey fillets grilled w	CFS	133	2	B
Nut bread	CBB	477	1	B
Nut bread	FFCB	487	2	B
Nut cake, steamed	JBGF	618	2	C
Nut tart	MSE	220	2	B
Nut turnovers	JBGF	607	1	C
Or berry angel pie	AC	632	1	
Orange bread	BCC	37	2	B
Orange bread	BHGN	78	1	B
Orange compote	AC	464	1	
Orange relish	BHGN	362	2	C
Orange relish	FFCB	282	1	B
Orange relish, spiked	YGM	233	1	C
Orange sherbet	KIS	324	1	B
Orange upside down cake, quick	FFBB	354	2	B
Pear cobbler	GHAC	289	1	C
Pear wine sauce	GHAC	206	1	B
Pie	FFBB	92	2	B
Pie	SC	345	1	B
Pineapple relish	GHAC	383	1	B
Poached pears	GHAC	147		
Poached pears, stuffed capon w	GHAC	147	2	B
Pot roast w acorn squash	GHAC	179	2	C
Preserves, baked	SC	442	2	
Pudding	SC	189	1	
Pudding, steamed	FFCB	618	2	B
Punch	SC	56	1	C
Hot	BCC	21	1	C
Sparkling	BCC	21	1	C
Wine	JBGF	288	1	C
Raisin apple pie	FFCB	584	2	B
Raisin bread	GHAC	365	2	C
Raisin pie	SC	345	1	
Red cabbage	VGCB	55	1	B

RECIPE	BOOK	PAGE	TD	S
Cranberry (*cont.*)				
Relish (see relish, cranberry)				
Ring	SC	370	2	
Ring, peach, spicy	EBE	142	2	B
Salad, beans, endive &	MCIC	415	1	B
Salad mold	JBGF	542	2	C
Salad, molded	JOC	102	2	B
Sauce	BHGN	359	1	C
◆	GHAC	383	1	B
◆	FFCB	282	1	C
◆	SC	261	1	
◆	PPLK	241	2	B
◆	NSD	329	1	C
◆	JOC	114	1	
Apples in	SC	262	1	
Home style	BTSB	213	1	B
Jellied	SC	261	1	
Tangy	BHGN	359	1	B
Tangy	BHGN	12	1	B
Whole	BHGN	131	1	B
Whole	JOC	114	1	
Sherbet	FFCB	635	2	B
Sherbet	JOC	724	2	B
Squash puree	GG	336	2	B
Strawberry compote	AC	464	1	
Swirl cheesecake	GHAC	340	2	C
Tangerine relish	GHAC	383	1	B
Tart, peach	MSE	247	2	B
Tartlets	MSE	197	2	C
Wine mold	GHAC	293	2	C
Wine punch	JBGF	288	1	C
Wine sauce	GHAC	195	1	B
Cravatta asparagus ties	GG	33	1	B
Crawfish or Crayfish				
All about	JOC	378		
Bisque	JOC	161	2	B
Bisque	MFC2	37	3	B
Bisque sauce, linguine w	CPPC	98	3	B
Boiled	SC	249	1	
Broth	LM	92	2	A
Cornbread dressing	PPLK	228	3	B
Eggs	MFC	54	2	A
Enchiladas con queso	PPLK	74	2	C
Etouffee	PPLK	75	3	B
Etouffee	GHAC	121	1	B
In light butter sauce	MFC	117	2	B
Magnifique a mirliton pirogue	PPLK	78	3	B
Pie	PPLK	80	3	B
Pie crusts	PPLK	81	2	B
Pike coulibiac	MFC	123	3	B
Quail w roasted cornbread	PPLK	144	3	B
Salad	CPMC	100	3	B
Sauteed	PPLK	77	2	A
Skewered	OC	154	1	B
Soup	MFC	72	2	B
Tails au gratin	LM	94	2	A
Tails, pizza w yellow tomatoes &	CPPC	159	3	B
Crazy cake	AC	677	1	
Cream cake	AC	656	1	
Cream cake, basic	SC	117	1	B
Cream cake, Hungarian	NYT	551	2	C
Cream cake, Sicilian	NYT	552	1	C
Cream cheese	BTSB	58	3	B
Appetizers, pickled	BB	115	1	A
Ball, salmon	FG	58	2	B
Balls	SC	42	1	
Canapes, hot	FFCB	66	1	C
Chocolate frosting	SC	144	1	
Cookies	BCC	100	1	C
Cookies, rolled	BHGN	166	2	C
Dessert	JOC	708	1	B
Dough	FFBB	65	1	B

RECIPE	BOOK	PAGE	TD	S
Dressing for fruit salad	JOC	318	1	B
Eggs, scrambled	JOC	200	1	B
Fig, nut &	SC	373	1	
French dressing	JOC	311	1	A
Frosting (see also frosting, cream cheese)				
Frosting	SP	296	1	C
Frosting for carrot cake	GHAC	323	2	C
Grape toss	BCC	297	1	B
Hard sauce	SC	219	2	
Herbed	BTSB	60	2	A
Herbed	NYT	53	1	B
Icing	JOC	678	1	A
Mints	BHGN	116	1	C
Mushroom appetizers	BB	115	1	A
Or Viennese pastry	AC	636	1	
Pastry	SC	342	1	
Pastry	JBC	41	2	
Pastry	NYTI	507	2	C
Pecan	SP	346	1	B
Pepper	BTSB	61	2	A
Pie	FFBB	105	2	B
Berry glazed	AC	620	1	
Florida	MHGD	174	2	B
Peanut butter	FFBB	108	2	B
Yogurt	MC	184	2	B
Pimiento	SC	38	1	
& Prune tart	MAFC	648	2	B
Rich	JOC	513	2	B
Ring, cheddar	SC	368	2	
Sandwiches, chicken &	JOC	248		
Sandwiches, pickled	BB	115	1	A
Spread	JOC	58	1	
Basic	SC	380	1	
Clam &	SC	380	1	

RECIPE	BOOK	PAGE	TD	S
Cucumber &	JOC	58	1	
Garden	BB	124	1	C
Liptauer	AC	11	1	
Olive	SC	380	1	
Pepper relish &	SC	380	1	
Pimiento	SC	380	1	
Pineapple	SC	380	1	
Sardine	BB	124	1	B
Watercress, nut &	SC	380	1	
Tart	MAFC	647	2	B
Tart	VE	270	1	B
Tomatoes stuffed w	NYT	425	1	B
Topping	BCC	135	1	
Vegetable	SC	373	1	
Watercress	SC	38	1	
Cream cornets	NYTI	286	1	C
Cream custard filling	SC	148	1	
Cream, different kinds of	FFBB	8		
Cream dressing, fluffy	SC	376	1	
Cream dressing, uncooked	SC	377	1	
Cream enrichment	MAFC	59	1	B
Cream filling				
Chicken or turkey	MAFC	203	1	B
For cream puffs	BCC	138	1	
French	FFCB	545	1	C
Shellfish or clams	MAFC	202	1	C
Swiss cheese	MAFC	201	1	B
Cream fruit juice sauce	SC	218	2	
Cream fruit sauce	SC	218	1	
Cream horns	NYT	537	2	C
Cream horns	FFCB	600	3	C
Cream horns	MFC2	468	2	
Cream horns, making	MFC2	135		
Cream horseradish dressing	JOC	317	1	B
Cream meringue tart cockaigne	JOC	641	3	B

RECIPE	BOOK	PAGE	TD	S
Cream mushroom sauce	MAFC	392	1	C
Cream mushroom sauce w egg yolks	MAFC	392	1	C
Cream mustard sauce	MAFC	406	1	A
Cream of oatmeal bread	FFBB	450	2	C
Cream of tartar	FFBB	8		
Cream of wheat custard pie	FFBB	141	1	B
Cream pie	FFCB	591	2	B
Cream pie	JOC	609	2	B
Cream pies	AC	624	1	
Cream puff	FFBB	181	2	C
◆	FFCB	596	3	C
◆	FAIC	440	2	C
◆	BCC	138	1	C
◆	EBE	19	2	C
◆	LT	393	2	
◆	BHGN	177	1	C
◆	SC	140	1	
Cake	LT	399	3	
Cake	LM	356	3	
Chocolate	BCC	138	1	C
Dough	LT	391		
Dough, making (photographs)	LT	391		
Filled	SC	39	1	
Fried for Saint Joseph	NYTI	443	3	C
Making (photographs)	NYT	532		
Paste	MAFC	175	1	B
Paste	MFC	204	2	C
Pastry	FAIC	438		
Pastry	MHGD	50	1	B
Pastry	FAIC	440	1	B
Ring	LT	396	2	
Saint Joseph's	NYTI	444	1	C
Savory	FFCB	67	1	C
Shells	JOC	597	3	C
Shells	NYT	531	1	C

RECIPE	BOOK	PAGE	TD	S
Swans	LT	394	3	
Tiny	SC	140	1	
Cream pull, candy	JOC	735	2	B
Cream rolls	JOC	596	3	B
Cream rolls	MFC2	468	2	
Cream, Russian	BBA	215	2	
Cream salad dressing, cooked	SC	377	1	
Cream sauce	SC	386	1	
◆	NYT	444	1	B
◆	JBC	261	1	
◆	AC	457	1	
Fresh	MAFC	458	1	B
Mix	JOC	323	1	C
Mock, making	FGCW	289		
Rich	JBC	261	1	
Thick	FFCB	265	1	B
& Variations	JOC	322	1	B
Cream soup, basic	JBC	279	2	
Cream vinaigrette	VGCB	6	1	A
Cream waffles, rich	AC	798	1	
Cream wine soup	SC	488	1	
Creams, three flavor, glazed	NSD	168	3	C
Creamy cheese	BBA	111	3	B
Creamy dressing for red or green lettuce	KIS	168	1	A
Creamy fruit dressing	BHGN	352	1	B
Creamy tarragon mustard dressing	SP	224	1	B
Creme a l'Anglaise	BBA	216	2	
Creme Anglaise (basic vanilla custard sauce)	GF	251	2	B
◆	FFCB	639	1	B
◆	MAFC	588	2	B
◆	MSE	257	3	B
◆	NYTI	308	1	B
◆	VE	284	1	B

RECIPE	BOOK	PAGE	TD	S
Creme Anglaise, making	NSD	20		
Creme au cafe	FGCW	384	1	B
Creme aux fruits	MIE	316	3	B
Creme brulee	FFCB	609	2	B
◆	BCC	140	2	B
◆	JBC	44	2	B
◆	NYT	594	2	B
◆	MAFC	588		
◆	EBE	191	2	B
◆	BHGN	173	2	B
◆	SP	307	2	B
◆	AC	729	2	
◆	NYTI	294	2	C
◆	JOC	685	2	B
Almond	NYTI	295	2	B
Basic method for making	NSD	168		
Ginger, making	NSD	169		
Ginger tart	NSD	174	3	B
Gingered	GHAC	297	2	
Maple berry tarts, individual	NSD	166	3	B
Mint, making	NSD	169		
Orange	AC	729	2	
Orange, making	NSD	169		
Tropical fruits	GHAC	297	2	B
Vanilla berry tarts, individual	NSD	166	3	B
Winter squash	GG	339	3	B
Creme caramel	JOC	685	2	B
Creme caramel	MSE	179	3	B
Creme chantilly	MAFC	580	1	B
Creme chantilly fillings w variations	JOC	645	1	C
Creme de cacao topping	BCC	79	1	B
Creme de menthe	EBE	193	1	B
Creme de menthe	JOC	711	1	B
Creme de menthe ice	SC	210	2	
Creme de menthe meringue	BCC	145	2	B
Creme de menthe topping	BCC	79	1	B
Creme du barry, cream of cauliflower soup	GG	100	1	B
Creme fraiche	GF	245	2	
◆	MHGD	386	1	B
◆	MIE	45	3	B
◆	YGM	172	3	B
◆	BTSB	62	2	A
◆	NYTI	298		B
◆	MSQC	17	1	A
◆	KIS	360	1	B
◆	JOC	487	2	
◆	NSD	122	1	C
◆	GRIL	39	1	B
◆	SP	339	3	B
Creme fraiche, coeur a la	MSE	224	2	B
Creme fraiche, gingered	MHGD	387	1	B
Creme frite	JOC	688	1	B
Creme glacee	JOC	716	2	B
Creme patissiere	MAFC	590	2	B
Creme patissiere	JOC	646	1	B
Creme patissiere	BBA	202	1	B
Creme patissiere, chocolate	BBA	202	1	B
Creme patissiere, coffee	BBA	202	1	B
Creme plombieres				
A l'ananas	MAFC	596	2	B
Au chocolat	MAFC	595	2	B
Aux fruits	MAFC	595	2	B
Pralinee	MAFC	594	2	B
Creme praline	BBA	192	1	B
Creme renversee	MHGD	354	2	B

RECIPE	BOOK	PAGE	TD	S
Creme renversee au caramel	EBE	192	3	B
Creme Saint Honore	MAFC	591	2	C
Creme Saint Jacques	NYTI	125	1	B
Creme St. Jacques	NYT	78	2	B
Creole				
Beef liver	JOC	440	1	B
Casserole, cucumber	JOC	276	1	B
Champagne punch	FFCB	742	1	C
Chicken dumplings	PPLK	154	2	B
Chicken, quick	JOC	235	1	B
Eggplant, stuffed	JOC	278	2	B
Eggs	SC	224	1	
Eggs	AC	111	1	
Eggs, scrambled	FFCB	347	1	B
Filling	PPLK	130	2	B
Fried chicken	AC	194	1	
Gumbo	BHGN	372	1	B
Lima beans	BCC	336	1	B
Lima beans	NYT	356	1	B
Louisiana hamburger	GHAC	187	1	
Okra	SC	422	1	
Okra	NYT	385	1	B
Omelet, shrimp	GHAC	112	1	A
Pork chops	AC	410	1	
Pork chops, braised	JOC	424	2	B
Pork sausage	NYT	147	1	C
Pork steaks	GHAC	190	2	B
Red snapper	GHAC	140	2	C
Red snapper	NYTI	557	1	B
Sauce	CF	34	1	B
◆	SC	388	1	
◆	BB	151	1	C
◆	GHAC	112		
◆	PPLK	248	2	B
◆	JOC	336	1	B
Chicken livers in	SMG	68	1	B
Chipped beef in	JOC	232	1	A
Eggplant in	SMG	111	1	B
Quick	JOC	333	1	B
Seafood casserole w	JOC	237	1	B
Shrimp in	SMG	164	1	B
Tongue baked in	JOC	446	1	B
Seafood cream	SC	257	1	
Shrimp	AC	155		
Shrimp	PPLK	95	2	C
Shrimp casserole	SC	256	1	
Soup	FFCB	86	1	B
Sprouts	SC	413	1	
Steak sauce	BB	146	1	
Style pork steaks	GHAC	190	2	B
Summer squash	JOC	303	1	
Sweet potatoes, scalloped	SC	430	1	
Tomatoes	FFCB	417	1	B
Tomatoes	JOC	306	1	B
Turkey soup	GHAC	105	2	C
Veal chops	SC	285	2	
Crepe, basic recipe	NYT	607	1	C
Crepes	MC	113	1	B
◆	SC	95	2	
◆	NYTI	439	1	
◆	FFCB	497	2	B
◆	BCC	138	1	B
◆	BBA	102	2	B
◆	JBC	48	1	
◆	PPLK	125	1	B
◆	PPLK	47	1	C
Alaska	NYT	609	1	B
Almond	VE	189	1	B
Almond cream	MAFC	652	2	B
Apples, mound of	MAFC	653	2	B
Asparagus & carrot	FG	100	1	B
Au fromage	VE	188	1	B
Basic	BHGN	222	1	C
Basic	FG	97	1	C
Basic	JBGF	502	2	B
Basic, dessert	BHGN	182	1	B

RECIPE	BOOK	PAGE	TD	S
Batter	MFC	204	1	B
Batter	MAFC	191	1	B
Batter for grand marnier crepes	MSQC	173	1	B
Buckwheat	SP	318	2	B
Buckwheat	CPMC	32	2	C
Buckwheat, tangerines in glaceed fruit butter	CPMC	60	2	B
Cheese filling for	FFCB	498	2	
Cheese, raisins &	MFC	234	1	B
Chestnut flour	FAIC	481	1	C
Chicken	FFCB	296	2	B
Chicken & cheese	BHGN	304	2	B
Chicken dinner	FG	99	2	B
Chicken & tomato	BBA	71	3	B
Chicken & vegetable	JBGF	504	1	B
Chocolate	JBC	48	1	
Chocolate, frozen	BBA	216	2	C
Cooking	MAFC	648		
Corn	LT	182	2	C
Corn, w tacoese filling	VGCB	89	2	B
Corn, w two fillings	GG	137	2	C
Crabmeat	EBE	17	3	C
Dessert	NYTI	290	1	C
Dessert	FFCB	614	1	B
Dessert pears	NYTI	291	2	C
Filled w papaya & banana	GF	113	2	C
Filling for herbed caviar roulade	SP	35	1	C
w Fines herbes	NYTI	148	1	C
Florentine	BBA	109	2	B
French	VE	184	1	B
Fresh berry	FFCB	614	1	B
Fruited buckwheat	JBGF	624	2	B
Gateau	JOC	212	2	
Gil blas	NYT	609	1	B
w Gruyere & white truffles	NYTI	439	2	B
Herb	JBGF	503	2	C
w Ice cream, Dolly Madison	GHAC	303		
Jelly	FFCB	614	1	B
Lemon filled	BHGN	182	1	C
Making	VE	183		
Making	MAFC	191		
Marcelle	NYT	610	1	B
Mushroom	FFCB	297	2	B
Mushroom & watercress	GG	197	1	C
Orange w almond butter	MAFC	651	2	B
Orange w honey butter sauce	PPLK	321	2	B
Parmesan	VE	185	1	B
Pepper, onion, tomato & cheese	MFC2	408	1	B
Pineapple	NYT	611	1	B
Puffy pecan meringue	PPLK	322	1	B
Raised batter for stuffed	MAFC	650	2	C
Raspberry	BCC	139	2	B
Ratatouille	JBGF	504	1	B
Salmon & broccoli	BHGN	222	2	B
Savory	NYTI	228	1	C
Seafood	NYTI	148	2	C
Seafood	FFCB	296	2	B
Seafood	PPLK	52	2	B
Shrimp, curried	JBGF	505	1	C
Soup noodles	FG	100	1	
Spinach	VGCB	266	2	B
Spinach, cream cheese & mushroom	MAFC	193	3	B
Spinach & salmon	FGCW	334	1	B
Stuffed	JOC	212	2	

RECIPE	BOOK	PAGE	TD	S
Crepes (*cont.*)				
Stuffed, Italian style	FG	98	2	B
Stuffed, rolled	MAFC	195	2	B
Stuffed w tomatoes, prosciutto & cheese	MCIC	343	1	B
Surprise	MFC	46	2	
Suzette	SC	95	1	
◆	NYT	609	1	B
◆	FFCB	614	2	B
◆	JOC	213	2	B
◆	BBA	226	2	B
◆	BHGN	182	1	B
◆	JBC	48	2	
◆	MAFC	650	2	B
◆	LT	448	2	
Suzette w light batter	MAFC	649	1	C
Swiss cheese & bacon	FG	99	1	B
Turkey	FFCB	296	2	B
w Various fillings	MAFC	195	2	B
Vegetable	VE	187	1	B
Vegetable stuffed spinach	FGCW	95	2	B
Watercress & mushroom	GG	197	1	C
Whipped cream	FFCB	614	1	B
Yeast batter for stuffed	MAFC	649	1	C
Crescent rolls	NYT	474	2	
◆	SC	75	2	
◆	BCC	48	2	C
◆	LM	260	3	C
Crescents	SC	82	2	
◆	NYT	536	2	
◆	FFCB	560	2	B
◆	SC	73	2	C
◆	AC	780	2	
Almond	FFBB	246	1	C
Almond	YGM	176	2	C
Embassy's nut	MHGD	222	2	C
Filled sweet	JOC	568	3	C
French	JOC	567	3	C
Viennese	FFCB	561	2	C
Viennese	NYT	586	1	C
Viennese	NYTI	17	3	C
Walnut	SC	82	2	
Crests, sauce of chicken livers, wattles and	FAIC	75	1	B
Cretons Francais	NYTI	27	2	B
Crinkle cookies	AC	714	1	
Crinkle cookies, chocolate	AC	714	1	
Crinkle cookies, spice	AC	714	1	
Criossant	MFC	205	3	C
◆	BHGN	74	3	C
◆	MFC2	96	3	C
◆	NYT	474	2	C
◆	FFBB	527	2	C
◆	JOC	567	3	C
All about	CBB	657		
Beth's	FFBB	523	3	C
Brioches	CBB	674	3	C
Brioches, making (photographs)	NYT	472	2	
Dough	FFBB	529	3	C
Forming	MFC2	100		
French	CBB	658	3	C
Ham & Swiss	GHAC	372		
Lobster or crab	MFC	39	3	B
Swiss	CBB	526	3	C
Swiss gipfelteig	CBB	526	3	C
Veggie filled	BCC	325	1	B
Crookneck squash	SC	432	1	
Crookneck squash, grilled	GRIL	95	1	B
Croque madame	BBA	104	2	B
Croque monsieur a la mornay	BBA	104	2	B

RECIPE	BOOK	PAGE	TD	S
Croque monsieur, French	FGCW	300		
Croquembouche (cream-filled pastry with caramel)	MSE	214	3	C
Croquembouche	JOC	598	3	C
Croquembouche miniature	GF	86	3	B
Croques	FFBB	264	1	C
Croquettes	MAFC	203	2	C
Cheese	JOC	219	3	C
Cheese	AC	117	1	
Cheese rice	NYT	325	2	B
Cheese rice	JOC	219	3	C
Chestnut	SC	186	1	
Chicken (see chicken, croquettes)				
Ham & corn	JOC	218	3	B
Lullworth	GG	259	1	B
Making	JOC	218		
Mushroom	JOC	219	3	B
Of cooked food	JOC	218	3	C
Oyster & chicken	JOC	220	3	C
Rice	SC	181	1	
Rice	JOC	219	3	B
Rice	FFCB	320	2	B
Rice w apricot sauce	WC	143	2	C
Salmon	SC	240	1	
Salmon	CFS	223	1	B
Salmon	JOC	220	3	C
Salmon w dill sauce	GHAC	141	1	B
Salmon & potato	JBGF	381	1	B
Sweet rice	JOC	219	3	C
Veal	JOC	219	3	
Crostini w anchovy butter	FAIC	92	2	C
Croutes (toasted bread cases)	MAFC	200	1	
Croutons	SMG	103	1	B

RECIPE	BOOK	PAGE	TD	S
◆	CBB	600	1	B
◆	NYTI	129	1	B
◆	MFC2	16	1	B
◆	JBC	25	1	
◆	NYTI	549	1	
◆	SMG	99	1	B
◆	JOC	342	1	
◆	SMG	101	1	B
Baked	SC	406	1	
Baked	FFCB	492	1	
Caesar	BHGN	331	1	
For soup	JOC	174	1	
Fried	SC	406	1	
Garlic	CPMC	95	1	B
Garlic	NYTI	119	1	
Garlic	FFCB	492	1	
Herb	FFCB	492	1	
Italian	FAIC	46	1	B
Preparing	GHAC	103		
Round square heart, making	LT	57		
Rye	BHGN	348	1	B
Sauteed	FFCB	492	1	
Triangles	NYTI	136	1	
Crudites, arranging festive	GHAC	94		
Crudites, blanching vegetables for	MSE	68		
Crudites sauce	GF	176	1	C
Crullers	FFCB	480	3	C
◆	AC	801	1	
◆	JOC	706	2	B
◆	FFCB	499	3	C
Crullers, French	SC	100	1	
Crullers, raised	SC	101	1	
Crullers, rice	JOC	707	2	B
Crumb				
Buttered	JBC	266	1	
Buttered	JOC	342	1	
Cake	SC	116	1	B

RECIPE	BOOK	PAGE	TD	S
Crumb (*cont.*)				
Cake	AC	653	1	
Crust	NYT	522	1	B
Crust	FFCB	578	1	B
Crust	JOC	592	1	
All about	FFBB	67		
Blender method	NYT	548	1	
Directions for	MHGD	137	1	
For pies	AC	637	1	
Unbaked	GHAC	321		
Different kinds of	JOC	501		
Filling, fruit	JOC	573	1	B
Nut cake	NYT	552	1	C
Nut crusts	GHAC	321		
Or gravel pie	AC	630	1	
Pie	AC	615	1	
Pie	JOC	605	2	B
Pie lemon	FFCB	588	2	B
Pie, or gravel	AC	630	1	
Topping	SC	83	1	
Topping	BCC	332	1	A
Basic	FFBB	77	1	B
Garlic	BCC	332	1	A
Nutmeg	BCC	332	1	A
Oregano	BCC	332	1	A
Crumbling foods	JOC	501		
Crumbly cake	CIC	432	1	B
Crumpets	JOC	568	3	C
◆	CBB	578	2	B
◆	BTSB	112	3	B
◆	NYT	474	2	C
Crunchy snack bars	GHAC	349	1	C
Crust				
Almond	NYT	521	1	B
Baked crust shells from one crust	AC	634		
Brazil nut	NYT	521	1	B
Bread crumb	JOC	593	1	B
Butter	BCC	88	1	

RECIPE	BOOK	PAGE	TD	S
Cake	JOC	593	1	B
Cereal	FFBB	69	1	B
Cereal pie	JOC	593	1	B
Chocolate coconut	FFCB	578	1	B
Chocolate coconut	FFBB	70	1	B
Chocolate crumb	FFBB	69	1	B
Chocolate wafer crumb	GHAC	321		
Cookie crumb	JOC	593	1	B
Corn flake crumb	GHAC	321		
Country bread	BBA	174	2	B
Crisped	SC	406	1	
Crumb	NYT	522	1	B
Crumb	JOC	592	1	
Crumb	FFCB	578	1	B
Blender method	NYT	548	1	
For pies	AC	637	1	
Luxury	JOC	593	1	B
Nut	GHAC	321		
Nut	NYT	548	1	
Flour paste pie	SC	342	1	
For pate	JOC	434	2	
Ginger snap	JOC	593	1	A
Gingersnap cookie crumb	GHAC	321		
Gingersnap crumb	FFBB	69	1	B
Graham cracker	BHGN	290	1	B
◆	JOC	593	1	A
◆	NYTI	563	1	
◆	FFBB	68	1	B
Graham cracker crumb	GHAC	321		
Ground nut	GHAC	321		
Hot water pie	AC	635	1	
Macaroon crumb	FFBB	69	1	B
Meringue	NYT	522	1	B
Meringue	BHGN	288	2	B
Nut	FFBB	70	1	B
Nut crumb	NYT	548	1	

RECIPE	BOOK	PAGE	TD	S
Nut perfect	MSE	236	2	C
Old fashioned lard vinegar	GG	166	2	B
Pastry, short	NYTI	288	1	
Peanut butter cookie crumb	GHAC	321		
Peanut butter pie	SC	342	1	
Pie	MAFC	139	2	
Pie	BBA	201	3	B
Baking filled one crust	AC	633		
Butter pastry for two crust 9 inch	AC	635	1	
One crust	AC	633	1	
Pastry for one crust 9 inch	AC	635	1	
Pastry for two crust 9 inch	AC	634	1	
Two crust flour paste method	AC	635	1	
Putting on the top only	AC	633		
Quick pie pastry for apple pie	MSQC	125	2	B
Rye crumb	FFBB	69	1	B
Sugar	MAFC	633	2	B
Sweet tart for strawberry tart	MSQC	85	2	B
Toasted coconut	FFBB	70	1	B
Two oil pastry	AC	635	1	
Unbaked crumb	GHAC	321		
Vanilla wafer	FFBB	69	1	B
Vanilla wafer crumb	GHAC	321		
Walnut pastry	GHAC	321		
Wheat flake crumb	GHAC	321		
Zwieback	JOC	593	1	A
Crustaceans, all about	JOC	363		
Crustaces, fondue au	MAFC	202	1	C
Crustless greens pie	GG	195	2	B

RECIPE	BOOK	PAGE	TD	S
Crystal Bay fizz, Brad Hill's	BBA	26	1	A
Crystallized mint leaves	FFCB	692	2	C
Crystallized mint leaves	BTSB	260	2	B
Crystallized violets	BTSB	261	3	
Cuba libre	JOC	46	1	A
Cuba libre	SC	63	1	
Cuban				
Black bean soup	FGCW	108	2	B
Black beans	NYTI	68	2	C
Black beans	FG	112	2	B
Bread	NYT	462	2	C
Bread	CBB	44	1	C
Style bread	JBC	16	2	B
Cubana (drink—brandy, rum, sugar)	JOC	39	1	
Cube, how to	BHGN	429		
Cucumber				
A la Grecque	MAFC	538	1	
All about	VGCB	93		
Appetizer	SC	47	1	
Appetizer	NYT	39	2	B
Aspic	FFCB	443	2	B
Avocado soup, cold	MIE	80	2	B
Baked	MAFC	499	1	B
w Basil cream	GG	151	1	B
Chicken, ham &	GG	153	2	A
Potato stuffed w	GG	151	1	B
& Stuffed	VGCB	99	1	B
Basque	GG	152	1	B
& Bay scallop slaw	GG	146	1	B
& Beet soup, chilled	VGCB	25	1	B
Blanched	VGCB	97	1	A
& Carrot ring, crabmeat	AC	59	2	
Casserole	JOC	276	1	B
Cheese sauce	MAFC	501	1	B

RECIPE	BOOK	PAGE	TD	S
Cucumber (*cont.*)				
Chicken & ham, baked	GG	153	2	A
Chilled salmon steak, marinated	GHAC	141	2	B
Chinese	NYT	421	1	A
Combination salads	VGCB	96	1	B
Cooking	AC	515		
Crab salad, Japanese	FG	79	1	B
Cream	FFCB	274	1	B
& Cream cheese spread	JOC	58	1	
Cream of	CBSS	270	2	B
Cream sauce	SC	392	1	
Creamed	MAFC	500	1	B
Creamed mushrooms &	MAFC	501	1	B
w Creme fraiche	CF	63	1	B
Creole casserole	JOC	276	1	B
Cups, shrimp &	AC	31	2	
& Dill	MFC	171	1	B
& Dill dressing	BBA	149	1	B
& Dill salad	SMG	285	1	B
& Dill sauce	MIE	53	2	B
Dilled yogurt	GHAC	276	1	
Filling	SC	382	1	
French fried	SC	420	1	
Fried	FG	199	1	
Gelatin on tomato slices	JOC	100	2	B
Green tomato, pickle, sweet	NYT	500	3	C
Herb soup, cream of chilled	JOC	158	1	B
Herbed	YGM	139	1	B
In mustard yogurt sauce	YGM	43	1	B
In orange sauce	KIS	200	1	A
In tumeric (atjar ketimun)	NYT	376	2	C

RECIPE	BOOK	PAGE	TD	S
Lily	JOC	69	1	
Mayonnaise	SC	392	1	
Mint relish	GHAC	384	1	C
Mint yogurt	KIS	147	1	A
Mousse	VGCB	98	2	B
Mousse	JOC	100	2	B
Mulled	JOC	276	1	B
Mushrooms	BCC	351	1	B
& Onions	AC	48	1	
& Onions, sauteed & sliced	VGCB	98	1	B
Oriental	KIS	171	1	B
Parsleyed	MAFC	500	1	B
& Peas in sour cream	NYT	391	1	B
Peeling seed	LM	30		
Pesto & pasta salad	VGCB	97	1	B
Pickled	EBE	117	3	C
Pickled	NYTI	83	2	B
Pickled, sweet ripe	SC	453	2	
Pickling	VGCB	99	2	B
Piquant	KIS	103	1	A
Preparing	GG	144		
Raita	MIE	55	1	C
& Red onion vinaigrette	CPMC	106	1	
& Red pepper salad	YGM	93	1	B
Relish	BHGN	362	3	C
Relish	SC	457	3	
Relish, mold	BCC	289	2	B
Rigadon	GG	150	2	B
Ring supreme	BHGN	337	2	C
Risotto	GG	145	2	B
Salad	FG	349	1	B
◆	NYT	422	1	B
◆	MSQC	113	1	B
◆	LT	184	1	B
◆	BCC	286	2	B
◆	FFCB	427	1	B
◆	LT	184	1	
◆	JBC	245	1	B

RECIPE	BOOK	PAGE	TD	S
Cucumber Salad (*cont.*)				
◆	SC	358	1	
◆	JOC	85	1	
Balkan	MC	62	1	B
Basic	VGCB	95	1	B
Chicken, Chinese	MIE	291	1	B
Chinese	BBA	142	1	B
Cool & creamy	GG	147	2	B
Creamy	BCC	286	2	B
w Creme fraiche dressing	MSE	104	3	C
Danish	NYTI	83	1	B
Dilled	MIE	267	2	B
Dressing for	VGCB	96	1	B
Hungarian	KIS	216	1	B
Indian, pachadi	GG	149	1	B
Minty	SP	216	2	B
Molded	GHAC	277	2	C
Molded	SC	369	2	
Orange &	MCIC	414	1	B
Pineapple &	SC	366	1	
Potato julienne, truffles &	GF	28	2	C
w Sesame dressing	CF	143	1	B
Shad roe &	SC	364	1	
Shrimp &	SC	364	1	
Shrimp &	AC	53	1	
Sour cream	SC	358	1	
w Sour cream dressing	BB	139	2	B
Swedish	NYTI	533	2	C
Sweet & sour	BB	139	2	B
Sweetbreads &	SC	362	1	
Sweetbreads &	AC	72	1	
Wilted	FFCB	427	1	B
Salted for future use	SC	450	3	
Sandwich	AC	812	1	
Sandwiches	GF	44	1	B
◆	BCC	12	1	
◆	JOC	60	1	
◆	FFCB	58	1	B
Sauce	BHGN	355	1	B
◆	NYT	448	1	B
◆	FG	316	1	B
◆	OC	166	1	B
◆	FFCB	274	1	B
◆	JOC	317	1	B
Cold	CFS	318	1	B
Cold	VGCB	97	1	B
Fish molded w	SC	371	2	
Salmon braised w	VGCB	99	1	B
Sauteed	KIS	140	1	A
Sauteed	SMG	145	1	B
Sauteed	VGCB	97	1	A
Sauteed braised	VGCB	97	1	A
& Shrimp	BCC	286	2	B
& Shrimp salad	AC	53	1	
& Shrimp sandwiches	BCC	12	1	
Shrimp soup, M.F.K. Fisher's	GG	146	2	B
Smothered	AC	48	1	
Sorbet	GF	137	2	B
Sorbet, dill sauce for	GF	137	1	B
Soup				
Chilled	AC	97	2	
Chilled	GHAC	99	2	B
Cockaigne, quick	JOC	166	1	B
Cold	FFCB	90	1	B
◆	BCC	314	2	B
◆	NYT	83	2	B
◆	MFC2	18	1	B
Cold, Bulgarian	JOC	158	1	A
Cream of	FFCB	88	1	B
Cream of	MFC2	17	1	B
Cream of	VGCB	98	1	B
Iced	VE	77	1	B

RECIPE	BOOK	PAGE	TD	S
Cucumber Soup (*cont.*)				
Shrimp, chilled	SP	53	2	B
Quick, cold	JOC	166	1	B
Sour cream	GHAC	276	1	B
◆	BBA	142	1	A
◆	VE	103	2	B
◆	JBC	245	2	
◆	BHGN	335	1	A
Sour cream dip	MSE	70	1	C
Sour cream mousse	JOC	100	2	B
Sour cream salad	NYTI	316	1	B
Spaghetti, cool	GG	148	2	B
Steamed	VGCB	97	1	A
Stewed	FFCB	381	1	B
Stuffed	FFCB	305	2	B
Stuffed	JBGF	298	1	B
Stuffed, cold	JOC	86	1	
Stuffed w green mayonnaise	NYT	421	1	B
& Sweetbread salad	AC	72	1	
& Tomato juice	JOC	32	1	B
& Tomato salad	JOC	89	1	
& Tomato, topping for pasta, cold	VGCB	96	1	B
& Tomatoes	BCC	285	2	B
Turtles, sculpting (photographs)	LM	61		
Wilted	SC	358	1	
Wilted	JOC	86	2	A
& Yogurt	NYT	422	1	B
& Yogurt	NYTI	361	1	B
& Yogurt	FG	370	1	B
& Cheese	GG	144	3	B
w Dill dressing	KIS	128	1	A
Dressing	BCC	302	1	A
For curry	NYTI	360	1	B
Greek-style	NYTI	323	2	B
Salad, Greek	FG	341	1	B
Sauce	SMG	191	1	B

RECIPE	BOOK	PAGE	TD	S
Sauce	JBGF	641	1	B
Soup	MIE	82	3	B
Soup, chilled	MC	30	1	B
Soup, cold	JBGF	326	2	B
Cumberland (sauce for ham & game)	JOC	312	1	A
Cumberland sauce	BBA	59	1	B
Cumberland sauce, chicken baked, imperial	EBE	69	1	B
Cumberland sauce, hot	JOC	331	2	B
Cumin bread	CBB	456	3	C
Cumin butter for corn on the cob	KIS	141	1	A
Cumin dressing	BCC	282	1	
Cumin rice, eggplant w	NYTI	247	1	B
Cumin rice pignoli	YGM	59	2	A
Cumin sauce, lamb w wine &	FGCW	223	1	B
Cumin vinaigrette, new potatoes in	YGM	55	1	A
Cup custard, baked	VE	270	1	B
Cup custard, unmolded	MAFC	611	1	B
Cupcakes	AC	647		
Cupcakes	BHGN	92	1	C
All about	FFBB	377		
All about	AC	647		
Angel	JOC	633	1	C
Banana	FFBB	382	1	C
Boston	FFCB	529	1	C
Brown-sugar walnut, chewy	FFBB	383	1	C
Caramel	JOC	633	1	C
Chocolate	GHAC	331	1	
Chocolate	JOC	633	1	C
Chocolate	SC	140	1	C
Chocolate, enough	FFBB	378	1	C
Cocoa	SC	140	1	C
Cocoa fudge	BCC	67	1	C

RECIPE	BOOK	PAGE	TD	S
Coconut	JOC	634	1	C
Frog, making	GHAC	343		
Ginger	SC	141	1	
Jam	JOC	633	1	C
One egg	JOC	632	1	C
Peanut butter	SC	141	1	C
Peanut butter	GHAC	323	2	C
Peanut butter	FFBB	379	1	C
Pecan	SC	141	1	
Raisin	SC	141	1	C
Sour cream almond	FFBB	382	1	C
Sour milk spice	JOC	633	1	C
Spice	FFBB	378	1	C
Spice crumb	FFBB	380	1	C
Sponge	JOC	632	1	C
Vanilla	SC	140	1	C
Whipped cream vanilla	FFBB	384	1	C
Yellow	FFBB	377	1	C
◆	BCC	69	1	C
◆	JOC	632	1	C
◆	BHGN	93	1	C
Cups, cookie serving for ices, fruits, creams	MFC2	419	3	B
Curacao cocktail	JOC	40	1	
Curd, almond	NYTI	93	2	C
Currant	AC	753		
Black, preserves, pork chops &	SP	98	1	B
Bread, almond	CBB	643	3	C
Buns	SC	80	2	
Cake	JOC	631	2	B
Cheesecake	MHGD	39	1	C
Chicken w apricots &	SPGT	104	1	B
Chocolate truffles	NSD	76	3	C
Event bread	JBGF	566	3	C
Glaze, chicken w	BHGN	314	2	B

RECIPE	BOOK	PAGE	TD	S
Glazed ham steak	GHAC	203	1	B
Jam, black	FFCB	704	2	B
Jam, raspberry	FFCB	703	2	B
Jam w honey (bar le duc jam)	JOC	776	2	
Jelly (see also jelly, currant)				
Black	SC	448	1	
Cherries	SC	448	1	
Cold process	SC	447	2	
Raspberry	JOC	774	2	
Raspberry	SC	447	2	
Raspberry	FFCB	702	2	C
Sauce	SC	98	1	
◆	JOC	331	1	B
◆	AC	457	1	
◆	SC	391	1	
Tapioca pudding	SC	198	1	
Without cooking	SC	447	2	
Orange sauce	GHAC	206	1	A
Pie	SC	345	1	
Rabbit, pine nuts &	SPGT	56	3	B
Raspberry jelly	JOC	774	2	
Raspberry jelly	FFCB	702	2	C
Raspberry jelly	SC	447	2	
Raspberry jelly, black	SC	449	1	
Raspberry juice	SC	436	1	
Refrigerator cookies	AC	701	2	
Sauce				
Black, pears wine poached w	MSQC	193	1	B
Orange	GHAC	206	1	A
Raspberry	BCC	154	1	B
Walnut cranberry	MSE	188	1	C
Scones	MSE	132	2	C
Scones, buttermilk	FFBB	582	1	C
Sunshine	SC	439	3	
Wine	SC	438	3	

RECIPE	BOOK	PAGE	TD	S
Curried				
Almonds	BTSB	288	1	C
Beef kebabs	CFS	95	2	B
Broccoli soup, cream	JBGF	314	1	B
Bulgur saute	BHGN	326	1	B
Cheese roll	EBE	35	2	B
Chicken (see also chicken, curried)				
Balls	EBE	35	1	C
Chowder	CBSS	142	2	B
Livers	FFCB	249	1	B
Salad	MIE	289	1	B
◆	BCC	264	2	B
◆	VGCB	314	1	
◆	BHGN	346	2	B
Soup, cream of	SP	63	2	B
Sweet & sour	NYTI	356	2	B
Coconut chips	BTSB	290	1	C
Coleslaw	JBGF	542	2	B
Corn, creamy	BHGN	396	1	B
Crabmeat	JBC	78	1	
Cranberry glaze	BHGN	254	1	B
Duckling, broiled	BB	45	1	B
Egg, artichoke	FG	57	1	B
Eggs (see also eggs, curried)				
Eggs, stuffed	FFCB	308	1	A
Fish, baked	FG	300	2	B
Fishwiches	BHGN	215	1	B
Goat, Jamaican	NYTI	448	2	C
Haddock	NYT	238	1	B
Kidneys, English style	NYTI	87	1	B
Kidneys, English style I	NYTI	88	3	B
Kidneys, English style II	NYTI	89	2	B
Lamb a la Francaise	NYTI	180	2	C
Lamb madras	BHGN	267	1	B
Lamb peas	WC	96	1	B
Lamb rice, cooked	JOC	229	2	B
Lamb snow peas	WC	110	1	B
Lentils	NYT	359	1	B
Lentils	JBGF	523	1	B
Lentils, pineapple &	VE	120	2	B
Nuts	JOC	66	1	
Omelet, chicken	MSE	92	1	C
Omelet, Spanish	JBC	56	1	
Pea soup, cream of	NYT	71	1	B
Pea soup, green	CBSS	324	1	B
Peanut soup	SC	397	1	
Peanuts	FFCB	72	1	B
Peas	BCC	355	1	B
Pepper strips, sweet	SMG	163	1	B
Pippin soup	CBSS	158	2	C
Pork	BHGN	250	1	B
Pork & noodles	WC	119	1	B
Potatoes	FFCB	404	1	B
Pumpkin soup	BBA	41	2	B
Pumpkin soup	CBSS	341	1	B
Rice	SC	181	1	
Rice, lamb &	WC	107	1	B
Shrimp crepes	JBGF	505	1	C
Squash soup, winter	GG	334	2	B
Turkey, apples & peanuts	GHAC	163	1	B
Walnut chicken, phyllo triangles filled w	MSE	52	3	C
Curry	JOC	527	1	
A word about	VE	251		
Almond sauce	GHAC	206	1	B
Almond spread	EBE	36	2	B
Almonds, sauteed crabmeat w	AC	150	1	
Apple, golden rice w	GHAC	268	1	B
Apple sauce, pork w	BHGN	249	2	C
Barley	FFCB	311	1	B

CURRY

RECIPE	BOOK	PAGE	TD	S
Beef	SC	275	1	
Beef	NYTI	31	2	B
Beef, tongue, sliced, braised	MFC2	240	2	B
Beef, vindaloo	NYTI	353	1	B
Bread honey	SPGT	86	3	B
Brown rice salad w fruit	MIE	279	2	B
Bryani	VE	262	1	B
Butter	AC	190		
Butter	SPGT	140	1	B
Butternut squash soup	SP	47	2	B
Carrot	VE	257	1	B
Cauliflower	VE	255	1	B
Cauliflower, Satyamma's famous	MC	136	2	B
Cheese canapes	NYT	43	1	C
Chicken (see also chicken curry)				
Chicken	JBC	220	2	B
Glazed apricot	WC	58	1	B
Parsley	BHGN	299	1	B
& Shrimp	SMG	154	1	B
Tomato cups	GHAC	280	1	B
Chutney butter	SP	116	1	
Cream sauce	FFCB	265	1	B
Deem sum, baked	NYTI	35	2	C
Dhal	NYTI	33	2	B
Dip honey	MSE	70	1	C
Dressing	BCC	266	1	
Dressing for fruit salad	JOC	318	1	B
Duck	SPGT	83	2	B
Duck honey	FG	141	2	B
Duck roast honey	JBC	230	1	B
Dunk, fruit w	AC	32	1	
Egg madras	NYT	312	1	B

RECIPE	BOOK	PAGE	TD	S
Eggplant	NYTI	32	1	B
Eggplant	MC	142	1	B
Eggplant pea	VE	258	1	B
Eggplant potato	VE	259	1	B
Fruit grilled	GHAC	226	1	B
Lamb (see also lamb, curry)				
Lamb bengal	NYT	125	2	B
Lamb rice	JOC	423	2	B
Lentil	NYTI	33	2	B
Lobster (see also lobster, curry)				
Lobster	EBE	94	1	B
Lobster	JOC	238	2	B
Lobster saute w	AC	146	1	
Marinade, lamb steaks w	BB	28	1	A
Mayonnaise (see mayonnaise, curry)				
Mushroom	MC	98	1	B
Of eggplant & peas	VE	258	1	B
Of eggplant & potatoes	VE	259	1	B
Orange	VE	254	1	B
Popcorn parmesan	BCC	14	1	C
Pork, Indonesian style	WC	115	1	B
Potato	VE	256	1	B
Powder	NYTI	33	1	C
Powder	BTSB	196	1	C
Powder	FGCW	227	1	
Powder, hot	BBA	165	1	
Powder, mild	BBA	165	1	
Puffs	NYTI	35	2	C
Refrigerator cookies	FFBB	216	1	C
Rice (see also rice, curry)				
Rice apple	GHAC	268	1	B

RECIPE	BOOK	PAGE	TD	S
Curry (*cont.*)				
Sauce	NYT	448	1	B
◆	JOC	325	1	B
◆	BCC	326	1	B
◆	MAFC	261	2	B
◆	AC	458	1	
◆	BHGN	355	1	B
◆	JBC	265	1	
◆	NYTI	270	1	B
Almond	GHAC	206	1	B
Brown	MAFC	73	1	B
Crabmeat mornay	JBC	77	1	
Creamy	JBC	262	1	
Creamy	BHGN	238	1	B
Dip	JBC	4	1	
Fish fillets poached in	JBC	69	1	
For pasta salad	JBGF	550	1	B
For tomato sorbet	GF	135	2	B
Herring in	NYTI	78	2	B
Japanese	BBA	161	1	B
Light	MAFC	63	1	B
Pickle	JOC	783	3	C
Sour cream	AC	11		
Traditional	AC	461		
Scallops	JBC	87	1	
Seafood	JOC	238	2	B
Shrimp (see also shrimp, curry)				
Shrimp	JBC	91	1	
Pilaf	AC	157	1	B
Salad	BCC	266	1	B
Salad	JBGF	407	1	A
Soup, chicken, easy	BHGN	380	1	A
Stuffed eggs	FFCB	308	1	A
Tomato	FFCB	417	1	B
Tomato	WC	38	1	B
Tomato, bisque	NYTI	130	1	C
Tomato, salad	KIS	256	1	A
Tomatoes, green	FFCB	418	1	B
Tomatoes, onion	YGM	111	1	A
Tuna	BCC	184	1	B
Tuna	WC	70	1	B
Turkey	JBC	236	1	
Turkey, apples & peanuts	GHAC	163	1	B
Turkey salad, brioche	BBA	148	2	B
Veal rice	JOC	229	2	B
Vegetable	VE	260	1	B
Vegetable	JBGF	396	2	B
Vegetable tofu	YGM	90	1	A
Winter squash, bisque	GG	334	2	B
Yams, cold	GG	358	1	B
Yogurt & cucumbers	NYTI	360	1	B
Yogurt dip	JBGF	296	2	B
Yogurt dip	JBGF	296	2	B
Cushion rolls	SC	73	2	C
Custard	JOC	684	2	B
Amaretti mascarpone	CF	39	1	B
Angel food cake	AC	686	1	
Apple pie	GHAC	311	2	B
Apple tart, Swiss	FFBB	170	1	B
Apricots, golden raisins	MSQC	205	1	B
Baked	BHGN	173	1	B
◆	AC	728	1	
◆	BCC	140	1	B
◆	JOC	684	2	B
◆	SC	199	1	
◆	FFCB	609	1	B
Baked coffee	BHGN	173	1	B
Baked coffee	GHAC	296	2	B
Banana sauce, velvety	GHAC	296	2	B
Boiled	FFCB	608	1	B
Boiled (soft custard)	AC	728	1	
Brandy, fresh berries	CW	93	1	B

RECIPE	BOOK	PAGE	TD	S
Bread & butter	NYTI	295	1	B
Broccoli	VGCB	32	1	B
Broccoli & cheese	FFCB	367	1	B
Cake, St. Valentine	LT	441	3	
Caramel (see caramel, custard)				
Carrot	CW	28	1	
Cauliflower	VGCB	64	1	B
Chicken	SC	488	1	
Chicken liver	LM	164	2	B
Chicken liver, unmolded	MAFC	174	2	B
Chocolate (see also chocolate, custard)				
Chocolate almond	MAFC	608	2	C
Chocolate rennet	SC	200	1	
Cinnamon, old fashioned	FAIC	436	2	B
Coconut	SC	199	1	
◆	AC	729	1	
◆	FFCB	609	1	B
◆	MHGD	352	2	B
Coffee	FFCB	609	1	B
Coffee	SC	199	1	
Coffee & chocolate	JOC	685	1	B
Collard green (green timbale)	GG	192	2	B
Corn pudding	GHAC	236	2	B
Cream	FAIC	430	1	B
Cream	SC	148	1	
Cream ice cream	MCIC	449	2	B
Cream pastry filling	JOC	646	1	B
Cream sauce, Italian	MCIC	423	1	B
Cup	JOC	684	2	B
Cup, unmolded	MAFC	611	1	B
Doughnuts, Florentine	FAIC	454	2	C
Egg	SC	410	1	
Eggplant	LM	133	2	B
English	NYT	595	1	B
English	FFCB	639	1	B
English, w chestnuts	NYTI	295	1	B
English cream	LT	333	1	
Filling	MAFC	590	2	B
Almond	SC	147	1	
Almond	MAFC	591	2	B
w Beaten egg whites	MAFC	591	2	C
Creamy	GHAC	344		
For vegetable timbales	JOC	207	2	B
French baked	MHGD	347	1	B
Fruit juice	JOC	686	1	B
Glaceed fruit, unmolded, warm, or cold	MAFC	612	2	B
Glaze	SC	83	1	
Glaze, nut	SC	83	1	
Grape, nut	MHGD	348	1	B
w Ham & onions	FG	263	1	A
Ice cream, old fashioned	FFCB	630	3	C
Leek	GG	251	1	B
Lemon sponge	JOC	687	2	B
Lemon sponge	NYTI	296	2	B
Luncheon	FFCB	345	1	B
Macaroon cup, unmolded	MAFC	611	1	B
Mexican	NYTI	479	2	C
Orange	MHGD	349	1	B
Baked	AC	729	1	
Baked	NYT	595	2	B
Filling	SC	148	1	
Meringue	JOC	686	2	B
Sponge	JOC	687	2	B
Pecan almond	CF	17		

RECIPE	BOOK	PAGE	TD	S
Custard (*cont.*)				
Pie	JBC	40	1	
◆	BCC	93	1	B
◆	SC	349	1	
◆	BHGN	283	1	B
◆	JOC	609	2	B
Apple honey	MC	194	1	B
Cheese	JOC	227	2	B
Date	FFBB	138	2	B
Pumpkin or squash	AC	627	1	
Slipped	FFBB	130	1	B
Slipped	FFCB	591	2	B
Sweet potato	AC	627	1	
Tips for making	BHGN	283		
Topped, chocolate	JOC	609	2	B
Translucent, all about	FFBB	142		
Pineapple, unmolded, cold	MAFC	631	1	B
Pineapple sponge	JOC	687	2	B
Pudding, baked	JBC	44	1	B
Raspberry	BCC	140	1	B
Raspberry rennet	SC	200	1	
Rennet	SC	488	2	
Rice cake	FAIC	486	2	B
Rich	JOC	685	1	B
Ring noodle	SC	335	1	
Royal	NYT	59	1	
Rum	NYTI	296	1	B
Rum brandy	MHGD	350	2	B
Rum pudding	NYTI	449	2	B
Salvaging a curdled	NSD	21		
Sauce	JOC	710	2	B
◆	SC	216	1	
◆	GHAC	290		
◆	BBA	211	1	A
Blackberries w stewed	JBC	99	1	
Blueberries w	JBC	99	1	
Brown sugar	NYT	614	1	B
Creamy	JBC	267	1	
Light	MAFC	588	2	B
Peaches & strawberries in	GHAC	290	2	B
Soft	NYT	614	1	B
Soft	JBC	266	1	
Sherry	NYT	614	1	B
Soft	FFCB	608	1	B
Soft	SC	198	1	
Soft, boiled	AC	728	1	
Soft, chocolate	SC	199	1	
Spiced	JBC	44	1	B
Steamed, egg	NYTI	456	1	B
Stirred	BHGN	173	1	B
Stirred	SC	199	1	
Tapioca, butterscotch	JOC	699	2	B
Tapioca, quick	JOC	699	2	B
Tart, blackberry	NSD	104	2	B
Tarts, fruit	JOC	609	2	B
Tomato	JOC	307	1	B
Vanilla cream	LT	333	1	
Wine	FGCW	392	1	B
Wine	JOC	686	1	B
Cutlet, paprika	JOC	404	1	
Cutlet Kiev, basic variations	AC	216	2	
Cutleti	NYTI	511	1	B
Cutlets for the village festival	OC	108	1	B
Cutting, chopping, slicing, dicing, mincing	MAFC	26		
Cutting (drawings)	MFC	14		
Cutting up foods	JBGF	254		
Cymling (patty-pan squash)	SC	432	1	

RECIPE	BOOK	PAGE	TD	S
Czarina sauce (w butter, shrimp and vegetables)	PPLK	310	2	B
Czarina sauce, shrimp or crawfish	PPLK	265	2	B
Czarina sauce, veal paneed	PPLK	117	2	B

D

RECIPE	BOOK	PAGE	TD	S
Daffodil cake	SC	122	1	B
◆	FFBB	300	2	C
◆	JOC	622	1	B
◆	FFCB	519	2	C
Daikon, braised	MIE	216	1	B
Daily loaf	CBB	253	3	C
Daily loaf, Sister Virginia's	CBB	61	3	C
Dainty sandwiches, variations	AC	815	1	
Daiquiri	NYT	649		
◆	SC	60	1	A
◆	JOC	39	1	
◆	BB	165	1	A
Blender, frozen	JOC	39	1	
Fresh fruit	SP	330	1	
Mango	JBGF	289	1	B
Mango	MSE	158	1	B
Pineapple frozen	MSQC	108	1	A
Sherbet, strawberry	NSD	232	1	B
Strawberry	JBGF	289	1	B
Dairy products, definitions	BHGN	427		
Dairying, notes on	BTSB	53		
Daisy cream candy	SC	171	1	
Daisy torte	SC	127	1	B

RECIPE	BOOK	PAGE	TD	S
Dal, spiced	VE	263	1	B
Dampf nudeln (baked kuchen dough with stewed prunes)	SC	193	2	
Dandelion	AC	559		
Frittella	GG	193	2	B
Greens	SC	420	1	
Greens w bacon dressing	AC	516	1	
Greens w prosciutto	GG	191	1	B
Greens, wilted	NYT	417	1	A
Salad	VGCB	247	1	B
◆	LM	148	1	B
◆	AC	39	1	
◆	GF	186	1	B
Bacon &	FFCB	431	1	B
Duck &	SPGT	38	3	B
Tuna &	AC	68	1	
Wilted	AC	39	1	
Soup	CBSS	272	3	B
Soup, spinach &	FG	49	2	B
Wine	SC	438	3	
Dandelions & potatoes, wilted	GG	189	1	B
Danish buns, filled	FFBB	533	2	B
Danish Christmas fruit loaf	CBB	307	3	B
Danish cones w whipped cream	NYTI	86	2	C
Danish dessert	SC	197	1	
Danish Easter duck	BBA	180	3	B
Danish kringle	BCC	54	2	C
Danish margarine	FFBB	529	3	C
Danish Mary ice	SP	317	3	B
Danish meatballs w caper sauce	FG	187	2	B
Danish open face sandwich	FGCW	299		
Danish pastry	SC	78	2	

RECIPE	BOOK	PAGE	TD	S
Danish pastry	NYT	533	3	C
Cheese filled	NYTI	85	3	C
Cheese filling for	NYT	535	1	
Dough	FFBB	528	3	C
Dough	BCC	52	3	C
Making (photographs)	NYT	534		
Danish strip	BCC	52	3	B
Danish twists	BCC	53	3	C
Dark bread	SC	68	2	C
Dark grains bread	CBB	223	2	C
Darnes, broiled	JOC	359	1	
Dashi (seaweed stock)	NYTI	451	1	A
Dashi	CBSS	56	2	C
Date				
Almond kisses	SC	163	1	
Apple coffee bread	BHGN	77	1	B
Banana bread	GHAC	366	1	B
Bars	BCC	105	1	C
◆	JOC	654	1	C
◆	FFBB	233	2	C
◆	SC	166	1	
Bread	SC	86	1	
Bran, deluxe	CBB	505	1	
Bran, quick	JOC	576	1	C
Quick	JOC	574	1	B
Vel's	CBB	486	1	B
Butterscotch pie	AC	626	1	
Cake	BHGN	95	1	C
Cake	SC	112	1	B
Cake, one bowl, quick	SC	107	1	B
Cake, quick	FFCB	528	1	B
Centers	JOC	740	2	B
Chocolate chip cake	BCC	72	1	C
Chocolates	SC	173	1	
Coffee cake, orange	BHGN	80	1	B
Cookie filling	AC	716	1	
Cookies, nut &	JOC	671	1	C
Custard pie	FFBB	138	2	B
Filled bars	FFBB	232	2	C
Filled oatmeal cookies	FFCB	562	2	B
Filling, cookie	AC	716	1	
Filling for coffee cake	JOC	573	1	B
Fondant, stuffed	SC	176	1	
Ginger nut, stuffed	SC	176	1	
Honey	NYTI	361	2	B
& Lemon chutney	BBA	167	1	B
Loaf candy	SC	176	1	
Loaf, uncooked	JOC	704	2	C
Muffins (see muffins, date)				
Nut				
Bars	NYT	579	1	C
Bars, honey	FFCB	567	1	C
Bread	GHAC	364	2	B
◆	SP	248	1	B
◆	BTSB	120	1	B
◆	FFCB	486	1	B
◆	AC	791	1	
Bread, orange	EBE	105	2	B
Cakes	FFCB	530	1	C
Cakes	FFBB	381	1	C
Loaf	MHGD	257	1	B
Pudding	SP	310	1	B
Sticks	SC	166	1	
Stuffed	SC	176	1	
Torte	AC	667	1	
Torte	MC	183	1	B
Orange bars	BHGN	155	1	C
Persimmon pudding	GHAC	298	2	B
Pinwheels	SC	156	1	
Pudding, steamed	AC	731	2	
◆	SC	190	2	
◆	JBC	46	1	
◆	JOC	703	2	C
Pudding cake	FFBB	340	2	B
Refrigerator cookies	AC	701	2	

RECIPE	BOOK	PAGE	TD	S
Rolls batter	SC	74	2	
Rye bread, sour	CBB	148	2	B
Sauce	BCC	326	1	B
◆	BHGN	359	1	B
◆	VE	92	1	
◆	MAFC	95	1	A
◆	JBC	262	1	
Easy	BHGN	359	1	B
Fish braised, wine	MIE	160	1	B
Fish, poached	BHGN	212	1	B
Fish, poached, cucumber w	FG	241	2	B
For cucumber sorbet	GF	137	1	B
Mustard	BBA	163	1	B
Mustard	MIE	47	2	B
Shrimp chilled	NYT	24	3	B
Soup	VE	74	2	B
Vinegar	SC	437	3	
Watercress sauce	MIE	52	2	B
Dilled ricotta dressing	JBGF	552	1	A
Dilled salmon dip	BHGN	13	1	B
Dilled soup, chilled	MC	36	2	B
Dilly casserole bread	CBB	443	2	B
Dinner, New England, boiled	JOC	412	2	B
Dinner rolls (see rolls, dinner)				
Dip				
Avocado	SP	21	1	B
Caviar	SP	36	1	B
Green peppercorn mustard	SP	22	1	B
Roquefort	SP	21	1	B
Sauces, Japanese	FGCW	359	1	
Tapenade	SP	22	1	B
Diplomas	AC	682	2	
Diplomat pudding	JBC	46	3	
Diplomat pudding, frozen	SC	214	2	
Dipping chocolates	BHGN	112		
Dipping fruit, do's & don'ts	BBA	210		
Dipping sauce for tempura	SC	258	1	
Divinity	BCC	117	3	C
◆	FFCB	683	2	B
◆	BHGN	111	3	C
◆	JOC	731	2	B
Almond	NYT	636	2	C
Coconut	NYT	636	2	C
Fruit	NYT	636	2	C
Fudge	AC	832	2	
Ginger	NYT	636	2	C
Vanilla	NYT	635	2	C
Dobos (many-tiered chocolate torte)	JOC	638	3	B
Dobos filling	SC	128	3	B
Dobos filling, chocolate	SC	128	3	
Dobos torte	SC	128	3	B
Dock (edible weed, similar to spinach)	AC	559		
Dog biscuits	CBB	716	2	C
Dolmadakia (stuffed grape leaves)	NYTI	322	1	C
Dolmadakia yialandji	NYTI	323	2	C
Dolmades (stuffed grapevine leaves)	VE	225	2	B
Donburi (Japanese omelet on rice)	FGCW	361	1	A
Doneness, testing for	GHAC	360		
Double broiler cookery	JOC	132		
Double chocolate pie	EBE	164	1	B
Double cream	MIE	45	3	C
Double cream chiffon pie, basic	FFBB	118	3	B

RECIPE	BOOK	PAGE	TD	S
Double diabolo	MSE	256	2	B
Double fudge chip cake	MIE	331	1	B
Double Gloucester cheese soup	CBSS	155	2	B
Doubletons	SC	73	2	C
Dough				
Basic pie	FFBB	54	1	B
Buckwheat	FFBB	60	1	B
Cake	AC	691	1	
Cheddar cheese	FFBB	66	1	B
Cornmeal	FFBB	59	1	B
Cottage cheese	FFBB	64	1	B
Cream cheese	FFBB	65	1	B
Cream puff, making (photographs)	LT	391		
Croissant	FFBB	529	3	C
Danish pastry	BCC	52	3	C
Danish pastry	FFBB	528	3	C
Egg pastry dough for cases & turnovers	MFC2	104	2	C
For individual pizzas	MSQC	48	2	B
For shortcake biscuit	SC	196	1	
For soft rolls	SC	74	2	
Galette	JOC	592	2	
Hot water	FFBB	58	1	B
Kneading	CBB	35		
Kneading (drawings)	FFCB	460		
Lard	FFBB	56	1	B
Leftover, reconstituting into pastry	MFC2	134		
Lining the mold w	MFC2	328		
Making better, Clancy's clues	BBA	175		
Nutty chocolate	FFBB	63	1	B
Oatmeal	FFBB	62	1	B
Pastry rolling out	NSD	25		
Pie, cutting & forming	JOC	589		
Pie, rolling	JOC	589		
Pockets, stuffed pierogi	FG	372	1	C
Process, starting, stopping action	MFC2	67		
Roll	BCC	48	2	
Rolling out the (drawings)	MAFC	141		
Rye caraway seed	FFBB	61	2	B
Shortcake	JOC	584	1	C
Sour cream	FFBB	64	1	B
Stirred	FFBB	59	1	B
Sweet roll	FFBB	513	1	C
Sweet roll	BCC	50	2	
Sweet roll potato	FFBB	514	2	C
Sweet roll whole wheat	FFBB	514	1	C
Sweet tart	FFBB	165	2	B
Tart	FFBB	166	2	B
Whole wheat	FFBB	57	1	B
Doughnut (see also beignets)				
All about	JOC	705		
Brazil nut	SC	99	1	
Buttermilk	BCC	34	2	C
Buttermilk	BHGN	83	2	C
Buttermilk	SC	99	1	
Buttermilk, New England	NYT	485	1	C
Cake	BHGN	82	2	C
Cake	BCC	34	2	C
Cake	AC	799	1	
Chocolate	FFCB	499	3	C
Chocolate cake	BHGN	82	2	C
Chocolate yeast	BHGN	69	2	C
Custard, Florentine	FAIC	454	2	C
Drops	SC	100	1	

RECIPE	BOOK	PAGE	TD	S
Drops, orange	SC	100	1	
Filled	AC	800	2	
Filled (Berliner pfannkuchen)	SC	100	1	
Frying	SC	99		
Holes, coffee	SPGT	128	3	C
Jelly	FFCB	480	3	C
Jelly	AC	800	2	
Nutmeg sugar	GHAC	369	2	C
Old fashioned	FFCB	498	3	C
Plain	SC	99	1	
Potato, quick	JOC	705	2	C
Potato, raised	VGCB	227	1	C
Raised	BCC	40	2	C
◆	SC	100	1	
◆	AC	800	2	
◆	FFCB	480	3	C
Sour cream	JOC	705	2	C
Sour cream	SC	99	1	
Sweet milk	JOC	705	2	C
Variations	JOC	706	2	C
Whole wheat	BTSB	242	3	C
Yeast	BHGN	69	2	C
Dove, delicious, charcoaled	OC	140	2	A
Dove pigeons	JOC	481	2	A
Doves, broiled	AC	245		
Doves, marinated & grilled	OC	141	2	B
Drawn butter sauce	SC	391	1	
Dream bars	FFBB	228	1	C
Dream bars	AC	713	1	
Dresden sauce	JOC	317	1	B
Dresdner stollen	BBA	180	3	C
Dressing				
Anchovy	JOC	311	1	A
Anchovy French	NYT	437	1	B
Andouille, smoked sausage w	PPLK	226	2	B
Apple	JOC	458	1	C
Apple onion	JOC	458	1	C
Apple prune	JOC	458	1	C
Apple sage	BBA	83	1	B
Apricot	JOC	458	1	C
Balsamic vinegar	MSQC	56	1	B
Boiled, preserving	SC	376		
Bread, egg, old fashioned	NYT	223	2	B
Bread, for fish	JOC	457	1	B
Bread, mushrooms, oysters & nuts	JOC	456	2	B
Chestnut, for game	JOC	457	2	C
Cornbread	PPLK	227	3	B
Crab Louis	AC	58	1	
Dry	JOC	456	1	
Fennel	JOC	457	1	B
For chicken salad, snow peas & water chestnuts	MSQC	88	1	B
For cornish hen or pigeon	JOC	458	2	
For hot escarole & pancetta	MSQC	33	1	B
For shrimp, Chinoise	MSQC	108	1	B
For spicy sesame noodles	MSQC	100	1	B
For spinach mushroom salad	MSQC	184	1	B
For three cabbage slaw	MSQC	140	1	B
For warm salad of winter vegetables	MSQC	177	1	B
Fruit	BBA	59	1	B
Greens for fish or fowl	JOC	457	1	B
Ham or turkey	JOC	458	1	C
Liver	JOC	458	1	C

RECIPE	BOOK	PAGE	TD	S
w Turnips	VGCB	332	2	B
Wild	JOC	478	2	
Breast				
Charcoal grilled	CPMC	159	1	B
Grilled	MSQC	160	2	A
Grilled w red wine marinade	GRIL	95	2	B
Grilled w roasted pepper mayonnaise	CFS	138	2	B
Of Muscovy limes	GF	237	2	B
w Port wine	MFC	91	3	B
Broiled, wild	BB	50	1	
Broiled, wild	JOC	478	2	
Broiled, wild	FFCB	262	2	B
w Cabernet sauce	FGCW	184	3	A
Casserole w pinto beans	AC	230	3	
Casserole w pork sausage	FGCW	305	3	C
Casserole, roast, w turnips	MAFC	279	1	B
Chinese (see also Chinese duck)				
Chinese, sauce	MC	70	1	B
Chinese (Peking) sauce	NYTI	57	1	A
Confit	BTSB	25	3	C
◆	CPPC	176	3	B
◆	FGCW	198	2	B
◆	CPMC	91	3	B
Confit, pizza w pearl onions &	CPPC	162	3	B
Curry	SPGT	83	2	B
Curry, honey	FG	141	2	B
& Dandelion, green salad w	SPGT	38	3	B
Danish, Easter	BBA	180	3	B
Etouffee	PPLK	168	3	B
Fermiere	NYTI	231	2	B
Five spice	NYTI	59	2	B
w Forty cloves of garlic	SP	186	3	A
Fruit complement for (photographs)	OC	60		
Galantine of	NYTI	108	3	C
Giblet soup	NYT	60	2	B
Gizzard sauce, papperdelle batolo	CPPC	132	3	B
Glazed	WC	54	3	B
Goose, chicken, timetable for roasting	BCC	241		
w Green peppercorns	MFC	88	3	B
Julienne, breast w truffles, pears & orange cream	GF	58	3	C
Lasagne, the style of arezzo	FAIC	195	2	C
Legs w turnips, green onions or leeks	MFC	89	3	A
Liver				
Bacon &	AC	25		
Chicken, bacon &	AC	25		
Fresh American	SPGT	248		
Green beans, walnut, pasta w	CPPC	112	2	B
Grilled, pasta, mustard w herb butter	CPPC	130	2	A
Sauteed w celery root	CPMC	87	3	B
Long Island, w olives & pistachios	GF	222	3	B
Mallard, bing cherries w	NYT	179	2	B
Marinated	OC	138	3	B

RECIPE	BOOK	PAGE	TD	S
Duck (*cont.*)				
Marinated w red wine, charcoal grilled	CPMC	142	3	B
Mary Hamblet's famous roast	AC	250	1	
Mock	SC	275	2	
Montmorency	NYTI	232	2	B
Mousse	MAFC	560	1	C
Mustard, leeks w	FGCW	188	2	B
Nivernaise	NYTI	233	2	B
w Olives	FGCW	186	2	B
w Olives, braised	FFCB	251	3	B
On a spit	OC	138	2	B
Orange aspic	FFCB	447	3	B
Orange sauce	FAIC	323	2	B
Orange sauce for	AC	457	1	
Orange sauce for	JOC	326		B
Pate w pistachio nuts	CPMC	42	3	C
w Peanut stuffing, wild	FFCB	262	2	B
& Pear salad w mango chutney dressing	SP	206	2	B
Pears & pink peppercorn sauce	MFC	92	3	B
Peking	FG	306	3	B
Pickled	FGCW	187	3	B
Pilaf	JOC	236	2	B
w Pineapple	JBC	231	2	B
& Pork sausage casserole	FGCW	305	3	C
Preparing for roasting	MAFC	272		
Preserved	MFC2	315	3	C
Rare roast wild	AC	249		
Ravioli	MFC	93	3	B
Ravioli w fresh herbs	MFC	94	3	B
w Rice	NYT	219	1	B
w Rice	PPLK	176	2	B
Rillettes	MSE	274	2	B
Roast	BCC	241		
◆	FFCB	250	3	B
◆	MCIC	323	1	B
◆	BB	78	1	
A simple	AC	229	2	
California	GHAC	165	2	B
Cantonese	NYTI	58	2	B
w Cherries	MAFC	278	2	B
Chinese	NYTI	60	2	B
Chinese style	JBC	230	3	B
Cold	JBC	232	2	B
Curry w honey	JBC	230	1	B
Domestic	JOC	473	2	A
w Olives	JBC	230	2	B
w Orange sauce	MAFC	276	2	B
w Peaches	MAFC	279	2	B
Peking	NYTI	56	3	B
Sage & onion stuffing	AC	229	2	
Sausage & apple stuffing	MAFC	275	2	B
Wild	BB	82	1	
◆	FFCB	262	2	B
◆	SC	323		
◆	JOC	477	2	B
Wild, spiced w apple rings	GHAC	167	2	B
Wild w wine sauce	BB	83	1	
Roasted rice, sweet potato & eggplant gravy	PPLK	173	3	B
Roasting, how to	JOC	464		
Roasting, timetable for	MAFC	273		
Rotisserie, Chinese	NYT	217	2	B
Rutabaga stew	NYTI	234	2	B
Salad	MFC	186	2	A

RECIPE	BOOK	PAGE	TD	S
Dumplings (*cont.*)				
Apple (see apple dumplings)				
Apricot	SC	104	1	
Baking powder	SC	407	1	
Baking powder	SC	102	1	
Bread	SC	103	1	
Bread & meat	SC	407	1	C
Broth & cheese	NYTI	377	3	B
Butter	JOC	172	1	A
Caraway seed soup w	NYTI	341	1	B
Cheese	JOC	191		
Cheese, quick	JOC	191	1	C
Chicken	FFCB	245	2	B
Chicken fricassee	GHAC	150	1	B
Chicken fricassee	SC	309	1	
Chicken fricassee	GHAC	150	1	B
Chicken, old fashioned	AC	205	2	
Cockaigne	JOC	192	2	B
Corn meal	JOC	192	2	
Cooking in stew	SC	102		
Cracker	SC	103	1	
Cracker meal	JOC	171	1	B
Cracker & parsley	SC	407	1	
Egg	SC	407	1	
Egg, German	JOC	192	2	B
Fried, Chinese	NYTI	62	3	C
Fried, stuffed	MCIC	79	3	B
Fruit	JOC	608	3	B
German	FGCW	162	2	B
Greens cornmeal	GG	190	1	B
Herbed	JBC	20	2	
Hor gwo sauce for one w	NYTI	64	1	A
Huckleberry	AC	725	1	
Liver	SC	300	1	
Liver leberkloesse	JOC	171	1	B
Liver sausage	JOC	173	1	A
Liver in soup	NYT	59	1	B
Matzo meal	JOC	171	1	B
Matzos	SC	104	2	
Matzos	SC	408	1	
Matzos, almond	SC	408	1	
Matzos, filled	SC	104	1	
Parsley	NYT	206	1	
Parsley	JBC	20	2	
Plain	SC	102	1	
Plum	SC	104	1	
Pork, hot sauce	FGCW	329	2	B
Potato	SC	103	1	
Potato	VGCB	221	1	B
Potato (Kartoffelkloesse)	JOC	192	2	
Croutons	SC	103	1	
Farina	SC	103	1	
& Matzo meal	SC	103	1	
Raw	SC	104	1	
Raw	JOC	193	2	B
Raised	JOC	608	3	C
Semolina	FGCW	160	2	B
Semolina, ham	FGCW	161	2	B
Shrimp, steamed	NYTI	61	2	C
Soup meat	MCIC	118	1	B
Spinach	BBA	110	2	B
Spinach	GG	315	1	B
Spinach & ricotta	NYT	337	1	B
Sponge	SC	408	1	
Sponge	SC	103	1	
Sponge parsley	SC	408	1	
Sponge rich	SC	408	1	
Stone griddled	MCIC	74	3	B
Yeast	SC	103	2	
Dundee cake	NYT	553	1	B
Dutch apple cake	FFCB	523	2	B
Dutch apple cake	SC	197	1	
Dutch apple pie	BCC	83	1	B
Dutch babies	MIE	62	1	A

RECIPE	BOOK	PAGE	TD	S
Dutch butter cookies	GHAC	348	2	C
Dutch honey bread	MHGD	267	1	C
Dutch roggebrood	CBB	170	3	C
Duxelle of mushrooms	LM	28	1	A
Duxelles (mushroom paste)	NYTI	497	1	
◆	MFC	174	1	B
◆	JOC	540	1	
◆	SP	170	2	C

E

RECIPE	BOOK	PAGE	TD	S
East Indies sauce for barbecue	GHAC	226	1	C
Easter				
Biscuit bunnies	JOC	585	1	
Bread	NYTI	337	2	C
Bread, Finnish	CBB	345	2	C
Bread, Russian	FFBB	506	3	C
Bread, Russian	CBB	317	3	B
Bunnies, chocolate glazed	MSE	229	3	B
Cheesecake	SPGT	60	2	C
Duck Danish	BBA	180	3	B
Egg bread, Italian	BBA	181	3	B
Egg dessert	SC	202	3	
Ham, baked	MSE	228	2	C
Lambs, chocolate glazed	MSE	229	3	B
Soup, Greek	NYTI	326	2	B
Torta	FAIC	234	2	C
Turkeys, chocolate glazed	MSE	229	3	B
Eastern greens salad	BBA	144	1	B
Eclair	FFCB	597	3	C

RECIPE	BOOK	PAGE	TD	S
◆	BHGN	177	2	C
◆	BCC	138	1	C
◆	NYT	533	2	
Caviar	SP	36	3	C
Chocolate	JOC	598	3	
Chocolate	SC	140	1	
Deep fried	WC	130	2	B
Deep fried, making	WC	131		
Fillings	JOC	598	2	
Making (photographs)	NYT	532		
Economy cake	SC	107	1	B
Ecrevisses (crawfish)	MAFC	213		
Ecrevisses	JOC	378		
Edam cheese, filled	JOC	66	1	
Edam nuggets	JOC	67	1	C
Eel				
A l'Orly	NYT	235	2	B
Grilled	OC	144	2	B
In green herb sauce (anguilles quo vadis)	NYT	18	2	B
In tomato sauce	NYT	235	1	B
Preparing	JOC	355		
Spit roasted	OC	144	1	B
Stifle (eel chowder)	AC	180	1	
Egg (see also huevos rancheros)				
A la flamande	BBA	123	1	
A la king	BHGN	194	1	B
A la king, easy cheese	BHGN	194	1	B
A la Livingston	AC	109	1	
A la Russe	NYT	25	1	B
A la Suisse	FFCB	347	1	B
A la tarcat	SC	222	1	
A la tripe	NYT	310	1	A
A nest	JOC	201	1	A
A nest	SC	223	1	
All about	FFBB	9		

RECIPE	BOOK	PAGE	TD	S
Egg, All about (*cont.*)				
◆	JBC	49		
◆	BCC	156		
◆	FFCB	335		
& Almond spread	BBA	20	1	B
w Anchovy butter, poached	SC	223	1	
Anchovy stuffed	FFCB	308	1	A
& Apples	JOC	68	2	
& Asparagus cockaigne, creamed	JOC	202	2	B
Asparagus w	AC	473	1	
Au gratin	SC	222	1	
Au gratin, creamed	JOC	202	2	B
& Bacon	AC	25	1	
& Bacon	SC	223	1	
Asparagus w	AC	106	1	
Baked	BCC	163	1	B
Scalloped	BHGN	195	1	B
Smoked	CFS	278	2	B
Bake, country	GHAC	109	1	B
Baked	JOC	201	2	A
◆	BCC	158	1	
◆	NYT	301		
◆	BHGN	190	1	A
A la Columbus	SC	223	1	
w Bacon rings	JOC	201	1	A
In mornay sauce	FFCB	348	2	B
Ramekins	MAFC	123	1	A
Ramekins w herbs	MAFC	124		
Zucchini &	VE	165	2	B
& Barley, baked	SC	337	2	
& Barley manfrigul	MCIC	174	3	
Basin Street	PPLK	303	2	C
& Beans, zesty Mexican	GHAC	109	1	B
Beating	JOC	515		
Beating	MAFC	127		
Beating	BHGN	427		
Beating sugar to form a ribbon	MAFC	579		
Beating to a ribbon	NSD	17		
& Beets salad	AC	47	1	
Benedict	FFCB	344	2	A
◆	NYT	303	1	A
◆	JBC	52	1	
◆	JOC	197	1	B
◆	GHAC	109	1	B
◆	AC	106	1	
◆	BBA	122	2	B
◆	BHGN	192	1	B
◆	BCC	159	2	B
◆	SC	223	1	
Benedict casserole	BCC	158	2	C
Boiled	JBC	50	1	
Boiled	AC	101	1	
Boiled, six minute	MAFC	118	1	B
& Brains, scrambled	FFCB	215	1	B
Bread	MFC2	83	3	C
Bread	BHGN	64	2	B
Bread, braided challah	BBA	173	3	C
Bread, Italian Easter	BBA	181	3	B
Bread raisins in	MFC2	84	3	C
Breads	AC	787		
& Broccoli, poached	MFC2	339	1	
Buckingham	SC	225	1	
Buns	BCC	323	1	B
& Butter cookies	SC	152	1	
Cake I	AC	657	1	
Cake II	AC	651	1	
& Catsup, deviled	BCC	14	3	B
& Caviar	AC	17		
& Caviar appetizer	SC	44	1	
& Caviar salad, molded	JOC	90	2	

RECIPE	BOOK	PAGE	TD	S
Chasseur	FFCB	344	2	B
& Cheese, gratin	JOC	343	1	B
& Cheese, poached	SC	222	1	
Cheese sandwich w tomato sauce	JOC	247	1	B
Chicken livers &	WC	47	1	B
Cocotte cream	LM	53	1	B
Coddled	JOC	195		
Coddled	BCC	279	1	
Cold poached w artichoke	GG	21	2	B
Cooked, truffles &	CPMC	100	3	B
Cooking	JOC	514		
& Corn, scrambled	SC	224	1	
Corned beef hash &	GHAC	110	1	B
Cowboy	JOC	197	2	B
Crayfish or shrimp w	MFC	54	2	A
& Cream sauce	JOC	323	1	B
Creamed	BHGN	194	1	B
Creamed	BCC	163	1	B
Creamed	FFCB	344	1	B
Creamy poached	BHGN	192	1	B
Creole	SC	224	1	
Creole	AC	111	1	
Creole, scrambled	FFCB	347	1	B
Crespelle Renaissance	FAIC	465	1	C
Cressonniere	NYT	26	1	
Curried	FFCB	344	1	B
◆	AC	113	1	
◆	JOC	202	2	B
◆	BHGN	194	1	B
◆	SC	222	1	
Curried, stuffed	VE	164	2	B
Curried, stuffed	NYT	312	1	B
Curry madras	NYT	312	1	B
Custard	SC	410	1	
Custard, baked, maple	MC	197	1	B
Custard, steamed	NYTI	456	1	B
Cutlets	SC	222	1	
Deep fried	LM	56	1	A
Desert Easter	SC	202	3	
Deviled	BCC	14	3	B
◆	BHGN	196	1	C
◆	AC	17		
◆	SC	45	1	
◆	JOC	203	3	B
Dill &	VE	163	1	
Italian style	BHGN	196	1	C
Olives &	BCC	14	3	B
Red caviar &	MSE	273	2	C
Sauce	JOC	203	3	B
& Variations	GHAC	90	1	C
Double boiler, scrambled	SC	224	1	
w Dried beef	SC	224	1	
w Dried shrimp gumbo	PPLK	199	3	B
Drop soup	CBSS	105	2	B
Drop soup	BCC	305	1	B
Drops	SC	409	1	
Drops, Chinese	SC	409	1	
Drops, hard-cooked	JOC	170	1	
Dumplings	SC	407	1	
En cocotte	JOC	201	2	A
Esau	BBA	123	1	
Florentine	BBA	123	1	
◆	BHGN	194	1	B
◆	JBC	53	1	
◆	AC	106	1	
◆	NYT	311	1	B
◆	VE	163	2	A
Florentine, the Florentine way	FAIC	287	1	B
Fluff	SC	409	1	
Foo yung	BHGN	192	2	A
Foo yung	BCC	162	1	A

RECIPE	BOOK	PAGE	TD	S
Egg (*cont.*)				
Foo yung	AC	110	1	
Foo yung I	SC	226	1	
Foo yung II	SC	227	1	
Foo yung, crab meat &	WC	67	1	B
Foo yung, ham &	BHGN	192	2	A
Foo yung, shrimp &	JOC	199	1	
Foo yung, shrimp &	BHGN	192	2	A
For aioli, hard-cooked	NYTI	135	1	B
Fried	BCC	157	1	
◆	JBC	53	1	
◆	NYT	302		
◆	FFCB	339	1	A
◆	JOC	195	1	B
◆	BHGN	190	1	A
Fried in butter	JBC	53	1	
Fritters	MCIC	85	1	B
Garin, scrambled	MFC	57	1	B
& Garlic soup	FGCW	366	1	B
Garnish of hard cooked	SMG	115	1	B
Garnished soups	JOC	169		
Georgette	BBA	123	1	
Goldenrod	BHGN	194	1	B
Goldenrod	FFCB	344	1	B
& Green sauce	NYTI	371	1	A
Gruyere, baked	NYT	301	1	A
Ham (see also ham, eggs)				
& Ham	SC	226	1	
& Ham	AC	448	1	
Appetizer	SC	45	1	
Cakes	JOC	201	1	B
Creamed	BCC	163	1	B
Italian	AC	452	1	
Stuffed	FFCB	308	1	A
Stuffed	AC	18		
Harbor bread	CBB	46	3	C
Hard boiled	FFCB	337	1	
Hard boiled, clown style	LM	57	1	B
Hard boiled, piquant sauce	CIC	45	1	B
Hard cooked	BCC	157	1	
◆	SC	221	1	
◆	BHGN	190	1	A
◆	JOC	195		
◆	NYT	302		
Hard cooked, quail	CPMC	19	2	B
Hard cooked, removing shells	BHGN	190		
Herbed, stuffed	AC	17		
Hors d'oeuvre, stuffed	JBC	10	1	
Iberian	BBA	123	1	
In aspic	JOC	99	2	
In aspic	LT	97	2	
In aspic	NYTI	110	2	B
In aspic cockaigne	JOC	99	2	
In aspic w tarragon	NYT	26	2	B
In black butter	LM	52	1	A
In Denver omelet	AC	109	1	
In nest, fluffy	FFCB	343	2	B
In wine sauce	BCC	323	1	B
Italian	JBC	52	1	
& Lemon soup	VE	50	2	B
& Lemon soup	FG	344	1	C
& Lemon soup, Greek	NYT	66	1	B
Marbled	GHAC	113	2	C
Marbleized & hard-boiled	MSE	226	2	B
Masked	JOC	202		
& Mayonnaise	FGCW	132	1	
Measuring broken	NSD	21		

RECIPE	BOOK	PAGE	TD	S
Medium boiled	FFCB	337	1	
Mexican	AC	17		
Milk punch	SC	63	1	
Molded	SC	222	2	
Mollet	NYT	302		
Mornay	JBC	52	1	
Mornay, poached	SC	223	1	
& Mushroom sauce	BHGN	193	2	A
& Mushrooms	SC	222	1	
& Mushrooms, scrambled	FFCB	347	1	B
& Noodle nests	JBC	52	2	
Norman, beans w	GG	353	1	B
Olive stuffed	AC	17		
Omelet	AC	104		
On English muffins	BCC	158	1	B
On toast baked	JOC	201	1	A
On tortillas	BCC	159	1	B
Onion rings, herb &	FGCW	313	1	B
& Pancakes	NYTI	363	1	C
Parsleyed on the half shell	VE	162	2	B
Party, creamy	GHAC	111	2	B
Party, deviled	BCC	14	3	B
Pastry dough for shells cases, turnovers	MFC2	104	2	C
Pastry sweet murbeteig or pate sucree	AC	636	1	
Paulette	PPLK	307	2	B
Pickled	NYT	312	1	B
◆	BCC	14	3	B
◆	JOC	203	3	B
◆	CF	79	3	B
◆	GHAC	113	3	C
Poached	JOC	196	1	A
◆	MAFC	116	1	B
◆	BHGN	190	2	
◆	FFCB	339	1	A
◆	BCC	157	1	
◆	NYT	303	1	
◆	JBC	51	1	
Aspics	MAFC	547	2	B
Blackstone	JOC	197	1	B
w Chili-tomato sauce	CF	135	1	B
w Corned beef hash	JBC	52	1	
Different suggestions	SPGT	122		
In soup	JOC	196	2	B
In wine	JOC	196	1	B
Lobster &	SC	223	1	
Mushrooms &	SC	223	1	
Mushrooms & bernaise sauce	MAFC	120	2	B
On artichoke bottoms	MAFC	118	2	B
On canapes	MAFC	118	2	B
On canapes w cheese fondue sauce	MAFC	118	2	B
On mushroom caps	MAFC	118	2	B
& Pastry shells	MAFC	118	2	B
w Red wine	MAFC	121	2	B
w Red wine	MFC	56	3	B
w Tomatoes	FAIC	286	1	B
Poaching, how to	LT	94		
& Pork noodles w coriander, stir-fried	YGM	148	2	A
& Potatoes, sliced	VGCB	215	1	
Ranch style	GHAC	111	1	B
& Rice	SC	181	1	
& Rice	WC	43	1	B
& Rice bake	BHGN	195	1	B
& Romaine salad	JBC	245	1	

RECIPE	BOOK	PAGE	TD	S
Egg (*cont.*)				
Roquefort, stuffed	AC	18		
Rosy, pickled	BHGN	196	3	C
Salad	SC	362	1	
Salad	FFCB	438	1	B
Salad	BBA	14	1	A
& Asparagus	AC	46	1	
& Asparagus	JOC	84	1	B
& Bacon & horseradish	SPGT	81	1	C
Beet &	AC	47	1	
Dill &	SP	221	1	B
Filling	SC	380	1	
Filling	BCC	321	1	B
Lettuce, chopped	CF	47	1	B
Liver &	SC	362	1	
Mexican	SPGT	82	2	C
On water biscuits	CF	122	1	B
w Poppy seeds	SPGT	81	2	B
Triangles	BHGN	15	1	C
w Salmon & sorrel	MFC	53	3	A
w Salmon, stuffed	AC	17		
Sandwich	FFCB	295		
Sandwich	AC	812	1	
Sandwiches, Mexican	BCC	323	1	B
& Sardine filling	SC	381	1	
Sardine & tomato	SC	45	1	
& Sardines	SC	45	1	
Sauce	FFCB	265	1	B
◆	AC	455		
◆	JBC	262	1	
◆	NYT	447	1	
◆	MC	68	1	B
Sauce, creamy	SC	392	1	
Sauce, fish fillets poached w	JBC	69	1	
Sauce, gribiche	NYTI	111	1	B
Sausage	SC	225	1	
Sausage casserole	BHGN	195	1	B
Sauteed	JOC	195	1	B
Scotch	JOC	202	2	A
Scrambled	LM	55	1	A
◆	BCC	157	1	
◆	MSE	131	1	C
◆	AC	101	1	
Basic	SC	224	1	
w Brains	AC	359	1	
w Caviar	MFC	59	2	A
w Caviar tartlets	GF	113	2	C
w Chipped beef	AC	307	1	
w Crabmeat	NYT	278	1	A
w Cream cheese	JOC	200	1	B
Different suggestions, making	SPGT	122		
Italian-style	WC	42	1	B
Matzos w	SC	224	1	
Skillet	JBC	54	1	
w Tomato sauce	SC	224	1	
Using double boiler	JBC	53	1	
& Variations	MAFC	125	1	B
◆	JOC	200	1	A
◆	FFCB	340	1	A
◆	BHGN	191	1	A
Various seasonings	JBC	54	1	
Western	GHAC	110	1	B
Scrambling	NYT	307	1	A
& Seafood, creamed	BCC	163	1	B
Separating	BHGN	423		
Separating, how to (photographs)	LT	93		
Shirred	SC	223	1	
◆	NYT	301		
◆	MAFC	122	1	A
◆	FG	110	1	A
◆	BCC	158	1	
◆	JOC	201	2	A
w Black butter sauce	MAFC	123		

RECIPE	BOOK	PAGE	TD	S
Browned, cheese &	MAFC	123		
Chicken livers &	FFCB	338	1	A
Cream	FFCB	338	1	A
Cream	MAFC	123		
Crumbs &	FFCB	338	1	A
Florentine	FFCB	339	1	A
Gratines	MAFC	123		
Ham &	FFCB	339	1	A
Herb butter &	MAFC	123		
Mornay	FFCB	339	1	A
Piperade	MAFC	123		
Sausage &	FFCB	338	1	A
w Tomato sauce	SC	223	1	
Tomatoes, onions & peppers &	MAFC	123		
& Variations	FFCB	338	1	A
Shrimp, Bombay-style	WC	46	2	B
Sieved w cauliflower & parsley	SMG	195	1	B
Skillet, peppers &	GHAC	112	1	A
& Smoked beef	SC	226	1	
& Smoked salmon	JOC	197	1	B
Soft boiled	FFCB	337	1	
Soft cooked	BHGN	190	1	A
◆	JOC	195		
◆	NYT	302		
◆	SC	221	1	
◆	BCC	157	1	
Soft cooked, cold water method	SC	221		
Soft cooked, hot water method	SC	221		
Soup, garlic &	FGCW	366	1	B
& Spaghetti	BTSB	302	2	B
w Spanish sauce	BHGN	195	1	B
Spiced	GHAC	113	3	C
& Spinach casserole	GHAC	110	1	B
& Spinach pie	NYT	28	1	B
Spreads, hard-cooked variations	JOC	59	1	A
St. Denis	AC	110	1	
Steamed for breakfast	FG	264	1	
Storing	JOC	516		
Stuffed	AC	16	1	
◆	FFCB	308	1	A
◆	JOC	203	3	B
◆	FAIC	94	1	B
◆	FGCW	90	1	
◆	NYT	25	2	C
◆	LT	100	1	
w Anchovy	FFCB	308	1	A
w Cheese	FFCB	308	1	A
Curried	FFCB	308	1	A
Curry	FFCB	308	1	A
w Ham	FFCB	308	1	A
Garnishing	NYT	25		
On rosettes w savory sauce	JOC	203	2	B
Stuffing, how to	LT	100		
Sunny, baked	SPGT	122	1	A
Surprise	MFC	58	1	A
Suzette	AC	108	1	
Terrine, chicken &	FG	138	3	B
Timbales	SC	223	1	
Timbales, herbed	NYT	311	1	B
& Tomato	FGCW	135	1	
Appetizer	SC	45	2	
Baked	AC	107	1	
w Mushrooms, making	LT	24		
Sandwiches	GF	45	1	C
Shells	NYTI	237	1	B
Tongue &	SC	226	1	
& Tongue in aspic	AC	321	3	
& Tuna sauce	FG	353	1	
Tuopinel, poached	MFC	55	2	B
& Vegetable, stir-fry	WC	47	1	B

EGGPLANT

RECIPE	BOOK	PAGE	TD	S
Arlesienne	NYTI	246	1	B
Au gratin	GG	160	1	B
Bake, midi-poche	GG	167	2	B
Baked	AC	518	1	
Baked	JBC	310	1	B
Broiled whole	VGCB	104	1	A
Mold	VGCB	113	2	B
w Parsley, garlic & bechamel	MFC2	348	1	
Stuffed	AC	520	1	
Stuffed	SC	420	1	
Stuffed	FFCB	382	2	B
Whole	VGCB	104	1	A
Barbecued	OC	93	1	B
Basil, sauteed	MFC2	351	1	B
Batter, shrimp St. Bernard	PPLK	99	3	B
Bayou teche	PPLK	64	3	B
& Beef casserole	NYT	109	1	B
& Beef salad	BCC	272	2	B
& Beef stuffed	WC	101	2	A
Blanched	VGCB	105	1	
Blanching & sauteeing	MFC2	355	1	B
Boats, baked shaklemeshi	GG	164	1	B
Braised	VGCB	106	1	
Braised	YGM	73	1	A
Broiled	YGM	135	1	B
◆	OC	93	1	B
◆	BCC	349	1	B
◆	JBC	310	1	
◆	NYT	378	1	B
Broiled, piquant	JBC	310	1	B
Broiled, slices & variations	MFC2	346	1	
Buying	MFC2	344		
& Capers	VE	136	1	B
Caponata (see caponata)				

RECIPE	BOOK	PAGE	TD	S
Casserole	JOC	278	2	B
◆	SC	421	1	
◆	NYT	379	2	B
◆	AC	518	1	
Baked	BB	134	1	B
Lamb	JOC	430	1	B
Lamb, fennel w sausage	FGCW	304	2	B
Tomatoes, zucchini &	MAFC	503	2	B
Caviar	MSE	71	2	B
Caviar	AC	16	2	
Caviar	FFCB	53	1	B
Caviar filling w walnuts	MFC2	353	1	B
& Cheese pie w zucchini crust	JBGF	392	1	B
Cheese rolls	FGCW	273	2	B
Cheese w tomato sauce, broiled	YGM	84	1	A
& Chicken	JBGF	427	1	B
Chinese style	FGCW	272	2	B
Chunks, baked	VGCB	105	1	A
Chutney, smoked	NYTI	360	2	B
Cold, a la Grecque w tomatoes & basil	MFC2	352	1	B
Cooking	SP	165		
Creole sauce	SMG	111	1	B
Creole, stuffed	JOC	278	2	B
Croquettes, golden	GG	163	1	B
Cubes, broiled	VGCB	105	1	A
& Cumin rice	NYTI	247	1	B
Curry	MC	142	1	B
Curry	NYTI	32	1	B
Custards	LM	133	2	B
Dip	FG	338	1	B
Dressing, shrimp, rice	YGM	189	2	C

RECIPE	BOOK	PAGE	TD	S
Eggplant (*cont.*)				
Farcie	JOC	278	1	B
Filled w shrimp or crawfish w oyster sauce	PPLK	101	3	B
Fingers, deep-fat-fried	VGCB	104	1	A
Fish stew	VGCB	112	1	B
Foil	AC	518	1	
French fried	JBC	311	1	B
French fried	BB	131	1	
Fried	PPLK	34	1	A
Fried	SC	420	1	
Fried	CIC	372	1	B
Fried, pappardelle	CPPC	111	2	B
Fritters	JOC	222	1	B
Fritters	NYT	380	1	B
w Garlic, appetizer (baba ghanouj)	NYTI	541	1	B
Garlic, sauteed, bread crumbs	MFC2	347	1	
Garlicked, grilled	CFS	240	1	B
Golden, fried	FFCB	383	1	B
Gratin	MFC	170	1	B
Gratin	BBA	62	1	B
Greek	NYTI	334	2	C
Grilled	SC	334	1	
Grilled, Japanese	GRIL	76	2	B
Grilled, whole small	VGCB	105	1	A
Halves, baked	JOC	277	1	B
Halves, baked	VGCB	104	1	A
Hamburger	BB	24	1	B
w Herbs	SP	168	1	A
Herbs, baby	VGCB	109	1	B
Imam bayildi	VGCB	110	1	B
In gruyere cheese sauce (aubergines Boston)	NYT	377	2	B
w Lamb, braised	NYTI	330	1	B
w Lamb casserole	NYT	131	1	B
w Lamb noisettes, zucchini &	MFC	144	2	B
Lamb w pine nuts	FG	368	1	B
& Lamb stuffing	VGCB	204	1	
Lasagne	MC	125	1	B
Livia, marinated	SP	326	3	B
Loni Kuhn's, baked & stuffed	GG	168	2	B
Lupescu	BBA	20	3	B
Main course, tomato, casserole	MFC2	356	1	B
Marinated	FAIC	90	2	B
& Meatballs	FGCW	278	1	B
Mold, lamb &	MAFC	349	2	B
Moussaka	JBC	191	2	B
Mozzarella, baby	MCIC	383	1	B
Mutton	SC	290	2	
Neapolitan	EBE	111	2	B
New England, stuffed	AC	520	1	
Oven crisp	EBE	115	1	B
Parmesan	MC	125	1	B
Parmesan	VGCB	108	1	B
Parmesan	CIC	373	1	B
Parmigiana	GHAC	237	1	B
◆	AC	518	1	
◆	SP	169	2	B
◆	BHGN	397	1	B
◆	NYTI	432	2	B
◆	EBE	112	1	B
◆	VE	137	1	B
◆	NYT	379	2	B
Parmigiana, baked	SMG	269	1	B
Parmigiana, easy	NYT	378	1	
Pasta	NYT	331	1	B
Pasta, sauce &	VE	246	1	B
Pasta w	FGCW	276	1	B
Pate	MC	92	2	B

RECIPE	BOOK	PAGE	TD	S
Patties, fried	MCIC	387	1	B
Patties, variation I	MCIC	388	1	B
Patties, variation II	MCIC	389	1	B
& Pea curry	VE	258	1	B
Peeling, salting, blanching	MFC2	345		
Pepper & pasta salad	CPPC	64	3	B
& Pepper salad	OC	93	1	B
& Peppers	FAIC	418	1	B
& Peppers, coal-roasted	MSE	286	2	C
& Peppers, deep-fried	MCIC	385	1	B
Pickled	VGCB	114	2	B
& Pine nuts, cold	NYTI	541	1	B
Pirogue, crab, shrimp au gratin	PPLK	97	3	B
Pizza, mozzarella &	CPPC	155	3	B
Pizza, pesto &	CPPC	155	3	B
Pizza, tomatoes, parmesan &	CPPC	155	3	B
& Potato curry	VE	259	1	B
Preparing	BCC	348		
Preparing	GG	158		
Preparing	FGCW	268		
Quiche, tomatoes, olives &	FFCB	301	2	B
Rabbit rhode IV	PPLK	159	3	B
Ratatouille	AC	519	1	
Ratatouille & shrimp pie	GG	165	2	B
Rayatha, Indian	NYTI	359	1	C
& Red pepper pother	GG	159	2	B
Red, white & blue-black	VGCB	108	1	B
Relish, spicy	MC	93	1	B
& Rice Provencale	NYTI	247	1	B
Ricotta, eggless	MC	105	1	B
Ricotta, spaghetti w	MCIC	138	1	B
Rollatini	GG	161	2	B
Rolls, Marie Caratelli's	VGCB	112	2	B
Salad	VGCB	111	1	B
Basil	SP	166	1	B
Fried	GG	160	1	B
Greek	JBGF	544	1	B
Greek melitzanosalata	GG	158	1	A
Lamb, Greek	SP	208	1	B
Moroccan	BBA	143	2	B
Oriental	VGCB	111	1	B
Sammy's	FGCW	274	1	B
Sandwiches	VGCB	111	1	B
Sausages	FGCW	277	2	B
Sauteed	AC	517		
Sauteed	JBC	309	1	B
Sauteed	VGCB	104	1	A
& Diced	CIC	374	1	B
w Garlic & bread crumbs	MFC2	347	1	
Mediterranean, vegetables &	VGCB	106	1	B
Tomatoes, garlic, basil &	MFC2	351	1	B
& Scallions	MSQC	101	1	B
Scalloped	FFCB	382	1	B
Scalloped	JOC	277	1	B
Scallopini	MC	168	1	B
Seafood, stuffed	BBA	91	3	B
Sesame	VE	138	1	B
Shells, stuffed	VGCB	113	1	B
& Shrimp souffle	GG	169	2	B
& Shrimp, stuffed	SC	256	1	
Sliced, baked w cheese & tomatoes	MFC2	354	1	B
Slices				
Baked	JOC	277	1	B
Baked	VGCB	105	1	A

RECIPE	BOOK	PAGE	TD	S
Eggplant Slices (*cont.*)				
Broiled	VGCB	105	1	A
Broiled w bread crumbs	VGCB	105	1	A
Crisp fried	MCIC	384	1	B
Deep fried	JOC	277	1	B
Grilled	BB	131	1	
Sauteed	NYTI	169	1	
Sauteed	JOC	278	1	B
Variations	JOC	277	1	
Souffle	NYTI	240	1	B
♦	JOC	206	2	B
♦	VE	177	2	A
♦	MFC2	349	1	B
Souffle, shrimp &	GG	169	2	B
Soup w red pepper garnish	CPMC	172	2	B
Spaghetti	NYTI	425	1	B
Spaghetti, ricotta &	MCIC	138	1	B
Spaghetti	CIC	98	1	B
Spicy, stuffed	BHGN	396	2	B
Sticks, fried	CW	36	1	C
w Strange flavor	MSE	124	2	C
Stuffed	FFCB	306	3	B
Stuffed	JOC	278	1	B
Stuffed	NYT	377	1	B
All'Italiana	NYTI	433	1	B
& Baked	VE	135	2	B
& Baked New Orleans	FGCW	271	2	B
Greek style	MC	115	1	B
Hippie style	MC	115	1	B
Mimi's eggplant	MC	115	1	B
w Mushrooms	MAFC	501	2	B
w Mushrooms & cheese	VGCB	107	2	B
Ravioli	JBGF	390	2	B
w Rice	VGCB	107	1	B
w Sausage & red gravy	PPLK	187	3	B
w Seafood & shrimp sauce	PPLK	67	3	B
w Shrimp	SC	256	1	
Vegetable cases	VGCB	107	1	B
Style of parma	FAIC	412	1	B
Summer, tomato & basil casserole	SPGT	164	2	B
& Sweet red pepper condiment	CW	73	1	B
Szechwan style	MIE	217	1	B
Tahini spread (baba ghanoush)	JBGF	293	1	B
Thin spaghetti w	CIC	98	1	B
Tofu, Szechwan	MC	135	2	B
& Tomato casserole	JBC	311	1	B
& Tomato casserole	VE	134	1	B
Tomatoes in cream	VGCB	106	1	B
Toppings for baked	VGCB	105	1	
Toppings for sauteed	VGCB	104	1	
& Tuna salad	BBA	142	2	B
Turkish style	FGCW	269	2	B
& Ziti parmesan	JBGF	353	2	B
& Zucchini casserole	SC	420	1	
Zucchini, potato & whole garlic	MSQC	144	1	B
Egyptian cheese salad	BBA	140	1	B
Eier kringel or egg yolk cookies	AC	714	1	
Eight yolk cake	JOC	626	2	C
Einlauf (egg drop soup garnish)	SC	409	1	
El Harirah (Morrocan soup)	NYTI	482	3	C
El Presidente (drink—vermouth, rum, curacao)	JOC	39	1	
Elderberry cordial	SC	438	1	
Elderberry jam	JOC	776	2	
Elderberry jelly	SC	448	1	
Elderberry pie	AC	619	1	

RECIPE	BOOK	PAGE	TD	S
& Pork chops	MSQC	136	1	B
& Pork chops	FG	357	1	A
& Pork roast	BHGN	248	3	C
& Pork sausage	NYTI	402	2	B
& Potato hash, home fried	GG	178	1	B
Preparing	GG	172		
Puree	GG	177	1	B
Puree of	MSE	182	2	C
Raw celery, artichoke pinzimonio	FAIC	83		
Red onion, salad vinaigrette	CPMC	190	1	B
Red pepper & endive appetizer	VGCB	117	1	B
Salad, chicory &	NYT	416	1	B
Salad, lamb & hazelnut dressing	SPGT	158	2	B
Salad, mushroom &	YGM	219	2	C
Salad, red onions, sun dried tomatoes &	MSQC	53	1	B
Sausage, fresh	CFS	197	1	B
Sausage, lamb & eggplant casserole	FGCW	304	2	B
Sauteed	VGCB	122	1	
Sauteed w butter	FAIC	414	1	B
Sauteed, potatoes &	MSQC	28	1	B
Seed rock bass, broiled	FFCB	117	1	B
Seeds w tomato sauce	NYT	342	1	B
Sicilian, cold braised	GG	174	2	B
Soup, cream of	VGCB	123	1	B
Soup, fragrant	GG	172	1	B
Steamed	VGCB	122	1	
Stuffed, roast turkey w	GG	178	3	C
w Tomato garnish	MFC2	23	1	
w Tomato sauce, winter	FAIC	414	1	B
& Walnut salad	BBA	143	2	B
Winter w tomato sauce	FAIC	414	1	B
& Zucchini, sauteed	YGM	75	1	A
Fenneled chicken	FAIC	300	1	B
Feta				
Angel's hair pasta w	GHAC	260	1	B
Biscuits	CBB	589	1	B
& Onions, marinated	FG	209	2	B
Pancakes, zucchini &	MC	146	1	B
Phyllo triangles w spinach filling	SP	9	1	C
Phyllo triangles w spinach filling	MSE	284	3	C
Pizza, shrimp &	JBGF	476	2	B
Quiche, spinach &	FG	106	2	B
Salad, Egyptian	JBGF	543	1	B
& Shrimp	YGM	167	2	C
Shrimp baked w fresh	NYTI	328	1	A
& Spinach strudel	NYT	30	2	C
& Walnut dip	MC	90	1	B
Fettuccine				
Al burro	JOC	188	1	B
Alfredo	NYTI	410	2	A
◆	GHAC	261	2	B
◆	NYT	328	3	B
◆	JBC	211	2	
◆	CF	122	1	B
Alfredo w tomato & snow peas	MSE	144	2	C
Alla Romana	NYTI	411	1	A
w Broken garlic & peas	CPPC	37	1	A
Carbonara	MIE	182	1	B
Con fetti	GG	271	1	B

RECIPE	BOOK	PAGE	TD	S
Fettuccine (*cont.*)				
w Cranberry, beans, savory & olive oil	CPPC	80	2	B
Due verdi	GG	272	1	B
w Fava beans, saffron & creme fraiche	CPPC	28	2	A
Four cheese	BCC	61	1	B
w Fried zucchini	MCIC	194	3	B
w Gorgonzola sauce	CIC	134	3	B
Green	BCC	59	3	B
w Green thyme, blossoms & oysters	CPPC	45	2	A
w Green tomatoes, chicken & prosciutto	GG	378	1	B
w Louisiana shrimp sauce	CPPC	76	3	A
w Mussels	SPGT	64	2	B
& Mussel sauce	JBGF	358	2	B
Pasta shells, stuffed w spinach	CIC	145	3	B
w Prosciutto & artichoke hearts	CPPC	105	2	B
& Rabbit, stewed w red wine	CPPC	134	3	B
Salad, beef, vegetable &	JBGF	411	2	B
w Smoked salmon & fresh peas	MSQC	197	1	B
Souffle	CW	141	1	B
& Tomato, anchovy & caper sauce	MSE	177	1	C
& Tomato concasse	MSQC	149	1	B
Tossed w butter cream	MSQC	217	1	A
Tossed w cream & butter	CIC	130	3	B
& Veal, paneed	PPLK	115	2	B
& White clam sauce	CIC	135	3	B
White or green	JOC	172	2	B
Wild mushrooms & prosciutto	CPPC	24	2	A
Feuding cake, moonshine or whiskey	AC	666	2	
Fiddlehead soup	SPGT	37	2	B
Fiddleheads (coiled tips of ferns)	SPGT	37		
Fiddleheads	AC	559		
Fig				
Bars	FFBB	230	2	C
Bars	JOC	654	1	C
Bars	MHGD	313	1	C
Bread	MHGD	272	1	C
California fresh	MHGD	403	1	B
Chocolate almond	BBA	216	2	B
& Chocolates	SC	173	1	
Conserve	CW	41	1	B
Cookie filling	AC	716	1	
Cookies	SC	153	1	
Cream	JBC	101	1	
Creme de cacao	NYT	619	1	B
Curacao, fresh	NYT	619	1	B
Dates, walnuts w sherried whipped cream	CF	7	1	B
Dried	JOC	116	1	
Filling (see also filling, fig)				
◆	SC	149	1	
◆	JOC	647	1	B
◆	FFBB	231	2	C
Cookie	AC	716	1	
For coffee cake	JOC	573	1	B
Meringue	SC	149	1	
Paste	SC	149	1	

RECIPE	BOOK	PAGE	TD	S
Fillets w lemon butter	KIS	143	1	A
Fillets w mustard, broiled	JBGF	450	1	B
Fillets of fish, broiled & variations	AC	126	1	A
Fillets, pan fried	BB	53	1	
Fillets, shrimp, filled	GHAC	138	2	B
Fillets steaks, baked	BHGN	209	1	B
Filling				
Almond	JOC	647	1	B
Almond	BCC	33	1	B
Custard	SC	147	1	
Custard	JOC	648	1	B
Custard	MAFC	591	2	B
Paste for coffee cake	SC	83	1	
Paste for Danish pastries	NYT	535	1	
Anchovy	NYTI	507	2	C
Apple	FFBB	538	2	C
Apple coffee cake	JOC	573	1	C
Apple lemon	SC	149	1	
Apple strudel	NYT	541	1	
Apricot	FFBB	538	2	C
Cookie	AC	716	1	
Custard	JOC	647	1	B
For coffee cake rolls	JOC	573	1	B
Or sauce using canned apricots	MFC2	507	1	
Avocado	SC	382	1	
Banana cream	FFBB	414	1	C
Basic cream	FFBB	415	1	C
Blue cheese nut	SC	380	1	
Bourbon	FFBB	414	2	C
Butter cream	NYTI	285	1	B
Butter cream, cooked	FFBB	412	1	C
Butter cream, uncooked	FFBB	412	1	C
Butter creams	MFC2	508		
Butter custard	SC	148	1	
Butterscotch	FFCB	545	1	B
◆	JOC	646	1	B
◆	FFBB	414	1	C
◆	BHGN	70	1	B
Cabbage	BBA	16	1	C
Caramel	SC	148	1	
Chantilly cream	SC	147	1	
Cheddar cheese anchovy	SC	380	1	
Cheese	FFBB	540	2	C
Cheese for blintzes	SC	94	1	
Cheese for Danish pastries	NYT	535	1	
Cherry	BHGN	98	1	
Cherry & pineapple	SC	382	1	
Cherry strudel	NYT	543	1	
Chestnut chocolate	NYTI	290	1	
Chicken, for knishes	SC	95	1	
Chicken nut	SC	382	1	
Chocolate	SC	148	1	
Chocolate	BHGN	70	1	B
Butter cream	FFBB	412	1	C
Butter cream	FFBB	312	1	B
Butter cream, cooked	FFBB	413	1	C
Cream	GHAC	344		
Cream	FFBB	414	1	C
Custard	SC	148	1	
Walnut	GHAC	344		
Citrus butter cream	FFBB	412	1	C
Citrus butter cream, cooked	FFBB	413	1	C
Clam	BBA	15	1	A
Coconut raisin	FFBB	405	1	C
Coffee butter cream	FFBB	412	1	C
Coffee butter cream, cooked	FFBB	413	1	C

RECIPE	BOOK	PAGE	TD	S
Coffee custard	SC	148	1	
Cottage cheese	SC	380	1	
Crab meat	SC	381	1	
Crabmeat avocado	BBA	14	1	A
Cranberry	FFBB	407	2	C
Cream, basic	FFCB	542	1	B
Cream, custard	SC	148	1	
Creamy custard	GHAC	344		
Crumb fruit	JOC	573	1	B
Cucumber	SC	382	1	
Custard cream pastry	JOC	646	1	B
Date cookie	AC	716	1	
Date, for coffee cake	JOC	573	1	B
Deviled ham	NYTI	507	2	C
Dobos	SC	128	3	
Egg salad	SC	380	1	
Egg sardine	SC	381	1	
Eggplant, caviar & walnut	MFC2	353	1	B
Fig	FFBB	538	2	C
Fig	JOC	647	1	B
Fig	SC	149	1	
Cookie	AC	716	1	
For coffee cake	JOC	573	1	B
Meringue	SC	149	1	
Paste	SC	149	1	
For				
Cake rolls & variations	FFBB	306	2	C
Cakes, butter	FFCB	531	1	B
Cakes, chocolate	FFCB	531	1	B
Cakes, coffee	FFCB	531	1	B
Cakes, lemon	FFCB	531	1	B
Coffee cakes, nuts & variations	JOC	573	1	B
Cream puff shells	JOC	598	2	
Creme chantilly & variations	JOC	645	1	C
Eclairs	JOC	598	2	
Grilled cheese, anchovy paste & sardines	SC	385	1	
Grilled cheese, brick cheese & ham	SC	385	1	
Grilled cheese, brick cheese & tomatoes	SC	385	1	
Grilled cheese, chicken & mushrooms	SC	385	1	
Grilled cheese & chicken salad	SC	385	1	
Grilled cheese, peanut butter & tomato	SC	385	1	
Grilled cheese, sweetbread & cheese	SC	385	1	
Jelly roll	FFCB	522	1	B
Omelettes	MAFC	135		
Stuffed tomatoes	JOC	89		
Tart shells, fully baked	FFCB	69	2	C
Tart shells, partially baked	FFCB	69	1	C
Frosting for cakes	FFBB	393		
Fruit, chopped	JOC	647	1	B
Fruit nut	SC	382	1	
Fruit, whipped	SC	150	1	
Ginger fruit	JOC	647	1	B
Gingerbread, for coffee cake	SC	83	1	
Golden, sour cream	SC	148	1	
Ham	SC	381	1	
Hazelnut custard	JOC	648	1	B
Horseradish	SC	382	1	

RECIPE	BOOK	PAGE	TD	S
Filling (*cont.*)				
Jam	FFBB	539	1	C
Jam, whipped	SC	150	1	
Jelly	NYTI	11	1	B
Lady Baltimore	FFBB	407	2	C
Lady Baltimore	AC	654	2	
Lemon	BHGN	92	1	
◆	JOC	646	1	B
◆	NYT	570	1	
◆	FFCB	545	1	A
Butter	MAFC	676	1	B
Butter custard	FFBB	415	1	C
Cornstarch	SC	148	1	
Custard	SC	148	1	
For cakes	FFCB	531	1	B
Fresh	GHAC	344		
Or orange cream	MFC2	484	1	
Orange custard	JOC	647	1	B
Liqueur butter cream	FFBB	412	1	C
Liqueur butter cream, cooked	FFBB	413	1	C
Lord Baltimore	FFBB	407	2	C
Meringue butter cream frosting	MFC2	489	1	B
Mocha	JOC	646	1	B
Mohn	JOC	574	1	C
Mushroom	SC	382	1	
Mushroom rice	BBA	16	1	C
Nut	FFBB	539	1	C
Nut fruit meringue	SC	149	1	
Nut paste for coffee cake	SC	83	1	
Orange	FFCB	545	1	B
Orange cream	JOC	647	2	B
Orange custard	JOC	647	1	B
Orange custard	SC	148	1	
Pate de foie gras, mock	SC	382	1	
Peanut butter	SC	382	1	
Pear alligator	SC	382	1	

RECIPE	BOOK	PAGE	TD	S
Pecan	SC	149	1	
Pecan, toasted	JOC	648	1	A
Pennsylvania Dutch	NYT	223	1	B
Pineapple cookie	AC	716	1	
Pineapple marshmallow	SC	149	1	
Poppy seed	JOC	574	1	C
Poppy seed cockaigne	JOC	573	1	B
Poppy seed for coffee cake	SC	83	1	
Pot cheese	JOC	574	1	B
Potato, for blintzes	SC	94	1	
Potato, for knishes	SC	95	1	
Prune	FFBB	539	2	C
Prune	SC	149	1	
Cookie	AC	716	1	
For coffee cake rolls	JOC	573	1	B
For Danish pastries	NYT	535	1	
For pie or kuchen	SC	83	1	
Raisin	JOC	647	1	B
Raisin	SC	149	1	
Ricotta	JOC	574	1	B
Ricotta	NYTI	443	1	
Ricotta chocolate	JOC	646	1	C
Ricotta for cream puffs	NYTI	444	1	
Ricotta green cannelloni	FAIC	186	2	C
Roquefort	BBA	15	1	A
Roquefort cheese	NYTI	507	2	C
Salmon	SC	381	1	
Seafood	SC	381	1	
Smoked beef	SC	381	1	
Smoked salmon kasha	BBA	16	1	C
Sour cream	SC	148	1	
Strawberry cream	NYT	552	1	
Strawberry cream	SC	149	1	

RECIPE	BOOK	PAGE	TD	S
Sweetbread	SC	382	1	
Tuna fish	SC	381	1	
Vanilla				
Chiffon cream	FFBB	416	1	C
Cream	FFBB	413	1	C
Cream for Danish pastries	NYT	535	1	
Cream rich	NYTI	290	1	
Custard	SC	147	1	
Walnut	SC	150	1	
Walnut for coffee cake	SC	83	1	
Walnut toasted	JOC	648	1	A
Whipped cream	SC	147	1	
Whipped cream nut brittle	SC	147	1	
Whipped cream pineapple & nut	SC	147	1	
Fines herbes dressing	NYT	437	1	B
Finger bowl, preparing a	GHAC	194		
Finger roll fillings	JOC	245		
Finger rolls	FFCB	474	2	B
Finger rolls	NYT	474	2	
Finger rolls	SC	75	2	
Fingerhuetchen (noodle puffs for soup)	SC	409	1	
Finnan haddie (fish)	SC	245	2	
A la creme	NYTI	137	2	B
Baked	JOC	356	2	B
Baked milk	FFCB	150	1	B
Broiled	SC	246	1	
Cream	SC	246	1	
Creamed	JOC	356	1	
Creamed	SC	245	1	
Delmonico	NYT	236	1	B
Delmonico	FFCB	150	1	B
Finnish polar bear's eye w beets	GG	46	2	B
Finocchio				
Braised w olive oil	CIC	378	1	B
Fried	CIC	378	1	B
Salad	CIC	407	1	B
Sauteed w butter & cheese	CIC	377	1	B
Sea bass	MCIC	206	1	B
Fireless cooking	JOC	133		
First loaf	CBB	39	2	C
Fish				
A l'orange, baked	BHGN	213	1	B
A la meuniere	BCC	183	1	B
All about	JBC	62		
Aspics, a fine court bouillon for	AC	135	1	
Au bleu, about cooking	JOC	348		
Au citron	NYTI	483	2	B
Baked	FG	337	1	B
Baked	AC	140	1	
Baked	BCC	177	1	A
A la Maurice	SC	239	1	A
Ashes	OC	153	3	B
Curried	FG	300	2	B
w Garlic confit	CPMC	113	2	B
In a covered dish	JOC	352	1	B
In a crust boned whole	FAIC	259	3	B
In foil	JOC	352	1	A
w Mushrooms	BHGN	209	1	B
w Onions	VGCB	183	1	B
Small whole	JBC	67	1	B
w Sour cream	JOC	352	1	B
& Stuffed	JOC	352	2	B
& Stuffed	BCC	179	2	B
& Stuffed whole	JBC	67	2	B
Unstuffed	JOC	350	1	
Whole	SC	236	1	

RECIPE	BOOK	PAGE	TD	S
Old fashioned	FFCB	99	2	C
Old fashioned New England	AC	179	1	
Superb	AC	179	2	
Cleaning	FFCB	108		
Cleaning & preparing	JOC	344		
Consomme	CBSS	60	3	C
Cooked in a paper bag	FAIC	245	1	B
Cooking time for	ACCB	123		
Cooking tips on	JOC	346		
Creamed & variations	FFCB	144	1	B
Creole	BHGN	211	1	B
Curing & smoking	SC	247		
Deep fat	JOC	350	1	
Deviled sauce	WC	70	1	A
Elvira	SP	122	2	A
Extract	BTSB	39	2	C
Filled noodles, toasted	FG	326	1	
Fillet poached w white wine & cream sauce	MAFC	211	2	B
Filleting	JOC	345		
Filleting, flat, how to	MFC	16		
Filleting, whole	MFC	18		
Fillets	WC	75	1	B
A la bonne femme	JOC	351	1	B
Baked	JBC	67	1	B
Baked	SMG	92	1	B
Baked in wine	JOC	352	1	B
Bonne femme	NYT	264	1	B
Broiled	SMG	95	1	B
Broiled	JBC	64	1	B
Broiled amandine	JBC	64	1	
Broiled w anchovy butter	SMG	94	1	B
Broiled & cheesed	JBC	64	1	
Broiled w crusty top	JBC	64	1	
Broiled mornay	JBC	65	1	
Broiled w mushrooms	JBC	64	1	
Broiled w shrimp sauce	JBC	64	1	
Broiled w tomato	JBC	64	1	
Broiled in wine	JBC	64	1	
Chinese	KIS	156	1	A
Cold poached	JBC	70	1	
Corn husks in	GHAC	223	1	B
Easy, baked	BHGN	209	1	B
Ecrevisses	MAFC	216	2	B
En papillotes & variations	JBC	71	2	
Fried	CW	112	1	B
Ginger	NYT	264	1	B
Grilled	SC	332	1	
Herb broiled	MIE	153	1	B
In foil	SC	332	1	
In foil, cooked	BB	53	1	
Marguery, baked w seafood sauce	JOC	351	2	B
Marinara	KIS	123	1	A
Molded & filled	JOC	352	2	B
Mushrooms &	MAFC	216	2	B
Mussels, shrimp &	MAFC	214	2	B
Nicoise	JBC	70	1	
On spinach, shrimp, mushrooms &	JOC	351	2	A
Oven fried, small	JOC	350	1	
Pan fried	BB	53	1	
Pan fried	CF	42	1	B
Piemontese	NYTI	380	1	B
Plaza Athenee	NYT	263	1	B
Poached	JBC	69	1	B

RECIPE	BOOK	PAGE	TD	S
Fish Fillets (*cont.*)				
Poached & cheese sauce	SC	235	1	
Poached & curry sauce	JBC	69	1	
Poached & egg sauce	JBC	69	1	
Poached & milk smoked	AC	136	1	
Poached mornay	JBC	70	1	
Poached w mushroom sauce	JBC	69	1	
Poached w seafood sauce	JBC	69	1	
Poached w white wine	MAFC	208	1	B
Poached w white wine & mushrooms	MAFC	210	2	B
Poached w white wine & vegetables	MAFC	211	2	B
Poached in wine sauce	JBC	69	1	
Quick baked	JOC	351	1	A
Ratatouille	JBGF	450	1	B
Sauteed amandine	JOC	350	1	
Sauteed, Palm Beach	JOC	350	1	A
Shellfish & mushrooms	MAFC	215	2	B
Shellfish & truffles	MAFC	215	2	B
Skewered	SC	333	1	
Stuffed	MAFC	216	2	B
Veronique	MIE	158	1	B
w Walnut coating	GHAC	142	1	B
Fillings for sandwiches	FFCB	288	1	A
Flambe	BB	52	1	
Flambe w fennel	BBA	86	1	B
Flambeed	AC	127	1	
Florentine	BHGN	215	1	B
For appetizers, smoked	AC	27		
Freezing	BHGN	143		
Fresh season	SC	235		
Freshness, checking	FG	64		
Fried	JOC	349	1	
Deep	AC	131	1	
Deep	BCC	183	1	B
Deep, fat	SC	236	1	
Deep, marinated	JOC	350	1	A
New Orleans	FGCW	118	1	B
Oven	BCC	183	1	B
Oven	BHGN	208	1	A
Pan	BB	53	1	
◆	BHGN	208	1	A
◆	SC	236	1	
◆	BCC	183	1	B
◆	AC	128	1	
Skillet	BHGN	38	1	B
Toys for children	FG	317	1	B
Wrapped in paper	NYTI	41	1	B
Frozen, cooking	JOC	347		
Fry Hawaiian style	WC	65	1	B
Frying, suitable for	SC	236		
& Garlic & green pepper	FG	258	2	A
Garlic & salsa	BCC	180	1	B
Grilled, whole	OC	144	3	B
◆	SC	332	1	
◆	OC	147	2	B
◆	BB	52	1	
Grilling	GR	50		
Hash	FFCB	145	1	B
Hash, deluxe	WC	65	1	B
Head sauce, spaghetti &	MCIC	133	2	B
House punch	FFCB	743	2	C
House punch	JOC	49	1	

RECIPE	BOOK	PAGE	TD	S
House punch	BB	165	1	C
In a basket	BHGN	38	1	B
In aspic cockaigne	JOC	353	2	B
In champagne sauce	FGCW	121	1	B
In foil	BCC	180	1	A
Kebab	BBA	86	1	B
Kebab Egyptian style	OC	142	2	B
Kebabs	JOC	349	1	B
Kebabs, marinated	BHGN	39	2	B
Kippered	AC	28		
& Lettuce soup	FG	316	1	B
Lettuce wrapped stuffed fillets of	VGCB	253	2	B
Loaf, quick	JOC	239	1	B
Marinara sauce	JBC	214	1	
Mediterranean	NYTI	368	1	B
Mold, layered	SC	371	2	
Mold, Swedish	NYT	269	2	B
Molded, celery & olive salad	SC	371	2	
Molded, creamed	JOC	98	2	B
Molded w cucumber sauce	SC	371	2	
Mousse	JOC	209	2	B
◆	MAFC	562	2	C
◆	FFCB	146	1	B
◆	FFCB	450	2	B
Mousse, smoked	MFC	29	3	B
Mussel soup Normandie	CBSS	195	3	B
Mustard-topped	BCC	182	1	B
Nicoise, sauteed	JBC	66	1	
w Noodles, stuffed	FG	326	1	
w Onions, stuffed	NYT	389	1	B
Orly	NYTI	147	3	C
Oyster chowder	SMG	130	1	B
Oyster sauce for	JOC	324	1	B
Packs, barbecue, preparing	GHAC	224		

RECIPE	BOOK	PAGE	TD	S
Parcels	OC	153	2	B
Parmigiana, baked	NYT	263	1	B
Paste, Chinese	FG	314	1	B
Pate, tricolor	LM	108	2	C
Paupiettes w spinach	VGCB	266	2	B
w Pecan butter sauce	PPLK	54	2	B
& Pepper salad	BCC	268	2	B
& Peppers, stir-fried	BHGN	208	1	B
& Peppers, stuffed	JOC	289	2	
& Peppers, stuffed	NYT	392	1	B
Pickled	JOC	353	3	
Pickled	SC	235	3	
Pickled, onions &	GG	239	3	C
Pickled, raw	NYTI	465	2	B
Pie	AC	170	1	
Pie w biscuit crust	AC	170	1	
Pie, mushrooms &	AC	170	1	
Planked	JOC	352	1	B
Planked	SC	237	1	
Planking the fish (cooking in fireplace) (photographs)	OC	70		
Planking, suitable for	SC	236		
Poached	FAIC	239	1	
Poached	AC	134	1	
Poached	SC	235	1	
Center cut of	JBC	71	1	
Center slice of	JBC	70	1	
w Cold avocado mayonnaise	GG	40	1	B
w Cucumber dill sauce	FG	241	2	B
w Dill sauce	BHGN	212	1	B
Whole	JBC	71	1	
Poaching, how to	JOC	348		
Portuguese-style	NYTI	501	1	B
& Potato supper, quick	BHGN	215	1	B

RECIPE	BOOK	PAGE	TD	S
Fish (*cont.*)				
Preparing for cooking	SC	234		
Pudding, Danish	NYTI	76	2	B
Quenelles	MAFC	185	3	B
Quenelles & oysters	MAFC	188	2	B
Ragout w garlic croutons	CPMC	95	2	B
w Rainbow sauce	NYTI	41	1	B
Ravioli, naked	FAIC	228	1	B
Roasted	FAIC	244	1	B
Roe ramekins, canned	JOC	242	1	A
Salad	SC	363	1	C
Salad, raw, seviche	FB	67	2	B
Salad, smoked	BCC	268	2	B
Salt	AC	144		
Sauce for boiled or poached	SC	236		
Sauce, Vietnamese	CFS	85	1	A
Sauteed fillets meuniere	JBC	66	1	B
Sauteed whole meuniere	JBC	66	1	B
Scaling, removing fins from	FFCB	108		
Scalloped	FFCB	146	1	B
Scalloped	SC	242	1	
Serbian	NYTI	550	2	B
Shellfish, about (chart)	FFCB	105		
Skewered	OC	150	2	B
Skinning	FFCB	108		
Skinning	SC	234		
Skinning, whole	SC	234		
Smoked	JBC	8	1	
Smoked, making	LM	111		
Souffle	FFCB	146	1	B
Souffle	MAFC	168	3	B
Souffle baked on a platter	MAFC	170	3	B
Souffle, cooked	JOC	206	2	B
Soup	SMG	99	1	B
◆	MCIC	210	1	B
◆	NYTI	117	2	B
◆	SC	404	1	
◆	CIC	235	2	B
All shellfish	MCIC	238	2	B
Au cognac	NYTI	117	1	B
Billi Bi	CBSS	205	2	B
w Clams, French	SMG	100	1	B
Creamed	NYTI	120	1	B
Garlic based (bourride aioli)	GF	218	2	C
Italian	JBGF	342	1	B
Quick	BCC	308	1	B
Southampton rouille w croutons	GF	152	2	B
Straight Wharf	VGCB	320	1	B
Strained	MAFC	50	1	B
w Trout cappelletti, smoked	CPPC	46	3	B
Tuscan Livorno style	FAIC	257	2	B
w Vegetables	SMG	102	2	B
Spicy, coating mix (shake it & bake it)	KIS	359	1	C
Spread, smoked	SC	38	2	
Steaks				
Baked	JBC	67	1	B
Broiled	JBC	65	1	
Broiled	BCC	180	1	A
En papillotes & variations	JBC	71	2	
Foil cooked	BB	53	1	
Grilled	SC	332	1	
Grilled	BB	52	1	

RECIPE	BOOK	PAGE	TD	S
Grilled w chili butter	GHAC	223	1	B
Lemon basted	CFS	216	1	B
Marguery, baked w seafood sauce	JOC	351	2	B
Marinated	BB	53	1	
Poached	JOC	351	1	A
Steamed	NYTI	40	1	B
Steamed	AC	137		
Steamed between two plates	MCIC	218	1	B
Steamed w ginger	YGM	118	1	A
Steamed w lemon	FG	266	1	B
Steaming, how to	JOC	348		
Stew (cioppino)	AC	181	1	
Stew (cacciucco)	NYT	266	2	B
African	NYTI	74	1	B
Creamy	VGCB	208	2	B
Eggplant &	VGCB	112	1	B
Fish to use for	MFC2	42		
Normandy w sole, shellfish & wine sauce	MFC2	46	3	C
Provencale w aioli (garlic mayo)	MFC2	50	2	B
Solianka	AC	180	1	
Sticks, oven-fried, small	JOC	350	1	
Stock	JOC	491	2	
◆	GF	246	1	C
◆	GG	410	1	B
◆	FFCB	83	2	B
◆	JBGF	311	1	B
◆	LM	42	2	B
◆	CBSS	53	3	C
◆	NYT	229	1	C
◆	NYTI	116	1	C
◆	SP	343	2	C
◆	MFC	65	2	B
◆	NYTI	368	1	

RECIPE	BOOK	PAGE	TD	S
Stock, emergency	MAFC	115	1	B
Stock w white wine	MAFC	114	1	B
Strange flavor	MSE	125	3	C
Stuffed				
w Corn	BHGN	212	2	B
Whole	SC	242	2	
Whole aspic	FAIC	264	3	B
w Wild rice	BHGN	212	2	B
Stuffing for, easy	VGCB	126	1	B
Stuffing, tomatoes baked w	FFCB	417	2	B
Sweet & sour	SC	46	1	
Sweet & sour	BHGN	215	1	B
Tahiti style	NYT	261	2	B
Tandoori	OC	154	2	A
Terrine	MFC	29	3	B
Testing for doneness	BHGN	207		
Timbale	JOC	209	2	B
Tips selecting	BCC	176		
Tricolor pate of	LM	108	2	C
Under a bed of ratatouille	YGM	104	1	A
& Vegetable casserole	SC	241	1	
Veloute	NYT	445	1	B
Veloute, thick	BBA	19	1	B
w Vinegar sauce, baked	FG	68	1	B
Whole, serving	GHAC	140		
Whole, stuffed w seafood	PPLK	60	3	B
Fisherman's salad	MFC	189	2	B
Fishwiches, curried	BHGN	215	1	B
Five cup salad	BHGN	342	2	B
Five spice powder, Chinese	BBA	165	1	A
Five spice powder, Chinese	BTSB	200	2	C
Five spice powder, homemade	BHGN	311	1	

RECIPE	BOOK	PAGE	TD	S
Fizz	SC	62	1	
Flageolets Bretonne (French beans)	NYTI	241	3	B
Flageolets Bretonne style	NYT	358	2	B
Flageolets w red runner beans	MSQC	17	1	B
Flaky pastry	SC	342	1	
Flambeing fruits	JOC	108		
Flamiche (onion cheese tart)	GG	250	2	B
Flammifero broccoli	GG	58	2	B
Flan				
Apple	MAFC	657	1	B
Blackberry	MAFC	657	1	B
Blueberry	MAFC	657	1	B
Cherry	MAFC	655	1	B
Cherry & almonds	MAFC	658	1	B
Cherry liqueur	MAFC	656	1	B
Corn, hot	GG	137	2	B
De Naranja	BBA	211	3	B
Fruit	JOC	609	2	B
Pastry, rich	MHGD	187	2	B
Pear	MAFC	656	1	B
Pear & almonds	MAFC	658	1	B
Pineapple	WC	138	1	B
Pineapple	NYTI	504	2	B
Plum	MAFC	657	1	B
Rings, large shells or	AC	636	1	
Flank steak	JOC	401	1	
Barbecued	OC	99	1	B
Broiled	SC	271	1	
Carving (photographs)	LT	330		
Chili, Oriental	BB	20	1	B
Definition	AC	261		
Dressing	JOC	416	2	B
Greens butterflied	GG	196	2	B
Grilled	SC	328	1	
w Herb stuffing	NYT	92	2	B
Marinated	MIE	116	3	B
w Mustard marinade	FGCW	237	2	B
Oriental	BB	20	1	B
Oriental	NYTI	48	2	B
Rolled & stuffed w spinach	VGCB	268	2	B
Sandwiches, grilled	AC	22	2	
Sauteed, gingered	MSE	157	3	C
Sesame marinade	GRIL	83	2	B
Stuffing (photographs)	LT	274		
Tennessee	CFS	86	3	B
w Wine sauce	SC	271	2	
Flapjacks corn crisp	JOC	215	1	C
Flatbread	FFBB	595	3	C
w Bacon	MCIC	57	3	B
w Bacon Bolognese	MCIC	58	3	B
Italian country	CBB	686	2	C
Middle Eastern	CBB	691	2	B
Norwegian	CBB	689	1	B
w Onion topping	MCIC	53	3	B
Plain salt	MCIC	54	3	B
w Raisins	CBB	429	3	B
w Rosemary	MCIC	56	3	B
w Sage	MCIC	55	3	B
Stone griddled, Romagna style	MCIC	72	2	B
Flatfish fillets, making protective packets for	OC	72		
Flemish sauce for poached salmon or trout	NYT	449	1	A
Fleurons (puff-pastry puffs)	MFC2	132		
Flip (drink—egg, sugar, brandy)	JOC	48	1	A

RECIPE	BOOK	PAGE	TD	S
Flip	SC	60	1	A
Floating iceberg	MHGD	384	2	B
Floating island	GF	102	2	C
◆	MSE	253	3	C
◆	LT	336	2	
◆	JOC	685	2	B
◆	SC	199	1	
◆	MFC	233	2	B
◆	LM	326	1	C
◆	NYT	597	2	C
◆	AC	728	2	
◆	FFCB	608	2	B
Florentine sauce	JOC	323	1	B
Florentines	JOC	670	1	C
Florentines	NYTI	287	1	C
Florentines	FFBB	241	2	C
Flounder				
Asparagus stuffed	JBGF	452	1	B
Dressed & baked	JBGF	451	1	B
w Fennel, poached, shrimp &	GG	180	2	B
Filet of grapes	EBE	92	2	B
Fillets, broiled w mustard	SMG	96	1	B
Fillets, marinated	JOC	355	1	B
Fillets w red butter sauce	CFS	208	1	B
w Grapefruit	WC	75	1	B
w Green chili sauce	GHAC	138	1	B
w Mexican hot sauce	JBGF	453	2	B
w Orange sauce & pine nuts	YGM	126	1	A
Pickled	NYT	236	3	B
w Red hot nasturtium butter	CFS	226	2	A
& Shrimp filled fillets	GHAC	138	2	B
Stuffed	BHGN	211	2	B
w Crab	SMG	146	1	B
Gulf Coast	NYT	236	1	B

RECIPE	BOOK	PAGE	TD	S
w Seafood	PPLK	62	3	B
w Spinach	GHAC	138	1	B
& Tarragon, striped, w Pernod cream	CFS	225	1	A
Flour	FFBB	14		
Bread, all-rye	JOC	560	2	B
Definitions	BHGN	426		
Formula, Cornell triple-rich	JOC	556	1	
Measuring chart	MFC2	544		
Non-wheat	JOC	498		
Paste pie crust	SC	342	1	
Preparing, browned	AC	456		
Flouring foods	JOC	501		
Flouring seasoned	JOC	502	3	
Flower canapes	JOC	53		
Flower cups	SP	286	2	C
Flowers, candied	NYT	635	1	B
Flowers for salads	AC	74		
Fluffy cake	SC	109	1	B
Fluffy frosting	AC	693	1	
Flummery (almond white custard)	CF	151	1	B
Foamy sauce	AC	742	1	
Foamy sauce	JOC	714	1	B
Foamy sauce	FFCB	640	1	B
Foamy sauce, brandied	NYT	615	2	B
Focaccia (Italian flat-bread)	MSE	143	3	B
Foh opp (Chinese roast duck)	NYTI	60	2	B
Foie gras	SPGT	249		
Foie gras	SC	381	1	
Biscuits w	JBC	4	1	
Half-boned chicken stuffed w	MFC2	271	2	
Liver pastes	JOC	61	1	
& Pork sausages, veal, truffles	MFC2	295	3	

RECIPE	BOOK	PAGE	TD	S
Freezing (*cont.*)				
Meat	BHGN	143		
Process	BHGN	125		
Shellfish	BHGN	143		
Vegetables	BHGN	127		
Wrapping	BHGN	143		
French 75	SC	63	1	
French bread	FFCB	468	3	C
◆	BHGN	60	2	B
◆	VE	29	2	B
◆	NYT	463	2	B
◆	JBC	16	2	B
◆	BCC	45	2	C
◆	SC	67	2	C
◆	FFBB	445	2	C
◆	JOC	557	3	B
Barbecued	EBE	103	1	B
Blue ribbon	CBB	270	2	C
Classic	FG	232	3	C
w Egg whites	CBB	256	3	C
Equipment needed for making	MFC2	57		
Herbed	SMG	131	1	B
Herbed	BB	112	1	B
Monsieur Monfort's	CBB	626	3	C
Pan toasted	MSQC	29	1	A
Plain	MFC2	57	3	C
Problems making	MFC2	73		
Problems & solutions	MFC2	73		
Sourdough, homecoming	CBB	278	3	C
Stuffed	NYT	48	1	C
Technique for making	MFC2	59		
Yeast raised	JBC	17	2	B
French dressing	SP	222	1	B
◆	NYT	437	1	A
◆	BHGN	352	1	A
◆	SC	373	1	
◆	JBC	256		
◆	JOC	311	1	A
◆	BCC	300	1	B
Basic	BB	142	1	
Celery seed	SC	373	1	
Classic	BCC	300	1	A
Classic	GHAC	284	1	B
Cream cheese	JOC	311	1	A
Creamy	BHGN	351	1	B
Creamy	JBGF	550	1	B
For fruit salad	SC	378	1	
Garlic	SC	373	1	
& Variations	FFCB	450	1	B
French fries	JOC	295	1	
French fries	VGCB	218	1	
French fries	BHGN	400	1	
French ice cream	SC	205	2	
French loaves, individual	BHGN	60	2	B
French pancakes (see pancakes, French)				
French puffs	BCC	31	1	C
French quarter sauce	NYT	449	1	A
French spice bread	MHGD	265	2	C
French toast	FFCB	491	1	B
◆	SC	72	1	
◆	BCC	30	1	C
◆	GHAC	371		
◆	JOC	587	1	
◆	BHGN	88	1	B
Cheese	JOC	247	1	B
Cholesterol-controlled	JBGF	510	1	B
Fabulous	SPGT	122	1	B
Matzos	SC	72	1	
Tomato	JOC	247		
French vanilla ice cream	NYTI	307	3	B
French vanilla ice cream	FFCB	629	3	C

RECIPE	BOOK	PAGE	TD	S
Fritter (*cont.*)				
Batter	JOC	221		
Batter, beer	FFCB	358	1	B
Batter for fruit	JOC	221	2	C
Batter, rich	SC	101	1	
Beans	SC	407	1	
Cherry	SC	102	1	
Clam	GHAC	119	1	B
Clam	FFCB	65	1	C
Corn (see also corn fritters)				
Corn, Dorothy Shank's Amish	GG	133	1	B
French	JOC	706	2	B
Fritterra	GG	248	1	B
Fruit	SC	102	1	
Fruit	FFCB	647	3	C
Fruit, Dutch	CBB	587	2	C
Frying	SC	101		
Garnish	JOC	172	1	A
Matzos	SC	193	1	
Matzos, filled	SC	194	2	
Matzos, fruit	SC	193	1	
Okra & corn	CW	93	1	C
"Ole Miss" okra	GG	226	3	B
Pancake	FAIC	467	1	B
Pineapple	SC	101	2	
Pineapple, crushed	SC	102	1	
Queen	SC	102	1	
Rice	FAIC	485	1	B
Rice	GHAC	370	2	C
Ricotta	MCIC	436	1	B
Rye	NYT	489	1	A
Sweet pastry	CIC	433	1	B
Unsweetened choux paste	JOC	221	2	
Zucchini	FGCW	93	2	B
Fritto dolce	NYTI	375	3	C
Fritto misto	WC	71	1	B
Fritto misto	NYT	272	2	B
Fritto misto	BBA	69	3	B
Frog's legs	LM	79	2	A
A la creme	NYTI	159	2	B
All about	JOC	379		
Braised	JOC	379	2	B
Broiled	OC	159	2	B
Forestiere	JOC	380	2	
Fried	AC	184	1	
Fried in deep fat	JOC	380	2	
Mousseline w watercress sauce	MFC	118	3	B
w Mushroom sauce	JOC	380	2	A
Newburg	SC	249	2	
Provencale	NYTI	159	2	B
Provencale	NYT	296	2	B
Sauteed	AC	184	1	
Sauteed	SC	249	2	
Frogs in the hole (sausages baked in batter)	FAIC	355	2	B
Fromage Romanesque	VE	205	1	B
Frosted snowmen	GHAC	352	1	C
Frosting				
A cake	NSD	23		
Banana butter	BHGN	160	1	
Black walnut fudge	NYT	575	1	B
Boiled	AC	693	1	
Brandy	SC	144	1	
Brown				
Beauty	SC	146	1	
Butter	SC	144	1	
Butter & brandy	SC	144	1	
Sugar	FFBB	403	1	C
Sugar & marshmallow	SC	145	1	
Browned butter	BHGN	161	1	
Butter	BHGN	104	1	B

RECIPE	BOOK	PAGE	TD	S
Butter	JBC	37	1	
Butter	FFBB	275	1	B
I	FFCB	539	1	A
II	FFCB	539	1	B
Basic	SC	143	1	
Cream	GHAC	344		
Cream & variations	AC	695	1	
Fluffy	FFCB	539	1	B
Quick	NYT	573	1	B
Buttercream	NYTI	11	2	B
Cakes	BCC	79		
Caramel	AC	694	1	
◆	NYT	576	1	B
◆	FFCB	540	1	B
◆	FFBB	406	1	C
◆	BCC	78	1	C
◆	SC	146	1	
Butter	SC	143	1	
Economy	SC	147	1	
Fudge	SC	147	1	
Quick	SC	147	1	
Quick	FFCB	537	1	B
Chocolate	SP	290	1	B
◆	BCC	78	1	C
◆	BBA	189	1	B
◆	BCC	99	1	
◆	SC	139	1	
◆	BCC	138	1	
◆	NYTI	287	1	B
◆	FFBB	275	1	B
◆	AC	694	1	
◆	JBC	37	1	
◆	BHGN	154	1	
◆	FFCB	536	1	B
Brandy	SC	146	1	
Butter	FFBB	398	1	C
Butter	SC	143	1	
Butter	BHGN	104	1	B
Butter cream	FFBB	312	1	B
Butter cream, orange	AC	695	1	
Caramel	SC	146	1	
Chip	FFBB	400	1	C
Cream	NYT	574	1	B
Creamy	SC	146	1	
Creamy	FFCB	536	1	B
Fluffy	SC	144	1	
For cream puffs & eclairs	FFCB	536	1	B
Fudge	AC	694	1	
Hungarian	SC	144	1	
Meringue	SC	145	1	
& Molasses	SC	146	1	
Mousse	BBA	188	2	C
Nut	SC	146	1	
Rich	BBA	187	1	B
& Sour cream	BHGN	106	1	B
& Sour cream	GHAC	331	1	
Union Hotel	FFBB	398	1	C
Whipped	SC	146	1	
& Whipped cream	FFBB	401	1	C
Cinnamon	AC	693	1	
Coconut	FFBB	406	1	C
Coconut	SC	145	1	
Coconut	FFCB	540	1	B
Broiled	SC	144	1	
Pecan	NYT	576	1	B
Pecan	BHGN	105	1	B
Raisin	FFBB	405	1	C
Coffee	FFBB	406	1	C
Coffee	FFCB	540	1	B
Coffee butter	SC	143	1	
Confectioners' for decoration	FFBB	397	1	C
Confectioners' I	FFCB	535	1	B
Confectioners' II	FFCB	535	1	B
Continental	FFBB	402	1	C
Continental chocolate	FFBB	403	1	C

RECIPE	BOOK	PAGE	TD	S
Frosting (*cont.*)				
Continental, rum	FFBB	403	1	C
Corn syrup	SC	146	1	
Cranberry	FFBB	407	2	C
Cream cheese	BCC	77	1	V
◆	BHGN	105	1	B
◆	FFBB	404	1	C
◆	SC	144	1	
◆	FFCB	538	1	B
◆	GHAC	323		
Cream cheese & chocolate	SC	144	1	
Creamy butter	BHGN	104	1	B
Creamy white	BHGN	104	1	B
Decorating w	GHAC	338		
Decorative I	NYT	576	1	B
Decorative II	NYT	577	1	B
Fluffy	AC	693	1	
Fluffy, boiled	GHAC	331	1	
Fluffy white	BHGN	105	1	B
For petit fours variations	FFCB	541	2	B
Four minute	SC	145	1	
Fudge	NYT	574	1	B
◆	FFBB	399	1	C
◆	SC	146	1	
◆	BCC	78	1	B
◆	FFCB	537	1	B
◆	BHGN	106	2	B
Fudge, quick	FFCB	537	1	B
Fudge, quick	GHAC	331	1	
Ginger	AC	693	1	
Golden butter	BHGN	98	1	
Jelly	FFBB	408	1	C
Lady Baltimore	FFBB	407	2	C
Lemon	FFCB	540	1	B
Lemon	FFBB	275	1	B
Lemon butter	SC	144	1	
Lemon butter	BHGN	104	1	B
Lemon fluff	SC	145	1	

RECIPE	BOOK	PAGE	TD	S
Lord Baltimore	FFBB	407	2	C
Maple	SC	145	1	
Maple	FFBB	406	1	C
Maple	FFCB	538	1	B
Maple butter cream	AC	695	1	
Marshmallow	SC	145	1	
Marshmallow	SC	139	1	
Marshmallow	AC	693	1	
Meringue	SC	145	1	
Meringue, butter cream filling &	MFC2	489	1	B
Mocha	SC	139	1	
Mocha	NYTI	286	1	B
Mocha	BHGN	161	1	
Butter	SC	144	1	
Butter	BHGN	104	1	B
Butter cream	GHAC	344		
Cream	NYT	575	1	B
Nutty coconut	FFBB	399	1	C
Orange	FFBB	275	1	B
Orange	FFCB	540	1	B
Orange butter	SC	144	1	
Orange butter	BHGN	104	1	B
Orange fluff	SC	145	1	
Ornamental	SC	145	1	
Ornamental cookie	GHAC	338		
Peanut butter	BHGN	104	1	B
Peanut butter chocolate	FFBB	400	1	C
Penuche	FFCB	538	1	B
Penuche	BHGN	105	1	B
Penuche	FFBB	405	1	C
Peppermint	FFCB	540	1	B
Peppermint	BHGN	104	1	B
Peppermint	AC	693	1	
Peppermint stick	BHGN	104	1	B
Pineapple butter	FFBB	402	1	C
Portsmouth	FFBB	396	1	C
Portsmouth	FFCB	535	1	B
Praline butter cream	AC	695	1	

RECIPE	BOOK	PAGE	TD	S
Rocky road	BHGN	106	1	B
Royal	FFCB	536	1	B
Rum	FFBB	275	1	B
Seafoam	SC	145	1	
Seafoam	AC	693	1	
Seafoam	BHGN	104	1	B
Seven minute	BHGN	104	1	B
◆	GHAC	344		
◆	SC	145	1	
◆	AC	694	1	
◆	FFBB	406	1	B
◆	FFCB	540	1	B
Seven minute (used for wedding cake —12 cups)	FFBB	389	1	C
Sour cream & caramel	SC	147	1	
Sugar icing for cakes & petits fours	MFC2	505	3	
Sultana nut	FFCB	538	1	B
Tomato butter cream	GG	380	2	C
Vanilla	GHAC	344		
Vanilla, boiled	NYT	573	1	B
Vanilla fudge	FFCB	537	1	B
Whipped cream honey	FFBB	402	1	C
White mountain	FFBB	291	1	C
White mountain	FFBB	396	1	C
Frostings butter creams	MFC2	508		
Frostings & fillings, list of	MFC2	508		
Frozen foods, all about	FFCB	725		
Frozen suckers	JOC	725	2	C
Frozen vegetables, grilling	BHGN	43		
Fruit				
Additions to, baked	JOC	107	1	
All about	FFCB	645		
Ambrosia	VE	282	1	B
Ambrosia	BCC	126	1	B

RECIPE	BOOK	PAGE	TD	S
Angel cake	SC	122	1	B
Appetizers, stuffed & dried	JOC	66	1	
Apple, wine, gelatin, summer	GHAC	293	2	C
& Avocado salad	JOC	93	1	
& Berries w spirits	SMG	277	1	B
Brandied	JOC	780	2	C
Brandied & dried	SC	459	3	
Bread, German	CBB	502	3	C
Brulee	JOC	108	2	B
Buttermilk ice cream &	JOC	719	2	B
Butters	AC	821	1	
Butting, citrus (photographs)	LT	29		
Cake	SC	116	3	
Cake	GF	93	3	C
Brandied	FFCB	517	2	B
Cockaigne	JOC	631	2	B
Cookies	AC	716	1	
Dark	JOC	631	2	B
Dark	FFCB	516	2	B
Fresh	LM	288	1	
Fried	AC	671	1	
Japanese	SC	114	1	B
Light	FFCB	515	2	C
w Pound cake base	AC	664	2	
White	SC	116	1	B
White	JOC	631	2	B
Cakes w fruit falling to bottom, what to do	MFC2	485		
Canned	FFCB	717	3	
& Cheese kabobs, ginger dip	BCC	16	2	C
& Cheese salad	BCC	296	1	B
& Chicken, summer	WC	63	1	B
Chiffon pies	SC	351	1	

RECIPE	BOOK	PAGE	TD	S
Hot, curried	BHGN	362	1	C
Ice	JOC	722	2	C
Ice, fresh	SC	210	2	
Ice, frozen	KIS	326	1	A
Ice cream	FFCB	631	3	C
Ice creams	JOC	716	2	C
Ice gems, crisp	FFBB	381	1	C
In deep fried batter	FAIC	497	2	B
In hard sauce	JOC	714	1	B
Jellies	SC	174	1	
Juice cocktail, minted	SC	44	1	
Juice custard	JOC	686	1	B
Juice icing	SC	143	1	
Juice sauce	SC	217	1	
Kebabs	FFCB	283	1	B
Kebabs	OC	97	2	B
Kebabs, fresh	JOC	107	1	
Kuchen	MSE	216	2	B
Kuchen	SC	352	1	
Layer pie	JBGF	628	2	B
Leather	FFCB	692	2	B
Leather, peach, apple, prune, plum, apricot	AC	832	2	
& Liqueurs	MSE	199	3	A
Loaf, Danish Christmas	CBB	307	3	B
Luncheon salad	GHAC	283	1	B
Macedoine	JOC	105	2	
Macedoine of	EBE	183	2	C
Macedoine w vermouth	NYT	625	2	B
Medley salad	BHGN	344	2	B
Melon baskets	GHAC	283	2	C
Milk shake	JOC	31	1	B
Milk sherbet	JOC	724	2	
Mixed	SMG	10	1	B
Mixed on skewers	OC	97	1	B

RECIPE	BOOK	PAGE	TD	S
Molded & stuffed	JOC	103	3	B
Mousse	JOC	720	2	C
Nut filling	SC	382	1	
Nut filling for filled sugar cookies	FFCB	550	1	C
Nut graham bread	CBB	113	3	C
Nut & rice casserole	JOC	183	1	C
Nut slices, candied	SC	177	1	
Nut stuffing, turkey, roast w	MSE	192	3	C
& Nut tropical slaw	BHGN	343	2	C
Nutrients, dictionary	JBGF	151		
Of the sea dip	EBE	36	2	C
Or berry ice cream	FFCB	632	3	B
Orange cream w	BCC	126	1	B
Oriental crackling	BBA	210	2	B
Pancakes	NYT	487	1	C
Pancakes	JOC	212	1	
Paradise	JOC	607	1	B
Paste	JOC	743	3	
Paste	AC	831	1	
Paste, Turkish	JOC	739	2	B
Patties	SC	172	1	
Pickled, canned	SC	459	3	
Pie, fresh, two crust	AC	614	1	
Pie, glazed	JOC	602	2	B
Pies	JOC	600	1	A
Pies, deep dish, all about	FFBB	92		
Pies, fresh, all about	FFBB	78		
Platter	BCC	296	2	B
Poached	SP	311	2	B
Poached	GF	215	2	C
Poached, pared	JOC	107	2	B
Poached, thick-skinned	JOC	107	1	
Poaching	NSD	24		
Pork potted	MIE	137	2	B
Preparing for jelly	SC	445		

RECIPE	BOOK	PAGE	TD	S
Souffle	JBC	272	1	B
Souffle	JOC	690	2	B
Souffle, light	JBC	272	1	B
Soup	MC	32	1	B
Soup	BCC	314	1	B
Soup cockaigne	JOC	109	1	B
Soup, iced	CBSS	171	1	B
Soup, Swedish	BHGN	379	1	C
Soups	JOC	149	1	B
Spirits	KIS	332		
Stewed, fresh	SC	263	1	
Stewed, pared	JOC	107	2	B
Stewed, thick-skinned	JOC	107	1	
Sticks	JOC	248		
Strata salad	BHGN	343	2	C
Stuffed & dried	JOC	740	2	B
Suet pudding, steamed	JOC	703	2	C
Sugar coated & stuffed	LM	360	2	
Sugar frosted	GHAC	294		
Sugar frosting, how to	GHAC	294		
Sundae sauce	SC	220	1	
Tapioca	AC	733	1	
Tart	VE	275	2	B
Tart	FFCB	595	2	B
Arranging	GHAC	316		
Fresh	SC	351	1	
Glaze	FFCB	579	1	C
Of French pastry w peekaboo jam	MFC2	459	2	B
Open face	NSD	106	2	B
Pinwheel	SP	304	1	C
Simple	MCIC	430	1	B
Small	LM	287	2	
Square	LT	427	2	
Strips	LT	425	2	
Tartlet	GF	48	3	C
Topped cake	BCC	71	3	B
Torte	EBE	154	1	B
Turnovers, mixed	FFBB	156	2	B
Upside down cake	AC	655	1	
& Vegetables, chart	BHGN	420		
& Vegetables w peanut sauce	YGM	241	2	C
Velvet	NYT	631	2	C
Walnut salad	BCC	295	1	B
Whip, blender	JOC	697	2	B
Whip, eggless	JOC	698	2	A
Whips	JOC	697	2	B
Whips	CIC	451	1	A
Wine compote	BCC	127	1	B
Yogurt w apple butter, summer	KIS	326	1	A
Yogurt bowl	BBA	143	1	B
Yogurt w pear butter, summer	KIS	326	1	A
Fruitcake				
Black, Jamaica spiced	NYT	554	2	C
Black, Nova Scotia	NYT	557	3	C
Chocolate	GHAC	342	3	C
Dark	FFBB	361	3	C
Dark	BHGN	99	2	C
Italian w thyme & fig	FFBB	363	3	B
Jeweled	BCC	74	1	C
Light	MHGD	82	3	C
Light	BHGN	99	2	C
Light, Jamaica	NYT	555	3	C
Mrs. Maus's	MSE	201	2	C
Orange	NYT	556	2	B
Pearl's Southampton	MHGD	79	2	C
Pumpkin	GG	332	2	C
Watermelon pickle	NYT	556	2	C
White	FFBB	362	3	C
White	NYT	555	2	B

RECIPE	BOOK	PAGE	TD	S
Fruited slaw	JBGF	541	2	C
Fruited yogurt desserts	MC	191	1	B
Fruity ginger ale mold	BHGN	339	2	B
Frying, deep	MCIC	12		
Frying, deep fat	JOC	124		
Frying, pan	JOC	127		
Fudge	AC	833	1	
Almond bark	BCC	116	2	C
Almond opera	BHGN	110	1	B
Brown sugar	AC	833	1	
Brownies, Moosewood	MC	192	1	B
Cake	AC	675	1	
Cake	SC	111	1	B
Cocoa	BCC	67	1	C
High altitude	JOC	649	1	B
Minnesota	NYT	550	1	C
Pie	FFBB	150	2	B
& Sour cream	NYT	550	1	C
Triple	BCC	67	1	C
Cherry opera	BHGN	110	1	B
Chocolate (see also chocolate fudge)				
Chocolate, sour cream	FFCB	679	2	B
Chocolate coated	SC	173	1	
Cockaigne	JOC	730	2	B
Cocoa	BCC	116	2	C
Cocoa	JOC	730	2	B
Cream	SC	169	1	
Cream cheese, quick	SC	169	1	
Cupcakes, cocoa	BCC	67	1	C
Divinity	AC	832	2	
Easy	BCC	115	1	C
Easy	BHGN	114	2	B
Frosting (see frosting, fudge)				
Hot	NSD	241	1	C
Layer cake	FFCB	508	2	B
Layer cake	JOC	627	2	B
Marshmallow, peanut butter &	FFCB	681	1	B
Meringue cake	JOC	627	1	B
Mexican	SC	169	1	
Million dollar	FFCB	680	1	B
Mint ice cream, cake	SC	209	2	
Never fail	AC	834	3	
Nut	SC	169	1	
Nut cake	JBC	34	2	B
Old time	BHGN	109	1	B
Opera	FFCB	680	2	B
Opera	BHGN	110	1	B
Orange	AC	833	1	
Peanut butter	GHAC	354		
◆	AC	833	1	
◆	BCC	116	2	C
◆	JOC	738	1	B
◆	FFCB	680	1	B
Pie, dense	FFBB	149	2	B
Quick	SC	169	1	
Remarkable	BHGN	110	1	B
Ribbon pie	BHGN	285	3	B
Roll	AC	834	1	
Sauce	BCC	153		
Sauce	FFCB	638	1	B
Hot	EBE	193	1	B
Hot	FFBB	420	1	C
Milk chocolate	SC	219	1	
Old fashioned	SPGT	134	1	B
Orange	BCC	153		
Sour cream	AC	833	1	
Sunday cake, hot	BCC	133	1	C
Twenty minute	FFCB	679	2	B
Fudged nuts	AC	833	1	
Fudgy meringue mallow	BCC	144	3	C
Fudgy oatmeal bars	BCC	105	1	C
Fuji foo young	NYTI	452	2	
Fumet stock	JOC	491	2	

GARLIC

RECIPE	BOOK	PAGE	TD	S
Chicken, 40 clove	JBGF	436	2	B
Chicken, garlic, garlic, garlic	FGCW	174	2	A
Cleaning	FG	277		
Confit, fish baked w	CPMC	113	2	B
Croutons	NYTI	119	1	
Croutons	CPMC	95	1	B
Croutons	FFCB	492	1	
Crumb topping	BCC	332	1	A
Dressing	BBA	149	1	B
Dressing	FGCW	129	1	B
Dressing	SP	220	1	B
Egg soup	FGCW	366	1	B
Eggplant baked w parsley, bechamel &	MFC2	348	1	
Everything you want to know about	SP	186		
Fried, deep	NYTI	365	1	
Getting smell off your hands	FG	278		
Heads, roasted	GRIL	87	2	B
& Herb mayonnaise	AC	77		
Lamb, leg of	AC	369		
Lamb, leg of, roast	AC	367		
Marinade	SC	327	2	
Mayonnaise (see also aioli)				
Mayonnaise	AC	76		
Mushrooms, sauteed	CIC	379	1	B
Mushrooms, stuffed	VGCB	173	1	B
Mustard dressing	SP	230	1	C
Oil sauce	JBC	213	1	A
Olive oil	BHGN	331	1	
Olives	JOC	70	3	
Olives, black	NYT	36	2	
Parsley, mushrooms w	FGCW	335	1	B
Pasta	FG	279	1	B
Peeling & chopping (photographs)	LT	6		
Peppers	LM	126	2	
Peppers, sauteed	JBC	322	1	B
Piperade soup	VGCB	182	1	B
Piperade soup	JBGF	317	1	B
& Potatoes, scalloped	MSE	228	2	C
Prawns, sauteed w wine	FGCW	116	1	A
Rice	AC	578	1	
Roast leg of lamb	AC	367		
Roasted chicken	BB	75	1	B
Salad, Russian	FG	277	2	
Salsa	BCC	180	1	
Salt	BTSB	202	2	C
Sauce	JOC	314	1	B
◆	FAIC	81	2	B
◆	FG	338	1	B
◆	BCC	316	1	
Sauce for roast lamb	MAFC	334	1	A
Sauce, herb	BHGN	355	1	B
Sauce, risotto w	FAIC	214	1	B
Sausage	BTSB	12	3	C
Sausage	KIS	255	1	B
Sausage	NYTI	245	1	A
Sausage, grilled	CFS	200	2	B
Sauteed, eggplant w bread crumbs &	MFC2	347	1	
Sauteed, zucchini w olive oil &	MFC2	365	1	B
& Scallops	FGCW	329	1	A
& Scallops & parsley	KIS	152	1	B
& Scallops, sauteed	MCIC	87	1	B
& Scallops, sauteed	JBC	86	1	
Shrimp, oil	FGCW	89	2	
Sliced potatoes sauteed w lemon	MFC2	390	1	B

RECIPE	BOOK	PAGE	TD	S
Garlic (*cont.*)				
Souffle	CPMC	112	3	B
Soup	MAFC	46	1	B
Cream of	VGCB	182	1	B
Mexican	CPMC	154	1	B
Poached eggs in	MAFC	47	1	B
Potatoes, saffron-flavored, in	MAFC	48	1	B
Spicy	CBSS	276	1	B
Spread	BHGN	41	1	
Stewed tomatoes, lemon &	AC	548	1	
Stuffing, rice, herbs &	MFC2	161	1	B
Sweet peppers, peeled, sliced, oil	MFC2	411	1	B
Toast (see also bruschetta)				
Toast	SMG	141	1	C
Toast, real	FGCW	341	1	
Tomato sauce w	BCC	161	1	
Tomato sauce w	FGCW	289	1	B
Turnip, rice puree	MFC2	405	1	B
Using fresh	BHGN	424		
Vinegar (made in 20 days)	SC	437	3	
Vinegar (made in 8 days)	SC	373	3	
Whole, baked w white cheese & peasant bread	CPMC	24	2	B
Wine	FGCW	372	3	
Zucchini, grated, sauteed in olive oil	MFC2	370	1	B
Zucchini, tomatoes & basil	MFC2	368	1	B
Garlicked hamburger	AC	314		
Garnish choux paste	JOC	171	2	B

RECIPE	BOOK	PAGE	TD	S
Garnish cocktail corn	GHAC	160		
Garnish fritter	JOC	172	1	A
Garnishes	BHGN	440		
Garnishes for soup	CBSS	410		
Garnishes, lemon	GHAC	135		
Garnishings for omelettes	MAFC	135		
Garnishings for onion soup	MAFC	44	1	B
Gateau Bretonne	NYTI	284	1	B
Gateau l'ermitage	BBA	188	3	C
Gaufrettes (French ice cream cones)	JOC	667	3	C
Gazpacho	GHAC	100	1	B
◆	MC	31	1	B
◆	NYT	81	1	B
◆	SP	55	1	C
◆	BHGN	379	2	C
◆	AC	97		
◆	FGCW	364	1	B
◆	VE	76	1	B
◆	MFC	76	2	B
◆	BCC	314	2	B
◆	VGCB	318	1	B
◆	JOC	148	2	B
I	SC	399	1	
II	SC	399	1	
Avocado	GG	39	1	B
Blender	JOC	165	1	B
California	AC	98	1	
Fruit	SPGT	146	2	B
Grande	JBGF	327	2	B
Green	SPGT	145	2	B
Malaga	NYTI	518	2	B
Pale almond	SPGT	146	2	B
Salad	VE	104	2	B
Salad	BHGN	335	2	B
Seafood	SPGT	147	2	C
Spanish	MIE	85	3	B
Verde	CBSS	279	3	B

RECIPE	BOOK	PAGE	TD	S
Cupcakes	SC	141	1	
Date & nut, stuffed w	SC	176	1	
Dill slaw, Donald Sack's	GG	78	2	B
Dip	BCC	16	1	C
Dip, Japanese	FGCW	359	1	
Divinity	NYT	636	2	C
Dressing	BCC	297	1	
Figs	SC	262	1	
Figs	NYT	620	1	B
Filling, fruit w	JOC	647	1	B
Fish fillets	NYT	264	1	B
Fish, steamed	YGM	118	1	A
Flank steak, sauteed	MSE	157	3	C
Frosting	AC	693	1	
Ham slice w	BCC	231	2	B
Honey dressing	BCC	300	1	A
Ice cream	FFCB	630	3	C
◆	FGCW	399	3	B
◆	NSD	207	1	B
◆	MHGD	433	1	C
Ice cream, pumpkin &	VGCB	235	2	B
Marinade	GHAC	223		
Marinade, sesame Korean	CFS	290	1	B
Marmalade	FFCB	707	2	C
Marmalade, yogurt &	MHGD	388	1	B
Melon	AC	759		
Muffins	MSE	133	1	C
Parfait	NSD	310	3	B
Pastry	NSD	85	2	C
Peach salad	SC	365	1	
Peanut barbecue sauce	GHAC	226	1	C
Pear preserves	SC	440	3	
Pears	NYT	623	1	B
Pears	MHGD	422	1	B
Pears, baked	JBC	108	1	B
Pears, poached	JBC	108	1	B
Pears, poached	NSD	94	1	B
Pepper sauce	NYTI	55	1	A
Pineapple	BCC	129	2	B
Plum sauce, spareribs w	NYT	15	3	C
Pork balls w	NYT	14	1	C
Pork chops w apples, prunes &	YGM	138	1	B
Pound cake	FFBB	365	1	B
Preserves, apple &	SC	439	3	
Pudding, steamed	AC	731	2	
Pumpkin mousse	SP	286	2	B
Punch, lemon	SC	57	1	
Raisin wheat bread	FFBB	460	2	B
Rhubarb sauce, turkey breast grilled w	CFS	130	2	B
Rice pork, fried	NYTI	60	1	B
Roll	NYT	564	2	C
Rutabaga	GG	391	1	B
Rye sour dough	FFBB	482	3	B
Sauce	BBA	91	2	B
Sauce	NSD	331	1	C
Crab fritter w	BBA	91	2	C
Orange	MC	81	1	B
Saffron oysters w	YGM	229	3	C
Soy shrimp foo yung	KIS	160	1	A
Squid w mustard	FGCW	124	2	A
Sausage balls	AC	21	1	
Scallops	MFC	136	3	A
Scallops, broiled	BCC	189	1	A
Sherbet	VE	267	2	B
Sherbet	FFCB	635	2	C
Shrimp w brussels sprouts	GG	72	1	B
Shrimp toasts	MSE	40	1	C
Souffle	NYT	604	1	B

RECIPE	BOOK	PAGE	TD	S
Ginger (*cont.*)				
Souffle	NYT	604	1	B
Souffle w rhubarb ginger sauce	SPGT	40	2	B
Soup, carrot &	SPGT	48	1	B
Soup, pear &	MSQC	140	1	B
Soy sauce for steamed shellfish, herbs	MSQC	92	1	B
& Spinach, stir fried	VGCB	263	1	B
Syrup	SC	53	3	
Thins	KIS	346	1	C
Thins	JOC	656	1	C
Upside down cake, pear &	NSD	136	2	B
Wafers	SC	154	1	
Wafers, thin	FFBB	252	1	C
Watermelon pickle	FFCB	716	2	B
Yogurt	BBA	227	1	B
Yogurt dressing, broccoli, cold &	YGM	213	1	C
Ginger ale salad	JOC	102	2	C
Ginger ale salad ring	SC	370	2	
Ginger ale syrup for home style	BTSB	217	1	C
Gingerbread	SC	113	1	B
◆	FFCB	513	2	B
◆	BHGN	95	1	B
◆	NYT	562	1	B
◆	AC	792	1	
◆	BTSB	245	1	B
◆	KIS	354	1	C
◆	JOC	636	2	B
◆	BCC	135	1	C
◆	SP	308	1	C
Boys	KIS	355	1	C
Card	SC	165	1	
Cookies	NYT	580	1	
Filling for coffee cake	SC	83	1	

RECIPE	BOOK	PAGE	TD	S
High altitude	JOC	650	1	B
Mansion	MSE	202	3	C
Mansion, making a	MSE	202		
Marmalade	MHGD	282	1	B
Men	FFCB	561	2	B
◆	NYT	579	1	C
◆	GHAC	353	2	C
◆	JOC	662	3	C
◆	AC	717	1	
Mix	BTSB	245	1	C
Mix	KIS	354	1	C
Moosehead	FFBB	326	1	B
Old fashioned	JBC	36	1	
People	BCC	114	2	C
Persons	FFBB	272	2	C
Pumpkin	MHGD	283	1	B
Ring, maple cream	GHAC	342	2	C
Soft	FFBB	325	1	B
w Sour cream	FFBB	327	1	B
w Sour cream	FFCB	513	2	B
Sugar	SC	113	1	B
Upside down cake	FFCB	525	2	B
Waffles	SC	98	1	B
w Warm vanilla ice cream	CF	123	1	C
Wheatless	JOC	636	1	B
Whole wheat from New Orleans	MHGD	280	1	C
Whole wheat, yogurt, date nut	MHGD	279	1	C
Yellow	FFBB	326	1	B
Gingersnap	BCC	106	2	C
◆	AC	717	1	
◆	FFBB	213	1	C
◆	SC	154	1	
◆	JOC	662	1	C
◆	SC	159	1	
Chutney cream cheese w	MSE	191	3	C

RECIPE	BOOK	PAGE	TD	S
Salad w green beans	YGM	190	1	C
Salad w lentils	YGM	179	1	C
Scramble, watercress &	GG	198	1	A
Souffle	CPMC	130	2	B
Spinach salad	GG	311	3	B
Spinach salad, warm	GG	311	3	B
Stuffed, endive &	CFS	241	2	B
& Sun dried tomatoes	GHAC	92	1	C
Tart, leek &	CPMC	147	3	B
Tomatoes, basil &	YGM	129	1	A
Zucchini, squash blossoms &	GG	404	2	B
Zucchini, squash, filled w	GG	404	2	B
Goat, curried Jamaican	NYTI	448	2	C
Goat, oven roasted (cabrito asada)	NYTI	471	2	C
Gobhi musallam Indian (Indian cauliflower dish)	NYTI	358	1	C
Goetta (pork scrapple)	JOC	438	2	B
Gold cake	SC	107	1	B
Gold cake, quick	FFCB	528	1	B
Gold coin eggs	MSE	124	1	C
Gold layer cake	JOC	625	2	B
Gold leaf, decorating w	NSD	341		
Gold nugget bread	FFBB	459	2	C
Gold rush brunch	BHGN	193	1	B
Golden buck	GHAC	115	1	B
Golden chiffon cake	SC	122	1	B
Golden chiffon cake	BHGN	100	2	C
Golden eagle	FFCB	295	1	B
Golden egg pastry	SC	343	1	
Golden fizz	SC	63	1	
Golden fizz	BBA	26	1	A
Golden glow cake	AC	684	1	
Golden glow salad	SC	369	2	
Golden monkey ring	FFBB	515	3	B

RECIPE	BOOK	PAGE	TD	S
Golden nuggets	BCC	243	1	B
Goldenrod eggs	AC	111	1	
Goldenrod toast	SC	221	1	
Gomatare (Japanese sesame sauce)	NYTI	455	1	B
Goose				
All about	MAFC	282		
w Apples & prunes, roast	FFCB	251	3	B
Braised, breast, legs of	SC	321		
Braised, w chestnut & sausage stuffing	MAFC	285	3	B
Braised, parts of	JOC	474	2	
Charcoal roasted	AC	230	2	
Confit	FGCW	197	3	B
Confit w marsala, pasta &	FGCW	200	1	B
Cracklings	SC	321	1	
Danish roast &	NYT	221	2	B
Fat rendered	FFCB	252	2	
Fricasseed	SC	321		
Garlic-stuffed roast	BB	79	2	B
Garlicked	AC	231	1	
Liver	JOC	439	2	
Liver appetizer	SC	47	1	
Liver, chicken breasts stuffed w	MFC	86	3	B
Liver pate in aspic	LM	162	3	C
Livers, chopped	JOC	71	1	
Meat sandwiches	SC	381	1	
Neck sausage	MFC2	317		
Neck, stuffed	SC	322		
Orange sauce for	JOC	326		B
Oven roasted	AC	231	2	
w Potato stuffing, roast	FFCB	252	3	B

RECIPE	BOOK	PAGE	TD	S
Goose (*cont.*)				
Potted	JOC	474	3	
Preserved	MFC2	312		
Preserved w cooked fat, also pork, game	MFC2	315	3	C
Preserved fat	SC	321	3	
Roast	BBA	83	3	B
◆	BCC	241		
◆	SC	321	2	
◆	JOC	474	2	B
◆	BB	78	2	
w Chestnut fruit stuffing	AC	231	2	
w Chestnut stuffing, sausage & apples	GHAC	167	3	B
w Prune & foie gras stuffing	MAFC	283	3	B
Stuffed w candied oranges	GHAC	166	3	C
Wild	NYT	179	2	B
Roasted w smoked ham stuffing	PPLK	148	3	B
Roasting, how to	JOC	464		
Smoked	SC	321	3	
Soup	SC	395	3	
Stuffing a	NYT	225		
Timetable for roast or braised	MAFC	283		
Timetable for roasting duck or chicken	BCC	241		
Wild	JOC	480	3	
Gooseberry				
& Black raspberry jelly	JOC	775	2	
Conserve	SC	444	1	
Fool	AC	754	1	
Fool	JBC	102	1	B
Fool	CF	150	1	B
Jam	FFCB	704	2	C
Jelly	FFCB	702	2	C
Mousse	MSE	175	1	B
Pie	SC	346	1	
Pie	AC	616	1	
Pie	BHGN	279	1	B
Poached	JBC	102	1	B
Preserves	JOC	779	2	B
Spiced	SC	458	3	
Tapioca pudding	SC	198	1	
Goreng udang sambal (Indonesian shrimp dish)	NYTI	362	1	B
Gorgonzola				
Cream sauce, tortellini w	SP	74	2	B
Dip	NYT	52	1	A
Mascarpone layered w	CW	65	1	A
Mascarpone linguine w	CPPC	92	1	A
Pears w	FGCW	392	1	
Pizza w caramelized onions, rosemary &	CPPC	153	3	B
Polenta	CIC	207	1	B
Polenta	NYT	339	1	B
Pork w	FGCW	216	1	B
Romaine lettuce salad, walnuts &	MCIC	413	1	B
Salad	EBE	138	1	B
Sauce, fettuccine w	CIC	134	3	B
Stuffing, tortelli w	FAIC	170	2	B
Gorp trail mix	FFCB	72	1	B
Gosling, roast	JOC	474	2	B
Gouda edam soup, cream of	CBSS	154	1	B

RECIPE	BOOK	PAGE	TD	S
Gougere (cheese pastry appetizer)	BBA	15	3	B
Gougere	SP	10	2	C
Goulash	CBSS	387	2	C
Another	AC	298	1	
Au blanc, lamb	JOC	417	2	
Au blanc, pork	JOC	417	2	
Beef	JOC	417	1	B
Beef, Budapest I	NYT	105	2	B
Beef, Budapest II	NYT	105	2	B
Beef, Hungarian I	NYTI	343	2	B
Beef, Hungarian II	NYTI	343	2	B
Cabbage, Transylvanian	YGM	223	3	C
Frankfurter, a la Walter Slezak	NYT	145		B
Gulyas	AC	298	1	
Hungarian	SC	286	2	
Hungarian	FFCB	162	1	B
Hungarian	JBC	151	2	B
Pork	AC	413	2	
Pork	NYTI	345	1	B
Stew	FFCB	162	2	B
Three meat, Prague	NYT	105	2	B
Triple	NYTI	342	2	B
Veal	NYTI	346	2	B
Veal & pork	JOC	417	1	B
Veal, Viennese	NYT	164	2	B
Venison	NYT	181	2	B
Graham bread	FFCB	472	2	C
Graham bread	JBC	17	2	C
Batter for	SC	70	2	C
Brown, quick	SC	84	1	
Fruit nut	CBB	113	3	C
Maple syrup	CBB	132	1	C
Graham cracker	FFBB	590	1	C
Graham cracker	BTSB	235	2	C
Cake	SC	113	1	B
Crumb crust	GHAC	321		
Crust	FFBB	68	1	B
Crust	NYTI	563	1	
Crust	BHGN	290	1	B
Glorified	SC	158	1	
& Peanut butter pie shell	SC	344	2	
Shell	SC	343	2	
Torte	BCC	148	2	C
Grains	AC	576		
Grand marnier				
Mousse, frozen	MHGD	442	2	C
Sauce	NYT	615	1	B
Sauce	GF	116	2	B
Sauce, raspberry &	MSE	168	1	B
Souffle	JOC	689	2	B
Souffle	FFCB	619	3	B
Souffle, froid	EBE	195	3	C
Souffle, frozen	MFC	241	2	B
Granita, two melon	GHAC	306	3	C
Granola	JBGF	508	1	B
◆	BTSB	294	1	B
◆	BHGN	326	1	C
◆	FFCB	311	2	C
Granola bark	BCC	122	1	C
Granola & carrot cookies	FFBB	235	2	C
Granola cookies	BTSB	232	2	C
Grape				
Brown sugar & sour cream	AC	755	1	
Brown sugar in yogurt	KIS	331	1	
Butter, Concord	NYT	510	1	B
& Carrots	GHAC	234	1	B
Chicken &	EBE	70	1	B
Chicken breast &	SMG	22	1	B
Chocolate dipped	SC	173	1	
Clusters simmering, lemon cheese gel	GHAC	294	2	C

GREEN BEAN

RECIPE	BOOK	PAGE	TD	S
A la nicoise	NYT	355	1	B
Almonds &	FFCB	362	1	B
Almonds &	AC	476	1	
Amandine	BHGN	389	1	B
Au gratin	FFCB	362	1	B
Bake, onion &	BHGN	391	1	B
Beef, ground w	JBGF	466	1	B
& Beets, aioli, warm	CPMC	219	1	B
Blanched	MAFC	443	1	B
Boiled	JBC	289	1	B
Broasted	CFS	241	1	B
Buttered, cashews &	SP	155	1	B
Buttered I	MAFC	444	1	B
Buttered w lemon juice & parsley	MAFC	444	1	B
California style	AC	476	1	
& Carrots, smothered mortadella w	MCIC	368	1	B
Casserole	JOC	259	2	B
Casserole, chicken &	SC	315	1	
Cheese sauce &	AC	478	1	
Chickpea salad	JBGF	536	2	B
Cooking	CIC	360		
Cooking	AC	475		
Cream	AC	477	1	
Creamed I	MAFC	445	1	B
Creamed II	MAFC	445	1	B
Crisp pickled	BTSB	137	2	C
& Egg casserole	SC	413	1	
Especial	BHGN	389	1	B
Filbert salad	FGCW	138	1	B
French style	JBC	290	1	B
Fresh butter	MFC	168	1	B
Frozen	MAFC	449	1	B
Garlicky	JBGF	514	1	B
& Goat cheese salad	YGM	190	1	C
w Gratineed cheese sauce	MAFC	446	1	B
Gruyere, mushrooms &	MSE	104	1	C
Herbed	BHGN	389	1	B
Herbed	BCC	335	1	B
w Herbs	FFCB	362	1	B
Italian style	JBC	291	1	B
Joe's	AC	477	1	
& Lettuce	FG	194	1	B
& Mushrooms	AC	478	1	
& Mushrooms w walnut dressing	MFC	194	1	B
& New potatoes, pesto w	KIS	183	1	A
& Onion casserole	GHAC	231	1	C
w Onions vinaigrette	SMG	161	1	B
& Oregano	FG	190	1	B
w Parsley butter	SMG	65	1	B
w Peanut sauce	KIS	144	1	A
Peppers, tomatoes &	CIC	362	1	B
& Potato pie, Genoa-style	MCIC	369	1	B
& Potato puree	CW	148	1	B
& Potato soup	FG	51	1	C
Potatoes & smoked meat	JOC	259	1	B
Pudding	MCIC	330	1	B
Puree, pasta w	CF	119	1	C
Pureed	JOC	259	1	B
Salad	NYT	420	1	
◆	SC	359	1	
◆	CIC	412	1	B
◆	EBE	138	3	B
Celery root &	GG	121	1	B
Garlic almonds murcia &	BBA	144	2	B
Old fashioned, hot	AC	477	1	
w Rocket & garden lettuces, warm	CPMC	214	1	B

RECIPE	BOOK	PAGE	TD	S
Stuffed, Tuscany style	NYTI	390	1	B
Vegetarian, stuffed	FFCB	395	2	B
Green peppercorn butter, noodles w	SMG	253	1	B
Green peppercorn sauce	BBA	70	2	B
Green peppercorns, rabbit w wine sauce &	FGCW	234	2	B
Green quills	GG	188	1	B
Green salad	CW	45	1	B
Green salad	CF	11	1	B
Green salad, tossed	VGCB	246	1	B
Green salad, tossed, zucchini &	VE	99	1	B
Green sauce	FAIC	57	1	B
Green sauce	SMG	115	1	B
Green sauce	BCC	182	1	
Green sauce for asparagus	SPGT	29	1	B
Green sauce, walnuts w	FAIC	58	2	B
Green sausage, poached	GG	194	1	B
Green soybeans	JOC	260	1	
Green spinach sauce	BBA	87	1	A
Green timbale	GG	192	2	B
Green tomato chow chow	GHAC	383	3	C
Green tomato pie	FFBB	87	2	B
Green tomatoes, short term, pickles &	VGCB	324	2	B
Green vegetables w tarragon cream	MSE	57	1	C
Green wax beans w blue cheese sauce	GHAC	231	1	B
Green wax beans w mustard sauce	GHAC	274	2	B

RECIPE	BOOK	PAGE	TD	S
Green wax beans, preparing	BCC	335		
Greenfield or quick tea cake	AC	659	1	
Greengage preserves	JOC	778	2	C
Greens				
All about	VGCB	126		
An old southern recipe for	AC	522	1	
& Beets	FFCB	365	1	A
Blanched	VGCB	130	1	
Boiled	VGCB	130	1	
& Buttermilk dressing	YGM	85	1	A
Chicken &	BBA	66	2	B
& Chicken casserole	VGCB	133	2	B
Cooking	AC	521		
Cornmeal dumplings w	GG	190	1	B
Definitions	SP	227		
w Lemon vinaigrette	YGM	137	1	B
Mixed sautee	VGCB	130	1	B
Pot likker	AC	420	2	
Potatoes & onions	VGCB	131	1	B
Preparing	GG	185		
Preparing	BCC	349		
Sauteed, baby	VGCB	130	1	
Sauteed, braised	VGCB	130	1	
Sauteed for piandina	MCIC	390	1	B
Soup	VGCB	133	2	B
Soup, chilled	SPGT	103	2	B
Steamed	VGCB	130	1	
Steamed or blanched	VGCB	130	1	
Stir fried	AC	562		
Stuffed, pork chops	GG	195	2	B
Tossed	GRIL	84	1	B
Wilted	JOC	80	1	B
Wilted summer	GG	191	1	B

RECIPE	BOOK	PAGE	TD	S
Gumbo (*cont.*)				
Egg & dried shrimp	PPLK	199	3	B
File	FG	291	3	C
Game hen, okra & sausage	GG	230	2	B
Louisiana	GHAC	106	2	C
Old New Orleans	AC	182	2	
Oyster & chicken	GHAC	150	1	B
Seafood	CBSS	380	3	B
Seafood	SC	405	1	
Seafood & okra	GG	229	2	B
Shellfish	VGCB	166	2	B
Steak & okra	PPLK	206	3	B
Two way	CBSS	382	2	B
Gumdrop marshmallow bars	BCC	122	1	C
Guylas goulash (beef goulash)	AC	298	1	
Gyngerbrede (gingerbread)	MHGD	276	1	C
Gypsy eggs	AC	108	1	
Gypsy soup	JBGF	340	1	B
Gypsy soup	MC	5	2	B
Gyros (Greek beef/ vegetable sandwich)	BCC	318	1	B

H

RECIPE	BOOK	PAGE	TD	S
Haddock				
Baked & stuffed	JOC	356	1	B
Blacksmith shop	MIE	151	1	B
Curried	NYT	238	1	B
Fillet	SC	237	1	
Fillets baked w cream sauce	JOC	356	1	B
Fillets w cream sauce	NYT	237	1	B
Fillets, oven-fried	NYT	238	1	B
Italian-style	WC	72	1	A
Stuffed w clams	NYT	237	1	B
Haggis (Scottish liver mush)	SC	180	2	
Haleakala cake (Hawaiian pineapple coconut cake)	MHGD	65	3	C
Half & half dressing	JOC	316	1	B
Halibut				
Baked				
w Bread crumbs	SMG	120	1	B
w Cheese	SC	237	1	
w Cream	NYT	238	1	B
w Tomato sauce	SC	237	1	
California style, marinated	GHAC	139	2	B
w Cheese sauce	FFCB	112	1	B
Creole	FFCB	113	1	B
w Fennel	MSQC	84	1	B
Fillets, barbecued	OC	145	2	B
w Grapefruit sauce	BCC	177	1	B
Hollendon	FFCB	113	1	B
Poached w parsley sauce	CIC	214	1	B
Ring mold	JOC	210	2	B
Sherry-sauced	BHGN	213	1	B
& Shrimp newburg	SC	237	1	
& Shrimp ring	SC	238	2	
Souffle ring	SC	238	1	
Steak				
Baked	SC	237	1	
Broiled	SC	237	1	
Grilled, garlic flavored	AC	125	2	A
Hawaiian	GHAC	139	1	B

RECIPE	BOOK	PAGE	TD	S
w Lemon dill sauce, broiled	GHAC	139	1	B
Sesame	NYT	239	1	B
Stuffed	NYT	239	1	B
Timbales	SC	237	1	
w White wine & anchovy sauce	MCIC	212	1	B
w White wine, braised	AC	138	1	
Hallacas (Venezuelan tamales)	NYT	110	3	C
Halloween surprise pie	EBE	166	2	C
Ham (see also pancetta, prosciutto)				
Ham	MAFC	389		
A la king	JOC	231	2	B
& Apples (schnitz und knepp)	AC	445	3	
w Apricot maple glaze	GHAC	202	2	B
& Apricot patties	BHGN	256	1	B
& Asparagus	AC	473	1	
& Asparagus sandwich w cheese sauce, hot	SC	384	1	
& Asparagus toast rolls	JOC	246	1	B
Aspic	LT	291	3	
Aspic	MFC2	310	3	C
Aspic, parsleyed	FFCB	448	2	B
Aspic salad	JBC	253	2	
Avocado salad	WSP	201	1	B
Baked	SC	296	2	
◆	BCC	228	2	
◆	FFCB	204	2	B
◆	JBC	206		
Aged	JBC	207	2	
Aged, cooked	AC	440		
w Bread crust	AC	443	2	
w Cheese sauce, endive &	SMG	284	1	B
Country	SPGT	55	2	C
Country	MSE	57	2	C
Country	AC	440		
Country, crust	SC	296	2	
Country, in a crust	AC	442	2	
Easter	MSE	228	2	C
Glazed	NYT	148		
w Ground cloves	JBC	207		
Honey	JBC	207		
In a pastry crust, stuffed	MAFC	395	3	C
In beer	NYT	148	2	C
In cider	AC	443	3	
In cider	JBC	207		
In cola	AC	443		
In dry wine	JBC	207		
In milk, slice of	FFCB	206	2	B
Kentucky	SC	296	3	
Mushrooms stuffed	BHGN	13	1	C
w Peaches & bourbon	JBC	207		
w Pineapple	JBC	207		
Processed	JOC	410	2	
Ready to eat or tenderized	AC	440		
Sandwich	AC	807	1	
Savory, pastry	GF	106	2	C
w Tomatoes & cheese	JOC	411	1	A
Unprocessed	JOC	409	2	
Virginia	SC	296	3	
Baking	BHGN	254		
Baking chart	SC	295		
Ball, cheese &	BHGN	14	2	B
Balls, sweet & sour	AC	450	1	

RECIPE	BOOK	PAGE	TD	S
Ham (*cont.*)				
Bean & vegetable soup	BHGN	375	2	C
& Beans Bretonne	NYTI	392	2	C
Beer soaked, w mustard sauce	CFS	161	1	B
Biscuits	JBC	5	1	
Biscuits	NYT	478	1	C
Biscuits, Kentucky	GHAC	363	1	C
& Black-eyed pea salad	YGM	207	2	C
Boiled	NYTI	392	2	C
Boiled	SC	297	1	
Boiled	JBC	209		
Boiled, country	FFCB	205	2	
Braised	WC	125	1	C
w Cider	NYTI	187	3	C
w Madeira wine	MAFC	393	1	C
w Mushroom stuffing	MAFC	394	3	C
w Wine-cream mushroom sauce	MAFC	391	1	C
& Broccoli, stir-fry	WC	112	1	B
Broiled	SC	297	1	
Broiled	JOC	411	1	
Broiling, an old manuscript recipe for	AC	449	1	
Butt	JOC	411	1	
Butts, baked, smoked, small	JBC	208	1	
w Cabbage, boiled	AC	447		
Cabbage & dill	AC	493	1	
Cakes, eggs &	JOC	201	1	B
Cakes, pineapple & sweet potatoes	JOC	230	2	B
Caribbean	BHGN	255	1	B
Carving a whole	BCC	229		
Casserole, country-style	FFCB	206	1	B

RECIPE	BOOK	PAGE	TD	S
Chart (photographs)	BHGN	246		
& Cheese				
Appetizers	BB	114	1	B
Bites, sesame	SP	4	2	C
Chicken or turkey sandwich	AC	809	1	
Cups	GHAC	86	1	C
Dip	EBE	20	1	B
Feuillete	MSE	56	3	C
Salad w walnut dressing	BBA	144	2	B
Sandwich	AC	808	1	
Sandwich, French toasted	AC	808	1	
& Sandwich, sauteed	AC	808	1	
Sandwiches	BB	114	1	B
Souffle	AC	452	2	
Souffle	NYT	310	2	A
Souffle	AC	452	2	
Veal cutlets stuffed w	GHAC	210	1	B
& Chicken crammed, cucumbers, baked	GG	153	2	A
w Chicken, roast stuffed	JBC	224	1	
Christmas Swedish	NYTI	532	3	C
Chunks in hot sauce	FGCW	91	1	
Cider & beer, glazed in	GF	226	2	C
Cold, parsleyed	LM	225	3	C
& Corn bread, deviled	GHAC	367		
& Corn filling	GG	138	1	C
Cornets	LT	54	1	
Cornets, making (photographs)	LT	54		
& Cornmeal cake	SC	305	1	
Country	JOC	410	3	

HAM

RECIPE	BOOK	PAGE	TD	S
Country w four sauces	GHAC	195	3	C
& Cream cheese appetizers	BB	114	1	B
& Cream cheese sandwiches	BB	114	1	B
w Cream sauce	SMG	87	1	B
Creamed	AC	452		
Croquettes	FFCB	209	2	B
Croquettes w cheese sauce	BHGN	255	1	B
Croquettes, corn &	JOC	218	3	B
Crust	LM	221	3	C
Cured, raw country w prosciutto/ bayonne	LM	217	3	
Cuts (chart)	BHGN	254		
Decorated for a buffet, cold	AC	444	2	
Deviled	AC	449	1	
Deviled	BTSB	27	2	B
Deviled w corn bread	GHAC	367		
Deviled, sandwich	AC	808	1	
Dressing	JOC	458	1	C
Egg foo yung	BHGN	192	2	A
& Egg sandwiches	SC	384	1	A
& Eggs	SC	226	1	
& Eggs	SC	224	1	
& Eggs	AC	448	1	
Creamed	BCC	163	1	B
Deviled	WC	46	1	B
For breakfast	WC	42	1	A
Italian	AC	452	1	
Sauteed	JOC	411	1	
Sherried	BBA	123	2	B
Stuffed	FFCB	58	1	A
& Endive mornay	NYTI	188	2	C
& Endive salad	SMG	306	1	B
Filling	SC	381	1	
Filling, deviled	NYTI	507	2	C

RECIPE	BOOK	PAGE	TD	S
Fresh	JOC	408	3	
Fried	JBC	209		
Fried w red eye gravy	AC	448	1	
Fried, sauteed	AC	447	1	
Frittata w mushrooms & red pepper	FFCB	343	1	B
Frittata, onion &	GHAC	112	1	B
Fritters, corn &	JOC	222	2	B
Fritters, potato &	MCIC	400	1	B
& Fruit	AC	31		
Frying, an old recipe for	AC	447		
Garnish accompaniments for baked	AC	441		
Glazed w apricots, baked	SP	99	2	C
Glazed & sliced	GHAC	202	2	C
Glazed, Virginia, country	MSE	96	3	C
Glazes & garnishes	AC	441		
Glazes, garnishes for baked	AC	441		
Gratin, cauliflower &	GG	110	2	B
Gratin of endive	MAFC	156	1	B
& Green noodles	WC	113	1	B
Grits w red eye gravy	GHAC	195	1	B
Gumbo, chicken, okra &	GG	231	2	B
Hocks & collard greens	GHAC	203	2	B
Hocks w sauerkraut, braised	BBA	99	2	B
Hodgepodge	BHGN	370	2	B
Hominy, scalloped	JOC	176	2	B
& Kidney bean tureen	AC	603	1	
Leftover, dishes using	FFCB	207		

RECIPE	BOOK	PAGE	TD	S
Sandwiches, French-toasted	SC	384	1	B
Sandwich, frizzled or fried	AC	807	1	
Sandwiches, party	BHGN	15	1	C
Scalloped	FFCB	209	2	B
Scalloped potatoes w	AC	567	1	
Scalloped potatoes w	JBC	327	1	B
Scalloped potatoes w	BCC	231	1	B
Scalloped potatoes w	AC	451	1	
w Semolina dumplings	FGCW	161	2	B
Shank	JOC	411	1	
Shirred eggs w	FFCB	339	1	A
Shoulders, smoked & baked, small	JBC	208	1	
Slices	SC	297	1	
w Asparagus spears & egg sauce	NYT	151	1	B
Baked	JBC	208	1	
Baked	AC	445		
Baked	MSE	293	1	C
Baked w fruit	SC	297	2	
Baked w orange juice	SC	297	2	
Baked, tomatoes, onions, peppers &	MAFC	396	1	B
Broiled	JBC	59	1	
Broiled	AC	448	1	
California	AC	445	1	
Casseroled	JOC	411	1	A
w Champagne	AC	446	1	
Fried	JBC	58	1	
w Fruit	JOC	411	1	A
w Fruit, broiled	AC	449	1	
Ginger	BCC	231	2	B
Glazed	BHGN	34	1	B
Grilled w cream	JBC	208		
w Mustard crust	AC	446	2	
w Oranges	AC	446	1	
Sauteed w cream & madeira sauce	MAFC	397	1	B
Sauteed w fresh cream sauce	MAFC	398	1	B
Smithfield, sandwich	AC	807	1	
Smoked & cooked	BCC	229	1	
Smoked, cottage roll	JOC	411	1	
Smoked, lasagne, spinach &	MSE	144	2	C
Smoked, shoulder butt	JOC	411	1	
Smoking & brining	JOC	754		
Souffle	SC	305	2	
Souffle	FAIC	377	2	B
Soup, potato &	GG	294	1	A
Spiced w fruits	BCC	229	1	B
& Spinach	MAFC	470	2	B
& Spinach souffle	FFCB	208	2	B
& Spinach, stir-fry	WC	115	1	B
Spit roasted, fresh	OC	121	2	B
Spread	FFCB	55	1	B
Spread, cheese &	AC	12	1	
Spread, deviled	FFCB	55	1	B
Steak	BB	31	1	
Barbecued	BB	31	1	A
Barbecued	OC	124	2	B
Currant glazed	GHAC	203	1	B
Glazed	BB	31	1	
Marinated	BB	31	1	
Oven braised	MSQC	200	1	B
Pan-broiled	BB	32	1	
Stuffed eggs	FFCB	308	1	A
Stuffed eggs	AC	18		
Stuffed fruits & nuts	AC	444		
Stuffing	BCC	222	2	C

RECIPE	BOOK	PAGE	TD	S
Ham (*cont.*)				
Stuffing, braised beef &	MFC2	386	1	B
Stuffing, smoked roast goose &	PPLK	148	3	B
& Sweet potatoes	SC	297	2	
Sweet & sour	BHGN	34	2	C
& Swiss cheese salad	BCC	270	1	B
& Swiss croissant	GHAC	372		
Tidbits	JOC	71	1	
Timbales	JOC	208	2	B
Toast, deviled	AC	450	1	
Toasts	AC	451	1	
& Tomato cream	AC	451	1	
& Tongue mousse	EBE	56	2	B
& Veal loaf	SC	298	1	
& Vegetables	WC	121	2	B
Westphalian, sandwich	AC	808	1	
& White bean salad	SP	209	3	B
Wine glazed	OC	124	2	B
Haman pockets (purim cakes)	SC	81	2	
Hamburg steak, Mrs. Roter's	AC	315	1	
Hamburger	AC	804	1	
◆	BB	22	1	
◆	FFCB	166	1	B
◆	BHGN	243	1	B
◆	SC	279	1	
◆	JBC	157	1	
◆	BCC	317	1	B
◆	FFCB	289	1	A
A cheval	JBC	158	1	
Au poivre	JBC	158	1	
Au poivre	NYT	106	1	B
Bagel burger, Big Apple	GHAC	186	1	
Baking	BHGN	243	1	B
Barbecue	BCC	317	1	B
Barbecue	CFS	74	1	B
Barbecued w bacon	BHGN	28	1	B
Basic	CFS	73	1	B
Basic, grilled & variations	BHGN	28	1	B
BBQ	CFS	74	1	B
Beef, heart	AC	319	1	
Big Apple bagel burger	GHAC	186	1	
& Blue cheese	GHAC	185	1	B
& Blue cheese	BHGN	28	1	B
Broiled	JOC	427	1	B
Broiled	JBC	157	1	
Broiled & variations	AC	312		
Broiling	BHGN	243	1	B
Buns	FFBB	500	2	C
Buns	BTSB	80	3	C
Buns, sesame topped	BTSB	82	3	C
Burgundy	SC	279	1	
California	BCC	317	1	B
California goat cheese	GHAC	186	1	
Casserole	JOC	430	1	B
Channing's Greek	FGCW	209	1	B
& Cheese sandwich	BB	24	1	A
Chevre	BCC	207	2	B
Chicago pizza	GHAC	186	1	
Chili	BCC	317	1	B
Chili, the Tex-Mex	GHAC	187	1	
Corn bake	BHGN	245	1	B
w Cream sauce	MAFC	302	1	B
Deviled	SC	279	1	
& Dill	NYT	107	1	B
Double-decker	BHGN	243	1	B
Egg & anchovy	SMG	246	1	B
Eggplant	BB	24	1	B

RECIPE	BOOK	PAGE	TD	S
Florida surf n turf	GHAC	187	1	
Garlic	AC	314		
Giant	BCC	207	1	B
Gilded	CFS	77	1	B
Grilled	JOC	428	1	
Grilled	OC	107	1	A
Grilling	SC	327		
Help, chili style	KIS	363	1	B
Herbed	BB	24	1	A
Kebab	EBE	57	1	B
Lager	CFS	76	1	B
Louisiana Creole	GHAC	187	1	
Marseillaise	JBC	158	1	
Mexican	BB	24	1	A
Minestrone	BCC	306	1	B
w Mushrooms	JBC	158	1	
My favorite	AC	315	1	
Open-face	BCC	317	1	B
Pan-broiled w variations	JBC	158	1	
Panbroiling	BHGN	243	1	B
Patties	BCC	207	1	B
& Peas, stir fry	VGCB	199	1	B
w Peppercorn sauce	SMG	244	1	B
Pie	BHGN	245	1	B
Pizza	BCC	167	2	C
◆	BHGN	28	1	C
◆	AC	315	1	
◆	BCC	167	2	C
Potato roll	NYT	107	2	B
Preparing	JOC	426		
Rarebit	BB	25	1	A
Rolls	NYT	474	2	
Sandwich	SC	384	1	
San Francisco	GHAC	187	1	
w Sauerbraten	BHGN	243	1	B
Sauteed	JOC	427	1	B
Savory	BB	23	1	A
Savory	CFS	76	1	B
Scandi	CFS	78	1	B
Skillet	BHGN	244	1	B
Small	AC	26		
w Sour cream	SMG	242	1	B
Steak, Norman Foster's	AC	314	1	
Teriyaki	SC	279	1	
Tex-Mex	CFS	75	1	B
Tex-Mex chili	GHAC	187	1	
Vegetable soup	SC	397	1	A
Venison	AC	236		
Venison	JOC	455	2	
Hamburgerbabs, spicy	BBA	51	2	B
Hangtown fry (oyster-fry)	FG	69	1	A
Hangtown fry (oysters)	GHAC	123	1	B
Hangtown fry (oyster & variations)	AC	160		
Hard-boiled egg w hot pepper vinegar dressing	PPLK	274	1	B
Hard candy	JOC	735	2	B
Hard candy drops	BTSB	275	2	C
Hard rolls	FFCB	476	2	C
Hard rolls	JOC	568	3	C
Hard rolls	BCC	47	2	C
Hard sauce	JBC	266	1	
◆	FFBB	422	2	C
◆	FFCB	641	1	B
◆	NYT	615	1	B
◆	MSE	221	1	B
◆	BCC	143	1	
◆	AC	742	1	
◆	JOC	714	1	B
Basic	BHGN	186	2	B
Brandy	BHGN	278	1	
◆	BHGN	186	1	C
◆	FFCB	641	1	B
◆	GHAC	315		

RECIPE	BOOK	PAGE	TD	S
Hard sauce (*cont.*)				
Brown sugar	SC	98	1	
Brown sugar	JOC	714	1	B
Cream cheese	SC	219	2	
Fluffy	BHGN	186	1	C
Fluffy	JOC	714	1	B
Fruit	JOC	714	1	B
Lemon	FFCB	641	1	B
Lemon brandy	BBA	213	3	
Mocha	FFCB	641	1	B
Orange	BHGN	186	1	B
Orange	SC	98	1	
Plain	SC	219	1	
Raspberry	FFCB	641	1	B
Spicy	JOC	714	1	B
Strawberry	SC	219	1	
Wine	FFCB	641	1	B
Hard wheat bread	MCIC	50	3	B
Hare				
A la mode	JOC	452	3	
Civet	JOC	452	3	
Fricassee	JOC	453	3	
Hasenpfeffer	JOC	452	3	
Pate	NYT	9	3	C
Roast	JOC	453	3	
Saddle of	AC	247	3	
w Sauce pappardelle	FAIC	151	2	B
Smothered w onions	JOC	453	3	
Har-gow (steamed shrimp dumplings)	NYTI	61	2	C
Haricot de mouton (lamb stew w beans)	NYTI	179	2	B
Haricot mutton or lamb w beans	AC	393	2	
Haricot of mutton	AC	393	2	
Haricot of mutton or lamb	AC	392	2	
Harlequin canapes	SC	39	1	

RECIPE	BOOK	PAGE	TD	S
Harlequin pudding	SC	214	2	
Harvard beets (see beets, Harvard)				
Harvest preserves	JOC	779	2	C
Harvest tart	SP	304	2	B
Hasenpfeffer (marinated, then fried rabbit)	BHGN	270	3	B
Hasenpfeffer	SC	302	1	
Hasenpfeffer hare	JOC	452	3	
Hash				
Baked, an old recipe for	AC	283	1	
Beef, braised	WC	79	1	B
Beef, corned	NYT	117	1	B
Brown, omelet	BHGN	200	2	B
Browned	JOC	233	1	B
Browns	VGCB	215	1	
Browns	BHGN	400	1	B
Celery root w wild mushroom	GG	125	1	B
Corned beef (see corned beef hash)				
Country, turkey	GHAC	163	1	B
w Creamed cabbage	JOC	234		
w Home fried, fennel & potato	GG	178	1	B
Lamb	NYT	131	1	B
Mexican	BCC	212	1	B
Oven	BCC	205	1	B
Potatoes, baked & stuffed	JOC	292	2	B
Quick	JOC	233	1	B
Red flannel	VGCB	27	1	B
◆	FFCB	161	1	B
◆	SC	303	1	
◆	NYT	118	1	B
◆	GHAC	179		

RECIPE	BOOK	PAGE	TD	S
Red flannel w beets	GG	54	2	B
Red flannel, skillet	BCC	205	1	B
Roast beef	NYT	118	1	B
◆	FFCB	171	1	B
◆	GHAC	176	1	C
◆	AC	283	1	
Roast beef, skillet	SC	303	1	
Salt codfish, tomatoes & garlic	FFCB	149	1	B
Sauteed	JOC	233	1	B
Skillet	BCC	205	1	B
Texas	FFCB	167	1	B
Tongue	AC	321	1	
w Vegetables	JOC	233	1	B
Hashed Browns	BCC	361	1	B
Hassenpfeffer (rabbit)	NYT	177	3	B
Hasty pudding	NYT	587	2	B
Hawaiian bread, fauchons	CBB	622	3	B
Hawaiian candy	JOC	739	1	B
Hawaiian centers	JOC	739	1	B
Hawaiian cooler	BB	166	1	A
Hawaiian toast w bacon sandwich	JOC	246	1	B
Hazel dressing	PPLK	294	1	B
Hazelnuts	SP	289		
Bars	BCC	104	1	C
Bavarian cream	JOC	694	3	B
Butter balls	FFBB	271	1	C
Buttercream	SP	289	2	B
Cake, chocolate	NSD	172	2	C
Cake, chocolate	SP	288	2	B
Cake, chocolate	SPGT	75	2	C
Chiffon pie, toasted	FFBB	121	2	B
Chocolate sable cookies	NSD	64	2	C
Coffee torte	SC	128	1	B
Filling, custard	JOC	648	1	B

RECIPE	BOOK	PAGE	TD	S
& Green peppercorns, duck terrine w	MFC	32	3	C
Ice cream	MCIC	450	2	B
Macaroons cook bake	FFBB	220	1	C
Oil, chevre &	KIS	310	1	
Parfait	MFC	239	3	B
Parfait, chocolate, orange &	NSD	312	3	B
Souffle	JOC	691	2	B
Tarts w chocolate icing, Austrian	NYTI	16	2	C
Topped ice cream & variations	MIE	314	1	B
Topping	BCC	104	1	
Torte	SC	128	1	B
Torte	JOC	638	2	B
Torte, chocolate	FFBB	371	2	C
Wafers	JOC	669	1	C
Head cheese	AC	320		
Head cheese	NYT	176	3	C
Head cheese or brawn	JOC	449	2	B
Head cheese or brawn	AC	419		
Head cheese, rolled	LM	204	3	C
Health bread	AC	784	2	
Health bread	JOC	561	2	B
Health dip	FFCB	54	1	B
Health drink	FFCB	745	1	A
Health salad	AC	49	1	
Health salad	FFCB	430	2	B
Health sandwich	FFCB	294	1	A
Heart	BB	39	1	B
Baked & stuffed	JOC	447	2	A
Broiled	BB	40	1	A
Cooking	BCC	217	2	
En papillote	JOC	447	2	A
Sauteed	FFCB	216	1	B
Slices w braised sour sauce	JOC	447	2	B
Stuffed w vegetables	FFCB	216	2	B

RECIPE	BOOK	PAGE	TD	S
Heartburgers	BB	26	1	
Hearts of butter lettuce w citrus dressing	VE	100	1	B
Hearts of palm	JOC	286	1	
Hearts of palm salad	JOC	87	1	
Hearts of palm salad w avocado	FFCB	432	1	B
Heating foods	JOC	122		
Heating foods in dry heat	JOC	122		
Heating, moist	JOC	127		
Heavenly hash candy	JOC	737	1	B
Heidelberg sandwiches	BCC	321	1	B
Hen, a mature pot, roasted	AC	204	3	
Hen, Guinea, Burmese style	OC	139	2	B
Hen, Guinea, roast	OC	139	2	A
Hen hazel	JOC	480	1	
Hens, mud	SC	323	2	
Hens & pork	CFS	129	2	B
Hen, roasted, wallbanger	CFS	128	2	A
Herb				
Blend	FG	244	1	A
Bread	JBC	24	1	
Bread	EBE	105	1	B
Bread	FFCB	468	3	C
Briarpatch	CBB	444	2	C
Hot	VE	46	1	B
Hot	NYT	50	1	A
Six	CBB	435	2	B
Butter (see also butter, herb)				
Butter basting sauce	BHGN	32	1	B
Butter, mixed	MAFC	102	1	A
Butters	KIS	365	1	
& Cheese souffle	GHAC	116	1	B
Chiffonade of	JOC	540	1	
& Cream salad sauce	NYTI	264	1	A
Creamy pasta sauce w fresh	SP	73	1	B
Croutons	FFCB	492	1	
Croutons	VE	79	1	B
Different kinds of	MCIC	28		
Dressing	BHGN	352	1	B
Dressing, burgundy	FGCW	129	1	B
Dressing, mixed	GHAC	284	1	B
Flavored root vegetables	MSQC	205	1	B
For soup, chiffonade of	JOC	173	1	
Frozen	BTSB	204		
Garlic sauce	BHGN	355	1	B
Green soup	MFC2	10	1	B
Green soup, cold	MFC2	11	1	B
Growing & drying	JOC	529		
Growing essential	VGCB	344		
Jelly	NYT	514	1	C
Loaf, round	SC	70	2	C
Onion bread	VE	40	2	B
Salt	BCC	221	1	
Sauce (Aji sauce)	BBA	30	1	B
Sauce	AC	459	1	
◆	BHGN	355	1	B
◆	NYT	437	1	A
◆	NYTI	271	1	B
◆	GHAC	256		
Sauce, brown	MAFC	73	1	B
Sauce, dried	NYT	444	1	
Sauce, fresh	NYT	444	1	
Scented jellies	JOC	775	2	
Snipping fresh	BHGN	425		
Soup	CBSS	280	1	B
Soup w celery	CBSS	269	1	B
Soup pot	NYT	69	1	B

RECIPE	BOOK	PAGE	TD	S
Herring (*cont.*)				
Rolls	JOC	73	1	
Rolls	SC	246	3	
Rolls, baked	SC	246	1	
Salad	NYT	24	2	B
◆	AC	43	1	
◆	SC	363	1	
◆	NYTI	79	3	C
◆	JOC	90	2	C
Beets &	SC	363	3	
Pickled beef, potato &	CF	74	1	B
Potato &	JOC	87	1	B
Scandanavian	AC	69	1	
Salt	BTSB	42	2	
Salt	SC	246	3	
Salted & trout, baked	SC	241	1	
Scotch, fried	JOC	357	3	C
Sherry matjes	NYTI	80	1	B
Soup, cream of Russian	SC	405	1	
w Tomato sauce	NYTI	79	3	B
Hickory nut cake	SC	113	1	B
Hickory nut kisses	SC	163	1	
Hidden mint cookies	BCC	107	1	C
High altitude cooking	BCC	373		
High ball	SC	62	1	
High protein-low calorie dressing	MC	46	1	B
High-protein bread	NYT	464	2	B
Highballs Rickys	JOC	45	1	
Himmel torte (cream-filled torte)	SC	128	1	B
Hindu cream	AC	730	2	
Hinged basket, tomatoes & onions in	OC	20		
Hobo bread	CBB	598	3	C
Hocks	FFCB	200	2	B

RECIPE	BOOK	PAGE	TD	S
Hoisin, chicken nuts in	MIE	170	2	B
Hoisin, chicken, sweet peppers &	KIS	120	1	A
Hoko pot (Chinese hot-pot)	FGCW	310	3	
Holiday decorated spritz	BCC	114	1	C
Holiday green sauce	BBA	21	1	C
Hollandaise sauce	FFCB	272	1	B
◆	BB	153	1	
◆	FG	225	1	B
◆	BBA	122	2	B
◆	GHAC	385		
◆	BCC	327	1	C
◆	MAFC	79	2	B
◆	NYT	449	1	B
◆	VE	90	1	A
◆	SC	388	1	
◆	SP	340	2	B
◆	LM	48	1	
◆	JBC	263	1	
◆	PPLK	258	1	B
◆	MFC	105	1	B
Anchovy &	AC	460	1	
Artichoke &	PPLK	309	1	B
w Beaten egg whites	MAFC	83	2	B
Blender	JOC	329	1	B
◆	FFCB	272	1	B
◆	SC	389	1	
◆	BB	153	1	
◆	NYTI	272	1	B
◆	BHGN	356	1	B
◆	AC	460	1	
Celery root w	AC	510	1	
Chive	NYTI	272	1	B
Classic	BHGN	356	2	B
D'oeufs	MAFC	83	2	B
Easy	SC	389	1	
Easy	MIE	48	1	A

RECIPE	BOOK	PAGE	TD	S
Electric blender	MAFC	81	1	A
Fail safe & variations	GG	409	1	B
Food processor	FFCB	272	1	B
& Hazelnut, lamb medallions of	SPGT	70	2	B
Herbal	PPLK	260	1	B
Leeks w	JBC	312	1	
Mock	FFCB	265	1	B
◆	JOC	329	1	B
◆	BHGN	356	1	A
◆	SC	389	1	
◆	MAFC	64	1	B
Mustard	BBA	93	1	A
Mustard	JOC	263	1	
Never-fail	JOC	329	1	B
One cup	GG	423	1	B
Orange flavored	MAFC	83	2	A
Quick	NYT	450	1	A
Quick	JBC	263	1	
Quick	SC	389	1	
Red pepper	CFS	310	1	B
Stove	AC	460	1	
Tarragon	JBC	263	1	
Whipped cream	MAFC	83	2	B
& White wine, fish fumet w	MAFC	84	2	B
Hollendon halibut	FFCB	113	1	B
Homard a l'absinthe (lobster)	NYT	279	2	A
Homard a l'Americaine (lobster)	MAFC	223	3	B
Homard aux aromates (lobster)	MAFC	223	2	B
Homard thermidor (lobster)	MAFC	221	3	B
Home fries	VGCB	215	1	
Hominy	JOC	176	2	B
Buttered	AC	580	1	
Cakes	JOC	176	2	B

RECIPE	BOOK	PAGE	TD	S
& Cheese casserole	AC	581	1	
Creamed	AC	581	1	
Gems	FFCB	490	2	C
Green chilies & sour cream	AC	581	1	
Grits	FFCB	314	1	B
Grits	SC	180	2	
Grits, boiled	AC	581	1	
Grits spoon bread	AC	582	2	
Ham, scalloped	JOC	176	2	B
Mexican	JBGF	520	1	B
Mexican	JBGF	520		
Rolls, golden	FFBB	496	2	C
Stew, Indian	CBSS	271	2	B
Honey				
Almond ice cream	NSD	202	1	B
Apples	JOC	111	1	
Balls	NYT	560	2	C
w Barbecue glaze	GHAC	164		
Bars	SC	166	1	
Bars, German	JOC	653	1	C
Bran bread	BTSB	82	2	C
Bread	FFCB	485	2	B
Bread	PPLK	42	2	C
Bread	MFC2	481	2	
Bran &	FFCB	470	2	C
Milk &	VE	44	1	B
Orange	NYT	484	2	B
Portuguese	CBB	341	3	C
Buns	SC	81	2	
Butter	SC	98	1	
Butter, spiced	SC	98	1	
Butter toast	JOC	587	1	
Butter, whipped	FFBB	408	1	B
Cake	FFBB	319	1	C
Cake	NYT	561	2	C
Cake cockaigne, eggless, all rye	JOC	578	2	B

RECIPE	BOOK	PAGE	TD	S
Honey (*cont.*)				
Cakes, German	FFBB	266	2	C
Caraway dressing	GHAC	284	1	B
Carrots	CW	149	1	B
Cookies, German	JOC	657	1	C
& Cranberry barbecue sauce	GHAC	226	1	C
Cream sauce	FFCB	640	1	B
Crunchy cookies	FFBB	207	2	C
Curry bread	SPGT	86	3	B
Curry dip	MSE	70	1	C
Date nut bars	FFCB	567	1	C
Dressing	BCC	295	1	
Dressing	JOC	317	1	B
Dressing	BCC	265	1	
Dressing, ginger	BCC	300	1	A
Glaze for meat	JOC	341	1	
Glaze for onions	JOC	341	1	
Ham, baked	JBC	207		
Health bread	JBGF	590	1	B
Ice cream	MFC	240	2	B
Ice cream, lavender	CPMC	64	3	B
Lebkuchen	SC	154	1	
Lime dressing	BHGN	344	1	B
Marinade, orange	CFS	292	1	A
Mint sauce	JOC	713	1	A
Muffins (see muffins, honey)				
Mustard sauce	GHAC	195	1	B
Pineapple bread	CBB	482	1	B
Rub	CFS	285	1	A
Salad dressing	SC	378	1	
Salad dressing	PPLK	274	1	B
Sauce	JOC	713	1	B
Sour cream dressing	BCC	295	1	
Spice cookies	BCC	112	3	C
Squash pie	MSE	194	2	B
Starter	CBB	275	3	B
Wheat berry bread	VE	36	2	B
Wine sauce	BCC	128	1	
Yam pie	MHGD	160	2	B
Yogurt dressing	FFCB	454	1	B
Yogurt tofu sauce	KIS	329	1	B
Honeycomb tripe	SC	301	2	
Honeycomb tripe w parmesan cheese	CIC	293	2	B
Honeydew melon (see also melon)				
Honeydew melon salad, crescent	SC	365	1	
Honeydew & shrimp appetizer	JBGF	299	2	B
Honeydew sorbet	GF	130	2	B
Honeymoon bars	AC	713	1	
Honeynuts	SC	157	1	
Honolulu (drink—juices & gin)	BBA	27	1	A
Hooker's pasta, spaghetti alla puttanesca	FGCW	149	1	B
Hoosier cake, Florine Hudspeth's	FFBB	332	1	C
Hoppin John	BCC	174	2	C
Hoppin John black eyed beans	GHAC	232	2	B
Hops starter	CBB	276	3	C
Hor gwo (Chinese dumpling sauce for one)	NYTI	47	3	
Horehound candy	JOC	735	2	B
Horns, cream baked w cheese filling	MFC2	138	2	B
Horns, puff pastry in cream	MFC2	135	2	
Horseradish	FFCB	717	2	B
Horseradish	BTSB	183	1	C
Horseradish	BTSB	193	2	C
Aioli sauce	BBA	88	1	B
Applesauce	AC	746	1	
Applesauce	AC	464		

RECIPE	BOOK	PAGE	TD	S
Bacon & egg salad	SPGT	81	1	C
Beets &	BTSB	184	1	C
Bluefish &	CFS	210	1	A
Butter	GRIL	39	1	B
Butter	FFCB	57	1	B
& Cheese ring	SC	368	2	
& Chicken, grilled	CFS	109	2	A
Cream	FFCB	273	1	B
Cream	VGCB	6	1	A
Beets in	GG	50	1	B
Cheese dip	NYT	51	1	B
Corned beef cabbage in	GG	81	2	B
Dressing	SC	377	1	
Dressing	NYT	438	1	B
Frozen	SC	392	2	
Sauce, whipped	SC	392	1	
Summer squash w	FFCB	410	1	B
w Trout chevrons, smoked	MSE	51	2	C
Dressing	JOC	312	1	A
Dressing	JBGF	551	1	A
Beet salad in	JBGF	540	2	B
Cold	NYT	450	1	B
Sour cream &	JOC	317	1	B
Spinach, tomato, onion &	FFCB	428	1	B
Filling	SC	382	1	
Herring (matjes)	NYTI	80	1	B
Mayonnaise	AC	76		
Meatballs	EBE	21	2	B
Pickled	JOC	785	3	C
Prepared	SC	458	2	
Sauce	SC	387	1	
◆	BBA	162	1	A
◆	AC	464		
◆	BBA	14	1	B
◆	JOC	324	1	B
◆	CW	148	1	B
◆	SPGT	132	1	B

RECIPE	BOOK	PAGE	TD	S
◆	GHAC	385		
◆	NYT	450	1	B
◆	EBE	55	1	B
◆	GF	125	1	B
◆	JBC	262	1	
◆	BCC	328	1	B
A la Dresden, cold	NYT	450	1	B
Creamy	MIE	51	2	B
Fluffy	BHGN	358	1	B
Frozen	JOC	312	2	B
Hot	SC	390	1	
Salmon &	SC	239	2	
Sour cream	NYTI	276	1	A
Sour cream	MC	79	1	B
Sour cream	EBE	57	1	B
Horticultural beans, Boston, baked	VGCB	14	1	B
Hoska (Czechoslovakian braided bread)	CBB	314	3	C
Hot buttered rum mix	BHGN	51	2	B
Hot butterscotch sauce for ice cream	GHAC	306		
Hot cakes, combination	SC	92	1	B
Hot chocolate	JOC	31	1	A
Hot chocolate	BCC	24	1	B
Hot chocolate	BHGN	50	1	B
Hot chocolate sauce	KIS	366	1	B
Hot & cold salad	VE	106	1	A
Hot cross buns	BHGN	69	3	C
◆	NYTI	92	2	C
◆	SC	80	2	
◆	BBA	181	2	C
◆	CBB	554	3	C
◆	FFBB	507	2	C
Hot dog roll ups	BCC	318	1	B
Hot dogs	FFCB	290	1	
Hog dogs, millionaire's	WC	123	1	B
Hot fudge sauce	JOC	711	1	B
Hot fudge sauce	NYT	613	1	B

RECIPE	BOOK	PAGE	TD	S
Hot fudge sauce, the world's best	MHGD	54	1	B
Hot fudge sundae, old fashioned	GHAC	303		
Hot fudge sundaes	BHGN	185	1	B
Hot oil dip	JBC	4	1	
Hot pepper sauce	VGCB	206	1	B
Hot peppers, peeling	VGCB	202	1	
Hot pot, American	AC	394	2	
Hot pot, Chinese	NYTI	47	3	
Hot pot, traditional Lancashire	AC	394	2	
Hot sauce, Mexican	MC	78	1	B
Hot slaw	FFCB	371	1	B
Hot & sour Chinese soup	JBGF	318	2	A
Hot & sour soup	MC	8	1	B
Hot & sour soup	NYTI	37	2	
Hot sweet filling	PPLK	132	2	B
Hot water bread	AC	785	2	
Hot water bread, fried	CW	165	2	C
Hot water or milk sponge cake	AC	683	1	
Hot water pie crust	AC	635	1	
Huckleberries	AC	750		
Huckleberries	AC	757		
Huckleberry dumplings	AC	725	1	
Huckleberry pie	NSD	32	2	C
Huckleberry pie, wild	AC	618	1	
Huckleberry sauce	NSD	330	1	C
Huckleberry tart	JOC	603	2	B
Huevos rancheros	KIS	196	1	A
Huevos rancheros	JOC	197	2	B
Huevos rancheros	BHGN	193	2	A
Hummus (garbanzo bean paste)	FG	365	2	C
◆	MC	91	2	B
◆	NYTI	540	1	C
◆	KIS	311	1	B

RECIPE	BOOK	PAGE	TD	S
◆	BBA	21	2	B
◆	JBGF	292	1	B
Bi tahini	BBA	18	2	B
Bi tahini	SP	346	1	B
Bi tahini (garbanzos w sesame oil sauce)	AC	608	1	
& Chicken halves grilled	CFS	115	2	B
Marinade	CFS	289	1	B
Middle Eastern	CF	82	1	B
Shell bean	VGCB	15	1	B
Hungarian goulash	SC	286	2	
Hungarian goulash	FFCB	162	1	B
Hungarian goulash	JBC	151	2	B
Hungarian salad	FG	78	2	
Hungarian sauce	JOC	324	1	B
Hungarian white bread	CBB	77	2	B
Hunter chicken	FAIC	297	1	B
Hunter chicken	JOC	469	3	B
Hunter chicken	LM	40	3	B
Hunter's sauce	SMG	241	1	B
Hunter's sauce	JOC	327	1	B
Hunter's stew, traditional bigos	FG	375	2	C
Hurry up cake	JOC	635	1	B
Hurry up cake, cocoa	JOC	635	1	B
Hush puppies	JOC	580	1	C
Hush puppies	BHGN	86	1	C
Hushpuppies	PPLK	57	1	C
Hush puppies, fried fish &	GHAC	136	1	B
Hushpuppies, fried catfish w	PPLK	55	2	B
Husky health bread	FFBB	457	2	C
Hwang kua jo tang (cucumber, sliced pork soup)	NYTI	37	1	B

I

RECIPE	BOOK	PAGE	TD	S
Irish				
Bread	FFCB	494	1	B
Coffee	BHGN	53	1	A
Creme liqueur, homemade	MHGD	ix	1	B
Stew	FFCB	189	1	B
◆	JOC	423	2	B
◆	AC	389	3	
◆	JBC	188	2	B
Stew, farmhouse style	VGCB	332	1	B
Tea bread (barm bread)	CBB	322	2	C
Isfanakh fatira (spinach pancake)	GG	318	1	A
Isobe tamago yaki (omelet rolls)	BBA	21	3	B
Italian				
Batter bread	CBB	264	3	B
Bread	CBB	262	3	C
Cream cake	BHGN	102	2	C
Dressing	BHGN	351	1	B
Dressing	BCC	300	2	B
Dressing, creamy	BCC	300	2	B
Flag	GG	378	1	B
Fontina cheese & sweet red pepper salad	BBA	141	1	B
Salad	JOC	84	1	B
Sauce	BB	152	1	C
Sauce for spaghetti	SC	339	2	
Sausage (see sausage, Italian)				
Soups (passati)	FAIC	116		
Sweets	BCC	113	2	C

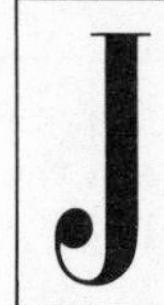

RECIPE	BOOK	PAGE	TD	S
Jack cheese pimiento spread	BBA	21	1	B
Jack o'lantern cookies	GHAC	248	1	
Jackaroo sauce, chicken, spit roasted w	CFS	260	2	A
Jade chicken	FGCW	358	3	B
Jalapeno				
Cheese bread	PPLK	46	2	C
Cheese rolls	PPLK	46	2	C
Corn bread	CW	153	1	B
Corn bread	CBB	193	1	C
Nachos, chicken, creamy &	SPGT	135	1	C
Pepper butter	SPGT	139	1	B
Jalousie (fruit tart)	MFC2	459	2	B
Jalousie	MHGD	61	3	B
Jam				
Apricot	SC	442	3	
Dried	SC	442	2	
& Pineapple	FFCB	703	2	B
& Pineapple, quick	JOC	777	2	
Bar le duc	JOC	776	2	
Bars	FFCB	568	1	C
Berry tarts	CW	61	2	B
Black currant	FFCB	704	2	B
Blackberry	FFCB	703	2	B
Blackberry	JOC	776	2	
Blueberry	JOC	776	2	
Blueberry	GHAC	381	3	C
Blueberry & crabapple	SC	442	1	

RECIPE	BOOK	PAGE	TD	S
Brandied, apricot	BTSB	167	2	C
Cake	FFCB	515	1	B
Cake	AC	668	1	
Cake, Rombauer	JOC	636	1	B
Cherry, sour	MSE	133	1	C
Cockaigne, five fruits	JOC	777	3	
Cupcakes	JOC	633	1	C
Elderberry	JOC	776	2	
Filling	FFBB	539	1	C
Filling, whipped	SC	150	1	
Freezer	BHGN	149	3	B
Gooseberry	FFCB	704	2	C
Grape	BHGN	150	2	B
Icing	SC	143	1	
& Jellies, canning	BHGN	148		
& Jellies, making	JOC	772		
Loganberry	JOC	776	2	
Muffins	FFBB	559	1	C
Pastries	BCC	53	3	C
Peach	BHGN	149	2	
Peach	SC	442	1	
Peach & banana	BHGN	149	2	
Peach & plum	BHGN	149	2	
Pear & pineapple, spiced	JOC	776	2	C
Plum	BHGN	150	2	B
Plum	SC	442	1	
Raspberry	FFCB	703	2	B
Raspberry	JOC	776	2	
Raspberry	MSE	133	1	C
Raspberry & currant	FFCB	703	2	B
Rose hip	JOC	777	2	
Sauce	JOC	710	1	A
Sauce	SC	219	1	
Sour cherry	GHAC	381	3	C
Strawberry	GHAC	381	3	C
Strawberry	BHGN	150	2	B
Freezer	SC	442	3	
& Pineapple	SC	442	2	

RECIPE	BOOK	PAGE	TD	S
Red red	JOC	776	2	
& Rhubarb	SC	442	2	
Sweet cherry	GHAC	381	3	C
Thimble buns	SC	80	2	
Thumbprints	BHGN	162	1	C
Toasts	LM	316	1	C
Tomato & orange	SC	443	1	
Tomato, yellow	GG	376	2	B
Turnovers	SC	352	1	
Uncooked, frozen	AC	821		
Jamaican punch	NYT	651	1	C
Jambalaya	BBA	100	2	C
◆	SC	257	1	
◆	NYT	320	2	B
◆	JOC	182	1	B
◆	FG	293	3	C
Chicken (see also chicken, jambalaya)				
Chicken	GHAC	153	2	B
Chicken & seafood	PPLK	218	2	B
Chicken tasso	PPLK	220	2	B
Fish	JOC	182	1	B
Meat	JOC	182	1	B
New Orleans style	WC	74	1	B
Pepper, all American	GG	286	1	B
Poorman's	PPLK	216	2	B
Rabbit	PPLK	217	2	B
Seafood	CBSS	391	3	C
Shrimp	GHAC	125	1	B
◆	FFCB	142	1	B
◆	JBC	90	1	B
◆	BCC	188	1	B
Janson's temptation	NYTI	533	1	B
Janson's temptation	NYT	270	1	B
Japanese				
Curry sauce	BBA	161	1	B
Eggplant, grilled	GRIL	76	2	B
Ginger dip	FGCW	359	1	

RECIPE	BOOK	PAGE	TD	S
Japanese (*cont.*)				
Omelet on rice donburi	FGCW	361	1	A
Pepper sauce	FGCW	359	1	
Jefferson Davis pie	FFBB	102	1	B
Jefferson Davis pie	JOC	605	2	B
Jefferson Davis pie & variations	AC	628	1	
Jellied consomme	CBSS	60	3	C
Jellied soup, Danish colors	NYTI	76	3	B
Jelly				
Apple (see apple jelly)				
Aspic	SC	367	2	
Bag, making a	SC	446		
Berry pectin	SC	447	1	
Berry, waterless	JOC	775	2	
Black currant	SC	448	1	
Black raspberry	SC	449	1	
Black raspberry & currant	SC	449	1	
Blackberry	FFCB	703	2	C
Blackberry	SC	449	1	
Blueberry & apple	FFCB	702	2	C
Cherry	SC	447	1	
Chocolate	SC	202	2	
Cinnamon & apple	BHGN	149	2	B
Coffee	SC	202	2	
Coffee	FFCB	621	2	B
Coffee & praline cream	AC	735	2	
Cooking	SC	445		
Crabapple	SC	446	1	
Crabapple	FFCB	702	2	C
Crabapple	JOC	775	2	
& Cranberry	SC	447	1	
& Plum	SC	447	1	
& Rosemary	MSE	199	2	B
Cranapple	GHAC	380	3	C
Cranberry	BTSB	169	2	C
◆	NYT	514	1	C
◆	SC	447	1	
◆	JOC	114	1	
◆	FFCB	282	1	B
Cranberry spiced	JOC	114	1	
Crepes	FFCB	614	1	B
Currant	SC	447	2	
◆	FFCB	702	2	C
◆	JOC	774	2	
◆	SC	448	1	
& Cherries	SC	448	1	
Cold process	SC	447	2	
& Raspberry	FFCB	702	2	C
& Raspberry	JOC	774	2	
& Raspberry	SC	447	2	
Sauce	AC	457	1	
Doughnuts	FFCB	480	3	C
Doughnuts	AC	800	2	
Elderberry	SC	448	1	
Filled cookies	SC	153	1	
Filling	NYTI	11	1	B
Fruit	SC	174	1	
Fruit, basic method for preparing	FFCB	701		
Fruit juice	BHGN	149	1	B
Fruit, suitable for	SC	446		
Glasses, filling & sealing	SC	446		
Gooseberry	FFCB	702	2	C
Gooseberry & black raspberry	JOC	775	2	
Grape	SC	448	1	
◆	GHAC	380	3	C
◆	BTSB	170	2	C
◆	JOC	775	2	
◆	NYT	514	1	C
◆	FFCB	702	2	C

RECIPE	BOOK	PAGE	TD	S
Kasha	JBC	119	1	B
◆	AC	584	1	
◆	FFCB	315	1	B
◆	KIS	100	1	A
◆	VE	223	1	A
◆	JOC	177	1	B
◆	MIE	202	1	B
Broth	FFCB	315	1	B
Cooking	JBGF	69		
Corn & cheese casserole	YGM	86	1	B
Filling, smoked salmon &	BBA	16	1	C
Knishes	VE	224	2	C
Lamb &	BCC	238	1	B
Mushrooms &	FFCB	315	1	B
Onion &	FFCB	315	1	B
Pilaf	KIS	117	1	A
Tex-Mex	JBGF	372	1	B
Varnishkas	JBGF	371	1	B
Kasseri flamed, Greek salad w	SPGT	152	2	B
Kedgeree (rice, fish & egg dish)	FFCB	145	1	B
Kedgeree	WC	67	1	B
Kefir (tangy cultured milk)	BTSB	68	2	A
Kefir, honey vanilla	BTSB	69	2	A
Kefir, strawberries &	BTSB	69	2	A
Kefta (sausages)	CFS	188	2	B
Keftedes (Greek meatballs)	NYT	14	2	C
Kentucky burgoo	BB	104	3	C
Kentucky ham biscuits	GHAC	363	1	C
Ketchup, tomato, spicy	NYT	498	2	B
Key lime pie	CW	29	1	
◆	GHAC	323	2	B
◆	EBE	167	2	B
◆	NYT	526	1	B
◆	MHGD	168	2	B
Key lime pie, Florida	FFBB	135	1	B
Key lime pie, frozen	MHGD	170	2	B
Kibbe (lamb loaf)	FG	171	2	B
Kibbee baked	NYTI	542	3	C
Kibbee raw	NYTI	539	1	B
Kibbeh, baked (lamb)	AC	391	1	
Kibbeh naye, lamb	AC	390	1	
Kid, garlic	OC	112	2	B
Kid, oven roasted	NYTI	471	2	C
Kidney	SC	301	1	
Kidney	LT	281	2	
All about	JOC	443		
Baked, veal	JOC	444	1	
Beef stew	JBC	161	2	B
Beef stew	AC	318	1	
Blazed w gin	JBC	177	2	B
Broiled	FFCB	217	1	B
Broiled	JBC	192	1	
Broiled	JOC	444	1	
Broiled, beef, tomatoes, onions &	JOC	445	1	A
Broiled, veal	BB	39	1	
Cooked in butter-mustard & parsley sauce	MAFC	417	1	B
Cooking	BCC	217	2	
Curried, English style	NYTI	87	1	B
Curried, English style I	NYTI	88	3	B
Curried, English style II	NYTI	89	2	B
Deviled	JBC	192	1	
Deviled	AC	362	1	
En brochette	JOC	445	1	A
In red wine	JBC	177	2	B
Kebab	OC	128	1	B
Kebabs, prunes &	OC	128	1	B
Lamb	AC	396		
Lamb, en brochette	AC	397	1	

RECIPE	BOOK	PAGE	TD	S
Lamb, plain, broiled	AC	397	1	
Lamb, preparing	MAFC	416	1	
Lamb, sauteed, onion &	MCIC	307	1	B
Lamb, sauteed w white wine	CIC	300	2	B
& Mushrooms en brochette	JBC	192	1	
Nuggets	JOC	444	1	A
On skewers	NYTI	371	2	C
Oyster & beefsteak pie	AC	327	2	
Pie, beefsteak &	JBC	148	3	B
Pie, beefsteak &	FFCB	164	2	B
Pie, beefsteak &	AC	326	2	
Pie, steak &	NYT	115	3	B
Pie, steak &	JOC	418	2	B
Pie, steak &	BHGN	269	2	C
Pudding, beefsteak &	JBC	149	3	B
Saute, middle western	AC	363	1	
Sauteed	FFCB	217	1	B
Sauteed	JOC	444	1	A
Sauteed w celery & mushrooms	JOC	444	1	B
Shallots	VGCB	183	1	B
Skewered, lamb	BB	88	1	B
Stew	FFCB	217	1	B
Stew	AC	363	1	
Stew	JOC	445	1	B
& Sweetbreads, broiled	AC	363	1	
Sweetbreads & sausages	AC	357	1	
Veal saute w wine	AC	364	1	
Veal (see veal kidneys)				
Kidney bean				
Boiled	AC	601	2	
Cheese, cazuela &	AC	602	1	

RECIPE	BOOK	PAGE	TD	S
Dish, quick	AC	603	1	
& Egg salad	NYT	428	1	B
Green bean salad	FFCB	436	1	B
In oil	FGCW	91	1	
Maitre d'hotel	AC	602	1	
Mexican style	SC	184	1	A
Salad	BCC	281	2	C
Salad & variations	AC	603	1	
w Sausage in red wine	AC	602	2	
Soup, split pea &	JBC	278	2	
& Tomatoes, canned	JOC	261	1	B
Tureen ham &	AC	603	1	
Kielbasa (Polish sausage)	FG	376	2	B
Cabbage	BBA	98	2	B
Fondue	BCC	17	2	B
w Red wine, poached	AC	433	1	
Roasted	MSE	228	1	C
& Sauerkraut	GHAC	212	1	B
Simmered in beer w onions	MSQC	176	1	B
Kiev chicken cutlet, variations	AC	216	2	
Kiewert (drink)	SC	60	1	A
Kim chee (Korean pickled cabbage)	NYTI	460	3	A
Kipfel (turnovers)	SC	81	3	
Kipfel (walnut crescents)	SC	82	2	
Kipfel, sour cream &	SC	352	1	
Kipfel, sour cream &	SC	82	2	
Kippered fish	AC	28		
Kippered herring, baked	NYT	240	1	B
Kippered herring, broiled	NYTI	87	1	B
Kippered herring in cream	FFCB	148	1	B

L

RECIPE	BOOK	PAGE	TD	S
Lacy ice cream shells	LM	312	2	C
Ladies cabbage	AC	493	1	
Lady Baltimore cake (egg white cake)	BHGN	92	1	C
◆	FFBB	315	1	C
◆	SC	109	1	B
◆	FFCB	510	1	B
◆	GHAC	327	2	C
◆	JOC	624	2	B
◆	AC	654	2	
Lady Baltimore filling	AC	654	2	
Lady Baltimore filling	FFCB	543	1	C
Lady Baltimore filling	FFBB	407	2	C
Lady Baltimore frosting	FFCB	543	1	C
Lady cake	JOC	627	1	B
Ladyfinger	MAFC	666	3	C
◆	LT	351	1	C
◆	FFCB	560	2	B
◆	SC	139	2	
◆	MSE	257	3	C
◆	FFBB	255	1	
◆	NYT	580	1	C
◆	JOC	633	1	C
◆	BTSB	230	2	C
◆	MFC	214	3	C
Almond torte	SC	129	1	B
Apple torte	SC	129	1	B
w Caramel pudding, steamed	SC	189	2	
Lining a mold w	MAFC	585		
Pudding, tipsy	FFCB	531	2	B
Torte	SC	129	1	B
Laggtarta (light pancakes used in desserts)	NYTI	534	2	B
Lalla rookh (ice cream dish)	MHGD	456	1	

RECIPE	BOOK	PAGE	TD	S
Lalla rookh cream	SC	215	2	
Lamb				
A la Breck	FFCB	192	1	B
A la Francaise, curried	NYTI	180	2	C
Artichoke stew	FG	172	2	B
Baked, kibbeh	AC	391	1	
Balls, zucchini &	WC	110	2	B
Bandit	BBA	55	3	B
& Barbecue sauce	FFCB	192	1	B
Barbecued	SC	329	1	
Barbecued, spicy	SC	329	1	
& Barley soup	CBSS	192	1	B
Basic marinade for shish kebab	AC	385	3	
Beans or okra	FG	367	1	B
Boned, stuffed & baked in pastry	MFC2	189	3	B
Breast	MFC2	197		
Barbecued	JBC	184	1	B
Barbecued & breaded	JBC	184	2	B
Braised	SC	290	1	
Braised	FFCB	187	2	B
Broiled	AC	386	1	
Marinated	AC	386	2	
Poached & breaded	AC	387	2	
Stuffed	AC	387	1	
Broiled	OC	129	1	A
Broiled	BCC	235	1	
Burgers	OC	106	2	B
Butterflied	CFS	182	2	B
Butterflied, buttermilk	CFS	183	2	B
Butterflied, piquant prodigal	CFS	184	2	B
Butterflying a (photographs)	OC	32		

RECIPE	BOOK	PAGE	TD	S
Lamb (*cont.*)				
Cakes, Turkish string beans &	GG	351	2	B
Carving	JOC	388		
Casserole, eggplant &	NYT	131	1	B
Casserole, wine, mushrooms, carrots &	MAFC	348	1	B
Casserole w roasted juniper berries	CIC	280	1	B
Charcoal grilled, spring	CPMC	204	2	B
Chart	SC	288		
Chart	CFS	172		
Chart (photographs)	BHGN	264		
Chick peas & cracked wheat	NYTI	542	1	B
Chinese	AC	395	1	
Chop	OC	108	2	B
Chop	JOC	406	1	
Apricots, broiled	YGM	132	1	A
Artichoke, endive &	SP	121	1	B
Baby, fried parmesan & cheese batter	CIC	283	1	B
Baked, stuffed	SC	290	1	
Breaded & variations	AC	383	1	
Broiled	JBC	185	1	
◆	SC	289	1	
◆	FFCB	185	1	B
◆	BHGN	266	1	B
◆	NYT	123	1	B
◆	AC	379	1	
◆	SMG	174	1	B
◆	BB	29	1	
Broiled, pan	SC	289	1	
Broiled, pan	SMG	174	1	B
Broiled, pan or sauteed	AC	380	1	
Broiled w tarragon	BB	29	1	
Broiling, extra thick English chops	AC	380	1	
Broiling, stove top, broiled pans	AC	380		
Cream of, shallots &	MFC	143	2	B
Cutting (photographs)	LT	249		
English	NYTI	89	1	B
Florentine style	FAIC	293	1	B
Garlic stuffed	BB	30	1	B
Grilled	SC	328	1	
Grilled & marinated	SC	328	2	
Herb stuffed	NYT	123	1	B
Herb stuffed	AC	381	1	
Herbed	NYT	123	1	B
Leeks, lemon, dill &	FG	256	3	B
Marinated	NYT	123	1	B
w Mint butter	MSQC	132	1	B
Minted	SC	328	1	
Mushroom stuffed	AC	381	1	
Mushroom stuffed	BB	30	1	B
Mustard &	BCC	236	1	B
Mustard & garlic butter	OC	113	1	B
w Olive paste	FGCW	226	1	B
On liver toast	SMG	186	2	B
Orange	YGM	134	1	B
Oregano	KIS	298	1	A
Oriental	SP	100	1	B
Planked	AC	381	1	
Provencal style	CFS	176	2	A
Provencale, garnish	SMG	184	1	B

RECIPE	BOOK	PAGE	TD	S
Ragout of chestnuts	AC	382	2	
Roasted, pan wine w lemon sauce	MCIC	286	1	B
Rosemary	FG	360	2	B
Rouennaise	NYTI	177	1	B
Saddle of	BB	29	1	
Shoulder, braised, onions & mushrooms	AC	383	1	
Shoulder, braised, onions & peppers	AC	382	1	
Skillet Italian	BHGN	267	1	B
Stuffed	JOC	406	1	B
Stuffed, chicken livers &	AC	381	1	
Supreme	BHGN	266	1	B
Teriyaki	AC	384	3	
Tiny	AC	26	1	
Tiny, hothouse	MSE	275	2	C
Tomatoes &	SC	290	1	
Vegetables & fruits	SP	118	1	B
Wrapping its apron	OC	28		
Chopped	JBC	190	1	
Chunky, bean soup	GHAC	101	2	C
Couscous	BCC	237	2	B
Crown roast, triple	SPGT	97	2	B
w Cumin sauce & wine	FGCW	223	1	B
Curry	FGCW	227	2	B
◆	EBE	58	2	B
◆	NYT	125	1	B
◆	PPLK	135	3	B
◆	BBA	56	2	B
◆	FFCB	190	1	B
◆	SC	304	1	
Early version of	AC	390	2	
Of Bengal	NYT	125	2	B
Peas &	WC	96	1	B

RECIPE	BOOK	PAGE	TD	S
Quick	FFCB	193	1	B
Rice &	WC	107	1	B
Snow peas &	WC	110	1	B
Cutlets	SC	290	1	
Cuts, chart	BHGN	266		
Cuts, chart	JOC	394		
Cuts (drawings)	FFCB	184		
Dijon, spitted	CFS	266	2	B
Dill	MIE	129	2	B
Dill	NYTI	531	2	B
Dill	SC	290	1	
Drawing	JBC	179		
& Eggplant, braised	NYTI	330	1	B
& Eggplant casserole	JOC	430	1	B
& Eggplant mold	MAFC	349	2	B
& Eggplant salad, Greek	SP	208	1	B
& Fennel salad w hazelnut dressing	SPGT	158	2	B
Fennel, sausage & eggplant casserole	FGCW	304	2	B
Fillets of	FFCB	187	2	B
Forestiere	JOC	422	3	
Fricassee of	FFCB	188	2	B
Fries	AC	399	1	
Fries	JOC	449	2	A
Fries, Basque style	AC	399	1	
w Garlic marinade	VGCB	179	1	B
Goulash au blanc	JOC	417	2	
Gravy	AC	367	1	
Greek w pork sausage	FGCW	248	2	B
Grilled, on skewers	OC	114	1	B
Haricot mutton, beans &	AC	393	2	
Haricot of mutton	AC	393	2	
Hash	NYT	131	1	B
Head	JOC	449	3	B

RECIPE	BOOK	PAGE	TD	S
Lamb (*cont.*)				
Hearts & peas, sauteed	VGCB	199	1	B
Hot house, Roman style	CIC	281	1	B
Hunter's style	BBA	56	2	B
In pocket bread, spicy	YGM	136	1	B
Javanese	BB	87	2	
Kale & barley stew	VGCB	146	1	B
Kapama	AC	390	2	
Kasha	BCC	238	1	B
Kebab	OC	114	2	B
Kebab	SMG	190	1	B
Broiled	JOC	406	1	B
Grilled	OC	115	2	B
Ground	OC	119	2	B
Ground	AC	386	1	
Miniature	SP	12	1	B
Kibbe naye	AC	390	1	
Kidney	AC	396	1	
Kidney	MAFC	416	1	
Broiled, plain	AC	397	1	
En brochette	AC	397	1	
Risotto w artichoke	CPMC	198	2	B
Sauteed & onion	MCIC	307	1	B
Sauteed, white wine &	CIC	300	2	B
Skewered	BB	88	1	B
Leg				
A la Molly Ellsworth	NYT	120	2	B
A more elegant, boiled	AC	372	2	
Baby roast	AC	371	1	
Baby & variations	AC	370		
Baked, w wilted escarole	CPMC	173	3	B
Balancing on a spit (photographs)	OC	42		
w Balsamic vinegar	FGCW	225	3	B
Barbecued	JOC	405	1	
Barbecued & butterflied	BBA	54	3	B
Boiled	JBC	182	2	B
Boiled w caper sauce	AC	372	1	
Boiled, rare	AC	373	1	
Boiled, sauce for	AC	373		
Boned & stuffed	AC	369	2	
Boning a	MFC2	186	1	
Braised	JOC	422	2	B
Braised	JBC	181	1	B
Braised w beans	MAFC	338	2	
Butterflied w Zinfandel sauce	GRIL	67	2	B
Carving a	GHAC	204		
Garlic	AC	369	1	
Garlic roast	AC	367	1	
Garlic, sauce for	MAFC	334	1	A
Gourmet	EBE	56	1	B
Grilled	AC	368	1	
Grilled & boned	SC	330	3	
Grilled & butterflied	FFCB	188	2	B
Indian style	OC	111	2	B
Kebab	OC	111	2	B
Marinated	AC	369	3	
Marinated	BHGN	40	3	C
Marinated	JBC	181	3	B
Marinated, butterflied	MIE	127	3	B
Marinated w red wine	MAFC	341	3	C
Middle Eastern style	NYT	122	1	B
Mustard roast	SC	289	1	
Pan roasted w vegetables	MSQC	42	1	B
Polynesian, stuffed	JBC	180	2	B

RECIPE	BOOK	PAGE	TD	S
Preparing for cooking	MAFC	329		
Roast	GHAC	204	2	C
◆	MAFC	332	1	C
◆	BBA	55	2	B
◆	NYT	119		B
◆	FFCB	183	1	B
◆	SPGT	54	2	B
◆	JBC	179	2	B
Roast, baker's style	JBC	180	2	B
Roast, French style	BB	63	1	
Roast, garlic & rosemary	MIE	126	2	B
Roast, garlic & guava glaze	MSE	174	1	B
Roast, Greek style (arni psito)	NYT	121	1	B
Roast, plain American	AC	366		
Roast, potatoes &	SC	289	1	
Roast, searing method	AC	367		
Spit, roasted	NYTI	390	3	B
Spit, roasted	OC	109	2	B
Spitted	JBC	182	2	B
Stuffed	MAFC	335		
Stuffed	JBC	180	2	B
Stuffed, curry, roasted	BB	63	1	
Stuffed, roast Italian style	BB	63	1	
Swedish	AC	369	1	
Trimming (photographs)	LT	250		
w Turnips	NYT	122		B
Weeping	AC	370	2	
Lemon, marinated & grilled	GHAC	218	3	B
Lemon, roast leg of	CFS	181	2	B
& Lentil casserole	JBC	343	2	B
& Lentils	FFCB	326	2	B
& Lettuce rocket salad	CPMC	202	1	B
Liver	AC	396	1	
Liver	JBC	192	1	
Loaves, individual herbed	BBA	56	2	B
Loin chops, stuffed	SC	290	1	
Loin chops w walnut glaze	BHGN	267	1	B
Loin of, crust	LM	238	3	B
Loin of, sauteed w walnut oil	CPMC	126	2	B
Loin, roasts	CFS	178	3	B
Madras, curried	BHGN	267	1	B
Making it taste like venison	AC	368	3	
Marinade for	SP	13	1	B
Marinated & grilled	OC	112	2	B
Marinated, Hunan style	YGM	194	2	C
Marrakech	NYTI	483	2	B
Medallions, breaded	SMG	188	1	B
Medallions of, w hazelnut hollandaise	SPGT	70	2	B
Mongolian, Lamb's Wool	FGCW	324	1	B
Mustard coating for roast	MAFC	335	1	B
Navarin of	SP	136	2	B
Noisettes	GHAC	206	1	B
Noisettes of zucchini & eggplant	MFC	144	2	B
& Okra stew	VGCB	165	2	B
On skewers	NYTI	462	3	B
On skewers w mint sauce	MSE	50	3	C

RECIPE	BOOK	PAGE	TD	S
Lamb (*cont.*)				
Onion, caper & tomato sauce, boiled leg of	MAFC	342	1	
Or beef vinaigrette, variations	AC	71	1	
& Parsley stew	NYT	126	2	B
Patties	JOC	428	2	C
Patties	MAFC	348	1	B
Broiled	SMG	180	1	B
w Dill sauce	BHGN	268	1	B
Savory	FFCB	189	1	B
w Sour cream & capers	SMG	182	1	B
& Pepper salad, cold	GG	279	1	B
& Peppercorn crust, roast	SP	100	2	B
Pie	AC	326	2	
Pie, herb crusted	BBA	62	3	B
Pinchitos	OC	117	2	B
& Pine nuts, eggplant &	FG	368	1	B
Pineapple & pepper, on skewers	OC	116	2	B
Pork, walnuts, pumpkin, prunes & white beans	CF	50	2	C
Provencal, charcoal grilled	NYTI	175	3	C
Rack of	MSE	223	2	A
A l'orange	WC	105	2	B
Baby, w herb crust	MSQC	16	1	A
Carving (photographs)	LT	327		
w Fresh mint sauce	MIE	130	1	B
w Parsley crust	GHAC	205	2	B
Parsleyed	SMG	178	2	B
Parsleyed	NYTI	176	1	B
Parsleyed, crumbed	AC	376	1	
Roast	JBC	180	2	B
Roast	BB	65	1	B
Roast	CFS	186	1	A
Roasted herbs	CPMC	44	2	B
Rosemary	SMG	176	1	B
Simple	AC	376	1	
Spring roast	GF	191	1	C
Trimming (photographs)	LT	244		
Ragout	BCC	238	2	B
Ragout	NYT	127	2	B
Dilled	BHGN	369	2	B
Spring	JBC	187	1	B
Spring	CPMC	199	3	B
Spring, Bretonne	JBC	188	2	B
Spring, Californian	JBC	188	2	B
Spring, French	JBC	187	2	B
Spring, Italian	JBC	188	2	B
Spring, Mexican	JBC	188	2	B
Spring, rice	JBC	187	2	B
Rib chops, stuffed	SC	290	1	
Riblets				
Barbecued	MIE	132	2	B
Breast, artichoke w mustard sauce	OC	110	3	B
Grilled	BBA	57	2	B
Saucy	BHGN	41	2	B
Sweet & sour	BBA	57	2	B
Rice casserole	AC	396	1	
Rice, cooked & curried	JOC	229	2	B
& Rice, curry of	JOC	423	2	B
Rice & pine nuts, Lebanese	AC	392	1	
Roast	JOC	405	2	B
Roast	BCC	234		
A la Francaise	NYTI	175	2	B
Artichoke for	NYTI	134	1	B

RECIPE	BOOK	PAGE	TD	S
Lamb, Shoulder (*cont.*)				
Roast	JBC	182	1	B
Roast, stuffed	BB	64	2	B
Roast, stuffed, Oriental	BB	64	2	B
Spitted	JBC	182	2	B
Stuffed	NYT	122		B
Stuffed	MAFC	335		
Stuffed	GHAC	204	2	B
Roast	JOC	406	2	B
Roast	AC	374		
Stuffed	BCC	235	2	C
Stuffed w grilled leeks	CPMC	208	3	B
Stuffed, smoked	OC	113	2	B
Shreds w cellophane noodles	NYTI	49	1	B
Skewered	OC	114	2	B
Skewered, Indochina	CFS	191	2	A
Skewered, minted	SC	331	2	
Soup, egg, lemon &	CBSS	191	2	B
Spiced, yogurt, okra &	BBA	98	3	B
Spit-roasted	SC	329	1	
Spring, w green vegetables	GHAC	205	1	B
Spring, roast, w white wine	CIC	278	1	B
Steaks	SC	289	1	
Steaks	AC	384		
Steaks	CFS	179	2	B
Steaks w curry marinade	BB	28	1	A
Steaks, grilled w olive butter	CFS	180	2	B
Stew	SC	290	2	
Stew	JOC	422	2	B
Stew	NYT	126	2	B
Caraway	NYT	127	2	A
Forestiere	NYTI	178	2	B
Greek	CBSS	193	2	B
Herbed	BHGN	369	1	B
Okra	NYT	127	2	B
Onions w mushrooms &	MAFC	348	1	B
Red wine, onions, mushrooms, bacon &	MAFC	347	2	B
Rice, onions, tomatoes &	MAFC	348	1	B
Sausage & sweet potato	VGCB	298	2	B
Spanish style	NYTI	522	2	B
Spring vegetables in	MAFC	345	2	B
Vegetables browned in	AC	388	2	
Vegetables, exceptional in	AC	388	3	
Vinegar, green beans in	MCIC	288	2	B
White wine, ham, pepper	MCIC	289	1	B
Stock, mixed	OC	167	2	B
& String beans	AC	391	2	
Stuffed w kohlrabis	VGCB	152	2	B
Stuffed Persian style	CFS	187	1	B
Swedish	NYT	120	2	B
Ta nissia (w ham)	BBA	57	3	B
Tartare	BBA	54	2	C
Terrapin	JOC	229	2	B
Tidbits, skewered & marinated	MCIC	91	2	B
Tomato greens stew	VGCB	132	2	B
Tomatoes & rice Oriental	WC	97	1	B

RECIPE	BOOK	PAGE	TD	S
Tongue	MFC2	242	2	B
Boiled	AC	398	1	
Fricassee of	AC	398	1	
Pickled	AC	398	3	
Paper cases	OC	129	2	B
Variety, meats skewered	OC	131	2	B
& White beans	WC	93	1	B
Whole, spit-roasted	OC	110	2	B
Wine & cumin sauce	FGCW	223	1	B
Lamburgers	BB	26	1	B
Lamburgers, filled	JOC	428	1	B
Lamburgers, savory	BHGN	268	1	B
Lane cake	AC	659	2	
Lane cake	MSE	214	2	C
Lane cake	GHAC	327	2	C
Langue de chat (waffer cake)	JOC	633	1	C
Lapin gibelotte (French rabbit stew)	NYTI	205	2	B
Lard	FFBB	13		
All about	JOC	510		
Crust, vinegar, old fashioned	MSQC	125	2	B
Dough	FFBB	56	1	B
Leaves for terrine pates, making	LT	53		
Meat, how to	NYT	100		
Seasoned	JOC	542	1	
Larder, stocking your	JBGF	242		
Larding a piece of meat (drawings)	MFC2	170		
Larding strips & leaves (photographs)	LT	48		
Lardons	MSQC	45	1	B
Lardoons	JOC	383	2	
Lasagne	FFCB	333	2	B
◆	VE	239	2	C
◆	EBE	60	2	B

RECIPE	BOOK	PAGE	TD	S
◆	NYT	330	3	C
◆	JOC	190	2	C
◆	SC	337	2	
◆	GHAC	264	1	B
◆	BHGN	259	1	C
◆	BTSB	302	2	B
◆	MC	124	1	B
w Artichoke	MCIC	184	3	B
Baked	AC	587	2	
Baked, northern Italian style	FAIC	189	2	C
w Bean sauce, quick	JBGF	354	2	B
Duck, style of Arezzo	FAIC	195	2	C
Eggplant	MC	125	1	B
For a crowd	NYTI	412	2	C
Green	SP	76	2	B
Imbottita	JBC	212	2	B
Italian sausage	BCC	232	2	B
Leek	SPGT	170	2	B
w Meat sauce, baked, green	CIC	143	3	B
Monterey cheese	GHAC	264	1	C
Mushrooms & ham	MCIC	187	3	B
Pesto	CPPC	72	3	B
Ricotta pesto	MCIC	190	3	B
Roll ups	BCC	213	1	B
Seafood	BCC	192	2	C
Spinach	BBA	109	2	B
Spinach & smoked ham	MSE	144	2	C
Stuffed	JBC	212	2	B
Stuffed, cheese only	JBC	213	2	B
Stuffed, fish	JBC	213	2	B
Stuffed, meat balls	JBC	213	2	B
Tomato & cheese	CPPC	68	3	B
Vegetable	JBGF	356	2	B
Vegetable	GHAC	264	1	C
Vegetarian	YGM	80	1	B

RECIPE	BOOK	PAGE	TD	S
& Artichoke, braised	CIC	348	1	B
& Barley soup	VGCB	159	1	B
Blackened red onions &	MSQC	24	1	A
Boiled	JBC	312	1	B
Braised	AC	523	1	
◆	FFCB	387	1	A
◆	NYT	382	1	B
◆	MAFC	495	1	B
Braised & parmesan cheese	MCIC	392	1	B
Browned, cheese &	MAFC	496	1	B
Browned w cheese sauce	MAFC	496	1	B
Charcoal grilled	CPMC	210	1	B
Cheesed	JBC	312	1	
Chicken breasts &	VGCB	160	1	B
& Chicken in cream	FG	139	2	B
Chowder, potato &	JBGF	322	1	B
Cooking	AC	523		
Creamed	JBC	312	1	
Custard	GG	251	1	B
w Dill sauce, cold	BBA	133	2	B
& Duck legs	MFC	89	3	A
Duck w mustard &	FGCW	188	2	B
Finishing touches for, whole braised	VGCB	157	1	
Frittata	SPGT	169	1	B
Frittata of	FAIC	97	2	B
Frittata, potato &	FFCB	342	1	B
& Goat cheese tart	CPMC	147	3	B
& Ham, gratin of	MAFC	155	1	B
Hollandaise	JBC	312	1	
Lamb chops, lemon dill	FG	256	3	B
Lamb, shoulder of, stuffed, w grilled	CPMC	208	3	B
Lasagne	SPGT	170	2	B
Leftover, boiled beef w	FAIC	272	2	B
Loaf, chicken, carrot &	CW	60	1	B
Nicoise	SP	184	2	B
Nicoise, cold	BBA	144	2	B
Omelet, creamed	MSE	92	1	C
& Oranges, chicken breasts stuffed w	SPGT	89	3	B
Oysters & pancetta, linguine &	CPPC	107	2	A
Panade	CBSS	348	1	B
Party, potatoes w	GHAC	243	1	C
& Pepper soup, Catalonian	MFC2	21	1	B
Pheasant w pecan stuffing	SP	109	3	B
Pie	FAIC	99	2	C
Pie	JOC	227	2	B
Pie, ham & cheese &	SC	232	1	
Pie, pork &	VGCB	160	2	B
Pizza w pancetta, goat cheese &	CPPC	155	3	B
Poached w pink peppercorn mayonnaise	SPGT	53	2	B
& Pork pie	VGCB	160	2	B
& Potato puree	SP	197	1	B
& Potato soup	FFCB	95	1	C
◆	JOC	159	1	B
◆ (English)	CBSS	281	1	B
◆	CBSS	339	1	B
◆	MAFC	37	1	B
◆	JBGF	329	2	B
◆	NYTI	125	1	B
◆	VGCB	158	1	B
& Potato soup, an old	AC	92	1	
& Potato soup, cold	MAFC	39	1	B

RECIPE	BOOK	PAGE	TD	S
Leek (*cont.*)				
& Potatoes, party	GHAC	243	1	C
Prassa	GG	246	1	B
Preparing	GG	239		
Preparing	BCC	350		
Puree of	JOC	279	1	
Quiche	FG	105	2	B
Quiche	MAFC	151	2	B
& Red wine, drunken	GG	247	1	B
Salad vinaigrette	VE	102	1	B
& Sausage pie	NYT	29	2	B
& Scallops, baked	VGCB	160	1	B
& Scallops w pernod	SMG	134	1	B
& Shrimp, stir fried	VGCB	159	1	B
& Smoked salmon quiches, miniature	MSE	44	3	B
Soup	FAIC	115	1	B
Cabbage &	MSQC	212	1	B
Chicken &	BCC	305	1	B
Chicken &	CBSS	283	2	B
Chicken, cream (cock-a-leekie)	JOC	155	1	B
Pepper, Catalonian	MFC2	21	1	B
Pumpkin &	BBA	41	3	B
Vegetable &	SC	400	1	
& Squid in red wine	CPMC	43	3	B
Steamed, red onion &	CW	116	1	B
Stewed, tomatoes &	GG	246	1	B
Stuffed	JOC	70	2	C
Sweet peppers & mushrooms, broiled	GHAC	255	2	B
Tart	VGCB	158	1	B
Tartlets	VGCB	158	1	C
Timbales	MFC	173	2	B
& Tomato sauce	BCC	350	1	B
& Tomatoes, stewed	GG	246	1	B
Veal kidneys in vinegar sauce	MFC	159	3	B
Vinaigrette	NYT	422	2	B
Vinaigrette	VGCB	158	1	B
A la Lucas	GG	248	1	B
Cold	JBC	313	2	
Julienne of	GF	226	1	C
Whole, boiled	VGCB	157	1	
Whole, braised	VGCB	157	1	
Whole, chopped, braised	VGCB	157	1	
Whole, steamed	VGCB	157	1	
Wrapped shrimp w cheese filling	GHAC	125	2	B
Leftover cake, chocolate dessert made from	MFC2	493	1	C
Leftover salad soup	MIE	86	2	B
Leftovers in bacon	JOC	230		
Legumes, dried, all about	JOC	259		
Legumes, types of, chart	BCC	170		
Lekach (honey cake)	NYT	561	2	C
Lemon				
Almond tart	MAFC	646	2	B
Almond tart	MHGD	214	2	C
Angel pie	SC	131	3	B
Angel trifle	EBE	197	3	B
Applesauce	AC	746	1	
Basting sauce	CFS	295	1	A
Batter	AC	132	1	
Black walnut bread	SP	252	2	B
Blancmange	AC	726	1	
Blueberry mold	EBE	134	2	C
Blueberry tart	SP	281	2	B
& Broccoli, stir fried	KIS	131	1	A
Butter (see also butter, lemon)				

RECIPE	BOOK	PAGE	TD	S
Butter cream icing	MAFC	676	1	C
Butter filling	MAFC	676	1	B
Butter, foaming	LM	131		
Butter frosting	SC	144	1	
Butter sauce	BCC	190	1	
◆	PPLK	242	1	B
◆	MAFC	98	2	B
◆	GHAC	256	1	
Buttermilk cake II	MHGD	115	1	C
Cake	AC	652	1	
Cake, glazed	SP	298	2	C
Cake pudding	AC	727	1	
Cake roll	BCC	76	2	C
Cake, the best damn	MHGD	113	1	B
Cake, white	FFBB	357	1	B
Caramel souffle	LM	320	1	B
Champagne ice	FGCW	397	3	B
Champagne sherbet	FGCW	396	3	B
Cheese gel, grape clusters in	GHAC	294	2	C
Cheesecake	JBGF	616	2	C
Cheesecake	BCC	137	2	C
Chess pie	BHGN	282	2	B
Chess pie	NYTI	565	1	B
Chicken	SP	93	3	B
◆	SPGT	104	3	B
◆	FG	245	1	
◆	NYTI	491	3	B
◆	NYTI	53	2	B
Broiled	AC	189	1	
Broiled	BCC	246	1	
Herbs &	SP	123	1	B
Roast	MCIC	311	1	B
Steamed	FG	266	1	B
Chiffon cake	BCC	76	2	C
Chiffon pie	FFCB	593	2	B
◆	FFBB	126	2	B
◆	AC	622	2	
◆	SC	350	1	

RECIPE	BOOK	PAGE	TD	S
◆	JOC	614	2	B
◆	BCC	93	2	B
Chive sauce	BHGN	355	1	B
Clove cookies	CPMC	79	1	C
Coconut cream filling	FFCB	543	1	B
Coconut pie	BCC	93	2	B
Cookie sandwiches	BCC	110	2	C
Cornstarch filling	SC	148	1	
Cream				
Dressing	SC	378	1	
Frozen	BCC	149	2	B
Frozen	NYTI	308	3	B
Pie	FFBB	111	2	B
Pie	JBC	43	1	
Pie, eggless	JOC	613	2	B
Pie, frozen	JOC	613	2	B
Tartlets	JBC	43	1	
Crepes	BHGN	182	1	C
Crisps	BBA	190	3	C
Crumb pie	FFCB	588	2	B
Curd	JBC	43	1	
Curd	BTSB	249	1	B
Curd, making	NSD	119		
Custard filling	SC	148	1	
Custard tartlets	MSE	92	2	C
Dill sauce, broiled halibut steaks w	GHAC	139	1	B
Dressing, north African	NYT	438	1	B
Egg sauce	SC	389	1	
Extract	BTSB	297	2	
Filled icebox cake	SC	135	1	B
Filled yellow cake	BCC	69	1	C
Filling (see filling, lemon)				
Frosting	BCC	99	1	
Frosting, creamy	BCC	77	1	C
Frosting, fluff	SC	145	1	

RECIPE	BOOK	PAGE	TD	S
Lemon (*cont.*)				
Garnish, making	GHAC	135		
Garnishes	GHAC	135		
Gelatin	JOC	695	2	B
Gelatin, fruit molded	JOC	696	2	B
Ginger cookies	YGM	203	1	C
Ginger punch	SC	57	1	
Glaze (see glaze, lemon)				
Glazed, potatoes, sweet	EBE	128	1	B
Hard sauce	FFCB	641	1	B
Hard sauce w brandy	BBA	213	3	
Ice	FFCB	636	2	C
◆	SC	210	2	
◆	JOC	723	2	C
◆	SP	310	2	B
◆	MHGD	441	1	C
Ice, champagne	FGCW	397	3	B
Ice, rum	CF	47	2	B
Icing	SC	143	1	
Orange	SP	271	1	B
Quick	JOC	678	1	B
Seven minute	JOC	676	1	B
Ideas for	SP	93		
Jelly	SC	201	1	
Jelly	FFCB	620	2	B
Lima beans &	AC	600	1	
Lime milk sherbet	GHAC	306	3	B
Lime tart	NSD	96	3	B
Loaf cake	AC	650	1	
Macaroon layer	NSD	316	3	B
Marinade	GRIL	36	1	B
Marinade, spicy	SC	327	1	
Marmalade	JOC	779	2	C
& Marshmallow meringue pie	SC	349	1	
Mayonnaise	SPGT	151	1	C

RECIPE	BOOK	PAGE	TD	S
Mayonnaise, caper &	MIE	250	1	B
Mayonnaise, garlic &	SP	209	1	B
Meringue pie	AC	621	1	
◆	SC	349	1	
◆	BHGN	281	2	B
◆	MHGD	164	2	B
◆	FFBB	145	2	B
◆	GHAC	322	2	C
◆	FFCB	589	2	B
◆	BCC	91	2	B
◆	JOC	612	2	B
◆	CF	143	1	B
◆	NYT	525	1	B
Meringue pie, mile high	MSE	244	3	B
Milk sherbet	FFCB	634	2	C
◆	NYT	627	2	B
◆	JOC	722	2	C
◆	SC	210	2	
Mint sorbet	GF	48	2	C
Mold, chicken	FGCW	295	2	B
Mousse	NYTI	305	2	B
Mousse	MC	213	2	B
Mousse	MHGD	356	2	B
w Berry puree	CF	119	2	B
Cake	NSD	268	3	B
Iced	MSE	98	2	C
Joan's frozen	MHGD	447	2	C
w Raspberry sauce, frozen	GF	168	2	A
Tartlets, iced	MSE	172	3	C
& Mushrooms, chilled	GHAC	238	1	B
Mustard sauce, brussels sprouts w	JBGF	514	1	B
Mustard sauce, roast breast of chicken w	GF	68	3	C

RECIPE	BOOK	PAGE	TD	S
Nut bread	CBB	471	1	B
Or orange cream filling	MFC2	484	1	
Or orange refrigerator cookies	AC	701	2	
Orange ice	JOC	722	2	C
Pastry	BHGN	289	1	B
Pastry	NSD	85	1	C
Peel, candied	NSD	77	2	C
Peel, candied	BTSB	255	2	C
Peel, glazed	MAFC	587	1	A
Pepper steak	GHAC	173	1	
Pickled	NYTI	491	3	B
Pie	JBC	41	2	B
Cockaigne	JOC	613	2	B
Fresh or lemon slice	AC	621	1	
Frozen	EBE	195	2	C
Frozen	BCC	94	2	B
Grant's	AC	622	1	
Mile high	FFBB	128	2	C
Old fashioned	SP	302	2	B
Pineapple	FFBB	146	1	B
Shaker	FFBB	87	2	B
Pig, making a (photographs)	LT	34		
Pilaf	BCC	56	1	B
Pork chops	BCC	223	1	B
Potatoes & chives	GHAC	243	1	B
Potatoes, new	GG	296	1	B
Potatoes, parsleyed	BHGN	401	1	B
Pound cake	BCC	69	1	C
Preserves	NYT	504	1	B
Pudding	FFCB	612	1	B
Pudding cake	FFBB	339	1	B
◆	BCC	133	1	B
◆	SC	188	1	C
◆	BHGN	174	1	B
Pudding, steamed	JBC	45	2	B
Punch, ginger	SC	57	1	
Rice (see also rice, lemon)				
Rice salad, scallops in	BBA	146	2	B
Ring, cherry	BHGN	339	2	B
Roll	JOC	642	1	B
Roll, nutted	JBC	43	1	
& Rum applesauce	GG	389	1	A
Sable cookies	NSD	62	2	C
Salad dressing	BCC	279	1	
Salad, frozen	BHGN	342	2	C
Salad, zucchini &	GG	400	2	B
Sauce	JOC	709	1	B
◆	PPLK	313	1	B
◆	FFBB	421	1	C
◆	BCC	154	1	B
◆	SC	217	1	
For desserts	FFCB	644	1	B
For vegetables	FFCB	266	1	B
Greek	MC	80	1	B
Old fashioned	MHGD	421	1	B
Schaum torte	BCC	144	3	C
Sherbet	JOC	723	2	B
Sherbet	AC	739	3	
Sherbet, champagne	FGCW	396	3	B
Sherbet ice	AC	739	3	
Sherry dressing for fruit salad	JOC	318	1	A
Slice or fresh lemon pie	AC	621	1	
Slices for fish	LT	36		
Sorbet	SPGT	141	2	B
Souffle	SC	195	1	
◆	FFCB	620	1	B
◆	JOC	690	2	B
◆	NYTI	303	2	B

RECIPE	BOOK	PAGE	TD	S
Lemon Souffle (*cont.*)				
◆	BCC	147	2	C
◆	JBC	273	1	B
Caramel	LM	320	1	B
Cold	VE	278	2	C
Cold	EBE	190	2	C
Cool	GHAC	300	2	B
Hot	MHGD	378	2	B
In lemon shells	BBA	210	2	B
Pie	SC	349	1	
Pie, Helen's	FFBB	146	1	B
Rum, frozen	MHGD	450	2	B
Tart	MAFC	645	2	B
Soup & celery, chilled	VGCB	81	2	B
Soup, chicken &	CBSS	100	1	B
Soup, egg, Greek	NYT	66	1	B
Soup, Greek	SP	55	2	B
Soy dressing	FFCB	455	1	B
Sponge	SC	201	1	
Sponge, custard	NYTI	296	2	B
Sponge, custard	JOC	687	2	B
Squares	MIE	327	1	C
◆	FFBB	230	1	C
◆	BCC	104	1	C
◆	BHGN	156	1	C
Squares, sour	MHGD	321	1	C
Sticks	SC	172	1	
String beans	GG	348	1	B
Sugar cookies	FFCB	550	1	C
Sundae 1, 2, 3, 4 cake	AC	651	1	
Surprise, frozen	JOC	723	2	
Syrup	SC	53	1	B
Tartlets	MHGD	162	2	C
Tartlets	GF	235	2	B
Tarts	FFCB	595	2	B
Tea cookies	BHGN	161	1	C
Tea loaf, rich	CBB	476	3	B

RECIPE	BOOK	PAGE	TD	S
Terrine w creamy strawberries	NSD	183	3	C
Thyme sherbet	NSD	233	2	B
Topping for cookies or bars	JOC	678	1	B
Torte	SC	129	2	B
Torte	BHGN	176	3	B
Torte, frozen	AC	740	3	
Velvet torte	SC	129	1	B
Wafers	BTSB	241	1	C
Wafers, old fashioned, jumbo	MHGD	324	1	C
Water ice	SC	211	2	
Yogurt cookies	BHGN	159	1	C
Yogurt dressing	BBA	147	1	A
Yogurt souffle, frozen	FFCB	627	3	B
Lemonade	SC	54	1	
◆	BCC	23	1	B
◆	JOC	34	1	
◆	BHGN	52	1	B
Best sparkling	GHAC	196	1	
For 100 people	JOC	34	1	C
Fresh fruit	SC	54	1	A
Fruit punch	SC	55	1	C
Hot, spiced	SC	57	1	B
Minted	BCC	23	1	B
Picnic	SC	54	1	B
Pink	BCC	23	1	B
Punch, fruit	SC	55	1	C
Syrup	JOC	34	1	B
Torte	SC	129	1	B
Lemony vinaigrette	GHAC	210	1	
Leniwe pierogi (cottage cheese dumpling)	VE	204	1	B
Lenten buns	FFBB	504	3	B
Lentil	JOC	262	2	B
Boiled cotechino sausage w	CIC	287	1	B

LENTIL

RECIPE	BOOK	PAGE	TD	S
Brown, & rice soup	JBGF	344	2	C
Bulgar salad	JBGF	405	1	B
Bulgar patty sandwiches	JBGF	493	1	B
Bulgar salad	JBGF	405	1	B
Casserole	JBC	343	2	B
Cheese &	JBC	344	2	B
Ham &	JBC	344	2	B
Lamb &	JBC	344	2	B
Pork chops &	JBC	344	2	B
Sausage &	AC	609	1	
& Cheddar cheese loaf	NYT	360	1	B
Cheesy	BCC	173	1	B
& Chevre	CF	63	1	B
& Collard soup	VGCB	132	1	B
Curried	JBGF	523	1	B
Curried	NYT	359	1	B
Curried, pineapple &	VE	120	2	B
Curry	NYTI	33	2	B
& Frankfurter soup	GHAC	101	2	C
& Goat cheese salad	YGM	179	1	C
& Ham	FFCB	326	1	B
Italian sausages &	FGCW	345	2	B
Lamb &	FFCB	326	2	B
Lamb shoulder, braised &	AC	374	2	
& Lamb, shoulder of, braised	AC	374	2	
Maitre d'hotel	AC	609	1	
Mrs. Rorer's Egyptian	AC	610	1	
& Onion	AC	48	1	
Pickled pork ribs w	FGCW	217	3	B
Pilaf, veal w	WC	103	1	B
Prunes &	JOC	262	1	B
Puree	AC	610	1	
Salad	FFCB	435	1	B

RECIPE	BOOK	PAGE	TD	S
◆	SMG	317	1	B
◆	NYT	427	1	B
◆	FG	371	1	B
◆	JBC	344	2	B
◆	AC	609	1	
◆	NYTI	257	3	B
◆	BB	142	1	B
Salad, goat cheese &	CPMC	189	2	B
Salad, marinated	VE	114	3	B
& Sausage	FFCB	326	2	B
& Sausage casserole	JOC	232	1	B
Sauteed	AC	608	1	
& Short rib stew	NYT	114	2	A
Soup	CIC	73	1	B
◆	NYTI	353	3	C
◆	JBC	279	2	
◆	NYT	63	2	B
◆	SC	397	1	
◆	MC	23	3	B
◆	BHGN	375	1	C
◆	JOC	153	2	B
◆	CBSS	285	2	C
◆	SP	156	2	B
◆	FG	45	2	B
Blonde	VE	64	1	A
w Chard & lemon	AC	96	2	
Chicken &	CBSS	287	2	B
Cream of	FGCW	103	1	B
Creole	VE	65	2	B
My favorite	JBGF	343	2	B
Rice &	CIC	75	1	B
Rice, lamb &	NYT	64	2	B
Texan	CBSS	289	2	C
Watercress &	CF	142	1	B
& Spinach soup	BCC	313	2	B
Tomato sauce	SC	185	3	
Tomato soup	VE	63	2	B
& Tomatoes	NYTI	542	1	A
Vinaigrette, pink	MSE	106	2	C

RECIPE	BOOK	PAGE	TD	S
Lentil (*cont.*)				
Walnut burgers	MC	106	2	B
Walnut salad	SP	160	3	B
& White bean salad	GF	162	1	B
Les courgettes Florentine (zucchini & spinach dish)	NYT	409	2	B
Les oiseaux sans tetes (steak dish)	JBC	145	2	B
Les oranges aux liqueurs	NYTI	280	2	B
Les truffes au mouton (Moroccan truffles w lamb)	NYTI	485	1	B
Lettuce				
All about	VGCB	244		
Balls, stuffed	NYTI	187	1	C
Blanched or steamed	VGCB	248	1	
Braised	MAFC	489	1	B
◆	LT	186	2	
◆	JBC	313	1	
◆	AC	522	1	
◆	NYTI	248	2	B
Braised, oven	NYT	382	1	B
Broth, braised	VGCB	249	1	B
Custard	VGCB	249	1	B
Egg salad, chopped	CF	47	1	B
Finishing touches for sauteed	VGCB	248	1	
Leaf dolmathis	VGCB	251	1	B
& Mushroom salad	BCC	279	1	B
& Oyster appetizer	VGCB	250	1	B
Packets of sole w smoked salmon	VGCB	253	1	B
Pie	VGCB	252	1	B
& Rice dish	JOC	267	1	B
Rolls, stuffed	JOC	90	1	
Salad w dill, wilted	BCC	279	1	B
Salad, wilted	BCC	279	1	B
Sandwiches	SC	382	1	
Sauteed	VGCB	248	1	B
Smothered, pancetta w	MCIC	393	1	B
Soup	FG	44	1	B
Soup	VGCB	251	1	B
Cream of	JOC	160	1	B
Cream of	SC	402	1	
Cream of	CBSS	290	1	B
Fish &	FG	316	1	B
Pea &	NYT	69	1	B
Romaine	NYT	70	1	C
Steamed	VGCB	248	1	
Stuffed	NYT	383	2	B
Stuffed broth-braised	VGCB	249	2	B
Wilted	JBC	314	1	B
Wilted	SC	358	1	
Wilted, peas &	GG	268	1	B
Wrapped, stuffed fillets of fish	VGCB	253	2	B
Leverpostej (chicken liver pate)	NYTI	492	2	C
Lichee nuts	AC	757		
Lichee nuts	JOC	520	1	
Light beer bread	MIE	300	2	B
Light stock	JOC	490	2	B
Lima bean	FFCB	364	1	B
Lima bean	JOC	262	1	B
Baby, prosciutto &	MIE	219	1	B
Bacon &	AC	483	1	
Bacon, onions, mushrooms &	AC	483	1	
Bake	EBE	113	1	B
Bake, herbed	BHGN	391	1	B
Baked, dried	SC	184	2	
Barbecued	FFCB	326	3	B
Boiled	JBC	292	1	A
Boiled, bacon &	JBC	292	1	A

RECIPE	BOOK	PAGE	TD	S
Boiled, mushrooms &	JBC	292	1	A
Boiled, sour cream &	JBC	292	1	A
Buttered	AC	599	1	
Buttered	AC	483	1	
Buttered, crumb	GHAC	231	1	B
Casserole	SC	184	2	
Casserole	BB	135	1	B
Casserole	JOC	263	1	B
Casserole, pork &	FFCB	202	2	B
Casserole, pork &	AC	600	2	
Cheese &	AC	483	1	
Cheese &	JOC	263	1	B
Chili &	JOC	263	2	B
Cooking	AC	482	1	
Corn &	SC	420	1	
Cream	NYT	356	1	B
Creole	NYT	356	1	B
Creole	BCC	336	1	B
Fermiere	FFCB	325	3	B
French	JOC	263	1	B
Fresh	NYT	356		
Gingersnaps &, baked	SPGT	105	1	B
Green	SC	413	1	
In piquant sauce	JOC	263	1	B
In sour cream	AC	483	1	
Italian	BCC	172	2	B
Lemon	AC	600	1	
Mexican style	SC	184	1	A
Mushrooms &	JOC	263	2	B
w Mushrooms	AC	600	1	
Mushrooms & bacon	AC	483	1	
& Mushroom salad	FG	117	2	B
Pears baked w	CW	164	1	B
& Pork casserole	AC	600	2	
Preparing	BCC	336		
Pureed	JOC	259	1	B
Rosemary	NYT	356	1	
Salad, radicchio &	MSQC	153	1	B

RECIPE	BOOK	PAGE	TD	S
Soup, hearty	FGCW	110	2	C
Soup, lamb shank &	CBSS	186	2	B
Spicy	EBE	118	1	B
Steamed, w brown butter	CW	97	1	B
Tomato sauce in	AC	601	1	
& Vegetable casserole	SC	184	3	
Lime				
Angel pie	AC	632	1	
Butter, red snapper w	GHAC	140	2	B
Chicken	KIS	85	1	A
Chicken w basil, slivered	BBA	70	2	C
Chicken, broiled	NYT	119	2	B
Chicken pieces	FG	136	1	B
Chiffon pie	BCC	93	2	B
Chiffon pie	JOC	614	2	B
Chiffon pie	FFCB	593	2	B
Clove cookies	NSD	69	3	C
Cream pie, eggless	JOC	613	2	B
Cream pie, frozen	JOC	613	2	B
Dessert, Rocky Mountain	BBA	202	3	C
Dressing	BCC	295	1	
Dressing	FFCB	452	1	A
Dressing, mint	GHAC	284	1	B
Honey dressing	BCC	298	1	B
Ice sherbet	AC	739	3	
Juice, orange	JOC	33	1	B
Marmalade	NYT	511	2	C
Marmalade	JOC	780	2	C
Mint dressing	NYT	438	1	B
Mint sherbet	NSD	234	2	B
Mold, pineapple &	EBE	140	2	B
Mousse	SP	283	2	B
Mousse, sour, strawberries &	MHGD	364	2	B

RECIPE	BOOK	PAGE	TD	S
Liver, Calf's (*cont.*)				
Sauteed, Tuscan style	FAIC	358	1	B
w Vinegar	SMG	214	1	B
Chicken (see also chicken liver)				
& Chicken breasts on a skewer	OC	135	1	B
& Chicken canapes	SC	39	1	
Chicken & mushroom canapes	SC	39	1	
Chopped	EBE	33	1	B
Cockaigne, wine, braised	JOC	440	2	B
Deep fried	FG	159	1	
Dressing	JOC	458	1	C
Duck in bacon	AC	25	1	
w Duck, fresh American	SPGT	248		
w Duck, sauteed w celery root	CPMC	87	3	B
Dumplings (see also dumplings, liver)				
Dumplings	SC	300	1	
Dumplings leberkloesse	JOC	171	1	B
Dumplings soup	NYT	59	1	B
& Egg salad	SC	362	1	
Foie Gras (roulade)	SPGT	249		
Forcemeat, pork &	LT	297	3	
Fried w onions & bacon	GHAC	211	1	B
Fried, pan, w bacon & onions	GHAC	211	1	B
Goose	JOC	439	2	
Appetizer	SC	47	1	
Chopped	JOC	71	1	
Pate in aspic	LM	162	3	C
Preparing	JOC	439		
Lamb	AC	396	1	
Lamb	JBC	192	1	
Loaf	JOC	432	1	B
Loaf	FFCB	224	1	B
Loaf, an old New England	AC	425	1	
Loaf, veal, to be eaten cold	AC	354	2	
Mousse, poultry &	LT	21	2	B
Mushrooms stuffed w	NYT	37	1	B
Mustard, herbs & bread crumbs	MAFC	407	1	B
On skewers	AC	354	1	
& Onions	BCC	217	1	B
& Onions, sauteed	BHGN	269	1	B
& Onions, stuffed	NYT	389	1	B
Paste	SC	381	1	
Canapes w juniper berries	FAIC	91	1	B
Foie gras &	JOC	61	1	
Mushrooms &	SC	381	1	
Pate	NYTI	105	2	C
Pate	JOC	435	2	
Pate	MFC2	319		
Baked	AC	12	2	
Chicken & quick	NYT	11	1	B
Fine	NYT	7	2	C
Goose in aspic	LM	162	3	C
Pork &	MFC2	321	2	C
Quick	AC	13	1	
Souffle	JOC	435	3	
Swedish	NYTI	532	1	B
Patties	SC	300	1	
Patties	JOC	428	1	B
Pepper, onions & olives on skewers	JOC	440	1	B

RECIPE	BOOK	PAGE	TD	S
& Peppers, stir fry	WC	107	1	B
& Peppers, stuffed	NYT	390	1	B
& Pork, Florentine style	FAIC	359	1	B
Pork pate	MFC2	320	2	C
& Pork pate, veal or chicken	MFC2	321	2	C
Pork sausage & greens	MFC2	304	3	C
Roast beef	AC	317		
Rolls, stuffed	BB	39	1	
Sauce, squab roasted w	CPMC	114	3	B
& Sausage, fried	SC	302	1	
Sausages & pork w greens	MFC2	304	3	C
Sauteed	SC	300	1	
Sauteed	JBC	175	1	B
Sauteed in butter	FFCB	223	1	B
Skewered	BB	87	1	
& Steak, beef	AC	317		
Steak, broiled	JBC	176	1	B
Steak, broiled	BB	38	1	
Steak, broiled pan	BB	38	1	A
Swiss sour	JBC	176	1	B
Toast, lamb chops on	SMG	186	2	B
Veal loaf, to be eaten cold	AC	354	2	
& Vegetables, braised	JOC	440	1	B
Venetian style	FFCB	224	1	B
Liverwurst	BTSB	16	3	B
Dip	JBC	3	1	
& Frankfurters	BB	28	1	B
Franks	BB	28	1	B
Pate	BB	125	1	C
Pate	MIE	28	2	B
Pate, parsleyed	FFCB	63	2	B
Sandwich	AC	809	1	

RECIPE	BOOK	PAGE	TD	S
Loaf cake	AC	649	1	
Brown sugar	SC	112	1	B
Danish	NYTI	84	2	C
Golden onion	GG	243	1	B
Lemon	AC	650	1	
Nut	AC	650	1	
Orange	AC	649	1	
Raised	AC	691	1	
Rum or brandy	AC	649	1	
Spicy	AC	650	1	
White bride's cake	AC	658	2	
Yellow w rum, raisins & cherries	MFC2	485	2	
Loaf, perfect equipment for	CBB	21		
Loaf, spiral, making a (photographs)	NYT	468		
Lobster	MSE	136	1	C
Lobster	MAFC	213		
Lobster	MFC2	25		
A l'Americaine	GHAC	122	2	B
◆	NYT	282	2	B
◆	FFCB	134	2	B
◆	JBC	81	2	B
A la Thackeray	SC	251	1	
All about	JOC	372		
Americaine	JOC	374	2	A
Americaine	NYTI	150	2	B
Aspic	MAFC	549	2	B
Au gratin	AC	147	1	
Avocado & tomato buffet salad	AC	62	1	
Baked	SC	250	1	
Baked & stuffed	JOC	375	2	A
Barbecued	BB	90	2	
Barbecued, special	OC	155	2	B
Bisque	SC	403	1	
◆	MFC	70	3	B
◆	JOC	162	2	B

RECIPE	BOOK	PAGE	TD	S
Lobster Bisque (*cont.*)				
◆	MFC2	32	3	B
◆	FFCB	100	3	B
◆	NYT	76	2	B
◆	NYTI	122	2	C
Bisque, rosy	SC	403	1	
Boiled	BCC	190	1	A
◆	JOC	373	2	
◆	JBC	80	1	
◆	LT	122	1	
◆	AC	144	1	
◆	BHGN	216	3	A
Boiled, live	FFCB	132	2	
Boiling	SC	250		
Bordelaise	SC	251	1	
Broiled	JBC	80	1	
◆	FFCB	133	2	
◆	LT	119	2	
◆	JOC	374	2	A
◆	AC	145		
California style	OC	155	2	A
Live	SC	250	1	
Split	BB	54	1	
Whole	BB	53	1	
Butter	NYTI	269	1	
Butter	JOC	339	2	A
Butter sauce	SC	391	1	
Buying	MFC2	25		
Cabbage leaves & roasted peppers	CPMC	202	3	B
Canapes	SC	40	1	
Canapes, hot	JOC	62	2	
Cantonese	NYTI	42	2	B
Cardinal	NYTI	381	2	B
& Cauliflower salad	AC	62	1	
Chaud froid	MAFC	553	3	B
& Cheese souffle	NYTI	239	2	B
& Chicken salad	AC	63	1	

RECIPE	BOOK	PAGE	TD	S
Chowder	CBSS	137	3	B
Chowder	AC	177	1	
Chowder, quick	JOC	168	1	B
Chunks, buttered	SC	250	1	
Cold, poached w sauce verte	MSE	284	1	A
Cooked, removing meat from	MFC2	28		
Cooked in seawater	NYTI	151	1	B
Creamed	SC	251	1	
Creamed	FFCB	134	1	B
Creamed	SC	249	1	
Croissants, crab &	MFC	39	3	B
Croquettes	SC	252	1	
Croquettes	FFCB	135	1	C
Curried	JBC	80	1	
Curry	EBE	94	1	B
Curry	JOC	238	2	B
Curry	AC	146	1	
Cutting up a raw	MFC2	26		
Dealing w live	MFC2	26		
Deviled	JBC	82	2	B
Eating a	GHAC	201		
& Eggs, poached	SC	223	1	
En Bellevue Parisienne	NYT	16	3	B
Farci	SC	251	1	
Fiesta salad	SPGT	156	1	B
Fra diavolo	AC	146	1	
Fra diavolo	JBC	81	2	B
Fra diavolo	NYTI	383	2	B
Franco American	AC	145	1	A
Grilled w basil butter	OC	155	2	A
Grilled, charcoal	CPMC	148	2	B
Grilled & split	SC	332	2	
Grilled, whole	SC	332	2	
Herbs &	MFC	119	3	B
Hot, in sherried brioche	BBA	91	2	B

RECIPE	BOOK	PAGE	TD	S
Julienne of mixed vegetables	VGCB	342	1	B
Kedgeree	JOC	237	1	B
Killing a live	MFC	20		
Linguine &	NYTI	383	2	B
Live, boiling	NYT	279		
& Macaroni imperial	EBE	95	1	B
w Marinara sauce	JBC	214	1	
Marseillaise	NYTI	150	2	B
& Meat, sauteed	JBC	80	1	
Moana	NYT	281	2	B
Mold	JOC	91	1	B
Mongole, quick or crab meat	JOC	238	1	B
Mongole, quick (soup)	JOC	168	1	B
Mornay	SC	252	1	
Mornay	JBC	80	1	
Mousse	JOC	98	2	B
Mousse, cold	NYT	434	2	B
Mousse w vinaigrette, garden salad	CPMC	196	3	B
Mushroom casserole	SC	251	1	
Newburg	AC	147	1	
◆	JBC	82	2	B
◆	BHGN	219	2	B
◆	JOC	238	1	B
◆	SC	250	1	
w Popovers	BCC	191	1	B
Quick	SC	251	1	
Quick	JBC	82	1	B
Opening boiled	SC	250		
Parfait	JOC	239	2	B
Pasta w asparagus &	CPMC	207	3	B
Poached	JOC	373	2	
& Potatoes, twice baked	SP	178	2	B
Potted	JOC	377	2	
Preparing for cooking (photographs)	LT	119		
Puff balls	JOC	61	2	
Quenelles	MAFC	189	2	B
Quiche	MAFC	149	2	B
Ravioli, scallops &	CPPC	138	3	B
Removing insides (drawings)	FFCB	133		
Rice salad	AC	62	1	
Ring, hot	JOC	239	1	B
Rissoles	SC	252	1	
Rumaki	NYT	16	2	
Salad	GHAC	279	2	A
◆	JOC	91	2	B
◆	JBC	80	1	
◆	JOC	90	1	
◆	SC	363	1	
◆	AC	61	1	
◆	FFCB	440	2	B
Salad, warm	MFC	188	2	B
Sandwiches	JOC	249	1	
Sandwiches, crabmeat, shrimp &	AC	812	1	
Sauce	SC	390	1	
Sauce, fish quenelle w	JOC	194	3	B
Saute, curry	AC	146	1	
Savannah baked	EBE	90	1	B
Shrimp or crabmeat sandwiches	AC	812	1	
Simmered w wine, tomatoes, garlic & herbs	MAFC	223	3	B
Souffle	MAFC	170	3	B
Souffle Plaza Athenee	LM	84	3	B

RECIPE	BOOK	PAGE	TD	S
Lord Baltimore egg yolk cake	AC	654	2	
Lord Baltimore filling	FFCB	543	1	C
Lord Baltimore filling & frosting	FFBB	407	2	C
Lord Baltimore frosting	FFCB	543	1	C
Lorenzo dressing	BCC	300	1	B
Lorenzo dressing	JOC	311	1	A
Lorenzo dressing	SC	373	1	
Lost bread	CBB	601	1	B
Lotus root salad	JOC	86	2	
Louis dressing	BHGN	348	1	B
Louis dressing	AC	58	1	
Louisiana chicken casserole	GHAC	154	1	B
Louisiana court bouillon	AC	181	1	
Louisiana gumbo	GHAC	106	2	C
Louisiana maquechoux w corn & vegetables	GG	136	1	B
Lovage leaves, red snapper grilled w	GF	156	1	B
Lover's morsels	AC	713	1	
Low fat cooking techniques	JBGF	173		
Low cal dressing, creamy	BCC	302	1	B
Lox	AC	143		
Loyalist bread	CBB	498	1	C
Luau kabobs	GHAC	202	1	
Luccan sweet bread	FAIC	42	2	B
Luffen (bread)	CBB	358	3	C
Luganega (pork sausage)	MCIC	30		
Lumpia goreng (fried egg rolls)	NYTI	366	1	B
Lunch basket pita & variations	FFCB	293	1	B
Lunch box sandwiches & variations	AC	814	1	
Lyonnaise potatoes	AC	568	1	
Lyonnaise sauce	JOC	327	1	B

M

RECIPE	BOOK	PAGE	TD	S
Macadamia				
Bars, coconut	BCC	100	1	C
Cookies, coconut	BCC	100	1	C
Meltaways	GHAC	351	1	C
Nut glaze w white chocolate	FFBB	411	2	C
Nut roll ups	CF	95	2	C
Macaroni	JBC	212		
Macaroni	KIS	282	1	A
w Asparagus, cream & ham	MCIC	142	1	B
Baked	JOC	186	1	B
Baked w sour cream	JOC	187	1	B
w Basil	MFC	173	1	B
w Beans	NYTI	414	2	B
Boiled	SC	338	1	
& Bologna salad	BCC	266	2	B
Casserole	BCC	253	1	B
& Cheese	BHGN	204	1	B
◆	AC	588	1	
◆	KIS	345	1	A
◆	FFCB	332	1	B
Baked	GHAC	259	1	B
Baked	VE	242	2	B
Baked w red sauce	SC	338	1	
Boiled	JOC	186	1	B
Nouvelle	KIS	200	1	A
Salad	BCC	266	2	B
& Variations	BCC	167	1	B

RECIPE	BOOK	PAGE	TD	S
Macaroni (*cont.*)				
& Chicken	SC	315	1	
& Chicken salad	BCC	266	2	B
& Chicken, stuffed	NYT	205	1	B
& Chipped beef, baked	SC	339	1	
& Frank salad	BCC	266	2	B
w Greek lamb sauce	NYTI	331	2	B
Homemade	CIC	170	2	
Leonardo	NYTI	413	1	B
Loaf	JOC	187	2	B
& Meat, Greek	NYTI	332	2	C
Mexican style	BCC	62	1	B
Mousse	FFCB	333	1	B
& Mushrooms	SC	338	1	
& Oysters	SC	338	1	
Peas & peppers	MCIC	144	1	B
Pudding	SC	338	2	
Quattro formaggi	SPGT	67	1	B
Salad	JBC	250	1	B
Salad	JOC	90	1	B
Salad	FFCB	434	1	B
w Cheddar	BHGN	334	2	B
w Chicken	BCC	269	2	B
w Salmon	BCC	269	2	B
& Shellfish	JOC	187	2	B
& Shrimp salad	BCC	266	2	B
& Squab in pastry drum	FAIC	206	2	B
Tomatoes, livers, mushrooms & cheese	JOC	187	1	B
Tomatoes & mushrooms	SC	338	2	
Whole wheat Russian style	MC	101	1	B
Woodsman style w mushrooms	MCIC	145	1	B
Macaroons	AC	720	1	

RECIPE	BOOK	PAGE	TD	S
◆	SC	163	1	
◆	JOC	671	2	C
◆	FFCB	556	2	C
Almond	FFBB	218	1	C
◆	FFCB	556	2	C
◆	NYT	577	1	C
◆	SC	163	1	
Baked apples w	MCIC	441	1	B
Bombe	JOC	718	2	B
Brown sugar	SC	164	1	
Cherry	FFCB	556	2	C
Children's mock	FFBB	238	1	C
Chocolate	SC	164	1	
Chocolate	BBA	189	2	B
Chocolate & coconut	JOC	659	1	C
Chocolate & coconut	EBE	175	1	C
Chocolate & cornflake	SC	164	1	
& Chocolate pudding	SC	204	2	
Coconut	SP	256	1	B
◆	JOC	658	1	C
◆	BHGN	161	1	C
◆	BCC	100	1	C
◆	FFBB	220	1	C
◆	GHAC	351	1	C
Coconut & cornflake	SC	164	1	
Cornflake	SC	164	1	
Cornflake	FFCB	556	1	B
Cream	FFCB	623	2	B
Crumb crust	FFBB	69	1	B
Crumb pie, cherry, canned	FFBB	91	2	B
Cup custard, unmolded	MAFC	611	1	B
Custard meringue	SC	200	2	
Dessert	SC	204	2	
Filbert	SC	163	1	
Filbert, golden	SC	163	1	
For soup	SC	408	1	

RECIPE	BOOK	PAGE	TD	S
Madeira Sauce (*cont.*)				
Mushrooms, sauteed, brown w	MAFC	515	1	B
Quick	AC	456	1	
Squab stuffed w	NYTI	236	2	B
Steak fillet w	MAFC	297	1	B
w Truffles	MAFC	75	2	B
Wine sauce, filet mignon w	SMG	226	1	B
Madeleines (cookies)	MSE	168	2	C
◆	NYT	581	1	C
◆	FFBB	257	1	C
◆	JOC	633	1	C
Madeline's almond honey	FFBB	258	1	C
Madelines, scented	SPGT	109	2	C
Madrasi kari (sweet potatoes, beef & pork dish)	GG	361	1	B
Madrilene ring shad roe	JOC	97	2	B
Mahashes (stuffed spiced vegetables)	NYTI	355	2	C
Mahogany cake	AC	677	1	
Mai Tai cocktail	MSE	158	1	A
Maiden's prayer	SC	60	1	A
Maids of honor	AC	648	2	
Mail order guide for equipment, gadgets	MIE	339		
Mais noix (spicy corn nut & peanut mix)	GG	130	1	B
Mallow sundae cake	BCC	133	1	C
Malt shake syrup, chocolate	JOC	31	1	C
Maltaglianti, making (drawings)	CIC	122		

RECIPE	BOOK	PAGE	TD	S
Maltaise rice mold	NYT	602	3	B
Maltaise sauce	BCC	327	1	A
Maltaise sauce	JOC	329	1	B
Maltaise sauce	AC	460	1	
Malted milk, chocolate egg	SC	51	1	
Malts, chocolate	BCC	24	1	A
Mama's yeast bread	PPLK	44	2	C
Mandarin orange				
Mold	EBE	139	2	C
Salad	BCC	280	1	B
Souffles	BBA	215	3	B
Soup	NYTI	37	3	B
Teriyaki	BBA	52	3	B
Mandel kloese (almond dumplings)	SC	407	1	
Mandel torte or almond torte	AC	688	1	
Mandelbrot (almond cookies)	BBA	190	2	C
Mandelchen (almond cookies)	SC	152	1	
Mandeltorte (lemon filled dessert)	NYT	570	2	C
Manfrigul egg barley	MCIC	174	3	
Mangetout (peas)	AC	539	1	
Mango	AC	757		
Chutney	JOC	785	3	C
Chutney	WC	114	2	C
Chutney dressing	SP	207	1	B
Chutney dressing, pear duck salad w	SP	206	2	B
Cocktail	JBGF	288	1	B
Compote	CPMC	33	2	C
Coriander sherbet	NSD	233	2	B
Cream kiwi tart	FFBB	170	2	B
Creamy, filled	BCC	127	1	B
Daiquiri	MSE	158	1	B
Daiquiri	JBGF	289	1	B

RECIPE	BOOK	PAGE	TD	S
Key West style	MHGD	425	1	
Rice tart	NSD	102	3	B
Sauce	NSD	330	1	C
Sliced, Indian style	MSQ	133	1	B
Soup, cream	SP	58	2	B
Spiced	BBA	169	3	B
w Strawberries, macerated white wine	MCIC	445	1	B
Tart w pastry cream	FFBB	170	2	B
Upside down cake	FFBB	329	1	B
Manhattan	JOC	38	1	
Manhattan	SC	61	1	A
Manhattan	NYT	648	1	
Dry	SC	61	1	A
Perfect	JOC	38	1	
Perfect	SC	61	1	A
Manhattan clam chowder (see clam chowder, Manhattan)				
Manicotti	JOC	190	3	C
Manicotti	VGCB	320	2	B
Manicotti	BCC	168	1	B
I	NYTI	437	2	C
II	NYTI	438	2	C
Beef, spinach, stuffed w	FFCB	299	3	B
Cheese, filled w	GHAC	263	1	B
Cheese stuffed w	FFCB	298	3	B
Chicken, stuffed w	FFCB	299	3	B
Pancakes	NYTI	438	1	
Stuffed	NYT	329	1	C
Stuffed	VE	235	1	B
Manjar blanco (caramel dessert spread)	NYT	596	1	B
Maple				
Bars	AC	800	2	
Bavarian cream	JOC	694	3	B
Bran muffins	GHAC	368	1	B
Bread pudding	GHAC	298	2	B
Butter cream frosting	AC	695	1	
Butternut squash	GHAC	245	1	C
Caramels	JOC	732	1	B
Charlotte	JOC	644	2	C
Cream candy	JOC	729	1	B
Cream pie	FFBB	111	2	B
Curls	JOC	668	1	C
Fluffs	SC	170	1	
Frosting	SC	145	1	
Gelatin chiffon pie	JOC	615	2	B
Glazed pork tenderloins	GHAC	218	2	B
Ice cream	SC	206	2	
Icing, quick	JOC	679	1	B
Icing, sugar	JOC	677	1	B
& Maple walnut ice cream	FFCB	630	3	C
Meringue squares	SC	167	1	
Mousse	FFCB	627	3	B
Mousse	SC	213	2	
Nut frosting	BCC	77	1	C
Nut Hubbard squash puree, Laura's	MSE	188	1	C
Oatmeal bread	CBB	218	3	C
Parfait	JOC	721	2	B
Pecan cookies	NSD	54	1	C
Pecan pie	FFBB	144	1	B
Rice pudding	AC	734	2	
Sugar ice cream	NSD	205	1	B
Sugar pie	AC	629	1	
Sugar sauce	JOC	712	1	B
Sundae sauce	SC	220	1	
Syrup cookies	FFBB	234	2	C
Syrup cream pie	FFBB	135	2	B
Syrup dressing	SC	378	1	
Syrup, fig-in	GHAC	370	1	B
Syrup graham bread	CBB	132	1	C
Syrup ice cream	NSD	206	1	B
Syrup sauce (dessert)	JOC	712	1	A

RECIPE	BOOK	PAGE	TD	S
Marinating sauce for meat & vegetables	VGCB	337	1	B
Marjolaine (almond meringue dessert)	NSD	296	3	B
Marjolaine	MFC	218	3	C
Marlborough pie (apple cream pie)	FFBB	97	2	B
Marlborough pie	AC	625	1	
Marmalade				
Apple & tomato	NYT	512	1	B
Bars	FFCB	568	1	C
Biscuits	JBC	19	1	
Bitter orange	BTSB	164	2	C
Carrot	SC	443	1	
Citrus	SC	443	3	
English	NYT	511	2	C
Ginger	FFCB	707	2	C
Gingerbread	MHGD	282	1	B
Golden chip	SC	443	3	
Grapefruit	JOC	779	2	C
Green tomato	NYT	512	1	B
Lemon	JOC	779	2	C
Lime	JOC	780	2	C
Lime	NYT	511	2	C
Old fashioned parsnip	GG	260	1	B
Onion	GG	241	3	C
Orange	JOC	779	2	C
◆	FFCB	706	2	C
◆	SC	443	3	
◆	BHGN	150	2	B
Orange & peach	SC	443	1	
Parsnip, old fashioned	GG	260	1	B
Pineapple	NYT	512	1	B
Pineapple & apricot	SC	443	3	
Pineapple & grapefruit	SC	443	2	

RECIPE	BOOK	PAGE	TD	S
Pudding cake	WC	142	1	B
Rhubarb & fig	FFCB	706	2	C
Ripe tomato	NYT	512	1	B
Sauce	SC	219	1	
Sauce	MHGD	380	1	
Souffle	FFCB	620	1	B
Tamarind	JOC	780	2	C
Three fruit	FFCB	707	2	C
Tomato	FFCB	706	2	C
Marmite petite (chicken, beef & vegetables in broth)	NYTI	173	2	B
Marquise de chocolat (chocolate mold cake)	NYTI	298	3	C
Marrons glaces (glazed chestnuts)	JOC	743	2	
Marrons glaces	SC	175	3	
Marrow	JOC	451	2	
Balls	JOC	173	2	A
Balls, beef bouillon w	FFCB	80	3	C
Bones, baked	JOC	421	2	A
Consomme	NYTI	116	3	B
Hors d'oeuvre	JOC	71	1	
Preparing	LM	51		
Preparing (photographs)	LM	51		
Poached	JBC	162	1	
Sauce	NYT	373	1	B
Sauce, celery braised w	NYT	373	2	B
Steak, Marchand de Viande	LM	39	3	A
Veal kidneys w red wine sauce &	MAFC	419	1	B
Marsala				
Beef stew w	FG	356	1	B
Chicken	FGCW	170	1	B
Chicken & grapes	KIS	89	1	A

RECIPE	BOOK	PAGE	TD	S
Chicken gizzards w	FGCW	344	2	B
Chicken livers in	NYT	211	1	B
Fruit biscuit bread	SPGT	79	2	B
Marinade	GRIL	37	1	B
Mushroom sauce	FGCW	285	1	B
Pasta w confit of goose &	FGCW	200	1	B
Pork chops, braised	MCIC	294	1	B
Sauce, mushroom w	FGCW	285	1	B
Turkey cutlets	GHAC	162	1	B
Marshmallow	JOC	730	2	B
Marshmallow	SC	174	1	
Marshmallow	BTSB	273	2	C
Apple dessert	SC	192	1	
Balls, chocolate	SC	177	1	
Bars	BCC	122	1	C
Chocolate	BCC	122	1	C
Coconutty	BCC	122	1	C
Gumdrop	BCC	122	1	C
Peanut butter	BCC	122	1	C
Cole slaw, pineapple &	BCC	282	2	B
Covered w caramel	SC	170	1	
Filling, pineapple	SC	149	1	
Frosting	SC	139	1	
Frosting	AC	693	1	
Frosting	SC	145	1	
Frosting, brown sugar	SC	145	1	
Fudge, chocolate	FFCB	679	2	B
Fudge, chocolate	GHAC	354	1	C
Ice cream	SC	207	2	
Chocolate	SC	207	2	
Coffee	SC	208	2	
Mocha	SC	208	2	
Pineapple	SC	207	2	
Icebox dessert, chocolate	SC	136	2	B
Icebox pudding	SC	135	3	B
Icing, brown sugar	JOC	677	1	B
Lemon meringue pie	SC	349	1	

RECIPE	BOOK	PAGE	TD	S
Meringue topping	SC	344	1	
Mint sauce	SC	220	1	
Mocha sauce	SC	220	1	
& Peanut butter fudge	FFCB	681	1	B
Pudding	JOC	697	2	B
Sauce	JOC	713	1	B
Sauce	BCC	153		
Sauce, chocolate	SC	219	1	
Sauce for ice cream, chocolate	GHAC	306	1	
Sundae sauce	SC	220	1	
Sweet potatoes &	SC	431	1	
Martha Washington pie	AC	657	1	
Martini	JOC	37	1	
Martini	SC	61	1	
Martini	NYT	648	1	
Dry	SC	61	1	
On the rocks	SC	61	1	
Perfect	JOC	37	1	
Sweet	SC	61	1	A
Vodka	SC	61	1	
Maryland fried chicken	AC	193	1	
Marzipan	FFCB	688	1	B
Marzipan	JOC	729	2	A
Cake w a sweet crust	NSD	185	3	C
Cookies	SC	158	1	
Cookies, rolled	NYT	577	1	
Tart, figs &	NSD	86	2	B
Tart, raspberries &	NSD	86	2	B
Tart, strawberries &	NSD	86	2	B
Torte pastry	SC	130	1	B
Mascarpone w Gorgonzola cheese, layered	CW	65	1	A
Mash sausages	AC	431	1	
Mashed potatoes	JOC	290	1	B
Mashed sweet potatoes	GG	360	1	B
Maste khiar (cucumbers & yogurt)	NYT	422	1	B

RECIPE	BOOK	PAGE	TD	S
Matalote (fish soup)	FG	283	1	B
Matchsticks (puff pastry)	MFC	215	3	C
Matelote (fish soup)	JOC	164	2	B
Matjes herring w horseradish	NYTI	80	1	B
Matjes herring w sherry	NYTI	80	1	B
Matsu kage yaki (Japanese broiled chicken)	BB	93	2	B
Mattar paneer (peas & cheese)	EBE	114	1	B
Matzo				
Almond dumplings	SC	408	1	
Apple pudding	SC	194	1	
Balls	SC	408	1	
Batter pudding	SC	194	2	
Charlotte	SC	194	1	
Charlottes w apples	SC	194	1	
Cookies	SC	155	1	
Dumplings	SC	408	2	
Dumplings	SC	104	2	
Dumplings, almond	SC	408	1	
Dumplings, filled	SC	104	1	
& Eggs, scrambled	SC	224	1	
French toast	SC	72	1	
Fritters	SC	193	1	
Fritters, filled	SC	194	2	
Fritters, fruit	SC	193	1	
Kloese (dumplings)	SC	104	2	
Lemon sponge cake	SC	124	1	B
Meal almond torte	SC	130	1	B
Meal apple torte	SC	131	2	B
Meal pancakes	SC	96	1	
Meal pancakes, puff	SC	96	1	
Meal torte, chocolate	SC	130	1	B
Pancakes	SC	96	1	
Pfarvel	SC	409	1	
Pie shell	SC	344	2	
Pie topping	SC	344	1	
Spice sponge cake	SC	124	1	B
Sponge cake	SC	124	1	B
Sponge cake, lemon	SC	124	1	B
Sponge roll	SC	124	1	B
Max's loaf (bread)	CBB	107	2	B
May wine	JOC	50	1	
Mayeritsa avgolemono (Greek Easter soup)	NYTI	326	2	B
Mayonnaise	BCC	301	2	B
◆	CIC	27	2	B
◆	MC	46	1	B
◆	JOC	314	1	B
◆	JBC	257	1	
◆	LT	45	1	
◆	MFC	102	1	B
◆	BB	142	1	
◆	NYT	438	1	B
◆	AC	75	1	
◆	GF	245	1	
◆	SC	374	1	
◆	NYTI	265	1	B
◆	FGCW	131	1	B
◆	MAFC	86	2	B
All about	JOC	313		
Anchovies, pickles, capers, herbs w	MAFC	91	1	B
Anchovy	AC	77	1	
Anchovy	MSE	70	1	C
Applesauce	FFCB	453	1	B
Avocado	FFCB	455	1	B
Avocado	GG	40	1	B
Base, cooked	SC	375	1	
Basic, blender	MIE	247	1	B
Basil, technique	OC	14	1	
Basil & variations	OC	165	1	B
Bearnaise	SPGT	155	1	B

MAYONNAISE

RECIPE	BOOK	PAGE	TD	S
Beef	PPLK	269	2	B
Blender	BCC	301	1	B
◆	FFCB	453	1	B
◆	BHGN	352	1	B
◆	BBA	62	1	B
◆	GHAC	284	1	B
Blueberry	SP	118	1	B
Buttermilk dressing	BCC	301	2	B
Cake	AC	674	1	
Chantilly	JOC	315	1	B
Chicken salad	LM	171	3	
Chocolate cake	FFBB	336	2	C
& Cognac sauce for shrimp	NYT	451	1	A
Collee (gelatin)	JOC	341	1	
Cream	FFCB	453	1	B
Cream	JOC	315	1	B
Cresson	MFC	102	1	B
Cucumber	SC	392	1	
Curry	MIE	249	1	B
◆	JBC	257	1	
◆	JOC	315	1	B
◆	AC	77	1	
Dill	MIE	250	1	B
Dill	AC	77	1	
Dressing, boiled	SC	375	1	
Dressing, frozen	SC	378	1	
Dunk	BB	121	1	B
w Egg, hard cooked	JOC	315	1	C
& Eggs	FGCW	132	1	
Fixing when it breaks down	LT	47		
Food processor	FFCB	453	1	B
Fruit salad	JOC	315	1	B
Garlic (see also aioli)				
◆	FG	278	1	B
◆	PPLK	270	1	B
◆	AC	76	1	
◆	GG	324	1	B

RECIPE	BOOK	PAGE	TD	S
Garlic & herb	AC	77	1	
Garlic Provencal	MAFC	92	2	B
Gelatin	JOC	341	1	
Gelatin for decorating cold dishes	MAFC	91	1	B
"Good old way"	FAIC	55	1	C
Green	NYT	439	1	B
◆	FFCB	453	1	B
◆	MC	46	1	B
◆	SMG	315	1	B
◆	JBC	257	1	
◆	JOC	315	1	B
◆	BB	143	1	
◆	BBA	164	1	B
◆	GHAC	385	1	B
Herbal	MAFC	89	1	B
Herbed	AC	77		
Herbs	MAFC	89	1	B
Machine made	FFCB	453	1	B
Pickles, capers, anchovies &	MAFC	90	1	B
Grenache	JOC	315	1	B
& Hard cooked eggs	SC	375	1	
Hard yolk	MAFC	90	1	B
Herb	SP	140	1	B
Herb, flavored	MSE	156	1	B
Herbal	GG	311	1	B
Herbal, w eggs, soft boiled	MAFC	93	2	B
Homemade	SP	339	1	C
◆	PPLK	268	1	B
◆	BHGN	352	1	B
◆	CW	153	1	B
Homemade, basic	FFCB	452	1	B
Horseradish	AC	76	1	B
Large quantity	SC	375	1	
Legere	MFC	102	1	B
Lemon	SPGT	151	1	C
Lemon & capers	MIE	250	1	B

RECIPE	BOOK	PAGE	TD	S
Cantonese	SC	280	1	
Caper sauce, Danish	FG	187	2	B
Chafing dish	EBE	13	1	C
Chinese	JOC	429	1	B
Cocktail	BHGN	12	1	C
Cocktail	GHAC	86	1	C
Cocktail	BCC	9	1	C
Cream, Norwegian	NYTI	493	1	B
Eggplant	FGCW	278	1	B
Finnish	GG	97	1	B
For couscous, sweet	NYTI	486	1	B
For Italian meat sauce	JBC	215	2	B
For soup	JOC	173	3	B
For spaghetti	AC	590	1	
German	SC	281	1	
German	JOC	428	3	B
Greek	FG	160	1	B
Greek	NYT	14	2	C
Green grain	JBGF	459	1	B
Green pepper heroes	WC	103	1	B
Grilled Arab	OC	118	2	B
Hearty	GHAC	183	1	B
Hero	FFCB	293	1	B
Hors d'oeuvre	JOC	71	1	
w Horseradish	EBE	21	2	B
Hot	JBC	5	1	
Italian	JOC	429	1	
Italian	SC	281	1	
Koftas in sour cream	NYTI	354	2	B
Lion's heads	MSE	124	2	C
Little	NYT	14	2	
Mexican style	GHAC	183	1	B
Middle Eastern style	NYTI	462	1	B
Moist, making them	FG	360		
Near Eastern	JBC	6	1	
Olive stuffed	SMG	278	1	B
On skewers, Turkish	NYTI	552	2	B
w Onions & sour cream	FFCB	168	1	B
w Paprika	NYTI	69	1	B
Paprikash	NYTI	344	2	B
Porcupine	SC	282	2	
Porcupine	BHGN	241	1	B
Remoulade	FFCB	62	2	C
Rice coated	NYTI	51	2	C
Sandwich	FFCB	295	1	
Sauce for spaghetti	FFCB	171	1	B
Saucy	BCC	209	1	B
Sauerbraten	SC	43	1	
Sausage & spinach	FG	359	1	B
Sicilian	NYTI	390	2	C
Smitane	NYTI	344	1	B
Spaghetti	SMG	292	1	B
Steamed	FG	267	1	A
Stew w spinach & dumplings	BHGN	368	2	B
Stroganoff	SC	280	1	
Swedish	FFCB	170	1	C
◆	JOC	429	1	B
◆	SC	281	1	
◆	NYT	108	1	B
◆	BHGN	12	1	C
I	NYTI	529	1	B
II	NYTI	529	1	B
III	NYTI	531	1	C
Easy	SC	281	1	
Sweet & sour	WC	90	1	B
Sweet & sour	SC	283	1	
Sweet & sour, Israeli	NYTI	369	1	C
Turkish, kale & barley	GG	207	2	B
Winter, savoy cabbage	MCIC	258	1	B
Meatless meal in a bowl	BHGN	348	1	B
Meaux mustard sauce	MFC	107	1	B
Mechana meat sauce	GG	304	2	B

RECIPE	BOOK	PAGE	TD	S
Media dolma (mussel dish)	NYTI	551	2	B
Mediterranean bourride	VGCB	223	1	
Mediterranean salad	BCC	270	2	B
Melba cheese rounds	JOC	174	1	
Melba sauce	JOC	709	2	B
Melba sauce	BCC	88	1	
Melba sauce	SC	217	1	
I	FFCB	641	1	B
II	FFCB	642	1	B
For ice cream	GHAC	306	1	
Melba toast	SC	72	1	
Melba toast	JOC	587	1	
Baskets	JOC	223	2	C
Homemade	MSE	274	1	C
Making (photographs)	LT	61		
Melitzanosalata (Greek eggplant salad)	GG	158	1	A
Melon (see also honeydew)				
Alaska	AC	759	1	
Balls				
Lemon ice w	JBC	105	1	
Lime ice w	JBC	105	1	
w Liqueur	JBC	104	1	
w Mint	CF	131	1	
w Other fruits	JBC	104	1	
w Wine	BCC	127	1	B
Baskets	JOC	117	1	B
Baskets, fruit in	GHAC	283	2	C
Berries	AC	759		
Bowls in strawberry soup, chilled	BBA	45	3	B
Cocktail	SC	44	1	
Coupe	SC	211	2	
Freezing	BHGN	131		
w Ginger	AC	759	1	
Glorious	GF	133	2	A
w Ham	AC	760	1	
Ice cream	AC	759	1	
Ice w vodka	CF	59	2	B
w Mint	BCC	128	2	B
w Mint cups	EBE	183	2	B
Plain	JBC	104	1	
w Plum wine or port	NSD	122	1	C
w Port	AC	759	1	
w Prosciutto	BCC	6	1	C
w Prosciutto	MSQC	72	1	B
w Prosciutto	MSE	166	1	B
Salad	SC	365	1	
Salad	JOC	94	1	
Salad, frosted	JOC	103	2	B
w Salt & pepper	AC	759	1	
Sherbet	MFC	244	2	B
Sherbet	LM	302	2	B
Soup, champagne &	CBSS	165	3	B
Soup, chilled	CBSS	163	2	B
Soup, true	CBSS	166	3	B
Soup, two	JBGF	328	2	B
Surprise or melon Alaska	AC	759	1	
Swan	LM	298		
Swan, making (photographs)	LM	298		
& Tomato soup, summer	SP	57	2	B
Vinaigrette w red & green salad	GG	188	1	B
Melting tea cake	AC	684	1	
Melton Mowbray pie	NYTI	90	3	B
Menus, sample	FFCB	746		
Meringue	BBA	227	2	C
◆	JOC	600	2	C
◆	LT	338	1	
◆	BCC	91	1	B
◆	FFBB	222	1	C
◆	FFCB	559	2	B
Almond cake, individual petits fours	MFC2	504	3	

RECIPE	BOOK	PAGE	TD	S
Mille feuilles a la fondue de fromage	MFC2	139	3	B
Millet				
Cakes	JBGF	506	1	B
Chickpea & vegetable stew	JBGF	373	1	B
Cooking	JBGF	71		
Supreme	JBGF	524	1	B
Milt, all about	JOC	359		
Mimosa	SP	331	1	
Mincing, how to	BHGN	429		
Mincemeat	SC	346	2	
Mincemeat	NYT	510	2	B
Mincemeat	JOC	603	3	B
Bars	BCC	105	1	C
Classic	FFBB	151	3	B
Cookies	AC	721	1	
Cookies	FFBB	274	2	C
Cookies	FFCB	558	2	C
Dark	FFBB	152	3	C
Lattice tart	MSE	244	3	B
Light	FFBB	153	3	B
Mock	SC	457	3	
Pie	SC	346	1	
◆	FFCB	585	3	B
◆	GHAC	315	3	C
◆	JOC	603	2	B
◆	JBC	39	2	B
◆	FFBB	154	3	B
Flambe	JOC	603	2	B
Homemade	BHGN	278	3	B
Mock	AC	623	1	
Mock	JOC	604	1	B
Pudding	WC	129	2	B
Tart	FFCB	586	3	B
Tartlets	MSE	196	2	B
w Wine	SC	346	2	
Minestrone	BHGN	375	2	B
◆	NYTI	379	3	B
◆	GHAC	101	1	C
◆	VE	61	1	B
◆	NYT	60	2	B
◆	JOC	153	2	B
I	CBSS	294	2	C
II	CBSS	296	2	B
Alla Milanese	VE	62	1	B
Country style, Tuscan	FAIC	122	3	B
Hamburger	BCC	306	1	B
Le Alpi	CBSS	301	2	B
Low sodium	CBSS	302	2	B
Peasant style	CBSS	299	2	B
w Pesto, hot or cold	CIC	69	1	
Reboiled, Tuscan	FAIC	124	3	B
Rice Tuscan	FAIC	121	2	B
Rich	FGCW	102	2	B
Soup	MC	7	1	B
w Sweet sausage & tortellini	SPGT	47	2	C
Mingle mangle warm zucchini salad	GG	399	1	B
Mint	AC	831	3	
Bars	BCC	101	1	C
Brownies, chocolate	GHAC	345	1	C
Butter lamb chops	MSQC	132	1	B
Cantaloupe	GF	157	1	B
Carrots	SMG	271	1	B
Chocolate meringues	SPGT	101	2	B
Cold pea soup w	AC	93	2	
Cookies, chocolate	NSD	46	3	C
Cookies, chocolate	BCC	98	1	C
Cookies, hickory	BCC	107	1	C
Cream (candies)	FFCB	687	2	B
Cream, asparagus in	GG	30	1	B
Cream cheese	BHGN	116	1	C
Creme brulee, making	NSD	169		

RECIPE	BOOK	PAGE	TD	S
Cucumber salad	SP	216	2	B
Fresh tortelli	FAIC	168	2	B
Frittata	CW	44	1	B
Fruit ice	SC	210	2	
Ice	JOC	724	2	C
Ice cream	FFCB	630	3	C
Ice cream cake, fudge	SC	209	2	
Ice cream, chocolate	NSD	212	1	B
Jelly	FFCB	702	2	C
◆	SC	173	1	
◆	BTSB	171	2	C
◆	SC	448	1	
Almost homemade	CFS	175	1	B
Apple	BHGN	149	2	B
Apple	NYT	513	3	
Julep	JOC	46	1	A
Julep	SC	63	1	
Julep	BB	166	1	A
Leaves, crystallized	FFCB	692	2	C
Leaves, crystallized	BTSB	260	2	B
Leaves, glazed	JOC	741	2	B
Lemonade	BCC	23	1	B
Lime dressing	GHAC	284	1	B
Macaroons	BCC	100	1	C
Melon	BCC	128	2	B
Melon cups	EBE	183	2	B
Parfait	NYT	632	2	B
Pea salad	SPGT	151	1	B
Pea soup	CBSS	323	1	B
Pea soup, puree of	GF	73	1	C
Peas	GHAC	239	1	B
Peas, new	BHGN	398	1	B
Peas, new	GG	267	1	B
Peas, orange	EBE	114	2	C
Potatoes & peas	SPGT	168	2	B
Pulled	JOC	734	2	B
Ring	SC	367	2	
Sandwich cookies, chocolate	SPGT	110	2	C
Sauce	JOC	330	1	B
◆	SC	391	1	
◆	BHGN	360	1	A
◆	NSD	335	2	C
◆	FFCB	275	1	A
Chocolate	JOC	712	1	B
Chocolate	NYT	613	1	B
Honey	JOC	713	1	A
Hot spicy	CFS	311	1	B
Lamb on skewers	MSE	50	3	C
Lamb, rack of, w	MIE	130	1	B
Marshmallow	SC	220	1	
Orange	BCC	330	1	B
Rum	NYT	616	1	B
Sorbet	JOC	724	2	C
Sorbet, lemon &	GF	48	2	C
Stuffing	FFCB	280	1	B
Sweet pea & spinach soup	SP	46	2	B
Tangy beets	GG	50	1	B
Tomato soup, cream of	SPGT	129	2	C
Tortelli	FAIC	168	2	B
Truffles	NSD	75	3	C
Velvet chocolate	BHGN	184	3	C
Vinegar	SC	437	3	
Wafers	BCC	120	2	C
Yogurt bread	CBB	452	2	B
Yogurt w spinach	YGM	63	1	A
Minute steak, definition	AC	261		
Mirepoix matignon (vegetable blend)	JOC	541	1	A
Mirepoix of vegetables & clams, linguine w	CPPC	97	3	A
Mirliton, fried	PPLK	34	1	A

RECIPE	BOOK	PAGE	TD	S
Mirliton pirogue stuffed w shrimp or crawfish	PPLK	104	3	B
Mirliton, stuffed, w shrimp & crab butter cream sauce	PPLK	72	2	B
Misaquatas (bean dish)	FG	287	1	B
Miso chicken w bean paste	FGCW	358	3	B
Miso soup	MC	9	2	B
Miso soup	FGCW	356	2	B
Miso soup	CBSS	292	2	B
Mixed beef stock	OC	167	2	B
Mixed chicken stock	OC	167	2	B
Mixed fry, Florentine style	FAIC	280		
Mixed grain bread	VE	39	2	B
Mixed grand, boiled dinner	FAIC	271		
Mixed green salad	SMG	199	1	B
Mixed greens, Southern style	FFCB	378	2	B
Mixed grill	FFCB	186	2	B
Garnished English	JOC	406	1	A
Tuscan style	OC	125	2	B
Woodcutter's style	OC	120	2	B
Mixed lamb stock	OC	167	2	B
Mixed meats, boiled	CIC	322	2	C
Mixed salad	CIC	408	1	B
Mixed veal stock	OC	167	2	B
Mixed vegetable				
A la Grecque	VGCB	335	2	B
Antipasto	VGCB	336	1	B
Grilled	VGCB	336	1	
Pickles	VGCB	342	2	B
Stew	VGCB	341	1	B
Mizutaki (Japanese vegetable & chicken dish)	NYT	208	1	A

RECIPE	BOOK	PAGE	TD	S
Mocha				
Almond cakes	YGM	220	2	C
Angel food cake	AC	686	1	
Butter cream frosting	GHAC	344	1	
Butter frosting	SC	144	1	
Cake	NSD	276	3	C
Cake, chocolate, quick	FFCB	528	1	B
Cake multilayered	LT	363	2	
Chiffon cake	AC	691	1	
Chiffon oil cake	JOC	634	2	B
Chiffon pie	EBE	169	2	B
Cream frosting	NYT	575	1	B
Filling	JOC	646	1	B
Fluff	BCC	79	1	C
Freezer cake, quick	JOC	644	1	C
Frosting	SC	139	1	
Frosting	NYTI	286	1	B
Frosting	BCC	78	1	C
Fudge cake	AC	675	1	
Gelatin	JOC	696	2	B
Gelatin, chiffon cream pie w	JOC	615	2	B
Hard sauce	FFCB	641	1	B
Ice cream	SC	206	2	
Ice cream	JOC	718	2	B
Icebox cake	SC	135	1	B
Icing	JOC	679	1	B
Icing	SC	143	1	
Icing	PPLK	330	1	B
Icing, chocolate cake w	PPLK	328	2	C
Layer cake	SC	119	1	B
Marshmallow ice cream	SC	208	2	
Mousse	SP	284	2	B
Mousse w praline sauce	EBE	198	2	B
Nut loaf, Penni's	MHGD	35	1	C
Pie	BBA	202	2	B

RECIPE	BOOK	PAGE	TD	S
Pudding, nut	WC	141	2	B
Punch	JOC	35	2	
Sauce	JOC	712	1	B
Sauce	BTSB	160	1	C
Sauce, marshmallow	SC	220	1	
Sponge cake	WC	142	1	B
Velvet cake	WC	147	2	C
Mock drumsticks	MSE	154	3	C
Mock strudel	EBE	176	3	C
Mohrenkoepfe (cake)	JOC	640	2	
Molasses				
Bars	JOC	653	1	C
Beans	AC	594	3	
Bran bread, quick	JOC	576	1	C
Bread, shredded wheat	CBB	613	3	B
Cake, oatmeal	BCC	68	1	C
Cake, pumpkin	BHGN	94	1	C
Candy	SC	171	1	
Cookies	FFCB	551	1	C
Cookies	AC	721	1	
Cookies	SP	261	1	C
Joe Froggers'	MHGD	308	2	C
Jumbo	BCC	114	2	C
Spiced	FFCB	551	1	C
Cover	CFS	286	1	A
Crisps cockaigne	JOC	660	1	C
Frosting, chocolate	SC	146	1	
Hermits	SC	154	1	
Lace cookies	SC	160	1	
Marbled cake	FFBB	317	1	C
Muffins, apple	GHAC	368	1	C
Nut wafers	JOC	669	1	C
Oatmeal bread	BHGN	60	2	B
Pie	AC	627	1	
Pie, pumpkin	MSE	196	2	B
Pudding, apple steamed	JOC	704	2	C
Pudding, steamed	BCC	143	2	B
Rolls, oat	JOC	566	3	C

RECIPE	BOOK	PAGE	TD	S
Spirals	GHAC	347	1	C
Syrup	JOC	738	1	B
Taffy	FFCB	685	3	B
Taffy	JOC	734	2	B
Taffy	AC	839	1	
Wheat bread	CBB	126	2	C
Mold, cranberry wine	GHAC	293	2	C
Mold, lining w caramel	MAFC	584	2	
Mold, lining w lady fingers	MAFC	585		
Mold, orange flavored w rice & cherries	MFC2	444	1	C
Mold, red & white blueberry	GHAC	293	2	C
Mold, spinach	LM	122	1	B
Molded almond cream	MFC2	446	2	C
Molded cookies, making	BCC	96		
Molded strawberries 'n' cream	GHAC	300	2	C
Molding a salad	JOC	95		
Molding salads	BCC	288		
Molds, dessert	JOC	692		
Molds, souffle, all about	MAFC	162		
Molds, preparing	SC	212		
Mole sauce, turkey (salsa mole poblano)	FGCW	192	2	C
Mole sauce, turkey w	BB	108	2	C
Mollusks, all about	JOC	363		
Mona Lisa dressing	NYT	439	1	A
Mondo bizzaro sauce	MC	69	1	B
Mongolian grill	NYTI	454	1	B
Mongolian lamb w Lamb's Wool	FGCW	324	1	B
Monkey bread	CBB	67	2	C
Monkfish sauce rouille	CFS	210	1	B
Mont blanc (chestnut cake)	BBA	227	3	C

RECIPE	BOOK	PAGE	TD	S
Moussaka (*cont.*)				
◆	JBC	191	2	B
◆	SC	291	2	
◆	BHGN	268	2	C
I	FFCB	190	2	B
II	FFCB	191	2	B
A la Grecque	NYT	130	2	C
A la Turque	NYT	128	3	B
Artichoke	BBA	100	3	C
Mushroom	MC	116	1	B
Mushrooms w pine nuts	JBC	191	2	B
Sliced eggplant	JBC	191	2	B
Souffle	GG	162	3	B
Mousse				
Amaretto	SP	285	2	C
Apple w apple brandy sauce	SP	269	2	C
Apple, Bretonne	BBA	208	2	B
Apricot	VE	283	2	C
w Evaporated milk	JOC	720	2	B
Frozen	FFCB	625	3	B
Frozen	NYT	632	2	B
w Molded sherbet or ice cream	MFC2	417	3	C
Artichoke	MFC	168	2	B
Au chocolat	EBE	199	1	B
Au chocolat I	NYT	596	2	B
Au chocolat II	NYT	597	2	B
Chestnut	NYTI	305	2	B
Chestnut cream	GHAC	299	3	C
For Jane's chocolate mousse tart	MSQC	165	2	B
Fruit	JOC	720	2	C
Legere	GF	166	2	B
Lemon (see lemon mousse)				
Molded	MAFC	558	3	C
Orange	MAFC	603	3	B
Orange	BCC	148	2	B
Orange & blueberries	MHGD	360	2	B
Orange & pineapple w orange peel, molded	MFC2	442	3	B
Poultry & liver	LT	21	2	B
Pumpkin	GG	331	3	B
Pumpkin, super easy	VGCB	234	1	B
Salmon (see salmon mousse)				
Sweetbread roast loin of veal, w	GF	38	3	C
Testing for taste	MFC	20		
Trout (see trout mousse)				
Mousseline				
Broccoli	GG	63	1	B
Of scallops w white butter	LM	80	3	B
Of shellfish	JOC	98	2	B
Sauce (see also sauce, mousseline)				
◆	FFCB	272	1	
◆	JBC	263	1	
◆	JOC	329	1	B
◆	BCC	326	1	A
Sauce, green	SC	377	1	
Mowbray pie, melton	NYTI	90	3	B
Mozzarella				
"In a carriage"	FAIC	88	1	B
In carrozza	NYT	317	1	B
In carrozza	NYTI	408	2	B
Chicken cutlets w sun dried tomatoes &	GHAC	158	1	B
& Eggplants (baby)	MCIC	383	1	B
Parmigiana, veal scaloppine &	SMG	205	1	B

RECIPE	BOOK	PAGE	TD	S
Mozzarella (*cont.*)				
Salad, tomato &	KIS	164	1	B
Salad, tomato &	FAIC	392	1	B
& Sun dried tomatoes, smoked	YGM	177	3	C
& Tomato salad	FAIC	392	1	B
& Tomato salad	SP	194	1	B
Mucver (Turkish squash cakes)	GG	326	1	C
Mud cake, Union Hotel	FFBB	336	2	C
Mud pie	MIE	335	2	B
Muenster cheese, banana &	KIS	318	1	
Muenster gin ball, sesame coated	YGM	188	1	C
Muerbe (butter cookie)	SC	152	1	
Muerbe Teig (rich egg pastry)	SC	342	1	
Muerbeteig	JOC	591	2	B
Muffaletta from New Orleans	FGCW	300	3	B
Muffin	BHGN	83	1	C
Muffin	KIS	350	1	C
Muffin	JOC	581	1	C
About	JOC	580	2	
Acorn squash	FFBB	560	1	C
Almond bran	CBB	573	1	C
Apple	BCC	31	1	C
Apple	SC	90	1	
Apple raisin	BHGN	87	1	C
Apple whole wheat	FFBB	567	1	C
Applesauce	JBGF	595	1	C
Bacon	NYT	481	1	C
Bacon	FFCB	489	1	C
Banana	PPLK	38	1	C
Banana nut	BHGN	87	1	C
Basic	NYT	480	1	C
◆	FFCB	488	1	C
◆	BHGN	87	1	C
◆	FFBB	558	1	C
Berkshire	FFCB	489	1	C
Berry	FFBB	563	1	B
Blueberry	JOC	582	1	C
◆	FFCB	489	1	C
◆	JBGF	599	1	C
◆	BHGN	87	1	C
◆	BCC	31	1	C
◆	SC	90	1	
◆	GHAC	368	1	B
◆	JBC	22	1	
◆	MHGD	285	1	C
Corn	SPGT	126	1	B
Lemon	CBB	574	1	C
Sugarless	JBGF	600	1	C
Whole wheat	YGM	243	1	C
Bran	JBGF	596	1	C
◆	PPLK	39	1	C
◆	BTSB	127	1	B
◆	MHGD	286	1	C
◆	SC	89	1	
◆	FFBB	563	1	C
◆	AC	795	1	
◆	JOC	581	1	C
◆	FFCB	489	1	C
Honey glazed	BBA	179	2	B
Maple	GHAC	368	1	B
Raisin	BCC	31	1	C
Refrigerator	JBGF	598	1	C
Bread, English	CBB	52	2	B
Buckwheat	NYT	481	1	C
Buttermilk	JOC	581	1	C
Buttermilk, bran flake	JBGF	597	1	C
Carrot	PPLK	40	1	C
Cheese	NYT	481	1	C
Cheese	BHGN	87	1	C

RECIPE	BOOK	PAGE	TD	S
Cheese	JOC	582	1	C
Chocolate	SC	90	1	
Cooked cereal	JOC	582	1	C
Corn	FFBB	559	1	C
◆	BCC	36	1	C
◆	FFCB	493	1	C
◆	GHAC	367	1	C
◆	JOC	578	1	C
◆	BTSB	126	1	B
◆	JBC	22	1	
◆	BBA	174	1	C
Green chilies	GRIL	98	1	B
Meal	SC	89	1	
Sandwich	CBB	197	2	B
Cornbread	PPLK	41	1	C
Cornmeal	AC	795	1	
Cornmeal	JBC	21	1	
Cornmeal & pumpkin	FFBB	561	1	C
Corny corn	JBGF	600	1	C
Cranberry	JOC	582	1	C
Cranberry	NYT	481	1	C
Cranberry	BHGN	87	1	C
Cranberry & orange	BCC	31	1	C
Cranberry & pumpkin	VGCB	236	1	C
Date	NYT	481	1	C
Date	FFCB	489	1	C
Date	SC	90	1	
Date nut	BHGN	87	1	C
Date nut	BCC	31	1	C
Eggless graham	JOC	581	1	C
English	CBB	568	2	C
◆	BTSB	111	3	C
◆	BCC	41	2	C
◆	SC	76	2	
◆	FFCB	476	3	C
◆	JOC	568	3	C

RECIPE	BOOK	PAGE	TD	S
Crabmeat &	FFCB	295	1	B
Eggs &	BCC	158	1	B
Honey &	BBA	181	2	C
Gayla's orange raisin	MSQC	88	1	B
Ginger	MSE	133	1	C
Ginger whole wheat	FFBB	566	2	B
Health	FFBB	565	1	C
Honey bran	CBB	539	1	C
Honey nut bran	SC	90	1	
Honey wheat	BHGN	87	1	C
Jam	FFBB	559	1	C
Jelly	BHGN	87	1	C
Maple w bran & maple butter sauce	FFBB	564	1	C
Mix	BTSB	126	1	C
Mix, bran	BTSB	127	1	C
Mix, corn	KIS	350	1	C
Mixing properly (photographs)	NYT	480		
Molasses apple	GHAC	368	1	C
New Orleans black	PPLK	43	1	C
Nut	NYT	481	1	C
Oatmeal	SC	89	1	
Oatmeal	FFCB	489	1	C
Oatmeal raisin	JBGF	601	1	C
Oatmeal raisin	BCC	31	1	C
Orange rice	FFBB	562	2	C
Orange wheat	JBGF	602	1	C
Parsnip	VGCB	192	1	B
Pecan	FFCB	489	1	C
Plain	SC	88	1	
Potato flour	SC	89	1	
Prune & pumpkin, whole wheat	FFBB	561	1	C
Pumpkin	BHGN	87	1	C
Pumpkin	FFBB	560	1	C
Pumpkin w raw grated pumpkin	VGCB	236	1	C

RECIPE	BOOK	PAGE	TD	S
Muffin (*cont.*)				
Raised	JOC	568	3	C
Raisin	FFCB	489	1	C
Raisin bran	BTSB	127	1	B
Raspberry streusel	SPGT	125	2	B
Rice	SC	89	1	
Rice flour	JOC	581	1	C
Rye applesauce	FFBB	566	2	C
Simple	AC	794	1	
Sour cream	SC	89	1	
Sour cream	JOC	581	1	C
Sour cream & corn	SC	90	1	C
Southern biscuit	PPLK	38	1	C
Sticky orange	FFBB	561	1	C
Sunflower seed	BHGN	87	1	C
Sunshine	BHGN	87	1	C
Sweet potato	BBA	183	2	C
Twin mountain	SC	90	1	
Upside down	NYT	481	1	C
Wheat walnut	JBGF	602	1	C
Whole grain	JOC	581	1	C
Whole wheat	FFCB	489	1	C
Zucchini basil	CBB	418	1	C
Zucchini gems	GG	403	1	C
Zucchini oatmeal	GHAC	368	1	C
Muffuletta (olive sandwich)	CF	71	3	B
Mullet parcels	OC	147	1	B
Mulligan stew	GHAC	207	2	B
Mulligatawny (spicy chicken & rice dish)	CBSS	103	2	B
Mulligatawny	BHGN	374	1	B
Soup	SC	398	1	
◆	JOC	154	1	B
◆	BCC	305	2	B
◆	GHAC	104	1	B
◆	FFCB	92	2	B
I	NYTI	351	1	B
II	NYTI	352	1	A
III	NYTI	352	2	B
Multigrain bread	CBB	228	3	C
Murbeteig or pate sucree (sweet egg pastry)	AC	636	1	
Muscatel sauce	FFBB	421	2	C
Mush cake	FFBB	320	1	C
Mush, cornmeal	BHGN	325	1	B
Mush, fried	BHGN	325	1	B
Mushkazunge (meringue cake)	SC	131	1	B
Mushroom	MAFC	258	2	B
A bordelaise, garnish	SMG	237	1	B
A l'Algonquin	FFCB	388	2	B
A la Grecque	MAFC	537	1	C
A la Grecque	NYT	36	3	B
A la provencale	FG	202	1	B
A la Schoener	JOC	281	1	B
& Asparagus sauce	MC	67	1	B
& Asparagus, sauteed	MCIC	366	1	B
& Bacon, sauteed	AC	525	1	
Baked	KIS	299	1	A
Baked	SC	422	1	
Baked, tenderloin of beef w	MFC2	178	1	C
Barley casserole	BB	137	1	B
Barley soup	MC	25	2	B
& Beef loaf	SC	278	1	
& Beef, red wine &	FGCW	203	2	C
Beefsteak w	AC	270	1	
Berkeley	VE	140	1	B
Bibb salad	AC	38	1	
Bisque	MC	21	2	B
Bisque	NYT	70	1	B
Broccoli & noodle casserole	MC	107	1	B

MUSHROOM

RECIPE	BOOK	PAGE	TD	S
Broiled	SC	421	1	
◆	AC	526	1	
◆	JOC	281	1	
◆	JBC	316	1	B
◆	SC	47	1	
Cheese	JBC	316	1	B
Leeks, sweet peppers &	GHAC	255	2	B
& Stuffed	NYT	38	1	C
& Stuffed cockaigne	JOC	281	1	B
Broth	JOC	148	1	B
Broth	FFCB	83	1	B
& Brussels sprouts	JBC	297	1	
Bulgur baked w onions &	MIE	201	1	B
Butter	NYT	458	1	B
Butter, blender	JOC	57	1	
Canapes	JOC	60	1	
Canned	MAFC	517	1	A
Canned, uses for	AC	558		
Caps				
Baked & stuffed	MCIC	86	2	B
Broiled	MAFC	512	1	
Broiled	NYT	384	1	A
w Parsnip puree	VGCB	189	1	
Poached eggs on	MAFC	118	2	B
Stuffed w broccoli	EBE	110	1	B
Stuffing (photographs)	OC	18		
Casserole, Italian	VE	143	1	A
Casserole, spinach	AC	528	1	
& Cauliflower w cheese sauce	JOC	271	1	B
Caviar	YGM	170	2	C
Cereal bake	BHGN	324	1	C
Chanterelle soup under puff pastry	CBSS	308	3	B

RECIPE	BOOK	PAGE	TD	S
Chanterelles, pizza w garlic puree &	CPPC	154	3	B
Cheese canapes	EBE	14	1	B
Cheese salad	CIC	47	1	B
& Cherry tomatoes, marinated	YGM	208	3	C
Chicken				
Breasts w cream &	MAFC	269	1	B
Breasts stuffed w	FFCB	247	1	B
Livers &	SC	318	1	
Livers &	EBE	79	1	B
Livers w madeira wine sauce &	SMG	76	1	B
Livers, spaghetti w	WC	50	1	B
Roast, stuffed w	JBC	224	1	
Chilled, lemony	GHAC	238	1	B
Clam bisque	JOC	162	1	A
Cleaning a	FG	201		
Consomme	JBC	275	2	
Cream baked	NYTI	249	1	B
& Cream cheese appetizers	BB	115	1	A
& Cream cheese sandwiches	BB	115	1	A
Cream soup	BBA	44	2	B
Creamed	MAFC	514	1	B
◆	SP	172	1	B
◆	AC	525	1	
◆	FFCB	388	1	B
◆	JOC	281	1	B
Creamy, stuffed	YGM	181	1	C
Crepes	FFCB	297	2	B
Crepes w chicken, Florentine	NYTI	228	2	B
Crepes, watercress &	GG	197	1	C
Croquettes	JOC	219	3	B
Croquettes, chicken &	FFCB	259	2	B

RECIPE	BOOK	PAGE	TD	S
Mushroom (*cont.*)				
Cucumbers	BCC	351	1	B
Curry	MC	98	1	B
Cutting	MAFC	509		
Deep fried	NYTI	112	1	B
Deviled	AC	526	1	
Different kinds of	SP	170		
Dill	AC	525	1	
Dried	JOC	541	1	
Dried	BTSB	201	2	C
Dried, risotto w	FAIC	215	1	B
Duxelles	MAFC	515	1	A
Duxelles	FFCB	389	1	B
Eggs	SC	222	1	
Eggs, scrambled &	FFCB	347	1	B
Elegante	BHGN	397	2	B
Enoki	CF	115	1	B
Essence	MAFC	512	1	
Fennel salad	YGM	219	2	C
Filled puffs in broth, little	FAIC	110	2	B
Filling	SC	382	1	
Filling, rice &	BBA	16	1	C
Fines herbes	MFC	174	1	B
Fish				
Baked	BHGN	209	1	B
Fillets &	MAFC	216	2	B
Fillets, broiled &	JBC	64	1	
Fillets on spinach w shrimp &	JOC	351	2	A
Sculpting into (photographs)	LM	59		
Florentine	JOC	282	1	B
Fluted, making	BHGN	440		
Fluted (photographs)	LT	25		
Fried	MCIC	396	1	B
Frittata, ham, red pepper &	FFCB	343	1	B
Garlic & parsley	FGCW	335	1	B
Garlic, stuffed w	VGCB	173	1	B

RECIPE	BOOK	PAGE	TD	S
Giant, stuffed	VE	139	2	B
Gratin, potato &	CPMC	159	2	B
Gravy, creamy	GHAC	166	1	B
& Green beans	AC	478	1	
Grilled	SC	334	1	
Grilled	GRIL	80	2	B
Hamburger	JBC	158	1	
Hash, wild, w celery root	GG	125	1	B
Hot, stuffed	VE	141	1	B
In brandy cream chicken &	WC	49	2	B
In cream sauce	SC	387	1	
In herbs w cream	AC	525	1	
Kebabs, Tyrolean style	OC	94	2	B
Lima beans	JOC	263	2	B
Lima beans w	AC	600	1	
Lima beans w	AC	483	1	
Lima beans, boiled	JBC	292	1	A
Liver pate	BBA	21	1	B
Loaf, carrot &	MC	99	1	B
Macaroni	SC	338	1	
Marinated	OC	94	1	B
◆	FG	205	1	B
◆	CW	45	1	
◆	BCC	7	2	C
◆	BTSB	142	1	C
◆	JOC	70	2	
Marinated w red peppers	MSE	106	1	C
Marinated w red wine & fennel	SP	173	3	B
Marsala sauce	FGCW	285	1	B
Meringue (see also meringue, mushroom)				
Meringue, making	LT	340	2	
Minced, sauteed in butter	MAFC	515	1	A

RECIPE	BOOK	PAGE	TD	S
Moussaka	MC	116	1	B
Moussaka w pine nuts	JBC	191	2	B
Mousse	JOC	282	2	B
Mustard & kale	BBA	133	1	B
Mutton chops, English	JBC	193	1	
Newburg	VE	142	1	B
Noodles	WC	35	1	B
Oil	FGCW	91	1	
Omelet (see omelet, mushroom)				
On toast w puffed cheese	JOC	247	1	B
Onions & wine	SC	422	1	
Onions & wine	JOC	282	1	B
Oriental, marinated	VE	141	1	B
Orzo & onions	MIE	205	1	B
Oysters	SC	247	1	
Oysters, creamed	JOC	370	1	B
Paprika	NYT	384	1	B
Parmigiana	NYTI	372	1	B
& Parsley, sole w	LT	151	2	
Pasta con funghi	VE	237	1	B
Paste	NYTI	497	1	
Pepper topping	GHAC	185	1	
Pickled	NYTI	500	1	B
Pie	NYT	383	2	B
Pie, potato &	AC	527	1	
Pilaf	FFCB	318	1	B
Pilaf	JBC	116	1	B
Piroshki	NYTI	497	2	C
Pizza	NYTI	440	2	
Pizza w pancetta, garlic &	CPPC	158	3	B
Pork chops	AC	411	1	
Pork chops	KIS	267	1	A
Pot roast, port &	FGCW	202	2	B
& Potato pie	AC	527	1	
& Potatoes, baked	MCIC	398	1	B
& Potatoes dauphinoise, wild	MSE	224	2	A
& Potatoes, mashed	NYT	395	1	B
Powder	FG	202	1	
Powdered, dried	BTSB	202	2	C
Preparing	BCC	351		
Preparing	JOC	280		
Puree	NYTI	249	1	B
Puree for seasoning	AC	528	2	
Puree for stuffing artichoke bottoms	MFC2	412	1	B
Quail w	GHAC	167	1	A
Quiche	FG	206	1	B
Quiche	MAFC	152	2	B
Quiche	BCC	166	1	B
Ragout, chicken liver w	GHAC	168	1	B
Raw, marinated	NYT	37	2	B
Reconstituting dry	SPGT	254		
Rice bake	BHGN	324	1	C
Rice ring	NYT	325	1	B
Ring	JOC	282	2	B
Ring	SC	422	2	
Ring mold, chicken &	JOC	210	2	B
Ring mold, sweetbreads &	JOC	210	2	B
Risotto	FGCW	155	1	B
Risotto w	FGCW	155	1	B
Risotto, dried wild	CIC	185	1	B
Risotto, fried	FAIC	215	1	B
Risotto, white	NYTI	410	2	B
Rolls, toasted	EBE	27	2	C
Rutabagas	AC	554	1	
Salad	JBC	245	1	B
Salad	LM	155	1	B
Salad	VE	101	1	B
Salad, lima bean &	FG	117	2	B

RECIPE	BOOK	PAGE	TD	S
Mushroom (*cont.*)				
Salad, spinach, bacon &	FFCB	429	1	B
Sandwiches, hot	SC	384	1	
Sauce	JOC	327	2	B
◆	BCC	339	1	
◆	JBC	213	1	A
◆	FFCB	270	1	B
◆	AC	456	1	
◆	NYT	452	1	B
◆	NYTI	273	1	B
◆	NYTI	139	1	B
◆	BCC	327	1	B
◆	FAIC	68	1	B
Artichoke bottoms w	NYT	350	1	B
Beef, scallions &	FFCB	173	1	B
Brown	SC	388	1	
Brown	MAFC	74	1	B
Cheese sandwich w	JOC	247	2	B
Creamed, black	VE	87	1	B
Creamy	BHGN	358	1	B
Deviled	SMG	71	1	B
Fish fillets w	JBC	69	1	
For pasta	VE	247	2	B
Ham braised in wine-cream &	MAFC	391	1	C
Quick	BHGN	357	1	B
Tomato &	SMG	73	1	A
Tomato &	MAFC	256	1	
Sauced eggs	BHGN	193	2	A
Sausages	JOC	231	1	B
Sauteed	FFCB	387	1	B
◆	AC	525	1	
◆	JOC	281	1	B
◆	MAFC	513	1	B
◆	BCC	351	1	B
◆	JBC	315	1	B
◆	SC	421	1	

RECIPE	BOOK	PAGE	TD	S
w Brown madeira sauce	MAFC	515	1	B
w Garlic & parsley	CIC	379	1	B
w Heavy cream	CIC	381	1	B
& Herbed	GHAC	177	1	C
Of well seasoned	NYT	384	1	A
Red snapper w	CIC	217	2	B
Shallots, garlic, herbs &	MAFC	513	1	B
Two	FG	204	2	A
Woodsy & wild	SP	170	2	C
Scallion salad	KIS	286	1	A
Shallot & madeira, omelets w	MSE	97	1	C
Shrimp shells	JBC	91	1	B
Smitane	NYTI	514	1	B
Smothered	MCIC	397	1	B
Soup	SC	310	1	
Soup	MFC	68	1	B
Soup	NYTI	6	3	B
Chicken &	FG	47	1	B
Cold	MFC2	13	1	B
Cream of	MFC2	12	1	B
◆	FG	203	3	C
◆	AC	96	1	
◆	GHAC	98	1	B
◆	JBC	280	2	
◆	SC	402	1	
◆	JOC	158	1	B
◆	NYT	71	1	B
◆	MAFC	40	1	B
◆	FFCB	88	1	A
◆	BCC	310	1	B
Cream of, wild	CBSS	305	1	B
French	MSE	114	1	C
Green onion	CBSS	315	2	B
Hot Oriental	MIE	76	1	B
Hungarian	MC	14	2	B
Mother's	MSE	192	3	C

MUSHROOM
401

RECIPE	BOOK	PAGE	TD	S
Parmesan cheese	CBSS	304	2	B
Quick	JOC	167	1	B
Wild	SP	171	2	B
Wild	NYTI	498	2	B
& Sour cream	NYTI	514	1	B
& Sour cream	SC	422	1	
Spaghetti &	BCC	61	1	B
Spaghetti & two	FC	126	1	B
Spinach &	NYT	400	1	B
Spinach, boiled	JBC	332	1	
& Spinach casserole	AC	528	1	
& Spinach souffle	MAFC	166	2	B
Spread	BCC	17	2	C
Spread	BB	62	1	A
Sprouts in mustard vinegar	KIS	271	1	A
Steak sauce	BHGN	238	1	B
Steamed	SC	421	1	
Steamed	JOC	281	1	
Steamed	AC	525	1	
Steamed, custard	FG	204	1	A
Stewed	MAFC	511	1	
Stir fried	GHAC	238	1	B
Straw & baby corn	FG	205	1	B
Strudel	MC	122	2	B
Stuffed	BCC	7	1	C
◆	FFCB	388	2	B
◆	OC	166	1	C
◆	MAFC	516	1	B
◆	AC	527	1	
◆	NYTI	373	1	B
◆	LT	194	1	
◆	GHAC	88	1	C
◆	JBC	316	1	B
w Anchovies	NYTI	373	1	B
w Baked ham	BHGN	13	1	C
Basted w wine	JBC	316	1	
w Bechamel sauce	CIC	46	1	B
Breast of veal	GHAC	208	2	B

RECIPE	BOOK	PAGE	TD	S
w Garlic herb cheese	MIE	31	1	B
w Liver	NYT	37	2	C
Meat	JBC	316	1	
w Pork & veal	NYTI	374	1	C
w Seafood	JBC	316	1	
w Seafood	AC	527	1	
w Seafood	JOC	282	2	B
w Snails	JOC	282	2	B
w Snails	NYT	37	1	B
w Tomatoes	GG	373	2	B
w Walnuts & cheese	SP	12	2	B
Stuffing, grilled bass fillets w	GHAC	224	1	B
Stuffing, ham braised w	MAFC	394	3	C
Stuffing, baked tomatoes w	FFCB	416	2	B
Tangy	EBE	121	1	B
Timbales	JOC	207	2	B
Tomato sauce	KIS	186	1	A
Turnips w	AC	553	1	
Turnovers	NYT	32	2	C
Under glass	AC	526	1	
Under glass	JOC	283	2	B
Under glass	NYT	36	2	B
Under glass, creamed	AC	526	1	
Veal chops or steaks braised w cream &	MFC2	206	1	B
Veal chops w	GHAC	209	1	B
Vichyssoise	MSE	284	2	C
& Walnut salad	CW	37	1	B
Wild	MCIC	35		
Drying	NYTI	498		
On croutons	CPMC	58	2	B
Red snapper, chives &	MFC	128	3	B

RECIPE	BOOK	PAGE	TD	S
Mushroom, Wild (*cont.*)				
Rice &	BCC	56	1	B
Rice, peas &	GHAC	268	1	C
Rice & stuffing	FFCB	279	1	B
Rice stuffing	GHAC	159	1	
w Veal stock & red wine, ragout of	CPMC	90	2	B
w Wine sauce	NYT	452	1	B
Muskellunge (fish, similar to pike)	JOC	358	1	
Muskrat	JOC	454	2	A
Muslim kebabs	NYT	123	1	B
Mussala (chicken & beef dish)	NYTI	484	2	B
Mussel	MAFC	226		
A la mariniere I	MAFC	227	1	B
A light Italian sauce	FG	363	2	B
All about	JOC	366		
Bacon	NYT	18	2	B
Baked, buttered	JOC	367	1	
Baked w cream pineau de charentes	CPMC	94	2	B
Bisque	SPGT	144	2	C
Canned	MAFC	226		
w Celeriac mayonnaise sauce	SMG	304	1	C
& Clams fra diavolo	GHAC	126	1	B
Cleaning	LT	110		
w Cream egg sauce	SMG	140	1	B
Directions	MAFC	213	1	
Fettuccine w	SPGT	64	2	B
Fish fillets, shrimp &	MAFC	214	2	B
Hors d'oeuvre, cold	JOC	73	1	
In white wine	SMG	310	1	B
Maine, baked	AC	165	1	
Marinara linguine w	NYTI	384	2	B
Marinated in oil & herbs	MAFC	229	1	B
Marinated on the half shell	GHAC	89	2	C
Mariners (moules mariniere)	AC	165	1	
Mariniere	NYT	282	2	B
On the half shell, cold	FFCB	136	2	B
On the half shell, gratineed	MAFC	228	2	B
On the spit	OC	154	3	B
w Pesto	MSQC	148	2	B
w Pesto sauce	MSQC	148	2	B
Pilaf of	LT	113	2	
Pilaf of	NYTI	153	2	B
Pizza, fennel &	CPPC	159	3	B
Provencale	JBGF	455	2	B
Risotto	NYTI	409	2	B
Sailor style	LT	112	1	B
Salad & variations	AC	64	1	
Sauce, fettuccine &	JBGF	358	2	B
Sauce, linguine & red	GHAC	260	2	B
Sauced in a rice ring	MAFC	231	1	
Sauced, served in scallop shells	MAFC	230	2	B
Scrubbing & soaking	MAFC	226		
& Shrimp soup	CBSS	206	3	B
Souffle	GF	168	2	A
Soup	MAFC	231	1	
Soup	MFC	71	2	B
Soup	CIC	56	1	B
Cold	GF	38	2	C
Cream of	NYTI	124	1	B
Fish Normandie	CBCC	195	3	B
Spaghetti w	NYTI	423	2	B
Steamed	JOC	367	1	A
Steamed	AC	164	1	
Steamed open in wine & flavorings, fresh	MAFC	227	1	B

RECIPE	BOOK	PAGE	TD	S
Steamed in white wine	FFCB	135	2	B
Steamed w wine, flavorings & bread crumbs	MAFC	228	1	B
Stuffed	NYTI	552	2	B
Taglierini, radicchio, anchovy cream &	CPPC	146	2	B
Trimming	LT	115		
Vinaigrette	VGCB	203	2	B
◆	NYTI	152	1	C
◆	GF	159	1	B
◆	MSE	287	2	C
Vinaigrette on the half shell	SMG	311	1	B
Mustard				
Anchovy dunk	BB	123	1	
Basil butter	SP	116	1	
Bluefish w baked apples &	SP	114	2	B
Bluefish fillets w	CFS	209	1	A
Bread	BB	113	1	B
Butter	NYT	457	1	
Butter	MAFC	100	1	A
Butter sauce	SC	391	1	
Butter steaks w	GHAC	173	1	A
Caper sauce	FG	242	1	A
Cheddar spread	BB	123	1	
Cheese appetizers	BB	113	1	
Cheese sandwiches	BB	113	1	
Chicken				
Breasts, grilled & boneless	MIE	103	1	B
Breasts, many	GRIL	90	2	B
Broiled w herbs, bread crumbs &	MAFC	265	1	B
Crusty	MSQC	144	1	B
Grilled	CFS	111	2	A
Grilled	SMG	56	1	B
w Wine sauce	FGCW	171	1	A
Coarse ground w red wine & garlic	BTSB	192	2	C
Coating for roast lamb, herbal	MAFC	335	1	B
Crust, ham slice w	AC	446	2	
Danish	NYTI	83	1	B
Different kinds of	SP	230		
Dill mayonnaise	GHAC	89	1	
Dill sauce	BBA	163	1	B
Dill sauce	MIE	47	2	B
Dip, Brooke's	MSE	70	2	C
Dip, green peppercorn &	SP	22	1	B
Dressing	BCC	279	1	
Cheese &	BCC	280	2	
Creamy tarragon for seafood salad	SP	223	1	B
Dijon	FGCW	131	1	A
Dijon	FG	82	1	A
Garlic	SP	230	1	C
Duck w leeks &	FGCW	188	2	B
Egg sauce	NYTI	273	1	C
Fish fillets, broiled w	JBGF	450	1	B
Ginger sauce, squid in	FGCW	124	2	A
Glaze	GHAC	164	1	
Glaze	SP	14	1	B
Glaze, easy	BHGN	254	1	A
& Green peppercorn	BTSB	191	2	C
Greens, cooking	AC	521		
Greens or escarole, braised	AC	522	1	
Herb butter	MSQC	24	1	A
Herb toast	MIE	297	1	C
Hollandaise	AC	460	1	
Hollandaise sauce	BBA	93	1	A
Hollandaise sauce	JBC	263	1	
Horseradish	BTSB	193	2	C

RECIPE	BOOK	PAGE	TD	S
Mustard (*cont.*)				
Hot, Chinese	BHGN	358	1	A
Hot, homemade	NYTI	279	1	A
& Kohlrabi	BCC	368	1	B
Lamb chops w	BCC	236	1	B
Marinade	GRIL	36	1	B
Marinade, flank steak in	FGCW	237	2	B
Mayonnaise (see mayonnaise, mustard)				
New potatoes in	GG	296	1	B
Parsley spread	BHGN	41	1	
Peas, ham &	GG	270	1	B
Pickle	JOC	783	3	C
Pickles (see also pickles, mustard)				
Pork chops w	NYTI	184	1	B
Pork chops w cream, tomato sauce &	MAFC	387	1	B
Pork chops, dill sauce &	MIE	133	2	B
Potatoes, new	GG	296	1	B
Rabbit, young, spit-roasted w	OC	127	2	B
Relish	FFCB	285	2	B
Ring w coleslaw	AC	497	2	
Russian	NYTI	515	1	B
Sauce	SC	294	1	
◆	CF	114	1	B
◆	JBC	262	1	
◆	SMG	119	1	B
◆	MAFC	66	1	B
◆	PPLK	281	1	B
◆	JOC	325	2	B
◆	BCC	243	1	
◆	FFCB	273	1	B
Artichoke w	GHAC	229	1	B
Beery	CFS	319	3	B
Beets in	GG	51	1	B
Brown	MAFC	72	1	B
Celery root	MAFC	540	1	B
Chinese	BBA	164	1	B
Cold & variations	JOC	313	1	B
Cooked	SC	389	1	
Cream	MAFC	382	1	B
Cream	BCC	328	1	B
Dijon	MFC	107	1	B
w Dijon	AC	455	1	
Dill	SP	17	1	B
Easy	BCC	224	1	B
For seafood (besetti sauce)	SC	45	1	
Green wax beans &	GHAC	274	2	B
Ham, beer soaked w	CFS	161	1	B
Herbs, cold w	MAFC	95	1	A
Herring in	NYTI	78	3	B
Honey	GHAC	195	1	B
Meaux	MFC	107	1	B
Melting, parsnips in	GG	258	1	B
Orange	BCC	330	1	A
Pork in	FGCW	214	1	B
Pork tenderloin	SC	294	2	
Rabbit in	FGCW	231	1	B
Rabbit tenderloin	PPLK	280	3	B
Scallions braised	SP	183	1	B
Steak w green peppercorns &	BBA	50	2	A
Sweet & sour	JOC	330	1	B
w White sauce	AC	459	1	
w White sauce	BCC	326	1	B
Shish kebabs w	BBA	55	2	B
Shrimp &	MFC	35	1	B
Sour cream dressing	VGCB	71	1	B

N

RECIPE	BOOK	PAGE	TD	S
Nasturtium (*cont.*)				
Capers, pickled	BBA	167	3	B
Pods, pickled	JOC	785	3	C
Navarin (French lamb ragout)	JBC	187	2	B
Navarin printanier	JOC	422	2	B
Navy bean soup	AC	94	1	
Navy bean soup	BCC	313	2	B
Nectar				
Apricot	BTSB	214	2	C
Dressing, spicy	BHGN	344	1	B
Nectarine	BTSB	214	2	C
Peach	BTSB	214	2	C
Pear	BTSB	214	2	C
Nectarine	AC	760		
Chutney	BTSB	148	2	C
Compote, grape &	KIS	319	1	B
Nectar	BTSB	214	2	C
Seafood &	KIS	140	1	A
Spiced	VE	299	3	B
Vermont	KIS	320	1	B
Negroni (drink—campari, vermouth & gin)	SPGT	65	2	A
Negus in quantity (mulled wine)	JOC	51		
Neruppu vazhai (Indian banana dessert)	NYTI	361	1	C
Nesselrode				
Frozen	SC	215	2	
Pie	NYT	526	2	B
Pudding	JOC	694	3	B
Pudding	SC	203	2	
Sauce	JOC	711	3	C
Nettle soup, cream of	JOC	159	1	B
Neufchatel (soft cheese)	JOC	513	3	B
Never fail fudge	AC	834	3	
New England boiled dinner	BCC	199	2	B
New England boiled dinner	AC	304	2	
New England boiled dinner	GHAC	179	2	C
New England clam chowder (see clam chowder, New England)				
New Orleans rice sausage	FGCW	243	2	B
New potato	YGM	139	1	B
Baked	MSE	59	1	
Boiled	KIS	212	1	A
◆	JOC	290	1	B
◆	KIS	147	1	A
◆	YGM	105	1	A
◆	SC	425	1	
Boiled, tiny	JBC	325	1	
Boiled, tiny	KIS	82	1	A
w Cumin vinaigrette	YGM	55	1	A
w Dill	YGM	49	1	A
w Dill seed & sour cream dressing	NYT	395	1	B
Dilled	CFS	246	2	B
Dilled	SP	176	1	B
w Fresh peas, herbed	NYT	395	1	B
Fried	JBC	329	1	B
Parchment	CPMC	25	1	B
Parsleyed, boiled	FFCB	398	1	B
Sauteed	JBC	329	1	B
Sauteed	JOC	293	1	B
Steamed	FFCB	397	1	B
Steamed in butter	JBC	329	1	B
New Year's cookies	AC	716	1	
New York ice cream	SC	206	2	
New York steak w four peppers & port wine	MFC	150	2	B

RECIPE	BOOK	PAGE	TD	S
Newburg sauce	JOC	323	1	B
Newburg sauce	SC	389	1	
Newburg sauce, quick	SC	390	1	
Newport centers	JOC	728	2	B
Newport creams	JOC	728	2	B
Nicoise, cauliflower	GF	223	1	B
Nicoise sauce	NYT	439	1	B
Nine grain crunch cookies	FFBB	236	2	C
Nine hole dish, Korean	NYTI	460	3	B
No oil dressing	BCC	302	2	A
Noodle	GF	191	1	C
Noodle	KIS	267	1	A
A la Neapolitan	SC	336	1	
Alfredo's	FFCB	330	1	B
Almond, poppy seed	EBE	123	1	C
& Apples	SC	336	1	
Bake, chicken chilled w	BHGN	310	1	B
Baskets	JOC	188	3	
& Beef casserole	FFCB	331	2	B
& Blue cheese	FG	125	1	B
Boiled	JOC	188	1	B
Buckwheat	BTSB	302	2	B
Buckwheat, Swiss chard, potatoes &	MCIC	200	3	B
Buttered	JOC	188	1	B
Buttered	SMG	207	1	B
Buttered, fine	SMG	53	1	B
Caraway seeds & buttered	SMG	217	1	B
Carrots, dill &	SMG	155	1	B
Carrots, poppy seeds &	SMG	133	1	B
Casserole, chicken &	FFCB	331	2	B
Cheese	SMG	35	1	B
& Cheese loaf, quantity	JOC	189	2	C
& Cheese ring	SC	336	1	
w Cheese & yogurt	YGM	141	1	B
Cheesed	JBC	211	2	
w Chicken campanini	NYTI	415	1	B
& Chicken w wine sauce	NYTI	210	1	B
Chinese	YGM	145	1	A
Chinese	SC	335	1	
Cold sesame	JBGF	303	2	C
w Consomme	JBC	275	2	
Cooking	AC	586		
Cooking	ACCB	586		
Creamy tomato-cheese	YGM	115	1	A
Crumb, egg topping &	SMG	75	1	B
Custard ring	SC	335	1	
Dill	SMG	279	1	B
Dough	SC	335	1	
Dough, egg	NYT	327	3	
Dough, white or green	JOC	172	2	B
Dutch	NYT	328	1	A
Egg	BTSB	300	2	B
◆	BCC	58	2	B
◆	CF	39	1	B
◆	KIS	134	1	B
Broad	KIS	215	1	B
For soup	SC	409	2	
Thin	KIS	292	1	B
Filled w cheese	SC	337	2	
Filled w meat	SC	337	2	
Florentine I	NYTI	416	1	B
Florentine II	NYTI	416	1	B
w Fresh tomato sauce	SMG	197	1	B
w Fresh tomatoes	SMG	27	1	B
Fried	JOC	188	1	
Frying	SC	335		
Garlic & green	NYTI	416	1	B

RECIPE	BOOK	PAGE	TD	S
Noodle (*cont.*)				
German	NYT	328	1	B
Green	LT	207	2	
◆	JBC	212	2	
◆	BHGN	319	2	B
◆	YGM	85	1	A
◆	KIS	125	1	A
Green, making (photographs)	LT	207		
& Green peppercorn butter	SMG	253	1	B
Homemade	FG	128	2	B
Homemade	BHGN	319	2	B
American style	FFCB	329	3	B
Boiling	SC	335		
Italian	FFCB	328	3	B
Machine	NYTI	415		
In cheese sauce	JBC	211	1	B
Kugel	SC	337	1	
Kugel	MC	112	1	B
Lisa's	KIS	144	1	A
Making	BTSB	298		
Making	AC	586		
Making	ACCB	586		
Mushrooms	WC	35	1	B
Nests, eggs in	JBC	52	2	
Nutmeg	SMG	43	1	B
Nutmeg	SMG	183	1	B
Oriental, cold	YGM	217	3	C
Parsley	SMG	77	1	B
Pfarvel	SC	409	1	
Poppy seed	KIS	251	1	A
Poppy seeds	FFCB	330	1	B
Pork casserole, Romanian	JOC	189	2	B
& Prunes, scalloped	SC	336	1	
Pudding	MIE	190	1	B
◆	SC	187	1	
◆	SC	337	1	
◆	FFCB	331	1	B
Apples & nuts	SC	188	1	
Marian's	EBE	128	2	C
Raisin	BCC	143	1	B
Souffle	SC	188	1	
Viennese	NYT	329	2	B
Puffs	SC	409	1	
Puffs, baked	SC	409	2	C
Rarebit	JOC	189	1	B
Ring	NYT	336	1	B
Ring, baked	JOC	188	2	B
Ring w whipped cream	JOC	189	1	C
Roman	NYT	328	1	B
Romanoff	BCC	61	1	B
Salad, Chinese w chicken	KIS	102	1	A
Salad, cold, Chinese	YGM	172	3	C
Salad, Oriental	MIE	277	2	B
Scalloped	SC	336	1	
& Sesame ginger dressing, chicken w	YGM	65	2	A
Sour cream &	FFCB	330	1	B
Spicy sesame	SP	79	1	B
Spicy sesame	MSQC	100	1	B
Spinach	MIE	189	1	B
Spinach	BTSB	301	2	B
Spinach & cheese	JBGF	362	1	B
Square	SC	409	1	
Butter & rosemary	MCIC	198	3	B
Homemade tonnarelli	MCIC	176	3	
w Mushroom sauce	MCIC	196	3	B
Stewed prunes & croutons	JOC	189		
Stir fry, buckwheat	JBGF	352	2	B
Szechuan w peanut sauce	JBGF	359	2	B
Thin	YGM	143	1	B
Vienna	SC	336	1	

RECIPE	BOOK	PAGE	TD	S
White	JBC	210	2	
White, w parsley	JBC	211	2	
Whole wheat	BTSB	301	2	B
Whole wheat	BHGN	319	2	B
Yellow & green w cream, ham & mushroom sauce	CIC	132	3	B
Yellow green w sweet peppers & sausage	MCIC	192	3	B
Noels (chewy cookie)	FFCB	567	1	C
Noisettes d'agneau a l'estragon (lamb chop dish)	NYTI	176	1	B
Norwegian lefse sandwiches (dough sandwiches)	FGCW	299	1	
Nougat	JOC	732	2	B
Nougat	NYT	638	2	C
Nougat, French	FFCB	686	2	B
Nougatine almonds	NSD	352	2	B
Nougatine, coconut	NSD	352	2	B
Nougatine ice cream w coconut	NSD	221	2	B
Nuss torte (nut torte)	AC	688	2	
Nut				
All about	JOC	518		
Balls, chocolate	BHGN	115	2	C
Balls, flourless	JOC	669	1	C
Bars	JOC	665	1	C
Bars	SC	178	1	
Brazil	BCC	103	1	C
Date	NYT	579	1	C
Layered	NYT	582	1	C
Bread	FFCB	484	1	B
◆	AC	781	2	
◆	CBB	499	3	C
◆	BHGN	79	2	B
◆	JOC	556	1	
Apricot	SC	85	1	
Apricot	CBB	487	2	C
Banana	FFCB	488	1	B
◆	BHGN	79	1	B
◆	MIE	302	2	B
◆	GHAC	366	1	B
Bran	CBB	93	1	B
Brown	SC	85	1	
Cheese	BHGN	79	2	B
Chocolate	FFBB	550	2	C
Date	GHAC	364	2	B
◆	FFCB	486	1	B
◆	SP	248	1	B
◆	AC	791	1	
For All Saints' Day	FAIC	44	2	B
Lemon	CBB	471	1	B
Loaf, cheese & bread	JOC	243	1	B
Orange	CBB	493	1	C
Orange	SC	86	1	
Pumpkin	BHGN	79	1	B
Quick	JOC	574	1	B
Raisin	CBB	489	3	B
Raisin	FFCB	471	2	C
Sesame	CBB	121	2	C
Squash, Lynn Wilson's	VGCB	292	1	B
White	SC	85	1	
Winchester	FFCB	485	2	C
Brittle	BHGN	113	1	B
◆	JOC	736	2	B
◆	NYT	634	1	B
◆	SC	174		
Bisque	FFCB	628	3	B
Brown sugar	BHGN	113	1	B
Creamy	SC	174	1	
Glazed w nuts & praline for garnish	JOC	736	2	B

RECIPE	BOOK	PAGE	TD	S
Nut Brittle (*cont.*)				
Ice cream	BCC	152	3	
Sauce, chocolate	JOC	712	1	B
Butter				
Balls	AC	699	1	
Balls	FFBB	271	1	C
Balls, chocolate	FFBB	271	1	C
Cookies	GF	91	1	C
Buying & storing	JBGF	114		
Cake	VE	303	2	B
Banana	BCC	73	1	B
Chocolate, meringue &	LT	347	2	C
Crumb	NYT	552	1	C
Date	FFCB	530	1	C
Date	FFBB	381	1	C
Fabulous	AC	666	2	
Greek	NYT	553	1	C
Hickory	SC	113	1	B
Orange	EBE	155	2	B
Candied	AC	833	1	
Cheese balls	JOC	67	2	
Chews, children's	FFBB	237	1	C
Chicken roast, stuffed	JBC	224	1	
Chiffon cake	AC	691	1	
Chips, Brazil	FFCB	690	1	
Chocolate sauce	JBC	267	1	
Clusters, raisin	BCC	120	2	C
Coffee, candied	SC	174	1	
Cookies	FFCB	553	1	C
Cookies	FFCB	550	1	C
Cookies, big breakfast	FFBB	234	2	C
Cookies, raisin &	MHGD	316	1	C
Creams	JOC	67	1	
Creams	SC	172	1	
Crunch	JOC	735	2	B
Crust	FFBB	70	1	B
Crumb	GHAC	321		
Crumb	NYT	548	1	
Perfect	MSE	236	2	C
Strawberry tart w	MSE	241	3	B
Curried	JOC	66	1	
Custard glaze	SC	83	1	
Date cookies	JOC	671	1	C
Drop cakes	SC	139	1	
Filling	FFBB	539	1	C
Filling, blue cheese	SC	380	1	
Fillings for coffee cakes & variations	JOC	573	1	B
Frosting, chocolate	SC	146	1	
Fruit bread, Portuguese	CBB	363	2	C
Fruit meringue filling	SC	149	1	
Glaceed	SC	175	1	
Glazed	BHGN	113	1	B
Horns	SC	81	2	
Kinds of uses for	SPGT	134		
Kinds & processes	FFBB	19		
Kisses, hickory	SC	163	1	
List of definitions	JBGF	118		
Loaf	JOC	180	1	B
Banana Hana	CBB	466	1	B
Cake	AC	650	1	
Cake, blueberry	MHGD	106	1	C
Date	MHGD	257	1	B
Zucchini	BHGN	78	1	B
Logs, chocolate	BCC	108	2	C
Meringue	FFCB	560	2	B
Mix, raisin &	FFCB	72	1	B
Muffins	NYT	481	1	C
Onions, stuffed	NYT	389	1	B
& Orange, candied	SC	174	1	
Oriental style	BCC	14	1	C
Pancakes	NYT	487	1	C

RECIPE	BOOK	PAGE	TD	S
Pascagoula dressing	FFCB	451	1	A
Paste filling for coffee cake	SC	83	1	
Patties	SC	161	1	
Pie	AC	631	1	
Pilaf	JBC	117	1	B
Potato croquettes	FFCB	399	2	B
Pudding, date &	SP	310	1	B
Refrigerator cookies	AC	702	2	
Refrigerator cookies	FFCB	562	1	C
Rice pilaf, raisins &	AC	579	1	
Roll	FFCB	522	2	C
◆	FFBB	306	2	C
◆	AC	679	2	
◆	NYT	564	2	C
Roll ups	BCC	113	2	C
Rolled cookies	AC	703	1	
Salted	SC	41	1	
Seeds, protein in	JBGF	113		
Souffle	SC	195	2	
Souffle	JOC	691	2	B
Soy	BBA	17	3	B
Spiced	VE	299	1	B
Spiced	JOC	737	2	B
Spiced	FFCB	690	1	B
Spiced caramel	JOC	737	2	B
Sticks, date &	SC	166	1	
Strudel, raisin, cheese &	SC	355	2	
Stuffing, Brazil, tomatoes &	NYT	406	1	B
Sugared	FFCB	72	1	B
Tarts, individual	JOC	665	1	C
Toasting	NSD	25		
Torte	NYTI	369	1	B
Torte	FFCB	520	1	C
Date	MC	183	1	B
Date	AC	667	1	
Or nuss torte	AC	688	2	

RECIPE	BOOK	PAGE	TD	S
Twists	NYT	473	2	C
Velvet	NYT	631	2	C
Wafers	JOC	669	1	C
Wafers, curled	JOC	668	1	C
Waffles	JOC	217	1	B
Nutmeat pate in brioche	VE	294	3	C
Nutmeg				
Butter, asparagus w	SMG	81	1	B
Cake, toasted w meringue topping	BHGN	94	2	C
Crumb topping	BCC	332	1	A
Doughnuts, sugar &	GHAC	369	2	C
Noodles	SMG	183	1	B
Noodles w	SMG	43	1	B
Refrigerator cookies	FFCB	562	1	C
Sauce	BCC	153	1	
& Spinach, creamed	BHGN	404	1	B
Sugar doughnuts	GHAC	369	2	C

O

RECIPE	BOOK	PAGE	TD	S
Oat				
Bars, caramel	BCC	105	1	C
Bread, steel cut	JOC	561	2	B
Molasses rolls	JOC	566	3	C
Wheat bread	JBGF	570	2	C
Oatcakes	BBA	177	3	C
Oatmeal				
Bars				
Apricot filled	BHGN	155	1	C
Fudgy	BCC	105	1	C
Peanut butter	BHGN	157	2	C
Prune filled	BHGN	155	1	C
Raisin filled	BHGN	155	1	C

RECIPE	BOOK	PAGE	TD	S
Oatmeal (*cont.*)				
Bread	SC	70	2	C
Bread	FFCB	466	2	C
Bran	BCC	46	3	C
Cinnamon	CBB	220	2	C
Crusty whole wheat	GHAC	357	2	B
English	CBB	210	3	B
Honey	FFCB	467	2	C
Maple	CBB	218	3	C
Molasses	BHGN	60	2	B
Old fashioned	NYT	465	2	C
Orange	CBB	217	1	B
Raisin	CBB	216	1	B
Scotch	CBB	213	3	C
Sourdough	CBB	281	3	C
White	VE	33	2	B
Cake	AC	670	1	
Cake	MHGD	103	1	C
Carrot cookies	AC	712	1	
Coconut slices	BCC	109	3	C
Cookies	SC	161	1	
◆	GHAC	351	1	C
◆	BCC	97	1	C
◆	BHGN	162	1	C
Apple filled	BHGN	160	1	C
Cape cod	FFCB	552	1	C
Carrot	JBGF	605	1	C
Carrot & honey	MHGD	318	1	C
Chocolate chip	FFCB	553	1	C
Coconut	MHGD	305	1	C
Crisp	FFBB	199	1	C
Date filled	FFCB	562	2	B
Quick	JOC	657	1	C
Soft	FFBB	200	1	C
Crackers, Swedish	CBB	701	1	C
Crispies	BCC	97	1	C
Crisps	SC	159	1	
Crisps	FFBB	198	1	C
Crumb topping	FFBB	78	1	C
Date pudding, steamed	SC	190	2	
Dough	FFBB	62	1	B
Gems	JOC	657	1	C
Griddle cakes	JOC	215	1	C
Griddle cakes	FFCB	497	1	B
Hearty	JBGF	509	1	B
Lace cookies	SC	161	1	
Molasses cake	BCC	68	1	C
Muffins	SC	89	1	
Muffins	FFCB	489	1	C
Muffins, raisin	JBGF	601	1	C
Muffins, raisin	BCC	31	1	C
Pancakes	JBGF	500	1	C
Raisin bread, sweet	VE	44	1	B
Raisin cookies	SP	258	1	C
Raisin cookies, spicy	BHGN	159	1	C
Raisins, spicy	BHGN	325	1	B
Refrigerator cookies	BHGN	168	2	C
Scotch chews, children's	FFBB	238	1	C
Shortbread	MSQC	177	1	B
Soup	CBSS	177	1	B
Spice cookies, giant	MHGD	302	1	C
Spice cookies, giant	YGM	239	1	C
Squares	BCC	97	1	C
Squares filled w dates	SC	166	1	
Wafers, crisp	MHGD	304	1	C
Wafers, flourless	JOC	658	1	C
Wafers, glazed	JOC	658	1	C
Walnut pie, creamed	FFBB	140	1	B
Ocean perch fillets filled & baked	FFCB	115	1	B
Ocean sunrise (drink—tequila & cranberry juice)	MSE	158	1	A
Octopus, all about	JOC	357		
Octopus, casseroled	JOC	358	2	

RECIPE	BOOK	PAGE	TD	S
Okra (*cont.*)				
Sauteed	VGCB	164	1	
Sauteed, fresh	GRIL	83	2	B
& Shrimp, Cross Creek	GG	227	1	B
Skewered	CFS	243	2	B
Skillet	BCC	352	1	B
Snappy pickled	GG	223	3	B
Soup	VGCB	164	1	B
Steamed	VGCB	163	1	
Steamed tomato vinaigrette	CW	65	1	B
Stew, lamb &	VGCB	165	2	B
Stewed	JOC	284	1	A
Stewed apricots (bamiya)	GG	227	1	B
Stewed tomatoes, Mediterranean	GG	225	2	B
Stewed vegetables	VGCB	163	1	
Tomato	BHGN	405	1	B
& Corn	AC	530	1	
& Corn	FFCB	390	1	B
& Corn, sauteed	CW	140	2	B
& Lemon	AC	529	1	
Mediterranean stewed w tomatoes	GG	225	2	B
Salad	GG	224	1	A
Stew	VGCB	165	1	B
Ol' Myra's salad dressing	PPLK	276	1	B
Old fashioned (bourbon drink)	SC	61	1	A
Old fashioned	NYT	649	1	
Old fashioned	JOC	38	1	
Olive	FGCW	91	1	
in Bacon	AC	24	1	
Bay & rosemary	BTSB	141	1	C
Beef stew, potatoes &	MFC2	153	2	B

RECIPE	BOOK	PAGE	TD	S
Black, broccoli w	NYT	366	1	B
Black, chicken w	FAIC	294	1	B
Black, Grecian style	NYT	35	3	C
Bread, Italian	CBB	512	3	B
Bread, w	FAIC	40	2	B
Brining & curing green	CPPC	179		
Butter	CFS	317	1	A
Butter	SC	379	1	
Butter, lamb steaks grilled w	CFS	180	2	B
Butter, salmon poached w basil &	CPMC	220	2	B
Casserole, rice &	AC	580	1	
& Cheese nuggets	EBE	22	2	C
Cheeses & plums	CW	33	1	B
Chicken &	FGCW	178	1	B
Chicken stuffed w potatoes &	FG	133	2	B
& Cream cheese spread	SC	380	1	
Deviled	SC	41	1	
Deviled w bacon blankets	SC	42	1	
Different kinds of	SP	6		
Dill	NYT	35	3	C
Dip, ham &	SC	37	1	
Duck w	FGCW	186	2	B
& Duck, braised	FFCB	251	3	B
Duck roast w	JBC	230	2	B
Garlic	JOC	70	3	
Garlic & black	NYT	36	2	
Golden rice &	GHAC	268	1	B
In pasta salad, black, tricolor	MSE	296	1	C
In pasta salad, crab, piquant	YGM	200	2	C
Marinated, Sicilian style	SPGT	68	3	B

RECIPE	BOOK	PAGE	TD	S
Meatballs, stuffed	SMG	278	1	B
Mixed Italian	NYT	35	3	C
Mosaic, spiced	SPGT	22	3	C
Oil	MCIC	30		
Garlic	BHGN	331	1	
Pickles	AC	823	3	
& Sauternes cake	CPMC	45	2	B
Onions	BCC	7	2	C
Pasta w	FGCW	148	3	
Pasta, pistachio, pesto &	SPGT	62	1	B
Paste	FGCW	94	3	
Paste, lamb chops w	FGCW	226	1	B
Peas	EBE	116	1	B
& Pistachios, Long Island duck &	GF	222	3	B
Pork tenderloin, mushrooms &	JOC	424	1	B
Rabbits, making (photographs)	LT	28		
& Rice casserole	AC	580	1	
& Rum, beef stew w	CF	118	2	C
Salad				
Molded fish, celery &	SC	371	2	
Orange &	KIS	251	1	A
Orange & black	SMG	171	1	B
Spiced	YGM	168	2	C
Sandwich, cheese &, broiled	SC	384	1	
Sauce	AC	457	1	
Sauce, shrimp &	GHAC	385		
Soup, black, chilled	CBSS	167	3	B
Spiced Spanish	NYT	35	2	
Stuffed	SC	42	1	
Stuffed eggs	AC	17	1	
Stuffed Mexican	NYTI	466	1	B
Stuffing, Italian	NYTI	407	1	B

RECIPE	BOOK	PAGE	TD	S
& Whole garlic, marinated w cheese	CPMC	19	2	B
Yogurt dip	FFCB	53	1	B
Omelet	AC	104		
All about	JOC	197		
All about	MAFC	126		
Almond dessert	SC	227	1	
Alternate way to stuff an (photographs)	LT	100		
Apple	FG	95	1	A
Apple Roquefort	VE	169	1	A
Asparagus	SC	225	1	B
Asparagus	MSE	88	1	C
Asparagus & cheese	SC	225	1	B
Aux confitures	JOC	691	1	A
Bacon	BCC	160	1	A
Bacon & asparagus	BHGN	197	1	A
Baked	JOC	199	1	B
Baked w chicken sauce	BHGN	201	2	B
Basic	FG	91	1	A
Basic rules for a good	FG	91		
Bread	SC	226	1	A
Brie & parsley	MSE	88	1	A
Broccoli oven	BCC	161	1	B
Chasseur	NYT	305	1	B
Cheese	SC	225	1	
Cheese	BCC	160	1	A
Cheese	JBC	56	1	
Fluffy	JBC	57	1	
French	BHGN	200	1	A
& Herb	BHGN	197	1	A
& Pepper	VE	169	1	A
& Tomato	FG	93	1	A
Chicken	SC	226	1	B
Chicken	JBC	56	1	
Chicken, tomato & cheese	SMG	82	1	B

RECIPE	BOOK	PAGE	TD	S
Omelet (*cont.*)				
Chive	BCC	160	1	A
Country	JBC	57	1	
Crabmeat, cold	SMG	308	1	B
Creamed fish	JBC	56	1	
Creamed leek	MSE	92	1	C
Creamed spinach	MSE	91	1	C
Creamy	SC	225	1	A
Curried chicken	MSE	92	1	C
Curried Spanish	JBC	56	1	
D'amour	BBA	123	2	A
Dessert, fluffy	JBC	57	1	
Dried beef	JBC	56	1	
Easy bake cheese	BHGN	201	1	A
Filled w tomatoes & cream cheese	MAFC	136	2	B
Fillings	MAFC	135		
Fines herbes	MSE	97	1	C
Fines herbes	JBC	56	1	
Firm	JOC	199	1	B
Flat, potato & ham	SMG	84	1	B
Flour	SC	226	1	A
Fluffy	JOC	199	1	B
Fluffy	JBC	57	1	
For two, simple	VE	167	1	A
French	JOC	198	1	
◆	BCC	160	1	A
◆	JBC	57	2	
◆	BHGN	200	1	A
French, making (drawings)	FFCB	341		
French, & variations	FFCB	340	1	A
Fruited French	BHGN	200	1	A
Garnishings	MAFC	135		
Grated w gruyere & bacon	MSE	88	1	B
w Green chili	BCC	160	1	A
Ham & cheese	BHGN	197	1	A
Hash brown	BHGN	200	2	B
Herbed	BCC	160	1	A
Herbs	SC	225	1	A
Individual	VE	168	1	A
Italian, artichoke & crab	GG	20	1	B
Jelly	BCC	160	1	A
Making an	SP	315		
Making an (drawings)	GHAC	112		
Making (photographs)	LT	98		
Master recipe	MSE	84	1	A
Mushroom	FG	94	1	A
Mushroom	JBC	56	1	
w Fines herbes	NYTI	238	1	B
French	BHGN	200	1	A
Rolled	GHAC	113	2	B
Norwegian	JOC	692	2	C
On rice	FGCW	361	1	A
Onion	JBC	56	1	
Open faced, Italian, onions	MCIC	346	1	B
Open faced, onions, peppers, tomatoes & ham	MAFC	137	2	B
Open faced w pan fried potatoes	MCIC	348	1	B
Orange dessert	BCC	128	1	B
Orange souffle	SC	196	1	
Oven	BCC	161	1	B
Oyster, Palace Hotel	AC	109	1	
Oyster, for small oysters only	AC	109	1	
Plain	LT	98	1	
Plain	JBC	56	1	
Plain	NYT	303	1	
Plain, making a	NYT	303	1	
Plain, making a (photographs)	NYT	304		
Poached w chicken	SMG	80	1	B
Potato	YGM	213	2	C

RECIPE	BOOK	PAGE	TD	S
Potato & garlic, French	FG	92	1	A
Potato & onion	NYT	305	1	B
Puffy	AC	104	1	
◆	BHGN	197	1	A
◆	BCC	161	1	A
◆	FFCB	342	1	A
Ratatouille	MSE	96	2	C
w Red caviar & sour cream	MSE	91	1	C
Rolls (isobe tamago yaki)	BBA	21	3	B
Rolled	MAFC	132	2	A
Rolled w mushroom	GHAC	113	2	B
Sandwich puff	BHGN	200	2	A
Scrambled	MAFC	129	2	A
Shrimp Creole	GHAC	112	1	A
Simple mushroom	VE	168	1	A
Souffle	SC	226	1	
Souffle	LT	353	3	C
Souffled	JOC	199	1	B
Spanish	VE	170	1	B
◆	NYT	306	1	B
◆	AC	108	1	
◆	SMG	83	1	B
◆	SC	226	1	A
Spinach w sour cream	NYT	305	1	B
Sweet	JOC	199		
Sweet	FFCB	614	1	A
w Berries & cream	FFCB	614	1	A
w Jam	FFCB	614	1	A
w Rum	FFCB	614	1	A
Sweetbread	SC	226	1	B
Swiss cheese	MSE	91	1	C
w Swiss cheese & sour cream	FG	93	1	A
Tomato sauce	JBC	56	1	
True, plus fillings	AC	104	1	
Two mushroom	FG	94	1	A
Vegetable	JBC	56	1	
Vegetable French	BHGN	200	1	A
Watercress	JBC	57	1	
Western	BCC	160	1	A
Western Denver	AC	109	1	
w Wild mushrooms	MSQC	28	1	A
Zucchini	SC	226	1	B
One crust pies	SC	341		
One egg cake	JOC	636	1	B
One egg cake, quick	SC	107	1	B
Onion				
A la Grecque	MAFC	539	1	
Almond soup	CBSS	313	2	B
Apple & bacon, chicken livers w	GHAC	168	1	B
& Apple casserole	JOC	286	1	B
& Apples	SC	423	1	
Au gratin	SC	423	1	
Au gratin	NYT	387	1	B
& Avocado salad	JBC	241	1	
& Avocado salad	KIS	180	1	A
Bake, Swiss	BHGN	193	1	B
Baked	GHAC	238	2	C
◆	FFCB	391	1	B
◆	JBC	319	2	B
◆	VGCB	174	1	
◆	SC	423	1	
Au gratin	FGCW	260	1	B
Cheese	AC	531	1	
Cinders	FG	212	1	C
Foil	VGCB	174	1	
Glazed	GG	245	2	B
In their skins	NYT	386	2	
White	GG	245	2	B
Whole	FG	213	1	
Whole	BCC	352	1	B
Whole	JOC	285	1	

RECIPE	BOOK	PAGE	TD	S
Onion (*cont.*)				
Beans	KIS	219	1	A
Beef	FGCW	236	2	A
Beets	JBC	294	1	A
& Endive salad	CF	15	1	B
& Herbs	AC	485	1	
Salad	JBC	244	1	B
Salad	NYTI	257	1	C
Bites	FFCB	66	1	B
Boiled	SC	423	1	
Boiled	VGCB	173	1	
Boiled, white	JBC	317	1	B
Braised, small	JOC	285	1	
Braised, small	AC	532	1	
Braised, white baby	FFCB	391	1	B
Bread	FFBB	446	2	C
Bread	FG	233	2	B
Bread, herb &	VE	40	2	B
Broccoli, savory	YGM	141	1	B
Brown, braised	MAFC	483	1	B
Brown, braised	VGCB	174	1	B
Brushes, making	BHGN	440		
Butter	SC	379	1	
Butter	BHGN	361	1	A
Cake, Hunan	FG	301	1	B
Canned	MAFC	484	1	B
Canned, uses for	AC	558		
Carrots	BCC	353	1	B
Casserole	BB	136	1	B
Casserole, green bean &	GHAC	231	1	C
Charcoal roasted	CFS	244	1	B
Cheddared	GHAC	239	1	B
w Cheese, steamed & sliced	AC	532	1	
Cheese bread	BBA	177	2	B
Cheese tart (flamiche)	GG	250	2	B
Chicken casserole	FGCW	322	2	B
Chopping	BHGN	423		
Cleaning in a hurry	FG	213		
Cooking	AC	530		
Coring & blanching	MFC2	377		
Corn bread & cheese	BCC	36	1	C
Corn & green peppers	FFCB	392	1	B
Crackers	CBB	697	2	C
Cream sherry	NYT	386	1	B
Creamed	MAFC	482	1	B
Creamed	JOC	284	2	B
Creamed	FFCB	391	1	B
Creamed & variations	NYT	386	1	B
Creamed, white	JBC	318	1	B
Cucumber	AC	48	1	
Deep fried	NYTI	365	1	
Dill casserole bread	BCC	47	3	B
Dinner rolls, Mrs. Culler's	VGCB	185	2	C
Dip				
Blue cheese &	BHGN	18	1	B
Creamy	BHGN	18	1	B
Green	EBE	36	1	B
Oriental	GHAC	94	1	B
Dressing	JOC	457	1	C
Dressing, orange &	BCC	300	1	A
Escalloped	VGCB	177	1	B
Family, all about	VGCB	167		
Finishing touches for cooked, whole	VGCB	174	1	
Fish, pickled	GG	239	3	C
Flake biscuits	EBE	105	1	B
Flowers, green	NYTI	57	2	
French fried	BCC	353	1	B
◆	BB	132	1	
◆	JBC	319	1	B
◆	NYT	387	1	

RECIPE	BOOK	PAGE	TD	S
Fried	SC	423	1	
In deep fat	VGCB	175	1	
Old fashioned	AC	532	1	
Tomatoes, corn, olives &	AC	551	1	
Frittata, ham &	GHAC	112	1	B
& Garlic butters	VGCB	178	1	
Glazed	NYT	388	1	B
◆	BHGN	397	1	B
◆	MAFC	481	1	B
◆	JBC	318	1	B
◆	NYTI	163	1	C
◆	GHAC	239	1	B
◆	FFCB	391	1	B
◆	JOC	285	1	B
Glazing (photographs)	LT	14		
Gourmet	BHGN	397	1	B
Green				
Cooking	AC	533		
Crested	GG	244	1	B
Forest, mushroom soup &	CBSS	315	2	B
Pasta salad &	FGCW	134	1	
Preparing	BCC	353		
Tart	AC	533	1	B
Young	JOC	284	1	
& Green peppers	JOC	288	1	B
Griddle cakes	JOC	216	1	C
Grilled	BB	132	1	
Grilled	JBC	319	1	B
Grilled	SC	334	1	
Grilled, spring	VGCB	174	1	
Herbed & barbecued	OC	94	1	B
w Herbs & wine	FGCW	259	1	B
& Herring appetizer, cold	VGCB	180	2	B
In onions	AC	532	1	
Jewish, stuffed	FG	210	2	C
Kuchen, quick	NYT	388	1	B
Leaves, stuffed	FG	208	3	
Liver &	BCC	217	1	B
Liver, sauteed	BHGN	269	1	B
Loaf cake, golden	GG	243	1	B
Lover's bread	CBB	409	3	B
w Madeira	FGCW	258	1	B
Marinated	JOC	70	3	
Marinated w feta	FG	209	2	B
Marmalade	GG	241	3	C
Marmalade, veal medallions w	MFC	147	2	B
Monegasque	VE	144	2	C
Olives	BCC	7	2	C
Omelet	JBC	56	1	
Pan fried, liver, bacon &	GHAC	211	1	B
Parsleyed	MAFC	484	1	B
Parsleyed	MAFC	482	1	B
Parsleyed, dried beans w	VGCB	176	1	B
Pasta, anchovy &	FGCW	147	1	B
Peeling	FG	212		
Peeling an (photographs)	LM	25		
& Peppers, stir fried	YGM	53	1	B
Pickled	SC	454	3	
◆	JOC	784	3	C
◆	FFCB	711	3	C
◆	NYT	501	2	B
◆	AC	825	3	
Pie	JOC	227	2	B
Pie, savory cheese &	VE	210	1	B
Pizza	FAIC	48	2	B
& Potato soup	MAFC	37	1	B
& Potatoes, mashed	CF	55	1	B
Potatoes, scalloped, tomatoes & anchovies	MAFC	525	1	B

RECIPE	BOOK	PAGE	TD	S
Onion Soup (*cont.*)				
◆	LM	158	1	B
◆	VE	68	2	B
Chablisienne	NYTI	126	1	B
Cream of	MFC2	14	1	B
Cream of	JOC	159	2	B
Cream of, Harvest	CBSS	317	2	B
Creamy	VGCB	182	1	B
Cyrano	NYT	71	1	B
French	SC	396	1	
◆	BCC	312	1	B
◆	FG	44	1	B
◆	JBC	276	1	
◆	BHGN	377	1	B
◆	MIE	73	2	B
Garnishings for	MAFC	44	1	B
Gratinee	GHAC	97	1	B
Gratinee	NYTI	126	1	B
Gratineed cheese	MAFC	44	1	B
Gratineed de luxe	MAFC	45	1	B
Karen Chewning's remarkable	GG	240	1	B
Les Halles	CBSS	310	2	C
Lyonnaise style	NYTI	127	2	B
Modern Tuscan	FAIC	114	1	B
Potato &	CIC	59	1	B
Quick	JOC	167	1	B
Renaissance	FAIC	113	1	B
Variations	AC	91	2	
Watercress & spring	CBSS	369	1	B
Squares	NYT	479	1	C
Steamed	JOC	284	1	B
Steamed	VGCB	173	1	
Steamed w butter	JBC	318	1	B
Steamed w butter, green	JBC	318	1	B
Stew, chicken &	FFCB	246	1	B
Stew, veal &, pearly	SP	188	2	C

RECIPE	BOOK	PAGE	TD	S
Stuffed	SC	423	2	
Stuffed	FFCB	307	3	B
Stuffed	JOC	286	2	
w Fish	NYT	389	1	B
w Liver	NYT	389	1	B
w Meat	NYT	389	1	B
w Nuts	NYT	388	1	B
w Poultry	NYT	389	1	B
w Rice, cheese & herbs	MFC2	376	2	B
w Sauerkraut	JOC	286	1	B
w Sausage	AC	533	1	
w Swiss chard	MSE	194	2	C
w Wild rice	VGCB	176	2	B
Stuffing	FFCB	279	1	B
Sweet & sour	CIC	382	1	B
Sweet & sour, braised w raisins	MFC2	410	1	B
& Swiss cheese soup	MC	13	1	B
Tart				
w Anchovies & black olives	MAFC	151	2	B
French	NYTI	113	2	B
Lyonnaise	VE	145	1	B
Red	CPMC	78	2	A
Sour cream &	AC	531	1	
Swiss	JBC	30	1	B
Topping, flat bread w	MCIC	53	3	B
Topping, sauteed	GHAC	185	1	
Triticale bread	CBB	225	3	B
Twist bread	CBB	416	2	C
Veloute	JOC	159	2	B
Vinaigrette, roast, w chopped red onion	CF	139	1	B
White, braised	VGCB	173	1	
White, braised	MAFC	481	1	B
White w cheese	JBC	318	1	B

RECIPE	BOOK	PAGE	TD	S
Onion (*cont.*)				
Opera centers (candy)	JOC	728	2	B
Opera creams	JOC	728	2	B
Opossum, all about	JOC	454		
Optimist's salad (okra & tomato)	GG	224	1	A
Orange				
Alaska	BBA	211	2	B
Almond snails	SPGT	100	3	C
Almond spongecake	MAFC	676	3	B
Angel pie	AC	632	1	
Angel pie	MHGD	171	2	B
Applesauce	AC	746	1	
Apricot bread	BHGN	78	1	B
Apricot ribs, spiced	BHGN	36	2	B
Avocado salad	BCC	298	1	B
Avocado salad	JBC	241	1	
Baby carrots	GHAC	178	1	
Baked Alaska	AC	740	2	
Bars, carrot &	VGCB	59	1	C
Baskets, making (photographs)	LT	31		
Bavarian	BCC	147	2	B
Bavarian cream	MAFC	596	3	C
Beef	YGM	200	2	C
Beets	NYT	365	1	B
Berry cocktail	SC	44	1	
Biscuits	FFBB	573	1	C
Blancmange	AC	726	1	
Blossom	SC	61	1	A
Blossom	BB	167	1	A
Bran cookies, breakfast	FFBB	236	2	C
Bread	CBB	495	3	C
Bread	AC	782	2	
Bread	AC	791	1	
Barley	CBB	177	1	B
Blueberry	MIE	304	1	B

RECIPE	BOOK	PAGE	TD	S
Cranberry	BCC	37	2	B
Peanut butter	FFBB	555	1	B
Pudding	NYT	587	2	B
Quick	JOC	575	1	C
Whole wheat	CBB	133	1	B
Yam	FFBB	556	1	C
Brulee w julienne of orange	GF	192	1	C
Butter	BHGN	361	1	A
Butter	SP	249	1	
Cake	FFBB	302	2	C
Cream	FFBB	388	2	C
Cream icing	MAFC	674	1	C
Frosting	SC	144	1	
Cake	NSD	171	2	C
◆	AC	652	1	
◆	SP	297	1	C
◆	SC	119	1	B
French	EBE	153	1	C
Princeton	FFCB	516	2	B
Sour cream	MC	185	2	B
Williamsburg	BCC	73	1	C
Campari ice	SP	309	2	B
Candy, Mexican	NYT	637	1	C
Cardamom cookies	NSD	67	2	C
Carrot bread	JBGF	571	2	C
Carrot soup, chilled	BBA	44	2	B
Carrots & cardamom	YGM	99	1	B
Charlotte Russe	SC	137	2	B
Chicken	KIS	117	1	A
Chicken, chilled	GHAC	156	2	C
Chicken salad	EBE	83	1	B
Chiffon cake	SC	122	1	B
◆	AC	690	1	
◆	BCC	76	2	C
◆	MHGD	120	2	C
Chiffon cake, California	FFBB	304	2	C

ORANGE

RECIPE	BOOK	PAGE	TD	S
Chiffon pie	BCC	93	2	B
◆	SC	351	1	
◆	JOC	614	2	B
◆	GHAC	323	2	B
◆	FFCB	593	2	B
Chiffon pie, pumpkin &	JBGF	631	2	B
Chip cookies	BHGN	168	2	C
Cider, hot	BCC	21	1	C
Cinnamon sourdough rolls	BHGN	76	2	C
Cinnamon swirl bread	CBB	462	2	C
Coconut pound cake	BCC	69	1	C
Coffee cake, date &	BHGN	80	1	B
Coffee cake, prune, caraway &	FFBB	580	2	B
Compote, cranberry &	AC	464	1	
Cookies	SC	155	1	
Cranberry compote	AC	464	1	
Cream filling (or lemon)	MFC2	484	1	
Cream pie	JOC	611	2	B
Cream sauce	SC	219	2	
Cream sherbet	FFCB	634	2	C
Creme brulee	AC	729	2	
Creme brulee, making	NSD	169		
Crepes w almond butter	MAFC	651	2	B
Crepes w honey butter sauce	PPLK	321	2	B
Crust pastry	GG	412	2	B
Cucumber salad	MCIC	414	1	B
Curd	BTSB	249	1	B
Currant sauce	GHAC	206	1	A
Curry	VE	254	1	B

RECIPE	BOOK	PAGE	TD	S
Custard	MHGD	349	1	B
Baked	NYT	595	2	B
Baked	AC	729	1	
Filling	SC	148	1	
Meringue	JOC	686	2	B
Date nut bread	EBE	105	2	B
Dessert omelets	BCC	128	1	B
Dip, Mexican	KIS	311	1	B
Doughnut drops	SC	100	1	
Dressing	SC	378	1	
Dressing	BCC	298	1	
Drops, Mexican	JOC	739	1	B
Duck in aspic	FFCB	447	3	B
Eggnog	JOC	34	1	B
Espresso checkerboards	NSD	56	3	C
Filled cake	JOC	641	2	C
Filling	FFCB	545	1	B
Filling, cream	JOC	647	2	B
Filling, custard	JOC	647	1	B
Flavored icing	NYTI	444	1	
Fluff frosting	SC	145	1	
Freeze	SC	54	1	
Frosting, creamy	BCC	77	1	C
Fruit soup	JOC	109	3	B
Fudge	AC	833	1	
Fudge sauce	BCC	153	1	
Gelatin	JOC	695	2	B
Gelatin, fruit, molded	JOC	696	2	B
Ginger sauce	MC	81	1	B
Glaze	SP	297	1	C
◆	BHGN	82	1	
◆	BCC	78	1	C
◆	FFBB	410	1	B
Glaze, marmalade	FFBB	410	1	C
Grape cooler	BHGN	51	1	C
Grape sauce	BHGN	360	1	B
Grapefruit & avocado salad	SC	365	1	

RECIPE	BOOK	PAGE	TD	S
Orange (*cont.*)				
Grapefruit salad	JOC	94	1	
Hard sauce	SC	98	1	
Hard sauce	BHGN	186	1	B
Hazelnut & chocolate parfait	NSD	312	3	B
Hollandaise	MAFC	83	2	A
Honey bread	NYT	484	2	B
Ice	SC	211	2	
Ice	MHGD	441	1	C
Ice	FFCB	636	3	C
Angelica	JOC	725	2	B
Lemon	JOC	722	2	C
Pineapple	BHGN	12	1	B
Ice cream	SC	205	2	
Ice cream	FFCB	633	3	C
Ice cream	JOC	717	2	C
Bitter	NSD	218	1	B
w Black raspberry sauce	MSQC	49	1	B
Chocolate	AC	739	3	
Palm Beach	MHGD	434	1	C
Icebox cake	SC	135	1	B
Icing	SC	143	1	
Butter cream	MAFC	674	1	C
Flavored	NYTI	444	1	
Luscious	JOC	676	1	B
Quick	JOC	678	1	B
Seven minute	JOC	676	1	B
Jam, tomato &	SC	443	1	
Jellies	BTSB	274	2	C
Jelly	FFCB	621	2	B
Jelly	SC	201	1	
& Jicama salad	BCC	298	1	B
Juice	SC	54	1	A
Juice	AC	761	1	
Ham slice baked in	SC	297	2	
Strawberries in	AC	773	1	
Sweet potatoes &	JOC	299	1	

RECIPE	BOOK	PAGE	TD	S
Lamb chops	YGM	134	1	B
& Leeks, chicken breasts stuffed w	SPGT	89	3	B
& Lime juice	JOC	33	1	B
Liqueur	BTSB	220	2	C
Loaf cake	AC	649	1	
Macaroon, layer	NSD	316	3	B
Mandarin salad, carrot &	MSQC	213	1	B
Marinade	CFS	292	1	A
Marinade, trout sauteed cold, in	CIC	220	2	B
Marmalade (see also marmalade, orange)				
Drops	JOC	658	1	C
Pie, open face	FFBB	147	2	B
Tarts	FFBB	176	2	B
Meringue pie	FFCB	590	2	B
Milk sherbet	SC	212	2	
Milk sherbet	JOC	722	2	C
Mint peas	EBE	114	2	C
Mint sauce	BCC	330	1	B
Mold, coconut	EBE	136	2	C
Mousse	MAFC	603	3	B
Mousse	BCC	148	2	B
Mousse, blueberries &	MHGD	360	2	B
Mousse, molded, w pineapple & orange peel	MFC2	442	3	B
Muffins, rice &	FFBB	562	2	C
Muffins, sticky	FFBB	561	1	C
Muffins, wheat	JBGF	602	1	C
Mustard sauce	BCC	330	1	A
Nut bread	CBB	493	1	C
Nut bread	SC	86	1	
Nut cake	EBE	155	2	B
Nuts, candied	SC	174	1	
Oatmeal bread	CBB	217	1	B

RECIPE	BOOK	PAGE	TD	S
Olive salad	KIS	251	1	A
Omelet souffle	SC	196	1	
Onion dressing	BCC	300	1	A
Onion salad	YGM	67	1	B
◆	KIS	247	1	A
◆	JOC	94	1	
◆	SP	215	1	B
◆	JBC	246	1	B
Or lemon refrigerator cookies	AC	701	2	
Pancakes, whole wheat	VE	192	1	A
Pastry	NSD	85	1	C
Pastry cream	NSD	295	2	C
& Peach marmalade	SC	443	1	
& Pears	KIS	323	1	B
Pecan bread	SP	249	2	B
Pecan dressing	BCC	300	1	A
Peel bread	FFCB	486	2	C
Peel cake, Victorian	BBA	188	3	C
Peel, candied	SC	175	1	
◆	BTSB	255	2	C
◆	NYTI	287	2	
◆	SC	175	1	
Peel, glazed	MAFC	587	1	A
Peel, julienne	LT	33		
Pie, yam, date &	FFBB	133	1	B
Pineapple, Bavarian	GHAC	294	2	C
Pineapple bundt cake	WC	133	1	C
Poppy seed cake	NSD	292	3	B
Poppy seed bundt cake	SP	297	2	C
Pork chops	SMG	272	1	B
Pound cake, coconut &	BCC	69	1	C
Pudding, lemon	WC	136	1	B
Puff cake	SC	120	2	B
Punch, pineapple &	NYT	649	1	B
& Radish salad	BBA	145	2	B
Radishes	VGCB	241	1	B
& Red onion salad	YGM	224	1	C
& Red pepper salad	YGM	107	1	B
Relish, cranberry &	BHGN	78	1	B
Relish, cranberry, spiked	YGM	233	1	C
Rice & cherry mold	MFC2	444	1	C
& Rice, herbed	GHAC	266	1	B
Rind	LT	33		
Rolls	EBE	106	1	C
Rolls	FFCB	478	3	C
Rolls	BCC	50	2	C
Rolls, quick	SC	87	1	
Roughy w tarragon	BCC	182	1	A
& Rum sherbet	NYT	628	2	B
Rye cake	FFBB	356	1	B
Sabayon	BBA	213	1	
Salad	BCC	298	1	B
Salad	SC	365	1	
Salad for game	JOC	94	1	B
Salad, shrimp &	AC	52	1	
Salad, tripe	BCC	292	2	B
& Salmon patties	KIS	133	1	B
Sambuca sherbet, fresh	SPGT	78	3	C
Sauce				
◆	JOC	709	1	B
◆	SC	217	1	
◆	KIS	133	1	
◆	BHGN	186	1	C
◆	BCC	154	1	B
Bitter	NSD	334	2	C
Brown sugar	JOC	713	1	B
Duck in	FAIC	323	2	B
Duck roast	MAFC	276	2	B
Flounder & pine nuts in	YGM	126	1	A
For desserts	FFCB	640	1	B
For duck	JOC	326	2	B

RECIPE	BOOK	PAGE	TD	S
Oxtail				
Braised	NYT	115	2	B
Braised	FFCB	164	2	B
Braised	JOC	450	2	B
Braised w wine & vegetables	CIC	291	2	B
Consomme or bouillon	AC	86	2	
Ragout	AC	323	2	
◆	NYTI	199	2	B
◆	JBC	150	2	B
◆	AC	323	2	
Ragout of	CBSS	68	3	B
Soup	JOC	154	2	B
◆	FFCB	91	2	C
◆	SC	398	2	
◆	NYTI	458	1	B
Soup, clear	CBSS	70	3	B
Soup w wine, quick	JOC	167	1	B
Stew	SP	138	3	B
◆	JOC	418	2	B
◆	SC	276	1	
◆	NYT	115	2	A
Stew w bread for sopping	FG	161	3	B
Oyako domburi (Japanese rice & chicken dish)	NYTI	457	1	A
Oyako domburi	BBA	72	2	A
Oysters	BB	89	2	
A la king	NYT	284	1	B
All about	JOC	363		
Appetizer, lettuce	VGCB	250	1	B
Bacon	FFCB	71	1	B
Bake w cheese, Long Island	BBA	92	2	B
Baked	JBC	83	1	
Baked	JOC	364	1	A
Baked in oil w parsley	CIC	32	1	B
Baked w parmesan cheese	CIC	33	1	B
Balls, an Illinois recipe for	AC	161	1	B
Baltimore	NYT	284	1	B
Bayou teche, fried	PPLK	85	3	B
Beef Ming's	FG	161	1	B
Benedict	SC	254	1	
Bienville	FG	295	3	C
Bisque	SC	403	1	
Bisques	JOC	162	2	B
Blanket, beefsteak &	AC	266		
Blankets	SC	42	1	
& Brie soup	PPLK	198	2	B
Broiled	JOC	364	1	
Broiled	SC	253	1	
Broiled au gratin	OC	156	1	B
Broiled, pan	SC	252	1	
Cakes	JOC	240	2	B
Canapes, creamed, hot	JOC	62	2	
Casino	JOC	366	1	
◆	FFCB	137	2	B
◆	JBC	84	1	B
◆	NYT	19	1	B
◆	AC	162	1	B
Casserole, mock	JOC	276	1	B
Caviar	SP	36	1	B
Celery	JOC	365	1	B
w Champagne sauce	FGCW	122	1	B
Charcoal baked	BB	55	1	
Charcoal grilled	CPMC	124	3	B
Chicken, creamed w	AC	201	1	
& Chicken croquettes	JOC	220	3	C
& Chicken, for a chafing dish	FFCB	259	2	B

RECIPE	BOOK	PAGE	TD	S
& Chicken pie	AC	213	2	
Chowder	NYT	77	1	B
Chowder, fish	SMG	130	1	B
& Clams, barbecued	BB	89	2	
& Clams, pan fried	JBC	9	1	
& Clams, scalloped	SC	247	1	
Cocktail	BHGN	15	1	B
Cocktail	SC	46	1	
Cooked	SC	252	1	
Creamed	JOC	365	2	B
Creamed, chicken w	AC	201	1	
Creamed & smoked salmon w noodles	SMG	128	2	B
Crepes, veal &	PPLK	123	3	B
Croquettes, chicken &	JOC	220	3	C
Crust case	SC	253	1	
Deviled	FFCB	138	2	B
Dressing	PPLK	178	2	B
Dressing	JOC	457	1	B
Dressing & ginger, boneless half chicken w	PPLK	177	3	B
En brochette	NYT	283	1	B
En brochette	PPLK	82	2	B
Fettuccine, green w thyme blossoms &	MSQC	197	1	B
& Fish quenelles	MAFC	188	2	B
Florentine	FG	73	1	
French fried	NYT	283	1	B
Fricassee	FFCB	138	2	B
Fried	FFCB	139	2	B
◆	AC	159	1	
◆	SC	253	1	
◆	BHGN	217	1	B
Fried in deep fat	JOC	364	1	A
Fried sandwiches	MSQC	212	2	A
Grilled	GRIL	101	1	B
Grilled	JOC	364	1	
Grilled	SC	333	1	
Gumbo, chicken &	GHAC	150	1	B
Gumbo, shrimp, crab &	JOC	163	1	B
Hangtown fry	GHAC	123	1	B
Hangtown fry, variations	AC	160		
Hollandaise tasso	PPLK	106	2	B
Hors d'oeuvre, cold	JOC	73	1	
In butter, grilled	SC	333	1	
Italian	FG	73	1	C
Leeks & pancetta linguine	CPPC	107	2	A
Lettuce, appetizer	VGCB	250	1	B
Lettuce bundles	MFC	33	2	B
Loaf	AC	163	1	
Loaf from New Orleans	FGCW	300		
Manhattan style	SC	253	1	
Mayonnaise	PPLK	270	1	B
Miniature	AC	159	1	
Mushrooms	SC	253	1	
Mushrooms au gratin	JOC	365	2	B
Mushrooms, creamed	JOC	370	1	B
My favorite quick	FG	72	1	A
Omelet for small oysters only	AC	109	1	
Omelet, Palace Hotel	AC	109	1	
On the half shell	GHAC	123	1	C
◆	AC	159	1	
◆	FFCB	136	2	B
◆	JOC	364	1	
On the half shell w champagne & sausages	CPMC	74	2	A

RECIPE	BOOK	PAGE	TD	S
Oysters (*cont.*)				
On the half shell w mignonette sauce	CPMC	86	2	B
Opening	SC	252		
Opening	JOC	363		
Opening (photographs)	LT	105		
Or clam cocktails, individual	AC	26		
Pan roast, variations	AC	163		
Pan roast, variations	JBC	84	1	
Panned	SC	252	1	
Panned	FFCB	138	2	B
Parmesan	BCC	6	1	A
Patties	AC	161	1	B
Peppers, stuffed & creamed	JOC	289	1	B
Pickled	FG	284	1	B
Pickled	JOC	73	3	
Pie	AC	161	1	B
Pie	AC	171	1	
Pie	NYT	285	1	B
Beef &	GHAC	181	2	B
Beefsteak kidney &	AC	327	2	
w Biscuit crust	AC	171	1	
Chicken &	AC	213	2	
Simple	AC	171	1	
Sweetbread &	AC	171	1	
w Pink butter	MSQC	184	2	B
Plant	AC	542		
Plant	SC	423	1	
Plant, a blanc	JOC	286	2	
Plant, sauteed	JOC	286	2	
Poulette	SC	253	1	
Puffs	BBA	14	2	C
Rarebit	SC	254	1	
Rarebit	JOC	366	1	B
Rockefeller	FFCB	137	2	B
◆	EBE	22	1	
◆	JOC	366	1	
◆	BHGN	11	1	B
◆	GHAC	123	2	B
◆	BCC	6	1	A
◆	JBC	84	1	B
◆	AC	162	1	B
◆	SC	253	1	
Rockefeller I	NYT	19	1	B
Rockefeller II	NYT	20	2	B
Saffron & ginger sauce	YGM	229	3	C
Salad	AC	65	1	
Sauce	FFCB	275	2	B
For beef	PPLK	246	2	B
For fish	JOC	324	1	B
Shrimp &	FG	322	2	B
Spaghetti &	AC	164	1	
Sausage	NYT	18		
Sauteed	JOC	364	1	A
Sauteed	JBC	83	1	
Scalloped	JBC	84	1	
◆	EBE	97	1	B
◆	FFCB	139	2	B
◆	AC	162	1	A
◆	JOC	365	1	B
◆	GHAC	123	1	B
◆	BCC	191	1	B
◆	SC	254	1	
Scalloped, in canned soup	JOC	365	1	B
Scalloped, old fashioned	NYT	285	2	B
& Scallops, poached, w truffle, saffron & mustard	GF	184	3	B

P

RECIPE	BOOK	PAGE	TD	S
Pale greens w watercress dressing	SPGT	95	1	B
Palermo cassata	NYT	631	2	C
Palm cookies	FFCB	601	3	C
Palm cookies	LT	430	2	
Palm cookies	FFBB	262	1	C
Palm leaf caramelized sugar cookies, from pastry	MFC2	478	2	
Palm leaves	AC	639	1	
Palm leaves	NYT	540	2	
Palm leaves	JOC	596	2	C
Palmiers (palm leaves)	LT	430	2	
◆	FFBB	262	1	C
◆	NYT	540	2	
◆	MFC	216	3	C
◆	MSE	251	2	C
◆	MFC2	478	2	
Palmiers w honey mustard & prosciutto	SPGT	24	3	C
Palusami (stuffed cabbage)	NYTI	95	2	B
Pan roast Grand Central	NYT	284	1	A
Panade au riz	MFC2	318		
Panade w leek	CBSS	348	1	B
Panade vegetable soup	JOC	155	2	B
Pancake	BHGN	88	1	B
◆	BCC	30	1	B
◆	BTSB	122	1	A
◆	BHGN	83	1	C
Apple	BBA	208	2	B
Apple & cheese	MC	147	1	B
Apple puffed	JBGF	623	1	B
Austrian (nockerln)	JOC	214	1	A
Baked	SC	93	1	B
Basic	NYT	486	1	C

RECIPE	BOOK	PAGE	TD	S
Beer	NYT	486	1	C
Blueberry	BCC	30	1	B
Bohemian	SC	94	1	C
Buckwheat	BHGN	88	1	B
Buckwheat	BCC	30	1	B
Buttermilk	AC	797	1	
◆	NYT	487	1	C
◆	BCC	30	1	B
◆	BTSB	122	1	A
◆	BHGN	88	1	B
Cabbage	GG	81	1	B
Chinese I	SC	226	1	
Chinese II	SC	227	1	
Chocolate, Italian (cannoli Sicilian)	NYTI	444	2	C
Corn meal	JOC	215	1	C
Cottage cheese	VE	191	1	B
Cottage cheese	JBGF	499	1	B
Cottage cheese	JOC	213	2	B
Country brunch	GHAC	370	1	B
Dessert	NYT	486	1	C
Dessert	SC	94	1	
Desserts	JOC	702	1	B
Egg	NYTI	363	1	C
For manicotti	NYTI	438	1	
French	SC	93	1	
◆	JOC	212	1	C
◆	FFCB	497	2	B
◆	FFCB	614	1	B
w Cream cheese, spinach & mushrooms	MAFC	193	3	B
Molded, w various fillings	MAFC	195	2	B
Stuffed	JOC	212	2	
Stuffed & rolled	MAFC	195	2	B
Fritters	FAIC	467	1	B
Fruit	JOC	212	1	
Fruit	NYT	487	1	C

RECIPE	BOOK	PAGE	TD	S
Garnish	SC	409	1	
German (pfannkuchen)	JOC	214	1	A
German	SC	96	1	B
German	AC	797	1	
German apple	VE	192	2	B
German & variations	AC	797	1	
Ham	BCC	30	1	B
Italian	CIC	175	1	B
Italian, filled w meat sauce	CIC	178	2	B
Italian, filled w spinach	CIC	177	2	B
w Jerusalem artichoke, lacy	VGCB	138	2	B
Korean	NYTI	461	1	C
Lettuce & cheese	CFS	242	1	B
Making	VE	183		
Matzo meal	SC	96	1	
Matzo meal, puff	SC	96	1	
Matzos	SC	96	1	
Mile high	JBGF	510	1	A
Mix	BTSB	121	1	A
Mix, buckwheat	KIS	341	1	C
Multigrain & variations	JBGF	498	2	B
Norwegian	SC	93	1	
Nut	NYT	487	1	C
Oatmeal	JBGF	500	1	C
Orange whole wheat	VE	192	1	A
Pepper, onion, tomato & cheese	MFC2	408	1	B
Potato (see potato pancakes)				
Pumpkin & oat	JBGF	500	1	B
Russian	SC	93	1	
Russian, raised, w blini	JOC	214	2	C

RECIPE	BOOK	PAGE	TD	S
Scotch	SC	93	1	B
Silver dollar	GHAC	370	1	C
Simple breakfast	VE	186	1	A
Souffle	SC	93		
Sour cream	BB	116	1	A
Sour cream	NYT	487	1	C
Sour milk	JOC	214	1	C
Spinach	MAFC	474	2	B
Spinach	GG	318	1	A
Steamed	NYTI	57	3	C
Swedish	NYT	611	1	C
Whole wheat	BCC	30	1	B
Zucchini (see zucchini pancakes)				
Pancetta				
Braised, celery, tomatoes, onions &	MCIC	380	1	B
Chicken, fava beans, tagliatelle &	CPPC	29	2	A
Dressing for hot escarole	MSQC	33	1	B
& Egg sauce, spaghetti	FAIC	155	1	B
& Escarole salad, hot	MSQC	33	1	B
Italian bacon	MCIC	32		
& Lettuce, smothered	MCIC	393	1	B
Oysters & leeks, linguine &	CPPC	107	2	A
Pizza				
w Artichoke hearts, garlic &	CPPC	154	3	B
w Artichoke, thyme &	CPPC	162	3	B
w Leeks, goat cheese &	CPPC	155	3	B

RECIPE	BOOK	PAGE	TD	S
Paradise jelly	JOC	775	2	
Paradise jelly	SC	449	1	
Paraffin wax, sealing w	BTSB	155		
Paratha (Indian bread)	BBA	15	1	B
Parchment, cooking in	FB	254		
Parchment new potatoes	CPMC	25	1	B
Parchment, red snapper baked in	MSQC	112	2	B
Parfait				
Angel	SC	213	2	
Angel	FFCB	626	3	B
Angelica	JOC	721	2	C
Butterscotch	JOC	721	2	B
Caramel	JOC	720	2	C
Coffee	JOC	720	2	B
Coffee	NSD	318	3	B
Coffee	SC	213	2	
Maple	JOC	721	2	B
Mint	NYT	632	2	B
Pineapple	SC	214	2	
Raspberry	JOC	721	2	C
San Francisco, strawberry	GHAC	303		
Strawberry	FFCB	626	3	C
Tutti frutti	JOC	720	2	B
Paris-Brest (dessert bread)	MHGD	49	3	B
Paris-Brest	BBA	192	3	C
Parker House				
Chocolate cream pie	AC	657	1	
Rolls	GHAC	361	2	C
◆	JBC	16	2	B
◆	FFBB	489	2	C
◆	JOC	563	2	C
◆	AC	780	2	
◆	SC	75	2	
◆	NYT	474	2	
Rolls, making	BHGN	71		
Rolls, quick	SC	87	1	

RECIPE	BOOK	PAGE	TD	S
Parkin (cake)	JOC	636	1	B
Parmesan				
Bread, zucchini	JBGF	593	1	B
Brussels sprouts	BCC	340	1	B
Carrots	CIC	365	1	B
Cauliflower	GHAC	235	1	B
Cheese canapes	NYT	44	1	C
Cheese & fennel	VGCB	122	1	B
Cheese sauce	GHAC	262		
Cheese souffle	JBC	270	1	B
Cheese, veal cutlet breaded w	JBC	166	1	B
Chicken	BHGN	299	1	B
Chicken	NYTI	405	1	B
Chicken saute	NYTI	212	1	B
Cream sauce, chicken w	NYT	196	1	B
Crepes	VE	185	1	B
Dressing	BCC	270	1	
Eggplant (see also eggplant, parmesan)				
Eggplant	CIC	373	1	B
Mushrooms	NYTI	372	1	B
Peas	BCC	355	1	B
Popovers	BBA	178	1	B
Potatoes	EBE	128	1	B
Puffs, Sherley's	EBE	23	1	
Pumpkin	JBGF	527	2	B
Risotto	CIC	181	1	B
Sauce	BHGN	355	1	B
Spread	BHGN	41	1	
Parsley				
Butter (see also butter, parsley)				
Butter sauce	SC	391	1	
Chicken, roast	FG	139	2	B
Dressing	BCC	271	1	
Fried	LM	128	1	
Fried	NYTI	249	1	B

RECIPE	BOOK	PAGE	TD	S
Parsley (*cont.*)				
Fried, deep	JOC	287	1	
w Fried soft shell crabs	GF	229	1	B
Mayonnaise	FAIC	65	1	B
Sauce	AC	455		
Soup	BBA	45	1	B
Sponge dumplings	SC	408	1	
Parsnip	VGCB	185		
Parsnip	JOC	287	1	B
Parsnip	SC	424	1	
& Apple sauce	GG	259	1	B
Baked fruit	VGCB	189	1	B
Boiled	VGCB	188	1	
Buttered	NYT	390	1	
Cakes	BCC	354	1	B
Cakes	AC	535	1	
Candied	NYT	390	1	B
Candied	FFCB	393	1	B
Caramel, chicken w	GG	260	1	B
& Carrot, chicken casserole w	VGCB	191	1	B
& Carrots, combined	MIE	212	1	B
Chowder	VGCB	190	1	B
Chowder	CBSS	147	1	B
Cooking	AC	534		
Cream, unparalleled	GG	257	1	B
Finishing touches for, cooked	VGCB	188	1	
French	JOC	287	1	B
Fried, pale	GG	256	1	B
Fritters	FFCB	393	1	B
Glazed	BCC	354	1	B
Hawaiian style	BHGN	398	1	B
In ginger cream	GG	258	1	B
In melting mustard sauce	GG	258	1	B
Marmalade, old fashioned	GG	260	1	B
Mashed	FFCB	393	1	B
Muffins	VGCB	192	1	B
Oven braised w brussels sprouts	MSE	188	2	B
Patties, sauteed	VGCB	189	2	B
Pecan cake	VGCB	192	1	B
Pie	FFBB	133	2	B
Pie	VGCB	192	1	B
Pie	FFCB	588	2	C
& Pork	BCC	223	1	B
Potato & carrot puree	VGCB	189	1	B
& Potatoes, scalloped	AC	535	1	
Preparing	BCC	354		
Preparing	GG	255		
Puff, whipped	BHGN	406	1	B
Pumpkin, pureed, & cannelini beans	VGCB	230	1	C
Puree w madeira	AC	535	1	
Puree w mushroom caps	VGCB	189	1	
Puree w zucchini halves	VGCB	189	1	
Pureed	FFCB	393	1	B
Pureed	VGCB	188	1	B
Salad, grated	VGCB	191	1	B
w Scalloped potatoes	AC	535	1	
Slices, sauteed	VGCB	188	1	B
Soffritto soup	VGCB	190	1	B
Soup	AC	82		
Soup, cream of	VGCB	190	1	B
Soup, curried	CBSS	321	1	B
Steamed	VGCB	188	1	
Stew	FFCB	96	1	B
Stew w celeriac	VGCB	73	1	B
Tart	VGCB	191	1	B
Partridge				
About	JOC	479		
Broiled	BB	48	1	

RECIPE	BOOK	PAGE	TD	S
Cabbage	NYTI	28	3	B
Giblets, pate of	BB	48	1	
Roast	SC	323		
Roast	AC	244	1	
Roast	BB	81	2	
Sauteed	BB	48	1	
Spit-roasted	OC	140	2	A
Party creamy eggs	GHAC	111	2	B
Party mix, crunchy	BHGN	17	1	C
Paschka (Russian dessert)	NYTI	516	3	C
Pashka	MSE	150	3	C
◆	FFBB	506	3	C
◆	GF	106	2	C
◆	NYT	607	2	C
◆	BBA	227	3	C
Passatelli (bread sticks in beef broth)	CIC	70	1	B
Passati (Italian soups)	FAIC	116		
Passion fruit sherbet	NSD	231	2	B
Passover desserts	SC	193		
Passover potato pudding	SC	194	1	
Pasta	YGM	71	1	B
Pasta	MFC	208	2	B
Pasta	KIS	286	1	A
A la caprese	GG	378	2	B
Al cavolfiore	MC	165	1	B
Al pesto	MIE	184	1	B
Al pesto	FG	128	2	C
Alfredo	CPPC	144	1	A
w Anchovy & onion	FGCW	147	1	B
Angel hair				
Broccoli & three cheeses	FG	123	1	B
w Feta	GHAC	260	1	B
& Ricotta custard	CF	109	2	B
Sesame & shrimp	YGM	107	3	B
Artichoke	GG	17	2	B

RECIPE	BOOK	PAGE	TD	S
Arugula, basil & pesto	SPGT	63	2	B
Asparagus	VGCB	7	1	B
August	MIE	180	1	B
Bagna cauda	FGCW	149	1	B
Bake, cottage	BHGN	320	1	B
& Bean soup	CBSS	243	2	B
& Bean soup	FAIC	127	3	B
Beet, spinach & greens	CPMC	223	2	B
Broccoli	VGCB	32	1	B
Broccoli	MIE	187	1	B
& Broken garlic, barbecued artichokes	CPPC	104	2	B
Broth	FAIC	109	2	B
w Brown sauce	CW	36	2	C
Buckwheat, w chard & goat cheese	CPPC	125	2	B
Buckwheat, w roasted peppers & endive	CPPC	89	2	B
Buckwheat, rocket w goat cheese	CPMC	217	2	B
w Caraway seeds, whole wheat	KIS	110	1	A
Carbonara	FG	130	1	C
Carbonara sauce	BHGN	320	2	C
Caviar	GF	96	1	A
Cheese & parsley	NYT	334	1	B
& Chick peas	CIC	87	1	B
& Chick peas soup	FAIC	128	3	B
& Chicken livers	FG	127	2	B
& Chicken salad, party	GHAC	281	1	B
Chu chu	PPLK	185	3	A
w Clam sauce	BBA	102	1	B
w Clam & vegetable sauce	FG	122	1	B

RECIPE	BOOK	PAGE	TD	S
Pasta (*cont.*)				
Soup (see also pasta e fagioli)				
Soup, chickpea &	JBGF	339	1	B
Spinach	CIC	126	3	
Summer vegetable ragout	CPPC	81	2	B
Tasso, oysters cream	PPLK	84	2	B
Thin w spring vegetables	CPMC	58	2	B
w Three meats & peas	FGCW	146	1	C
Timbale, broccoli &	GG	64	2	B
w Toasted bread crumbs	SPGT	66	1	B
w Tomato sauce	CW	36	1	C
Truffle, chanterelle & endive	CPPC	143	2	B
w Truffles	MFC	38	3	B
w Veal, oysters & artichoke	PPLK	126	3	B
Walnut sauce for	GHAC	265		
What you need to make	CIC	112		
& White bean soup	CPPC	147	2	B
w White truffles	CPPC	115	1	
Whole wheat	KIS	289	1	B
Whole wheat, grilled tomato sauce &	CPPC	101	1	B
Whole wheat w hot red sausage & red peppers	CPPC	90	2	B
Zucchini	VGCB	279	1	B
Paste half puff	JOC	596	2	
Paste rough	JOC	596	2	
Pastel de choclo (beef, chicken, corn casserole)	NYT	112	2	C
Pastellios (cheese turnover)	NYTI	502	2	C
Pastels (pastry)	NYTI	481	1	C
Pasties (meat & vegetable turnover)	SC	283	1	
Pasties Michigan style	GHAC	182	2	B
Pastillage (gum paste for decorating)	JOC	738	2	B
Pastisto (macaroni)	EBE	61	1	B
Pastitsio (Greek macaroni with meat)	NYTI	332	2	C
Pastitsio	VE	240	3	B
Pastitso	FG	342	1	B
Pastrami	BTSB	28	3	C
Pastrami, homemade	AC	306	3	
Pastrami, sandwich, hot	AC	806	1	
Pastries benne	FFCB	67	1	C
Pastries, jam	BCC	53	3	C
Pastries, stamped	FAIC	459	2	C
Pastry	BCC	225	1	
Pastry	BBA	60	2	A
Bag, making your own (drawings)	FFCB	534		
Bag tube, using (photographs)	LT	90		
Bag, using a	NSD	27		
Bag, using a	BHGN	425		
Bags for decorating cakes, using	FFBB	395		
Baked tart shells	BCC	82	2	B
Basic	FFCB	575	1	B
Basic pie	NYT	520	2	B
Basic shortcrust	VE	285	1	B
Basics	BCC	81		
Brisee	VE	286	1	B
Brisee sweet	VE	286	1	B

RECIPE	BOOK	PAGE	TD	S
Catherine's	FFCB	577	2	B
Cottage cheese or pot cheese	AC	636	1	
Cream	FAIC	431	1	A
◆	SP	337	2	B
◆	MHGD	52	2	B
◆	GF	251	1	B
◆	MFC	147	2	B
◆	NYT	533	1	
Cream cheese	SC	342	1	
Cream chocolate	FAIC	432	1	B
Danish	NYT	533	3	C
Decorating w	GHAC	309		
Double crust pie	BHGN	288	1	B
Dough	MAFC	139	2	
Dough	MFC2	103		
For palm leaf caramelized sugar cookies	MFC2	478	2	
Formulas, reference chart for	MFC2	108		
Rolling out	NSD	25		
Tongue shaped caramelized cookies	MFC2	477	1	
Drum of polenta filled w quails	FAIC	371	3	B
Drum, whole poached pears in a	FAIC	449	2	B
Edges, making	BCC	81		
Egg yolk	SC	342	1	
Electric mixer	BHGN	289	1	C
Flaky	SC	342	1	
Flaky	NSD	130	1	C
Flaky, making	GHAC	310		
Golden egg	SC	343	1	
Hearts	NYTI	507	2	C
Hot water	FFCB	577	1	B
Into the pan	AC	632		
Large shells or flan rings	AC	636	1	
Lattice top	BCC	82	2	B
Lattice top pie	BHGN	288	1	B
Nuggets, deep fried	FAIC	443	1	B
One crust pie, 9 inch	AC	635	1	
w Orange crust	GG	412	2	B
Puff	NSD	175	3	C
Puff	AC	637	2	
Puff	MFC2	110		
Apple or pear tart baked in	MFC2	457	2	B
Cheese tart, peekaboo	MFC2	140	3	B
Classic French for vol-au-vent	MFC2	118	3	B
Cocktail shells	MFC2	133		
Cream rolls	MFC2	139		
For decorations	MFC2	132		
Frenchy almond cream in	MFC2	468	3	B
Horns	MFC2	135	2	
Sausages baked in	MFC2	304	3	C
Shells for fruit tarts, forming	MFC2	454		
Simple flaky	MFC2	113	3	B
Putting on a top crust only	AC	633		
Quick	SC	342	1	
Raised egg	SC	343	2	
Rich egg	SC	342	1	
Ring, my grandmother's	MCIC	428	1	B
Rolling out	MFC	13		
Rolling out	GHAC	310		
Rules for making	SC	341		
Savory	GF	247	1	C
Scandinavian	JOC	572	3	B

RECIPE	BOOK	PAGE	TD	S
Hare	NYT	9	3	C
Homemade	NYTI	492	2	C
Weighing a	NYT	7		
Liver (see also liver pate)				
Liver	NYT	7	2	C
Liver	MFC2	319		
Liver, quick	AC	13	1	
Loaf country	GHAC	91	3	C
Maison	SP	27	2	C
Maison a la sardi	NYT	9	1	B
On apple slices	MSE	45	2	C
Partridge giblets	BB	48	1	
Pheasant crust	LT	303	3	
Pork liver	MFC2	320	2	C
Pork & liver in brioche dough	MFC2	322	3	C
Pork, liver, veal or chicken	MFC2	321	2	C
Porkless	MFC2	324	2	C
Rabbit	NYT	9	3	C
Seafood	SP	28	3	C
Shells, stuffed	JOC	55		
Sucree	JOC	591	2	B
Sucree or murbeteig, sweet egg pastry	AC	636	1	
Truffled	NYT	6	3	C
Unmolding a	GF	65		
Patty shells	NYT	537	2	C
◆	MFC2	123		
◆	AC	638	1	
◆	JOC	596	2	C
Dessert	AC	639	1	
Individual	LT	418	1	
Individual servings	MFC2	124	3	B
Large	SC	343	3	
Large	MFC2	126	3	B
Making	MFC2	123		
Puff paste	SC	343	2	
Pattypan squash, grilled	GRIL	68	1	B
Paupiettes (beef rolls)	JOC	418	1	
Paupiettes de boeuf	MAFC	318	2	B
Paupiettes de veau	NYTI	194	2	B
Pave au chocolat (chocolate pudding)	NYT	599	2	B
Pavlova (dessert)	BCC	144	2	B
Pavlova	SP	275	2	B
Pawnhaas (scrapple)	NYT	145	2	C
Pea				
A la Francaise green	NYTI	250	1	B
All about	VGCB	193		
Aspic	LM	168	2	
Baby w butter lettuce	MSQC	64	1	A
w Bacon	AC	539	1	
Beef, onions	FFCB	172	1	B
Beets stuffed w	SC	359	1	
Black eyed	FG	113	1	B
Black eyed salad, ham &	YGM	207	2	C
& Black olives	EBE	116	1	B
Blanched	VGCB	195	1	
Blanched & braised, methods for overaged	VGCB	195	1	
Boiled, green	JBC	320	1	B
Boiled, green & herbs	JBC	321	1	B
Boiled, green & mushrooms	JBC	321	1	B
Boiled, green & onions	JBC	320	1	B
Braised	FFCB	394	1	B
Artichoke w	GG	16	1	B
In butter	VGCB	195	1	
w Lettuce, French style	VGCB	196	1	B
w Lettuce & onions	MAFC	465	1	B

RECIPE	BOOK	PAGE	TD	S
Pea (*cont.*)				
Buttered	NYT	390	1	
Buttered (for large tender fresh green peas)	MAFC	463	1	B
Buttered (for large tough fresh green peas)	MAFC	464	1	B
Buttered (for tender sweet fresh green peas)	MAFC	462	1	B
Canned	MAFC	467	1	B
Canned, uses for	AC	558		
& Carrots	SC	417	1	
◆	FFCB	372	1	B
◆	JOC	288	1	
◆	AC	503	1	
& Carrots, 80's style	VGCB	196	1	B
& Cheese	EBE	114	1	B
& Chicken, wine w	FGCW	326	1	B
Clam soup	MCIC	100	2	B
Consomme	JBC	275	2	
Cooking	AC	537	1	
Cream cloaked, chicken &	GG	270	1	B
Cucumbers & sour cream	NYT	391	1	B
Curried	BCC	355	1	B
& Dried beans	VGCB	197	1	B
Dried, green	SC	184	2	
& Egg soup	FG	320	1	B
Finishing touches for cooked	VGCB	195	1	
Florentine manner	FAIC	415	1	B
French style	NYT	390	1	B
Frozen	MAFC	466	1	B
Green	JOC	287	1	A
Green, canning	BHGN	139		
Green, freezing	BHGN	139		
& Green onions	GHAC	239	1	B
Green pasta	GG	271	2	B
Green, preparing	BCC	355		
Green salad, tortellini &	FGCW	139	1	
Ham, mustardy	GG	270	1	B
Knepp	GG	267	1	B
Lettuce	JOC	287	1	A
Lettuce soup	NYT	69	1	B
Lettuce, wilted	GG	268	1	B
Minted	GHAC	239	1	B
Minted, new	BHGN	398	1	B
& Mushrooms deluxe	BHGN	398	1	B
& New potatoes, creamed	BHGN	398	1	B
Newly minted	GG	267	1	B
Onions	BCC	355	1	B
Onions, buttered	MAFC	464	1	B
Oriental	EBE	117	1	B
Parmesan	BCC	355	1	B
Pasta	MIE	185	1	B
Pasta	FG	355	1	B
Pasta	VGCB	199	1	B
Pasta, red beans &	FG	115	1	B
Pasta souffle, green	GG	272	2	B
Pie	AC	538	2	
Pod soup	MFC2	7	1	B
Podded	JOC	288	1	
Pods w almonds	BHGN	398	2	A
Pods Chinese, preparing	BCC	345		
Pods & peppers	BCC	345	1	B
Potatoes in cream	SMG	113	1	B
Preparing	GG	266		
Puree	SC	184	2	
Puree	AC	538	1	
Puree of	MSE	229	1	C
Puree of	JOC	288	1	
Pureed	VGCB	196	1	

RECIPE	BOOK	PAGE	TD	S
Pureed	JOC	259	1	B
Pureed	NYTI	75	3	B
Pureed green	NYT	391		B
Rice	FGCW	157	1	B
Rice	SMG	177	1	B
Rice w	AC	579	1	
Rice spicy	VGCB	197	1	B
Ring	SC	424	1	
Salad, bacon &	FG	85	1	B
Salad, black eyed	FG	116	1	B
Salad, black eyed	JBGF	538	1	B
Salad, minty	SPGT	151	1	B
& Sauteed lamb hearts	VGCB	199	1	B
Sauteed w prosciutto, Florentine style	CIC	383	1	B
Sauteed w veal hearts	VGCB	199	1	B
Sesame	BCC	355	1	B
Shrimp	NYTI	75	3	B
Skinned	VGCB	196	1	
Soup				
w Butter dumplings	VE	59	2	B
Canadian	NYT	63	3	B
Chicken, cold	NYT	84	2	B
Cold, curried	MIE	84	3	B
Cream of	FFCB	94	1	B
Cream of, curried	NYT	71	1	B
Croutons	MSQC	52	1	B
Curried green	CBSS	324	1	B
Dried	SC	396	3	
Dutch	BBA	41	3	B
Fresh	VGCB	198	1	B
Green	JOC	154	1	B
Hearty split	GHAC	103	2	C
Mint	CBSS	323	1	B
Mint cold	AC	93	2	
Puree of mint	GF	73	1	C
Quick	JOC	166	1	B
Toklas, green & gold cream of	GG	266	1	B
Yellow Canadian	NYTI	26	2	B
Split	SC	185	2	
Split, puree of	AC	610	2	
Steamed	VGCB	195	1	
Steamed, French	JBC	321	1	B
Steamed, French green onions	JBC	321	1	B
Steamed French herbs	JBC	321	1	B
Sugar snap, sauteed	MSQC	73	1	B
Sugar snap, stir fried	GHAC	239	1	B
Timbales	SC	424	1	
Tomato sauce	AC	537	1	
Turnip caps	AC	537	1	
& Walnuts, sauteed	GG	268	1	B
& Water chestnuts	EBE	116	1	B
& Watercress puree, green	CF	39	1	B
Peach				
& Almond tart	MHGD	212	2	C
& Apricot pie	BCC	87	1	B
& Apricots, pickled	GHAC	379	3	C
Baked	AC	764	1	
Baked I	JBC	106	1	
Baked II	JBC	106	1	B
& Banana cream	BCC	125	1	B
& Blueberries w mint sauce	JBGF	612	1	B
& Blueberry casserole	MHGD	406	1	B
Brandied	MHGD	406	1	B
◆	FFCB	708	2	B
◆	JOC	786	3	C
◆	SC	459	1	
◆	AC	764	1	
◆	MSE	228	3	B

RECIPE	BOOK	PAGE	TD	S
Peach (*cont.*)				
Brandied I	NYT	508	3	B
Brandied II	NYT	508	3	B
Brandied III	NYT	509	3	B
Brandy	SC	438	3	
Brandy hot	KIS	321	1	A
w Brandy sauce, baked	SC	263	1	
Broiled	BB	159	1	
Broiled	FFCB	283	1	B
Broiled	AC	764	1	
Brown Betty	FFCB	651	1	B
w Brown sugar	AC	763	1	
Butter	GHAC	379	1	B
Butter	JOC	777	2	C
Buttermilk soup	CBSS	168	3	B
Cake	SP	300	1	B
Cake cockaigne	JOC	606	2	B
Cake French	JOC	607	1	B
Canning	BHGN	132		
Canning (photographs)	BCC	385		
Cheese salad	JOC	94	1	B
Cherry ice cream	BHGN	182	3	C
Chianti wine	FAIC	496	2	B
& Chicken, stir fry	WC	60	1	B
Chutney (see chutney, peach)				
Cobbler	SP	308	1	B
◆	SC	196	1	
◆	FFBB	95	2	B
◆	FFCB	524	2	B
◆	BHGN	180	2	B
Cobbler, fresh	BCC	125	1	B
Cobbler w whipped cream	CW	141	2	B
Cognac	BB	159	1	B
Compote, fresh	SC	263	1	
Cranberry ring, spicy	EBE	142	2	B
& Cranberry tart	MSE	247	2	B
& Cream cheese balls	FFCB	442	1	B
Crisp	BCC	124	1	B
Crumb pie, canned	FFBB	89	2	B
Custard tart w sour cream	NSD	100	2	B
& Duck, roast	MAFC	279	2	B
Dumplings	FFBB	158	2	B
Filled	JOC	118	1	B
Flambe	BCC	131	2	B
Freezing	BHG	132		
w Ginger berry sauce	YGM	238	2	C
Glace pie	BCC	89	2	B
Glaze, pickled for ham	AC	441		
Glazed Canadian bacon	GHAC	203	1	B
Halves, broiled	JBC	106	1	
& Ham, baked w bourbon	JBC	207		
Ice	JOC	722	2	C
Ice cream	BBA	229	2	B
◆	SC	205	2	
◆	NYT	625	2	B
◆	JOC	717	2	C
Ice cream, fresh	BCC	152		
In red wine	AC	763	1	
Jam	SC	442	1	
Jam	BHGN	149	2	
Jam, banana &	BHGN	149	2	
Jam, plum &	BHGN	149	2	
Jellied	AC	764	1	
Jelly	SC	449	1	
Juice	SC	436	1	
Kuchen	SC	353	1	
Leather	AC	832	2	
Leather	JOC	740	1	B
Liqueur	JBC	106	1	

PEACH

RECIPE	BOOK	PAGE	TD	S
Marmalade, orange				
&	SC	443	1	
Melba	BCC	131	1	B
◆	JBC	107	1	
◆	SC	208	2	
◆	NYT	620	1	B
Georgia	GHAC	302		
Ice cream cake	SC	208	2	
Mousse	SP	284	2	B
Tarts	BCC	88	2	B
Meringue, coffee	BCC	145	2	B
Mold spiced	BCC	292	2	B
Nectar	BTSB	214	2	C
& Other fruits	JBC	105	1	
Pecan tart	BCC	88	2	B
Peppered	CW	100	1	B
Pickled	SC	458	3	
Pickled, apricots &	GHAC	379	3	C
Pickled, baked	SC	458	2	
Pie	BCC	87	1	B
◆	JOC	601	1	B
◆	FFBB	85	2	B
◆	JBC	39	2	B
Canned	FFBB	88	2	B
w Crunchy top	MC	212	1	B
Deep dish	BHGN	278	2	B
◆	AC	614	1	
◆	FFCB	582	2	B
◆	FFBB	94	2	C
Down home	GHAC	313	2	C
Easy	BCC	87	1	B
French crunch	BHGN	278	1	B
Fresh	FFCB	580	2	B
No bake	JBGF	630	2	B
Two crust	AC	614	1	
Pineapple conserve	SC	444	1	
Plum soup, brandied	CBSS	169	2	B
& Plums w lime				
juice	MSQC	81	1	B

RECIPE	BOOK	PAGE	TD	S
Poached	JBC	106	1	B
w Liqueur	JBC	107	1	B
Orange-flavored	JBC	107	1	B
w Raspberry sauce	LM	292	1	B
w Red peppercorn				
sauce	GF	234	2	B
Variations	AC	763	1	
w Zabaglione				
cream,				
pistachios &	GF	143	2	B
Port or madeira	AC	763	1	
Preserves	FFCB	704	2	B
Preserves	JOC	778	2	C
Preserves	GHAC	381	3	C
Puree	KIS	322	1	A
Puree, frozen	KIS	321	1	A
Raspberries	AC	763	1	
Raspberry puree,				
compote	MAFC	630	1	C
Rum or brandy				
syrup	BTSB	156	2	B
Rum mousse	BBA	212	2	C
Salad	SC	365	1	
Salad, ginger	SC	365	1	
Salad porcupine	SC	366	1	
Salad stuffed	SC	366	1	
Sauce	CFS	303	1	B
Sauce	BHGN	186	2	C
Sauce, pears poached				
w	JBGF	612	1	B
Sauce spareribs w	GHAC	219	2	B
Sherbet	FGCW	397	3	B
Sherbet, creamy	JBGF	636	2	B
Shortcake	BHGN	179	2	B
Shortcake	SC	196	1	
Shortcake	JBC	107	2	
Sliced	AC	763		
Sliced w brown sugar				
& cognac	MSQC	157	1	B

RECIPE	BOOK	PAGE	TD	S
Peach (*cont.*)				
Sliced chicken	EBE	86	1	B
Snow	SC	198	1	
Sorbet	GF	130	2	B
Sour cream	BB	159	1	
Spiced	BHGN	132	1	
Spiced, dried	SC	263	1	
Spirits	AC	763	1	
Stewed	MHGD	404	1	B
Stewed w brandy	MHGD	405	1	B
Strawberry & custard sauce	GHAC	290	2	B
Stuffed	FAIC	492	1	B
Stuffed w almonds	FAIC	493	2	B
Stuffed w toasted almond & cheese	KIS	322	1	B
Sundae, strawberry	KIS	325	1	B
Tart	FFBB	165	2	B
Tart	MAFC	639	2	B
Turnovers	FFBB	155	2	B
Upside down cake	FFBB	329	1	B
Wine	BCC	127	1	B
Peanut				
Bars, chocolate, children's crispy	FFBB	239	1	C
Batter bread	CBB	509	2	B
Beef	WC	87	1	B
Brownies	AC	712	1	
Cake	BCC	69	1	C
Caramel apples	BHGN	113	1	C
Caramel corn &	BTSB	271	2	C
Cheesecake	BCC	136	2	B
Chicken on skewers	GRIL	97	2	B
Choco nuggets	GHAC	350	2	C
Chocolate chip pie	BCC	92	2	B
Cookies, chocolate	BHGN	159	1	C
Curried	FFCB	72	1	B
Curried turkey apples &	GHAC	163	1	B
Dip Indian	JBGF	295	1	B
Ginger barbecue sauce	GHAC	226	1	C
Ice cream	SPGT	134	2	B
Icebox cookies	SC	159	1	
Loaf, nubby	CBB	474	2	B
Macaroons	FFCB	556	1	B
Marinade	GRIL	34	1	B
Noshes	SPGT	102	1	C
Pickles &	EBE	40	1	B
Puree, carrot &	SPGT	57	1	C
Ring cake	NYT	562	1	B
Salad pasta	JBGF	414	1	B
Sauce	YGM	52	1	C
Sauce, beef & vegetable kabobs w	GHAC	220	2	B
Sauce, chicken & glass noodle salad w	FG	305	2	B
Sauce, green beans w	KIS	144	1	A
Soup	CBSS	322	1	B
Soup cream of	GHAC	102	1	B
Soup, curried	SC	397	1	
Stuffing, duck, wild w	FFCB	262	2	B
Peanut brittle	SC	174	1	
◆	BTSB	269	2	C
◆	BCC	117	2	C
◆	FFCB	684	2	B
◆	AC	834	2	
◆	GHAC	354	1	C
◆	JOC	736	2	B
Ice cream	FFCB	630	3	C
Mousse	SC	213	2	
Old fashioned	FFCB	684	2	B
Peanut butter	BTSB	291	1	A
Peanut butter	JOC	521	1	
& Bacon sandwich	JOC	248	1	B
& Bacon sandwiches, hot	SC	384	1	

RECIPE	BOOK	PAGE	TD	S
Bars, chocolate crispy	BHGN	157	2	C
Bars, oatmeal	BHGN	157	2	C
Beer bread	CBB	504	1	B
Bites, chocolate	SP	294	1	C
Bread	FFCB	487	2	B
Bread	GHAC	365	1	B
Bread	SC	85	1	
Butter cookies	FFBB	202	2	C
Cake or cupcakes	AC	668	1	
Candy bars	BCC	120	2	C
Candy, coconut	SC	178	1	
Candy tops	GHAC	350	1	C
Centers	JOC	738	1	B
Chewies	FFCB	693	1	A
Chiffon pie	SC	351	1	
Cookie crumb crust	GHAC	321		
Cookies	KIS	347	1	C
◆	JOC	658	1	C
◆	BHGN	162	1	C
◆	AC	700	1	
◆	FFCB	553	1	C
◆	NSD	43	1	C
◆	BCC	106	2	C
Cookies, criss-cross	SC	156	1	
Cream cheese pie	FFBB	108	2	B
Cream pie	FFBB	113	2	B
Cupcakes	FFBB	379	1	C
Cupcakes	SC	141	1	C
Cupcakes	GHAC	323	2	C
Cups	BCC	120	2	C
Filling	SC	382	1	
Fingers	BCC	106	2	C
Frosting	BCC	77	1	C
Frosting	BCC	104	1	
Fudge (see also fudge, peanut butter)				
Fudge, marshmallow	FFCB	681	1	B
Jelly cookies	BCC	106	2	C
Marshmallow bars	BCC	122	1	C
Oatmeal bars	BHGN	157	2	C
Orange bread	FFBB	555	1	B
Pie, chocolate	GHAC	324	2	C
Pie crust	SC	342	1	
Pie shell, graham cracker	SC	344	2	
Prunes, chocolate	BBA	225	2	C
Rounds	JBGF	608	1	C
Slices	BHGN	167	1	C
Soups	SC	403	1	
Squares	BCC	104	1	C
Tomato sandwich	JOC	248		
Vegetable & chicken soup	JBGF	337	1	B
& Vegetable soup, pureed	JBGF	319	1	B
Peanutty sundae cake	BCC	133	1	C
Pear	AC	765		
A la bordelaise	NYT	621	1	B
A la bressane, braised	BBA	212	1	B
A la joinville	NYT	599	2	B
Almond tart	MSE	246	2	B
Almond tart	MHGD	206	2	C
Almond tart	MAFC	642	2	B
Apple conserve	SC	444	1	
Apple pie, old fashioned	GHAC	312	2	C
Apple salad	BCC	297	2	B
Apricot, glazed	BCC	131	1	B
Baked	SC	263	2	
◆	JBC	107	1	B
◆	MSE	115	1	A
◆	FFCB	667	1	B
In cognac	JBC	108	1	B
w Cream	MSQC	221	1	B
w Creme fraiche	NSD	124	1	B
w Custard sauce	GF	227	1	C
w Ginger	JBC	108	1	B

RECIPE	BOOK	PAGE	TD	S
Pear, Baked (*cont.*)				
w Macaroons	MAFC	630	1	B
Variations	AC	766	1	
Brandied	SC	459	1	
Butter	AC	821	1	
Canning	BHGN	132		
Caramel on puff paste	LM	285	2	B
Cardinal	WC	147	1	B
Champagne sabayon	MFC	234	1	B
Chestnuts, poached	NYTI	281	1	B
Chips	NYT	509	1	C
Chocolate sauce	FFCB	667	1	B
Chocolate sauce, spiced	GHAC	291	2	B
Chutney	AC	827	1	
Chutney	BBA	168	1	B
Cinnamon	JOC	111	2	B
Cobbler	FFBB	96	2	B
Cobbler, cranberry &	GHAC	289	1	C
Cobbler w whipped cream	CW	125	1	B
Cointreau	FFCB	667	2	B
Compote, fresh	SC	263	1	
Conserve	SC	444	3	
Conserve	NYTI	291	1	C
Cooked custard cream sauce, chocolate	MCIC	439	2	B
Country cake	MCIC	432	1	B
Cream	JBC	107	1	
Crepes dessert	NYTI	290	2	C
Crisp	JBGF	622	1	B
Crumble pie	BHGN	280	1	B
Custard tart	FFBB	173	2	B
Different kinds of	SPGT	280		
Dumplings	FFBB	158	2	B
& Figs poached in Zinfandel & cassis cream	CPMC	92	2	B

RECIPE	BOOK	PAGE	TD	S
Filling, alligator w	SC	382	1	
Flambe	NYT	621	1	B
Flan	MAFC	656	1	B
Flan w almonds	MAFC	658	1	B
Frangipane tart	MSE	240	3	B
Ginger	MHGD	422	1	B
Ginger	NYT	623	1	B
Ginger brown butter tart	NSD	90	2	B
Ginger crisp	MHGD	423	1	B
Ginger upside down cake	NSD	136	2	B
Glazed w chocolate	SP	291	2	B
Gorgonzola	FGCW	392	1	
Grape salad	JOC	94	1	
Grilled	GRIL	80	2	B
Helene	FFCB	667	1	B
◆	BCC	131	1	B
◆	JBC	108	1	
◆	NYT	622	1	B
In port wine	FFCB	667	2	B
In wine sauce, cranberry &	GHAC	206		
Jam, pineapple, spiced	JOC	776	2	C
Kuchen	SC	353	1	
& Lima beans, baked	CW	164	1	B
Liqueur	JOC	119	1	B
Mary Garden	NYT	621	2	B
Melba	JBC	108	1	
Nectar	BTSB	214	2	C
Or apple tart baked in French puff pastry	MFC2	457	2	B
& Orange sabayon	BBA	212	2	B
& Orange sauce	EBE	193	1	B
Oranges, golden	KIS	323	1	B
Pear & cranberry cobbler	GHAC	289	1	C

RECIPE	BOOK	PAGE	TD	S
Pickled	SC	459	3	
Pickled seckel	NYT	505	2	B
Pie	FFBB	82	2	B
Pie, two crust	AC	614	1	
w Pigeon & red wine	MFC	95	3	B
Pink	SC	261	1	
w Pink peppercorn sauce, duck	MFC	92	3	B
Poached	MIE	323	1	A
◆	JBC	108	1	B
◆	AC	766	1	
◆	MSE	255	2	B
w Cognac	JBC	108	1	B
Cranberry	GHAC	147	2	B
Cranberry, for stuffed capon	GHAC	147	2	B
Flamed	JBC	108	1	B
Ginger	NSD	94	1	B
Ginger	JBC	108	1	B
Orange flavored	JBC	108	1	B
w Peach sauce	JBGF	612	1	B
w Port	FGCW	391	1	B
w Raspberry sauce, pistachios	GF	238	1	B
Red wine & basil	YGM	214	1	C
In Riesling, caramel glazed	NSD	108	2	B
Spicy	JBGF	613	1	B
w Wine	FAIC	495	3	B
Polenta tart, Rick O'Connell's	FFBB	171	3	B
w Port wine	NYTI	281	1	B
Preserves, ginger	SC	440	3	
Preserves, pineapple &	SC	440	1	
Preserves, seckel baked	SC	441	2	
Puff paste caramel	LM	285	2	B
Raspberry puree	NYT	622	1	B
Red wine	AC	766	1	
Relish, hot	BBA	169	2	B
Relish, pepper	GHAC	384	1	C
Saint Honore	MFC	227	3	B
Salad	JOC	94	1	
Salad	BCC	298	1	B
Salad, duck w mango chutney dressing	SP	206	2	B
Salad, molded	JOC	102	3	B
Sauce	NSD	332	1	C
Sauce, pork chops, barbecued, w tangy	GHAC	220	1	B
Seckel w red wine	GF	94	1	B
Slices, candied	BTSB	259	2	C
Sorbet	GF	130	2	B
Souffle	MFC	235	2	B
Soup, ginger	MSQC	140	1	B
Spiced	NYT	506	2	B
Spiced	JOC	786	3	C
Stewed	FFCB	667	1	B
Stuffed	KIS	323	1	B
Stuffed	JOC	118	2	B
Stuffed capon w cranberry poached	GHAC	147	2	B
Tart	BCC	88	2	B
Tart	MAFC	638	2	B
Tart	FFBB	164	2	B
w Caramel sauce	MFC	226	3	B
Country	BBA	204	2	B
In baked puff pastry	MFC2	457	2	B
Puff pastry, free form	FFBB	180	2	B
Tatin	CPMC	70	3	C
Torte, Helen Knopf's	FFBB	375	1	C
Turnip puree	CW	132	1	B
Upside down cake	FFBB	329	1	B
Waldorf salad	BCC	297	1	B
w White turnip puree	GF	81	1	C

RECIPE	BOOK	PAGE	TD	S
Pear (*cont.*)				
Whole, poached in a pastry drum	FAIC	449	2	B
Wine-poached, baked in meringue (sabayon)	MFC2	440	2	B
Wine-poached w black currant sauce	MSQC	193	1	B
Pearl balls	NYTI	51	2	C
Peasant bread	CPMC	232	2	C
Peasant bread	BHGN	66	2	B
Peasant loaf	CBSS	402	3	C
Peasant loaf, braided	CBB	268	3	C
Peasant loaf, Madame Doz's	CBB	249	3	C
Pease porridge	FG	198	1	B
Pecan				
Asparagus &	YGM	167	1	C
Balls	SC	372	1	
Biscuit spirals	BHGN	84	2	C
Bourbon pie	BBA	204	3	B
Bread cherry	CBB	497	1	B
Bread cherry	BHGN	78	1	B
Bread Georgia	MHGD	270	1	B
Brittle	SC	174	1	
Buns cinnamon	GHAC	362	2	C
Butter w brussels sprouts	GG	69	1	B
Butter sauce	PPLK	55	1	B
Butterscotch squares	MIE	326	1	C
Cabbage company	BHGN	394	1	B
Cake	SC	114	1	B
Cake, parsnip &	VGCB	192	1	B
Cake w spiced pecan icing	PPLK	330	2	B
Chicken salad w red grapes &	SPGT	148	2	B
Cinnamon buns	GHAC	362	2	C
Cookies	CW	121	1	C
Cookies maple	NSD	54	1	C
Crumb coffeecakes	GHAC	329	2	C
Crunch	GHAC	349	1	C
Crunch pumpkin pie	GHAC	318	2	
Crust, chicken breasts in a	GHAC	156	1	B
Cupcakes	SC	141	1	
Deviled	SC	41	1	
Dressing, orange	BCC	300	1	A
Drop cookies	JOC	668	1	C
Drops	EBE	177	1	C
Filling	SC	149	1	
Filling, toasted	JOC	648	1	A
Fingers	SC	158	1	
Frosting	PPLK	332	1	B
Frosting, coconut	BCC	67	1	
Frosting, coconut	NYT	576	1	B
Hot pepper	GHAC	92	1	B
Ice cream w sundae sauce	PPLK	334	2	C
Icebox cake	SC	135	3	B
Icing for pecan cake, spiced	PPLK	330	2	B
Kisses	AC	711	1	
Kisses	SC	163	1	
Kisses, chocolate	SC	163	1	
Loaf, blueberry	CBB	468	1	B
Meringue crepes, puffy	PPLK	322	1	B
Muffins	FFCB	489	1	C
Pastry	BHGN	289	1	B
Penuche	FFCB	681	2	B
Pepper, hot	GHAC	92	1	B
Peppery	KIS	312	1	
Pie	MSE	244	2	B
◆	BHGN	282	1	C
◆	NYTI	563	1	B
◆	SC	349	1	
◆	FFCB	583	2	B
◆	SP	302	1	B

RECIPE	BOOK	PAGE	TD	S
Pecan Pie (*cont.*)				
◆	AC	631	1	
◆	JOC	605	2	B
◆	BCC	92	2	B
Brandy	BCC	92	2	B
Chocolate	BCC	92	2	B
Dark	FFBB	142	2	B
Down south	EBE	165	1	B
Golden	FFBB	143	1	B
Maple	FFBB	144	1	B
Raisin, spiced	FFBB	144	1	B
Sweet potato &	PPLK	319	2	B
Pralines	PPLK	324	1	C
Pralines chocolate	PPLK	326	2	C
Puffs	JOC	669	1	C
Rolls	SC	81	2	
Rolls caramel	BHGN	68	2	C
Slices	JOC	666	1	C
Spiced	NSD	72	1	B
Spongecake, grated	CW	165	1	B
Squares	SP	256	1	C
Squares	FFCB	566	1	C
Squares, Americana	MHGD	332	2	C
Sticky buns	MSE	98	3	C
Stuffing	GHAC	160		
Stuffing, pheasant, leeks w	SP	109	3	B
Stuffing, turkey roast w	GHAC	160	2	C
Tart, Georgia w cream cheese pastry	GHAC	324	2	C
Tart, peach	BCC	88	2	B
Tartes, grapefruit, chocolate &	YGM	235	3	C
Tartlets	NSD	146	2	B
Tartlets, chocolate	MSE	197	2	B
Tarts	FFCB	595	2	B
Tassies	BHGN	163	1	C
Tidbits	SC	41	1	

RECIPE	BOOK	PAGE	TD	S
Topping, coconut	BCC	137	1	
Torte	JOC	638	1	B
Torte, cocoa	BCC	65	1	C
Wafers	JOC	669	1	C
Waffles	SC	97	1	
Waffles, buttermilk	GHAC	371		
Whiskey cake	FFBB	369	1	C
Peccary (game)	JOC	454	2	
Pectin apple, homemade	SC	446	2	
Peekaboo jam or fruit tart of French pastry	MFC2	459	2	B
Peel candied citrus	JOC	742	2	
Peel chocolate, dipped & candied	SC	175	1	
Peel grapefruit, candied	SC	175	1	
Peel orange, candied	SC	175	1	
Peel orange, candied	NYTI	287	2	
Peixada (Brazilian fish dish)	NYT	269	3	B
Peking duck	FG	306	3	B
Peking duck roast	NYTI	56	3	B
Peking duck sauce	NYTI	57	1	A
Penne (tubular pasta)				
Broccoli de rabe	VGCB	134	1	B
Cauliflower w garlic & oil	MCIC	149	1	B
Ricotta & spinach sauce	MCIC	147	1	B
Sauce, tomatoes, dried wild mushrooms &	CIC	108	1	B
Pennsylvania Dutch corn chicken soup	GHAC	104	2	C
Pennsylvania Dutch filling	NYT	223	1	B

RECIPE	BOOK	PAGE	TD	S
w Meat stuffed, green	NYT	391	1	B
Mediterranean, stuffed	AC	541	1	
Mis toklas, braised & stuffed	GG	283	1	A
Oil, making your own	FG	303		
Onion shortcake	MC	88	2	B
Onions	JOC	288	1	B
Onions & mushrooms	KIS	259	1	A
Onions, sauteed	FG	211	1	B
Onions, stir fried	YGM	53	1	B
Oven braised, stuffed	VGCB	204	1	
Packet, poached	CFS	245	1	B
Pea pods	BCC	345	1	B
& Pear relish	GHAC	384	1	C
Peeled oil	VGCB	206	1	B
Peeling, hot	VGCB	202	1	
Pickled, red	SC	454	3	
Pickled, red sweet	NYT	502	2	B
Pickled, stuffed	NYT	502	3	C
Pieces, baked	VGCB	204	1	
Pieces, broiled	VGCB	204	1	
Pieces, grilled	VGCB	204	1	
Pot	JOC	155	1	B
Pot	AC	90	2	
Pot, Philadelphia	GHAC	102	2	C
Pot, Philadelphia	CBSS	74	3	B
Pot soup	SC	398	1	
Pot soup	FG	286	3	C
Potatoes & onions, baked	VGCB	206	1	B
Potatoes & pimentos	SMG	245	1	B
Preserved in vinegar	VGCB	210	2	B
Provencal	SP	6	1	B
Puree, red	YGM	174	2	C
Puree, yellow	SPGT	165	1	B
Red, butter	GG	277	1	B
Red, onions &	YGM	45	1	B

RECIPE	BOOK	PAGE	TD	S
Relish (see also relish, pepper)				
Relish & cream cheese spread	SC	380	1	
Rice & cheese stuffing	VGCB	205	1	
Rice & herb stuffing	VGCB	205	1	
Roasted, Italian	NYTI	374	1	B
Roasted, ratatouille in	GHAC	241	2	C
Roasted, red w anchovies	CPMC	18	1	B
Salad				
Cold lamb &	GG	279	1	B
Fish &	BCC	268	2	B
Grilled	FAIC	389	1	B
Hot tuna &	GG	279	1	A
Italian	NYT	423	1	B
Red	YGM	81	1	B
Tangy, stuffed	BHGN	336	2	B
Sauce	JOC	328	2	C
Green	JOC	288	1	
Hot	NYTI	488	1	
Hot	VGCB	206	1	B
Japanese	FGCW	359	1	
Red, smoked tongue &	GG	285	2	B
w Sausage, stuffed	AC	541	1	
Sauteed	VGCB	203	1	
◆	AC	540	1	
◆	BCC	356	1	B
◆	JBC	322	1	B
w Garlic	JBC	322	1	B
w Green onions	JBC	322	1	B
Sweet red & green	FFCB	395	1	B
w Tomatoes	FAIC	419	1	B
Sherry	BTSB	185	1	C
Sherry for soup	FGCW	105	3	
Slaw	AC	498	2	

RECIPE	BOOK	PAGE	TD	S
Pepper (*cont.*)				
Slaw	VGCB	207	1	B
Slices, broiled	JBC	323	1	
Slices fillings	JOC	87	1	C
Soup, red bell	MSQC	180	1	B
Soup, savory	VE	66	1	A
Spice bread	CBB	432	3	C
Steak	NYT	90	1	B
Steak	SC	270	1	
Steak, Chinese	NYTI	48	1	B
Steak, grilled	SC	328	1	
Steak, lemon	GHAC	173	1	
Strips, curried sweet	SMG	163	1	B
Stuffed	VE	222	1	B
◆	BCC	214	2	B
◆	JOC	288	1	
◆	AC	540	1	
◆	JBC	323	1	
◆	FAIC	94	1	B
◆	SC	424	2	
w Anchovy dressing	JOC	289	1	B
w Beef	SC	425	1	
w Chicken	SC	425	1	
w Corn	AC	541	1	
w Corn	NYT	392	1	B
w Corn	SC	425	1	
w Corn a la king	JOC	289	1	B
w Creamed oysters	JOC	289	1	B
w Fish	JOC	289	2	
w Fish	NYT	392	1	B
Green	LM	126	2	
Green	BHGN	244	1	B
w Liver	NYT	390	1	B
w Meat	JOC	289	2	
w Meat & rice	JOC	289	1	B
w Rice	JOC	289	1	B
w Spaghetti	SC	425	1	
Sweet	EBE	65	1	B

RECIPE	BOOK	PAGE	TD	S
w Tomato, basil & chevre	SPGT	167	1	B
Sweet	JOC	288	1	
Canning	BHGN	139		
Freezing	BHGN	139		
w Leeks, mushrooms & broiled	GHAC	255	2	B
Peeled, sliced w garlic oil	MFC2	411	1	B
Rigatoni Neapolitan style w	MCIC	152	1	B
Sauteed, Italian style	SMG	295	1	B
Tamale pie, stuffed	GG	284	2	A
Tex Mex, stuffed	SPGT	166	2	B
Tomato w crumb stuffing	VGCB	205	1	
Tomato soup	VGCB	207	1	B
Tuna antipasto	VGCB	207	1	B
w Tuna stuffing	VGCB	204	1	
w Vegetable stuffing	VGCB	204	1	
& Zucchini w lamb stuffing	VGCB	204	1	
Zucchini salad, cold	VGCB	205	1	B
Peppercorn				
Chicken salad Madame Chu's	MIE	288	1	B
Different kinds of	SP	100		
Green, breast of duckling w	GHAC	165	2	A
Green wine sauce, rabbit in	FGCW	234	2	B
Pink, calf's liver w ginger &	MFC	156	2	B
Sauce, hamburger w	SMG	244	1	B
Sauce, peaches poached w	GF	234	2	B

RECIPE	BOOK	PAGE	TD	S
& Shallot butter, green	CF	115	1	B
Shrimp	MFC	137	2	B
Peppered meat loaf	GG	285	2	B
Peppered tenderloin sandwiches	BB	61	1	
Peppergrass wild (greens)	AC	560		
Peppermint				
Bonbons	BHGN	115	1	C
Candy, Bavarian cream	AC	736	2	
Candy cake	AC	652	1	
Candy canes	BCC	108	2	C
Candy ice cream	FFCB	630	3	C
Cream wafers	JOC	729	1	B
Fluff	BCC	79	1	C
Frosting	AC	693	1	
Frosting	BCC	98	1	
Frosting	BCC	77	1	C
Ice cream	BCC	152		
Ice milk	CW	100	2	B
Patties	SC	172	1	
Souffle w bittersweet chocolate sauce	SPGT	98	2	B
Stick ice cream	SC	207	2	
Stick ice cream	JOC	716	2	C
Sticks	SC	172	1	
Taffy	BCC	119	2	B
Tea ice cream	NSD	208	1	B
Peppernuts	FFBB	267	2	C
Peppernuts or pfeffernusse	AC	700	1	
Pepperoni calzones	BCC	319	2	B
Pepperoni con rigatoni	FGCW	145	1	B
Pepperoni pizza	NYTI	440	2	
Pepperoni pizza	BCC	167	2	C
Peppery hot sauce for barbecue	GHAC	226	1	C

RECIPE	BOOK	PAGE	TD	S
Peppery rice pasticcio	FAIC	86	2	B
Peppery sauce for boiled meats	MCIC	241	1	B
Peppery sauce for roast birds	MCIC	242	1	B
Perch fillets, ocean, filled & baked	FFCB	115	1	B
Perch fillets, oven fried w tartar sauce	SC	238	1	
Perch, grilled	OC	147	1	B
Perdrix au choux (partridge with cabbage)	NYTI	28	3	B
Perfect protein salad	MC	49	2	B
Perfection salad	AC	40	1	
Periwinkles baked	NYT	295	2	B
Pernod cream, tarragon striped flounder w	CFS	225	1	A
Pernod & oysters w spinach	SMG	132	1	B
Pernod, scallops & leeks	SMG	134	1	B
Pernod shrimp saute	SMG	156	1	B
Persian balls	JOC	740	1	C
Persian centers	JOC	740	1	C
Persian cream	JOC	697	2	B
Persimmon	AC	767		
Cookies	FFBB	210	2	C
Date pudding	GHAC	298	2	B
Ice cream	JOC	719	2	B
Pudding	JOC	702	1	B
Salad, Japanese	JOC	94	1	
Pesto (see also basil sauce)				
◆	JBGF	642	1	B
◆	MC	74	1	B
◆	NYTI	436	1	B
◆	SP	80	1	C

RECIPE	BOOK	PAGE	TD	S
Pfeffernusse German Christmas cookies	BTSB	233	2	C
Pheasant				
w Apples	BHGN	302	2	B
Braised	JOC	478	3	
Braised	SC	323	1	
Braised w sauerkraut	AC	241	2	
Braised, choucroute w	GF	206	3	C
Broiled & variations	BB	47	1	
Casserole of	AC	242	2	
Cream	GHAC	168	2	B
Fried	AC	240	2	
w Game sauce	JOC	478	3	C
Gravy	BCC	259	2	A
w Juniper berries, orange zest & sage	GF	80	2	C
w Leek & pecan stuffing	SP	109	3	B
Pate in crust	LT	303	3	
Pioneer style	BB	47	1	
Roast	SC	323		
◆	BB	80	1	
◆	AC	241	2	
◆	MSQC	152	1	B
◆	JOC	478	2	A
◆	NYT	178	2	A
Roast w cream sauce	BB	80	1	
Roast w sauerkraut	BB	81	2	
w Sauteed cabbage	AC	241	2	
Smitane	JOC	479	2	A
Terrine of	NYTI	106	2	C
Philadelphia ice cream	SC	206	2	
Philadelphia ice cream	FFCB	629	3	C
Philadelphia pepper pot	GHAC	102	2	C
Philadelphia pepper pot	FFCB	89	2	B
Philly beef sandwiches	BCC	316	1	B
Phyllo				
Crabmeat wrapped in	NYTI	324	2	B
Kisses, chevre	SPGT	116	2	C
Rolling the dough	BCC	13		
Seafood & basil	YGM	193	3	C
Triangles	SP	8	3	C
w Feta & spinach	MSE	284	3	C
Filled w curried walnut chicken	MSE	52	3	C
Roquefort & pistachio filling for	SP	8	1	C
Rosemary & prosciutto filling for	SP	9	1	C
Spinach & feta filling for	SP	9	1	C
Working the dough	SP	8		
Piandina, sauteed greens for	MCIC	390	1	B
Picadillo (meat dish served with tortillas)	YGM	76	2	B
Picadillo California	KIS	208	1	B
Picadillo rice & beans	NYT	364	3	B
Picadinho a Brasileira	NYTI	24	1	B
Picante de Gallina	NYTI	496	2	C
Piccalilli (Spanish pickle)	SC	457	2	
◆	FFCB	713	2	C
◆	VGCB	324	1	B
◆	AC	825	3	
◆	JOC	783	3	C
Piccalilli relish	GHAC	384	2	C
Pickerel (fish)	JOC	358	1	
Pickle (see also cornichons)				
All about	FFCB	709		
Bread butter	BTSB	134	2	C

RECIPE	BOOK	PAGE	TD	S
Pickle, Bread butter (*cont.*)				
◆	JOC	782	3	C
◆	BHGN	146	2	
◆	FFCB	710	3	B
◆	GHAC	377	3	C
Bread butter, old fashioned, sliced	AC	824	3	
Capers w brown sauce	MAFC	72	1	B
Celery	SC	452	3	
Cherry leaf	SC	452	3	
Chow chow	AC	826	3	
Cucumber, ripe	SC	452	3	
Curry sauce	JOC	783	3	C
Dill	AC	823	3	
◆	GHAC	377	3	C
◆	BHGN	147	3	
◆	JOC	786	3	C
◆	FFCB	710	3	C
Crisp	SC	450	3	
Hot pack	AC	824	3	
Kosher	BHGN	147	3	
Kosher	JOC	786	3	C
Kosher	BTSB	131	2	C
Kosher style	NYT	500	3	C
Quick I	NYT	501	3	B
Quick II	NYT	501	3	B
Small	SC	451	3	
Summer	SC	450	3	
Sweet	AC	824	3	
Sweet	SC	452	3	
Sweet dill oil	SC	452	3	
Winter	SC	450	3	
Dip hot	JBC	4	1	
Green tomato	SC	458	3	
Green tomato	JOC	783	3	C
Icicle	FFCB	711	3	C
Indonesian	NYTI	367	1	B
Jerusalem artichoke & mustard	BBA	168	2	B
Mixed	BHGN	147	3	
Mixed	SC	455	3	
Mustard	JOC	783	3	C
◆	FFCB	711	3	B
◆	AC	826	3	
◆	SC	454	3	
Mustard, easy	SC	451	3	
Mustard, Nana's	VGCB	323	2	B
Mustard, quick	BHGN	147	1	
Nutty	BBA	169	1	B
Oil	AC	823	3	
Oil sliced	SC	452	3	
Out of this world outhouse	GG	149	3	C
& Peanuts	EBE	40	1	B
& Relishes, canning	BHGN	145		
Rings, nine day	SC	453	3	
Saccharin	JOC	783	3	C
Saccharin	SC	452	3	
Sandwich	SC	451	3	
Slices, sweet	BHGN	146	3	
Sour half	VGCB	100	2	B
Sour, lazy housewife	AC	825	3	
Spanish	SC	457	2	
Spicy, watermelon	GHAC	378	3	C
Sunchoke	GHAC	377	3	C
Sweet	SC	451	3	
Sweet green bean	GG	350	1	B
Sweet sour	SC	451	3	
Sweet & sour mustard	SC	451	3	
Sweet & sour spiced cucumber	JOC	782	3	C
Sweet & sour yellow cucumber	JOC	782	3	C
Tarragon	SC	450	3	
Vegetable, mixed	VGCB	342	2	B
Watermelon rind	AC	822	2	
Yellow cucumber	JOC	782	3	C
Zucchini	GG	402	2	B

RECIPE	BOOK	PAGE	TD	S
Salad w walnuts	MFC	185	2	B
Wood	JOC	481	2	A
Piggies tied up	FGCW	215	1	B
Pignoli rice cumin (pine nuts & rice)	YGM	59	2	A
Pigs'				
Ears	FFBB	262	1	C
Feet	FFCB	200	2	B
Baked	JOC	450	2	
Boiled	FFCB	201	2	B
Breaded, mustard	GF	160	2	B
Court bouillon for	AC	421	1	
Grilled	BB	35	2	
Grilled	NYT	143	2	B
Grilled	AC	421	2	
Jellied	AC	422	3	
Jellied	JOC	450	2	B
Jellied	FFCB	201	2	B
Pickled	AC	422	3	
Pickled	FFCB	201	2	B
Remoulade sauce, cold	AC	422	3	
Sainte-Menehould	NYTI	199	2	B
Stewed	JOC	450	2	B
Stuffed	LM	202	3	B
Hocks jellied	AC	423	3	
Hocks vinaigrette	AC	423		
Knuckles sauerkraut	AC	422	2	
Knuckles sauerkraut	NYT	142	2	B
Tail, barbecued	OC	130	2	C
Tails, barbecued	AC	424	2	
Pike	JOC	358	1	
A la tartare	SC	238	1	
Baked herbs	NYT	241	1	B
Crayfish, coulibiac of	MFC	123	3	B
w Lemon sauce, cold	SC	238	1	
Quenelles	LT	127	3	
Sauteed, walleyed	NYT	241	1	B
Steamed w chive butter sauce	MFC	122	3	B
Veloute poached	SC	238	1	
Pikelets	CBB	578	2	B
Pilaf (see also rice pilaf)				
Pilaf	JOC	183	1	B
Pilaf	JBC	116	1	B
w A purpose	JBGF	377	1	B
Bulgur	BCC	57	1	B
Bulgur, basic	JBGF	515	1	B
Bulgur mix	KIS	342	1	C
Chicken	FFCB	318	1	B
Greek	MC	102	2	B
Greek style	NYT	321	1	B
w Green pepper	JBC	116	1	B
Herbs	JBC	117	1	B
Indian	EBE	59	1	B
Lemon	BCC	56	1	B
w Mushrooms	FFCB	318	1	B
w Mushrooms	JBC	116	1	B
Mussels	NYTI	153	2	B
Nuts	JBC	117	1	B
Oat groat	JBGF	525	1	B
Of mussels	LT	113	2	
Seafood	JBGF	456	2	B
Turkish I	FFCB	318	1	B
Turkish II	FFCB	319	1	B
Pimento cheddar spread, spicy	BB	124	1	C
Pimento sauce, cheese &	NYT	447	1	B
Pimiento	JOC	288	1	
Butter	SC	379	1	
w Cream cheese	SC	38	1	
Cream cheese spread	SC	380	1	
Filled	JOC	87	1	B
Mold, shrimp &	AC	54	2	
Peppers oil	VE	115	1	B
Sauce, trout w	WC	73	1	B
Soup, cold	CF	15	1	B

PINEAPPLE

RECIPE	BOOK	PAGE	TD	S
Fritters	SC	101	2	
Fritters, crushed	SC	102	1	
Frosting	BCC	77	1	C
Gelatin	JOC	696	2	B
Gingered	BCC	129	2	B
Glaze for ham	BCC	228	1	
Glaze for ham	AC	441		
Glazed	JOC	742	1	
Glazed spareribs	GHAC	194	1	B
Grapefruit cocktail	SC	44	1	
Grapefruit juice	JOC	33	1	B
Grapefruit marmalade	SC	443	2	
Grilled	JOC	120	1	B
& Ham, baked	JBC	207		
& Ham sandwiches	BCC	321	1	B
& Honey dressing	FFCB	452	1	A
Ice	SC	210	2	
Ice	JOC	722	2	C
Icing	JOC	680	1	B
Island	MHGD	408	1	B
Jam, apricot &	FFCB	703	2	B
Jam, apricot &, quick	JOC	777	2	
Jam, pear &, spiced	JOC	776	2	C
Jam, strawberry &	SC	442	1	
Jelly	SC	202	2	
Juice, cocktail	SC	44	1	
Juice, fresh	JOC	33	1	B
Lemon pie	FFBB	146	1	B
Lime mold	EBE	140	2	B
Maraschino strudel	SC	355	2	
Marmalade	NYT	512	1	B
Marshmallow filling	SC	149	1	
Marshmallow ice cream	SC	207	2	
Meringue dessert	SC	138	1	
Meringue pie	FFCB	590	2	B
Milk shakes	BCC	24	1	A
Milk sherbet	JOC	722	2	B
Milk sherbet	SC	211	2	
Mousse, frozen	FFCB	626	3	B
On toasted rusk	SC	44	1	
Orange Bavarian	GHAC	294	2	C
Orange bundt cake	WC	133	1	C
Orange ice	BHGN	12	1	B
Orange punch	NYT	649	1	B
& Other fruits	JBC	109	1	
& Papaya, upside down cake	FFBB	360	2	B
Parfait	SC	214	2	
Pear jam, spiced	JOC	776	2	C
& Pear preserves	SC	440	1	
Pie	BHGN	280	1	B
Pie, apricot, deep dish	FFBB	94	2	C
Pink	SC	261	1	
Plain fresh	JBC	109	1	
Poached	AC	768	1	
Pork en adobo, Philippine style	WC	119	1	B
Portuguese	MHGD	409	1	B
Preserves	SC	441	3	
Preserves, strawberry &	JOC	778	2	C
Pudding, baked	SC	197	1	
Punch	JOC	35	1	
Punch, orange	NYT	649	1	B
Punch, rum	NYTI	504	2	C
& Raspberries	BB	159	1	
Relish, cranberry &	GHAC	383	1	B
Rhubarb	SC	263	1	
Ring, molded	JOC	103	2	B
Ring salad	BCC	298	1	B
Rum punch	NYTI	504	2	C
Rum small	AC	768	1	
Salad	SC	366	1	
Salad	JOC	95	1	

RECIPE	BOOK	PAGE	TD	S
Pineapple (*cont.*)				
Salad	BCC	285	1	B
Avocado &	SC	364	1	
Carrot &	BCC	289	2	B
Chicken &	SPGT	149	1	B
Shrimp &	SC	364	1	
Zucchini &	BCC	289	2	B
Sauce, cookies w	AC	710	1	
Sauteed	JBC	110	1	
Shell, chicken in a	NYT	201	2	B
Sherbet	LM	304	2	B
Sherbet	BHGN	185	3	C
Sherbet	JBGF	637	2	C
Sherbet w champagne sabayon & candied petals	CPMC	88	3	B
Slaw	SC	358	1	
Slices, broiled	JBC	110	1	
Slices, broiled w flamed rum	JBC	110	1	
Slices, ham w	JOC	230	1	B
Slices, maraschino &	CIC	453	1	A
Snow	JOC	697	2	B
Snow, watercress	GG	199	1	B
Snow, watercress	GG	199	1	B
Souffle	JOC	690	2	B
Souffle, sweet potato &	JOC	205	1	B
Spareribs, glazed	GHAC	194	1	B
Sponge custard	JOC	687	2	B
Star fruit	MSE	157	3	C
Stuffed, small	AC	768	1	
Surprise	JBC	109	1	
Surprise	EBE	184	1	A
Sweet potatoes	BCC	364	1	B
Sweet potatoes	SC	431	1	
Sweet potatoes, ham cakes w	JOC	230	2	B

RECIPE	BOOK	PAGE	TD	S
Sweet potatoes, w pecans, mashed	FFCB	406	1	B
Tapioca, coconut	GHAC	295	1	B
Tart	MAFC	644	2	B
Tart Martinique	NYTI	289	2	B
Tidbits	JOC	119	1	B
Tomato juice	JOC	33	1	B
Tomato salad	SC	366	1	
Tomatoes, stuffed	JOC	307	1	B
Tropic	JOC	47	1	A
Turkey	BCC	258	2	C
Upside down cake	FFBB	328	1	B
◆	FFCB	524	2	B
◆	BCC	71	2	B
◆	GHAC	328	2	C
◆	SPGT	87	2	B
◆	MHGD	108	1	B
◆	SC	115	1	B
◆	BHGN	93	1	B
Upside down cake, cornmeal &	FFBB	359	2	C
Wedges, grilled	GHAC	292	1	B
White cake	AC	656	1	
Pineappleade	SC	54	1	A
Pink colada	BCC	23	1	C
Pink grapefruit cassis granite	NSD	235	1	B
Pink grapefruit tequila sherbet	NSD	231	1	B
Pink lady	JOC	38	1	
Pink lady	SC	61	1	A
Pink lentil vinaigrette	MSE	106	2	C
Pinto beans				
Baked	BCC	171	2	B
& Duck casserole	AC	230	3	
Frijoles bolitas	AC	605	3	
Or bolitas frijoles, boiled	AC	605	3	

RECIPE	BOOK	PAGE	TD	S
Pita (*cont.*)				
Herbed	KIS	128	1	A
Meat pies	JBGF	304	1	C
Pizza	JBGF	475	1	B
Pocket fillings	BBA	104		
Toast	MIE	296	1	C
Whole wheat	BTSB	92	3	C
Whole wheat w carrot	JBGF	578	3	C
Pithiviers	MFC2	468	3	B
Pithiviers	LM	273	2	
Pizza	BHGN	259	2	B
◆	FFCB	302	3	C
◆	SC	385	2	
◆	NYTI	440	2	B
◆	JOC	226	2	
Anchovy filling	FFCB	302	3	C
Apple pie	FFBB	175	2	C
Avocado tomato	GHAC	374	1	B
Basil & extra cheese	GHAC	374	2	B
Bites	BCC	10	1	B
Broccoli, deep dish	VGCB	33	2	B
Burger, the Chicago	GHAC	186	1	
Caramelized onions, gorgonzola, rosemary	CPPC	153	3	B
Cheese	BCC	167	2	C
Cocktail	NYT	33	2	C
Corn bread	KIS	352	1	B
Crawfish tails & yellow tomatoes	CPPC	159	3	B
Crusts, pan	BHGN	259	2	
Crusts, thin	BHGN	259	2	
Deep dish, Chicago	GHAC	374	1	B
Dough	CPPC	151	3	B
◆	MCIC	60	2	B
◆	BCC	319	1	
◆	SP	135	2	C
Dough for individual	MSQC	48	2	B
w Dried tomato puree & mozzarella	CPPC	156	3	B

RECIPE	BOOK	PAGE	TD	S
w Dried tomatoes, mozzarella & olives	CPPC	158	3	B
w Duck confit & pearl onions	CPPC	162	3	B
w Eggplant & dried tomato puree	CPPC	156	3	B
w Eggplant & pesto	CPPC	155	3	B
w Eggplant, tomatoes & parmesan	CPPC	155	3	B
w Escarole, capers & Fontina	CPPC	161	3	B
w Fennel & mussels	CPPC	159	3	B
Frank sandwiches	BHGN	33	1	B
w Fresh anchovies, garlic & red onions	CPPC	160	3	B
w Fresh & dried wild mushrooms	CPPC	158	3	B
w Fresh herbs	CPPC	161	3	B
w Fresh mozzarella, tomatoes & basil	CPPC	157	3	B
w Garlic, pancetta & artichoke hearts	CPPC	154	3	B
w Garlic, tomatoes & olive oil	MCIC	65	3	B
w Grilled artichoke, pancetta & thyme	CPPC	162	3	B
w Grilled eggplant & pesto	CPPC	155	3	B
w Grilled radicchio & pancetta	CPPC	162	3	B
Hamburger	BCC	167	2	C
Hamburger	AC	315	1	
Hamburgers	BHGN	28	1	C
w Hot peppers, coriander & sausage	CPPC	156	3	B
Individual	MSQC	48	2	B

RECIPE	BOOK	PAGE	TD	S
w Italian sausage	BCC	167	2	C
w Leeks, pancetta & goat cheese	CPPC	155	3	B
Loaf	AC	781	2	
Miniature	EBE	23	1	C
w Mozzarella & anchovies	MCIC	66	3	B
w Multicolored peppers & fresh sausage	CPPC	156	3	B
w Mushrooms	NYTI	440	2	
Napoli	SPGT	69	2	B
Neapolitan style	FAIC	46	2	B
w Onion & cheese	JBGF	474	2	B
w Onion confit, walnuts & anchovies	CPPC	153	3	B
w Onions	FAIC	48	2	B
w Onions, garlic & herbs	CPPC	153	3	B
w Pancetta, mushrooms & garlic	CPPC	158	3	B
w Pepperoni	NYTI	440	2	
w Pepperoni	BCC	167	2	C
Pissaladiere	CPPC	153	3	B
Pita	JBGF	475	1	B
w Polenta	MC	162	1	B
Pot pie	SP	135	2	C
Provencale style	LM	258	2	
Ratatouille, pita	JBGF	305	1	C
w Rice crust	JBGF	480	1	B
w Roasted eggplant & mozzarella	CPPC	155	3	B
w Roasted garlic puree & chanterelles	CPPC	154	3	B
w Roasted new potatoes & pesto	CPPC	161	3	B
w Roasted tomato sauce	CPPC	157	3	C
w Rosemary	FAIC	49	2	B
Rustica	VE	211	2	B
w Sausage	FFCB	302	3	C
w Shrimp & feta	JBGF	476	2	B
w Shrimp, green onion & tomato	CPPC	160	3	B
Slices, pepperoni	BCC	320	1	B
Special	FAIC	48	2	B
w Spinach, deep dish	JBGF	478	3	B
w Squid & roasted peppers	CPPC	159	3	B
w Stewed garlic, pancetta & herbs	CPPC	154	3	B
w Stewed whole garlic	CPPC	154	3	B
w Tapenade & mozzarella	CPPC	161	3	B
Tiny, plus suggested fillings	AC	22	1	
w Tomato & mushroom filling	FFCB	302	3	C
w Tomatoes, herbs & quail eggs	CPPC	157	3	B
w Tomatoes, mozzarella, olive oil & parmesan	MCIC	62	3	B
w Tortilla crust, Mexican	JBGF	473	1	B
w Truffles	CPPC	160	3	B
w Wild mushrooms	CPPC	158	3	B
Zucchini	BBA	17	1	
Zucchini crust	JBGF	481	2	B
Pizzaburgers grilled	SC	328	1	
Pizzaiola sauce	KIS	285	1	A
Pizzaioula sauce	BB	17	1	B
Plaetzchen	SC	409	1	
Plain rolls	SC	76	2	
Plaky	NYT	38	2	C

RECIPE	BOOK	PAGE	TD	S
Sauteed Italian	GF	116	1	A
Sherbet	YGM	204	2	C
Sorbet	MHGD	444	1	B
Soup, peach brandied	CBSS	169	2	B
Sweet & sour sauce	BCC	187	1	
Tart	NSD	92	2	B
Tart, almond Viennese	BBA	205	2	B
Tartlets, Italian	MSE	240	2	B
Turnovers	FFBB	155	2	B
Upside down cake	FFBB	329	1	B
Whole green, baked	MSQC	73	1	B
Wine, melons in	NSD	122	1	C
Wine sherbet	NSD	229	1	B
Plymouth bread	CBB	190	2	C
Po'boy sandwich	AC	814	1	
Po'pottage (potato & ham soup)	GG	294	1	A
Poached eggs	AC	101		
Poached eggs, deviled	AC	107	1	
Poached eggs w tomato	AC	107	1	
Poaching	JOC	129		
Pocket bread sandwiches	FGCW	298		
Pocketbook steak	AC	266		
Podarakia arniou (baked lamb shanks)	NYTI	330	2	B
Poi (tard root paste)	JOC	276	3	B
Poireaux nicoise, stewed, leeks, tomatoes &	GG	246	1	B
Poisson cru Tahitian	NYTI	543	2	B
Poivrade sauce	NYTI	314	2	C
Poivrade sauce	JOC	328	2	C
Pokeweed	AC	559		
Polenta (cornmeal mush)	JOC	177		

RECIPE	BOOK	PAGE	TD	S
◆	FAIC	367	1	A
◆	VE	248	1	B
◆	AC	596	1	
◆	BHGN	325	1	B
◆	JBC	120	1	B
◆	FFCB	314	2	B
◆	CIC	204	1	A
Baked	VE	249	1	B
Baked, meat sauce w	CIC	208	2	B
Baked, variations	FGCW	161	1	B
Basic	NYT	339	1	B
Bel Paese	NYT	339	1	B
Butter & cheese	CIC	206	1	B
Cheese	JBC	120	1	B
w Cottage cheese & tomato sauce	KIS	185	1	A
Fried	CIC	206	1	B
Fried, appetizer	FAIC	84	1	
Gorgonzola	NYT	339	1	B
Gorgonzola	CIC	207	1	B
Grilled	NYT	339	1	B
Grilled, pesto	GRIL	68	2	B
Herring	FAIC	370	1	B
Layers	NYT	339	2	B
Pastry drum filled w quails	FAIC	371	3	B
Pizza	MC	162	1	B
Plus	GG	135	2	B
Sauce	JBC	120	1	B
Sausage	CIC	205	1	B
Sausages	FAIC	369	1	B
Shortcake w dried fruit & pine nuts	MCIC	433	1	B
Spicy, vegetables &	MC	118	1	B
Tart, pear &	FFBB	171	3	B
Polish sausage (see sausage, Polish)				
Polka dot brownies	AC	712	1	
Pollo alla cacciatore	NYTI	406	1	B

RECIPE	BOOK	PAGE	TD	S
Pollo con calabacitas	NYTI	474	2	B
Pollo estofado	NYTI	475	3	B
Polonaise sauce	JOC	340	1	B
Polonaise topping for vegetables	BHGN	388	1	
Pomegranate seeds w Grand Marnier	MSQC	197	1	B
Pomegranate sorbet	GF	130	2	B
Pommes Anna	MSQC	164	1	A
Pommes Anna	MFC2	395		
Pommes Anna	CPMC	103	2	B
Pommes Anna, all about	MFC2	393		
Pommes Anna, making (photographs)	LT	197		
Pommes duchesse, individual nests or mounds	MFC2	402		
Pommes souffles	SC	429	2	
Pompano (fish)				
A la Siepi	NYT	242	1	B
Baked, w wine	NYT	242	1	A
En papillote	BBA	86	2	B
En papillote	JOC	358	1	
En papillote	FFCB	115	1	B
Sauteed fillets of	AC	129	1	
Whole, roasted	FFCB	115	1	B
Pone sweet potato	GG	360	2	B
Ponzu (soy & lemon sauce)	NYTI	455	1	B
Poor boy sandwich	JOC	247	1	B
Poor Knights of Windsor	CF	151	1	B
Poor man's cakes	AC	715	1	
Poor boy sandwich	FFCB	292	1	B
Popcorn	BCC	14	1	C
◆	FFCB	73	1	B
◆	JOC	738	1	B
◆	SC	177	1	

RECIPE	BOOK	PAGE	TD	S
Balls	AC	836	2	
Balls	FFCB	690	1	C
Balls	BCC	121	1	B
Caramel	BCC	121	1	B
Caramelized	SC	177	1	
Chocolate	BCC	121	1	B
Old time	BHGN	114	1	C
Candied	JOC	738	1	B
Parmesan curry	BCC	14	1	C
Seasoned	JOC	66	1	
w Sherry wine sauce, Cajun	PPLK	281	2	B
Sugared	BHGN	115	1	B
Popovers	JOC	582	1	C
◆	AC	795	1	
◆	VE	46	1	B
◆	EBE	106	1	B
◆	FFCB	492	1	C
◆	JBC	22	1	
◆	BBA	178	1	B
◆	BHGN	88	1	B
◆	BCC	35	1	B
◆	CBB	577	1	B
◆	NYT	481	1	B
◆	FFBB	567	1	C
◆	NSD	141	2	B
Beef & burgundy	BCC	205	2	B
Cheese	JOC	582	1	C
Cheese	SC	91	1	
Crab Newburg	BCC	191	1	B
Custardy	MC	177	1	C
Freezer to oven to table	KIS	362	1	C
Giant	GHAC	364	1	B
Gluten	SC	91	1	
Goat cheese	SPGT	59	1	C
Lobster Newburg	BCC	191	1	B
Parmesan	BBA	178	1	B
Plain	SC	90	1	

RECIPE	BOOK	PAGE	TD	S
Quick	MIE	299	1	B
Rye	SC	91	1	
Whole grain	JOC	582	1	C
Whole wheat	FFBB	568	1	C
Whole wheat	FFCB	492	1	C
Poppadums (spiced Indian bread)	BBA	16	2	C
Poppy cheese bread	EBE	107	1	B
Poppy seed				
Bread	FFBB	549	1	C
Bubble loaf	CBB	67	2	C
Bundt cake, orange	SP	297	2	C
Cake	NSD	291	2	B
◆	AC	661	1	
◆	SC	115	1	B
◆	MHGD	118	2	C
◆	BHGN	102	1	C
California	FFBB	350	2	B
Orange	NSD	292	3	B
Ukrainian	MC	190	1	C
Caramel parfait	NSD	307	3	B
Custard torte	JOC	639	2	B
Dressing	BCC	299	2	B
◆	AC	79		
◆	SP	222	1	C
◆	GHAC	284	1	B
Dressing for summer fruits	YGM	208	1	C
Dressing, framboise	SPGT	391	2	B
Egg salad	SPGT	81	2	B
Filling	JOC	574	1	C
Filling cockaigne	JOC	573	1	B
Filling for coffee cake	SC	83	1	
Horns	SC	73	2	C
Noodles	FFCB	330	1	B
Noodles	KIS	251	1	A
Noodles, almond	EBE	123	1	C
Noodles & carrots	SMG	133	1	B
Orange cookies	NSD	52	1	C
Pinwheels	GHAC	351	2	C
Rolls	FFCB	476	2	C
Straws	MSE	274	2	C
Torte	SC	132	2	B
Torte, chocolate	SC	132	2	B
Porc braise aux choux rouges	MAFC	384	1	B
Porc braise avec choucroute	MAFC	385	1	B
Porc Sylvie	MAFC	385	2	C
Porchetta casalinga	CFS	264	2	B
Porcini (see also mushrooms)				
Porcini risotto	GF	200	1	B
Porcini risotto	MSQC	32	2	B
Porcupine icebox cake	SC	135	3	B
Porcupine meatballs	BHGN	241	1	B
Porcupine peach salad	SC	366	1	
Porcupines	JOC	430	1	B
Porgies broiled	NYT	243	1	B
Porgies, pan roasted, w marjoram & lemon	MCIC	213	1	B
Porgy, pan fried	FFCB	116	1	B
Porgy saute meuniere	NYT	243	1	B
Pork				
& Apple w curry sauce	BHGN	249	2	C
& Apple grill	GHAC	193	1	B
& Apple patties, spicy	BHGN	251	1	B
& Apple skewered	OC	126	2	B
& Asparagus	OC	92	1	B
Au vin blanc, roast loin of	NYTI	181	2	B
Au vin rouge, ragout of	NYTI	182	3	C
Backbone stew	PPLK	200	3	B

RECIPE	BOOK	PAGE	TD	S
Pork (*cont.*)				
Baked w cabbage & cream	FFCB	201	1	B
Bakonyi	NYTI	345	1	B
Balls				
Danish	NYT	144	1	C
Ginger	NYT	14	1	C
& Sauerkraut	NYTI	243	2	B
Steamed	NYTI	52	2	B
w Tomato sauce	JOC	429	1	B
Barbecued, Southern style	CFS	276	3	B
& Beans en adobo	WC	111	1	B
& Beans island	GHAC	233	2	B
& Beans w tomato sauce, baked	AC	594	3	
& Beans Vermont	GHAC	193	2	C
Beef, chicken & sausage, vegetables	MAFC	306	3	C
Beef, sweet potatoes, Madras style	GG	361	1	B
& Beef terrine, ham	FG	178	3	C
Birds	JOC	425	2	B
Boulettes	NYTI	244	1	C
Braised				
Hungarian style	NYTI	346	2	B
w Red cabbage	MAFC	384	1	B
w Sauerkraut	MAFC	385	1	B
Shoulder of	JBC	198	2	B
w Wild mushrooms & juniper berries	MCIC	297	1	B
Broiled	BCC	222		
Broiling fresh	BCC	222		
Burgers	BHGN	251	1	B
Butt				
Boiled w vegetables	CW	136	2	B
Smoked, boiled dinner	SMG	276	1	B
Smoked w stuffed greens	VGCB	132	2	B
Steaks, smoked	CFS	162	2	B
Butterflied, south of the border	CFS	158	2	B
& Cabbage, casserole roasted	MAFC	383	1	B
& Cabbage w noodles	WC	115	1	B
& Cabbage soup, old country	CBSS	262	2	C
Cake	AC	674	1	
Carving	JOC	388		
Casserole				
Chicken, Philippine	FGCW	307	2	B
w Duck sausage	FGCW	305	3	C
Roasted	MAFC	380	1	B
Roasted cabbage &	MAFC	383	1	B
Roasted, potatoes, onions &	MAFC	382	1	B
Roasted w turnips	MAFC	383	1	B
Cassoulet	BHGN	370	1	B
Chart	CFS	142		
Chart	SC	292		
Chart (photographs)	BHGN	246		
& Cheese pie	MCIC	341	2	B
& Chicken stew	GHAC	193	1	B
Chili sauce	NYTI	470	2	B
& Chinese cabbage	WC	120	2	B
Chinese style	NYT	139	1	B
Chinese style w plum sauce	WC	14	1	C
w Chinese vegetables	WC	116	1	B
Chop suey	SC	294	1	
Chops	BB	33	1	
Chops	MAFC	385		
Chops	JOC	408	1	
A l'orange	CFS	147	2	B
w Apple, cabbage & cumin	KIS	263	1	A

RECIPE	BOOK	PAGE	TD	S
Apple dappled	CFS	146	2	B
w Apples, braised	SC	294	1	
w Apples, loin	SMG	262	1	B
Baked w sour cream	JOC	424	2	B
Baked, stuffed	GHAC	191	2	B
Barbecued	OC	122	3	B
Barbecued	BB	34	1	
Barbecued w tangy pear sauce	GHAC	220	1	B
w Basil	NYT	133	2	B
w Black currant preserves	SP	98	1	B
Black forest	BBA	59	2	B
Braised	BB	34	1	
Braised au gratin	JBC	205		
Braised butterfly	NYT	136	1	B
Braised, deviled	JOC	424	2	B
Braised w fresh tomato sauce	MAFC	388	1	B
Braised w green pepper	JBC	205		
Braised, w marsala red wine	MCIC	294	1	B
Braised, Mexican	FFCB	198	1	B
Braised w mushrooms	MCIC	291	1	B
Braised w sage & tomatoes	MCIC	293	1	B
Braised w sweet potatoes	FFCB	197	1	B
Breaded	JOC	409	1	B
◆	SMG	258	1	B
◆	AC	410	1	
◆	BCC	222	1	B
w Broccoli de rabe	VGCB	134	1	B
Broiled	AC	409	1	
Broiled	JBC	203		
w Cabbage & sherry vinegar sauce	MFC	155	2	A
Cantonese	SC	294	1	
Caramelized w walnuts & raisins	MSQC	40	1	B
Casserole, sauteed	MAFC	386	1	B
Charcutiere	NYT	135	1	B
Chili flavored	OC	121	2	B
Chilied	AC	410	1	
Chinese style	WC	111	1	A
Classic	CFS	145	2	B
Cockaigne, braised & stuffed	JOC	425	2	B
Country fried	JBC	203	1	B
Country style	BB	33	1	
w Cream gravy	AC	409	1	
w Creamy gravy	GHAC	189	1	B
Creole	AC	410	1	
Creole, braised	JOC	424	2	B
Deviled	JBC	204	2	B
◆	BB	33	1	
◆	CFS	145	1	B
◆	KIS	250	1	A
Fennel	MSQC	136	1	A
Fennel	FG	357	1	A
Flambe	JBC	204	1	B
w Fruit, braised	JOC	425	2	
Gingered w apples & prunes	YGM	138	1	B
Glazed w cheese	SMG	270	1	B
Golden, glazed	GHAC	189	1	B
w Gravy, Italian	FGCW	343	2	
w Greens, stuffed	GG	195	2	B
Grilled	SC	328	1	
Grilled	NYTI	183	1	B
Grilled Hawaiian	SC	329	2	
Grilled & marinated	OC	122	2	B

RECIPE	BOOK	PAGE	TD	S
Pork (*cont.*)				
Herb stuffed w wine sauce	NYT	137	2	B
Herbed	NYT	133	1	B
Inebriated	FAIC	345	1	B
Italian style	BB	34	1	B
Kale &	FAIC	346	1	B
Key West	NYT	134	2	B
Lemon	BCC	223	1	B
& Lentil casserole	JBC	343	2	B
Malayan	NYT	138	2	B
Mexicali	BHGN	252	1	B
& Mushrooms	AC	411	1	
& Mushrooms	KIS	267	1	A
Mustard	NYTI	184	1	B
Mustard w cream tomato sauce	MAFC	387	1	B
w Mustard & dill sauce	MIE	133	2	B
Neapolitan	NYT	135	1	B
& Onions	AC	411	1	
Orange	SMG	272	1	B
"Outdoor," w roasted apples	OC	122	2	B
Pan broiled	BB	34	1	
Pan browned	SC	294	1	
& Paprika	NYT	133	2	B
w Paprika cream sauce	SMG	266	1	B
Piquant	AC	412	1	
Plain, sauteed	AC	409	1	
Polish	NYT	135	1	B
Polish	KIS	281	1	A
Poppy	CFS	148	2	B
Potato, scallop &	AC	413	1	
Roasted	BHGN	35	1	B
w Rye-bread stuffing	NYT	136	2	B
w Sauerkraut	BB	34	1	
& Sauerkraut casserole	AC	413	1	
Sauteed	SMG	260	1	B
Sauteed w apples	BBA	59	2	B
Sauteed w thyme & apple slices	MSQC	105	1	B
Scotch	CFS	149	2	B
Shoulder	JBC	205		
Skillet fried	FFCB	196	1	B
Snap	CFS	148	2	B
Sour cream, stuffed	NYTI	71	1	B
Stuffed	PPLK	184	3	B
Stuffed	AC	412	1	
Stuffed aux pistaches	NYTI	190	2	B
Stuffed w corn	BHGN	35	1	B
Stuffed w greens	GG	195	2	B
Stuffed, Italian	NYTI	391	2	B
Stuffed w sour cream gravy	NYT	137	1	B
Stuffed w sour sauce	LM	228	2	B
Sweet potato & apple casserole	FFCB	197	2	B
Sweet & sour	MIE	135	1	B
Teriyaki	NYTI	456	1	B
w Tomato sauce & oregano	SMG	268	1	B
Veracruz	NYTI	470	2	B
w Wine	SC	294	1	
Zingara	NYT	134	1	B
Chow mein	BCC	227	1	B
◆	WC	124	2	B
◆	SC	313	1	
◆	BHGN	250	1	B
Chow yuk	FG	320	2	B
& Clams, Portuguese	YGM	211	3	C

RECIPE	BOOK	PAGE	TD	S
Coating mix	BCC	222	1	B
Coating mix, shake it & bake it	KIS	358	1	B
Cold, loin of	AC	403		
Confit of	FGCW	199	1	B
Cooking liquid	BCC	223		
Crisp noodles, Thai	SC	295	2	
Crown of, smoked	AC	407		
Crown roast w cranapple stuffing	GHAC	188	3	C
Crown roast of	AC	403		
◆	JOC	407	1	
◆	FGCW	219	1	B
◆	MSE	219	3	B
◆	BBA	59	3	C
Cubes, sweet & pungent	NYT	140	1	B
Curried	BHGN	250	1	B
Curried w noodles	WC	119	1	B
Curry, Indonesian style	WC	115	1	B
Cutlets w paprika sour cream	SMG	264	1	B
Cuts				
Chart	SC	291		
Chart	BHGN	248		
Chart	JOC	396		
Drawing	FFCB	195		
For roasting or braising	MAFC	378		
Drawing	JBC	195		
Drunk roast	MCIC	296	1	B
Dry, curing at home	MFC2	308		
& Duck sausage casserole	FGCW	305	3	C
Dumplings w hot sauce	FGCW	329	2	B
& Egg noodles w coriander, stir fried	YGM	148	2	A
Egg rolls w shrimp	NYTI	63	2	C
En adobo w cabbage	WC	113	1	B
En adobo w pineapple, Philippine style	WC	119	1	B
Espanol, chicken &	NYTI	523	2	B
w Fennel, roast	BHGN	248	3	C
Filling for cocktail turnover	WC	22	1	C
Fried rice	WC	124	1	B
Fried rice	BCC	227	1	B
Fried rice	GHAC	267	1	B
w Fruit, potted	MIE	137	2	B
& Fruit ragout, winter	SP	132	3	B
Fruit stuffed loin of	SP	105	2	B
Fruited Chinese	WC	116	1	B
Gayettes w Swiss chard	VGCB	308	2	B
w Gorgonzola	FGCW	216	1	B
Goulash	AC	413	2	
Goulash	NYTI	345	1	B
Goulash au blanc	JOC	417	2	
& Grapes w wine sauce	FGCW	336	2	B
& Green beans, stir fried	JBGF	470	1	B
Greens & pot likker	AC	420	2	
Ground, w cellophane noodles, Szechwan style	MIE	174	1	B
Hibachi	BB	94	2	B
Hocks				
In brown sauce	NYTI	27	2	B
w Potatoes	GHAC	192	2	B

RECIPE	BOOK	PAGE	TD	S
Meatballs	SMG	275	1	B
Meatballs w marinara sauce	SMG	298	1	B
Medallions, barbecued, Vietnamese	CFS	151	2	B
Medallions of	MFC	154	2	B
Mexican style	FG	165	1	B
Mushrooms stuffed w veal &	NYTI	374	1	C
w Mustard sauce	FGCW	214	1	B
Neck bones, stewed	JOC	426	2	
New Orleans, grilled	FGCW	216	2	B
Normandy, roast	MFC	153	2	B
Northern Chinese	FG	164	1	B
w Paprika	NYTI	345	1	B
w Parsnips	BCC	223	1	B
Pate, chicken &	FFCB	60	2	C
Pate, veal &	FG	180	3	B
& Peas, stir fry	VGCB	199	1	B
& Peppers	VGCB	209	1	B
& Peppers, skewered	CFS	169	1	B
Piccata	FG	354	1	B
Piccata	BCC	225	1	B
Pickled	JOC	755	2	
Pie	BCC	225	1	B
Pie	NYT	144	2	B
Pie	AC	326		
Pie, French Canadian	NYTI	28		B
Pie, veal &	JOC	420	1	B
& Pork liver pate in brioche dough	MFC2	322	3	C
& Potato chowder	JBGF	345	1	B
w Potatoes & onions, casserole roasted	MAFC	382	1	B
Potted cracklings	NYTI	27	2	B
Preserved	MFC2	315	3	C
& Prune skewers	OC	125	2	A

RECIPE	BOOK	PAGE	TD	S
& Prunes, boneless loin of	MSE	182	2	C
& Prunes, loin of	AC	402		
Ribs, pickled, lentils &	FGCW	217	3	B
Roast	FFCB	194	2	B
◆	BCC	220		
◆	JOC	407	2	
◆	MAFC	378		
◆	NYT	132	2	B
Amagansett	CFS	156	2	B
Chinese	NYTI	50	2	B
w Rosemary	BCC	221	2	C
Santiago	NYTI	68	3	C
Stuffed w sauerkraut	JOC	408	1	
Stuffed w sausage & spinach	FG	358	2	B
Temperature, timing for	MAFC	379		
w Thyme	NYT	132	2	B
Trinidad	NYTI	546	2	C
Roasted	PPLK	183	2	B
Roasted w bay leaves	CIC	286	1	B
Roasting	BHGN	248		
Roasting chart	SC	293		
Roasting, timetable for	BCC	220		
Rolls, Polish fashion	JBC	202	2	B
Salad	AC	70	1	
Salt	JOC	755	2	
Salt	BTSB	24	1	
Salt	AC	419		
Baked	AC	420	2	
Marinade w herbs & spices	MAFC	376		
Midwestern style	AC	420	1	
& Milk gravy	JOC	426	1	B

RECIPE	BOOK	PAGE	TD	S
Pork (*cont.*)				
Sandwich, barbecued	FFCB	292	1	B
Sandwich, cold	AC	807	1	
Sandwiches, barbecued	BHGN	250	1	B
Satay	NYT	138	2	B
Sate	KIS	270	1	A
& Sauerkraut	NYTI	312	2	B
& Sauerkraut meats	NYT	141	2	B
& Sauerkraut supper	GHAC	191	2	B
& Sauerkraut, Transylvanian	NYTI	512	2	B
Sausage	OC	167	1	C
Creole	NYT	147	1	C
& Fennel	NYTI	402	2	B
Fried	SC	302	1	
Greek lamb &	FGCW	248	2	B
& Liver sausage w greens	MFC2	304	3	C
& Sauerkraut	FGCW	332	2	C
Spicy Italian	FGCW	249	2	B
Veal, truffles, foie gras &	MFC2	295	3	
Scrapple	JOC	438	2	B
Shoulder of, or picnic shoulder	AC	406		
Shoulder, roast	JBC	197	2	B
Shoulder, roast, baker's fashion	JBC	198	2	B
Shoulder, roast, country style	GHAC	188	2	C
& Shrimp, glass noodles w	FGCW	328	1	B
Shu mei	FG	265	2	C
Skewered, Indonesian	NYTI	364	3	B
Skewered, Indonesian style	OC	125	2	B
Smoked, timetable for roasting	BCC	228		
& Snow pea salad, Oriental, roast	MIE	285	1	B
Soup & cucumber, sliced	NYTI	37	1	B
Soup, South American	BHGN	370	2	B
Souvlakia	FG	166	1	B
Spareribs w Italian gravy	FGCW	344	2	B
& Spicy cabbage, hot pot w	GG	76	2	B
Spread	LM	199	3	C
Steak	BB	32	1	
Steak	MAFC	385		
Apple peanut buttered	BHGN	35	1	B
Braised	BHGN	252	1	B
Broiled	JBC	201	1	B
Creole style	GHAC	190	2	B
Garlic marinated	BB	33	1	A
Oriental	BB	32	1	A
Pan broiled	BB	32	1	
& Sauerkraut casserole, beer	JBC	202	1	
& Sauerkraut casserole, cider	JBC	202	1	
& Sauerkraut casserole w fried apple rings	JBC	202	1	
Stew w an onion sauce	VGCB	184	2	B
Stew, oven baked	BHGN	370	2	B
Strips, marinated	NYT	13	2	C
Stuffed cheese	MAFC	385	2	C
Sweet potatoes & beef madras style	GG	361	1	B

RECIPE	BOOK	PAGE	TD	S
Sweet & sour	BCC	226	1	B
◆	BHGN	250	2	B
◆	FFCB	203	2	B
◆	SC	295	1	
◆	JOC	409	2	B
◆	WC	118	2	B
Sweet & sour Chinese	SC	304	1	
Szechwan	NYTI	51	2	B
Tenderloin	JOC	408	1	
Tenderloin	SC	293	1	
Tenderloin	BB	35	1	
Apple glazed	GHAC	191	2	B
Breaded	BHGN	252	1	B
Broiled	AC	414	1	
Broiled	FFCB	194	1	B
Cooked on a spit	OC	119	2	B
Frenched	JOC	408	1	
& Fruit casserole	JOC	409	1	B
Grilled on skewers	OC	126	1	B
Maple glazed	GHAC	218	2	B
w Mushrooms & olives	JOC	424	1	B
w Mustard sauce	SC	294	2	
w Prunes or apricots	SC	294	2	
Sauteed	AC	414	1	
Teriyaki	FFCB	196	1	B
Tenderloin of	CFS	276	2	B
Timetable for braising	BCC	223		
Tongues	MFC2	242	2	B
Tonkatsu	FGCW	360	1	B
w Turnips, casserole roasted	MAFC	383	1	B
Turnovers	FFCB	202	2	B
& Veal pate, ham	MAFC	566	3	C
& Veal pate, liver	MAFC	568	3	C
& Veal pie tourtiere	AC	426	1	
& Veal roast, Bavarian	NYTI	311	2	B
& Vegetables, Wisconsin style	WC	123	1	B
& Vermouth	OC	123	2	B
& Watercress	NYT	140	1	B
w Wine gravy	BCC	221	1	
w Wine sauce, slow cooked, Chinese	FGCW	320	2	B
w Wine vinegar sauce	FGCW	213	2	B
Porkabobs, fruited	CFS	170	2	B
Porkless pate	MFC2	324	2	C
Porridge, spiced	BHGN	325	1	A
Port				
Cheese, walnut &	BBA	23	2	B
Chicken &	FGCW	175	1	B
Chicken breasts w	NYTI	501	1	B
Chicken in	FGCW	175	1	B
Duckling, Long Island in	NYT	217	2	B
Grape jelly &	NYT	515	1	C
& Melon	AC	759		
Melon in	NSD	122	1	C
Melon w	AC	759		
w Peaches or madeira	AC	763	1	
Pears poached in	FGCW	391	1	B
Pork loin, boneless w sherry vinegar &	GRIL	84	2	B
Pot roast mushrooms w	FGCW	202	2	B
Wine				
Chicken roast w cream	MAFC	245	2	B
Duck breast w	MFC	91	3	B
New York steak w four peppers &	MFC	150	2	B
Pears w	FFCB	667	2	B
Pears w	NYTI	281	1	B

RECIPE	BOOK	PAGE	TD	S
Potage				
A la caravelle	NYT	78	2	B
Creme de cresson	MAFC	41	1	B
Creme Normande	NYTI	120	1	B
Cressoniere	NYT	68	1	B
Les deux champignons	VE	52	2	B
Parmentier	MAFC	37	1	B
St. Germain	JOC	154	1	B
Sweet tater	GG	358	1	B
Veloute w champignons	MAFC	40	1	B
Vert (spinach vegetable soup)	GG	310	2	B
Potato	SC	333	1	
A la huancaina	NYTI	495	1	B
A lattice design (photographs)	OC	20		
In a parcel, cheese	OC	95	1	B
Alexandre	NYTI	514	1	B
All about	VGCB	210		
All about	JOC	290		
All about	FFCB	396		
Almond studded	AC	572	1	
American fried	BHGN	400	1	B
& Anchovies	NYT	270	1	B
& Anchovies au vin blanc	NYTI	113	1	B
& Anchovy casserole, Swedish	VGCB	224	1	B
& Anchovy salad	NYTI	258	1	B
Anglais	LT	199		
Anna	JOC	293	2	B
◆	AC	572	1	
◆	VGCB	221	1	B
◆	SC	426	1	
◆	JBC	327	1	B
& Arugula soup	MCIC	105	1	B
Au gratin	SC	427	1	
Au gratin	BCC	360	2	B
Au gratin	AC	568	1	
Au gratin, leftover	JOC	297	1	
& Bacon salad	AC	42	1	
Baked	NYT	393	1	
◆	BB	129	1	
◆	SC	426	1	
◆	AC	565	1	
◆	JOC	292	1	
◆	BHGN	400	1	
◆	FFCB	397	1	A
◆	MSQC	172	1	A
◆	JBC	326	1	
Au gratin	JBC	326	1	
w Bacon	JBC	327	1	
w Bay leaf	FG	215	1	A
& Chives	JBC	326	1	
Crunchy	GG	299	1	B
Eating a	AC	566		
French fried	JOC	295	1	B
w Grated cheese	JBC	326	1	
Leftover	JOC	297	1	
& Mushrooms	MCIC	398	1	B
& Onion salad	OC	94	1	B
Parsley	JBC	326	1	
Perfect	MIE	222	1	B
Roquefort cheese-stuffed	NYT	397	1	B
& Sour cream	JBC	326	1	
Stuffed	JBGF	385	1	B
◆	EBE	124	1	B
◆	FFCB	397	1	A
◆	AC	566	1	
Stuffed hash	JOC	292	2	B
Stuffed w vegetables	JOC	292	1	B
& Sweet orange glaze	EBE	124	1	B
& Variations	VGCB	215	1	

RECIPE	BOOK	PAGE	TD	S
& Carrots, pureed	SMG	259	1	B
& Carrots, scalloped, cream	MAFC	525	1	B
Casserole, artichoke &	GG	15	1	B
Casserole, creamed	JOC	291	1	
Casserole, Polish	JBGF	383	2	B
& Caviar	GF	177	1	C
& Celeriac cake	VGCB	73	1	B
& Celery, braised in olive oil	CIC	369	1	B
& Celery root puree	YGM	135	1	B
Chantilly	FFCB	398	1	B
Chantilly	JOC	291	1	B
Cheese gratin, celeriac &	VGCB	74	1	B
& Cheese w mayonnaise alla Romana	NYTI	375	2	B
& Cheese pancakes	YGM	236	1	C
& Cheese puffs, mashed	JOC	291	2	B
& Cheese soup	SP	60	2	B
& Cheese sticks	MAFC	198	2	C
Cheesy, scalloped	BHGN	401	1	B
Chicken salad w avocado, papaya &	GHAC	280	2	B
Chicken stuffed w olives &	FG	133	2	B
Chips	FFCB	400	1	
◆	JOC	296	1	
◆	JBC	330	1	B
◆	VGCB	218	1	
◆	BB	128	1	
Chicken &	BHGN	299	1	B
Loaf, tuna &	JOC	239	1	B
Oven baked	CF	35	1	B
Saratoga	SC	428	1	

RECIPE	BOOK	PAGE	TD	S
Chowder, pork &	JBGF	345	1	B
Ciro	NYTI	252	1	B
Cocotte	LT	199		
Cooking	JBGF	35		
Cornflaked	EBE	126	2	B
Cottage fried	FFCB	400	1	B
Country fried	SC	428	1	
Cream puff	LT	203		
Creamed	AC	565	1	
Creamed	FFCB	402	1	B
Creamed	SC	426	1	
Croquettes	FFCB	399	1	B
Croquettes	SC	429	1	
Croquettes	NYTI	537	2	B
Croquettes w crisp fried onions	CIC	385	1	B
Croquettes, nut &	FFCB	399	2	B
Cubes, sauteed	SMG	213	1	B
& Cucumber salad, julienne of truffle w	GF	28	2	C
Cups, stuffed	JOC	293		
Curried	FFCB	404	1	B
Curry	VE	256	1	B
& Dandelions, wilted	GG	189	1	B
Dauphine	JOC	296	1	
Dauphine	BBA	134	2	C
Dauphinoise	VGCB	219	1	B
Dauphinoise w wild mushrooms	MSE	224	2	A
Deep frying, basic rules for	AC	571	1	
Deerfoot	FFCB	405	1	A
Delmonico	GHAC	244	1	C
Delmonico	FFCB	404	1	B
Dipping	KIS	307	1	B
Doughnuts	VGCB	226	1	C
Doughnuts, Lynn's raised	VGCB	227	1	C

RECIPE	BOOK	PAGE	TD	S
Potato (*cont.*)				
Doughnuts, quick	JOC	705	2	C
Dressing	JOC	458	1	C
Duchesse	BHGN	401	1	B
◆	GHAC	244	1	C
◆	JOC	296	1	B
◆	SC	427	1	
◆	NYT	394	1	B
Dumplings (see also gnocchi, potato, dumplings, potato)				
Dumplings	VGCB	221	1	B
Fans, roasted	GHAC	244	1	B
& Fennel hash, home fried	GG	178	1	B
Filling for blintzes	SC	94	1	
Filling for knishes	SC	95	1	
Filling for pierogi	FG	374	1	
Filling & stuffing	AC	233	1	
Finishing touches for, boiled	VGCB	214	1	
Flour cake	SC	123	1	B
Flour sponge cake	JOC	621	1	B
Flowers, crisp	MFC	175	1	A
Foil baked	BHGN	400	1	
Foil baked, new	MSQC	188	1	B
Fondant	NYTI	252	1	B
Fontecchio	SPGT	168	1	B
For aioli	NYTI	135	1	B
Franconia	SC	427	1	
Franconia	JOC	293	1	
French fried	MSQC	133	1	B
◆	FFCB	400	1	
◆	SC	428	1	
◆	BCC	360	1	B
◆	JBC	330	1	B
◆	BB	128	1	
Fried	JBC	328	1	B
w Cheese	JBC	328	1	B
Cooked	JBC	329	1	
German	FFCB	440	1	B
German, leftover	JOC	297	1	B
w Green onions	JBC	328	1	B
Oven	JBC	328	1	B
Oven	SC	427	1	
Pan raw	SC	428	1	
w Parsley	JBC	328	1	B
w Parsley & chives	JBC	328	1	B
Skillet	SMG	175	1	B
w Sliced onions	JBC	328	1	B
Soft	JBC	328	1	B
w Suet (beef)	AC	569	1	
Sweet, crisps	GG	361	1	B
Frittata, leek &	FFCB	342	1	B
Galette	JBC	327	1	
Galette	AC	572	1	
Gnocchi (see gnocchi, potato)				
Grandmere	NYTI	251	1	B
Gratin a la Savoyarde	VGCB	219	1	B
Gratin of sliced endives	MFC2	389	2	B
Gratin Swiss	SP	177	1	B
Gratineed	MFC	175	2	B
Gratins	VGCB	218	1	
& Green bean salad	JBGF	545	2	B
& Green bean salad, warm	YGM	127	1	A
Green & white	KIS	131	1	A
Gridlocked	CFS	247	1	B
Grilled w caraway	OC	95	1	A
Grilled & scalloped	SC	333	1	
Grilled, whole	GRIL	83	2	B
Grilled, whole	BHGN	42	1	
Gruyere	NYTI	538	1	B
Gruyere en casserole	VE	146	2	B

RECIPE	BOOK	PAGE	TD	S
Ham, eggs & onions, gratin of shredded	MAFC	153	1	B
& Ham fritters	MCIC	400	1	B
& Ham scallop	BHGN	256	2	B
& Ham soup	GG	294	1	A
Hash brown	AC	569		
◆	JBC	329	1	B
◆	SC	428	1	
◆	NYT	394	1	B
◆	FFCB	400	1	B
◆	JOC	294	1	B
◆	BHGN	400	1	B
◆	BB	128	1	
◆	GHAC	242	1	B
Hash brown, tomatoes, herbs &	MFC2	391	1	B
Hashed in cream	JBC	330	1	
Hashed in cream	FFCB	402	1	B
Hashed in cream	BB	129	1	
Hashed in cream, variations	AC	570	1	
Heavenly, mashed	GG	301	1	B
Herbed	GRIL	84	2	B
Herbed & mashed w bechamel	GF	226	1	C
& Herring salad	JOC	87	1	B
Home fried	GHAC	242	1	B
Home fried	BB	128	1	
Home fried	AC	568	1	
Hors d'oeuvre, baked	AC	15	1	
Impaled on skewers (photographs)	OC	18		
In cream sauce	SMG	239	1	B
Julienne	BB	128	1	
Katherine Smith's small	AC	16	1	
& Kohlrabi, whipped	VGCB	151	1	B
Latkes, Myra's	GG	303	1	B
& Leek chowder	JBGF	322	1	B
& Leek soup (see leek & potato soup)				
& Leeks, party	GHAC	243	1	C
Leftover	JOC	297	1	
& Lemon, new	GG	296	1	B
& Lemon, parsleyed	BHGN	401	1	B
Lime & chives	BCC	357	1	B
Loaf, meat &	GHAC	184	2	B
Luncheon dish	NYT	395	1	B
Lyonnaise	JOC	293	1	
◆	SC	428	1	
◆	AC	568	1	
◆	BB	129	1	B
◆	MFC	176	1	B
◆	FFCB	402	1	B
◆	JBC	329	1	
Macaire	NYTI	253	2	B
Martinique	FFCB	404	2	B
Mashed	JOC	290	1	B
◆	FFCB	398	1	B
◆	BCC	359	1	B
◆	JBC	325	1	B
◆	NYT	394	1	B
◆	SC	426	1	
◆	BHGN	401	1	B
w Baked cheese	SMG	255	1	B
w Carrots	AC	503	1	
w Celery root	AC	510	1	
w Cheese	NYT	395	1	B
w Chives	JBC	325	1	B
w Eggs	SMG	233	1	B
For borders & decorations	MFC2	399	1	B

RECIPE	BOOK	PAGE	TD	S
Potato, Mashed (*cont.*)				
Garlic	MAFC	520	1	B
Italian style parmesan cheese	CIC	384	1	B
Leftover	JOC	297	1	
w Mushrooms	NYT	395	1	B
w Onions	SC	426	1	
w Parsley	JBC	325	1	B
Rutabagas &	GG	389	1	B
w Scallions	NYT	395	1	B
Sweet	MSQC	220	1	B
& Variations	VGCB	217	1	
& Variations	AC	566	1	
Meat bake	BHGN	34	2	B
Micro-baked	BHGN	400	1	
Mold of sliced, baked in butter	MFC2	394	3	B
Mold of sliced, cheese & butter	MFC2	397	3	B
& Mushroom pie	AC	527	1	
& Mustard, new	GG	296	1	B
Nest, straw	LM	145	2	A
Nest, waffle	LM	147	2	
New, lemon, chives &	GHAC	243	1	B
New, peas, mint &	SPGT	168	2	B
O'Brien	SC	428	1	
O'Brien	WC	37	1	B
O'Brien	AC	568	1	
O'Brien, leftover	JOC	297	1	B
Old French style	FG	219	1	B
Omelet	YGM	213	2	C
Omelet w ham, flat	SMG	84	1	B
On the half shell	SC	426	1	
& Onion soup	CIC	59	1	B
Onions & anchovies, gratin of	MAFC	154	1	B
& Onions, mashed	CF	55	1	B
& Onions w sausages, gratin of	MAFC	155	1	B
& Onions, scalloped	SC	427	1	
Orange, mashed	SP	177	1	B
Ovals, making (photographs)	LT	199		
Oven fried	FFCB	400	1	
Pan sauteed w fennel	MSQC	28	1	B
Pancakes	AC	573	1	
◆	FFCB	401	1	B
◆	JBGF	507	1	C
◆	VE	190	1	A
◆	NYT	396	1	B
◆	JOC	294	1	C
◆	SC	96	1	B
◆	MSQC	200	1	B
◆	JBC	331	1	B
Baked	SC	96	1	
Blender	VGCB	220	1	B
Grated	VGCB	220	1	B
Grated	MAFC	521	1	B
Mashed from leftovers	MFC2	402	1	B
Miniature	EBE	23	2	B
w Sour cream	SC	96	1	B
Straw	CPMC	155	1	B
Paprika	SMG	93	1	B
Parmesan	EBE	128	1	B
Patties	PPLK	302	2	B
Patties	BHGN	401	1	B
Patties, mashed	JBC	326	1	
& Peas in cream	SMG	113	1	B
& Peas in cream sauce	SMG	201	1	B
Peel broth	VE	48	2	B
Peelings, oven fried	YGM	216	1	C
Peppers & pimentos	SMG	245	1	B
& Pesto	FAIC	417	1	B

RECIPE	BOOK	PAGE	TD	S
Pie				
Genoa style, green bean &	MCIC	369	1	B
w Herbs & cream	MFC2	398	1	B
Meat &	BCC	208	1	B
Savory	AC	573	2	
Savory	VGCB	224	1	B
Pizza w pesto &	CPPC	161	3	B
Planks	BCC	359	1	B
Pommes duchesse, individual nests	MFC2	402		
Pork hocks &	GHAC	192	2	B
Preparing	GG	292		
Provencale	WC	34	1	B
Pudding	SC	428	1	
Pudding w cheese	VE	216	2	B
Pudding for Passover	SC	194	1	
Puffed	JOC	294	3	B
Puffed	SC	429	2	
Puffs	JOC	296	1	B
Puffs	SC	428	1	
Punts	GG	298	2	B
Puree w celeriac	MSE	182	1	C
Puree w chestnut	SP	195	1	B
Puree w green beans	CW	148	1	B
Puree w truffles	MFC	176	1	B
Pureed	SMG	215	1	B
Pureed	SMG	261	1	B
Ragout of	SMG	265	1	B
Ragout of	VE	147	1	B
Raita	VE	261	1	B
Red, & red onion gratin	CPMC	215	1	B
Riced	JOC	290	1	B
Ricotta ring w chicken liver sauce	FAIC	361	2	B
Ring burnished w carrots, glazed	BBA	134	2	B
Ring, ricotta, w chicken liver sauce	FAIC	361	2	B
Rissolees	NYT	396	1	B
Roast	BBA	134	2	C
Roast, pan, diced	CIC	387	1	B
Roasted				
Mustard &	CFS	247	1	B
On coals (photographs)	OC	19		
Pan	FFCB	398	2	B
Pan w anchovies	MCIC	401	1	B
Stuffed	NYT	396	1	B
Roesti, Swiss	AC	570	1	
Rolls	FFBB	492	1	C
Rolls, Karen's mashed	GG	301	2	C
Rolls, refrigerator	SC	76	2	
Romanoff	VE	144	1	B
Rose, making (photographs)	LT	18		
w Rosemary & garden vegetables	GF	40	1	C
Rosti	SMG	219	1	B
Rounds	LT	198		
Rounds, making (photographs)	LT	198		
Salad	BCC	287	2	C
◆	MSE	137	1	B
◆	BB	141	1	B
◆	JOC	87	2	B
I	JBC	249	2	B
II	JBC	250	2	B
III	JBC	250	1	B
American picnic	SP	180	3	C
Bacon &	AC	42	1	
Bacon, French	SP	180	1	B
Buttermilk	YGM	180	3	C

RECIPE	BOOK	PAGE	TD	S
Potato Salad (*cont.*)				
California style	BCC	287	2	C
Carried away	JBGF	546	1	B
Creamy	BHGN	334	2	B
Creamy	SC	360	1	
Endive &	SMG	307	1	B
Florentine style	FAIC	390	1	B
French	NYT	426	1	B
French	MAFC	541	1	C
French provincial	GG	294	2	B
Garden	BCC	287	2	C
German	FFCB	436	2	B
German	BHGN	334	1	B
German, hot	JOC	88	1	B
German, hot	BCC	286	1	B
German, hot	SC	360	1	
German sour cream	NYT	426	1	B
Greek	FG	219	1	B
w Green onion salad dressing	PPLK	237	1	B
Herbed	NYTI	258	1	C
Hot	KIS	255	1	A
◆	SC	360	1	
◆	FFCB	436	2	B
◆	KIS	278	1	A
Hot, new	AC	42	1	
Italian	MCIC	419	1	B
Kathe's	VGCB	223	1	B
Kristina's	MC	48	1	B
w Mayonnaise	SC	360	1	
Meal in a bowl	JBGF	378	1	B
Mideast	JBGF	546	1	B
Mother's	EBE	140	2	B
Nicoise	JOC	88	1	C
Nicoise	BHGN	334	2	C
w Oil & vinegar	AC	42	1	
Old fashioned	GHAC	273	1	B
Patriotic	SPGT	169	2	B
Peggy Martin's	AC	41	2	
Pesto	FG	219	1	
Picnic	AC	41	1	
Polly Hamblet's	AC	41	2	
Scandinavian	SP	181	2	B
Scandinavian style	BCC	287	2	C
Sour cream	NYT	426	1	B
Speck's famed	GG	295	1	B
Tangy & hot	GHAC	273	1	C
Variations	FFCB	436	2	B
Vinaigrette	VE	107	2	B
Vinaigrette	MSE	104	1	B
Warm	GF	195	1	C
Warm w fried potato skins	SPGT	133	2	B
& Salmon croquettes	JBGF	381	1	B
Salt rising bread	JOC	558	3	
Sausage salad	BBA	145	2	B
Sauteed	BB	127	1	
◆	SMG	251	1	B
◆	VGCB	216	1	
◆	SMG	247	1	B
Sauteed in butter	MAFC	526	1	B
Sauteed w onions	SMG	249	1	B
Sauteed w sage	FAIC	416	1	B
Scalloped	BHGN	401	1	B
◆	FFCB	401	1	B
◆	JOC	291	2	B
◆	JBC	327	1	B
◆	SC	427	1	
◆	VGCB	218	1	
◆	YGM	119	1	A
◆	BCC	361	2	B
w Butter	JOC	292	1	B
w Celery root	FFCB	401	1	B
w Celery root	AC	510	1	
w Cheese	JBC	327	1	B
w Chives & parsley	JBC	327	1	B
Creamy	SC	427	1	

RECIPE	BOOK	PAGE	TD	S
w Garlic	MSE	228	2	C
Ham w	SC	297	2	
◆	JBC	327	1	B
◆	BCC	231	1	B
◆	AC	451	1	
Milk, cheese, garlic &	MAFC	523	1	B
Old fashioned	VGCB	219	1	B
w Onions	JBC	327	1	B
w Onions, tomatoes, anchovies & garlic	MAFC	525	1	B
Parsnips &	AC	535	1	
Special	JBGF	384	2	B
& Variations	AC	567	1	
Shells, beef in	BCC	210	1	B
Shoestring	BB	128	1	
◆	JBC	330	1	B
◆	JOC	295	1	
◆	SC	428	1	
Skillet	SMG	203	1	B
Skillet, creamed	FFCB	402	1	B
Skillet, new	CW	124	1	B
Skins, baked	MIE	223	1	B
Skins, broiled	BCC	9	1	C
Skins, crimped	GG	293	2	A
w Sliced eggs	VGCB	215	1	
Sliced & sauteed w lemon & garlic	MFC2	390	1	B
Sliced & simmered in cream & basil	MFC2	388	1	B
Sliced, w tarragon cream, new	GG	297	1	B
Slices fried in olive oil	MSQC	161	1	A
Slices, puffed	LT	205		
Small, new, preparing	BCC	357		

RECIPE	BOOK	PAGE	TD	S
Soap shaped	LM	142	1	B
& Sorrel soup	VGCB	224	1	B
Souffle	VE	181	1	A
◆	AC	571	1	
◆	JOC	294	3	B
◆	JBGF	489	2	B
Souffle, Italian	EBE	127	1	C
Soup	JOC	159	1	A
◆	CBSS	335	1	B
◆	VE	60	1	B
◆	SC	399	2	
Cantaloupe &	GG	293	2	B
Carrots & celery, creamy	CIC	58	1	B
Cream of	SC	402	1	
Delicate older	VGCB	224	1	B
Green bean &	FG	51	1	C
Ham &	GG	294	1	A
Mashed	VGCB	213	1	
Onion &	CIC	59	1	B
Onion &	MAFC	37	1	B
Quick	SC	400	1	
Russian	CBSS	336	1	B
Simple	FAIC	125	2	B
Split green pea &	CIC	72	1	B
Tomatoes &	JOC	159	1	C
Staff	VGCB	215	1	
Starter, cooked	CBB	274	3	C
Starter, raw	CBB	275	3	B
Starter, white bread	CBB	404	3	C
Steamed	SMG	211	1	B
◆	SMG	275	1	B
◆	SMG	105	1	B
◆	SMG	107	1	B
◆	SMG	139	1	B
◆	VGCB	215	1	
Steamed cabbage &	VGCB	44	1	B
Stewed	SC	426	1	

RECIPE	BOOK	PAGE	TD	S
Zucchini, eggplant & whole garlic, tian of	MSQC	144	1	B
Pots de cream a la vanille	NYT	600	2	B
Pots de cream au chocolat	NYT	600	2	B
Pots de creme (custard)	JOC	687	2	B
Pots de creme	NYTI	297	1	B
Pots de creme, chocolate	BHGN	173	2	B
Pots de creme, chocolate	BCC	141	1	B
Pottage Esau's	FG	118	2	B
Potted cheese	JOC	708	1	A
Potted Edam	VE	217	1	
Poule-au-pot (soup)	JOC	147	2	B
Poulet a ma mere	MIE	98	1	B
Poulet au riesling	NYTI	221	1	B
Poulet au riz	NYTI	221	2	B
Poulet marengo	NYT	200	1	B
Poulette sauce	NYTI	275	1	B
Poulette sauce	JOC	324	1	B
Poultry				
All about	JOC	460		
All about	FFCB	228		
Boning	JOC	462		
Boning	SC	307		
Canning	BHGN	143		
Carving	JOC	464		
Carving	SC	307		
Carving, cooked	FFCB	234		
Chart	CFS	101		
Chart	MAFC	235		
Cleaning (photographs)	LT	213		
Disjointing	MFC2	313		
Disjointing, uncooked	SC	306		
Dressing, cleaning	SC	306		

RECIPE	BOOK	PAGE	TD	S
Easy stuffing for	VGCB	126	1	B
Freezing	BHGN	143		
Glazes	GHAC	164		
Grilling	GR	47		
Liver mousse	LT	21	2	B
On-a-spit, basted	BHGN	32	2	B
Onions, stuffed	NYT	389	1	B
Plucking & singeing	JOC	460		
Preparing undrawn for saute fricassee	JOC	461		
Roasting & preparing, undrawn	JOC	462		
Stock, brown	MAFC	110		
Stock, white	MAFC	109	2	C
Stuffing	NYTI	407	1	B
Stuffing (drawings)	FFCB	231		
Stuffing, Lebanese	FG	369	1	B
Trussing	SC	306		
Trussing	NYT	222		
Trussing	NYTI	217		
Pound cake	JOC	626	2	B
◆	MFC2	482	1	
◆	FFCB	511	2	B
◆	BCC	69	1	C
◆	SC	108	2	B
◆	BTSB	244	1	B
◆	AC	663	1	
◆	BHGN	93	1	C
Almond	BCC	69	1	C
Almond butter, crusted	FFBB	368	1	C
Bay leaf	FFBB	366	1	C
Brown sugar, Willard Scott's	YGM	186	2	C
Buttermilk & lemon	FFBB	366	1	C
w Cherries & raisins	MSE	260	2	B
Citron	FFBB	365	1	B

RECIPE	BOOK	PAGE	TD	S
Profiteroles (ice cream filled pastry puffs)	SC	140	1	
Profiteroles	JOC	598	3	
Profiteroles	SP	292	2	B
Profiteroles w chocolate sauce	BBA	192	3	C
Prosciutto				
All about	MCIC	32		
& Artichoke hearts, fettuccine	CPPC	105	2	B
Asparagus &	SP	148	1	B
Asparagus bundles &	MCIC	328	1	B
Asparagus tips w	NYT	354	1	B
Barley soup w	CBSS	175	1	B
Bayonne cured ham w	LM	217	3	
Bread, onion	GG	242	2	C
Chicken, tomatoes, fettuccini &	GG	378	1	B
Cornish game hens w	SMG	66	1	B
Crepes stuffed w tomatoes & cheese	MCIC	343	1	B
Dandelion greens w	GG	191	1	B
Figs w	AC	754	1	
Filling, phyllo triangles w rosemary	SP	9	1	C
Fruit	JOC	71	1	
& Gnocchi, pumpkin	GG	330	1	B
& Green tortellini w cream sauce	MCIC	178	3	B
& Gruyere, veal chops w	GRIL	68	2	B
Lima beans, baby w	MIE	219	1	B
Melon	MSE	166	1	B
Melon	BCC	6	1	C
Melon	MSQC	72	1	B
On toast, creamed crab w	SMG	144	1	B
Pasta w peas, spinach &	CPPC	33	1	B
Pudding of veal, chicken breast &	FAIC	375	2	B
Sandwich	AC	808	1	
& Shrimp skewered	SP	122	1	B
Veal scaloppine w	NYT	158	1	A
& Wild mushrooms, fettuccine w	CPPC	24	2	A
Prosnos (spinach casserole)	SC	432	1	
Provencal salad	NYTI	263	2	B
Provencale garnish	SMG	185	1	B
Provencale sauce	VE	93	1	
Provencale sauce	BCC	327	1	B
Provolone sandwiches, hot	BCC	325	1	B
Provolone sauce, yellow squash w	KIS	263	1	A
Prune				
& Apple stuffing	FFCB	279	1	B
& Apricot strudel	SC	355	2	
Armagnac ice cream	NSD	220	1	B
Baked	AC	769	1	
Bars	JOC	654	1	C
Bars, oatmeal	BHGN	155	1	C
Betty	JOC	701	2	B
Brandied	MHGD	426	1	B
Bread	JOC	556	1	
◆	SC	86	1	
◆	EBE	107	1	B
◆	FFCB	488	2	C
Bread, quick	JOC	575	2	B
Brisket, baked	SC	273	3	
Buns, bohemian	SC	80	2	
Cake	SC	115	1	B
Cake	FFBB	348	2	C

RECIPE	BOOK	PAGE	TD	S
Cake, chocolate spiced	JOC	628	1	B
Catsup	BBA	163	1	B
Cheese ring	SC	370	2	
Chestnuts	JOC	120	1	B
Chicken w hot peppers &	CF	58	3	B
Coffee cake, orange, caraway &	FFBB	580	2	B
Cookie filling	AC	716	1	
Cream	SC	203	2	
Dressing	JOC	458	1	C
Dried	JOC	120	1	
Filling (see also filling, prune)				
Filling	FFBB	539	2	C
Cookie	AC	716	1	
For brioche	CBB	671	3	B
For coffee cake rolls	JOC	573	1	B
For danish pastries	NYT	535	1	
For pie or kuchen	SC	83	1	
Glaceed	SC	175	1	
Ice cream	MCIC	452	2	B
Kidney kebabs	OC	128	1	B
Kuchen	FFBB	349	2	B
Kuchen	SC	354	1	
Kuchen	BHGN	67	2	B
Leather	AC	832	2	
Lentils	JOC	262	1	B
Loaf, cornmeal	FFBB	370	2	C
Loin of pork w	AC	402		
Muffins, pumpkin, whole wheat	FFBB	561	1	C
Noodles, scalloped	SC	336	1	
Peanut butter, chocolate	BBA	225	2	C
Pickled	JOC	120	1	
Pie	FFCB	584	2	B
Pie	JOC	604	1	B
Pie, deep dish	AC	614	1	
Pie, two crust	AC	615	1	
Plums, baked	JBC	111	1	B
Plums, fresh baked w custard	MFC2	436	1	B
Poached	NSD	157	1	B
Pork				
Chops w ginger, apples &	YGM	138	1	B
Loin of	NYT	132	2	B
Loin of, boneless	MSE	182	2	C
Skewers w	OC	125	2	A
Tenderloin w	SC	294	2	
Pucks	NSD	60	3	C
Pudding	SC	193	2	
Pudding, molded	SC	197	1	
Pudding, steamed	JBC	46	1	
Rabbit w	LM	192	3	B
Refrigerator cookies	AC	701	2	
Salad, stuffed	SC	366	1	
Sauce, cookies w	AC	710	1	
Sausage, stuffed	FFCB	211	1	B
Souffle	JOC	690	2	B
Spiced	GHAC	378	3	C
Spread	SC	380	1	
Stewed	SC	263	2	
Stuffed	SC	372	1	
Stuffed	SC	176	1	
Stuffed	FFCB	692	2	C
Stuffed w sausage	FFCB	211	1	B
Stuffing (see also stuffing, prune)				
Stuffing & foie gras, roast goose w	MAFC	283	3	B
Stuffing, pork loin chops w	GHAC	190	2	B
Tart w brioche crust	NSD	152	2	B
Tart w cream cheese	MAFC	648	2	B

RECIPE	BOOK	PAGE	TD	S
Prune (*cont.*)				
Torte	SC	132	2	B
Torte	NYT	571	1	C
Upside down cake, apricot &	BCC	71	2	B
& Walnut cake	BCC	73	1	C
Walnut & rum cake	FFBB	370	2	C
Walnut tart	FFBB	174	2	B
Whip	FFCB	670	1	B
Whip	AC	725	1	
Whip	JOC	690	2	B
Double boiler	SC	190	2	
w Port wine	NYT	623	1	B
Steamed	SC	190	2	
Wine	JOC	120	1	B
Ptarmigan (prairie chicken)	JOC	479		B
Ptarmigan, about	JOC	479		
Pudding				
Almond apple	MHGD	417	1	B
Apple	BCC	142	1	B
Apple	VE	268	2	B
Brandied	WC	145	2	B
Bread	MHGD	415	2	C
Cape cod	FFCB	650	1	B
& Molasses, steamed	JOC	704	2	C
Beefsteak	AC	328	2	
Birdie McSherry's Christmas	GF	92	2	C
Black	NYTI	20	2	C
Black	LM	208	3	C
Blueberry	SC	192	1	
Blueberry	MIE	319	1	B
Bread (see also bread pudding)				
Bread, glazed	CIC	431	2	B
Brown rice fruited	JBGF	635	1	B
Brown, steamed	JOC	703	2	C
Brownie	BHGN	174	1	B
Butterscotch	BCC	141	1	B
Cabinet	JOC	693	3	C
Cake, chocolate	SC	188	1	
Cake, lemon	FFBB	339	1	B
◆	SC	188	1	C
◆	BCC	133	1	B
◆	BHGN	174	1	B
Caramel				
& Almond, steamed	SC	189	1	
Custard & cornstarch	JOC	688	1	B
Frozen	SC	214	2	
Steamed	JOC	704	2	C
Steamed w ladyfingers	SC	189	2	
Carrot	SC	417	1	
Carrot	AC	732	1	
Carrot, savory	VGCB	53	1	B
Casserole	NYTI	503	2	C
Charleston	AC	724	1	
Cheese	JBC	29	1	B
Cheese w actual cheese	AC	727	1	
Cherry	SC	193	1	
Chocolate	BCC	141	1	B
◆	FFCB	610	1	B
◆	BHGN	172	2	B
◆	BTSB	250	1	B
◆	NYTI	16	2	B
◆	GHAC	297	2	B
Almond	SC	190	2	
Bread	MFC	230	2	C
Cornstarch	JOC	688	1	B
Cornstarch	SC	197	1	
Feather	JOC	702	2	B
Frozen	SC	214	2	
Steamed	SC	189	1	

RECIPE	BOOK	PAGE	TD	S
Pudding, Chocolate Steamed (*cont.*)				
◆	BCC	143	2	B
◆	JOC	703	2	C
◆	FFCB	615	2	B
◆	JBC	45	2	B
Steamed w whipped cream	MSE	88	2	C
Sweet, frozen	SC	214	2	
Christmas	NSD	192	2	C
Coconut	SC	188	2	
Coconut milk, chilled	NYTI	504	2	C
Coffee, frozen	SC	215	2	
Colonial cheese	AC	726	1	
Cornstarch (blanc mange)	SC	197	1	
Cornstarch & custard	JOC	688	2	B
Couscous	JBGF	634	2	C
Cranberry	SC	189	1	
Cranberry, steamed	FFCB	618	2	B
Custard, baked	JBC	44	1	B
Custard corn	GHAC	236	2	B
Date (see also date pudding)				
Date, steamed	JOC	703	2	C
◆	SC	190	2	
◆	AC	731	2	
◆	JBC	46	1	
Diplomat	JBC	46	3	
Diplomat, frozen	SC	214	2	
Down East Indian	WC	128	2	B
Farina	SC	187	1	
Farina	JOC	698	1	B
Farina mold	NYTI	299	2	B
Fig (see also fig pudding)				
Baked	JOC	701	1	C
Frozen	SC	215	2	
Steamed	SC	190	2	

RECIPE	BOOK	PAGE	TD	S
◆	AC	731	2	
◆	JBC	46	1	
◆	NYT	588	2	C
◆	FFCB	616	2	B
◆	JBC	46	1	
Finnish whipped fruit	MC	208	2	B
Fruit				
Dried	SC	193	2	
English	SC	201	3	
Suet, steamed	JOC	703	2	C
Gelatin	JOC	695		
Ginger, steamed	AC	731	2	
Gooseberry tapioca	SC	198	1	
Grant Thomas	SC	193	1	
Grape, chilled	MCIC	444	1	B
Grateful, w sour lemon sauce	MSE	195	2	C
Harlequin	SC	214	2	
Indian	NYT	588	2	B
◆	AC	732	2	
◆	JOC	698	2	B
◆	SC	187	2	
◆	FFCB	613	2	B
◆	JBC	47	2	B
◆	BBA	227	2	B
◆	FG	288	3	C
Indian, baked	GHAC	298	2	B
Lemon	FFCB	612	1	B
Lemon cake	AC	727	1	
Lemon, steamed	JBC	45	2	B
Macaroon chocolate	SC	204	2	
Macaroon fruit	SC	200	1	
Maple bread	GHAC	298	2	B
Maple rice	AC	734	2	
Marshmallow	JOC	697	2	B
Marshmallow icebox	SC	135	3	B
Matzo apple	SC	194	1	
Matzo batter	SC	194	2	
Mincemeat	WC	129	2	B

RECIPE	BOOK	PAGE	TD	S
Pudding (*cont.*)				
Mix, chocolate	BTSB	250	1	C
Mix, vanilla	BTSB	251	1	C
Mocha nut	WC	141	2	B
Molasses, steamed	BCC	143	2	B
Mold, farina	NYTI	299	2	B
Nesselrode	SC	203	2	
Nesselrode	JOC	694	3	B
Noodle (see noodle pudding)				
Oatmeal & date, steamed	SC	190	2	
Ohio	FFCB	615	3	B
Orange bread w vanilla sauce, molded	BBA	211	2	C
Orange & lemon	WC	136	1	B
Persimmon	JOC	702	1	B
Persimmon & date	GHAC	298	2	B
Pie, Tyler	FFBB	101	1	B
Pineapple, baked	SC	197	1	
Plum (see also plum pudding)				
Flaming	BBA	213	3	C
Regal	BHGN	174	3	C
Steamed	JOC	704	2	C
Potato for passover	SC	194	1	
Prune	SC	193	2	
Prune, molded	SC	197	1	
Prune, steamed	JBC	46	1	
Pumpkin	NYT	589	1	B
Pumpkin	AC	733	1	
Raisin, steamed	JBC	46	1	
Red fruit w frozen berries	NYTI	84	1	B
Rennet	JOC	695	3	B
Rice (see also rice pudding)				
Rice, creamy	MC	193	1	B
Rum custard	NYTI	449	2	B
Rum, frozen	SC	215	2	
Rum, raisin	WC	144	1	B
Sauce for plum & other puddings	AC	742	1	
Semolina, glazed	CIC	430	2	B
Snow	FFCB	622	2	B
Snow	SC	201	1	
Spinach dessert	AC	730	1	
Steamed	JOC	702		
Steamed	FFCB	603		
Steamed lemon	JBC	45	2	B
Steaming	SC	189		
Sterling	FFCB	616	3	B
Suet	AC	731	2	
Suet steamed	SC	191	2	
Summer	CF	151	1	B
Summer	AC	753	1	
Summer	FFCB	656	3	B
Sweet potato	JOC	702	1	B
Sweet potato	VGCB	299	1	B
Tapioca	AC	733	1	
w Crushed fruit	JOC	699	1	B
w Currant jelly	SC	198	1	
Fluff	BHGN	172	2	C
Gooseberry	SC	198	1	
Old fashioned	AC	733	1	
Pearl	JOC	700	1	B
Thanksgiving	FFCB	617	3	B
Tipsy	FFCB	531	1	B
Tipsy ladyfingers	FFCB	531	2	B
Vanilla	FFCB	610	1	B
◆	AC	725	1	
◆	BCC	141	1	B
◆	BTSB	251	1	B
◆	BHGN	172	2	B
Vanilla cream	SC	204	2	
Whole wheat, steamed	SC	191	2	

RECIPE	BOOK	PAGE	TD	S
Wine	FGCW	390	1	
Yorkshire (see Yorkshire pudding)				
Puerco en adobo (pork in chili sauce)	NYTI	470	2	B
Puff cakes, cornstarch	JOC	633	1	C
Puff pancake (see pancake, puff)				
Puff paste	SC	343	3	
Puff paste	JOC	593	3	
Almond cake	LM	273	2	
Cheese straws, crescent	LT	420	1	
Classic	LT	406		
Egg yolk	LM	265	2	
Fast	LT	411	1	
Glazed	LM	315	2	C
Patty shells	SC	343	2	
Pears in caramel on	LM	285	2	B
Pie shell	SC	343	2	
Rough	AC	640	1	
Sea trout or bass in	LM	105	3	C
Stuffed	JOC	55	3	
Tart shells	SC	343	2	
Zucchini	LM	136	1	B
Puff pastry (blaetter teig)	SC	343	3	
◆	MFC2	110	2	
◆	GF	249	2	C
◆	MFC	200	3	C
◆	NYT	536	3	
◆	SP	336		
◆	AC	637	2	
All about	FFCB	597		
All about	FFBB	71		
Almond cream baked in	MFC2	468	3	B

RECIPE	BOOK	PAGE	TD	S
Apple or pear tart baked in	MFC2	457	2	B
Basic	FFCB	598	2	B
Cheese tart, peekaboo	MFC2	140	3	B
Classic	FFBB	71	3	B
Classic French for vol au vent	MFC2	118	3	B
Cocktail shells	MFC2	133		
Cream	FAIC	440	1	B
Cream rolls	MFC2	139		
Horns	MFC2	135	2	
Kinds of	MFC2	111		
Making (photographs)	NYT	538		
Mock, for tarts	NYT	540	2	B
Perfect	MSE	237	3	C
Puffs for decorations	MFC2	132		
Sausages, baked in	MFC2	304	3	C
Shells for fruit tarts, forming	MFC2	454		
Shells, forming	MFC2	454		
Simple, flaky	MFC2	113	3	B
Whole wheat	FFBB	74	2	B
Puff ring, Gruyere	BCC	35	1	B
Puff shells, filling	MAFC	180		
Puff shells, freezing	MAFC	180		
Puffed eggs	AC	107	1	
Puffs, large	MAFC	179	2	C
Puffs, small	MAFC	178	2	C
Pulled bread	CBB	597	1	B
Pullman bread	LM	255	2	B
Pumpernickel	SC	69	2	C
Pumpernickel	BHGN	62	2	B
Bread	NYT	466	2	C
Bread	CBB	168	3	B
Bread	FFBB	476	2	C
Bread, American style	FFBB	477	2	C

RECIPE	BOOK	PAGE	TD	S
Pumpernickel (*cont.*)				
Bread, Red River	CBB	227	2	B
Cheese crisps	MIE	298	1	B
Cheese heart	CBB	544	3	B
Dark	BCC	45	2	C
Monday	VE	38	2	B
Rye bread	GHAC	358	2	C
Sourdough	NYT	467	2	C
Sourdough	CBB	295	3	C
Supreme	JBGF	575	2	C
Westphalian	CBB	150	3	B
Pumpkin	AC	542		
Pumpkin	SC	431	1	
All about	VGCB	228		
Baked	VGCB	230	1	
Baked Alaska	BBA	213	3	C
Baked w ginger	NYT	399	1	B
Bars	BHGN	157	1	C
Beef pot roasted w	GG	330	2	B
Bisque, velvety	GHAC	97	1	B
Boiled	VGCB	230	1	
Bread	JBGF	590	2	B
◆	FFBB	557	2	C
◆	GHAC	365	2	C
◆	SC	71	1	C
◆	MSE	298	2	B
◆	BBA	182	2	C
◆	FFCB	487	2	B
◆	BCC	36	2	C
Bread, grated	VGCB	236	1	B
Bread spicy	MIE	305	1	C
Brulee	VGCB	233	1	B
Cake	FFBB	346	1	C
Cake	BCC	68	1	C
Canned, uses for	AC	559		
Canning	BHGN	142		
Casserole	FFCB	407	2	B
Cheese pie	VGCB	235	1	B
Cheesecake	BCC	137	2	C
Cheesecake w a nut crust	YGM	234	3	C
Chiffon pie	VGCB	236	1	B
Chiffon pie	FFBB	123	2	B
Chiffon pie	EBE	170	1	B
Chiffon pie, coconut &	BBA	205	2	B
Conserve	BBA	169	1	B
Cookies	FFBB	209	2	C
Cookies	JBGF	609	1	C
Cranberry cookies	VGCB	236	1	C
Custard pie or squash	AC	627	1	
Drop cookies	BHGN	160	1	C
Freezing	BHGN	142		
Fruitcake	GG	332	2	C
Gelatin chiffon pie	JOC	615	2	B
& Ginger ice cream	VGCB	235	2	B
Gingerbread	MHGD	283	1	B
Gnocchi & prosciutto	GG	330	1	B
Ice cream	MHGD	435	1	C
Kebabs	OC	97	2	B
Keeping fresh	SC	431		
Leek soup	BBA	41	3	B
Loaf, Joan's	MHGD	258	1	B
Molasses cake	BHGN	94	1	C
Molasses pie	MSE	196	2	B
Mousse	GG	331	3	B
Mousse, ginger	SP	286	2	B
Mousse, super easy	VGCB	234	1	B
Muffins	FFBB	560	1	C
Muffins	VGCB	236	1	C
Muffins	BHGN	87	1	C
Cornmeal	FFBB	561	1	C
Cranberry	VGCB	236	1	C
Prune, whole wheat	FFBB	561	1	C
Nut bread	BHGN	79	1	B
Or squash custard pie	AC	627	1	

RECIPE	BOOK	PAGE	TD	S
Or squash pie	AC	626	1	
Or squash spice cake	AC	671	1	
Orange chiffon pie	JBGF	631	2	B
Pancakes, oat	JBGF	500	1	B
Parmesan	JBGF	527	2	B
& Parsnips pureed w cannellini beans	VGCB	230	1	C
Peas	JBGF	526	1	B
Pie	MHGD	158	2	B
◆	BHGN	282	1	B
◆	FFCB	587	2	B
◆	JBC	40	1	
◆	JOC	605	2	B
◆	JBGF	632	2	C
◆	SC	350	2	
◆	NYT	527	1	B
◆	SP	303	2	B
◆	BCC	92	2	B
◆	FFBB	131	2	B
Frozen	SC	350	1	
Frozen	BCC	94	2	B
No fault	MC	195	1	B
Or squash	AC	626	1	
Pecan crunch	GHAC	318	2	
Praline	BCC	92	2	B
Sour cream	NYT	527	2	B
Sour cream	FFBB	131	2	B
Sour cream	GHAC	318	2	C
Spice blend	BBA	165	1	
Ultimate	GG	332	1	B
Pot-roasted beef w	GG	330	2	B
Preparing	GG	322		
Prosciutto & gnocchi	GG	330	1	B
Pudding	AC	733	1	
Pudding	NYT	589	1	B
Puree	BBA	134	1	B
Puree of winter squash & white beans	MFC2	404	1	B
Puree, shrimp &	NYTI	468	1	B
Puree, white beans &	MFC2	404	1	B
Ring	NYT	398	1	B
Rolls	GG	329	2	C
Scramble, easy	VGCB	230	1	B
Seed				
Salted & roasted	BTSB	287	1	B
Sauce	BBA	161	1	B
Toasted	BBA	16	1	B
Variations	VGCB	230	1	
Shell, beef stew in	BBA	96	3	B
Shell, beef stew & pumpkin in a	VGCB	232	2	B
Shell w stuffed rice	VGCB	231	1	B
Shrimp, puree	NYTI	468	1	B
Souffle, chilled	VGCB	233	2	B
Souffle, cold	BBA	214	2	B
Soup	GF	79	2	C
◆	JBGF	322	2	B
◆	NYTI	127	1	B
◆	NYT	72	1	B
◆	JOC	160	1	B
◆	FFCB	85	1	B
◆	FGCW	106	2	C
Brandied	BBA	41	2	C
w Bread, Haitian	NYTI	339	1	B
Creamy	CBSS	345	2	B
Curried	CBSS	341	1	B
Curried	BBA	41	2	B
Iced, cream of	CBSS	340	3	B
In a pumpkin	MSE	188	2	B
Inside	VGCB	231	2	B
Served in a pumpkin	MFC2	361	2	B
Spice cake	AC	671	1	
Spice cake (or squash)	AC	671	1	
Steamed	VGCB	230	1	
Stuffed	MFC2	361	2	B

RECIPE	BOOK	PAGE	TD	S
Pumpkin (*cont.*)				
Stuffed	VE	159	2	B
Sweet potato dessert, chilled	VGCB	234	1	C
Things to do w	SPGT	226		
Tortelli, Modena style	FAIC	174	2	B
Walnut bread	CBB	412	1	C
Yeast bread, Toni Greenwald's	VGCB	237	1	C
Punch				
Base for a party	BHGN	48	2	
Basic fruit & variations	FFCB	743	1	B
Burgundy, sparkling	NYT	651	1	C
Champagne	JOC	49	2	
◆	NYT	652	1	C
◆	FFCB	742	2	C
◆	SC	57	1	
Bordelaise	NYT	650	1	
Creole	FFCB	742	1	C
Mock	SC	57	1	
Sherbet	SC	57	1	
Wedding	NYT	653	1	C
Cider	FFCB	743	1	C
Citrus rum	BHGN	47	1	C
Cranberry	SC	56	1	
Cranberry, hot	BCC	21	1	C
Cranberry, sparkling	BCC	21	1	C
Cranberry wine	JBGF	288	1	C
Creamy, reception	BHGN	49	1	C
Easy sherbet	BHGN	49	1	
Egg milk	SC	63	1	
Fish house	FFCB	743	2	C
Fish house	JOC	49	1	
Fish house	BB	165	1	C
Fruit	JOC	35	1	
For 50 people	JOC	35	2	C
Foundation	SC	55	1	
Hot	SC	57	1	B
Lemonade	SC	55	1	C
w Lemon ice	SC	55	1	B
Sparkling	SC	56	1	C
Grenadine	BHGN	49	1	C
Imperial	SC	64	1	
Jamaican	NYT	651	1	C
James Beard's	NYT	653	2	C
Lemon ginger	SC	57	1	
Milk	JOC	47	1	B
Milk, hot	JOC	48	1	B
Mocha	JOC	35	2	
Moonlight	SC	56	1	
Moselle	SC	57	3	C
Moselle	NYT	653	2	C
Nonalcoholic	BHGN	48	2	
Orange ice fruit	SC	55	1	B
Pastel	BHGN	49	1	
Pineapple	JOC	35	1	
Pineapple orange	NYT	649	1	B
Pineapple rum	NYTI	504	2	C
Planter's	JOC	46	1	A
Planter's	SC	63	1	
Regent	FFCB	742	1	C
Rum	JOC	46	1	A
Rum	FFCB	742	2	C
Rum	NYTI	20	1	C
Rum, French	NYTI	309	1	C
Slushy	BHGN	48	3	C
Spiked, party	BHGN	48	2	
Spiked, slushy	BHGN	48	3	C
Strawberry broth	SC	58	2	
Strawberry fruit	SC	56	1	C
Strawberry fruit	JOC	35	2	
Summer	NYT	650	1	B
Tea	SC	56	1	B
Tomato	JOC	34	1	C
Trinidad	NYTI	548	3	C
Tropical tea	NYT	651	3	C

RECIPE	BOOK	PAGE	TD	S
Quenelle (*cont.*)				
De brochet	NYTI	138	3	B
Fish	MAFC	185	3	B
Fish & oysters	MAFC	188	2	B
Fish w lobster sauce	JOC	194	3	B
For soup	JOC	173	3	
Gratineed w white wine sauce	MAFC	188	2	B
Lobster	MAFC	189	2	B
Poached	JOC	194	3	B
Salmon	MAFC	189	2	B
Shrimp	MAFC	189	2	B
Turkey	MAFC	189	2	B
Veal	MAFC	189	2	B
Quesados (Mexican tortilla sandwiches)	GHAC	87	1	C
Quiche	MFC	40	2	B
Artichoke, no crust	GHAC	114	1	B
Asparagus	GHAC	114	1	B
Asparagus	JBGF	486	2	B
Asparagus	FG	103	1	B
Basic, crustless	FG	107	1	C
w Bay scallops	NYT	28	1	C
w Broccoli & Swiss cheese	FG	104	2	B
w Broccoli, whole wheat crust	GHAC	114	1	B
California w chilies	GHAC	114	1	B
w Camembert cheese	MAFC	148	2	B
Casseroles, individual	BHGN	203	1	B
w Cheese & bacon	FFCB	301	2	B
w Cheese & beef	SC	232	1	
Chicken	BCC	166	1	B
Clam	AC	172	1	
Crab	BCC	166	1	B
Crab	MAFC	149	2	B
Crabmeat	EBE	18	2	B

RECIPE	BOOK	PAGE	TD	S
Crabmeat	NYT	27	1	C
Cream bacon	MAFC	147	2	B
Creamy zucchini	BBA	121	3	B
Crust	FG	102	1	B
Crustless	JOC	208	2	
Custard, basic	SP	5	1	C
Eggplant, tomatoes & olives	FFCB	301	2	B
Endive	MAFC	152	2	B
Fillings, favorite	SP	5	1	
Garden, crustless	FG	108	1	C
Individual crustless	FG	109	2	C
Kinds of	MFC	147	1	B
Leek	MAFC	151	2	B
Leek	FG	105	2	B
Lobster	MAFC	149	2	B
Lorraine	JOC	227	2	B
◆	NYT	27	1	C
◆	SC	232	1	
◆	MAFC	147	2	B
◆	BHGN	203	2	B
◆	JBC	30	1	B
◆	BCC	166	1	B
Making (drawings)	MAFC	143		
Miniature	SP	5	2	C
Mushroom	MAFC	152	2	B
Mushroom	FG	206	1	B
Mushroom	BCC	166	1	B
Onion	VGCW	183	1	B
Onion	MAFC	150	2	B
Onion & caraway, crustless	FG	107	1	C
Rich, cocktail	JOC	55		
Roquefort cheese	MAFC	148	2	B
Rules for a good	FG	102		
Seafood	BBA	121	3	B
◆	BHGN	203	2	B
◆	FG	104	2	B
◆	NYTI	115	2	B

RECIPE	BOOK	PAGE	TD	S
Shrimp	MAFC	149	2	B
Spinach	MAFC	153	2	B
Spinach	MIE	63	1	C
Spinach	GHAC	114	1	B
Spinach & feta cheese	FG	106	2	B
Swiss cheese	MAFC	147	2	B
Swiss cheese & mushroom	MC	111	1	B
Tomato, anchovies & olives	MAFC	148	2	B
w Tomato & chicken	BBA	72	2	B
Zucchini	VE	154	2	B
w Zucchini & rice	JBGF	487	1	B
Quick appetizers	GHAC	90		
Quick batter bread	AC	788	2	
Quick bread, basic, master recipe	FFBB	546	1	C
Quick breads	FFBB	541		
Quick breads, ingredients for	FFBB	544		
Quick on the side	KIS	367	1	A
Quick reuben salad	BHGN	348	1	B
Quick sauce for vegetables	BHGN	388	1	
Quick stock	JOC	490	1	B
Quick stock, household	JOC	490	1	
Quince				
Apple jelly	FFCB	703	2	C
Baked	JOC	121	1	
Baked	AC	769	1	
Beef stew w	NYTI	329	2	B
Compote	NYTI	336	1	B
Conserve	SC	445	1	
Glaze	GHAC	164	1	A
Jelly (see jelly, quince)				
Preserves	JOC	778	2	C
Preserves	SC	440	1	
Preserves	NYTI	336	2	B
Baked	SC	442	2	
Spicy	MSE	219	2	B
w Sweet apple	SC	440	2	
Spiced	NYT	505	2	B
Torte	NYTI	338	2	C

R

RECIPE	BOOK	PAGE	TD	S
Rabbit				
A la mode	JOC	452	3	
Beer	BHGN	204	1	B
Beer braised	BHGN	270	3	B
Buying & preparing for cooking	MFC2	246		
Chokes gibelotte	VGCB	140	3	B
Civet	JOC	452	3	
Forestiere, ragout of	SP	107	3	B
Fricassee	JOC	453	3	
Fried	FFCB	225	1	B
Fried, plain	FGCW	233	2	B
w Green peppercorns & wine sauce	FGCW	234	2	B
Grilling	SC	334		
w Hare sauce & pappardelle	FAIC	151	2	B
Hasenpfeffer	JOC	452	3	
Hasenpfeffer	NYT	177	3	B
In wine, stewed	CIC	320	2	B
Jambalaya	PPLK	217	2	B
Larding & basting (photographs)	OC	82		
Marinated vinegar, stewed in red wine	MFC2	247	3	B

RECIPE	BOOK	PAGE	TD	S
Rabbit (*cont.*)				
w Mustard sauce	FGCW	231	1	B
Paneed fettuccine	PPLK	163	3	B
Pate	NYT	9	3	C
Pine nuts & currants	SPGT	56	3	B
Prunes	LM	192	3	B
Prunes	LM	192	3	B
Red wine	FGCW	230	3	B
Roast	JOC	453	3	
Salad, white	MC	45	1	B
Sauce, piquant	PPLK	141	3	B
Sauce, tortelli &	FAIC	173	2	B
Sauteed	JOC	453	3	
Sauteed w bacon & sour cream	AC	246	1	
Sauteed w cream	FFCB	225	1	B
Smothered	PPLK	147	3	B
& Smothered onions	JOC	453	3	
Stew, French	NYTI	205	2	B
Stewed	BCC	260	2	B
Stewed in red wine w fettuccine	CPPC	134	3	B
Stewed w white wine	CIC	320	2	B
Stewing	SC	334		
Stock	JOC	491	2	B
Stuffed w artichoke & tarragon	FAIC	327	2	B
Sweet & sour sauce	FAIC	329	2	B
Tenderloin w mustard sauce	PPLK	280	3	B
Thawing	MFC2	247		
Tomato	VE	214	1	B
Vermouth	FGCW	232	2	B
Wine	NYTI	206	2	B
Young, broiled	OC	128	2	B
Young, spit roasted w mustard	OC	127	2	B

RECIPE	BOOK	PAGE	TD	S
Rabbit's carrot cake	FFBB	351	1	C
Rabbits out of olives, carving (photographs)	LT	28		
Raccoon	JOC	454	2	
Rachel sandwiches	BCC	316	1	B
Raclette (cheese)	SPGT	376		
Radicchio				
Buckwheat noodles, pancetta &	CPPC	91	2	B
& Endive, skillet braised	GHAC	256	1	B
Grilled	MSQC	189	1	B
& Lima bean salad	MSQC	153	1	B
Pizza, pancetta &	CPPC	162	3	B
Salad	GRIL	90	1	B
Salad, lima bean &	MSQC	153	1	B
Taglierini w mussels, in anchovy cream	CPPC	146	2	B
Radish				
Accordions, making	BHGN	440		
All about	VGCB	238		
Baby, raw	VGCB	239	1	
Bites	FFCB	58	1	B
Black, canapes	JOC	60	1	
Cheese salad	YGM	83	1	A
Chinese	NYT	423	1	A
Chinese style	VGCB	241	1	B
Cooked	JOC	300	1	
Dip, Susan Mayer's	VGCB	240	1	B
Finishing touches for cooked	VGCB	239	1	
Garnishes	VGCB	241	1	
Hors d'oeuvre	JOC	70	1	
Jerusalem artichoke & watercress salad	VGCB	140	1	B

RECIPE	BOOK	PAGE	TD	S
Oranges	VGCB	241	1	B
Preserves	SC	441	1	
Salad	NYT	423	2	B
Chinese	JBGF	547	1	B
Orange	BBA	145	2	B
Red	CF	94	1	B
Variations	VGCB	240	1	B
Sliced, sauteed	VGCB	239	1	
Snow peas, papaya & carrots	GF	209	1	B
Steamed	VGCB	239	1	
Sticks, beef w	FGCW	327	1	B
Top soup	VGCB	240	1	B
Vinaigrette & variations	VGCB	240	1	
Ragout				
Beef	NYTI	171	2	B
Beef of	NYT	97	2	B
De mutton	MAFC	344	2	
De pattes	NYTI	27	2	B
De poulet	NYTI	225	2	B
Des pauvres	NYTI	203	2	B
Fin	JOC	442	2	B
Mushroom, chicken liver	GHAC	168	1	B
Oxtail	AC	323	2	
Pasta, summer vegetable	CPPC	81	2	B
Pork au vin rouge	NYTI	182	3	C
Potatoes	VE	147	1	B
Rabbit forestiere	SP	107	3	B
Sauce	MAFC	69	1	C
Sweetbread	SPGT	96	3	B
Toulousaine	NYTI	226	3	B
Veal & chestnut	GHAC	211	2	B
Veal salsify	VGCB	259	2	B
Vegetable fall	CPMC	140	1	B
Winter pork & fruit	SP	132	3	B

RECIPE	BOOK	PAGE	TD	S
Rags (deep fried pastry snacks)	FAIC	457	1	B
Rainbow trout, broiled	FFCB	125	1	B
Raised egg pastry	SC	343	2	
Raised loaf cake	AC	691	1	
Raisin	FFCB	611	2	B
Almond braid	GHAC	359	2	B
Apple & cranberry pie	FFCB	584	2	B
Applesauce cake	SP	270	1	C
Apricot bread	SP	251	1	B
Bars	FFBB	233	2	C
Bars, oatmeal	BHGN	155	1	C
Bars, old fashioned	BHGN	156	1	C
Braised, sweet & sour onions	MFC2	410	1	B
Bread	AC	781	2	
◆	BHGN	64	2	B
◆	SC	68	2	B
◆	SC	86	1	
◆	MFC2	82	3	C
◆	JOC	556	1	
Familia	CBB	507	2	C
German	CBB	484	3	C
Glazed	CBB	479	3	B
Health food	MHGD	275	1	B
Brioche	MFC2	93	3	C
Brown bread	FFCB	495	2	B
Cake, apples &	MHGD	98	1	C
Cheese brioche	CBB	668	3	C
Cider	JOC	331	1	B
Clusters	BCC	120	2	C
Coffee cake	CBB	510	3	C
Coffee cake, spice	BCC	33	1	B
Cookies	FFCB	550	1	C
Oatmeal	SP	258	1	C
Oatmeal, spicy	BHGN	159	1	C
Whole wheat	JBGF	610	1	C

RECIPE	BOOK	PAGE	TD	S
Raisin (*cont.*)				
Cranberry bread	GHAC	365	2	C
Cream pie	AC	623	1	
Crepes, cheese	MFC	234	1	B
Crisscross pie	BHGN	277	1	B
Cupcakes	SC	141	1	C
Custard, apricot	MSQC	205	1	B
Egg bread	MFC2	84	3	C
Filling	JOC	647	1	B
Filling	SC	149	1	
Filling & frosting, coconut	FFBB	405	1	C
Flat bread	CBB	429	3	B
Icing	JOC	673	1	B
Muffins	FFCB	489	1	C
Muffins, bran &	BTSB	127	1	B
Muffins, bran &	BCC	31	1	C
Nut				
Bread	FFCB	471	2	C
Bread	FFBB	460	2	C
Bread	CBB	489	3	B
Clusters	BCC	120	2	C
Cookies	MHGD	316	1	C
Mix	FFCB	72	1	B
Oatmeal bread	CBB	216	1	B
Onions, sweet & sour braised w	MFC2	410	1	B
Orange bread	CBB	491	3	C
Pecan pie, spiced	FFBB	144	1	B
Pie	FFBB	91	2	B
◆	FFCB	584	1	B
◆	SC	346	1	
◆	MIE	337	1	B
◆	AC	623	1	
Buttermilk	AC	624	1	
Cranberry &	SC	345	1	
Lattice topped	GHAC	315	2	B
Sour cream	NYT	527	2	B
Sour cream	MSE	247	2	B
Sour cream	BHGN	282	3	C
Pork chops, caramelized, w walnuts	MSQC	40	1	B
Pudding, steamed	JBC	46	1	
Puff, steamed	SC	190	1	
Pumpernickel	SP	242	3	C
Refrigerator cookies	AC	701	2	
Rice w almonds &	SMG	51	1	B
Rice pilaf w nuts &	AC	579	1	
Rice pudding	SC	187	1	
Rye bread	CBB	146	3	C
Rye, Jewish	FFBB	478	2	B
Salad, carrot &	BCC	285	1	B
Sauce	BCC	330	1	B
◆	SC	391	1	
◆	BHGN	359	1	B
◆	SC	388	1	
◆	FFCB	273	1	B
◆	JOC	710	1	B
Sauce, buttered	GHAC	195	1	B
Schiacciata (cake)	FAIC	473	2	B
Sour cream pie	BCC	88	2	B
Spice cookies	SC	161	1	
Sundae cake	BCC	133	1	C
Tarts	FFCB	596	2	C
Waffles	JOC	217	1	B
Wheat bread, Beard's	JBGF	561	2	C
Wheat bread, ginger	FFBB	460	2	B
Wine	SC	438	3	
Raita (cucumbers w yogurt)	MC	72	1	B
Raita	BBA	142	1	B
Raita	NYTI	361	1	B
Raita sauce	CFS	318	1	B
Ramaki	EBE	24	2	C
Ramequin (hot puff cheese dish)	MFC2	130	3	B
w Artichoke puree	VE	179	2	B
Eggs baked in	MAFC	123	1	A
Three cheese	VE	178	1	A

RECIPE	BOOK	PAGE	TD	S
Ranch salad	AC	604	1	
Ranch salad w sauerkraut	AC	604	1	
Ranch style eggs	GHAC	111	1	B
Ranger cookies	BHGN	159	1	C
Rape sausage	FAIC	353	2	B
Rape, sauteed	FAIC	420	1	B
Rarebit	MC	84	1	B
Beer	SC	233	1	
Cheese & tomato	SC	233	1	
Hamburger	BB	25	1	A
Noodle	JOC	189	1	B
Oyster	SC	254	1	
Oyster	JOC	366	1	B
Tomato	FFCB	352	1	B
Tomato	BBA	111	2	B
Tomato	JOC	242	2	B
Raspberry				
Apple crumble	MSQC	129	1	B
Apple jelly	SC	449	1	
Bavarian	MHGD	367	1	B
Bavarian cream	MAFC	600	3	C
Bombe	JOC	719	2	C
Bombe glace	SC	215	2	
Brush	CFS	305	1	B
Cake, black	CW	69	1	B
Caramel Napoleon	NSD	180	3	C
Cassis	MHGD	401	1	B
Chicken	SP	87	2	B
Chicken cutlets	SPGT	88	1	B
Chiffon pie	BHGN	284	2	B
Chiffon pie	FFBB	125	2	B
Chocolate truffles	NSD	79	3	C
Cookies w cinnamon	NSD	68	3	C
Cordial	SP	280	3	B
Cordial	AC	770	1	
Cream	MSQC	105	1	A
Cream	MAFC	608	2	C
Cream	SC	204	2	
Cream freeze	JBC	112	1	B
Cream pie	JOC	602	2	B
Crepes	BCC	139	2	B
Currant				
Jam	FFCB	703	2	B
Jelly, black	SC	449	1	
Preserves	FFCB	705	2	C
Sauce	BCC	154	1	B
Custard	BCC	140	1	B
Custard, rennet	SC	200	1	
Custard tart	NSD	104	2	B
Dreams	EBE	178	1	C
Filled melon	EBE	185	2	B
Fool	VE	284	1	B
Frozen yogurt	BTSB	67	2	B
Glace pie	BCC	89	2	B
w Grand Marnier sauce	MSE	168	1	B
Hard sauce	FFCB	641	1	B
Ice	SC	210	2	
Ice	FFCB	636	3	C
Ice	FGCW	398	3	B
Ice I	JOC	722	2	C
Ice II	JOC	723	2	B
Ice cream	AC	737	3	
Ice cream	MFC2	418	2	B
Ice cream	JOC	717	2	C
Jam	MSE	133	1	C
Jam	JOC	776	2	
Jam	FFCB	703	2	B
Jam, currant	FFCB	703	2	B
Jelly	FFCB	703	2	C
Black	SC	449	1	
Currant	JOC	774	2	
Currant	FFCB	702	2	C
Currant	SC	447	2	
Gooseberry	JOC	775	2	
Juice, currant	SC	436	1	
Kirsch	BB	159	1	
Liqueur	JBC	111	1	

RECIPE	BOOK	PAGE	TD	S
Raspberry (*cont.*)				
Liqueur pound cake	FFBB	367	2	C
Marinade vinegar	GRIL	34	1	B
Marzipan tart	NSD	86	2	B
Mousse cake, chocolate	NSD	258	3	B
Muffins, streusel	SPGT	125	2	B
Other fruits	JBC	111	1	
Parfait	JOC	721	2	C
Peaches	AC	763	1	
Pie	BHGN	279	1	B
◆	SP	279	2	B
◆	AC	618	1	
◆	BCC	85	1	B
Pie, French	NYT	528	1	B
Pineapple	BB	159	1	
Poached carrots	SP	164	3	B
Preserves	SC	440	3	
Puff pastry	MFC	225	3	B
Puree	AC	770	1	
Puree, strawberries &	AC	773	1	
Rennet custard	SC	200	1	
Ribbons	FFBB	246	1	C
Romanoff	BCC	132	2	B
Rum cake	JOC	640	2	
Salad, frozen	BCC	293	3	C
Salad, shrimp, haricots verts &	SPGT	157	2	B
Sauce	FFBB	421	2	C
◆	JBC	43	1	
◆	GHAC	290	1	B
◆	BBA	215	1	
◆	GF	250	1	
◆	MHGD	377	1	B
◆	NSD	327	1	C
For figs stuffed w raspberries	MSQC	93	1	B
Fresh	NYT	616	1	B
Pears, poached & pistachios w	GF	238	1	B
Poached peaches w	LM	292	1	B
Rhubarb &	NSD	328	1	C
Strawberries, fresh w	MHGD	397	1	B
Strawberries, honeyed w	MHGD	398	1	B
Strawberry &	MHGD	380	1	
Sauternes dessert soup	SP	280	2	B
Sherbet	MFC	145	2	B
Sherbet	NYT	628	2	B
Sherbet	JOC	724	2	B
Sherbet, fresh	MFC2	418	2	B
Sherbet, red or black	SC	212	2	
Shrub	SC	54	1	B
Souffle	LM	318	1	B
Souffle, cold	FFCB	625	3	B
Souffle, frozen	FFCB	627	3	B
Soup	CBSS	170	1	B
Spareribs brushed w	CFS	265	2	B
Sparkling	BBA	214	1	B
Squares, Aunt Leah's	MHGD	248	2	C
Stuffed figs	MSQC	93	1	A
Supreme, strawberry &	EBE	185	1	B
Syrup	SC	54	1	
Tart	GF	224	2	B
Fig &	SP	279	2	B
Puff pastry shell	MSE	118	3	C
Royale	GHAC	317	2	C
Tea squares	MIE	329	1	C
Vinegar	BCC	299	1	B
◆	MIE	244	3	C
◆	AC	770	1	
◆	FGCW	379	3	B

RECIPE	BOOK	PAGE	TD	S
Whipped cream	FAIC	497	1	B
w Yogurt sauce	KIS	328	1	A
Raspberryade	SC	55	1	C
Ratatouille	SC	434	1	
◆	VE	155	2	B
◆	AC	519	1	
◆	MAFC	503	2	B
◆	NYTI	256	1	B
◆	VGCB	108	1	B
◆	JBGF	520	1	B
◆	SP	167	2	C
◆	BB	136	1	B
◆	BCC	349	1	B
◆	FG	333	1	C
◆	MC	119	1	B
◆	GF	232	3	C
A la nicoise	BBA	108	3	B
Base	YGM	47	1	B
Best	JBGF	520	1	B
Chicken breasts	YGM	46	1	B
Crepes	JBGF	504	1	B
Fish fillets	JBGF	450	1	B
Hot pepper	SPGT	140	1	B
Lemon basil	SPGT	165	2	B
Nicoise	NYT	411	2	B
Omelet	MSE	96	2	C
Pita pizza	JBGF	305	1	C
Provencale	JOC	278	2	B
Roasted peppers	GHAC	241	2	C
Salad	BCC	284	2	B
Sausage	BBA	98	2	C
Sausage Italian	CF	82	2	B
Shrimp & eggplant pie	GG	165	2	B
Shrimp pie	GG	165	2	B
Tartlets	GF	177	2	C
Ravani (cake)	NYTI	337	2	C
Ravigote butter	SP	116	1	B
Crab	FFCB	439	1	B
Sauce	JOC	311	1	B

RECIPE	BOOK	PAGE	TD	S
Sauce	SC	387	1	
Sauce, hot	JOC	325	1	
Ravioli	JOC	191	1	
Ravioli	NYTI	417	2	C
Ravioli	FFCB	300	3	C
Alla bardelli	NYT	332	3	C
Cheese	SC	337	2	
Cheese, duck soup &	MFC	75	3	B
Cheese filling for	GHAC	263	1	
w Chicken, ricotta & greens	CPPC	126	3	B
Duck	MFC	93	3	B
Duck & fresh herbs	MFC	94	3	B
Eggplant, stuffed	JBGF	390	2	B
Filling	JOC	191		
Filling, w veal, braised	NYTI	417	1	C
Fish, naked	FAIC	228	1	B
Five cheeses	BBA	103	3	B
Green garlic	CPPC	39	2	B
Intercontinental	JBGF	391	2	B
w Lobster & scallops	CPPC	138	3	B
Making	NYT	333		
Meat	SC	337	2	
w Mushrooms & sugar snap peas	MSQC	61	1	B
Naked	FAIC	228	1	B
Pan fried w bleu cheese dressing	FGCW	152	2	B
w Salt cod in fish broth	CPPC	140	3	B
Smashed potato	CPPC	128	3	B
w Spinach filling	GHAC	263	1	
Stuffing for veal	NYTI	417	1	B
& Swiss chard jumbo	GHAC	263	2	A
w Veal stuffing	NYTI	417	1	B
w Vegetable sauce	FGCW	152	1	B
Raw mushroom salad	MIE	269	1	B
Reception salad	AC	74	2	B
Red bean stew	AC	604	2	

RECIPE	BOOK	PAGE	TD	S
Red beans & rice	VGCB	14	1	B
Red butter peppers (burro rosso)	GG	277	1	B
Red butter sauce	MFC	106	1	B
Red cabbage w cranberries	VGCB	55	1	B
Red cabbage w pork, braised	MAFC	384	1	B
Red cake	SC	111	1	B
Red currant glaze	MAFC	594	1	A
Red currant glaze	SP	346	1	A
Red devil rub	CFS	285	1	A
Red devil's food cake	AC	677	1	
Red-eye gravy, ham w	FFCB	206	1	
Red-eye gravy, ham & grits w	GHAC	195	1	B
Red flannel hash	GHAC	179	1	B
◆	FFCB	161	1	B
◆	VGCB	27	1	B
◆	SC	303	1	
◆	GG	54	2	B
Red onion				
Bulgur	YGM	190	1	C
& Endive salad	MSQC	41	1	B
Quarters, grilled	GRIL	89	1	B
Salad, w fennel vinaigrette	CPMC	190	1	B
Salad, orange &	YGM	224	1	C
Wilted, & pickled beet salad	CW	100	2	B
Red pasta	FAIC	144	2	A
Red pepper				
& Basil w zabaglione sauce	CFS	314	1	A
& Broccoli salad	MSE	104	1	C
& Cheese bread	GG	281	2	C
Freezer jelly	GHAC	380	3	C
Frittata w mushrooms & ham	FFCB	343	1	B

RECIPE	BOOK	PAGE	TD	S
Hollandaise	CFS	310	1	B
Jelly	MSE	199	2	B
& Mushrooms, marinated	MSE	106	1	C
Pasta w red pepper strips & Parmesan	MSQC	37	3	B
Pother & eggplant (soup)	GG	159	2	B
Roasted	MSQC	148	1	B
Roasted sweet	CW	45	1	
Salad, orange	YGM	107	1	B
Sauce, spicy	GHAC	385	1	
Soup	CBSS	332	1	B
Soup, French	CBSS	333	1	B
& Zucchini saute & salad	VGCB	205	1	B
Red sauce	FAIC	59	1	B
Red sauce	CIC	30	1	B
Red sauce, Chinese	BBA	164	1	B
Red sauce, spicy	FAIC	61	1	B
Red snapper				
Antiboise	NYTI	143	1	B
Baked	NYT	252	1	B
Baked w grapefruit	NYT	252	1	B
Baked in parchment	MSQC	112	2	B
Baked, savory w tomato sauce	JOC	361	2	B
Butter w shallot sauce	SP	187	2	A
Chives & wild mushrooms	MFC	128	3	B
Creole	GHAC	140	2	C
Creole	NYTI	557	1	B
Fillets, Florida style	FFCB	117	1	B
Grilled w lovage leaves	GF	156	1	B
Grilled w tarragon butter	MSQC	96	1	B

RECIPE	BOOK	PAGE	TD	S
w Lime butter	GHAC	140	2	B
Marguery	SC	239	1	
Sauteed w mushrooms	CIC	217	2	B
Scallop mousse	MFC	130	3	B
Steamed fillet of tarragon butter	MFC	129	2	B
Stuffed & baked	FFCB	116	1	B
w Tarragon butter for grilled	MSQC	96	1	B
w Tomato sauce	SC	239	2	
Red velvet cake	AC	678	1	
Red & white blueberry mold	GHAC	293	2	C
Red wine				
Beef & mushrooms in	FGCW	203	2	C
Chicken w	BCC	247	1	B
Chicken in	FGCW	168	2	B
Dressing	BHGN	351	1	B
Drunken leeks in	GG	247	1	B
Onions, chicken, mushrooms & bacon in	MAFC	262	2	B
Rabbit in	FGCW	230	3	B
Sauce	JOC	711	1	B
Sauce, beefsteak w	GHAC	175	2	B
Soup	SC	405	1	
Soup	SC	488	1	
Red & yellow peppers, chicken w	SPGT	90	2	B
Redfish, blackened	PPLK	50	2	B
Reedbirds or ricebirds	AC	245		
Refried bean bake	BCC	174	1	B
Refried beans (frijoles refritos)	AC	605	3	
Refried beans	SC	183	3	
Refried beans, cheese &	FFCB	325	3	B
Refrigerator cakes	JOC	640	2	
Refrigerator cheesecake	SC	347	2	
Refrigerator cheesecake, rum	NYT	547	2	C
Refrigerator cookies	FFCB	562	1	C
Refrigerator cookies	BHGN	167	1	C
Butterscotch	AC	701	2	
Butterscotch	JOC	660	1	C
Chocolate	JOC	660	1	C
Chocolate	AC	701	2	
Chocolate	FFCB	562	1	C
Cinnamon	FFCB	562	1	C
Coconut	FFCB	562	1	C
Currant	AC	701	2	
Curry	FFBB	216	1	C
Date	AC	701	2	
Filled	AC	701	2	
Lemon or orange	AC	701	2	
Making	BCC	96		
Nut	AC	702	2	
Nut	FFCB	562	1	C
Nutmeg	FFCB	562	1	C
Oatmeal	BHGN	168	2	C
Or icebox	AC	700	2	
Orange or lemon	AC	701	2	
Pinwheel	AC	701	2	
Pinwheel	JOC	660	1	C
Prune	AC	701	2	
Raisin	FFCB	562	1	C
Raisin	AC	701	2	
Rolled oat	AC	701	2	
Spice	AC	701	2	
Sunflower seed	FFBB	218	2	C
Vanilla	JOC	659	1	C
Refrigerator doughs	JOC	569		
Refrigerator ice cream	FFCB	634	2	B

RECIPE	BOOK	PAGE	TD	S
Refrigerator lace cookies	JOC	660	1	C
Refrigerator rolls	FFBB	488	2	C
Refrigerator rolls	AC	780	2	
Bran	JOC	569	1	C
Ever ready	SC	75	2	
No knead	JOC	569	1	C
Potato	JOC	569	1	C
Whole grain	JOC	569	1	C
Refrigerator spice cookies	FFBB	216	1	C
Refritos (beans)	MC	143	2	B
Refritos	BBA	22	1	B
Regal fish shellfish	BBA	32	3	B
Regents torte	SC	132	2	B
Relish	BBA	166	1	A
Applesauce	SC	391	1	
Beet	FFCB	283	1	B
Beet	SC	456	3	
Beet & cabbage	NYT	493	1	C
Beets	VGCB	27	1	B
Cabbage-green	VGCB	49	2	B
Cabbage, green, tomato	NYT	493	3	C
Cabbage, marinated red	VGCB	49	2	B
Celery	FFCB	284	1	B
Celery	NYT	494	1	B
Celery	FFCB	713	2	B
Chili	OC	164	1	C
Corn	BHGN	146	1	
Corn	SC	456	2	
Corn	FFCB	712	2	C
Confetti	SC	457	1	
Ohio	NYT	495	1	B
Old fashioned	NYT	495	1	B
Quick	BBA	168	3	B
Quick, old fashioned	BBA	168	2	B
Tall grass	GG	130	2	B
Tangy	GHAC	385	2	C
Tart	JOC	784	3	C
Tomato	NYT	496	2	B
Cranberry	JBGF	646	1	B
Cranberry	PPLK	240	2	B
Apple	GHAC	383	1	B
Fresh	SC	261	3	
Mint	GHAC	384	1	C
Orange	FFCB	282	1	B
Orange, cooked	NYT	496	1	C
Orange, quick	MSQC	204	1	B
Pineapple	GHAC	383	1	B
Tangerine	GHAC	383	1	B
Uncooked	JOC	114	1	
Cucumber	SC	457	3	
Cucumber	BHGN	362	3	C
Cucumber tomato	BHGN	243	2	
Fireworks	SPGT	137	2	C
Green tomato	JOC	783	3	C
Green tomato	SC	457	3	
Herb tomato, hot	NYTI	490	1	B
w Hot chilies, a piquant	OC	12		
India	BTSB	144	3	C
Indian	JOC	785	3	C
Mustard	FFCB	285	2	B
Onion	NYT	497	1	B
Onion	NYTI	478	1	B
Pear, hot	BBA	169	2	B
Pear-pepper	GHAC	384	1	C
Pepper	SC	457	2	
Fresh, sirloin steaks w	GHAC	217	1	B
Green	FFCB	712	2	C
Pear	GHAC	384	1	C
Red	FFCB	712	2	C
Philadelphia	FFCB	284	1	B
Raw vegetable	OC	164	1	B

RECIPE	BOOK	PAGE	TD	S
For two	BBA	58	2	A
Georgia	CFS	167	2	B
Grown up	CFS	165	2	B
Korean, Seoul	CFS	92	2	B
Kraut, oven baked	BHGN	249	2	B
Of beef, au vin rouge	NYTI	162	3	C
Of beef w caraway, short	NYTI	82	2	B
Orange & apricot, spiced	BHGN	36	2	B
Orange glazed	BHGN	249	1	B
Shanghai style	CFS	168	1	B
Smoked, mustard glazed	BHGN	36	2	B
Smoked, short	BHGN	26	2	B
Spicy	BBA	58	1	B
Teriyaki	BBA	58	3	B
Teriyaki, appetizer	BHGN	44	2	C
Texas country	GHAC	219	2	C
Rice (see also arroz)				
◆	KIS	97	1	A
◆	MAFC	528	1	
◆	BCC	55	1	B
A la Grecque	NYT	320	1	B
Albufera	NYTI	222	1	B
Almond & bacon salad	BBA	146	2	B
Almonds & raisins	SMG	51	1	B
Andalouse	NYTI	524	1	B
Anise	KIS	161	1	A
Apple & raisin dressing	PPLK	229	2	C
Apricot	MIE	197	1	B
& Artichoke	BBA	131	1	B
& Artichoke	BCC	56	1	B
& Artichoke pie, Dolores Tottino's	BBA	99	2	B
Asian	KIS	271	1	A
Asparagus	NYT	325	1	B

RECIPE	BOOK	PAGE	TD	S
Bacon custard	JOC	181	2	B
Bacon, fried brown	GHAC	266	1	B
& Bacon stuffing	GHAC	164	1	
Bake, calico	BHGN	43	1	B
Bake, carrot &	BHGN	395	1	B
Bake, mushroom &	BHGN	324	1	C
Baked	MSQC	65	1	A
◆	JOC	178	1	B
◆	SMG	69	1	B
◆	SMG	135	1	B
◆	SMG	163	1	B
◆	NYTI	240	1	C
◆	FFCB	317	1	B
◆	SMG	157	1	B
Green	CW	61	1	B
Green	JOC	178	1	A
Pepper, ham &	FFCB	317	1	B
Pine nuts &	SMG	137	1	B
Balls, fried	FGCW	163	2	C
Barley	FFCB	311	1	B
Basic cooked	PPLK	224	1	B
Beans	AC	606	3	
Beans, company	JBGF	376	1	B
Beans, Italian style	NYT	319	2	B
Beans, Jamaican	NYTI	448	2	C
& Beef casserole, western	NYT	109	1	B
& Beet salad	MAFC	543	3	C
& Black beans	GHAC	232	1	B
Boiled	JBC	115	1	B
◆	NYT	318	1	B
◆	JOC	178	1	B
◆	SMG	165	1	B
◆	SC	180	1	
◆	FFCB	316	1	B
For hors d'oeuvres & salads	MAFC	532	1	B
Quick	SC	180	1	
White	VE	220	1	

RECIPE	BOOK	PAGE	TD	S
Rice (*cont.*)				
Bouillon, browned	NYT	319	1	B
Braised	MAFC	532	1	B
Bread	CBB	618	2	C
Brown	YGM	53	2	B
◆	YGM	43	2	B
◆	SC	180	1	
◆	BCC	55	1	B
◆	YGM	91	2	A
◆	AC	578	1	
◆	BHGN	321	1	B
◆	YGM	149	2	A
◆	JBC	118	1	
Fragrant	YGM	82	1	A
Fruit nut	BHGN	321	1	B
Oriental style	EBE	125	1	B
Plain	MIE	193	1	B
Plain, boiled	GHAC	266	1	B
Saffron	VE	221	1	
Steamed	VE	220	1	
Bujambura	NYTI	75	1	B
Buttered I	MAFC	530	1	B
Buttered II	MAFC	531	1	B
Buttered III	MAFC	531	1	B
Buttered, mushrooms &	MAFC	531	1	B
Cabbage dish	JOC	267	1	B
Cake	CIC	428	1	B
Cake	FAIC	484	1	C
Amaretti	FAIC	490	1	B
Calas	PPLK	314	2	B
Fried	AC	801	1	
Casserole	JOC	180	2	B
Chicken &	SC	315	1	
Olives, almonds &	WC	33	1	B
Shrimp &	SC	256	1	
Wild	FFCB	321	1	B
& Cauliflower casserole, Venetian	GG	108	1	B
& Celery soup	CIC	62	1	B
Cheese	JOC	179	1	B
Cheese	AC	577	1	
Cheese	FFCB	317	1	B
Cheese croquettes	NYT	325	2	B
& Cheese sauce	BB	130	1	B
Chicken	SC	313	1	
& Chicken livers	SMG	19	1	B
& Chicken livers, Italian	SC	181	1	
w Chicken & sausage	NYTI	525	1	B
& Chicken soup	GHAC	105	1	C
Chicken supper	BCC	254	1	B
Chili cheese	KIS	106	1	A
Chili peppers, cheese &	NYT	326	1	B
Chilies, cheese &	FGCW	159	1	B
Chinese	SC	180	1	
Chinese, fried	BHGN	324	1	B
Chinese, fried	SC	182	1	
Coconut	EBE	125	1	B
Cold, Mexican	BBA	17	1	B
Collards	JBGF	528	1	B
Confetti	BHGN	321	1	B
Consomme	JBC	275	2	
Converted	AC	577	1	
Cooked w broth	KIS	137	1	A
Cooked w chicken stock	JOC	179	1	A
Cookery, modern boiled rice	AC	577		
Cooking	BHGN	321	1	B
Cooking, the old fashioned way	AC	577		
Corn & cheese casserole	JBGF	375	1	B
Cream	FFCB	610	2	C
Croquettes	JOC	219	3	B
Croquettes	FFCB	320	2	B
Croquettes	SC	181	1	

RECIPE	BOOK	PAGE	TD	S
Croquettes w apricot sauce	WC	143	2	C
Crullers	JOC	707	2	B
Crumbed	AC	578	1	
Crust pizza	JBGF	480	1	B
Cumin w pignoli (pine nuts)	YGM	59	2	A
Curried	SC	181	1	
Curry	BCC	56	1	B
◆	FFCB	321	1	B
◆	SMG	233	1	B
◆	JOC	179	2	A
◆	MIE	196	1	B
◆	KIS	154	1	B
◆	BHGN	324	1	B
Curry, fried	WC	26	1	B
Curry w vegetables & shrimp, brown	JBGF	374	1	B
Custard cake	FAIC	486	2	B
Custard pudding	AC	734	1	
Custard pudding	JBC	47	1	B
Different kinds of	SPGT	115		
Dirty	PPLK	224	1	B
Dish Rombauer	JOC	182	2	B
Dressing	JOC	458	1	C
w Dried fruits & nuts	YGM	194	1	C
Eggs	SC	181	1	
Eggs & vegetables	CW	72	1	B
For rice cakes, cooked	PPLK	315	1	A
w Fresh basil & mozzarella	CIC	194	1	B
w Fresh corn	CW	157	1	B
w Fresh dill	CF	51	1	B
Fried	AC	579	1	
◆	MIE	198	1	B
◆	JBC	118	1	B
◆	FFCB	320	1	B
w Bacon, lettuce & tomato	WC	27	1	B
Chinese	JOC	179	1	B
w Leftover meat	JBC	118	1	B
w Mushrooms	JBC	118	1	B
w Onion & green pepper	JBC	118	1	B
w Seafood	JBC	118	1	B
Young jewel	NYTI	61	1	B
Fritters	GHAC	370	2	C
Fritters	FAIC	485	1	B
Fritters calas	GHAC	370	2	C
& Fruit cream	JOC	699	1	B
Fruit ring	GHAC	265	1	B
Fruited	EBE	126	1	B
Garlic	AC	578	1	
Garnish	SC	410	1	
w Ginger, pork fried	NYTI	60	1	B
Golden	GHAC	268	1	B
Almonds &	GHAC	268	1	B
Bacon &	GHAC	268	1	B
Curried apple &	GHAC	268	1	B
Olives &	GHAC	268	1	B
Onion &	GHAC	268	1	B
Greek style	YGM	133	1	A
Green	MSQC	84	1	B
◆	FFCB	318	1	B
◆	MIE	199	1	C
◆	AC	578	1	
◆	FGCW	158	1	B
Green, creamed	GG	315	1	B
& Green onions	BB	130	1	B
Grete	NYT	601	1	B
Griddle cakes	FFCB	497	1	B
Griddle cakes	SC	93	1	B
Griddle cakes, flour &	JOC	216	1	C
& Ham ring	JOC	181	2	B
Herbed	BHGN	321	1	B
Herbed	BB	130	1	B
Herbed	GRIL	71	2	B
Herbed, orange	GHAC	266	1	B

RECIPE	BOOK	PAGE	TD	S
Rice (*cont.*)				
Hot, steamed	GG	412	1	B
Indian w nuts, wild	JBGF	528	1	B
Italian	JOC	183	2	C
Italian style	GHAC	267	1	B
Jollof	BBA	135	2	B
Junk fried	BBA	135	2	B
Kinds of	FFCB	316		
& Kohlrabi soup	MCIC	109	2	B
& Lamb casserole	FFCB	193	1	B
& Lamb lentil soup	NYT	64	2	B
Lemon	BCC	55	1	B
◆	MIE	195	1	B
◆	CF	30	1	B
◆	SPGT	59	1	B
Lemon grass, coconut	GRIL	97	1	B
Lemon oven	BCC	190	1	
& Lentil soup	CIC	75	1	B
& Lettuce dish	JOC	267	1	B
& Liver w mushrooms	SMG	67	1	B
Loaf	JOC	180	2	B
Long grain, Carolina	AC	577	1	
& Meat salad	NYT	429	1	A
Mexican	SC	181	1	
Mexican or Spanish	AC	579	1	
Mexican style	WC	32	1	B
Mix, fruited	KIS	353	1	B
Mold	JOC	180	2	B
Mold, Maltaise	NYT	602	3	B
Muffins	SC	89	1	
Muffins, flour	JOC	581	1	C
Mushroom	BCC	55	1	B
Mushroom	KIS	296	1	B
Mushroom	BB	129	1	B
Bake	BHGN	324	1	C
Casserole	SC	422	1	
Onion	KIS	90	1	A
Ring	SC	182	1	

RECIPE	BOOK	PAGE	TD	S
Noodle pilaf	FG	120	2	B
& Nuts	AC	578	1	
Okra, bacon &	GG	225	1	B
& Olive casserole	AC	580	1	
& Onion	BCC	55	1	B
& Onion casserole	JOC	181	1	A
& Onions, baked	CF	107	1	B
& Orange	YGM	153	2	A
Orange-flavored, mold w cherries	MFC2	444	1	C
Oriental style	WC	27	1	B
Oven	BHGN	321	1	B
Oven, steamed	BCC	55	1	B
Paprika	WC	25	1	B
Parched w tomato sauce & cheese	FFCB	321	1	B
Parmesan	SMG	71	1	B
Parmigiana	VE	222	1	B
Parsley	BCC	55	1	B
Parsley	BHGN	321	1	B
Parsley	BBA	62	1	B
w Parsley & peas	SMG	153	1	B
Parsleyed	SP	345	1	B
Parsleyed	SMG	273	1	B
Parsleyed, brown	YGM	73	3	A
Pasticcio, peppery	FAIC	86	2	B
Peas	AC	579	1	
◆	SMG	177	1	B
◆	FGCW	157	1	B
◆	CIC	60	1	B
Peas & celery	VGCB	82	1	B
& Pecan loaf	FFCB	320	1	B
& Peppers	SMG	149	1	B
w Pigeon peas	NYTI	503	1	B
Pilaf (see also pilaf, rice)				
Pilaf	AC	578	1	
Pilaf	VE	227	1	B
Armenian	NYTI	2	1	B
Lebanese	FG	367	1	B

RECIPE	BOOK	PAGE	TD	S
w Nuts & raisins	AC	579	1	
w Pine nuts	MIE	194	1	B
w Pine nut stuffing	YGM	230	3	C
& Pineapple, baked	JOC	181	2	B
Pirogues	PPLK	193	2	B
Pork, fried	GHAC	267	1	B
Pudding	SC	187	1	
◆	PPLK	313	2	C
◆	BCC	142	1	B
◆	JBC	46	2	
◆	VE	269	2	B
◆	JOC	699	2	B
A la Francaise	NYTI	300	3	B
Baked	BHGN	172	1	B
Baked	FFCB	611	2	B
Basic	AC	734	2	
Carrot	GG	97	1	B
Cereal	JBGF	509	1	B
Chocolate	FFCB	611	2	B
Chocolate	SC	201	2	
Custard	JBC	47	1	B
Custard	AC	734	1	
Danish	SC	204	2	
w Fresh fruit, range top	GHAC	295	1	B
Fruited, brown	JBGF	635	1	B
Indian	NYT	590	2	C
Maple	AC	734	2	
Mold	BCC	142	2	B
Nut &	BCC	142	1	B
Old fashioned	NYT	589	2	B
Papuan	NYTI	300	2	C
Raisin &	SC	187	1	
Raisin &	FFCB	611	2	B
Raisin, old fashioned	SC	187	2	
Saucepan	BHGN	171	1	B
w Whipped cream	JOC	699	2	C
Raisin stuffing, rock cornish hens w	FFCB	253	3	B

RECIPE	BOOK	PAGE	TD	S
Ravigote, cold	NYT	429	1	B
Red	CFS	199	1	B
& Red beans	FG	292	3	B
& Red beans	NYT	358	2	B
& Red beans	BCC	174	2	C
& Red beans w ham hocks & Andouille smoked sausage &	PPLK	190	3	B
Ring	SC	181	1	
◆	AC	577	1	
◆	MAFC	534	1	
◆	JOC	180	2	B
Brown	SC	181	1	
Cheese	JOC	181	2	A
German	VE	226	1	B
Green	SC	182	1	
Indienne	BBA	135	2	B
Italian style	WC	25	1	B
Mushroom	EBE	129	1	B
Mushroom	JOC	181	1	B
Mushroom	NYT	325	1	B
Stuffed fruit	FAIC	487	2	B
Wild	JOC	179	1	B
Romanoff	NYT	602	2	B
Saffron	JBC	117	1	B
◆	SMG	167	1	B
◆	KIS	113	1	A
◆	BB	130	1	B
◆	AC	577	1	
Saffron, raisins & pine nuts	FFCB	317	1	B
Saffron, white	VE	221	1	B
Salad	NYTI	260	1	B
◆	JOC	88	1	B
◆	FAIC	85	1	B
◆	JBC	246	1	B
Celery &	VGCB	78	1	B
Cold	NYT	429	1	B

RECIPE	BOOK	PAGE	TD	S
Rice Salad (*cont.*)				
Nicoise	MIE	278	2	B
Sri Wasano's infamous Indonesian	MC	43	2	B
& Variations	FFCB	434	2	B
& Vegetables	AC	50	1	
w Zucchini flowers	GF	140	1	C
& Sausage, Mexican style	WC	35	1	B
Sausage stuffing	GHAC	169	1	B
Sauternes	FFCB	319	2	B
Savory, mixed	BCC	56	1	B
Savoy cabbage &	MCIC	120	1	B
& Shrimp, cold	NYT	428	1	B
& Shrimp, fried	NYT	319	1	B
& Shrimp, fried	SC	182	1	
Smothered cabbage soup	MCIC	108	1	B
Soup				
Celery &	CIC	62	1	B
Chick peas &	CIC	86	1	B
Egg &	CBSS	182	1	B
En croute, wild	CBSS	180	3	B
Escarole &	CIC	63	1	B
Sizzling	CBSS	179	3	B
Spinach	MCIC	103	1	B
Wild salmon	BCC	309	1	B
Spanish	JOC	180	2	A
◆	SC	182	1	
◆	FFCB	319	1	B
◆	BHGN	324	1	B
Spinach w chestnuts	JOC	181	1	B
Spinach salad	BCC	275	2	B
Spoon bread	JOC	580	1	B
Squash pie	FFCB	587	2	B
Steamed	FFCB	317	1	B
◆	NYT	318	1	A
◆	MAFC	529	1	B
◆	SC	180	1	
◆	JBC	116	1	B
Almonds &	JBC	116	1	B
Bacon, onion &	JBC	116	1	B
w Chicken broth	JBC	116	1	B
w Mushrooms	JBC	116	1	B
Stock	AC	577	1	
Stuffed chicken, spinach &	GG	317	2	A
Stuffing	BCC	257	1	B
Fruited	BCC	257	1	B
w Garlic & herbs	MFC2	161	1	B
w Mushroom, wild	FFCB	279	1	B
Nutty brown	GHAC	169	1	B
Summer garden	GHAC	268	1	B
Supper mold	GHAC	266	1	B
Swiss	SC	200	1	
Table or Rijsttafel	JOC	183	3	B
Tart w mango	NSD	102	3	B
Tex-Mex style	GHAC	267	1	B
Tibetan	EBE	130	1	B
Timbales	JOC	208	2	
Timballo stuffed w sausages	FAIC	222	2	B
Tomato casserole	NYT	326	1	B
Tomato soup, quick	BHGN	380	1	B
Turkish	EBE	130	1	B
Turkish	SC	182	1	
Turmeric	SMG	61	1	B
Turnip puree w herbs & garlic	MFC2	405	1	B
Valencian	NYTI	526	1	B
Vegetable	JOC	182	1	B
Vegetable, fried	EBE	131	1	C
Vegetable salad	SP	214	1	C
Vegetable salad, Italian	YGM	184	2	C
Vitamin, contents of, chart	JBGF	57		

RECIPE	BOOK	PAGE	TD	S
White, plain, the Chinese way	MIE	192	1	B
Wild (see also wild rice)	BHGN	321	1	B
◆	MSQC	41	1	B
◆	FFCB	321	1	B
◆	BCC	55	1	B
◆	JBC	118	1	
◆	GF	85	1	B
◆	MAFC	535	1	B
◆	JOC	179	1	B
◆	SC	180	1	
Boiled & variations	AC	585		
Casserole, chicken &	BHGN	309	1	B
Explanation	SP	345		
Fluffy	NYT	323	1	A
Minnesota style	NYT	324	2	B
Mushrooms	BCC	56	1	B
Mushrooms	BHGN	321	1	B
Mushrooms	JBC	118	1	
Nutted	SP	345	2	B
Party dish	EBE	131	2	B
Peas, mushrooms &	GHAC	268	1	C
Popped	JOC	66	1	
Salad, chicken &	BCC	266	2	B
Snow peas &	NYT	324	2	B
Steeped	AC	585	1	
Yellow	NYTI	32	2	C
Yellow loaf cake w rum, raisins & cherries	MFC2	485	2	
Ricebirds or Reedbirds	AC	245		
Riced potatoes	JOC	290	1	B
Rich egg pastry	SC	342	1	
Rich loaf, Lee's	CBB	81	3	C
Rickey (drink—gin)	SC	62	1	

RECIPE	BOOK	PAGE	TD	S
Ricotta	BTSB	54	3	B
Almond strudel	MC	210	1	B
Apple pie	JBGF	625	1	B
Broccoli souffle	JBGF	488	1	B
Cake	MC	198	1	B
Cannelloni stuffed w	FAIC	185	2	C
Cannelloni stuffed w spinach &	FAIC	184	2	C
Cheese pie	FFBB	108	2	B
Cheese pudding (ricotta budino di)	NYT	606	1	B
Cheese spread	BCC	17	1	B
Cheesecake	MCIC	434	2	B
Dressing, dill &	JBGF	552	1	A
Dumplings, spinach &	NYT	337	1	B
Filling (see filling, ricotta)				
Fried	FAIC	469	1	B
Fritters	MCIC	436	1	B
Gnocchi	MC	166	2	B
Gnocchi, spinach &	CIC	200	1	B
Pasta	NYTI	414	1	B
Pasta shells, bacon, peas &	MCIC	150	1	B
Penne w spinach sauce	MCIC	147	1	B
& Pesto lasagne	MCIC	190	3	B
Pie, spinach &	MC	123	2	B
Pie (torta di ricotta)	VE	273	2	C
Potato ring w chicken liver sauce	FAIC	361	2	B
Souffle	FAIC	491	1	B
& Spinach, tortelli stuffed w	FAIC	169	2	B
Sweet, for spooning or dipping	KIS	330	1	B

RECIPE	BOOK	PAGE	TD	S
Ricotta (*cont.*)				
Tomatoes stuffed w spinach &	SP	193	2	C
Torte	FAIC	448	2	B
Tortellini filled w	CIC	162	3	B
Rigatoni				
Con pepperoni	FGCW	145	1	B
Con quattro formaggi (w four cheeses)	NYTI	418	2	B
w Meat sauce, baked	CIC	110	2	B
Neapolitan style w roasted sweet peppers	MCIC	152	1	B
w Shrimp, Greek style	SMG	160	1	B
Stuffed	EBE	43	1	C
Tomatoes	BCC	62	2	B
Rigodon (custard dish)	CF	10	2	B
Rind, candied, oranges poached w	LM	293	1	B
Rinktum dity (egg & cheese dish)	SC	233	1	
Ripple ice cream, how to	GHAC	304		
Ripples, fried, Hester Liste	SC	100	1	
Ris de veau (see also sweetbreads)				
Ris de veau	MFC2	143	3	B
Ris de veau	LT	283	1	
Risi e bisi (rice & peas)	FGCW	157	1	B
Risi pisi (rice & vegetable dish)	BB	130	1	B
Riso verde (green rice)	FGCW	158	1	B
Risotto	MAFC	532	1	B
◆	CIC	179	1	
◆	FAIC	214	1	A
◆	NYTI	408	2	B
◆	MSE	172	1	B
◆	SC	181	1	
◆	JBC	117	1	
A la Milanese	JOC	183	2	C
A la Norton	NYT	322	1	B
A la Suisse	NYT	321	1	B
Alla marinara	NYT	322	1	B
Alla Milanese	VE	223	2	B
Alla Milanese	NYT	321	1	A
Artichoke	FAIC	216	1	A
Artichoke	GG	17	2	B
Artichoke & spring lamb kidneys	CPMC	198	2	B
Asparagus	CIC	189	2	B
Asparagus	GG	28	1	B
Cacciucco broth	FAIC	221	1	A
Celery	MCIC	122	1	B
Chicken	JBC	117	1	
w Chicken livers & mushrooms	NYT	322	2	B
w Clams	CIC	192	2	B
Cooked w vegetables & red wine	MCIC	125	1	B
w Cucumber	GG	145	2	B
Doug Edwards	VE	228	2	B
w Dried wild mushrooms	CIC	185	1	B
w Fish broth	FAIC	220	1	A
w Fried mushrooms	FAIC	215	1	B
w Garlic sauce	FAIC	214	1	B
w Luganega sausage	CIC	188	2	B
w Meat sauce	FAIC	217	2	A
w Meat sauce	CIC	187	2	B
Milan style	CIC	184	1	B
Milanese	NYTI	409	2	B
Molded, Parmesan & chicken liver sauce	CIC	183	2	B
w Mushrooms	FGCW	155	1	B
w Mushrooms, dried	FAIC	215	1	B

RECIPE	BOOK	PAGE	TD	S
Roberta Heart (chocolate cake)	MSE	250	3	C
Rock candy	JOC	735	2	B
Rock Cornish game hens (see also Cornish hens)				
Rock Cornish game hens w raspberry vinegar marinade	GRIL	80	3	B
Rock Cornish game hens w rice raisin stuffing	FFCB	253	3	B
Rock Cornish game hens w wild rice stuffing	FFCB	253	3	B
Rock lobster tails, boiled	FFCB	133	1	
Rock lobster tails, broiled	FFCB	133	1	
Rock salt shrimp, grilled	CPMC	172	1	B
Rockbass, broiled w fennel seed	FFCB	117	1	B
Rocket buckwheat pasta w goat cheese	CPMC	217	2	B
Rocket salad, tomato	CPMC	62	1	B
Rockfish charcoal grilled w onion tomato relish	CPMC	49	1	B
Rocks	AC	702	1	
Rocks	SC	161	1	
Rocks	JOC	656	1	C
Rocky Mountain high	CFS	307	1	B
Rocky road	AC	836	3	
Rocky road	BHGN	116	2	B
Rocky road ice cream	BBA	229	2	B
Roe				
All about	JOC	359		
Butter	GRIL	39	1	B
Preparing for caviar	JOC	756	3	
Sauce, making a	OC	67		
Sauteed	GHAC	136	1	B
Roesti (Swiss) potatoes	AC	570	1	
Roll cases	JOC	223	1	
Roll cookies	JOC	661	2	C
Roll cookies, rich	JOC	661	2	C
Rolladen (beef dish)	NYTI	311	2	B
Rolled cake	LT	359	1	
Rolled cookies	AC	702	1	
Rolled cookies	BCC	96	1	
Caramel	AC	703	1	
Chocolate	AC	703	1	
Nut	AC	703	1	
Rolled oat refrigerator cookies	AC	701	2	
Rolled rib roast	AC	279	1	
Rollmops (herring appetizer)	NYTI	507	3	C
Rollmops	JOC	73	3	
Rolls				
Aberdeen butter	CBB	571	3	C
Basic	NYT	473	2	C
Batter	BHGN	76	2	C
Batter dill	SC	74	2	
Biscuit	NYT	474	2	
Braided	SC	75	2	
Braided, miniature	FFBB	494	1	C
Bran pretzel	JBGF	580	2	C
Bran, refrigerator	JOC	569	1	C
Brown & serve	BHGN	70	2	B
Butter	FFCB	474	2	B
Butter	FFBB	490	2	C
Butter pecan	GG	303	2	C
Buttermilk	JOC	563	3	C
Buttermilk, butter	FFBB	491	1	C
Buttermilk, potato	JOC	565	3	C
Butterscotch, pecan	BCC	51	2	C
Button	CBB	637	3	C
Caramel	GG	302	2	C

ROLLS

RECIPE	BOOK	PAGE	TD	S
Caramel skillet	SC	80	2	
Caramel tea	SC	81	2	
Caraway rye	SC	73	2	C
Celery seed	CBB	559	3	C
Cheese	JOC	565	3	B
Chocolate filled	CBB	676	3	C
Cinnamon (see cinnamon rolls)				
Cloverleaf (see cloverleaf rolls)				
Crescent	NYT	474	2	
Crescent	SC	75	2	
Crescent	BCC	48	2	C
Cushion	SC	73	2	C
Dinner	SC	73	2	C
Dinner	FFBB	485	2	C
Dinner	BHGN	70	2	B
Egg shell	CBB	582	3	C
Feather	FFCB	474	2	C
Filled meat	JOC	224	3	B
Finger	FFCB	474	2	B
Finger	SC	75	2	
Finger	NYT	474	2	
Forming	GHAC	361		
Frankfurter	BTSB	82	3	C
Golden hominy	FFBB	496	2	C
Hamburger	NYT	474	2	
Hard	FFCB	476	2	C
Hard	BCC	47	2	C
Hard	JOC	568	3	C
Kaiser	CBB	542	3	C
Lemon parsley	FFBB	494	1	C
Mound	SC	75	2	
Mrs. Russo's	BBA	178	2	C
No knead, light	JOC	562	3	C
No knead, refrigerator	JOC	569	1	C
Oat & molasses	JOC	566	3	C
Orange	FFCB	478	3	C
Orange	BCC	50	2	C
Orange	EBE	106	1	C
Orange, quick	SC	87	1	
Overnight	JOC	564	3	C
Palm leaf	JOC	563	3	C
Pan	BCC	48	2	C
Parker House (see also Parker House rolls)				
Parker House	GG	302	2	C
Pecan	SC	81	2	
Pinwheel, filled	JOC	564	3	B
Plain	SC	76	2	
Poppy seed	FFCB	476	2	C
Potato, refrigerator	SC	76	2	
Pumpkin	GG	329	2	C
Refrigerator	FFBB	488	2	C
Refrigerator	AC	780	2	
Refrigerator, ever ready	SC	75	2	
Refrigerator potato	JOC	569	1	C
Rye	JOC	566	3	C
Crisp	FFBB	499	2	C
Inflation	FFBB	498	2	C
Yeast	SC	73	2	C
Sesame seed	FFCB	476	2	C
Shaping dinner	BHGN	71		
Sour cream	JOC	564	2	C
Square	BCC	48	2	C
S.S. France	CBB	633	3	C
Sweet	FFCB	478	3	C
Tea	SC	76	2	
Versatile	JOC	565	2	C
Vienna	SC	74	2	
Vienna	JOC	568	3	C
Water	FFBB	492	1	C
Whole grain	JOC	566	3	C
Whole grain, refrigerator	JOC	569	1	C

RECIPE	BOOK	PAGE	TD	S
Rolls (*cont.*)				
Whole wheat				
Brown	FFBB	496	2	C
Hard	FFCB	476	2	C
Quick	NYT	474	2	C
Soy	FFBB	497	2	C
Yeast	JBC	15	2	B
Romaine				
Leaves of heart of Boursault	GF	61	1	C
Lettuce w garlic & croutons	SMG	291	1	B
Lettuce salad w Gorgonzola & walnuts	MCIC	413	1	B
Salad w garlic dressing	KIS	239	1	A
Salad w Litchi nuts	MIE	258	1	B
Roman meal bread, home	CBB	86	2	C
Romano sauce	BHGN	355	1	B
Rombauer jam cake	JOC	636	1	B
Root soup	JBGF	323	2	B
Root vegetables, glazed	JOC	256		
Roots escabeche	GG	390	3	B
Roots & stalks, candied	JOC	743	3	B
Roots & stalks, crystalized	JOC	743	3	B
Roquefort				
Balls, cold	MAFC	196	1	B
Beet salad w walnuts	SP	218	2	B
Biscuits	MAFC	197	1	C
Blend, sour cream	AC	11		
Bread	CBB	367	2	C
Broiled steak	AC	263	1	
Butter w walnuts	KIS	313	1	B
Camembert spread	SC	334		
Cognac	NYT	51	1	C
Dip	FFCB	55	1	B
Dip	VGCB	335	1	B
Dip	SP	21	1	B
Dressing, anchovy, blender	JOC	312	1	B
Dressing for salad	SC	374	1	
Filling	BBA	15	1	A
Filling	NYTI	507	2	C
French dressing	JOC	312	1	A
Grapes	MSE	46	1	C
Grapes	GF	176	1	C
Ground steak w green pepper	MFC	151	2	B
Log	AC	15	1	
Mayonnaise cream	NYT	439	1	B
Mousse	VE	200	2	B
Omelet & apple	VE	169	1	A
Phyllo triangles w pistachio filling	SP	8	1	C
Quiche	MAFC	148	2	B
Shrimp, sole stuffed	BBA	89	2	B
Shrimp, stuffed	NYT	22	2	B
Soup, cold	CBSS	152	2	B
Spread	BB	123	1	
Spread	SC	38	1	
Spread	JOC	58	1	
Sticks, puffed	JOC	58	2	
Stuffed eggs	AC	18	1	
Stuffed potatoes, baked	NYT	397	1	B
Turnovers	MAFC	204	2	C
Vinaigrette for garden lettuce salad	CPMC	78	1	A
Rose blancmange	AC	726	1	
Rose hip jam	JOC	777	2	
Rose petal jelly	NYT	515	1	C
Rose petals, candied or crystallized	AC	837	2	

RECIPE	BOOK	PAGE	TD	S
Roselle sauce	JOC	121	1	
Rosemary				
Bread	FAIC	40	2	B
Butter	AC	189	1	
Butter sauce for barbecue	GHAC	226	1	C
Garlic bread	CBB	464	2	C
Wine sauce	JOC	328	1	B
Rosettes (fried cookies)	BCC	114	1	C
Rosettes	SC	101	1	C
Rosettes, making	BHGN	71		
Rosewater pound cake, almond	FFBB	365	2	C
Rotelle bacon sauteed w walnuts	MSQC	185	1	B
Rotelle mushrooms	NYTI	419	1	B
Roti de porc aux choux	MAFC	383	1	B
Roti de porc aux navets	MAFC	383	1	B
Roti de porc grand'mere	MAFC	382	1	B
Roti de porc poele	MAFC	380	1	B
Rotini (spiral macaroni)	KIS	164	1	B
Rotini w tomato sauce	YGM	102	1	B
Rotisserie cooking	CFS	254		
Rouille (spicy sauce)	MAFC	52	1	A
Rouille	CBSS	408	3	B
Rouille	VGCB	180	1	B
Rouille, processor	CFS	314	1	B
Rouille sauce	JOC	315	1	
Roulade	SPGT	249		
Roulade	JOC	418	1	
Chocolate	MSE	260	3	B
De boeuf	NYTI	170	2	B
Herbed caviar	SP	34	1	
Roulage Leontine or chocolate roll	AC	678	2	
Rouleaux (puff pastry cream rolls)	MFC2	139	2	
Rouleaux	MFC2	468	2	
Rounds, spiral-bordered	FFBB	533	3	C
Roux, brown (brown sauce)	AC	456		
Roux, making a	PPLK	27		
Roux, preparing	JOC	319		
Roux, white, drawn butter	AC	455	1	
Rowies, buttery (rolls)	CBB	571	3	C
Rub				
Chili bacon	CFS	283	1	A
Galveston	CFS	284	1	A
Garlic anchovy	CFS	283	1	A
Hotted honey	CFS	285	1	A
Red devil	CFS	285	1	A
Rosemary allspice	CFS	286	1	A
Sesame mustard	CFS	285	1	A
South Texas chuck wagon	CFS	286	1	A
Rub up cake, Jamaican	NYTI	450	2	C
Rugelach (cookies)	FFBB	250	2	C
Rum				
Apricot cake	BCC	71	3	B
Apricot dip	KIS	329	1	B
Babas	MAFC	660	3	C
Babas	FFBB	338	2	C
Balls	SC	178	1	
◆	FFCB	568	1	C
◆	AC	711	1	
◆	BCC	120	3	C
Banana ice cream w	MCIC	452	2	B
Black beans	NYT	357	2	B
Buns, rich & sticky	SPGT	126	3	C
Butter sauce	SC	217	1	
Butter sauce	CF	43	1	B
Buttered, hot	JOC	51	1	
Cake (see also baba au rhum)				

RECIPE	BOOK	PAGE	TD	S
Rum (*cont.*)				
Cake	WC	137	2	C
Cake	FFCB	530	1	B
Caramel custard flambee	MFC2	451	3	B
Florida	MHGD	90	2	C
Original Italian	FAIC	452	2	B
Raspberry &	JOC	640	2	
Walnut & prune	FFBB	370	2	C
Cassis cup	JOC	50	1	
Chiffon pie	NYT	529	2	B
Chiffon pie, coffee &	FFBB	120	2	B
Chocolate mousse	JOC	687	2	C
Chocolate sauce	JBC	267	1	
Coffee flavored chocolate layer cake	CIC	436	2	B
Cracker torte	BCC	134	1	C
Cream pie	NYT	529	2	C
Cream pie	BHGN	283	2	B
Custard	NYTI	296	1	B
Custard pudding	NYTI	449	2	B
Drops, uncooked	JOC	670	3	C
Flavored whipped cream	BCC	134	1	
Flavoring	SC	142	1	
Gelatin cream pie	JOC	614	2	B
Hot buttered	SC	63	1	
Macaroon souffle, unmolded	MAFC	620	2	B
Mint sauce	NYT	616	1	B
Mousse, peach &	BBA	212	2	C
& Olives, beef stew w	CF	118	2	C
Or brandy loaf cake	AC	649	1	
Papaya, glazed	KIS	320	1	B
Pineapple slices broiled & flamed w	JBC	110	1	
Pineapples, small	AC	768	1	
Pudding, frozen	SC	215	2	
Pudding, raisin &	WC	144	1	B
Punch	JOC	46	1	A
Punch	NYTI	20	1	C
Punch	FFCB	742	2	C
Citrus &	BHGN	47	1	C
French	NYTI	309	1	C
Pineapple &	NYTI	504	2	C
Raisin				
Banana bread	FFBB	551	2	C
Ice cream	NSD	219	1	B
Ice cream	BBA	229	2	B
Ice cream	KIS	327	1	A
Refrigerator cheesecake	NYT	547	2	C
Rich yellow loaf cake w raisins, cherries &	MFC2	485	2	
Sauce	SC	217	1	
Sauce	MHGD	454	2	B
Sauce	JOC	710	1	B
Sauce, chocolate souffle w	LM	322	1	B
Shake, papaya, banana &	MSE	158	1	A
Sherbet, orange &	NYT	628	2	B
Slices	SC	158	1	
Soaked brioche, strawberry shortcake made w	MFC2	448	2	B
Souffle, lemon, frozen	MHGD	450	2	B
Syrup	NYT	616	1	B
Syrup, peaches in	BTSB	156	2	B
Rumaki (marinated chicken livers)	AC	221	1	
◆	AC	25	1	
◆	MSE	156	2	C

RECIPE	BOOK	PAGE	TD	S
Rumaki (*cont.*)				
◆	NYT	16	2	B
◆	JOC	71	1	
◆	BCC	10	1	B
Rumaki, lobster	NYT	16	2	
Rumanian cheese	BBA	21	1	C
Rump roast	AC	280		
Rump roast	JBC	138		
Rump roast w caraway seeds	NYT	101	2	B
Rump roast w vegetables	BHGN	234	2	C
Rump steak, definition	AC	259		
Rusk, pineapple on toasted	SC	44	1	
Russian black bread	BHGN	63	3	B
Russian dressing	BHGN	352	1	B
◆	SC	377	1	
◆	JOC	316	1	B
◆	FFCB	453	1	B
◆	AC	78	1	
◆	GHAC	284	1	
◆	BB	143	1	
◆	BCC	301	2	B
A l'Audelan	NYT	440	1	B
Joe Hyde's	VGCB	335	1	B
Sharp	SC	377	1	
Russian Easter bread	FFBB	506	3	C
Russian salad	JOC	83	1	B
Russian salad I (vegetable Macedoine)	AC	42	1	
Russian salad II	AC	43	1	
Russian tea cookies	EBE	178	1	C
Russian teacakes	BCC	109	1	C
Russian torte	SC	137	1	B
Rutabaga	SC	434	1	
Rutabaga	BHGN	141		

RECIPE	BOOK	PAGE	TD	S
Rutabaga	JOC	300	1	B
All about	VGCB	324		
Apple	BHGN	403	1	B
Apple sauced	GG	389	1	B
Boiled	VGCB	327	1	
Braised	GG	388	1	B
Buttered	AC	554	1	
Disks, baked honeyed	VGCB	328	1	B
Gingered	GG	391	1	B
Glazed	BCC	368	1	B
Julienned accompaniments	VGCB	327	1	
Kohlrabi, turnips, preparing	BCC	367		
Mashed	JBC	340	1	B
Mashed	FFCB	419	1	B
Mashed	JBGF	529	1	B
Bacon	JBC	340	1	B
Cream	JBC	340	1	B
Potatoes	JBC	340	1	B
Potatoes	GG	389	1	B
Mushrooms	AC	554	1	
Ovals, glazed	VGCB	326	1	
Pie	VGCB	333	1	B
Potato whip	BCC	368	1	B
& Potatoes, mashed	GG	389	1	B
Preparing	GG	385		
Pudding	VGCB	329	1	B
Puff, whipped	BHGN	406	1	B
Puree of yellow turnips	MFC2	406	1	B
Pureed	NYT	408	1	
Pureed	FFCB	419	1	B
Roulade	VGCB	329	2	B
Salad, turnip tart &	VGCB	331	1	B
Scratch backs	GG	393	1	B
Shinbone soup w turnips	VGCB	331	2	B

RECIPE	BOOK	PAGE	TD	S
Rutabaga (*cont.*)				
Squash gratin	VGCB	288	1	B
Steamed or boiled	VGCB	327	1	
Stew, duck &	NYTI	234	2	B
Rye				
Bread	AC	785	2	
◆	CPMC	231	3	C
◆	FFCB	467	2	C
◆	BHGN	61	2	B
◆	FFBB	472		
American	FFBB	473	1	C
Brie	CBB	395	3	C
Corn	SC	69	2	C
Finnish	SC	68	2	B
Heavy sour	CBB	164	3	C
Herbed	BB	112	1	B
Milwaukee	SC	68	2	C
Norwegian	SC	69	2	C
Old Milwaukee	CBB	136	3	C
Onion	NYT	465	2	C
Onion	CBB	156	3	B
Pain Seigle	CBB	161	3	C
Raisin	CBB	146	3	C
Sauerkraut	CBB	158	2	C
Seeded	CBB	172	3	C
Sour cream	CBB	154	2	C
Sour dill	CBB	148	2	B
Sour dough	JOC	560	3	B
Sour dough for	SC	69	2	C
Sour yogurt	FFBB	479	2	B
Sourdough	FFBB	480	2	C
Spicy	CBB	166	2	C
Sticks	JOC	570	1	C
Stuffing	GHAC	166	1	B
Swedish	VE	35	2	B
Swedish	JOC	560	2	B
Torte	SC	132	2	B
Torte brandy	SC	133	1	B
Torte chocolate	SC	133	1	B
Triple	CBB	139	3	C

RECIPE	BOOK	PAGE	TD	S
Coarse sour yogurt	FFBB	480	2	B
Croutons	BHGN	348	1	B
Crumb crust	FFBB	69	1	B
Deli corn	BBA	174	2	C
Dough w caraway seeds	FFBB	61	2	B
Fried cakes	SC	100	1	
Fritters	NYT	489	1	A
Jewish raisin	FFBB	478	2	B
Popovers	SC	91	1	
Rolls	JOC	566	3	C
Caraway	SC	73	2	C
Crisp	FFBB	499	2	C
Inflation	FFBB	498	2	C
Salt flutes	BBA	178	2	B
Sour bread	CBB	136	3	C
Sourdough, ginger	FFBB	482	3	B
Sourdough starter	BTSB	104	1	
Sweet Swedish, American style	FFBB	476	2	C
Whole wheat bread, buttermilk	CBB	160	3	B
Yeast rolls	SC	73	2	C

S

RECIPE	BOOK	PAGE	TD	S
S'more bars	BCC	122	2	C
Sabayon (zabaglione)	JOC	686	2	B
Making	NSD	109		
Orange	BBA	213	1	
Pears & orange	BBA	212	2	B
Pears, wine-poached baked in meringue w	MFC2	440	2	B
Sauce (see also Zabaglione)				

RECIPE	BOOK	PAGE	TD	S
Sally Lunn bread	GHAC	358	2	B
Sally Lunn, quick	JOC	574	1	B
Salmagundi (salad w chicken)	VGCB	17	1	B
Salmagundi chef's salad	GHAC	278	1	B
Salmi of duck	FFCB	251	3	B
Salmi of duck, wild	AC	252	2	
Salmi of wild birds, about	JOC	477		
Salmi of wild duck	AC	252	2	
Salmon				
Archiduc	NYT	247	1	B
& Avocado salad	BBA	14	1	A
Baked w anchovy butter	CPMC	214	1	B
Baked w foil, whole	NYT	243	2	C
Baked, Seattle Indian	CFS	211	2	B
Baked & stuffed	FG	65	2	C
Baked, whole	MIE	150	3	B
Ball	FFCB	58	1	B
w Basil sauce	MFC	124	2	B
Bass & avocado	MFC	125	3	B
Beignets, fresh	SPGT	16	2	C
Braised w cucumber sauce	VGCB	99	1	B
Broccoli crepes	BHGN	222	2	B
Broccoli souffle	BBA	124	3	B
Broiled	NYT	245	1	B
Broiled	FFCB	118	1	B
Butter, smoked	SC	379	1	
Cakes	JOC	240	1	B
Canaped, smoked	SC	39	1	
Canapes, smoked	JOC	62	1	
Caper (dip)	KIS	313	1	B
Casserole	JOC	240	1	B
Casserole	SC	240	2	
& Caviar hearts	SPGT	112	2	C
& Chick pea salad	SMG	313	1	B
Cocktail croquettes	WC	13	1	B
Cold foam	CIC	33	1	B
Cold poached	BCC	182	2	B
Cold poached w lemon sauce	EBE	90	1	B
Cornets	LT	55	1	
Cornets, making (photographs)	LT	54		
Coubiliac of	CPMC	31	3	C
& Cream cheese ball	FG	58	2	B
Cream sauce & spinach, pasta w	SP	81	1	B
Crepes w broccoli	BHGN	222	2	B
Croquettes	JOC	220	3	C
Croquettes	CFS	223	1	B
Croquettes	SC	240	1	
Croquettes w dill sauce	GHAC	141	1	B
Croquettes, potato	JBGF	381	1	B
Dip, smoked	NYT	52	1	A
Eggs & sorrel	MFC	53	3	A
En gelee	FG	66	2	C
Fillet poached w vermouth	KIS	146	1	A
Fillets, grilled & dilled	SMG	112	1	B
Filling	SC	381	1	
Flemish sauce for poached	NYT	449	1	A
Florentine	NYT	245	1	B
Fondue, canned	SC	243	1	
Francoise	MFC	34	3	B
Fromage	NYT	246	1	B
Glazed, cold	JOC	359	3	
Gratin of, creamed	MAFC	156	1	B
w Green sauce	FGCW	114	2	B
Grilled red onions, charcoal grilled	CPMC	59	1	B
w Honey, cured & smoked	CFS	280	2	B

RECIPE	BOOK	PAGE	TD	S
Salmon (*cont.*)				
w Horseradish sauce	SC	239	2	
In puff pastry	MFC	125	3	B
Kippered	AC	143		
Loaf	AC	142	1	
◆	FFCB	147	1	B
◆	BCC	185	1	B
◆	BHGN	222	1	A
Baked	NYT	245	1	B
Canned	SC	243	1	
w Cheese sauce	JOC	241	2	B
Macaroni salad	BCC	269	2	B
Marinated w dill, Scandinavian	MIE	40	3	C
Mold, jellied	AC	67	2	
Molded in aspic	LT	143	3	
Mousse	BBA	90	2	B
◆	MAFC	562	1	C
◆	SP	18	3	C
◆	GF	137	1	B
◆	BCC	20	2	C
◆	GHAC	141	2	C
◆	BHGN	14	2	B
◆	FGCW	292	2	B
Aspic	NYT	435	3	B
w Cucumber sauce	MSE	296	3	C
Dieter's delight	JBGF	456	2	B
Double	MIE	38	3	B
In aspic, making a	NYT	434		
Smoked	CF	114	2	B
w Sour cream & dill sauce	NYT	435	2	B
Napoleon	MFC	43	3	B
& Olive, linguine &	YGM	129	1	A
w Parsley sauce, rice or noodle ring	JOC	241	2	B
Patties, orange	KIS	133	1	B
Patties, skillet, dilled	BHGN	222	1	B
Patty sandwiches	BCC	322	1	B
Pickled	NYTI	528	3	C
Pinwheels, smoked	EBE	42	1	C
Poached	FG	64	2	C
Poached	FFCB	118	2	C
Carving (photographs)	LT	314		
w Fresh basil & olive butters	CPMC	220	2	B
& Glazed in aspic	LT	138	3	
Pot pie	JOC	241	2	B
Potato cakes	JOC	240	1	B
Poupous	MSE	154	3	C
Provencal	MFC	126	3	B
Puff	BCC	185	1	B
Puffs	JOC	240	1	B
Quenelles	MAFC	189	2	B
Quiche, crustless	BCC	185	1	B
Quiche w smoked leek, miniature	MSE	44	3	B
Rice, canned	SC	244	1	
Ring	SC	240	1	
& Roasted red pepper, pasta w	CPPC	78	1	B
Roe & peas, linguine w	CPPC	35	2	B
Roe & smoked salmon pasta salad	CPPC	108	2	C
Rolls, smoked	BBA	17	1	B
Rolls, smoked	JOC	73	1	
Rolls, smoked	FFCB	57	1	B
Salad	SC	363	1	
Canned	AC	66	1	
Fresh, variations	AC	66	1	
Mixed	JBC	255	1	B
Mold	SC	372	2	
Plate	JBC	255	1	B
Scandinavian	JBGF	415	2	B

RECIPE	BOOK	PAGE	TD	S
Smoked	AC	67	1	
w Spinach	AC	66	1	
Salt-cured, w green peppercorns	LT	133	3	
Sandwich	AC	811	1	
Sandwich, hot, creamed	SC	384	1	
Sandwiches, sauteed	BBA	105	1	B
Scalloped	JBC	72	1	B
Scallops w sorrel sauce	MSE	171	2	B
Scotch sandwiches, open faced	BBA	105	1	B
Shortcakes	BCC	185	1	B
Smoked	LM	115	3	
◆	MSE	96	1	C
◆	AC	143		
◆	BTSB	33	3	B
w Boursin in cucumber cups	BBA	17	3	C
w Brie & tortilla triangles	GHAC	86	1	C
Butter	SC	379	1	
w Caviar cornucopia	SC	41	1	
Eggs &	JOC	197	1	B
Filling, kasha w	BBA	16	1	C
Linguine &	MIE	183	1	B
Lox, cream cheese &	AC	811	1	
Mousse	CF	114	2	B
& Peas, fettuccine	MSQC	197	1	B
Snacks, smoked	SC	41	1	
Souffle	MFC	36	2	B
Souffle	NYT	307	2	A
Souffle	JBC	271	1	B
Souffle, broccoli &	BBA	124	3	B
Souffle & variations	MAFC	166	2	B
Soup, cream of	SC	404	1	

RECIPE	BOOK	PAGE	TD	S
& Spaghetti, quick	JOC	185	1	B
Spiced	AC	135	1	
& Spinach crepes	FGCW	334	1	B
& Spinach salad	AC	66	1	
Spread	FFCB	56	1	B
Spread, smoked	SPGT	15	1	B
Steak				
w Anchovy lemon butter	WC	73	1	B
Barbecued	OC	148	2	B
Broiled	MSQC	64	1	A
◆	AC	124	1	A
◆	JOC	359	1	
◆	FG	67	1	B
w Chive butter	GRIL	76	2	B
Cold, poached	AC	136	1	B
w Dill butter	SC	239	1	
w Fried bread crumbs	SMG	122	1	B
Grilled	NYT	244	1	B
Grilled	BHGN	39	1	B
Grilled w Bearnaise sauce	OC	148	2	B
Lemon, marinated	BHGN	213	2	B
Marinated	CFS	218	2	B
w Marinated cucumber, chilled	GHAC	141	2	B
Poached	NYT	246	1	B
w Spinach sauce, cold poached	BBA	86	2	A
Stimpirata style	MCIC	220	1	B
Stuffed	BBA	87	3	B
Stuffed	SC	240	1	
Stuffed eggs	AC	17	1	
Sweet & sour	AC	137	1	
Sweet & sour, canned	SC	243	1	

RECIPE	BOOK	PAGE	TD	S
Salty sweet filling	PPLK	134	2	B
Sambal dip	NYT	53	1	B
Sambhar (Indian sauce for rice)	NYTI	359	2	C
Sambuca coffee ice cream	FGCW	385	1	
Sambuca ice cream, vanilla &	MSQC	21	1	B
Sambuca sorbet, fresh orange	SPGT	78	3	C
Samosas (yogurt curry vegetable turnovers)	MC	155	2	B
Sand tarts (cookies)	FFCB	555	1	C
◆	FFBB	250	1	C
◆	AC	704	1	
◆	JOC	662	2	C
Sand torte	SC	108	1	B
Sandbakelse (cookie shells)	AC	703	1	
Sandies (cookies)	BHGN	163	1	C
Sandwich	AC	802		
Alsatian	BBA	104	2	B
Big bread	SP	327	2	C
Broiled, open-faced	MC	83	1	B
California, open	GHAC	373	1	
Checkerboard	SC	383	1	
Club	AC	803	1	
Country club	GHAC	373	1	
Fillings	JBGF	496	1	
Fillings	MC	83	1	A
Fish fillings	FFCB	288	1	A
Glazed	JOC	56	1	
Grilled	JOC	244	1	
Ides of March	SPGT	49	2	B
In bacon, tiny	AC	25	1	
Kinds of	SPGT	224		
Loaf, a rye white bread	AC	816	1	
Loaf, ribbon	SC	383	2	
Loaves	JOC	54	1	
Loaves & variations	AC	815		
Meal for one	JOC	245	1	A
Meat fillings	FFCB	288	1	A
Melting	SPGT	225		
Milwaukee	SC	383	1	
Milwaukee, baked	SC	383	1	
Mosaic	SC	383	1	
Pinwheel	SC	383	1	
Ribbon	JOC	53	1	
Ribbon	SC	383	2	
Rolled	JOC	53	1	
Salad fillings	FFCB	289	1	A
Sauteed	JOC	244	1	
Savoyarde	JOC	246	1	A
Toasted	JOC	244	1	
Traditional	GHAC	373	1	
Variations	FGCW	298		
Zoo	JOC	54	1	
Sandwich cookies, Viennese	BBA	191	2	C
Sandy's salad	KIS	176	1	A
Sanford sauce	BBA	164	1	B
Sangria (drink)	BHGN	50	2	C
Sangria	FFCB	744	2	B
Sangria	SC	57	1	
Sangria mold	BCC	293	2	B
Sangria punch	BCC	21	1	B
Sangrita (drink—tequila)	NYTI	479	1	A
Sangrita Maria	BBA	27	1	A
Santa's whiskers	BHGN	168	2	C
Saparagua ties, cravatta	GG	33	1	B
Saratoga chips	JOC	296	1	
Sardine				
All about	JOC	359		
Appetizer, molded	SC	46	2	
Butter	SC	380	1	

RECIPE	BOOK	PAGE	TD	S
Avocado	OC	165	1	A
Barbecue (see also barbecue sauce)				
Barbecue	OC	160	1	B
Ferocious	OC	160	1	A
Hottish	OC	160	1	B
Italian	OC	159	1	B
New American, spicy	GRIL	38	2	C
Richmond pork or spareribs	OC	161	1	A
Spicy	OC	161	1	B
Traditional	GRIL	38	2	C
Bearnaise (see Bearnaise sauce)				
Bechamel (see Bechamel sauce)				
Belle aurore	NYTI	267	1	B
Beurre blanc l'ermitage	BBA	90	1	A
Black butter	MSQC	128	1	B
Blanche	JOC	324	1	B
Bourguignonne	JOC	331	1	B
Brune	MAFC	67	1	C
Butterscotch	BTSB	162	1	B
Chantilly	MAFC	83	2	B
Charcutiere	NYTI	269	1	B
Chasseur	JOC	327	1	B
Chasseur	MAFC	75	1	
Chasseur	NYTI	269	1	B
Chaud froid	NYT	444	1	B
Chaud froid	JOC	341	2	
Chicken livers, wattles & crests	FAIC	75	1	B
Chien Martinique	NYTI	272	1	B
Chili	BTSB	180	2	C
Chinese style, plum	BTSB	181	3	C
Chivry	MAFC	62	1	B
Chocolate mint	BTSB	160	1	C

RECIPE	BOOK	PAGE	TD	S
Chocolate orange	BTSB	160	1	C
Choron	MAFC	85	2	B
Choron	MFC	104	1	A
Colbert	MAFC	85	2	B
Color in	JOC	319		
Cranapple wine	GHAC	206	1	B
Cranberry, home style	BTSB	213	1	B
Cranberry, jellied	BTSB	168	2	C
Cranberry-pear wine	GHAC	206	1	B
Cranberry wine	GHAC	195	1	B
Cucumber	OC	166	1	B
Currant orange	GHAC	206	1	A
De sorges (herbal mayonnaise)	GG	311	1	B
Diable (devil sauce)	NYTI	270	1	B
◆	BHGN	357	1	A
◆	MAFC	71	1	B
◆	JBC	264	1	
◆	AC	456	1	
Diane	NYTI	271	2	B
Espagnole	JOC	326	3	C
For asparagus, cold	MAFC	438	1	
For asparagus, hot	MAFC	436	1	
For asparagus mold	MAFC	441	1	
For cauliflower, hot	MAFC	458	1	
For Chateaubriand	BB	19	1	B
For cold artichoke	MAFC	426		
For hot or warm artichoke	MAFC	426		
For ice cream	GHAC	306		
For light meat game	JOC	331		
For pasta	GHAC	265		
For plum & other puddings	AC	742	1	
For red pepper pasta w red pepper strips	MSQC	37	1	B
For smoked food	JOC	315	1	

RECIPE	BOOK	PAGE	TD	S
Sauce (*cont.*)				
For spaghetti	MSQC	156	1	B
For vegetables	GHAC	256		
For venison	AC	457	1	
Fudge, hot	BTSB	161	1	B
Georgian moppin'	CFS	288	1	B
Grand Marnier	MHGD	382	1	B
Gribiche	JOC	315	1	C
Hints for making	VE	81		
Honey mustard	GHAC	195	1	B
Jerome le Plat	BB	16	2	A
Johnny Reb	CFS	302	1	B
Keeping	JOC	319		
Lemon butter	GRIL	38	1	A
Liver, spaghetti w	JOC	335	1	B
Louis	JOC	316	1	B
Marinara (see marinara sauce)				
Mocha	BTSB	160	1	C
Moppin'	CFS	297	2	B
Mornay (see mornay sauce)				
Moscovite	MFC	105	1	A
Mousseline	NYT	451	1	B
◆	MFC	105	1	B
◆	MAFC	83	2	B
◆	AC	460	1	
Mousseline,sabayon	MAFC	169	1	
Moutarde	MFC	103	1	B
Nantaise	NYTI	274	1	B
Perigueux	JOC	327	1	B
Perigueux	MAFC	75	2	B
Piquante	NYTI	274	1	B
Piquante	MAFC	72	1	B
Plum	WC	54	1	B
Poivrade	NYT	452	1	B
Portugaise	NYTI	275	2	B
Praline	GHAC	195	1	B
Preparing	JOC	318		

RECIPE	BOOK	PAGE	TD	S
Provencale	BHGN	357	1	B
Quantity, making	JOC	319		
Ragout	MAFC	69	1	C
Raspberry, for figs stuffed w raspberries	MSQC	93	1	B
Ravigote	MAFC	95	1	A
Red pepper butter	GRIL	38	1	B
Red wine butter	GRIL	38	1	A
Remoulade	MAFC	91	1	B
Remoulade	BBA	163	1	B
Riviera	MAFC	90	1	B
Robert	JOC	328	1	B
Robert	FFCB	270	1	B
Robert	MAFC	72	1	B
Robert I	NYTI	276	1	B
Robert II	NYTI	276	1	B
Rouille	GG	22	2	B
Soppin'	CFS	300	1	B
Soubise	JBC	261	1	
Soubise, veal chops w	JBC	170	1	B
Suedoise	BBA	164	1	B
Supreme	AC	458	1	
Tartare	MAFC	90	1	B
Tartare	BBA	164	1	B
Tartare	MFC	103	1	B
Teriyaki	GRIL	38	1	B
Thickeners for	JOC	319		
Thickness of testing	MFC	13		
Tomato (see tomato sauce)				
Tonnato	BBA	162	1	B
Veloute (see veloute sauce)				
Verde	NYT	440	1	B
Verte	MSE	285	1	C
Verte	JOC	315	1	B
Verte	BBA	164	1	B

RECIPE	BOOK	PAGE	TD	S
Walnut dessert	BTSB	161	1	B
White (see white sauce)				
White wine butter	GRIL	38	1	A
Saucy pudding cake	BCC	133	1	B
Sauerbraten (beef dish)	SC	273	3	
◆	JBC	141	2	B
◆	JOC	415	3	B
◆	FFCB	161	3	C
◆	AC	290	3	
◆	NYTI	310	3	B
◆	BHGN	236	2	C
I	NYT	103	3	C
II	NYT	103	3	C
Czechoslovakia style	NYTI	70	3	B
Hamburgers	BHGN	243	1	B
w Knackwurst	GHAC	213	1	B
w Meatballs	SC	43	1	
Sauerkraut	SC	416	2	
◆	FFCB	370	1	B
◆	JOC	787	3	
◆	VGCB	49	2	C
◆	JOC	269	2	B
◆	BTSB	284	3	C
& Apples	MSQC	57	1	B
Balls	BCC	9	1	C
Balls	AC	21	1	
Balls	JOC	429	2	B
Braised	MAFC	498	1	B
Braised ham hocks w	BBA	99	2	B
Casserole				
Pork chops &	AC	413	1	
Pork steak, beer &	JBC	202	1	
Pork steak, cider &	JBC	202	1	
Pork steak, fried apples &	JBC	202	1	
Dressing for game	JOC	458	1	
Duck braised in	MAFC	280	2	B
Garnished meat	BBA	99	3	B
Homemade	AC	499	3	
In champagne	CPMC	68	3	B
In champagne, three day	NYTI	245	3	B
In glass jars	SC	455	3	
In sherry wine	NYTI	315	2	B
In tomato cream	SC	416	1	
Juice cocktail	SC	44	1	
Juice (Lumpensuppe)	JOC	32	1	B
w Kielbasa	GHAC	212	1	B
Lamb stew w	NYTI	1	2	B
Meats	SMG	274	1	B
Meats, pork &	NYT	141	2	B
& Mushroom filling for pierogi	FG	374	2	
Old fashioned	SC	455	3	
Onions stuffed w	JOC	286	1	B
Peas baked	VE	148	3	C
Pheasant, braised	AC	241	2	
Pheasant, roast	BB	81	2	
& Pigs' knuckles	AC	422	2	
& Pigs' knuckles	NYT	142	2	B
& Pork	NYTI	312	2	B
Balls	NYTI	243	2	B
Braised	MAFC	385	1	B
Chops	BB	34	1	
Hocks	BCC	227	2	B
Supper	GHAC	191	2	B
Transylvanian	NYTI	512	2	B
Pork roast, stuffed w	JOC	408	1	
Pork sausage w	FGCW	332	2	C
Ranch salad w	AC	604	1	
Rye bread w	CBB	158	2	C
Salad, cooked	AC	500	1	
Sausage, pork &	FGCW	332	2	C
Sausages w	AC	432	1	
Slaw	AC	500	1	

RECIPE	BOOK	PAGE	TD	S
Chicken	MFC2	290	3	C
Chicken	LT	232	3	
& Chicken liver in brioche dough	MFC2	296	1	B
& Chicken, roast & stuffed	JBC	224	1	
& Chickpea salad	FFCB	435	2	B
Chili	KIS	238	1	A
Chitterling	LM	211	3	C
Chocolate	SC	177	1	
Chowder, German	BHGN	369	1	B
Cocktail	BCC	9	1	C
Cocktails	AC	19	1	
Cooked	BCC	232	1	
Cooking fresh pork	BHGN	258		
Corn bread	BHGN	260	2	B
& Corn bread stuffing	GHAC	169	1	B
Country	JOC	437	2	
Country style	OC	127	2	B
Cream sauce, conchiglie w	CIC	109	1	B
Crust	BBA	60	3	A
Crust	AC	435	2	
Cured (cotechino)	AC	434		
Cuts of, chart	CFS	195		
Date	SC	176	1	
Different kinds of	SP	24		
Dressing	JOC	457	1	B
Dressing, andouille smoked w	PPLK	226	2	B
Duck, roast, w apple stuffing &	MAFC	275	2	B
& Eggplant	FGCW	277	2	B
Eggs	SC	225	1	
& Fennel, lamb & eggplant casserole w	FGCW	304	2	B
Filling, andouille smoked w	PPLK	130	2	C

RECIPE	BOOK	PAGE	TD	S
Forming cheesecloth casings	MFC2	286		
Frittata, pepper &	FFCB	343	1	B
& Game hen gumbo, okra	GG	230	2	B
Garlic	BTSB	12	3	C
Garlic	NYTI	245	1	A
Garlic	KIS	255	1	A
Garlic, grilled	CFS	200	2	B
Goose neck	MFC2	317	2	
Gratin, potato, onions	MAFC	155	1	B
Grilled	JBC	7	1	
Gumbo, andouille, chicken &	PPLK	202	3	B
Gumbo, chicken &	CBSS	384	3	B
Hard	JOC	755	3	
Hominy, smoked	AC	432	1	
Hot, baked	MIE	36	1	C
Hot, Italian	BTSB	10	3	C
Hot, Spanish	BTSB	11	3	B
In beer, Polish	BCC	232	1	B
Italian	FG	356	2	B
◆	BB	35	1	
◆	JBC	60	1	
◆	FG	181	2	B
w Cheese & red wine	FGCW	245	2	B
Gravy	FGCW	343	2	
Grilled, hot & sweet	OC	126	1	A
Grilled & poached	CFS	196	1	B
Pepper	NYT	147	1	C
Pepper & basil sauce	KIS	274	1	A
Peppers	AC	432	1	
Peppers	GHAC	212	1	B
Spinach	FGCW	346	1	B
& Kidney beans in red wine	AC	602	2	

RECIPE	BOOK	PAGE	TD	S
Sausage (*cont.*)				
Kidneys & sweetbreads	AC	357	1	
w Kraut	BHGN	263	1	B
w Krauters, Polish	BHGN	33	1	B
Lamb	FGCW	246	2	B
& Lamb, Moroccan	YGM	130	1	B
Lasagne, Italian	BCC	232	2	B
Lecso	YGM	178	2	C
& Lentil casserole	AC	609	1	
& Lentils	FFCB	326	2	B
& Lentils, Italian	FGCW	345	2	B
Link	JBC	59	1	
Breakfast	BTSB	8	3	C
Cooking	AC	431	1	
Making	AC	429		
Liver canapes	JOC	61	1	
Luganega, risotto w	CIC	188	2	B
& Macaroni, Mexican style	WC	114	1	B
& Macaroni, skillet	BHGN	261	1	B
Making	LT	286	3	
Making, hints on	FGCW	242		
Making, paraphernalia, about	BTSB	4		
Making (photographs)	LT	286		
Marchigiana Italian	NYTI	403	1	B
w Marinara sauce	JBC	214	1	
w Marinated quail, grilled	CPMC	222	3	B
Mash	AC	431	1	
Meat	FFCB	210	1	B
Baked apples filled w	JOC	112	1	B
Cooking	AC	430	1	
Herbed & spiced	FFCB	211	1	B
Making	AC	428		
Patties	JBC	60	1	
Patties, sauteed	JOC	437	1	B
Ring, baked	JOC	438	1	B
w Sweet potatoes & fruit, baked	JOC	438	2	B
Mexican	FGCW	250	2	B
Mixed grilled	GRIL	89	1	B
Mixture, southwestern	AC	430	2	
Muenster melts	GHAC	86	1	C
Mushroom strudel	CF	16	3	B
& Mushrooms	JOC	231	1	B
w Napoli noodles	WC	121	1	B
& Onion bread	CF	131	2	B
& Onions	JOC	231	1	B
& Onions, stuffed	AC	533	1	
& Orange	FG	182	1	C
Oven roasted, mixed	CF	46	1	B
w Oysters	NYT	18	1	
Pan fried w red wine & dried wild mushrooms	MCIC	305	1	B
Patties	MSE	131	1	C
Apple stuffed	BHGN	260	1	B
Breakfast	GHAC	213	1	B
Broiled	JOC	437	1	A
Chicken	CW	128	2	C
Peppers, Italian	GHAC	212	1	B
Peppers, pasta w	SP	71	2	B
Pie, leek &	NYT	29	2	B
Pie, quail, squab, chicken, tortelli &	FAIC	383	3	C
Pizza w	FFCB	302	3	C
w Hot peppers, coriander &	CPPC	156	3	B
w Italian	BCC	167	2	C
w Multicolored peppers &	CPPC	156	3	B

RECIPE	BOOK	PAGE	TD	S
Plain pork meat for cakes, chipolatas	MFC2	289	2	
Poached green	GG	194	1	B
Polenta	CIC	205	1	B
Polenta	FAIC	369	1	B
Polish	FG	376	2	B
Polish	BTSB	13	3	C
Polish, beer-poached	CFS	200	1	B
Polish & red cabbage	GHAC	213	1	B
Pork	OC	167	1	C
Fennel &	NYTI	402	2	B
Greek lamb	FGCW	248	2	B
& Liver greens	MFC2	304	3	C
Luganega	MCIC	30		
Roast stuffed w spinach	FG	358	2	B
& Sauerkraut	FGCW	332	2	C
Spicy, Italian	FGCW	249	2	B
Veal, truffles & foie gras	MFC2	295	3	
Provencale w leftover braised beef	MFC2	306	3	C
Prunes stuffed	FFCB	211	1	B
Puff pastry	MSE	131	3	C
Puff pastry, baked in	MFC2	304	3	C
Ragout	SP	131	1	B
Rape	FAIC	353	2	B
Rape & turnip	FAIC	353	2	B
Ratatouille	BBA	98	2	C
Ratatouille, Italian	CF	82	2	B
Ratatouille, squash &	GG	327	1	B
Recipe, basic	NYT	146	1	C
& Red cabbage	MCIC	302	1	B
Red hot, whole wheat pasta, red peppers &	CPPC	90	2	B
Red wine, kidney beans &	AC	602	2	
& Rice baked	SMG	280	1	B
& Rice, New Orleans	FGCW	243	2	B
Rice stuffing	GHAC	169	1	B
Rice timballo, stuffed	FAIC	222	2	B
Risotto	FAIC	218	1	A
Rolls	AC	20	1	
Rolls	AC	434		
Salad	FG	86	2	B
Salad, potato &	BBA	145	2	B
Salad & smoked kohlrabi, wilted	GG	215	1	B
Sauce, andouille smoked w	PPLK	250	2	B
Sauces	JOC	231	1	A
& Sauerkraut	AC	432	1	
Sauerkraut, pork &	FGCW	332	2	C
Savoy in brioche	LM	196	3	B
w Savoy cabbage	NYTI	402	1	B
Scramble w tomato	GHAC	110	1	B
Seafood	FGCW	250	2	C
Seafood, rosy	SPGT	18	3	B
Shellfish	LM	89	3	C
w Shirred eggs	FFCB	338	1	A
& Shrimp, grilled	CFS	198	2	B
Smoked				
Country	BTSB	7	3	B
Polish kielbasa, sauerkraut	GHAC	212	1	B
Salad, warm w kohlrabi	GG	215	1	B
White beans &	AC	598	1	
Smothered in onions	MCIC	303	1	B
Soup Micaele	BBA	41	2	B
Spaghettini	NYTI	429	2	B
Spanish, hot	NYT	147	1	B
Spicy, breakfast	SPGT	124	2	C
Spicy, country style	BTSB	6	1	B
& Spinach meatballs	FG	359	1	B

RECIPE	BOOK	PAGE	TD	S
Sausage (*cont.*)				
Spirals, crisped in a basket	OC	38	2	
Squash	BHGN	405	1	A
Stuffed				
w Apples	FFCB	212	1	B
Flank steak	BBA	51	2	B
Mushrooms	SP	11	2	B
Onions	VGCB	184	1	B
Peppers	AC	541	1	
Prunes	FFCB	211	1	B
Stuffing (see also stuffing, sausage)				
Stuffing	MFC2	285		
Stuffing	FFCB	280	1	C
Stuffing w chestnut, duck braised in	MAFC	281	3	B
Stuffing, procedure	BTSB	4		
Supper salad	BHGN	348	1	B
Swedish potato &	AC	430	2	
Sweet Italian	BTSB	9	3	C
Sweet Italian, & grilled green peppers	OC	127	2	B
Terrine, Italian	BCC	18	2	C
Tomato sauce, meatballs &	NYTI	393	3	B
Tomatoed, grilled	CFS	201	2	B
Tuscan	FAIC	350	2	C
Tuscan beans w	FAIC	354	1	B
& Veal birds	JBC	174	2	B
Venison	AC	239		
& White bean soup, peppers &	SP	159	3	B
& White beans	NYTI	403	2	B
White meat chicken, veal or pork w	MFC2	290	3	C
w White pudding	FGCW	244	2	B
w White wine	AC	431	1	
Winter greens, & semolina pasta w	CPPC	124	2	B
Wrapped in brioche w truffle butter	MFC	41	3	B
Saute				
Chinese style	MC	149	2	B
De boeuf a la bourguignonne	MAFC	326	1	B
De boeuf a la Provencale	MAFC	327	1	B
De veau (veal stew or Blanquette de Veau)	MAFC	359	2	
Meuniere (sauteed fish)	AC	130	1	
Sauteing	JOC	126		
Sauternes sabayon	SPGT	108	1	B
Savarin (dessert roll)	NYT	564	2	C
◆	JOC	640	3	
◆	FFCB	526	3	B
◆	MHGD	230	2	C
Babas yeast cake	LM	270	2	C
Chantilly	MAFC	662	3	B
Whipped cream	MAFC	662	3	B
Savory bread	CBB	434	3	C
Savory bread	EBE	107	1	B
Savory duckling, grilled	GHAC	222	2	B
Savoy cabbage & bacon	BCC	341	1	B
Savoy cabbage, creamed	AC	495	1	
Savoy cabbage, stuffed	AC	494	2	
Savoy sausage in brioche	LM	196	3	B
Savoy soup	NYTI	380	2	B
Savoyard gratin (leek & ham dish)	BBA	133	2	B
Savoyard gratin	MAFC	524	1	B
Sayadia tahini (sole dish)	BBA	18	2	B

RECIPE	BOOK	PAGE	TD	S
Sayur lodeh (vegetables w shrimp)	NYT	289	1	C
Sazerac (bourbon drink)	JOC	39	1	
Scalding	JOC	129		
Scallion	JOC	284	1	
Bean sprouts &	KIS	268	1	A
Beef	YGM	152	1	A
& Beef in mushroom sauce	FFCB	173	1	B
& Beets appetizer	NYT	41	2	B
Braised	FFCB	392	1	B
Braised, Jerusalem artichokes w	MSQC	217	1	A
Braised & Jerusalem artichokes	MCIC	363	1	B
Braised w mustard sauce	SP	183	1	B
Bread	MSE	123	3	C
& Cheese bread	YGM	103	1	B
& Cheese sauce	NYT	399	1	B
Chicken, Kerry w	GG	249	1	B
& Eggplant	MSQC	101	1	B
Grilled	GRIL	76	2	B
Lamb	MIE	173	1	B
Mayonnaise	SMG	123	1	B
& Mushroom soup	VGCB	170	1	B
Onions sauteed w	VGCB	175	1	
Potatoes mashed w	NYT	395	1	B
Quiche, cheese &	VE	206	1	B
Salad, mushroom &	KIS	286	1	A
Soup, cream of, w cheese	CBSS	319	1	B
Soup, noodles &	CBSS	320	1	B
Scalloped eggs, cheese	AC	111	1	
Scalloped oysters (see also oysters, scalloped)				
Scalloped oysters	EBE	97	1	B
Scalloped potatoes	JOC	291	2	B
Scalloped sweets	GG	359	2	B
Scallops	BB	90	1	
All about	JOC	369		
Au citron	NYTI	154	1	B
Baked	SC	254	1	
Baked leeks &	VGCB	160	1	B
Bay, quiche	NYT	28	1	C
Bay, sauteed w string beans	GG	352	1	B
Bay, slaw & cucumber	GG	146	1	B
Bisque	SP	52	2	B
Boiled	BHGN	217	1	B
Bouillabaisse of	MFC2	37	1	B
Breaded	NYTI	154	1	B
Broiled	SC	254	2	
◆	NYT	286	1	B
◆	JBC	86	1	
◆	AC	167	1	
w Ginger	BCC	189	1	A
w Lemon	NYTI	155	2	B
Marinated	JBC	86	2	B
& Celery in a vinaigrette sauce	VGCB	81	1	B
Ceviche	JBGF	297	2	B
Charcoal broiled	OC	158	1	B
w Cheese sauce	FGCW	117	1	B
Chowder, Nantucket	CBSS	136	2	B
Cold, poached	SP	118	1	B
Cream sauce	BCC	189	1	B
Cream sauce	MFC	135	2	B
& Cucumbers w dill, skewered	OC	158	1	B
Curried	MIE	165	1	A
Curried, sea	NYT	286	2	B
Curry	JBC	87	1	
Deviled	AC	169	1	
Deviled	FFCB	140	1	A

RECIPE	BOOK	PAGE	TD	S
Scallops (*cont.*)				
En brochette	NYT	285	1	B
En brochette	AC	168	1	
w English cucumbers	GF	46	1	B
w Fresh coriander	YGM	122	2	A
Fried	BHGN	217	1	B
Fried	FFCB	140	1	B
Fried	SC	254	1	
Deep	AC	168	1	
Deep fat	JOC	370	1	
Pan	GHAC	124	1	A
w Garlic	FGCW	329	1	A
w Garlic & parsley	KIS	152	1	B
Ginger	MFC	136	3	A
Gratineed w wine, garlic & herbs	MAFC	218	2	B
In puff pastry	MFC	45	3	B
In wine	JOC	370	1	B
Kabobs	GHAC	124	1	B
Kebab	BBA	91	2	B
& Leeks w Pernod	SMG	134	1	B
Lemon & rice salad	BBA	146	2	B
Marinara	SC	254	1	
Marinated	MSE	154	3	C
Meuniere	JOC	370	1	B
Mornay	JOC	370	2	B
Poached	JBC	87	1	B
Poached crabmeat &	JBC	87	1	B
Poached w creamed mushrooms	JBC	87	1	B
Mousseline w white butter	LM	80	3	B
Mushrooms w cream sauce	SMG	136	1	B
Mushrooms, creamed	JOC	370	1	B
Mushrooms w white wine sauce	MAFC	216	3	B
Newburg	FFCB	141	1	A
On a bed of red onions	YGM	114	1	A
On skewers	OC	158	1	B
Oysters, truffles & saffron, poached	GF	184	3	B
Pasta, pesto w	JBGF	413	1	B
Pesto	FGCW	125	1	A
Poached	AC	169	1	
Poached in a green sauce	LM	111	1	B
Poached, cold	JBC	88	1	
Provencale	WC	66	1	B
Quick fried butter	SMG	138	1	B
Ravioli & lobster	CPPC	138	3	B
& Roasted pepper, pasta w	CPPC	93	2	B
Saint Jacques, creme	NYTI	125	1	B
Salad	AC	63	2	
Salad	EBE	97	1	B
Salad, watercress &	MFC	190	2	B
Sauce verte	NYT	287	1	B
Saute	NYT	287	1	B
Sauteed	JBC	86	1	
◆	AC	168	1	
◆	SC	254	1	
◆	FFCB	139	1	B
w Chives & red peppers	GF	236	1	B
w Garlic	JBC	86	1	
w Garlic butter	NYT	287	1	B
w Garlic & parsley	MCIC	87	1	B
& Herbed	JBC	86	1	
Savoy	FFCB	141	1	B
Scalloped	JOC	370	2	B
Sea, sauteed w scallions	MSQC	156	1	B
Seviche	AC	169	2	B
Seviche, sea	NYT	21	2	B

RECIPE	BOOK	PAGE	TD	S
Skewered	CFS	220	1	B
Skewered	SC	333	1	
Soup, cream of	FFCB	103	1	B
Soup, cream of hot or cold	MFC2	39	1	B
Spaghetti w	MCIC	128	1	B
Stew w sole fillet & basil	MFC	132	3	B
Thin spaghetti w	MCIC	128	1	B
Toss	BHGN	347	1	B
& Vegetables	FG	257	3	B
Zucchini, artichoke hearts & salsa	GRIL	71	2	B
Scaloppine & mozzarella Parmigiana	SMG	205	1	B
Scampi	NYTI	385	1	B
Scampi	EBE	98	3	B
Grilled & frozen	SC	333	1	
Maltese	VGCB	198	2	B
Sauce	BBA	161	1	B
& Spaghetti	NYTI	385	1	B
Style fish	GHAC	137	1	B
Scandanavian gold cake	AC	662	1	
Scarlet runner beans, cooking	AC	482	1	
Schaum torte (meringue)	SC	131	1	B
Coffee	SC	131	1	B
Lemon	BCC	144	3	C
Lime	BCC	144	3	C
Or meringue shells	AC	689	2	
Pie	SC	133	1	
Scheherezade casserole	MC	141	2	B
Schiacciata (egg bread)	CBB	266	2	B
Schiacciata w raisins	FAIC	473	2	B
Schiacciata, sweet carnival	FAIC	472	2	B
Schlemmerschnitte a la luchow (beef, caviar appetizer)	NYT	44	1	B
Schnecken (caramel buns)	JOC	566	3	C
Schnecken (snail-cookies)	SC	82	2	
Schnecken (cinnamon rolls)	SC	80	2	
Schnecken, miniature	MHGD	226	3	C
Schneckendoodles (crinkle cookies)	AC	705	1	
Schnippel (vinegar bean soup)	CBSS	253	3	B
Schnitz und knepp (ham w apples)	AC	445	3	
Schnitzel paprika	JOC	404	1	
Schokoladendunstkoch (chocolate pudding)	NYTI	16	2	B
Scone	BCC	29	1	B
◆	GF	47	1	C
◆	JOC	586	2	C
◆	FFBB	581	1	C
◆	SC	88	1	
Buttermilk & currant	FFBB	582	1	C
Cheese, Hungarian	CBB	566	3	C
Cherry studded bannock	CBB	605	1	B
Cream	VE	45	1	B
Cream	FFCB	495	1	C
Griddle	SC	88	1	
Mrs. Macnab's	CBB	563	1	C
Scottish	BBA	183	2	C
Tea	NYT	479	2	C
Sconset sunrise	SPGT	124	1	A
Scotch	SC	180	2	
Scotch broth	BHGN	369	2	B

RECIPE	BOOK	PAGE	TD	S
Scotch broth (*cont.*)				
◆	CBSS	189	2	B
◆	BCC	307	1	B
◆	AC	89	2	
◆	SC	398	2	
◆	JOC	150	3	C
◆	FFCB	97	2	B
Scotch broth, Marie O'Day's	VGCB	57	1	B
Scotch eggs	AC	18	1	B
Scotch mist	SC	62	1	
Scotch oatmeal bread	CBB	213	3	C
Scotch pancakes	SC	93	1	B
Scotch shortbread	AC	704	2	
Scotch sling	SC	64	1	
Scotch woodcock	JOC	200	1	A
Scrambled eggs (see also eggs, scrambled)				
Scrambled eggs w brains	AC	359	1	
Scrapple	NYT	145	2	C
Scrapple	AC	426	1	
Scrapple	FFCB	201	2	B
Scrapple, Philadelphia	AC	426	1	
Screwdriver	SC	62	1	A
Screwnog (drink—vodka)	BBA	27	1	A
Scripture cake	FFBB	322	2	C
Scripture or bible cake	AC	669	2	
Scrod, broiled	FFCB	118	1	B
Scrod, broiled	JOC	355	1	
Sea bass				
Broiled	OC	143	2	B
w Fresh finocchio	MCIC	206	1	B
Oven steamed	GHAC	134	1	B
Poached Chinese style	NYTI	39	2	A
Sorrel, fillet of	MFC	115	2	B
Steamed	NYTI	40	2	A

RECIPE	BOOK	PAGE	TD	S
Stuffed & baked	GHAC	134	2	C
Stuffed w crabmeat	NYT	231	1	B
Sea fish skewers	OC	147	2	B
Sea foam	SC	170	1	
Sea foam frosting	SC	145	1	
Sea foam sauce	FFCB	639	1	B
Sea food, spaghetti sauce w	JOC	335	1	B
Sea scallops seviche	NYT	21	2	B
Sea soup	JBGF	334	2	B
Sea squab, about	JOC	359		
Sea squab, sauteed	FFCB	119	1	B
Sea trout or bass in puff paste	LM	105	3	C
Sea urchins, opening (photographs)	LT	108		
Seafoam frosting	AC	693	1	
Seafood				
A la king	JOC	237	2	B
Artichoke w	BBA	130	2	B
Aspic	SC	372	2	
Aspic	FFCB	447	2	B
Aspic, tomato &	JBGF	406	2	B
Au gratin creamed	JOC	237	1	B
Basil phyllo	YGM	193	3	C
Bisque	SC	403	1	
Bisque, quick	NYT	79	1	B
Casserole w Creole sauce	JOC	237	1	B
Casserole, quick	JOC	237	1	B
Casserole, San Francisco	GHAC	126	1	B
Chesapeake	FFCB	145	1	B
Cream Creole	SC	257	1	
Crepes	FFCB	296	2	B
Crepes	PPLK	52	2	B
Crepes	NYTI	148	2	C
Croquettes, Belgian	BBA	18	3	C
Curry	JOC	238	2	B

RECIPE	BOOK	PAGE	TD	S
Dirty rice	PPLK	51	2	B
Divan, quick	JOC	238	2	B
Dressing	JOC	458	2	
Eggs, creamed	BCC	163	1	B
File gumbo	PPLK	209	3	B
Filling	SC	381	1	
Filling, creamed	MFC2	145	1	
Flounder, stuffed	PPLK	62	3	B
Gazpacho	SPGT	147	2	C
Gumbo	SC	405	1	
Gumbo	CBSS	380	3	B
Gumbo, Cajun w andouille smoked sausage	PPLK	208	2	C
Gumbo, okra &	GG	229	2	B
Jambalaya	CBSS	391	3	C
Jambalaya, chicken &	PPLK	218	2	B
Lasagne	BCC	192	2	C
Mayonnaise, hot	FFCB	64	1	B
Mixed grill	CFS	231	3	C
Mold, jellied	JOC	98	2	B
Mousse	JOC	98	2	B
Mushroom, stuffed	AC	527	1	
Mushroom, stuffed	JOC	282	2	B
Mushrooms, stuffed	JBC	316	1	
Nectarines	KIS	140	1	A
Newburg	JOC	238	1	B
Newburg, baked	SC	249	1	
Newburg, skillet	GHAC	126	1	B
& Okra gumbo	GG	229	2	B
Orly	NYTI	147	3	C
Oysters, baked & creamed	JOC	365	1	B
Pancake pie	SC	249	1	
Pasta	NYTI	418	1	B
Pate	SP	28	3	C
Pilaf	JBGF	456	2	B

RECIPE	BOOK	PAGE	TD	S
Platter w meuniere sauce, sauteed	PPLK	58	3	B
Quiche (see quiche, seafood)				
Ramekins	NYT	295	1	B
& Rice salad	AC	64	1	
Ring, jellied	JOC	98	2	B
Risotto, chilled	GHAC	127	2	B
Salad	MSQC	60	2	B
Salad	BCC	263	2	B
Basic	JBC	255	1	B
Chinese	MIE	286	2	B
Chorus line	SPGT	130	1	B
w Creamy tarragon & mustard dressing	SP	223	2	B
Fish mold	SC	372	2	
Herb flavored	CIC	421	2	B
Mixed	AC	64	1	
w Pasta & basil	GHAC	281	1	B
& Tomato sandwiches, open-faced	JOC	249	1	
Salsify	VGCB	258	1	B
Sauce	SC	387	1	
Sauce	NYT	340	1	B
Sauce, fish fillets poached w	JBC	69	1	
Sausage	FGCW	250	2	C
Shrimp, stuffed	PPLK	93	3	B
Souffle, molded	SC	257	3	
Soup	NYTI	120	1	B
Soup, Oriental	BCC	308	1	B
Soup, summer squash &	GG	324	1	B
Stew (cioppino)	CBSS	197	3	B
Stew, Italian	NYT	266	2	B
Stew, Mediterranee	NYTI	149	1	B
Stock	PPLK	32	2	B

RECIPE	BOOK	PAGE	TD	S
Shad (*cont.*)				
Carving	JOC	360		
Old fashioned whole, boneless	FFCB	120	1	B
Planked	NYT	249	1	B
Planked w creamed roe	FFCB	121	1	B
Planked w shad roe dressing	NYT	249	2	B
Roe				
A l'oseille	NYT	250	1	A
Aux fines herbes	NYT	251	1	A
w Bacon blankets	SC	42	1	
Baked	JOC	360	1	
Broiled	JOC	360	1	
Broiled, canned	JOC	242	1	A
Broiled, fried	SC	240	1	
Creamed, baked	JOC	360	1	B
Creamed, canned	JOC	242	1	A
w Cucumber salad	SC	364	1	
In a chafing dish	FFCB	120	1	A
Parboiled	JOC	360	1	
Poaching, how to	NYT	250		
Salad	AC	69	1	
Salad	JOC	91	1	B
Sauteed	JOC	360	1	
Sauteed w bacon	SPGT	38	2	B
Souffle	JOC	207	2	B
Stuffed	FFCB	120	1	B
Toast points	NYT	250	1	B
& Shad roe in cream	SMG	104	1	B
Shake breakfast	JBGF	511	1	A
Shakle meshi (baked eggplant boats)	GG	164	1	B
Shallot				
Avocado salad, Peter McGhee's	VGCB	180	1	B
Butter				
w Green peppercorns	CF	115	1	B
& Red wine	MAFC	103	1	A
Sandwiches	CF	87	1	B
Sauce	VGCB	178	1	A
& White wine	MAFC	103	1	A
& Cherry tomatoes, sauteed	SMG	169	1	B
Chicken, tomatoes, vermouth &	FGCW	173	1	A
Definition of	SP	187		
Garden grass shrimp, green pasta w	CPPC	44	2	A
w Green beans	NYTI	241	1	B
Quail w parsley &	CPMC	213	2	B
Sauce	SP	37	1	B
Sauces, simple	VGCB	178	1	A
Souffle	AC	556	2	
Soup & carrot w chervil cream	CPMC	169	1	B
Spring, red onions, leeks & pappardelle	CPPC	43	2	B
Tarragon butter	BBA	152	1	A
Whole braised	MSE	168	1	B
Shamrock salad	SC	358	1	
Shandygaff (beer & ginger ale drink)	BB	168	1	A
Shanghai marinade	BBA	164	1	A
Shark				
About	JOC	360		
Barbecued	OC	149	2	B
Brochettes	OC	150	2	B
Steaks grilled w lettuce leaves	OC	151	2	B
Shashlik (Russian shish kebab, see also lamb)				
◆	JBC	190	3	B
◆	NYT	124	1	B

RECIPE	BOOK	PAGE	TD	S
Shashlik (*cont.*)				
◆	AC	385	3	
◆	SC	330	2	
I	BB	87	3	
II	BB	87	3	
Lamb w wine juniper	FGCW	222	3	B
Ukrainian	OC	104	1	B
Shchav chard (soup w greens)	GG	186	1	B
Shchi (sauerkraut soup)	CBSS	260	2	B
Shchi	NYTI	509	2	B
She crab soup	AC	177	1	
Sheep's trotters (lambs' tongues)	AC	398	3	
Shell bean				
& Bacon	AC	480	1	
Braised	VGCB	13	1	A
& Butter onions	AC	480	1	
Casserole	VGCB	18	1	B
Cooking	AC	480	1	
Hummus	VGCB	15	1	B
Steamed	VGCB	13	1	A
Succotash	VGCB	14	1	B
Shell for Jane's chocolate mousse tart	MSQC	165	2	B
Shell roast (boneless sirloin)	AC	279	1	
Shellfish				
All about	BCC	186		
All about	JOC	363		
All about, chart	FFCB	105		
Butter	MAFC	104	2	A
Buying, storing & cooking	BHGN	216		
Charcoal grilled w red wine sauce	CPMC	134	2	C
Cream filling	MAFC	202	1	C
Deep fried	BCC	192		

RECIPE	BOOK	PAGE	TD	S
Deep frying, timetable for	BCC	192		
Equivalents	BHGN	216		
Fish fillets w truffles	MAFC	215	2	B
Fish soup	MCIC	238	2	B
Gumbo	VGCB	166	2	B
Herbs, steamed	MSQC	92	1	B
w Macaroni	JOC	187	2	B
w Mixed rice	SMG	127	2	B
Mousseline	JOC	98	2	B
Preparing for freezing	BHGN	143		
Preparing for grilling (photographs)	OC	76		
Risotto	JBC	117	1	
w Sausage	LM	89	3	C
Soup, cream, for canned or frozen fish	MFC2	41	1	B
Shells, stuffed	FGCW	150	1	B
Shells w tuna sauce	FAIC	160	1	B
Shepherd's pie (meat & potato dish)	SC	304	2	
◆	FFCB	191	2	B
◆	JOC	234	1	
◆	AC	394	2	
Cajun	PPLK	119	2	B
For a crowd	VGCB	225	3	C
Vegetarian	JBGF	382	2	B
Sherbet				
Apple cider	CPMC	97	2	B
Apricot	NSD	230	1	B
Apricot	MFC2	415	3	B
Apricot	SC	212	2	
Berry parfaits	BCC	149	2	B
Champagne	JOC	724	2	B
Champagne punch	SC	57	1	
Lemon	AC	739	3	
Lemon	JOC	723	2	B
Lemon champagne	FGCW	396	3	B
Lemon lime milk	GHAC	306	3	B

RECIPE	BOOK	PAGE	TD	S
Sherbet (cont.)				
Lime ice	AC	739	3	
Melon	MFC	244	2	B
Melon	LM	302	2	B
Orange	AC	739	3	
Orange	JOC	723	2	B
Peach	FGCW	397	3	B
Peach, creamy	JBGF	636	2	B
Pineapple champagne	MFC	244	2	B
Pineapple (see pineapple sherbet)				
Strawberry (see strawberry sherbet)				
Sherried cheddar cheese spreads	KIS	314	1	B
Sherried chicken balls	JOC	71	1	
Sherry				
Almond souffle	EBE	199	3	C
Balls	AC	711	1	
Bread dressing	JOC	456	1	B
Cake orange (Williamsburg)	SPGT	106	3	C
Charlotte Russe	SC	137	2	B
Cheese dip	SC	376	1	
Cherry mold	EBE	141	2	B
Creme glace, frozen	BBA	229	2	B
Custard	NYT	614	1	B
Dressing for fruit salad	JOC	318	1	A
Fluff sauce	SC	218	1	
& Grapefruit jelly	JOC	102	2	C
& Grapefruit juice	NYT	650	1	B
Mayonnaise	SP	208	1	B
Pea soup, elegante	BHGN	380	1	C
Pepper for soup	FGCW	105	3	
Sauce	BHGN	355	1	B
Wine sauce	PPLK	282	1	B
Shinbone soup, turnip, rutabaga &	VGCB	331	2	B
Shirley Temple cake	FFBB	333	1	C
Shish kabob	GHAC	207	3	B
◆	SC	330	2	
◆	JBC	189	1	
◆	BB	86	2	
◆	FFCB	186	2	B
◆	EBE	64	2	B
◆	BCC	236	3	B
◆	OC	115	2	B
Lamb	AC	384	2	B
Marinated	JBC	190	2	B
Mustard	BBA	55	2	B
Russian	OC	117	2	B
Spicy	MIE	122	1	B
Traditional Armenian	CFS	189	2	A
Vegetarian	MC	164	1	B
Shoo fly pie	AC	631	1	
Shoofly pie	FFBB	98	2	B
Shoofly pie	GHAC	324	2	C
Short crust pastry	GG	412	2	B
Short paste	MAFC	139	2	
Short paste, directions for making	MAFC	140		
Short paste, sweet	MAFC	633	1	
Short pastry (pate sucree or pasta frolla)	SC	342	1	
Short pastry	FAIC	439		
Short rib				
A la Francaise	NYTI	171	2	C
Beef, savory	BCC	206	1	B
Boiled, Spanish style	SC	277	2	
Braised	FFCB	165	2	B
Broiled w red wine marinade	BB	21	1	B

RECIPE	BOOK	PAGE	TD	S
Deviled	MIE	123	2	B
Deviled	NYT	114	2	A
Dinner, old country	GHAC	180	2	B
Extraordinary, barbecued	OC	102	2	B
Judy Hyun's marinated Korean	OC	102	2	B
Mrs. Roter's	AC	294	2	
Mustard	BCC	206	2	B
w Mustard sauce, beer & lime	CFS	91	3	B
Of beef	JOC	417	2	A
Braised	NYT	112	2	A
Braised	AC	293	2	
Braised	SP	129	2	B
Southern style	WC	82	1	B
Oven barbecued	SC	274	2	
Recipe, another, braised	AC	294	2	
Short shortbread	MIE	332	1	C
Shortbread	BTSB	227	1	C
Shortbread	CW	101	1	B
Cheese	CBB	394	1	B
Hearts	SP	261	2	C
Helen Gustafson's	FFBB	215	1	C
Oatmeal	MSQC	177	1	B
Scotch	BCC	113	1	C
◆	FFBB	214	1	C
◆	NYT	583	1	C
◆	SC	167	1	
◆	JOC	663	2	C
◆	FFCB	561	2	B
Shortcake	FFCB	526	2	B
◆	BTSB	125	1	C
◆	JBC	20	2	B
◆	AC	793	1	
Banana	NYT	565	1	C
Biscuit dough, making	SC	196	1	

RECIPE	BOOK	PAGE	TD	S
Blueberry	BHGN	179	2	B
Dough	JOC	584	1	C
Fluffy	FFBB	576	1	C
Fruit, fresh w topping	FAIC	444	2	B
Individual	BHGN	179	1	B
Individual	JOC	644	2	A
Large	JOC	644	2	B
Peach (see also peach shortcake)				
Peach	JBC	107	2	
Pepper & onion	MC	88	2	B
Sour cream & fruit	BB	117	1	A
Strawberry (see strawberry shortcake)				
Tomato	GG	373	2	B
Shortening bread	FFBB	215	1	C
Shoulder chops w wine, sauced	BHGN	40	1	B
Shredded wheat molasses bread	CBB	613	3	B
Shredding finely, how to	BHGN	429		
Shrimp	MAFC	213		
Shrimp	BB	89	1	
Al pesto	MIE	164	1	B
All about	JOC	376		
w Anchovy butter, boiled	NYTI	100	1	B
w Anchovy tomato sauce & spaghetti	SMG	297	1	B
Appetizer, broiled	BB	54	2	B
Appetizer, honeydew &	JBGF	299	2	B
Appetizers, marinated	BHGN	44	2	C
& Apple brandy	KIS	127	1	A
Apples & snow peas	SP	113	2	B

RECIPE	BOOK	PAGE	TD	S
Shrimp (*cont.*)				
& Artichoke				
Aux capres	NYTI	99	1	C
Bottoms	NYT	23	2	B
Leaves	SC	47	1	
Salad	FFCB	439	2	B
Salad	SP	225	1	B
Au gratin	NYT	293	1	B
Au gratin, crab, eggplant pirogue	PPLK	97	3	B
Aux capres	NYTI	99	1	B
& Avocado cocktail	SC	46	1	
& Avocado salad	BHGN	346	1	B
& Baby butter lettuce salad	FGCW	137	1	A
& Bacon	EBE	25	1	C
& Bacon	AC	25	2	C
& Bacon bites	BCC	10	1	B
& Bacon blankets	SC	42	1	
Baked	AC	157	1	B
Balls, Chinese	SC	40	1	
Balls, fried	JOC	74	1	
Baratin	NYTI	100	1	B
Barbecued	FG	290	2	B
◆	AC	154	1	
◆	PPLK	88	2	A
◆	OC	157	2	B
I	BB	90	1	
II	BB	90	1	
In foil	BHGN	39	1	B
Bisque	FFCB	100	2	B
◆	CBSS	216	3	B
◆	JOC	162	1	B
◆	MFC2	36	3	B
Bisque w black bean	CBSS	248	1	B
Blazing Brussels sprouts & gingered	GG	72	1	B
Boiled	BHGN	217	1	B
◆	JBC	89	1	
◆	FFCB	141	1	B
◆	SC	255	1	
◆	NYT	288	1	B
Boiled in beer	NYT	288	1	B
Bread	LM	75	1	B
& Broccoli, sauteed	NYTI	45	2	B
Brochettes, Adriatic style	CIC	226	1	B
Broiled	JBC	92	1	B
◆	FFCB	144	1	B
◆	BHGN	217	1	B
◆	JOC	74	1	
Charcoal	OC	158	1	B
Dill flavored	BB	55	2	
Garlic	OC	157	1	B
Garlic	NYT	293	3	B
Garlic	BBA	93	2	B
Italian style	JBC	90	1	B
Olive oil & seasonings	SMG	162	1	B
Polynesian	AC	154	2	
w Sambal sauce	BBA	92	2	C
Soy soaked	BB	54	1	
w Brussels sprouts	VGCB	39	1	B
Butter	SC	379	1	
◆	FFCB	56	1	B
◆	AC	12	2	
◆	JOC	339	2	A
Butter cream sauce	PPLK	68	1	B
Butterfly	AC	155	1	
Butterfly	JOC	376	2	
Butterfly, how to	LM	74		
& Cabbage salad	AC	51	1	
Canapes a la suede	NYT	43	1	B
Casserole w snail butter	JOC	377	1	B

SHRIMP

RECIPE	BOOK	PAGE	TD	S
Cauliflower	AC	507	1	
& Cauliflower in a blanket of mayo	GG	103	1	B
Charcoaled	OC	157	1	B
Cheese delight	EBE	99	1	B
w Cheese filling, leek wrapped	GHAC	125	2	B
Cheese nibblings	EBE	25	1	C
& Cheese in onion sauce	JOC	237	1	B
Cheese strata	BCC	20	1	C
& Chicken, curried	SMG	154	1	B
Chinoise	MSQC	108	1	B
Chop suey	WC	72	1	B
Chop suey	GHAC	192	1	
Chow mein	BHGN	219	2	B
Chowder, southern	CBSS	126	2	B
Clam sauce for pasta, quick	JOC	336	1	B
Cloaked	CFS	222	1	B
Club sandwiches	BCC	322	1	B
Cocktail	AC	153	1	
Cocktail	BCC	6	1	B
Cocktail	BHGN	15	1	B
Cocktail sauce	EBE	41	1	B
Cocktail, tangy dip	GHAC	89	1	B
Coconut	MSE	155	3	C
Coconut beer, w sweet dipping sauce	PPLK	283	2	B
Cold	AC	28	1	
Cooked	BCC	186	1	A
Cooked	AC	153	1	
& Corn chowder	CBSS	134	2	B
Court bouillon	FFCB	142	1	B
& Crab w butter cream sauce	PPLK	254	2	C
Crab & oyster gumbo	JOC	163	1	B
Crabmeat madeira	BBA	92	2	A
Crabmeat or lobster sandwiches	AC	812	1	
Cream sauce	SMG	152	1	B
Cream sauce, baked	NYTI	95	1	B
Creamed, variations	AC	156	1	
Creole	PPLK	95	2	C
Creole	AC	155	1	B
Casserole	SC	256	1	
Omelet	GHAC	112	1	A
Sauce	SMG	164	1	B
Crepes, curried	JBGF	505	1	C
Appetizer spread	BHGN	14	1	B
Cups	AC	31	2	
Salad	AC	53	1	
Salad	SC	364	1	
Soup, chilled	SP	53	2	B
Soup, M.F.K. Fisher's	GG	146	2	B
Cucumber	BCC	286	2	B
Curried	JBC	91	1	
Curry	BCC	250	1	B
Curry	NYT	293	1	B
Hawaiian	EBE	94	1	B
Oriental	JBC	90	1	B
Pilaf	AC	157	1	B
w Sour cream	EBE	100	1	B
Dahomienne	NYTI	74	1	B
De Jonghe	JBC	89	1	
Diane	PPLK	86	2	A
& Dill in lemon sauce	NYT	23	2	B
w Dill sauce, chilled	NYT	24	3	B
Dip	JOC	75	1	
Dip sauce	JBC	9	1	
Dumplings, steamed	NYTI	61	2	C
Egg bake	BHGN	196	2	B
Egg foo yung	BHGN	192	2	A
Eggplant, stuffed	SC	256	1	
& Eggs	MFC	54	2	A

RECIPE	BOOK	PAGE	TD	S
Shrimp (*cont.*)				
& Eggs, Bombay style	WC	46	2	B
Eggs foo yung	JOC	199	1	
Etouffee	PPLK	75	3	B
& Fennel, poached flounder w	GG	180	2	B
& Feta	YGM	167	2	C
w Feta cheese, baked, fresh	NYTI	328	1	A
Filled fillets	GHAC	138	2	B
Filled, fillets of sole	GHAC	138	2	B
Fillets, filled	GHAC	138	2	B
Filling, turnover cocktail	WC	22	1	C
Fish cocktail croquettes	WC	13	1	B
Fish fillets w mussels &	MAFC	214	2	B
Fondue	SC	256	1	
Fondue	NYT	291	2	B
Foo yung w soy ginger sauce	KIS	160	1	A
French fried	BHGN	217	2	B
Fried	NYT	289	1	A
Fried	AC	30	1	
Batter	JOC	378	1	A
Butterfly	SC	255	1	
Chinese	BCC	187	1	B
Chinese style	FG	318	1	B
Deep, squid &	FAIC	250	1	B
In deep fat	JOC	377	2	A
In deep fat, stuffed	JOC	377	2	B
In egg batter	NYTI	458	1	B
In leavened butter	MCIC	224	1	B
Fungus	FG	206	2	B
& Garlic marinade	VGCB	179	1	B
w Garlic oil	FGCW	89	2	
& Gin	FG	309	1	B

RECIPE	BOOK	PAGE	TD	S
Ginger toast	MSE	40	1	C
Gingered w Brussels sprouts	GG	72	1	B
w Glass noodles, pork &	FGCW	328	1	B
Glazed aspic	JOC	73	2	
Granados	NYTI	519	1	B
Grape salad, dill	SP	224	2	B
Grass, & pasta, garden shallots	CPPC	44	2	A
Greek style	NYTI	328	1	B
Greek style rigatoni	SMG	160	1	B
w Green cheese sauce	BBA	19	1	B
Grilled	NYT	292	2	B
Grilled	SC	333	2	
Cannocchie style	MCIC	227	1	B
Coach House	CFS	221	1	B
On rock salt	CPMC	172	1	B
Gumbo	BCC	308	2	B
Gumbo, dried egg &	PPLK	199	3	B
Herb sauce	NYT	22	2	B
Herbed	JBC	92	1	B
Herbed oil, jumbo	SPGT	19	2	C
w Hoisin sauce	NYTI	43	2	B
w Hot fish sauce	NYTI	44	2	B
w Hot sauce	WC	74	1	B
In aspic	AC	55	1	
In aspic	MAFC	549	2	B
In beer	SMG	150	1	B
In beer batter, fried	GHAC	124	2	B
In black bean sauce	NYTI	43	1	B
In Bloody Mary aspic	BBA	146	3	B
In dill flavored cream sauce	NYT	291	1	B
In eggplant batter, St. Bernard	PPLK	99	3	B
In lettuce shells w lemon yogurt dressing	BBA	147	1	B

RECIPE	BOOK	PAGE	TD	S
In wine sauce, striped bass stuffed w	NYT	230	3	B
w Indian sauce	SMG	166	1	B
Italian	SC	255	1	
Italian style	NYT	292	1	B
Jambalaya	JBC	90	1	B
◆	GHAC	125	1	B
◆	FFCB	142	1	B
◆	BCC	188	1	B
Kebabs	OC	156	1	B
Kebabs, steak &	BHGN	26	1	B
Kiev	BBA	93	3	B
Leek wrapped w cheese filling	GHAC	125	2	B
& Leeks, stir fried	VGCB	159	1	B
& Lettuce salad, warm	VGCB	250	1	B
Luau islander	NYT	23	2	B
Marinara	NYTI	385	1	B
w Marinara sauce	JBC	214	1	
w Marinara sauce, lobster &	JBC	214	1	
Marinated	AC	29	3	B
Marinated in beer	NYT	288	3	B
Marinated, fresh corn &	CW	64	1	B
Marseillaise	NYTI	155	2	B
Mayonnaise	PPLK	272	2	B
Mayonnaise	FAIC	65	1	B
Mayonnaise sauce	SMG	151	1	B
Mix	EBE	41	1	B
Mold	JOC	91	1	B
Mold, Margaret's	EBE	95	2	B
Mornay	JBC	91	1	B
Mousse, zucchini flowers filled w	MFC	27	3	B
& Mushroom, artichoke casserole w	SC	256	2	

RECIPE	BOOK	PAGE	TD	S
& Mushrooms in shells	JBC	91	1	B
Mustard	MFC	35	1	B
Nam Prik	GRIL	93	2	B
New Orleans	JOC	378	3	B
Newburg	JOC	378	2	A
Newburg	BHGN	219	2	B
Newburg	FFCB	143	1	B
Newburg, halibut &	SC	237	1	
w Oil & lemon	CIC	39	1	B
Okra, andouille smoked sausage gumbo	PPLK	211	3	C
& Okra bisque	PPLK	196	3	B
& Okra, Cross Creek	GG	227	1	B
Olive-sauce	GHAC	385		
Omelet, Creole	GHAC	112	1	A
On a stick	AC	30	1	
On shells of pastry, chutney	BBA	92	3	B
& Orange salad	AC	52	1	
& Orange salad I	AC	52	1	
Oriental	NYT	294	1	B
& Oyster sauce	FG	322	2	B
Oysters on pasta w garlic	PPLK	89	2	A
Paprika & sour cream	NYTI	342	1	B
Paste, southern	AC	154	1	
Pate w dill sauce, cold	GF	64	3	C
Patties, barbecued & skewered	OC	156	2	B
Peas	NYTI	75	3	B
Peas & creme fraiche, spaghetti w	CPPC	36	1	B
Pickled	WC	19	2	C
Pickled	JOC	73	2	
Pickled	EBE	39	2	C
Pie	SC	255	1	

RECIPE	BOOK	PAGE	TD	S
Shrimp (*cont.*)				
Pie, asparagus &	GG	32	2	B
Pie, ratatouille	GG	165	2	B
Pie, ratatouille eggplant	GG	165	2	B
Pierre	NYT	292	2	B
Pilaf, curried	AC	157	1	B
Pimiento mold	AC	54	2	
Pineapple salad	SC	364	1	
w Pink peppercorns	MFC	137	2	B
Pizza, feta &	JBGF	476	2	B
Pizza, green onion, tomato &	CPPC	160	3	B
Platter, cold	SC	255	1	
Poached	JBC	89	1	
Poached	JOC	377	1	B
Poached, cold	JBC	89	1	
Pork egg rolls	NYTI	63	2	C
& Pork w glass noodles	FGCW	328	1	B
Potted	JOC	377	2	
& Prosciutto, skewered	SP	122	1	B
Puffed	NYTI	44	2	B
Puffs	JOC	62	1	C
Puree, pumpkin &	NYTI	468	1	B
Quenelles	MAFC	189	2	B
Quiche	MAFC	149	2	B
Raspberry salad w haricots verts	SPGT	157	2	B
Remoulade	PPLK	285	2	B
Rice	NYT	294	1	B
& Rice casserole	SC	256	1	
& Rice, Mexican	JBC	90	1	B
& Rice soup	BHGN	373	1	B
Risotto	FAIC	219	1	A
Roman	NYTI	384	1	B
Saffron	NYT	291	1	A
Saffron	NYTI	519	1	B

RECIPE	BOOK	PAGE	TD	S
Salad	SC	363	2	
◆	JOC	91	1	B
◆	LM	75	1	
◆	AC	52	1	
◆	GHAC	279	1	B
Asparagus &	GG	27	1	B
Celery root &	BBA	140	2	B
Curried	JBGF	407	1	A
Curried	BCC	266	1	B
Island	BBA	147	2	B
Macaroni &	BCC	266	2	B
Marinated	AC	56	2	
Molded	BHGN	337	2	C
Old fashioned	AC	51	1	
Perfect	AC	51	1	
Sandwiches w cheese sauce	JOC	249	1	A
Sandwiches, cucumber &	BCC	12	1	
Satay	OC	157	1	B
Sauce	FAIC	66	1	B
◆	SC	390	1	
◆	JBGF	367	1	B
◆	BHGN	210	1	
Cauliflower &	EBE	111	1	B
Fettuccine w	CPPC	76	3	A
Fillets of sole w	NYTI	143	2	B
Fish fillets, broiled w	JBC	64	1	
For fish	JOC	334	2	C
Piquant	PPLK	91	2	B
& Sausages, grilled, on red rice	CFS	198	2	B
Saute w Pernod	SMG	156	1	B
Sauteed	SC	46	1	
Sauteed	FFCB	143	1	B
Scorpio	NYTI	327	1	B
Sesame, angel hair pasta w	YGM	107	1	B

RECIPE	BOOK	PAGE	TD	S
Smitane sauce	JOC	325	2	B
Smoke, basic flavoring, chart	CFS	51		
Smoked (see also beef, brisket, canapes, chicken, fish, goose, ham, herring, lamb, pork, salmon, sausage, shrimp, tongue, trout, turkey, whitefish)				
Smoked beef (see also beef, smoked)				
Smoked beef, basil-buttered & cured	CFS	281	2	B
Smoked beef & tongue, boiled	AC	321	1	
Smoked fish	AC	143		
Fillets poached in milk	AC	136	1	
For appetizers	AC	27		
List of	AC	143		
Mousse	MFC	29	3	B
Smoked food, sauce for	JOC	315	1	
Smoked Polish sausage kielbasa w sauerkraut	GHAC	212	1	B
Smoked salmon (see also salmon, smoked)				
Smoked salmon, lettuce packets of sole &	VGCB	253	1	B
Smoked tongue, cold	AC	320		
Smoked trout, rillettes of	SPGT	17	3	B
Smoker, chart	CFS	271		
Smoking, home, a note on	BTSB	28		
Snack mix	SC	41	1	B
Snail	JOC	378	2	
Snail	FFBB	536	3	C
All about	JOC	378		
Butter	MAFC	103	1	A
Butter	NYT	297	1	
Butter	JOC	339	1	B
For aioli	NYTI	135	1	B
In celery cream	FGCW	334	1	B
Mushroom stuffed w	NYT	37	1	B
Mushroom stuffed w	JOC	282	2	B
Orange almond	SPGT	100	3	C
Pastry	SC	82	2	
Preparing (photographs)	LT	123		
Provencale on toast	NYTI	157	1	B
Sicilian style	NYTI	386	1	B
w Wine	NYT	297	1	B
Snap bean	JOC	258	1	B
& Beef, stir fried	VGCB	19	1	B
Puree	VGCB	15	1	B
Puree	GG	349	2	B
Salad	JOC	85	1	B
Salad, hot	JOC	85	1	B
Souffle	AC	556	2	
Soup, pureed	VGCB	16	1	B
& Tomatoes	VGCB	14	1	B
Snapper				
Grilled & poached & dressed w fennel	CFS	227	1	B
w Orange sauce	KIS	130	1	A
Red, Creole	GHAC	140	2	C
Red w lime butter	GHAC	140	2	B
Snappy cheese, potted	SC	38	1	
Snappy soup (beef soup w unusual ingredients)	BBA	42	2	A
Snickerdoodles, snipdoodles or schneckendoodles	AC	705	1	
◆	FFBB	212	1	C
◆	GHAC	347	2	C
◆	BHGN	162	1	C

RECIPE	BOOK	PAGE	TD	S
Snickerdoodle cupcakes	AC	649	1	
Snickerdoodle snipdoodle (quick coffee cake)	AC	648	1	
Snipdoodles (cookies)	AC	705	1	
Snipe (woodcock)	JOC	481	2	
Snow apples	GHAC	288	2	B
Snow pea	AC	539		
Snow pea	FFCB	394	1	B
Snow pea	JBC	321	1	B
& Almonds	JBC	322	1	B
Chicken &	JBC	322	1	B
Chicken salad, water chestnuts &	MSQC	88	1	B
Garlic	KIS	161	1	A
Papaya, radishes, carrots &	GF	209	1	B
& Red pepper salad	YGM	133	1	A
Salad	MIE	270	1	B
Salad & Oriental roast pork	MIE	285	1	B
Sassy	CFS	248	1	B
Sauteed	CF	23	1	B
& Shrimp	SP	16	2	B
St. Andre	MSE	44	1	C
Steamed	YGM	115	1	A
& Tomato, fettuccine Alfredo w	MSE	144	2	C
Snow pudding	SC	201	1	
Snow pudding	FFCB	622	2	B
Snowflake cookies	FFBB	257	1	C
Soba noodles, cold	GRIL	79	2	B
Soboro (veal & shrimp dish)	CF	83	2	B
Soda bread	SP	246	2	B
Irish	FFBB	571	1	B
Irish	BCC	35	1	B
Irish	VE	43	2	B
Irish, quick	JOC	575	1	B
Whole wheat, Irish	JBGF	592	1	B
Wholemeal, currant	FFBB	571	1	B
Wholemeal, raisin	FFBB	572	1	B
Soda cracker pie	FFBB	100	2	B
Soda crackers, plain	CBB	695	3	C
Soffritto soup, parsnip	VGCB	190	1	B
Sofrito (vegetable dish)	NYTI	68	1	
Soft shell crabs (see crabs, soft shell)				
Sole				
A la meuniere	BBA	89	2	B
Albert	NYT	253	1	B
Amandine, fillets of	BBA	87	2	B
Ambassador	JOC	361	2	
Baked				
Fillets of	BBA	87	3	B
w Herbed cream	FFCB	122	1	B
In cream & mushrooms	FFCB	123	1	B
w Lemon sauce	GHAC	142	1	B
w Mushrooms & parsley	LT	151	2	
w Wine, grapes & cream	FFCB	123	1	B
w Black butter & capers	MSQC	128	1	B
w Butter, lemon & parsley	FFCB	122	1	B
Deauville	NYT	254	1	B
Deep fried, strips of	SMG	118	1	B
Duglere	NYT	255	1	B
Duglere gray	VGCB	321	2	B
Fillet	LT	146	2	
w Celery cream sauce	MFC	131	2	B
w Crabmeat sauce	EBE	93	2	B
Creamy	GHAC	142	1	B
Marguery	NYT	256	2	B
w Mornay sauce	NYT	253	1	B

RECIPE	BOOK	PAGE	TD	S
Sorbet (*cont.*)				
Cucumber, dill sauce for	GF	137	1	B
Espresso	MSQC	149	1	A
Fruit w apricot puree	CF	11	1	B
Grapefruit	YGM	185	2	C
Honeydew	GF	130	2	B
Instant	MIE	313	2	B
Lemon	SPGT	141	2	B
Lemon mint	GF	48	2	C
Making fruit	GF	131		
Peach	GF	130	2	B
Pear	GF	130	2	B
Plum	MHGD	444	1	B
Pomegranate	GF	130	2	B
Rhubarb	SPGT	42	3	B
Strawberry	MHGD	440	1	C
Tomato	GF	135	2	B
Sorghum (a grain) all about	JBGF	73		
Sorrel	JOC	300	1	
Sorrel	AC	559		
Definition	SP	56		
Eggs, salmon &	MFC	53	3	A
Flan	SPGT	58	2	C
Sea bass fillet w	MFC	115	2	B
Soup	SP	56	2	B
Soup	CBSS	349	2	B
Soup	MSE	228	2	C
Cold	MSQC	112	1	B
Cold, cream of	MFC	69	1	B
Cream of	NYTI	128	1	B
Cream of	JOC	160	1	B
Cream of	MAFC	42	1	B
Cream of, cold	NYT	81	1	B
Polish	GG	187	1	B
Potato	VGCB	224	1	B
Soto ajam (chicken & potato soup)	NYTI	365	2	B
Soubise (onion & rice casserole)	VGCB	176	1	B
◆	FFCB	267	1	B
◆	MAFC	485	1	B
◆	JOC	325	2	B
Soubise w onion sauce	AC	459	1	
Souffle				
A l'orange	NYTI	304	2	B
All about	JBC	269		
Almond	MAFC	618	3	B
Apple	SC	191	1	
Applesauce & sweet potato	JOC	205	1	B
Apricot (see also apricot souffle)				
Cold	FFCB	624	3	B
Frozen	FFCB	627	3	B
Omelet	JOC	692	1	B
Salad	BHGN	339	2	B
Artichoke	GG	20	2	B
Asparagus	VE	173	1	B
Au Grand Marnier	NYT	604	1	B
Aux fromages	BBA	124	2	B
Banana	NYT	605	2	B
Basic	BBA	123	2	B
Basic	JBC	270	1	B
Basic dessert	FFCB	618	3	B
Beet	GG	53	2	B
Broccoli (see also broccoli souffle)				
Broccoli & ricotta	JBGF	488	1	B
w Brussels sprouts	BHGN	394	2	B
w Brussels sprouts	GG	71	1	B
Caramel almond	MAFC	622	3	B
Caramelized almonds or macaroons	MAFC	617	3	B
Carrot (see carrot souffle)				

RECIPE	BOOK	PAGE	TD	S
Celery	GG	120	2	B
Celery root	SC	418	1	
Chartreuse w creme Anglaise	GF	348	1	B
Checklist	BBA	124		
Cheese (see also cheese souffle)				
Cheese, low calorie	KIS	204	2	A
Chestnut	VE	174	2	B
Chestnut	SC	195	1	
Chicken & wild rice	GHAC	116	2	B
Chocolate (see chocolate souffle)				
Clam	JBC	271	1	B
Coffee	FFCB	618	3	B
Coffee	MAFC	617	3	B
Collar, making (photographs)	LT	76		
Corn (see corn souffle)				
Cornmeal	JBC	21	1	
Crab	AC	149	1	
Crab	MAFC	170	3	B
Dessert	JOC	689		
Dessert, facts about	FFCB	604		
Eggplant (see eggplant souffle)				
Escarole	LT	189	2	
Fish	MAFC	168	3	B
Fish	FFCB	146	1	B
Fish baked on a platter	MAFC	170	3	B
Fruit	JBC	272	1	B
Fruit	JOC	690	2	B
Fruit	FFCB	619	2	B
Fruit, light	JBC	272	1	B
Garlic	CPMC	112	3	B
Ginger	NYT	604	1	B

RECIPE	BOOK	PAGE	TD	S
Ginger w rhubarb ginger sauce	SPGT	40	2	B
Glace aux fraises	NYT	633	2	B
Glace w candied fruit	NYTI	306	3	B
Glace vanilla & variations	NYTI	306	1	B
Glaceed w fruits & kirsch	MAFC	617	3	B
Goat cheese	CPPC	130	2	B
Grand Marnier	JOC	689	2	B
Grand Marnier	MHGD	381	2	B
Green pasta	FAIC	150	2	B
Green pea pasta	GG	272	2	B
Greene's	GG	193	1	B
Half & half	MAFC	618	3	B
Ham	FAIC	377	2	B
Ham	SC	305	2	
Ham & cheese	AC	452	2	
Ham & cheese	NYT	310	2	A
Hazelnut	JOC	691	2	B
Herb	FFCB	346	2	B
Herb & cheese	GHAC	116	1	B
Hints for making	VE	172		
Individual apple, in apples	MFC2	437	2	B
Laurette	NYTI	239	1	B
Lemon (see also lemon souffle)				
Lemon, cool	GHAC	300	2	B
Liqueur	JBC	272	1	B
Lobster	MAFC	170	3	B
Lobster, Plaza Athenee	LM	84	3	B
Macaroon (auflauf)	SC	192	1	
Macaroon	SC	195	1	
Making	JOC	204		
Making (photographs)	NYT	308		
Mandarin	BBA	215	3	B

broccoli, brown, Brussels sprouts, buttermilk, cabbage, carrot, cauliflower, celery, champagne, cheese, cherry, chestnut, chick pea, chicken, chili, clam, corn, crab, crayfish, Creole, cucumber, dill, duck, Easter, egg, eggplant, eggplant & red pepper, endive, escarole, fennel, fiddlehead, fish, fruit, garlic, goose, greens, guacamole, gypsy, ham, herb, herring, hot & sour, Jerusalem artichokes, kale, kohlrabi, lamb, leek, lemon, lentil, lettuce, mandarin, mango, melon, milk, minestrone, mint, miso, mulligatawny, mush, mussel, navy bean, oatmeal, okra, onion, orange, oxtail, oyster, parsnip, parsley, pasta, pea, peanut, pepper, pimiento, pistou, potage, rice, Roquefort, root, salsify, sauerkraut, sausage, scallion, scallop, seafood, shellfish, shrimp, sorrel, spinach, split pea, squash, squid, strawberry, summer squash, Swiss chard, tomato, tuna, turkey, turnip, turtle, vegetable, watercress, white bean, won ton, yellow squash, yogurt, zucchini

RECIPE	BOOK	PAGE	TD	S
Soup				
A hearty main dish	AC	88	1	
All about	FFCB	74		
Beet zucchini	MSQC	104	1	B
Broccoli	MSQC	152	1	B
Cabbage & leek	MSQC	212	1	B
Clearing	SC	393		
Coloring	JOC	144		
Cream, all about	JOC	157		
Custard	JOC	170	2	
De maiz	BBA	42	2	B
w Egg, garnished	JOC	169		
Eggplant & red pepper pother	GG	159	2	B
Flavoring	SC	393		
Garnishes	GHAC	100		
Garnishes for	JOC	169		
Ginger pear	MSQC	140	1	B
Making, basics	BHGN	365		
Meat, roasted	SC	276	2	
Nockerln	JOC	171	1	A
Paysanne	JOC	150	1	B
Pea w croutons	MSQC	52	1	B
Red bell pepper	MSQC	180	1	B
Removing fat from	SC	393		
Removing grease from	JOC	144		
Royale	JOC	170	2	
Sauces, dried	JOC	333	1	B
Sauces, thick, canned	JOC	333	1	B
Seasonings for	JOC	144		
Spices, herbs, seasonings for stews &	CBSS	413		
Sticks	SC	406	1	
Stock	SC	393	3	
Sunday, cream of bean	CBSS	252	3	B
Thickenings for	JOC	145		
Thickness of, testing	MFC	13		
Three "C"	JBGF	315	1	B
Tomato Tuscan	MSQC	81	1	B
Vinegar bean (Schnippel)	CBSS	253	3	B
Soupe au pistou	MFC	74	1	B
Soupe aux pois Canadienne	NYTI	26	2	B
Soupe de poissons	NYTI	121	2	C
Sour (drink—liquor)	SC	62	1	A
Sour bread, dark	CBB	128	3	C
Sour cherry jam	GHAC	381	3	C

RECIPE	BOOK	PAGE	TD	S
Sour cream	BTSB	63	2	A
Almond cupcakes	FFBB	382	1	C
Apple cake cockaigne	JOC	691	2	B
Apple pie	SP	272	3	B
Beans	BCC	336	1	B
Beef stew w	CBSS	76	3	B
& Beets	JBC	244	2	B
& Beets	NYT	364	1	B
& Beets	AC	484	1	
& Beets, cold	JBC	294	1	A
Biscuits	BHGN	84	1	C
Biscuits	GHAC	363	1	C
Buns	SC	82	2	
Cabbage	BCC	343	1	B
Cabbage	NYT	367	1	B
Cake	JOC	625	2	B
Cake	AC	656	1	
Cake	SC	118	1	B
Caramel frosting	SC	147	1	
w Celery root	SC	360	1	
Cheesecake	JOC	611	2	C
Cheesecake	SC	348	2	
Cheesecake	BHGN	175	1	C
Cherry pie	JOC	602	2	B
Chicken	EBE	77	1	B
Chicken w tarragon	NYTI	212	1	B
Chile dip	KIS	314	1	B
Chili dip	AC	11		
Chocolate cake	BCC	66	1	C
Chocolate cake	BHGN	98	1	C
Coffee cake	SC	118	1	B
◆	SP	321	2	C
◆	MHGD	104	1	C
◆	BCC	33	2	B
◆	GHAC	329	2	C
◆	FFBB	579	1	B
Coffee cake, quick	JOC	577	1	B
Cookies	FFCB	550	1	C
Cookies	SC	155	1	
Cookies	BCC	110	1	C
& Cucumber salad	SC	358	1	
& Cucumber sauce	NYT	440	1	B
& Cucumbers	VE	103	2	B
◆	BBA	142	1	A
◆	JBC	245	2	
◆	GHAC	276	1	B
◆	BHGN	335	1	A
Cultured	JOC	486	3	
Curry sauce	AC	11	1	B
Custard tart, peaches &	NSD	100	2	B
Dill sauce	NYT	453	1	B
Dip	KIS	328	1	B
◆	FFCB	54	1	B
◆	AC	11		
◆	JBC	3	1	
◆	JOC	74	1	
Dough	FFBB	64	1	B
Doughnuts	JOC	705	2	C
Doughnuts	SC	99	1	
Dressing	FFCB	455	1	B
◆	MAFC	95	1	A
◆	BCC	296	1	
◆	JBC	258	1	
Cucumber salad w	BB	139	2	B
For vegetable salad	JOC	317	1	B
Honey	BCC	295	1	
Dunk, herbed	BB	122	1	B
Filling	SC	148	1	
Filling, golden	SC	148	1	
Fish, baked	JOC	352	1	A
Frankfurters	AC	436	1	
Frosting, chocolate	GHAC	331	1	
Frosting, chocolate	BCC	78	1	C
Fudge	AC	833	1	
Fudge cake	NYT	550	1	C
Fudge, chocolate	FFCB	679	2	B
Gingerbread	FFBB	327	1	B

RECIPE	BOOK	PAGE	TD	S
Gingerbread	FFCB	513	2	B
Grape kuchen	SC	353	1	
Gravy	SC	387	1	
Green beans in	NYT	355		
Griddle cakes	SC	92	1	
Herb dip	AC	11	1	
Herring	NYTI	79	3	B
Herring	FG	350	1	
Herring marinated in	JOC	357	3	C
Hominy green & chilies in	AC	581	1	
Horseradish dressing	JOC	317	1	B
Horseradish sauce	EBE	57	1	B
Horseradish sauce	MC	79	1	B
Horseradish sauce	NYTI	276	1	A
Kipfel	SC	82	2	
Lima beans, boiled	JBC	292	1	A
Lima beans in	AC	483	1	
Mayonnaise	AC	76		
Mock, making	FGCW	289	1	
Mousse, cucumber &	JOC	100	2	B
Muffins	JOC	581	1	C
Muffins	SC	89	1	
Muffins, corn &	SC	90	1	C
Mushrooms in	SC	422	1	
Mushrooms in	NYTI	372	1	B
Mustard sauce	GHAC	256	1	B
Nut drops	BHGN	161	1	C
Omelet, spinach &	NYT	305	1	B
Omelet, Swiss cheese &	FG	93	1	A
Onion tart	AC	531	1	
Orange cake	MC	185	2	B
Orange sauce	BBA	192	1	A
Pancakes	BB	116	1	A
Pancakes	NYT	487	1	C
Peas, cucumbers &	NYT	391	1	B
Pie, apple	BCC	83	1	B
Pie, banana	MC	203	2	B
Pork chops baked in	JOC	424	2	B
Pork chops, stuffed	NYTI	71	1	B
Potato salad	NYT	426	1	B
Potatoes, baked	JBC	326	1	
Pumpkin pie	NYT	527	2	B
Pumpkin pie	FFBB	131	2	B
Pumpkin pie	GHAC	318	2	C
Raisin pie	MSE	247	2	B
Raisin pie	BHGN	282	3	C
Raisin pie	NYT	527	1	B
Red caviar w	NYT	53	1	B
Reduced calorie	MIE	46	1	B
Ring	SC	368	2	
Rolls	JOC	564	2	C
Roquefort cheese blend	AC	11	2	B
Rye bread	CBB	154	2	C
Salad, cucumber &	NYTI	316	1	B
Sauce	JOC	714	1	B
Broccoli &	GHAC	234	1	
Chocolate &	NYT	613	1	B
For baked potatoes	JOC	317	1	B
Tangy	CFS	317	1	A
Slaw	AC	498	2	
Souffle	NYT	309	1	B
Spice cake	FFBB	344	1	C
Spice cake	BCC	74	1	C
Steak, pepper &	JBC	130	1	B
Strawberries, fresh, in	MHGD	393	1	B
Strawberry shortcake w	NYT	565	2	B
Strudel	SC	355	2	
Substitute	JOC	487	1	
Tart, apricot &	NSD	100	2	B
Tart, nectarine &	NSD	100	2	B
Topping	BCC	137	1	
Torte, chocolate	GHAC	331	2	C

RECIPE	BOOK	PAGE	TD	S
Sour cream (*cont.*)				
Twists	FFBB	519	2	C
Twists, German	CBB	517	3	C
Veal rump &	NYT	152	2	B
Venison chops &	BB	51	1	
Waffles (see waffles, sour cream)				
Yogurt sauce for beet sorbet	GF	136	1	B
Sour hot soup	CBSS	342	2	B
Sour milk				
1, 2, 3, 4 cake	AC	651	1	
Biscuits	SC	88	1	
Cake	AC	652	1	
Cookies	SC	155	1	
Making	BHGN	77	1	
Sour skons (caraway-flavored)	CBB	565	3	B
Sourdough				
All about	JOC	504		
Biscuits or buns	AC	789	2	
Bread	AC	789	2	
Bread	BHGN	76	2	B
Bread	GHAC	359	3	C
For rye bread	SC	69	2	C
French bread, homecoming	CBB	278	3	C
Ginger rye	FFBB	482	3	B
Loaf	CBB	286	3	C
Oatmeal bread	CBB	281	3	C
Potato bread	CBB	288	3	C
Pumpernickel	CBB	295	3	C
Pumpernickel	NYT	467	2	C
Rolls, blue cheese	YGM	99	1	B
Rye bread	JOC	560	3	B
Rye bread	FFBB	480	2	C
Rye, ginger	FFBB	482	3	B
Starter	FFBB	465	1	C
Starter	BHGN	76	2	
Starter	AC	789	3	
Starter, yeast	CBB	276	3	B
White bread	FFBB	465	3	C
Whole wheat bread	CBB	283	3	C
Whole wheat bread, California	CBB	292	3	C
Souse	NYTI	19	3	C
South of the border salad	BHGN	347	1	B
Soy				
Barbecue marinade & basting sauce	AC	463	1	B
Butter	SPGT	30	1	A
Dressing, lemon	FFCB	455	1	B
Fish, braised	NYTI	38	1	B
Gevult	MC	100	3	B
Lemon sauce	NYTI	455	1	B
Marinade sauce	OC	162	1	A
Marinade, sesame	GHAC	223	1	B
Nuts	BBA	17	3	B
Rolls, whole wheat	FFBB	497	2	C
Sauce				
Beef spiced w	NYTI	48	1	B
Dressing	BCC	275	1	B
Ginger, steamed shellfish w herbs &	MSQC	92	1	B
Green onion for barbecue	GHAC	226	1	C
Spareribs, roast w	JBC	200	2	B
Sesame marinade	GHAC	223	1	B
Soybean				
Baked chutney	VE	134	3	A
Casserole, herbed	VE	128	3	B
Croquettes	VE	130	2	B
Milk	JOC	487	1	
Waffles	SC	97	1	
Spaetzle (dough like dish)	GF	71	1	C

RECIPE	BOOK	PAGE	TD	S
Spaetzle (*cont.*)				
◆	AC	588	1	
◆	BCC	58	1	B
◆	JBC	172	1	B
◆	BHGN	319	1	B
◆	FGCW	162	2	B
◆	JOC	192	2	B
Spaghetti	JBC	212	1	
Spaghetti	KIS	275	1	A
All'ortolana	NYTI	425	1	B
Alla puttanesca	FGCW	149	1	B
Alla puttanesca w clams	SMG	290	1	B
Anchovies	BCC	62	1	B
Anchovy w clam sauce	NYTI	420	2	B
w Anchovy sauce	FAIC	159	1	B
Baked	JOC	185	1	B
Beef, quick	JOC	185	1	B
w Beef sauce	BCC	209	1	B
w Black truffles, norcia style	MCIC	140	3	A
Boiled	SC	339	1	
Boiled	JOC	185	1	B
w Bread crumb sauce	FAIC	158	1	B
Broccoli de rabe	VGCB	134	1	B
Carbonara	FFCB	332	1	B
Carbonara	KIS	259	1	A
Carbonara I	NYTI	420	1	B
Carbonara II	NYTI	422	2	B
Caruso	AC	591	1	
Casserole	SC	340	1	
Casserole, chicken &	NYT	336	1	B
& Chicken w gizzard sauce	FAIC	157	2	B
w Chicken livers	NYTI	422	2	B
w Chicken & mushrooms	NYT	335	1	B

RECIPE	BOOK	PAGE	TD	S
w Chicken sauce	BCC	209	1	B
w Chickpea sauce	JBGF	357	1	B
Chop suey	SC	340	1	
& Clams	FFCB	331	1	B
w Clams	AC	590	1	
Coachman's style	FAIC	156	1	B
Cooked by a new technique	SMG	299	1	B
Cooking	AC	589	2	
w Cucumber, cool	GG	148	2	B
w Egg & cheese	JOC	185	1	B
Egg w pancetta sauce	FAIC	155	1	B
Egg w pesto	MSE	138	1	C
w Eggplant	NYTI	425	1	B
w Eggplant & ricotta	MCIC	138	1	B
w Fish balls	NYTI	423	1	B
w Fish head sauce	MCIC	133	2	B
w Fresh peas	NYTI	425	1	B
Frittata	FG	354	1	A
Frittata	MCIC	349	1	B
Frittata, stuffed	MCIC	352	2	B
w Garlic oil	CIC	103	1	B
w Garlic, parsley & anchovy	CPPC	145	1	B
Hot w cold tomato sauce	SMG	288	1	B
Italienne	SC	340	1	
w Lobster	NYT	335	2	B
w Marinara sauce	BHGN	320	1	B
w Meat balls bracciolini	NYTI	424	2	C
Meat pie, quick	JOC	185	1	B
w Meat sauce for a big party	BB	106	2	C
w Meatballs	GHAC	259	2	B
◆	BHGN	244	2	B
◆	SC	339	1	
◆	SMG	292	1	B

RECIPE	BOOK	PAGE	TD	S
Spaghetti w Meatballs (*cont.*)				
◆	BCC	209	1	B
◆	CPPC	102	2	B
Mushrooms	BCC	61	1	B
w Mussels	NYTI	423	2	B
w Oil & garlic	SP	68	2	B
Or linguini w clams	AC	590	1	
w Oyster sauce	AC	164	1	
Pancake	JBGF	355	1	B
w Pancetta & raw eggs	MCIC	135	1	B
w Peas	NYTI	426	1	B
w Pesto & vegetables	NYTI	427	1	B
Puttanesca (hooker's pasta)	FGCW	149	1	B
w Raw eggs & Italian bacon	MCIC	135	1	B
Salad	JOC	90	1	B
w Anchovies & olives, cold	MCIC	93	1	B
Chinese	JBGF	412	2	B
Sesame	JBGF	416	2	B
Shrimp, Norwegian	FG	84	1	B
Salmon, quick	JOC	185	1	B
Sauce	BHGN	244	2	B
Sauce	GHAC	259	1	B
Sauce	MSQC	156	1	B
Bolognese	NYT	342	2	C
Chicken wings w	FG	148	1	
Italian	JOC	185	1	B
Sea food	JOC	335	1	B
w Scallops	MCIC	128	1	B
Scampi	NYTI	385	1	B
w Shrimp, anchovy & tomato sauce	SMG	297	1	B
w Smothered onions	MCIC	136	1	B
Soup w bacon, quick	JOC	186	1	B
Southern	SC	339	2	

RECIPE	BOOK	PAGE	TD	S
Spicy tomato & bacon sauce	CF	123	2	B
Stuffed peppers	NYTI	426	2	B
Superb	EBE	64	1	B
w Sweetbreads & mushrooms	SC	339	1	
Tarragon w meat balls & sausages	NYTI	427	1	B
Thin				
w Anchovy & tomato sauce	CIC	101	1	B
w Eggplant	CIC	98	1	B
w Fresh basil & tomato sauce	CIC	97	1	B
w Red clam sauce	CIC	100	1	B
w Scallops	MCIC	128	1	B
w Tuna fish, quick	JOC	185	1	B
w Tuna sauce	CIC	102	1	B
w Two mushrooms	FG	126	1	B
w Uncooked tomato sauce	MSQC	156	1	B
Spaghetti squash (see squash, spaghetti)	MC	158	1	B
Spaghettini				
w Clams & cream sauce	FGCW	145	1	B
Estivi	NYTI	429	1	B
w Little veal cubes	NYTI	430	1	B
w Sausages	NYTI	429	2	B
Spanakopetes (spinach cheese puffs)	NYTI	325	2	B
Spanakopita (spinach pastry)	VE	150	2	B
Spanakopita	MC	151	2	B
Spanakopita	NYTI	334	2	C
Spanish bun	SC	110	1	B
Spanish bun cake	AC	653	2	

RECIPE	BOOK	PAGE	TD	S
Spanish casserole, rice	JOC	430	1	B
Spanish cream	SC	204	2	
◆	AC	735	2	
◆	FFCB	623	2	B
◆	JOC	685	2	B
Spanish cream chiffon pie	FFBB	120	2	B
Spanish omelet (see also omelet, Spanish)				
Spanish omelet	AC	108	1	
Spanish rice (albufera rice)	NYTI	222	1	B
Spanish rice	AC	579	1	
Spanish sauce	NYT	453	1	B
Spanish sweets	SC	177	1	
Spareribs				
Another old way, baked	AC	415	2	
Baked, dressing	JOC	425	2	B
Baked w sauerkraut	JOC	425	2	B
Barbecue sauce for	AC	417	1	B
Barbecue, smoked	FG	272	2	B
Barbecued	FFCB	199	2	B
◆	SC	330	2	
◆	NYTI	558	1	C
◆	AC	416	1	
w Beer & honey	NYT	140	3	B
Cantonese style	OC	123	2	B
Chinese	NYT	15	2	C
Chinese	FG	273	2	B
Chinese style	OC	123	2	B
Country style	OC	124	2	B
Herbed	NYT	141	2	B
Spicy	OC	124	3	B
w Black beans, Chinese	NYTI	50	2	B
Boiled	JOC	426	2	
Broiled	JBC	199	1	B
Chinese style	EBE	53	3	B
w Gingered plum sauce	NYT	15	3	C
Glazed	AC	416	1	
Grilled & marinated	MCIC	299	1	B
Hunan steamed w hot black bean sauce	FG	303	1	B
Italian gravy	FGCW	344	2	B
w Kraut	NYT	142	2	A
Kun koki	OC	123	3	B
Mexican	NYTI	471	2	B
Mustard	BCC	224	2	B
Old fashioned	CFS	164	2	B
Oriental	AC	417	2	
Oven barbecued	GHAC	194	1	C
Pan roasted, treviso style	MCIC	301	1	B
w Peach sauce	GHAC	219	2	B
Pineapple glazed	GHAC	194	1	B
Precooked	JBC	200	3	B
Raspberry-brushed	CFS	265	2	B
Roast, Chinese	BB	72	2	A
Roast, Polynesian	BB	72	1	B
Roasted	JBC	199	2	B
w Honey	JBC	200	2	B
w Honey & lemon	JBC	200	2	B
w Sauerkraut	JBC	200	2	B
w Soy sauce	JBC	200	2	B
Rodeo	BBA	58	1	B
w Sauerkraut	FFCB	199	1	B
w Sauerkraut	SC	295	2	
w Sauerkraut, boiled	AC	415	2	
So good	WC	120	1	B
Special	MIE	139	2	B
Spit roasted	SC	330	2	
Spitted	BB	71	1	
Spitted & barbecued	AC	416	2	
Stuffed	AC	416	2	
Stuffed	FFCB	199	1	B

RECIPE	BOOK	PAGE	TD	S
Spareribs (*cont.*)				
Sweet & sour	JOC	426	2	
Sweet, spicy	SC	330	2	
Sweet, zesty	BCC	224	2	B
Teriyaki, barbecued	BB	92	1	A
Tex Mex, barbecued	GHAC	219	2	B
Vegetables	FFCB	198	1	B
Spatzen (plain dumplings)	SC	102	1	
Spatzen	JOC	192	2	B
Spatzen	SC	407	1	
Spatzen for soup	JOC	173	2	B
Spatzle (dough noodles)	NYTI	72	2	B
Special salad	FG	80	1	B
Speckle cake, Vienna	NYTI	8	2	C
Speckled bread	CBB	361	3	B
Speckled trout, broiled	FFCB	125	1	B
Speculatius (cookies)	JOC	664	3	C
Spekulaas (cookies)	AC	705	1	
Spencer steak, definition	AC	260		
Spice				
1, 2, 3, 4 cake	AC	651	1	
Angel cake, high altitude	JOC	649	1	B
Bread	MFC2	481	2	
Cake	MFC2	481	2	
◆	SC	116	1	B
◆	AC	652	1	
◆	FFCB	514	1	B
Brown sugar	JOC	629	1	B
Eggless & milkless	JOC	637	2	B
Hurry up	JOC	635	1	B
Mix	KIS	344	1	C
Old fashioned	GHAC	342	2	C
Pumpkin or squash	AC	671	1	
Roll	FFBB	306	2	C
Sour cream	BCC	74	1	C
Velvet	JOC	628	2	B
Cookies	SC	161	1	
Cookies, Christmas	SC	153	1	
Cookies, raisin	SC	161	1	
Crinkles	AC	714	1	
Crumb cupcakes	FFBB	380	1	C
Cupcakes	FFBB	378	1	C
Glaze	FFBB	275	1	B
Loaf cake	AC	650	1	
Nut cake	BHGN	95	1	C
Oil cake, quick	JOC	635	1	B
Parisienne	BTSB	198	1	B
Parisienne	JOC	541	1	
Pie	FFBB	137	2	B
Pointers	BBA	165		
Refrigerator cookies	AC	701	2	
Spritz	AC	708	2	
Yeast cake	SC	80	2	
Spiced eggs	GHAC	113	3	C
Spiced syrup for canned fruits	JOC	106	1	B
Spices, all about	JOC	526		
Spices, four	JOC	541	1	
Spices, herbs & seasonings for soups & stews	CBSS	413		
Spices, herbs, uses for	NYT	657		
Spices, using, whole	BHGN	425		
Spicy hard sauce	JOC	714	1	B
Spicy nectar dressing	BHGN	344	1	B
Spicy quince preserve	MSE	219	2	B
Spicy red sauce	FAIC	61	1	B
Spicy spiral loaf	SC	71	2	C
Spider bread or spider corn bread	AC	583	1	
Spinach	MAFC	467		
Spinach	JOC	300		
All about	VGCB	260		
Artichoke casserole	FG	193	1	C
Artichoke Cajun	GG	14	1	B

SPINACH

RECIPE	BOOK	PAGE	TD	S
Avocado &	GG	41	1	B
Bean bake Santa Fe	GG	316	2	B
Blanched	VGCB	262	1	
Blanched & chopped	MAFC	468	2	B
Blender	JOC	301	1	A
Boiled	JBC	331	1	B
Boiled	JOC	300	1	A
Boiled w mushrooms	JBC	332	1	
& Brains between layers of puff pastry	MFC	44	3	B
Braised				
Baby	FFCB	409	1	A
w Butter	MAFC	470	2	B
w Cream	MAFC	471	2	B
w Onions	MFC2	360	1	B
w Toasted almonds	GRIL	67	2	B
& Broccoli pie	FG	340	3	B
Bundles	YGM	196	3	C
Butter	SMG	25	1	B
Buttered	MAFC	470	2	B
Cannelloni stuffed w ricotta &	FAIC	184	2	C
Casserole	SC	432	1	
Casserole, egg &	GHAC	110	1	B
Celery, saute of	VGCB	262	1	B
& Cheese				
Baked	MIE	225	1	B
Canapes	MAFC	472	2	B
Puffs	NYTI	325	2	B
Squares	JBGF	306	1	C
& Chicken breasts	SMG	24	1	B
& Chicken filling for pasta	NYT	331	1	B
Chicken stuffed w cheese &	BBA	66	3	B
Chinese	BHGN	404	1	B
Chopped	SC	431	1	
Chopped	JBC	332	1	

RECIPE	BOOK	PAGE	TD	S
Coconut, moruga	GG	313	1	B
Cooked & chopped	MAFC	469	2	B
Cooking	AC	543		
Creamed	JOC	300	1	A
◆	MAFC	471	2	B
◆	KIS	89	1	A
◆	SC	431	1	
Creamed I	JBC	332	1	
Creamed II	JBC	332	1	
Crepes	VGCB	266	2	B
w Cream cheese & mushrooms	MAFC	193	2	B
Salmon &	FGCW	334	1	B
Vegetable stuffed	FGCW	95	2	B
Dessert pudding	AC	730	1	
Dip	BBA	22	1	C
Dip	BCC	15	1	C
Dumplings	GG	315	1	B
Dumplings	BBA	110	2	B
Dumplings, ricotta &	NYT	337	1	B
& Feta strudel	NYT	30	2	C
Fettuccine stuffed w yellow pasta shells &	CIC	145	3	B
Fillets of sole, wrapped	MSQC	192	1	B
Filling for ravioli	GHAC	263	1	
Finishing touches for blanched & steamed	VGCB	262	1	
Fish paupiettes w	VGCB	266	2	B
Flan w fresh tomato	MFC	177	2	B
Florentine style	FAIC	422	1	B
Four day	GG	313	3	B
Frittata	JBGF	484	1	C
Frittata & cheese	FFCB	343	1	B
Frozen	MAFC	475	1	B
& Garlic, pan sauteed	MSQC	173	1	A

RECIPE	BOOK	PAGE	TD	S
Spinach (*cont.*)				
& Ginger, stir fried	VGCB	263	1	B
Gnocchi & ricotta	CIC	200	1	B
w Gratineed cheese	MAFC	471	2	B
w Gratineed cheese sauce	MAFC	472	2	B
Greens, pasta w beet &	CPMC	223	2	B
Ground	JOC	301	1	A
Ham	MAFC	470	2	B
w Herb sauce	CFS	313	1	B
Hidden under a giant crepe	MAFC	473	2	B
Italian	NYT	400	1	B
w Italian sausage	FGCW	346	1	B
Italian style	SC	431	1	
Lasagne	BBA	109	2	B
Lasagne, smoked ham &	MSE	144	2	C
Leaf	LM	121	1	
Loaf, tuna &	MCIC	326	1	B
Mayonnaise	MIE	251	3	C
Meatballs & sausage	FG	359	1	B
Mold	MAFC	474	2	B
Mold	LM	122	1	B
Mornay	EBE	119	1	C
Mousse	BBA	90	2	A
& Mushroom casserole	AC	528	1	
& Mushrooms, salad dressing for	MSQC	184	1	B
& Mushrooms	NYT	400	1	B
Noodles	MIE	189	1	B
Noodles	BTSB	301	2	B
Noodles & cheese	JBGF	362	1	B
& Nutmeg, creamed	BHGN	404	1	B
Omelet, creamed	MSE	91	1	C
Omelet w sour cream	NYT	305	1	B
Orange toss	BHGN	332	1	B
Oysters & caviar	SP	37	3	C
Oysters & Pernod	SMG	132	1	B
& Oysters w white butter sauce	VGCB	264	2	B
Pancake (isfanakh fatira)	GG	318	1	A
Pancakes	JOC	301	1	
Pancakes	MAFC	474	2	B
Panned	JOC	301	1	A
Pasta	CIC	126	3	
Dough, egg &	MCIC	158	3	
w Prosciutto, peas &	CPPC	33	1	B
w Salmon & cream sauce	SP	81	1	B
Pie	BBA	110	2	C
w Egg	NYT	28	1	B
Greek	VGCB	265	2	B
Lebanese	NYTI	463	3	C
Piquant	KIS	134	1	B
Pizza, deep dish	JBGF	478	3	B
Preparing	GG	308		
Provencale	VE	149	1	A
Pudding (see pudding, spinach)				
Puree	AC	544	1	
Puree of	MAFC	469	2	B
Pureed	JBC	332	1	
Pureed	FFCB	409	1	A
Quiche	GHAC	114	1	B
Quiche, cheese &	MSE	55	3	C
& Rice casserole	MC	121	1	B
& Rice stuffed chicken	GG	317	2	A
& Ricotta pie	MC	123	2	B
& Ricotta, tomatoes stuffed w	SP	193	2	C
& Ricotta, tortelli stuffed w	FAIC	169	2	B

SPINACH

RECIPE	BOOK	PAGE	TD	S
Ring	SC	431	1	
Ring	NYT	400	1	B
Ring	AC	544	1	
Ring, Danish	NYT	401	1	B
Ring mold	JOC	209	2	B
Roll	AC	544	1	
Rolls (brummagems)	GG	308	1	C
Salad	MFC	187	1	B
◆	FG	78	1	B
◆	MIE	260	1	B
◆	EBE	142	1	B
◆	SC	358	1	
◆	NYT	417	1	B
◆	AC	49	1	
Almond &	YGM	89	1	B
Apple, walnut &	KIS	275	1	A
Avocado &	NYT	417	1	B
Basil, warm	SPGT	68	1	B
w Chicken livers	LM	150	2	B
Citrus	JBGF	548	1	B
Creamy dressing	MIE	261	1	B
Fresh	VGCB	264	1	B
Golden door dressing	KIS	193	1	A
Grapefruit &	MSQC	97	1	B
Jerusalem artichoke &	CIC	406	1	B
Mushroom &	MSQC	184	1	B
Mushroom &	BCC	278	1	B
Mushroom, bacon &	FFCB	429	1	B
Mushroom, bacon &	GHAC	271	1	B
Mushroom, hot	YGM	71	1	B
Salmon &	AC	66	1	
w Soy dressing	YGM	91	1	A
Tongue &	AC	72	1	
Warm goat cheese &	GG	311	3	B
Wilted	VGCB	264	1	B
Wilted	BHGN	332	1	B
Wilted	AC	49	1	
Sauce	BCC	265	1	
Sauce (for pasta)	GHAC	265	1	B
Ricotta penne w	MCIC	147	1	B
Salmon steaks, poached, cold w	BBA	86	2	A
Sauteed	CIC	388	1	B
Sauteed, veal w	LM	40	3	B
Sauteed, wax beans &	GG	347	1	B
w Sesame bean paste	FGCW	353	1	B
w Sesame seed dressing	GG	312	1	A
w Sesame seeds	FGCW	353	1	B
w Sesame seeds	KIS	121	1	A
w Sesame seeds & sesame bean paste	FGCW	353	1	B
Sicilian	JOC	301	1	A
w Sliced potatoes, anchovies gratin of	MAFC	474	2	B
Souffle	AC	557	1	
◆	MSQC	168	1	B
◆	BCC	350	2	B
◆	MAFC	165	2	B
◆	JBC	270	1	B
◆	FFCB	346	2	B
◆	VGCB	263	1	B
Ham &	FFCB	208	2	B
Ham &	MAFC	166	2	B
Mushrooms &	MAFC	166	2	B
Soup	CIC	65	1	B
◆	MFC2	9	1	B
◆	CBSS	347	1	B
◆	JOC	156	1	B
Cold	MFC2	10	1	B
Cream of	SC	402	1	

RECIPE	BOOK	PAGE	TD	S
Spinach Soup, Cream of (*cont.*)				
◆	JOC	160	1	B
◆	VGCB	265	1	B
◆	MC	18	1	B
◆	MAFC	43	1	B
Cream of I	NYTI	128	1	B
Cream of II	NYTI	128	1	B
Creamed	FAIC	118	1	B
Dandelion	FG	49	2	B
Fresh	VGCB	264	1	B
Lentil &	BCC	313	2	B
Quick	JOC	167	1	B
Rice &	MCIC	103	1	B
Vegetable	GG	310	2	B
Spread	KIS	315	1	B
Squid	FAIC	251	2	B
Steamed	VGCB	262	1	
Stir fried	MIE	224	1	A
Stir fry	WC	30	1	A
Stir fry, ham &	WC	115	1	B
Stir, sauteed	FAIC	421	1	B
Stuffed flounder	GHAC	138	1	B
Stuffing	GHAC	159	1	
Stuffing, meat loaf roll w	GHAC	184	2	B
Stuffing, veal breast w	NYT	161	2	B
Tart	EBE	119	1	C
Tart	MFC	178	2	
Tart, slow baked	GG	309	2	C
Timbales	JOC	208	2	B
Timbales	VGCB	263	1	B
Tomato & cheese loaf	JOC	301	2	B
Tomato & red onion w horseradish dressing	FFCB	428	1	B
Tomatoes	JOC	301	1	B
Tossed leaf	AC	544	1	
Tossed salad	BCC	278	1	B
Vermicelli	BCC	61	1	B
Viennese	NYT	401	1	B
Walnuts &	BBA	147	1	B
Washing	SC	431		
Whole sauteed	VGCB	262	1	B
Wilted	BCC	349	1	B
Wilted	JBC	332	1	
Wilted, rustic	CFS	248	1	B
w Wine & sesame	FGCW	325	1	B
w Yogurt & mint	YGM	63	1	A
Yogurt sauce	MC	67	1	B
Spiral bread	NYT	467	3	C
Spirals (bread)	FFBB	263	1	C
Spirit glaze for ham	JOC	340	1	
Spit roasting, chart	BHGN	24		
Split green pea soup, potato &	CIC	72	1	B
Split pea soup	JOC	153	2	B
◆	BHGN	375	2	C
◆	FFCB	98	2	C
◆	AC	92	2	
◆	JBC	278	2	
◆	MIE	70	2	C
◆	BCC	313	2	B
Best of	MC	17	2	B
w Black beans	JBC	278	2	
Blender	JOC	153	2	B
Cream of	CBSS	329	2	C
Dutch	NYT	64	2	C
Dutch	JBGF	346	2	B
Green	CBSS	325	2	B
Green w cheese	CBSS	326	2	B
Green w wine	CBSS	328	2	B
Hearty	GHAC	103	2	C
w Kidney beans	JBC	278	2	
Puree of yellow	GF	195	1	C
Pureed	JBGF	324	2	B
w White pea beans	JBC	278	2	

RECIPE	BOOK	PAGE	TD	S
Sponge cake	WC	134	1	B
◆	JOC	621	1	B
◆	FFCB	517	2	B
◆	AC	682	1	
◆	NYTI	10	2	B
◆	NYT	566	2	B
◆	JBC	35	2	B
Basic	LT	356	1	
Butter	MAFC	669	3	C
Butter	FFBB	301	2	C
Chocolate	MAFC	679	3	B
Chocolate	JOC	622	1	B
Chocolate	FFCB	518	1	B
Chocolate butter	FFBB	301	2	C
w Chocolate filling	EBE	156	2	B
Coffee	SC	119	1	B
Cold water	FFBB	297	2	C
Cream	FFCB	518	2	B
Four egg	SC	118	1	B
Golden	SC	119	1	B
High altitude	JOC	650	1	B
Hot milk	BHGN	100	1	C
Hot milk	FFBB	298	2	B
Hot water	FFCB	518	2	B
Hot water	SC	119	1	B
Italian	FAIC	450	1	B
Matzo	SC	124	1	B
Matzo lemon	SC	124	1	B
Orange	MAFC	671	3	B
◆	FFBB	299	2	C
◆	BHGN	100	1	C
◆	SC	120	2	B
◆	EBE	156	3	B
Orange almond	MAFC	676	3	B
Orange, w butter filling	MAFC	672	1	B
Potato flour	JOC	621	1	B
Rice flour	JOC	621	1	B
Simply	FFBB	296	2	B
Two egg	SC	118	1	B
Sponge candy	BCC	119	1	B
Sponge cookies	NYT	581	1	C
Sponge drops	SC	140	1	
Sponge dumplings	SC	408	1	
Sponge dumplings	SC	103	1	
Sponge dumplings, rich	SC	408	1	
Sponge jelly roll	NYTI	285	2	B
Sponge jelly roll	SC	123	2	B
Sponge layer	JBC	42	1	
Sponge layers	NYT	567	1	B
Sponge roll	JBC	42	1	
Sponge roll	NYTI	284	2	B
Chocolate	SC	123	1	B
Matzo	SC	124	1	B
Or sponge layer	AC	679	1	
Spicy	MHGD	76	2	B
Sponge sheet	FFBB	305	2	C
Spoon bread	BHGN	86	1	B
◆	FFCB	313	1	B
◆	CW	117	1	B
◆	NYT	482	1	B
◆	JBC	21	1	
◆	GHAC	366	1	B
◆	BBA	178	2	B
Alice's	FFCB	315	1	B
Bacon	CBB	185	1	B
Cheese	BHGN	86	1	B
Corn	JOC	580	1	B
& Corn meal souffle	VE	176	1	A
Cornmeal	AC	583	1	
Crusty	JOC	579	1	B
Green gold	GG	269	1	B
Hominy grits &	AC	582	2	
Light	FFCB	313	1	B
Pan baked	BB	118	1	B
Rice	JOC	580	1	B
Soft centered	JOC	579	1	B

RECIPE	BOOK	PAGE	TD	S
Spoon corn bread, southern, quick	SC	85	1	
Spoon-scalloped edge, forming for pies	GHAC	318		
Spread, mystery	EBE	37	2	B
Spring bean salad	MIE	272	1	B
Spring garden soup	VGCB	331	1	B
Spring salad	MFC	193	1	B
Springerle (spicy, hard cookie)	FFBB	268	2	C
◆	AC	706	2	
◆	SC	156	1	
◆	JOC	663	2	C
◆	NYT	584	3	C
Spritz (filled cookies)	BHGN	165	1	C
◆	GHAC	348	1	C
◆	BCC	114	1	C
◆	FFBB	253	2	C
Butterscotch	AC	708	2	
Chocolate	BCC	114	1	C
Chocolate	AC	708	2	
Cookies	JOC	664	2	C
Cookies	SC	158	1	
Cookies, white	NYTI	318	1	C
Holiday decorated	BCC	114	1	C
Holiday pineapple filled	BHGN	165	2	C
Krapfen	SC	100	1	
Or cookie press cookies	AC	707	2	
Spice	AC	708	2	
Spritzer	BB	168	1	
Sprout & fennel chowder	GG	70	1	B
Sprouting	BTSB	279		
Sprouts, Creole	SC	413	1	
Sprouts, growing your own	JBGF	109		

RECIPE	BOOK	PAGE	TD	S
Spumoni cookies	BCC	110	2	C
Squab	JOC	475	3	
w Anchovy & olive butter, spit roasted	CPMC	25	2	B
Boned & stuffed	LM	186	3	B
Broiled	BB	49	1	
Broiled	SC	322	1	
Broiled	JOC	475	2	
Butterflied & grilled w mustard sauce	MSQC	76	2	B
Chicken, grilled	FAIC	290	1	A
Chicken, roast	JBC	224	1	
Cleaning (photographs)	LT	213		
Cold	JBC	234	2	B
En casserole	SC	322	1	B
Grilled over charcoal	OC	138	2	B
Macaroni in a pastry drum	FAIC	206	2	B
On the spit	JBC	234	2	B
Pie, quail, chicken, sausage, tortelli &	FAIC	383	3	C
Potted	JOC	475	2	B
Roast	JBC	233	1	
Roast	BB	82	1	
Roast	NYT	180	2	A
Garlic & liver sauce	CPMC	114	3	B
w Sauterne sauce	CPMC	96	3	B
Stuffed	JBC	234	2	B
w Tarragon	JBC	233	1	
Roasted	SC	322	2	
Roasted pan	CIC	319	2	B
Salad w garden lettuces	CPMC	125	2	B
Sauteed w bacon	BB	49	1	
Sauteed w white wine	BB	49	1	

RECIPE	BOOK	PAGE	TD	S
Stuffed	NYTI	235	2	B
Stuffed w madeira sauce	NYTI	236	2	B
Toadlike	LT	216	2	
Whole, flattening for grilling	OC	50		
Squah cookies	VGCB	292	1	C
Squash				
Acorn				
Applesauce	EBE	109	1	B
Baked	SMG	267	1	B
◆	SC	432	1	
◆	MIE	227	2	B
◆	JBC	334	1	B
◆	NYT	402	1	
Baked w bacon	NYT	402	1	B
Baked w bacon	JBC	334	1	B
Baked w brown sugar	JBC	334	1	B
Baked halves	BHGN	405	1	A
Baked slices	KIS	86	1	A
Baked & stuffed	SC	432	1	
Baked w sugar	JBC	335	1	B
& Cranberry pot roast	GHAC	179	2	C
Flan	GG	333	2	B
Grilled	BHGN	42	2	B
Maple	BCC	362	1	B
Muffins	FFBB	560	1	C
Sesame chicken w	MSQC	124	1	B
Skillet, baked	GHAC	245	1	A
Sour cream	VGCB	289	1	B
Stuffed	VGCB	288	2	B
Stuffed	GHAC	245	1	A
Applesauce	BHGN	405	1	A
Baked	OC	96	1	A
Baked	VGCB	285	1	
Baked	VGCB	272	1	
Baked, mashed	VGCB	287	1	B
Bisque	CBSS	344	2	B
Bisque, curried, winter	GG	334	2	B
Blossoms				
Deep fried	CPMC	48	2	B
& Goat cheese, zucchini	GG	404	2	B
Stuffed	JOC	302	1	
Zucchini, goat cheese &	GG	404	2	B
Boats	GG	338	2	B
Boiled	VGCB	284	1	
Bundt, sweet, summer	GG	328	1	C
Butternut				
Anise	YGM	55	1	A
Baked	NYT	402	1	
Glazed	NYT	403	1	B
Mashed	SC	432	1	
Mashed	NYT	403	1	B
Raisins	YGM	137	1	B
Soup, curried	SP	47	2	B
Stuffed	NYT	402	2	B
Cake	VGCB	292	1	C
Cake, Turkish	GG	326	1	C
Candied	BHGN	405	1	A
Canned, uses for	AC	559		
Casserole, baked	BCC	363	1	B
Casserole of	AC	547	1	
& Cheese casserole, Arabian	MC	134	2	B
Chicken, corn &	NYTI	474	2	B
Chilean	MC	97	1	B
Cornbread	VGCB	292	1	B
Cream	NYTI	476	1	B
Creamed yellow	YGM	123	1	A
Creme brulee, winter	GG	339	3	B
Creme, winter, w caramel	VGCB	291	2	B

RECIPE	BOOK	PAGE	TD	S
Squash, Spaghetti (*cont.*)				
◆	KIS	175	1	A
◆	KIS	223	1	B
◆	YGM	71	1	B
Baked	MIE	229	2	B
w Clam sauce	JBGF	448	1	B
Primavera	GG	337	1	B
w Spicy meat sauce	GHAC	245	1	B
Tetrazzini	GG	336	1	B
Vegetable, variations	VGCB	286	1	
Spears, easy dilled	VGCB	282	1	B
Spice cake	AC	671	1	
Steamed	VGCB	284	1	
Steamed, ginger & apple	VGCB	287	1	B
Stew	VGCB	277	1	B
Stir-fried	AC	562		
Stuffed, small	VGCB	275	2	B
Stuffed, variations of fillings	MC	128	1	B
Stuffing	VGCB	289	1	B
Summer	AC	545		
A la Grecque	VGCB	271	1	
All about	VGCB	269		
Baked	JOC	303	1	B
Boiled	VGCB	272	1	
Boiled	JBC	333	1	B
Broiled	VGCB	273	1	
Buying & storing	MFC2	362		
Cake, orange	VGCB	281	1	B
Casserole	JBC	333	1	B
Casserole cockaigne	JOC	304	1	B
Casserole, Marylin Harris's	GG	327	1	B
Creole	JOC	303	1	
Deep fried	VGCB	273	1	

RECIPE	BOOK	PAGE	TD	S
Dill panned	BHGN	404	1	A
Grilled	VGCB	273	1	
w Horseradish cream	FFCB	410	1	B
Kate's, pan fried	GG	325	1	B
Loaf, two tone	VGCB	278	1	B
Onion	FFCB	410	1	B
Pepper slaw	GHAC	272	2	C
Preparing	BCC	361		
Sauteed	JOC	303	1	B
Sauteed	FFCB	410	1	B
Sauteed	VGCB	272	1	
Scalloped w cheese	NYT	403	1	B
Seafood soup	GG	324	1	B
Soup, curried	VGCB	279	1	B
Spice cake	VGCB	281	1	B
Steamed	VGCB	272	1	
Steamed	JOC	302	1	B
Stir fried straw & hay	MIE	226	1	B
Stuffed	VGCB	273	1	
Stuffed & cooked	JOC	303	1	B
Stuffed, raw	JOC	303	1	B
w Sun dried tomatoes	MSQC	96	1	B
w Tarragon cream	GG	326	1	B
Tomatoes	FFCB	410	1	B
Swiss	NYTI	538	1	B
Tomatoes filled w lamb &	VGCB	322	1	B
Winter	VGCB	282		
Baked	JOC	304	1	
Baked	FFCB	411	1	B
Braised, garlic	GG	335	1	B
Canning	BHGN	142		
Charcoal roasted	CFS	250	1	B
Cooking	AC	547	1	
Creme brulee	GG	339	3	B
Freezing	BHGN	142		

RECIPE	BOOK	PAGE	TD	S
St. Honore Gateau (cream puff cake)	LT	399	3	
St. Valentine custard cake	LT	441	3	
Stampfenbohnen (bean dish)	VGCB	15	1	B
Standard rolls	FFCB	473	2	C
Staples for the average family	JOC	745		
Staples for your kitchen, list of explanations	FFCB	11		
Starter				
Bread	CBB	273		
Brioche dough	CBB	663	3	C
Brioche dough, without	CBB	665	3	C
Honey	CBB	275	3	B
Hops	CBB	276	3	C
Potato, cooked	CBB	274	3	C
Potato, raw	CBB	275	3	B
Potato, white bread	CBB	404	3	C
Salt rising	AC	790	2	
Sourdough rye	BTSB	104	1	
Sourdough white flour	BTSB	110	1	
White bread	CBB	290	3	C
Stashi (cooked spinach w soy sauce)	NYTI	457	1	B
Steak				
A la creme	NYTI	165	1	B
An early Polish American recipe for	AC	267	2	
An old recipe for mignon fillets	AC	265	1	
Anchovy butter	GHAC	217	1	B
Au poivre	BBA	50	2	A
◆	NYTI	166	1	B
◆	OC	100	2	B
◆	NYT	91	1	B
◆	JBC	130	1	B
◆	JOC	401	1	
◆	AC	262	1	
Au poivre a la creme	NYTI	167	1	B
Au poivre w sour cream	JBC	130	1	B
Aux echalotes	NYTI	167	1	B
Baked	SC	270	1	
Baked w vegetables	SC	270	1	
Barbecued	OC	100	2	B
Barbecued	BB	15	1	
Barbecued, basic	BBA	49	1	B
Bert Greene's	CFS	81	2	B
Broiled	JOC	400	1	
Broiled	FFCB	157	1	
Broiled	SC	270	1	
w Bearnaise sauce	MSQC	172	1	A
Florentine way	CIC	238	1	A
Oven, basic	BBA	49	1	B
Pan	SC	270	1	
◆	JOC	400	1	
◆	MAFC	292	1	B
◆	FFCB	158	1	
Pan, basic	BBA	49	1	B
Pan, w Bearnaise sauce	MAFC	295	2	B
Pan, fillet	JOC	400	1	
Pan, w marsala & hot pepper sauce	CIC	239	1	B
Pan, mock	SC	280	1	
Pan, w red wine sauce	MAFC	295	1	B
Pan, w shallot & white wine sauce	MAFC	294	1	B
Pan, thin tomatoes & olives	CIC	241	1	B

STEAK

RECIPE	BOOK	PAGE	TD	S
Mock fillet	SC	280	1	
Mosaic, flank	SP	105	2	B
& Mushrooms	BCC	201	2	B
& Mushrooms	WC	88	2	B
w Mustard butter	GHAC	173	1	A
w Mustard cream sauce	SMG	234	1	B
Mustard, herb broiled	BBA	49	1	A
Neapolitan w tomato caper sauce	BBA	50	2	B
& Okra gumbo, seven	PPLK	206	3	B
w Onions, green pepper & tomatoes	BBA	50	1	B
Onion stuffed	BHGN	27	1	B
Pepper	BB	15	1	
◆	SC	270	1	
◆	FFCB	158	1	B
◆	NYT	90	1	B
Pepper w brandy sauce	MAFC	296	1	B
Pepper, Chinese	NYTI	48	1	B
Peppered	JOC	401	1	
Pizzaiola	AC	269	1	
Plain	JBC	130	1	B
Planked	AC	265	1	
Planked	SC	270	1	
Planked, presenting a	GHAC	217	1	
Pocketbook	AC	266	1	
Porterhouse, definition	AC	256		
Porterhouse w red wine sauce	SMG	238	1	B
Potted, burgundy style	NYTI	168	2	B
Quick, garlic cubed	BHGN	27	1	B
Rib	JBC	131	1	B
Rib, w French-fried parsley	JBC	131	1	B

RECIPE	BOOK	PAGE	TD	S
Roast w carrots	VGCB	58	1	B
Roquefort broiled	AC	263	1	
Roquefort broiled	BB	17	1	A
Rosemary	BB	15	1	
Round, Sicilian	NYTI	388	1	B
Round, vegetable stuffed	FG	155	2	B
Rump	JBC	133	1	B
Salad	FG	85	1	B
Salisbury	FFCB	167	1	B
Salisbury	BCC	208	1	B
Salisbury w onions & peppers	GHAC	185	1	B
Salt, broiled	AC	263	1	
Sandwich	AC	806	1	
◆	AC	262	1	
◆	BB	18	1	
◆	JBC	134	1	
Deluxe	GHAC	372	1	
Grilled flank	AC	22	2	
Grilled w tartar sauce	NYTI	170	1	B
Philadelphia	FGCW	302	1	
Sauce				
Anchovy	BB	145	1	
Creole	BB	146	1	
Simple	BB	144	1	
Tarragon	BB	145	1	
Sausages in sauce, fresh	FAIC	335	1	B
Shell, trimming (photographs)	LT	265		
Sherried, cubed	GHAC	174	1	B
Shrimp kebabs	BHGN	26	1	B
Skirt, soy marinated	YGM	212	3	C
w Sky ranch steak glaze	OC	99	2	B
Soppressata	CFS	201	2	B
Soup	CBSS	67	2	B
Spice & pepper	CFS	82	2	A

RECIPE	BOOK	PAGE	TD	S
Pineapple &	SC	442	2	
Red red	JOC	776	2	
Rhubarb &	SC	442	2	
Jamaica	BB	160	1	B
Jubilee	NYT	624	1	B
Kirsch pie	MHGD	151	1	B
w Lemon custard meringue	FFBB	138	2	B
Lemon preserves	SC	439	3	
Marinated	CW	153	1	B
w Marzipan tart	NSD	86	2	B
w Melon balls in bourbon	MSQC	77	1	B
Meringue dessert	SC	138	1	
Meringue pie	SC	350	1	
Milk shake	BHGN	51	1	A
Mousse	SC	213	2	
Mousse	BBA	214	2	B
Mousse	SP	285	2	C
Mousse, frozen	MFC	236	2	B
& Other fruits	JBC	113	1	
Parfait	FFCB	626	3	C
Parfait, San Francisco	GHAC	303	1	
Peach sundaes	KIS	325	1	B
Pie	PPLK	315	1	B
Pie	FFBB	83	2	B
Pie	AC	618	1	
Mile high	FFBB	127	2	B
Rhubarb &	BCC	89	1	B
Rhubarb &	GHAC	314	2	B
Rhubarb &	AC	618	1	
Pineapple jam	SC	442	1	
Pineapple preserves	JOC	778	2	C
Plain	JBC	113	1	
Preparing	GHAC	314		
Preserve	CW	41	1	B
Preserves	FFCB	704	2	B
Preserves	SC	439	3	
Six minute	AC	819	1	
Sunshine	AC	820	2	
Sunshine	JOC	778	2	C
Punch broth	SC	58	2	
Punch, fruit &	SC	56	1	C
Punch, fruit &	JOC	35	2	
Puree	GHAC	290	1	
'n' Puree	JBGF	614	2	B
w Raspberry puree	AC	773	1	
Raspberry sauce	MHGD	380	1	
Raspberry supreme	EBE	185	1	B
Red, glaceed w green grapes	MSE	217	1	B
Rhubarb				
Grunt	GHAC	289	1	B
Jam	SC	442	2	
Mold	EBE	143	2	B
Pie	GHAC	314	2	B
Pie	BHGN	280	1	B
Pies, deep dish, individual	MHGD	152	2	B
Preserves	JOC	778	2	C
Salad molds	JOC	104	2	C
Sauce	BCC	132	1	B
& Rhubarb	MHGD	399	1	B
& Rhubarb ring	AC	772	2	
Roll	NYT	563	2	B
Roll	EBE	157	3	B
Romanoff	FFCB	674	1	B
◆	SC	208	2	
◆	BBA	215	1	
◆	BB	160	1	B
◆	JOC	114	1	
Romanoff w Russian cream	BBA	215	2	B
Sauce	NSD	328	2	C
Sauce	NYT	617	1	B
I	FFCB	642	1	B
II	FFCB		1	B

RECIPE	BOOK	PAGE	TD	S
Strawberry Sauce (*cont.*)				
For ice cream, brandied	GHAC	306	1	C
Peaches in custard &	GHAC	290	2	B
Sherbet	NYT	629	2	B
◆	SC	211	2	
◆	LM	300	2	
◆	JOC	724	2	B
Sherbet, fresh	MFC2	418	2	B
w Sherry cream	FFCB	672	1	B
Short toast a la Helen Brown	BB	160	1	
Shortcake	BCC	132	2	B
◆	NSD	126	1	B
◆	SC	196	1	
◆	JBC	114	2	
◆	BHGN	179	2	B
◆	CW	85	2	B
◆	SP	276	2	B
◆	GHAC	341	2	C
Old fashioned	BBA	190	3	B
Rum soaked brioche	MFC2	448	2	B
w Sour cream	NYT	565	2	B
Torte	SC	133	1	
Sorbet	MHGD	440	1	C
Souffle	NYT	605	1	B
Cold	FFCB	625	3	B
Frozen	BBA	215	3	C
Frozen	FFCB	627	3	B
w Raspberry sauce	GF	210	2	B
Soup, chilled	CBSS	174	2	B
Soup in melon bowls, chilled	BBA	45	3	B
Southampton	MHGD	396	1	B
w Spicy yogurt	KIS	326	1	B
Spritzer	BHGN	52	1	C
Spritzer	BCC	23	1	B
Strip	LM	283	2	C
Sunshine	SC	439	3	
Surprise cake	BBA	189	3	C
Tart	MSQC	85	2	B
Tart	MHGD	202	2	B
Cold	MAFC	640	2	B
French	BCC	89	2	B
Glazed, fresh	FFCB	582	2	B
w Nut crust	MSE	241	3	B
Variations, fresh	JOC	114	1	
Vinegar	BCC	299	1	B
w Whipped cream sauce	SC	220	2	
White chocolate torte	NSD	264	3	B
w Wine	BCC	127	1	B
Wine soup	CBSS	173	2	B
Yogurt, frozen	BTSB	67	2	B
Yogurt mousse cake	NSD	272	3	B
Streusel (cake)	BCC	33	1	B
Apple	AC	751	1	
Apple	SC	192	1	
Blueberry	AC	751	1	
Coffee cake	BHGN	81	1	B
Coffee cake	BCC	33	1	B
Coffee cake, quick	AC	659	1	
Topping, basic	FFBB	77	1	B
Variations	JOC	681	2	B
String bean	MSE	220	1	B
Blanching	GG	343		
Boiled	FAIC	404		
Braised w garlic	GG	350	1	B
& Carrots, julienned	MSE	172	2	B
Fricassee	FAIC	404	1	B
Lemon	SMG	241	1	B
& Mushroom casserole	BB	134	1	B
Mushrooms	CF	35	1	B
& New potato salad, warm	CW	92	1	B
New style southern	WC	34	1	B
Potatoes	GG	346	1	B

RECIPE	BOOK	PAGE	TD	S
Preparing	GG	343		
Provencal	EBE	120	1	B
Salad	GF	140	1	C
Sauteed chartreuse	GG	348	1	B
& Tomato salad	LM	152	1	B
Tomatoes & basil	FAIC	405	1	B
Vinaigrette	MSE	287	1	C
Vinaigrette	VE	103	1	B
w Vinaigrette sauce	SMG	189	1	B
Striped bass (see also bass)				
Au vin blanc	NYTI	131	3	B
Baked				
w Artichokes, Riviera style	MCIC	205	1	B
My favorite	AC	140	1	
& Stuffed	FFCB	124	1	B
w Vegetables	FFCB	124	1	B
Grilled & stuffed	OC	143	2	B
Mayonnaise	NYTI	130	1	C
Moroccan style	NYTI	482	2	B
w Oysters & herbs	NYT	231	1	B
Paella, stuffed	CFS	228	1	B
Poached	FFCB	124	1	B
Poached	SMG	114	1	B
Poached, cold	JBGF	446	1	B
& Shellfish sealed & baked in foil	CIC	212	2	B
Steamed, whole	FFCB	123	1	B
Stir fried	JBGF	445	1	B
Stuffed				
& Baked	AC	140	1	
w Shrimp wine sauce	NYT	230	3	B
w Swiss chard	VGCB	307	1	B
w Tomatoes & mushrooms	NYT	232	2	B
w White wine	NYTI	133	1	A
Stroganoff (see also beef stroganoff)				

RECIPE	BOOK	PAGE	TD	S
w Beef, ground	WC	104	1	B
w Chicken livers	BHGN	303	2	B
Filet of beef	AC	273	1	
Lemon	CF	38	2	C
Meatballs	SC	280	1	
Strucla (holiday, spicy bread)	VE	296	3	C
Strudel	JOC	598	3	
Strudel	NYT	541	3	
Almond	SC	354	2	
Amaretti rhubarb	SPGT	41	3	B
Apple	NSD	194	2	B
Apple	SC	354	2	
Apple cheddar	MC	211	1	B
Apple filling	NYT	541	1	
Apple, making (photographs)	NYT	542		
Baking	SC	354		
Cabbage	JOC	267	2	C
Cheese	SC	354	2	
Cheese filling, variations	MC	160	3	B
Cheese, assembling	MC	161		
Dough	SC	354	1	
Filling, rolling & shaping	SC	354		
Mixing & kneading	SC	354		
Raisin, cherry & coconut	SC	355	2	
Ricotta & almond	MC	210	1	B
w Roquefort cheese	NYT	29	2	C
Savory	JOC	267	2	C
Spinach & feta	NYT	30	2	C
Stretching the dough	SC	354		
Stuffed lettuce soup	MCIC	115	2	B
Stuffing				
All about	FFCB	277		
Almond, for squabs	SC	324	1	
Almond, for turkey	SC	324	1	

RECIPE	BOOK	PAGE	TD	S
Stuffing (*cont.*)				
Apple				
Cornbread & sausage	SP	96	2	C
For goose or duck	SC	325	1	
Herb	GHAC	170	1	B
Raisin	BCC	257	1	B
Raisin whole wheat	JBGF	442	1	
Bacon rice	GHAC	164	1	
Baltimore	NYT	224	1	B
Bienville	PPLK	230	2	B
Braised beef & ham	MFC2	386	1	B
Brazil nut & mushroom	NYT	224	1	B
Bread	BCC	257	1	B
Bread	SC	324	1	
Bread	FFCB	278	1	B
Basic forcemeat & variations	AC	232	1	
Crumb basic	NYT	222	1	B
Crumb, chestnut	NYT	222	1	B
For goose or duck	SC	325	1	
Savory	SC	324	1	
Savory	FFCB	278	1	B
Bulgur raisin	JBGF	443	1	
Casserole	BCC	257	1	B
Chestnut	BHGN	315	1	C
Chestnut	GHAC	169	1	B
Chestnut	NYT	224	1	C
For sausage, apples, roast goose &	GHAC	167	3	B
For turkey	SC	324	1	
Sausage, braised goose w	MAFC	285	3	B
Chicken liver w rice & mushrooms & garlic puree	MFC2	274	1	
Corn bread	SC	324	1	
◆	NYT	222	1	B
◆	BCC	257	1	B
◆	AC	233	1	
◆	NYTI	561	1	B
◆	FFCB	279	1	B
Corn bread & bacon	BHGN	316	1	B
Corn bread & sausage	GHAC	169	1	B
For baked fish	SC	236	1	
For cabbage leaves, Armenian	NYT	369	2	B
For game	SC	325	1	
Fruit & nut	MSE	192	2	C
Garlic & herb	MAFC	336	1	B
Giblet	BCC	257	1	B
◆	FFCB	278	1	B
◆	NYT	222	1	B
◆	BHGN	315	1	C
Gorgonzola, tortelli w	FAIC	170	2	B
Ham & mushroom	MAFC	337	1	B
Ham & olive	NYT	225	1	C
Harvest	BHGN	315	1	C
Heated	JBC	236	1	
Herb	FFCB	279	1	B
Liver for squabs	SC	324	1	
Moist bread	GHAC	170	1	C
Mushroom	MAFC	249	1	B
◆	BCC	257	1	B
◆	NYT	222	1	B
◆	BHGN	315	1	C
Mushroom & bacon	OC	167	1	B
Mushroom, grilled, bass fillets w	GHAC	224	1	B
Nutty brown rice	GHAC	169	1	B
Old fashioned bread	BHGN	315	1	C
Olive & ground lamb	MAFC	338	1	B
Olive, pimento, garlic & herbs	MFC2	160	1	B

RECIPE	BOOK	PAGE	TD	S
Orange, for squabs	SC	325	1	
Oyster	GHAC	170	1	C
Oyster	BCC	257	1	B
Oyster	BHGN	315	1	C
Oyster, for turkey	SC	324	1	
Pecan	GHAC	160	1	
Pork crown roast w cranapple	GHAC	188	3	C
Pork w herb	MAFC	336	1	B
Pork w veal	MAFC	565	1	C
Pot to plate	KIS	356	1	C
Potato	AC	233	1	
Potato	SC	325	1	
Potato	JBGF	443	1	
Poultry	NYTI	407	1	B
Prune & apple for goose or duck	SC	325	1	
Prune, pork loin chops w	GHAC	190	2	B
Quantities, calculating	GHAC	170		
Raisin	BHGN	315	1	C
Raisin nut	FFCB	278	1	B
Rice, garlic & herb	MFC2	161	1	B
Rice & kidney	MAFC	337	1	B
Rye bread	GHAC	166	1	B
Salmon & anchovy	MAFC	338	1	B
Sausage	BCC	257	1	B
Sausage	NYT	222	1	B
Sausage & corn bread	GHAC	169	1	B
Sausage & rice	GHAC	169	1	B
Seafood & avocado	FFCB	437	2	B
Shrimp	NYT	230	1	
Spinach	GHAC	159	1	
Spinach, meat loaf roll w	GHAC	184	2	B
Summer vegetable, grilled trout w	GHAC	224	1	B

RECIPE	BOOK	PAGE	TD	S
Sweet potato & sausage	JOC	458	1	C
Tangerine for goose	NYT	225	1	B
Vegetable	BCC	257	1	B
White forcemeat mushroom duxelles	MFC2	275	1	
Wild rice & mushroom	GHAC	159	1	
Sturgeon				
Braised, sweet & sour	AC	139	1	
Kebabs	AC	128	1	
Kippered	AC	143		
Smoked	AC	143		
Su su curry (shrimp & rice curry dish)	BBA	93	2	B
Submarine sandwich	JOC	247	1	B
Submarine sandwich	AC	813	1	
Submarine sandwiches	BCC	321	1	B
Substituting ingredients, how to change recipes	JBGF	262		
Substitutions, emergency	BCC	373		
Substitutions, emergency	BHGN	433		
Substitutions for common foods	SC	33		
Succotash	GHAC	231	1	C
◆	VGCB	87	1	B
◆	JBC	293	1	B
◆	FFCB	379	1	B
◆	SC	420	1	
◆	BCC	336	1	B
Chowder	MC	10	1	B
Creamy	BHGN	391	1	B
Mexican	JBGF	519	1	B

RECIPE	BOOK	PAGE	TD	S
Summer punch	NYT	650	1	B
Summer salad	SC	358	1	
Summer salad w fresh tuna	MFC	187	1	B
Summer soup, Sarah's	SPGT	143	2	B
Summer squash (see squash, summer)				
Sun dried tomatoes	SPGT	252		
Chicken cutlets w mozzarella &	GHAC	158	1	B
w Fennel & red onion salad	MSQC	53	1	B
w Herbed goat cheese	GHAC	92	1	C
w Mozzarella, smoked	YGM	177	3	C
w Summer squash	MSQC	96	1	B
Sunchokes sauteed	KIS	85	1	A
Sundae, Mr. Stewart's favorite	FGCW	385	1	
Sunday soup (cream of bean soup)	CBSS	252	3	B
Sunflower loaf	JBGF	576	2	B
Sunflower seed muffins	BHGN	87	1	C
Sunflower seed refrigerator cookies	FFBB	218	2	C
Sunrise soup	BBA	45	1	A
Sunshine cake	FFBB	302	2	C
◆	FFCB	519	2	C
◆	SC	120	1	B
◆	JOC	622	1	B
Easy	SC	121	1	B
Filled	SC	137	1	B
Imperial	SC	119	1	B
Or golden glow cake	AC	684	1	
Rich	SC	121	1	B
Supreme sauce	JOC	325	1	B
Surprise balls	SC	305	1	

RECIPE	BOOK	PAGE	TD	S
Survival cake	MHGD	95	1	C
Sushi bites	BBA	22	3	B
Sushi, definitions	SPGT	16		
Suzette sauce	SC	95	1	
Suzette sauce, flambe	SC	95	1	
Swan apple, making (photographs)	LM	62		
Swan, melon	LM	298		
Swans, cream puff	LT	394	3	
Swedes, mashed	GG	388	1	B
Swedes & potatoes	AC	554	1	
Swedish almond wafers	FFCB	554	1	C
Swedish bread	FFCB	482	3	C
Swedish bread, braided	FFCB	482	3	C
Swedish glogg	NYT	652	3	C
Swedish hardtack	MHGD	338	2	B
Swedish layer cake	SC	119	1	B
Swedish leaf cakes	MHGD	245	2	C
Swedish limpa	AC	786	2	
Swedish limpa	BHGN	62	2	B
Swedish meatballs (see meatballs, Swedish)				
Swedish nut wafers	FFCB	554	1	C
Swedish sandwich, open faced	FFCB	294	1	A
Sweet braid, Grecian	CBB	334	3	C
Sweet bread				
For All Saints' Day	FAIC	471	2	B
Irish	NYT	484	2	B
Portuguese	CBB	84	3	C
Sticks	SC	74	2	
Sweet chocolate cookies	AC	713	1	
Sweet corn, grilled	GRIL	75	2	B
Sweet cream, fried	CIC	445	2	B
Sweet loaf type breads, all about	FFBB	545		

RECIPE	BOOK	PAGE	TD	S
Sweet pastry dough	MFC	199	3	C
Sweet pepper sauce	VGCB	206	1	B
Sweet peppers, peeling	VGCB	201	1	
Sweet potato	JOC	298	1	
All about	VGCB	293		
Apple	JBGF	530	2	B
◆	SC	431	2	
◆	KIS	298	1	A
◆	JOC	299	1	B
Or oranges, scalloped	SC	429	1	
Pie	AC	627	1	
& Scallops	FFCB	405	1	B
Applesauce souffle	JOC	205	1	B
Baked	AC	574	1	
◆	JBC	336	1	
◆	FFCB	405	1	A
◆	VGCB	296	1	
◆	JOC	298	1	
Candied	FFCB	406	1	B
Candied	GHAC	246	1	C
Mashed	BHGN	403	1	B
Batter bread	AC	788	2	
w Beef & pork, Madras style	GG	361	1	B
Beignets	GG	362	2	C
Biscuit	JOC	585	1	C
Biscuit crust	VGCB	301	1	B
Biscuits	VGCB	301	1	B
Boiled	JBC	335	1	B
◆	VGCB	296	1	
◆	SC	429	1	
◆	AC	574	1	
◆	FFCB	405	1	A
◆	JOC	298	1	
Bourbon cake, Lynn's	VGCB	301	1	B
Brandied	NYT	398	1	B
Bread	VGCB	301	1	B
Candied	SC	429	1	

RECIPE	BOOK	PAGE	TD	S
◆	PPLK	133	1	A
◆	JOC	298	1	B
◆	FFCB	406	1	B
◆	AC	574	1	
◆	JBC	336	1	
Candies	BCC	364	1	B
Cappellacci, filled	CIC	168	3	B
Caramelized	JOC	298	1	
& Carrot puree	SP	198	2	B
& Cashew bake	BHGN	403	1	B
Casserole	AC	574	1	
Casserole	SC	430	1	
Casserole, tangerine &	NYT	398	1	B
Chicken & fruit sauce	VGCB	298	1	B
& Chipped beef casserole	JOC	232	1	B
Chips, deep fried	VGCB	295	1	
& Chocolate nut cake	VGCB	300	1	B
& Coconut milk	FG	298	2	B
Creole, scalloped	SC	430	1	
Crisped	JBC	336	1	
Crisps, fried	GG	361	1	B
Croquettes	SC	430	1	
& Custard pie	AC	627	1	
Dessert, chilled pumpkin &	VGCB	234	1	C
Dressing, apple &	JOC	458	1	C
& Eggplant gravy	PPLK	175	3	B
Finishing touches for cooked	VGCB	296	1	
Fried	AC	574	1	
Fried	JBC	336	1	
Fried, deep	JOC	299	1	
& Fruits	JOC	299	1	
Georgian	FFCB	406	1	B
Glazed	SC	429	1	
Jersey sweets, yams, preparing	BCC	364		

RECIPE	BOOK	PAGE	TD	S
& Lamb sausage stew	VGCB	298	2	B
& Lime chiffon pie	VGCB	299	1	B
Mallow	BCC	365	1	B
& Marshmallows	SC	431	1	
Mashed	AC	574	1	
◆	SC	430	1	
◆	JBC	335	1	
◆	FFCB	406	1	B
◆	JOC	298	1	B
Mashed, pineapple, pecans &	FFCB	406	1	B
On half shell	SC	430	1	
Orange	BCC	364	1	B
& Orange juice	JOC	299	1	
Oven candied	BHGN	403	1	B
Pancakes	MC	169	1	B
Pecan pie	PPLK	319	2	B
Pie	FFCB	587	2	B
◆	AC	627	1	
◆	BCC	92	2	B
◆	FFBB	134	2	B
Pie spicy	VE	272	1	B
Pie w walnut crunch topping	GHAC	318	2	C
Pineapple	SC	431	1	
Pineapple	BCC	364	1	B
& Pineapple souffle	JOC	205	1	B
Pone	GG	360	2	B
Pone	VGCB	297	1	B
Pork & beef, Madras style	GG	361	1	B
Pot pie, chicken &	SC	316	2	
Preparing	GG	357		
Pudding	VGCB	299	1	B
Pudding	JOC	702	1	B
Puff, orange	SC	430	2	
Puffs	JOC	299	1	
Puffs	SC	430	1	
Puree of	GF	81	1	C

RECIPE	BOOK	PAGE	TD	S
Ring	SC	430	1	
Rolls	FFBB	493	1	C
Sauteed	JOC	299	1	
Sherry	BCC	364	1	B
Skillet, candied	BHGN	403	1	B
Slices	BCC	365	1	B
Slices, fried	CW	117	1	B
Souffle	MIE	231	1	B
Soup, tomato &	VGCB	297	1	B
Southern style	SC	429	1	
Spicy	BCC	364	1	B
Squares	VGCB	300	1	B
Steamed	VGCB	296	1	
Stuffed	JOC	298	1	B
Sugared	JBC	336	1	
w Sweet sauce	VGCB	297	1	B
Waffles	VGCB	297	1	B
Sweet roll	BHGN	68	2	C
Dough	FFBB	513	1	C
Dough, potato	FFBB	514	2	C
Dough, whole wheat	FFBB	514	1	C
Sweet & sour				
w Bacon sauce	JOC	330	1	B
w Basting sauce	BHGN	32	1	B
w Brown sauce	SC	388	1	
w Cream dressing	JOC	330	1	B
Dressing	BBA	149	1	B
Dressing	BCC	280	1	
Fish	SC	46	1	
Low calorie dressing	JOC	313	1	B
Mustard sauce	JOC	330	1	B
Relish	GHAC	384	1	C
Sauce	BCC	243	1	
◆	BCC	329	1	B
◆	BHGN	360	1	B
◆	FFCB	274	2	B
◆	CFS	306	1	B
Chinese	BB	151	1	C
Cornish hens w	GHAC	222	1	B
Rich	SC	388	1	

RECIPE	BOOK	PAGE	TD	S
Sweet & Sour Sauce (*cont.*)				
Tomato sauce, fresh tongue w	GHAC	214	1	C
Sweet & tangy dipping sauce	PPLK	284	1	B
Sweet tart dough	FFBB	165	2	B
Sweet tart plum dip	BBA	22	1	C
Sweet tater pottage	GG	358	1	B
Sweetbread	LT	283	1	
A la bechamel	AC	355	1	
A la creme	AC	355	1	
A la king	NYT	174	2	B
A la Napoli	FFCB	219	1	B
All about	MAFC	408		
Au gratin	MAFC	413	1	B
Baked	SC	298	1	
Blanching	MAFC	409		
Boiled	SC	298	1	
Boiled w chili sauce	SC	299	1	
Brains	MAFC	408		
Braised	NYT	171	1	B
◆	SC	299	1	
◆	MAFC	409	1	B
◆	JOC	442	1	A
w Brown mushroom sauce	MAFC	411	1	B
w Quenelles & truffles	MFC2	143	3	B
w Tomatoes & peas	CIC	295	2	B
Broiled	SC	47	1	
Broiled	FFCB	218	1	B
Broiled	JOC	441	1	A
Broiled, variations	AC	356	1	
& Chicken in patty shells	JOC	236	3	C
Country style	AC	356	1	
Creamed	FFCB	219	1	B
Creamed	BHGN	269	1	B
Creamed	MAFC	412	1	B
w Creamed mushrooms	MAFC	412	1	B
& Cucumber salad	SC	362	1	
Filling	SC	382	1	
Florentine	NYTI	201	3	B
Fried	SC	299	1	
Glazed	JOC	442	1	A
In patty shells	NYT	172	2	B
Kidneys & sausages	AC	357	1	
& Kidneys, broiled	AC	363	1	
Marechale	NYTI	203	3	B
Mousse, veal loin roast of	GF	38	3	C
& Mushroom ring mold	JOC	210	2	B
w Mushrooms	SC	47	1	
w Mushrooms	SC	299	1	
& Mushrooms, gratin of	MAFC	157	1	B
& Mushrooms on ham, sauteed	NYT	173	2	B
Omelet	SC	226	1	B
On skewers	JOC	442	1	A
& Oyster pie	AC	171	1	
Oysters & veal in pastry	AC	357	2	
Pate pie	BBA	63	3	B
Perigourdine	NYTI	202	3	B
Pie, crab &	AC	170	1	
Pie, oyster &	AC	171	1	
Preparing	JOC	441		
Ragout	SPGT	96	3	B
Salad				
Chicken &	SC	362	1	
Chicken, elegant	SC	362	1	
Cucumber &	AC	72	1	
Molded	SC	371	2	C
Warm	SPGT	31	3	B

RECIPE	BOOK	PAGE	TD	S
Sauced & poached	JOC	441	1	A
Sausages & kidneys	AC	357	1	
Sauteed	AC	358	1	
Sauteed	FFCB	218	1	B
Sauteed	JOC	441	1	A
Sauteed w butter	MAFC	413	1	
Savory	NYT	171	2	B
Smothered	AC	357	1	
w Sorrel sauce	MFC	161	3	B
Sous cloche	AC	356	1	B
Spaghetti, mushrooms &	SC	339	1	
Terrine	LT	300	3	
Tomatoes stuffed w creamed	JOC	308	1	B
Tourte	MFC	160	3	B
Virginia, broiled	NYT	173	1	B
Sweeteners	FFBB	21		
Sweeteners, definitions	BHGN	426		
Sweetmeats	SP	260	1	C
Swiss chard	JOC	272	1	
Swiss chard	SC	432	1	
All about	VGCB	302		
Blanched	VGCB	304	1	
Cooking	AC	521		
Custards, individual	VGCB	305	1	B
Filling, tortelloni w	NYTI	430	2	C
Gratin of	FFCB	413	1	B
Ham & cheese custard, layered	VGCB	306	2	C
Jumbo ravioli w	GHAC	263	2	A
Onions stuffed w	MSE	194	2	C
Pork, gayettes	VGCB	308	2	B
Ribs w sea trout	VGCB	307	1	B
Salad, broiled	CIC	414	1	B
Saute	JBGF	531	1	A
Sauteed	VGCB	304	1	
Soup	VGCB	306	1	B

RECIPE	BOOK	PAGE	TD	S
Soup, Chinese style	VGCB	306	1	B
Stalks w Parmesan cheese	CIC	370	1	B
Stalks, sauteed	MCIC	381	1	B
Steamed	VGCB	304	1	
Stuffed	BBA	110	2	B
Torta	VGCB	307	1	B
Tortelloni filled w	CIC	164	3	B
Swiss cheddar fondue	VE	202	1	B
Swiss cheese				
w Cream filling	MAFC	201	1	B
Crepes, bacon &	FG	99	1	B
Crust	NYT	316	2	B
w Ham spread	BHGN	13	1	B
& Onion soup	MC	13	1	B
Souffle	JBC	270	1	B
Souffle	AC	116	1	
Swiss croissants (gipfelteig)	CBB	526	3	C
Swiss onion bake	BHGN	193	1	B
Swiss raclette	VGCB	212	1	B
Swiss steak				
Baked	GHAC	174	2	B
& Tomatoes	AC	269	2	
Variations	AC	268	2	
w Wine	AC	268	2	
Swordfish				
Baked in foil	NYT	259	2	B
Broiled	FFCB	124	1	B
Garlic, Joe Hyde's	VGCB	183	2	B
Grilled	OC	151	1	B
w Herb butter	GHAC	143	1	B
On skewers	OC	150	1	B
Pasta & pecan salad	SPGT	154	2	B
& Pepper w cold cucumber sauce	CFS	212	2	B
w Portuguese sauce	VGCB	322	1	B
Provincetown, broiled	OC	151	1	B

RECIPE	BOOK	PAGE	TD	S
Swordfish (*cont.*)				
Russet	CFS	213	2	B
w Salmoriglio sauce	MCIC	216	1	B
Shish kebab	NYTI	550	2	B
Steak	SP	115	1	B
Steak	JOC	361	1	
Anchovied	OC	152	1	A
Broiled	AC	125	1	A
Broiled	NYT	257	1	B
w Cauliflower & cheese sauce	WC	71	1	B
Grilled	OC	150	2	B
Grilled & lettuce leaves	OC	151	2	B
Marinated & grilled	MIE	152	1	B
Peppered	AC	124	1	A
Poached in beer & sauced	NYT	258	1	B
Rosemary	NYT	258	1	B
Spanish style	NYTI	518	1	A
w Wine, tomatoes & herbs	MAFC	219	2	B
Stir fried	GHAC	143	1	B
Tidbits, fried	MCIC	215	1	B
Syllabub (chocolate cake)	GF	93	1	B
Syllabub	JOC	47	1	B
Syrup				
Bar	SC	54	1	
Blueberry pancake	BTSB	163	1	B
Brown sugar	SC	98	1	
Caramel	JOC	738	1	B
Caramel	MAFC	584	1	A
Caramel	SC	142	1	
Fig-maple	GHAC	370		
Ginger for home style ginger ale	BTSB	217	1	C
Light sugar	GF	250	1	B
Maple	SC	98	1	
Molasses	JOC	738	1	B
Praline	GHAC	370		
Soothing	CFS	302	1	B
Spiced	SC	54	1	B
Sugar	SC	54	1	
White sugar	JOC	738	1	B
Szechwan eggplant	MIE	217	1	B
Szechwan eggplant tofu	MC	135	2	B
Szechwan peanut sauce	YGM	52	1	C
Szechwan sauce	BBA	162	1	A
Szechwan sauce for dumplings	NYTI	64	1	A

T

RECIPE	BOOK	PAGE	TD	S
T bone steak, definition	AC	258		
Tabasco				
Butter	AC	189		
Butter	BB	153	1	
Cheese bread	CBB	379	2	B
Fried chicken	AC	193	2	
Tabbouleh (bulgur wheat)	MSE	296	1	C
I	NYTI	539	2	B
II	NYTI	540	2	C
Bulgur salad	JBGF	540	2	B
Raisin	YGM	63	1	A
Tomatoes	VGCB	318	1	B
Wheat pilaf salad	MIE	281	2	B
Table settings	FFCB	746		
Tabouli	MC	42	2	B
Taco	JOC	56	1	
Beef, filling for	FFCB	303	1	C
Con carne	BHGN	245	1	B
Dinner	BCC	211	1	B
Filling	FFCB	303	2	B

RECIPE	BOOK	PAGE	TD	S
Half the beef	JBGF	465	1	B
Salads	BCC	273	1	B
Sauce	FFCB	304	1	B
Tacoese filling for corn crepes	VGCB	90	1	B
Taffies	JOC	733		
Taffy	AC	837	2	
Taffy	BCC	119	2	B
Almond	BCC	119	2	B
Cream	NYT	636	2	C
Making	NYT	636		
Molasses	FFCB	685	3	B
Molasses	JOC	734	2	B
Molasses	AC	839	1	
Old fashioned molasses	BHGN	114	1	B
Peppermint	BCC	119	2	B
Salt water	SC	171	1	
◆	JOC	734	2	B
◆	BHGN	113	2	B
◆	AC	838	2	
Vanilla	JOC	734	2	A
Vinegar	AC	838	2	
White	NYT	636	2	C
White	SC	171	1	
Tagliatelle				
w Bolognese meat sauce	CIC	129	2	B
& Chicken liver sauce, fresh	FAIC	149	2	B
& Chicken w wild mushrooms & pine nuts	CPPC	110	2	B
w Cibreo sauce, fresh	FAIC	148	2	B
w Cream sauce, fresh	FAIC	147	2	B
w Dried tomatoes & green beans	CPPC	114	2	B
w Fava beans, pancetta & chicken	CPPC	29	2	A
w Fried prawns, garlic & parsley	CPPC	77	1	B
w Fried squid, yellow tomatoes & garlic	CPPC	59	3	A
w Meat sauce, fresh	FAIC	146	2	B
Primavera, whole wheat	MSE	145	2	C
w Spinach, fontina & Parmesan	MSE	145	2	C
Taglierini				
Basil & green beans, squid w	CPPC	57	3	B
w Fresh tomato sauce	FAIC	145	2	B
w Garden lettuce vinaigrette	CPPC	109	2	B
w Mussels, radicchio & anchovy creme	CPPC	146	2	B
Tahini	BTSB	292	1	A
Lemon sauce	MC	75	1	B
Sauce, yogurt	JBGF	645	1	B
Spread, eggplant (baba ghanoush)	JBGF	293	1	B
Tall drinks	NYT	649		
Tamale	JOC	275	2	C
Casserole	SC	317	1	
Chicken	WC	62	1	C
Green corn	BBA	108	3	B
Loaf	SC	278	1	
Pie	AC	329	2	
Chicken	NYT	193	2	B
Meatless	JBGF	389	2	B
w Stuffed peppers	GG	284	2	A
Tamarind marmalade	JOC	780	2	C
Tan abour (cucumber yogurt soup)	VGCB	98	1	B
Tan kisses	AC	711	1	
Tandoori chicken	NYTI	357	1	B

RECIPE	BOOK	PAGE	TD	S
Tiropetes (cheese pastries)	NYTI	326	2	B
Tiropites	VE	207	2	B
Tisanes (drink—herb)	JOC	30	2	
Toast				
Almond	BTSB	238	1	C
Anise crunchy	BTSB	239	2	C
Buttered	SC	72	1	
Melba	BTSB	118	1	
Mushrooms, rolled	SC	42	1	
Sardines, rolled	SC	42	1	
Sticks, rolled	SC	406	1	
Toastadas, chicken	GHAC	151	2	B
Toasted almond cream pie	FFBB	114	2	B
Toasted almond raisin bread	FFBB	461	2	C
Toasted hazelnut chiffon pie	FFBB	121	2	B
Toasted meringue topping	BHGN	94	1	
Toddy (drink)	JOC	47	1	A
Toffee	NSD	239	1	B
Toffee	FFCB	684	2	B
Almond	SC	171	1	
Bars	SP	257	1	C
◆	FFBB	228	1	C
◆	BCC	103	1	C
◆	BHGN	155	1	C
Chocolate	SC	165	1	
English	BHGN	155	1	C
Quick	SC	167	1	
Bisque, English	FFCB	628	3	B
Butter crunch	BHGN	114	2	B
English	JOC	736	1	B
English	SC	171	1	
Or English toffee	AC	839	3	
Squares w chocolate topping	EBE	179	1	C

RECIPE	BOOK	PAGE	TD	S
Tofu				
Beef loaf	JBGF	461	2	B
Eggplant, Szechwan &	MC	135	2	B
Marinated in sesame oil & rice vinegar, scallions &	GRIL	79	2	B
& Pasta sauce	KIS	175	1	A
Salad	MC	50	2	B
Stir fry, simple	JBGF	393	1	B
Toll House cookies	AC	713	1	
Tolls for grilling	GR	21		
Tom Collins	NYT	649	1	
Tom Collins	BB	168	1	A
Tom Collins	JOC	45	1	A
Tom & Jerry	NYT	653	1	C
Tom & Jerry	SC	63	1	A
Tom & Jerry, hot	JOC	47	1	B
Tom & Jerry, quantity	JOC	51		
Tomato	MAFC	505		
A la provencale, hot	VE	151	1	B
All about	VGCB	308		
w Anchovy, stuffed & baked	NYT	405	1	B
Apple tartin	GG	379	2	B
Aspic (see also aspic, tomato)				
Fresh	FFCB	446	2	B
Quick	SC	367	2	
Tasty centers	JOC	101	2	B
Vegetables &	FFCB	445	2	B
& Artichokes	BCC	366	1	B
& Bacon soup	CBSS	358	1	B
& Bacon, wrapped & broiled	GHAC	247	1	B
Baked	VGCB	315	1	

RECIPE	BOOK	PAGE	TD	S
Tomato, Baked (*cont.*)				
◆	BHGN	405	1	B
◆	FAIC	424	1	B
◆	JOC	305	1	B
w Chicken stuffing	FFCB	417	2	B
w Fish stuffing	FFCB	417	2	B
Herbed	GG	372	1	B
w Meat stuffing	FFCB	417	2	B
w Mushroom stuffing	FFCB	416	2	B
Plum	BCC	367	1	B
w Provencal crumble topping	VGCB	316	1	B
w Spinach & water chestnut stuffing	FFCB	417	2	B
& Stuffed	FFCB	416	2	B
◆	VGCB	315	1	
◆	BCC	367	1	B
◆	JBC	338	1	B
& Stuffed w couscous	SPGT	161	2	B
w Tuna stuffing	FFCB	417	2	B
Balls for garnish, making (photographs)	LT	13		
Basil & goat cheese	YGM	129	1	A
Basil salad	FGCW	377	1	B
& Basil sauce, fresh	JBGF	643	1	B
& Basil soup, iced	CBSS	354	1	B
Beefsteak, & onions	AC	44	1	
Beer cooler	BCC	23	1	B
Bisque	BBA	42	2	B
Bisque, curried	NYTI	130	1	C
Bisque, four minute	BBA	42	1	B
Bouillon	JOC	147	1	A
Bouillon, chicken &	AC	87	1	
Bouillon, jellied	JOC	149	2	B
Braised herb	FFCB	415	1	B
w Brazil nut stuffing	NYT	406	1	B
Broccoli	GG	60	1	B
Broiled	MSE	175	1	A
◆	JBC	339	1	B
◆	BBA	136	1	B
◆	FFCB	416	1	B
◆	VGCB	315	1	
◆	BHGN	405	1	B
◆	SC	433	1	
◆	SMG	187	1	B
◆	BBA	62	1	B
◆	MSQC	133	1	B
Basil	JBC	339	1	B
Breaded	JOC	306	1	
Cheese	JBC	339	1	B
Chives & parsley	JBC	339	1	B
French	FG	221	1	B
Garlic & marjoram	SMG	180	1	B
Italian	FG	221	1	
Onion	JBC	339	1	B
Broth chilled	VGCB	311	1	
Butter cream frosting for devil's food	GG	380	2	C
Candied	JOC	306	1	B
Canned	VGCB	316	1	
Canned, uses for	AC	559		
Canning	BHGN	140		
Canning (photographs)	BCC	386		
Caper salad	FAIC	392	1	B
Caper sauce	NYTI	437	2	C
Capers	KIS	183	1	A
Caraway bread	CBB	414	2	B
Catsup (see also catsup, tomato)				
Catsup	BHGN	141	2	
◆	OC	163	2	C
◆	BTSB	177	2	C
◆	JOC	784	3	C
◆	SC	456	2	
◆	FFCB	715	2	B

RECIPE	BOOK	PAGE	TD	S
Catsup, spiced	SC	455	2	
Cheese				
Bread	CBB	420	1	B
Pie	AC	552	1	
Pie	SC	232	2	
Salad, marinated	SPGT	152	2	B
Salads	BCC	287	1	B
Sauce, quick	JOC	333	1	B
Cherry				
Asparagus &	GHAC	230	1	B
& Parsnip garnish	VGCB	189	1	
w Smoked fish pate	VGCB	318	1	B
Stuffed, chicken quarters w	GHAC	153	2	B
Stuffed w sour cream & red caviar	MSE	41	2	B
Chicken bubbling w	GG	377	2	B
Chicken w shallots, vermouth &	FGCW	173	1	A
Chili & guacamole	BHGN	18	2	B
Chili sauce	VE	85	1	B
Chutney, apple &	BBA	168	2	B
Chutney, green	JOC	786	3	C
Cocktail	BTSB	211	2	C
Cold	NYT	407	1	B
Corn chowder, quick	JOC	167	1	B
Corn, okra &	AC	530	1	
Corn, olives & fried onions	AC	551	1	
Cottage cheese ring	SC	368	2	
Coulis	SP	191	2	C
Cream cheese ring	SC	368	2	
Cream soup, quick, chilled fresh	JOC	168	1	B
Creamed, canned	JOC	305	1	B
Creole	JOC	306	1	B
Creole	FFCB	417	1	B
Cuban	GG	370	1	B
& Cucumber juice	JOC	32	1	B

RECIPE	BOOK	PAGE	TD	S
& Cucumber relish	BHGN	243	2	
& Cucumber salad	JOC	89	1	
& Cucumber salad, platter	NYT	423	2	B
& Cucumbers	BCC	285	2	B
& Cucumbers, chunky	KIS	224	1	B
Cups, making	BHGN	349		
Curried, green	FFCB	418	1	B
Curry	FFCB	417	1	B
Curry	WC	38	1	B
Curry w egg	MC	167	2	B
Custard	JOC	307	1	B
Dal & dill	VE	153	1	B
Deep fried, green	FAIC	424		
Devil's food butter cream frosting	GG	380	2	C
Deviled	NYT	405	1	B
& Dill soup	SP	192	3	C
& Dill soup	NYT	73	1	B
Dressing	BCC	300	1	B
Dressing, no oil, spicy	MIE	255	2	B
Egg & mushrooms, making	LT	24		
Eggs poached in	FAIC	286	1	B
Escalloped	AC	548	1	
Essence of	BBA	162	2	B
Fennel, garnish	MFC2	23	1	
Filled w lamb & squash	VGCB	322	1	B
Filled w onions	JOC	308	1	B
Filled w peas	MIE	233	1	B
Fish bisque &	GG	370	1	B
Fondue, coulis	VGCB	312	1	A
For aioli	NYTI	135	1	B
Franks	BB	27	1	
Freezing	BHGN	140		
French toast &	JOC	247		
Fried	CIC	390	1	B

RECIPE	BOOK	PAGE	TD	S
& Okra salad	GG	224	1	A
& Olive casserole	JOC	306	1	A
& Olives, broiled	NYT	404	1	B
& Onion, curried	YGM	111	1	A
& Onion relish	YGM	95	1	A
w Onion rings, marinated	KIS	97	1	A
& Onion salad	SC	359	1	
◆	JOC	89	1	
◆	JBC	246	1	B
◆	MIE	273	1	B
◆	BB	141	1	
& Onions in vermouth	YGM	41	1	A
& Orange jam	SC	443	1	
Oven browned	CIC	389	1	B
Pan fried	BCC	366	1	A
Pan fried, cherry	GHAC	247	1	B
Pasta w olive oil, lemon zest &	GRIL	93	1	B
& Pasta salad	BCC	275	2	B
Paste	JOC	334	1	A
Paste, Italian	JOC	334	2	
Peeled	VGCB	313	1	
Peeling	MAFC	505		
Peeling	BHGN	423		
Peeling & seeding (photographs)	LT	12		
Peeling, two quick methods	FG	223		
Pennsylvania Dutch	BB	132		
Pennsylvania Dutch	AC	550	1	
& Pepper relish	BHGN	362	2	B
Pickle green	SC	458	3	
Pie	MIE	234	1	B
Pie, green	AC	622	1	
& Pine nut soup	CBSS	357	1	B
Piquant	AC	548	1	
Plum, scalloped	AC	549	1	

RECIPE	BOOK	PAGE	TD	S
Polish	VE	104	1	B
Preparing	GG	368		
Preparing	BCC	366		
Preserves	JOC	779	2	C
Preserves	SC	441	3	
Preserves, green	SC	441	2	
Provencale	KIS	296	1	B
Provencale	NYTI	253	1	B
Provencale	JOC	305	1	
Pudding	EBE	122	1	B
Pudding cockaigne	JOC	307	1	B
Punch	JOC	34	1	C
Puree	VGCB	313	1	
Puree w garlic & herbs	MAFC	78	2	B
Rabbit	VE	214	1	B
Rarebit	FFCB	352	1	B
Rarebit	BBA	111	2	B
Rarebit	JOC	242	2	B
Relish (see relish, tomatoes)				
Rellenos green	MC	132	2	B
& Rice soup, quick	BHGN	380	1	B
Ring	SC	434	2	
Ring sandwiches	SC	383	1	
Ring, shrimp &	AC	55	1	
Risotto	GG	371	2	B
& Rocket salad	CPMC	62	1	B
Roses	BHGN	440		
Salad	FAIC	391	1	B
Salad	JBC	246	1	
Salad	SC	358	1	
w Basil, sliced	MSE	293	1	C
Broiled	BCC	287	1	B
Curried	KIS	256	1	A
w Endive & fennel	VGCB	123	1	B
Italian	BBA	147	1	B
Italian	FG	80	1	B
Russe	NYTI	261	1	B

RECIPE	BOOK	PAGE	TD	S
Tomato Salad (*cont.*)				
Sliced	NYT	424	1	
w String beans	LM	152	1	B
Stuffed	FFCB	437	2	B
Stuffed w bacon	FFCB	437	2	B
Stuffed w tuna fish	FFCB	437	2	B
Stuffed, variations of	JBC	247		
& Salami, stuffed	EBE	117	1	B
Sambal	NYTI	181	1	B
Sandwich	AC	812	1	
Sandwich, ideas	VGCB	314	1	
Sandwiches	JOC	60	1	
Sauce	SC	390	1	
◆	SMG	281	1	B
◆	FG	227	1	C
◆	BHGN	259	1	
◆	MFC	109	2	C
◆	MAFC	76	2	B
◆	OC	163	1	A
◆	NYT	454	2	C
◆	AC	461		
◆	SMG	221	1	B
◆	FFCB	271	2	B
1	CIC	93	1	B
2	CIC	94	1	B
3	CIC	95	1	B
I	NYTI	278	1	B
II	NYTI	278	1	B
A favorite	AC	462	1	
Basic	GG	374	1	B
Basic	NYT	341	2	B
Beans	AC	594	3	
Beans, Greek style	FG	114	1	B
Beans & pork	AC	594	3	
Broccoli	JBGF	640	1	B
& Brussels sprouts tangy	KIS	93	1	A
Cold, w hot pasta	VGCB	320	1	B
Creamy	GG	375	1	B
Creamy	JBGF	643	1	B
Fall, freezer	VGCB	323	1	B
w Fennel seeds	NYT	342	1	B
w Fennel, winter	FAIC	414	1	B
For pasta, simple	VE	245	1	A
Fresh	FFCB	270	1	B
◆	FAIC	69	1	B
◆	NYT	454	1	B
◆	NYTI	279	1	B
◆	AC	461	1	
Garlic	FGCW	289	1	B
Garlic &	BCC	161	1	
Green	NYTI	477	1	B
Herring	NYTI	79	3	B
Hot	VGCB	313	1	
Hot, quick	BBA	104	1	B
Italian	MC	66	2	B
Italian	BCC	329	1	B
Italian	SC	390	1	
Italian I	NYTI	435	1	B
Italian II	NYTI	435	2	B
Italian gravy	FGCW	341	2	B
Long simmering	JBGF	644	2	B
w Marjoram & cheese	CIC	95	1	B
Meat	NYT	341	2	B
Meat balls & sausages w	NYTI	393	3	B
& Meat balls, Sicilian	NYTI	394	2	C
Mexican	NYTI	477	1	B
Mexican	FFCB	271	1	B
Mushrooms	NYT	341	1	B
Nice style	CFS	315	1	B
Provencale	YGM	88	1	B
Quick	SP	343	2	C
Quick	JOC	334	1	B
w Rosemary & pancetta	CIC	96	1	B
Rotini	YGM	102	1	B

RECIPE	BOOK	PAGE	TD	S
Simple	AC	590	1	
Spicy	SC	390	1	
Spicy	SP	344	2	C
Summer	FAIC	70	2	B
w Tarragon & veal balls	NYTI	400	1	B
Thickened	JOC	333	1	B
Uncooked	VGCB	313	1	
Unthickened	JOC	333	2	C
Variations	JBC	264	1	
Winter	FAIC	71	1	B
& Sausage scramble	GHAC	110	1	B
Saute	FG	222	1	B
Saute, yellow or red	SPGT	161	1	B
Sauteed	FFCB	415	1	B
◆	NYT	404	1	
◆	BB	132		
◆	BBA	136	2	B
Sauteed & crumbed	AC	551	1	
Sauteed & variations	VGCB	314	1	
& Scallion salad	YGM	119	1	A
Scalloped	BHGN	405	2	B
Scalloped	VGCB	317	1	B
Scalloped	JBC	338	1	B
Scalloped additional crumbs	JBC	338	1	B
Scalloped cheese	JBC	338	1	B
& Seafood in aspic	JBGF	406	2	B
Seasoned, sauteed	JOC	305	1	B
Seeding juice	MAFC	505		
Shells, double zapped	GG	369	1	B
Shirley's	KIS	153	1	B
Shortcake	GG	373	2	B
Shortcakes, Jill Gardner's	GG	373	2	B
Shrimp stuffed	AC	54	1	
Sicilian	BB	133		
Sicilian style, broiled	AC	549	1	
Skinning & seeding	SC	432		
Sliced	AC	44	1	

RECIPE	BOOK	PAGE	TD	S
Sliced	VGCB	313	1	
Sliced w lemon dressing	GHAC	276	1	B
Sliced w olive oil & basil	GRIL	83	2	B
Slices w garlic	BCC	287	2	B
Sorbet	GF	135	2	B
Souffle	GG	375	2	B
Souffle	CW	32	2	B
Soup	SC	400	1	
Soup	FG	222	1	B
Soup	NYTI	129	2	B
Bean, fennel &	VGCB	124	1	B
Broiled	BBA	42	2	B
Cake or mystery cake	AC	670	1	
Carrot &	CF	103	1	B
Celeriac &	VGCB	75	1	B
w Chervil, cold roasted	CF	70	1	B
Chilled (cascalilla)	MC	29	1	B
Clear	FFCB	94	1	B
Cold	FGCW	364	1	B
Cold	JOC	148	2	B
Cold I	NYT	82	1	B
Cold II	NYT	82	1	B
Cream of	FFCB	95	1	B
◆	AC	95	1	
◆	SC	402	1	
◆	JOC	160	1	B
◆	NYT	72	1	B
Cream of fresh	GHAC	98	1	B
Cream of mint	SPGT	129	2	C
Creamed cognac	VE	72	1	B
Dill	CBSS	352	1	B
Dressing	SC	374	1	
Fresh	VGCB	319	1	B
Hearty	BCC	311	1	B
Herbed	BHGN	377	1	B
Icy spicy	BBA	45	1	B

RECIPE	BOOK	PAGE	TD	S
Tomato Soup (*cont.*)				
Lentil	VE	63	2	B
My mother's standard cream of	AC	95	1	
Pepper	VGCB	207	1	B
Quick	JOC	167	1	B
Quick iced	AC	96	1	
Rice Mediterranean	MFC2	20	1	B
Savory	NYT	65	3	B
Spicy	MC	4	1	B
Supreme	VE	73	2	B
Sweet potato	VGCB	297	1	B
Sweet spicy	CBSS	353	1	B
Three one velvety	VGCB	319	1	B
Thyme cream of fresh	CBSS	355	1	B
Tuscan	MSE	114	1	B
Tuscan	MSQC	81	1	B
Steak sauce	EBE	55	1	B
Steamed, cherry	AC	551	1	
Stewed	BCC	366	1	B
◆	SC	433	1	
◆	VGCB	316	1	
◆	JBC	337	1	B
◆	AC	548	1	
◆	KIS	201	1	A
◆	FFCB	415	1	B
◆	JOC	305	1	B
Basil	JBC	337	1	B
w Basil	AC	548	1	
w Croutons	JBC	337	1	B
Fresh	GHAC	247	1	B
Green	JOC	305	1	B
Leeks &	GG	246	1	B
w Lemon & garlic	AC	548	1	
Onion	JBC	337	1	B
Onion	AC	548	1	

RECIPE	BOOK	PAGE	TD	S
w Sweet basil	NYT	404	1	B
Stuffed	BBA	136	2	B
◆	BCC	263	2	B
◆	AC	550	1	
◆	FAIC	225	1	B
◆	JBC	11	1	
◆	SC	433	1	
◆	BBA	147	3	B
w Anchovies	SC	361	1	
w Asparagus	SC	361	1	
w Baby string beans	MSQC	93	1	A
& Baked, variations	AC	552	1	
w Basil	NYT	424	1	B
w Bread crumbs & anchovies	JOC	308	1	B
w Bread crumbs, herbs & garlic	MAFC	507	1	B
w Chicken	BHGN	349	1	B
w Chicken livers	SC	433	1	
Cold	JOC	89		
Corn	JOC	307	1	B
Crab	BHGN	349	1	B
w Crab meat	JOC	308	1	B
w Crab meat & caviar	SC	361	1	
w Cream cheese	NYT	425	1	B
& Creamed, sweetbreads &	JOC	308	1	B
w Cucumbers	SC	361	1	
w Fresh corn	NYT	424	1	B
Middle Eastern style	FG	223	1	B
w Monterey Jack cheese	CFS	250	1	B
w Pineapple	JOC	307	1	B
w Rice, cold	NYT	425	2	B
w Rice, hot	VGCB	317	1	B
w Shrimp	CIC	39	1	B

RECIPE	BOOK	PAGE	TD	S
w Shrimp	NYT	406	1	B
w Shrimp	JOC	308	1	B
Sicilian	NYT	406	1	B
w Spinach & ricotta	SP	193	2	C
w Tuna	BHGN	349	1	B
w Tuna & capers	CIC	38	1	B
Variations	VGCB	314	1	
Variations	AC	45		
w Vermicelli pesto	MSE	286	2	C
Sun dried	SPGT	252		
Tart	JOC	307	1	B
Tart quick	JOC	228	2	B
Timbales petit	BBA	17	2	C
Tricks w	BBA	137		
& Tuna salad	FAIC	393	1	B
& Vegetable soup, cold	MFC	76	2	B
Vertis	SC	433	1	
Vinaigrette	NYTI	254	1	B
Vinaigrette oranges &	GHAC	276	1	B
& Vodka appetizer	FG	223	1	
Whole baked	MAFC	506	1	
& Wild rice soup	CBSS	351	1	B
w Wine sauce	NYT	341	2	B
w Wine sauce for pasta	VE	244	1	B
Tongue	JBC	160	2	B
All about	JOC	445		
Aspic	NYT	174	2	B
Aspic	JOC	447	2	B
Baked w Creole sauce	JOC	446	1	B
Basic preparation	FFCB	220	2	B
Beef				
A la jardiniere	SC	301	2	
Boiled	JOC	446	2	B
Boiled fresh	NYT	175	2	B

RECIPE	BOOK	PAGE	TD	S
Boiled w sweet & sour sauce	MFC2	233	2	B
Braised, whole w madeira sauce	MFC2	236	2	B
Sliced, braised curry	MFC2	240	2	B
Smoked, boiled	AC	321	1	
Boiled, New England dinner	JBC	155	2	B
Boiled, sauces to serve	MFC2	235		
Boiling	MFC2	232	1	B
Braised	FFCB	220	2	B
Braised, fresh	JBC	162	1	B
Calf's, braised w red wine & onions	MFC	157	3	B
Calf's w vinegar & capers	MFC	158	3	B
Cat's	FFBB	259	1	C
Cat's, cookies	JOC	633	1	C
& Chicken ring, variations	AC	208	2	
Cooking	BCC	218	2	
Corned, boiled	JOC	446	2	
Cornucopias	JOC	71	2	
Eggs	SC	226	1	
& Eggs in aspic	AC	321	3	
Fresh notes on	MFC2	231		
Fresh w sweet & sour tomato sauce	GHAC	214	1	C
Hash	AC	321	1	
Lamb	MFC2	242	2	B
Boiled	AC	398	1	
Fricassee of	AC	398	1	
In paper cases	OC	129	2	B
Pickled	AC	398	3	
& Lima skillet	BHGN	269	1	B
Mousse, ham &	EBE	56	2	B
w Mustard dill sauce	SMG	316	1	B

RECIPE	BOOK	PAGE	TD	S
Tongue (*cont.*)				
Peeling a	MFC2	233		
Pickled & boiled	JOC	446	2	
Pork	MFC2	242	2	B
Pork loaf, pressed	FGCW	294	3	B
w Raisin sauce, beef	JOC	446	2	
w Red pepper sauce, smoked	GG	285	2	B
Ring, chicken, variations	AC	208	2	
Salad	SC	362	1	C
Salad, molded	SC	371	2	C
Salad sandwich	JOC	246		
Sandwich	FFCB	295		
Sandwich, variations	AC	809	1	
Sauces to serve w	MFC2	235		
Shells, cat's (cookies)	LM	311	2	C
Smoked				
Beef	SC	300	3	
Beef, boiled	AC	321	1	
Boiled	JOC	446	3	B
Boiled	NYT	174		B
Cold	AC	320		
w Pepper sauce	GG	285	2	B
Spiced beef	NYT	175	2	B
& Spinach salad	AC	72	1	
Stuffed birds	AC	300	2	
Sweet & sour	FFCB	220	1	B
Sweet & sour	EBE	66	1	B
Sweet & sour w tomato sauce	GHAC	214	1	C
w Tarragon, grilled	OC	128	2	B
w Tomato sauce, braised	AC	322	2	
Veal	MFC2	242	2	B
Veal	BTSB	20	3	B
Veal, boiled	FAIC	269		
& Vegetables	FFCB	221	2	B

RECIPE	BOOK	PAGE	TD	S
& Vegetables, simmered, fresh	AC	322	2	
w White wine	FFCB	221	2	B
Tonic	SC	62	1	
Tonic	JOC	47	1	A
Tonnarelli (square homemade noodles)	MCIC	176	3	
Topini of potato chicken breast broth	FAIC	111	2	B
Topinka (broiled cheese & toast)	GRIL	101	1	B
Topping				
Almond	BCC	79	1	B
Crumb	SC	83	1	
Elaborate	JOC	343	1	B
For ice cream	BB	161	1	
For individual pizzas	MSQC	48	2	B
For meringue torte	SC	132	2	B
Lace	JOC	681	1	
Lazy daisy	FFBB	404	1	C
Lemon for cookies or bars	JOC	678	1	B
Marshmallow meringue	SC	344	1	
Matzos pie	SC	344	1	
Meringue (see meringue topping)				
Mushroom pepper	GHAC	185	1	
Sauteed onion	GHAC	185	1	
Streusel	FFBB	540	1	C
Terrific	BBA	228		
Torta di ricotta	VE	273	2	C
Torta lampo	AC	689	1	
Torta rustica	BBA	63	3	B

RECIPE	BOOK	PAGE	TD	S
Tostadas	MC	144	2	B
Tostadas, cheese	NYTI	466	1	B
Tostadas & guacamole	YGM	199	2	C
Tournedos, broiled	JOC	400	1	
Tournedos, definition	AC	260		
Tournedos Ismal Rayeldi	NYTI	169	1	B
Tournedos Rossini	NYTI	168	1	B
Tourtiere (French Canadian pork pie)	NYTI	28		B
Tourtiere	NYT	144	2	B
Tourtiere (pork veal pie)	AC	426	1	
Trail mix gorp	FFCB	72	1	B
Transparent pie	JOC	605	2	B
Treacle tart, Cornish	FFCB	583	2	B
Trenette w basil sauce	FAIC	153	2	B
Trenette con pesto	VE	236	1	B
Trenette potatoes & pesto	CIC	142	3	B
Triangle tip, Broder's	MIE	117	1	B
Triangles, brie & smoked salmon &	GHAC	86	1	C
Trieste cheese spread	BBA	22	2	B
Trifle	JOC	640	2	
Trifle	CF	150	2	B
Trifle	SC	136	1	C
Chocolate cake, individual	MSQC	29	1	B
English	BCC	141	2	C
◆	FFCB	531	1	B
◆	NYTI	93	2	C
◆	LM	289	2	B
Lemon angel	EBE	197	3	B
Tripe	AC	320		
Tripe	MFC2	243		
A la mode de Caen	NYT	176	3	C
A la mode de Caen	JOC	448	3	B

RECIPE	BOOK	PAGE	TD	S
All about	JOC	448		
w Baked onions & tomatoes Provencale	MFC2	244	2	B
Batter	FFCB	222	2	B
Beans	MCIC	309	1	B
Broiled	FFCB	222	2	B
Buying	MFC2	243		
Cooked	JOC	448	3	B
Florentine	FG	158	2	B
Florentine style	FAIC	365	2	B
Fried	JOC	448	3	
Honeycomb	SC	301	2	
Honeycomb w parmesan cheese	CIC	293	2	B
Lyonnaise	FFCB	223	2	B
Nicoise	MFC2	244	2	B
Soup	NYTI	549	3	C
Spanish	JOC	448	3	
w Wine & calvados	LM	214	2	C
Triticale bread, entire	FFBB	483	3	C
Triticale bread, toasted wheat	FFBB	484	3	C
Triticale, forms of	JBGF	72		
Triticale marmalade bread	FFBB	484	3	C
Tropical salad	EBE	186	3	C
Trotters (lamb shanks)	JOC	422	2	B
Trotters, sheep's	AC	398	3	
Trout				
Almonds	LT	160	2	
Amandine	NYTI	144	1	B
Amandine	BHGN	213	1	B
Aspic, cold	NYT	260	2	B
Baked	SC	242	1	
Baked w salted herring	SC	241	1	
Barbecued	SC	332	1	
Blue	JOC	362	2	

RECIPE	BOOK	PAGE	TD	S
Blue	AC	137		
Boiled mayonnaise	FAIC	241	1	B
Broiled, lake	JOC	362	1	
Brook meuniere	NYT	261	1	B
Brook, pan fried	FFCB	125	1	B
Cappelletti & smoked fish soup	CPPC	46	3	B
Chevrons smoked w horseradish cream	MSE	51	2	C
Citrus-barbecued	OC	152	1	B
Cleaning, boning (photographs)	LT	157		
Cooked on a plate	FAIC	242	1	B
w Dill sauce, cold	AC	136	1	B
Fillets in puff pastry	MFC	133	3	C
Fisherman's style	OC	152	1	A
Flemish sauce for poached	NYT	449	1	A
Grenobloise	NYTI	144	1	B
Grilled	OC	153	2	B
Grilled w summer vegetable stuffing	GHAC	224	1	B
Grilled, whole	GRIL	72	2	B
Loaf, baked	SC	241	1	
Luchow, blue	NYT	259	2	A
Meuniere	NYTI	144	1	B
Meuniere, brook	JOC	361	1	B
Mousse, smoked	YGM	165	3	A
Mousse, smoked w chervil butter	CPMC	66	3	B
Mousse, smoked, on cucumber slices	MSE	58	2	C
On a spit	OC	152	1	B
Pan fried w vegetable stuffing	GHAC	143	1	B
Pan, sauteed, stuffed w sage	MSQC	36	1	B
w Pimiento sauce	WC	73	1	B
Puff paste	LM	105	3	C
Rainbow, broiled	FFCB	125	1	B
Rolled, how to (photographs)	LT	159		
Sauteed w orange marinade, cold	CIC	220	2	B
Sea or bass in puff paste	LM	105	3	C
Smoked	BTSB	32	3	C
Smoked	LM	112	3	C
Smoked pasta w golden caviar &	CPMC	184	2	A
Smoked, rillettes of	SPGT	17	3	B
Stuffed w cream sauce	LT	163	3	
Stuffed w fish mousse	NYTI	145	3	B
Vegetables, cooked in foil	MFC	134	2	B
Truffle	BCC	116	3	C
All about	JOC	283		
Almond	BCC	116	3	C
Apricot	BCC	116	3	C
Black flowers, making	LT	20	2	
Black, spaghetti w	MCIC	140	3	A
Breast of duck, pears &	GF	58	3	C
Butter sausage wrapped in brioche w	MFC	41	3	B
Cake, chocolate	LM	328	3	C
Cashew	BCC	116	3	C
Cassis	NSD	76	3	C
Chanterelle & endive, pasta w	CPPC	143	2	B
Cherry	BCC	116	3	C
Chicken, steamed	NYTI	215	2	B
Chocolate	LM	345	2	C

RECIPE	BOOK	PAGE	TD	S
Tulsa toppin	CFS	300	1	C
Tuna				
A la king	BHGN	221	1	B
A la king, canned	SC	244	1	
Antipasto w pepper	VGCB	207	1	B
& Asparagus casserole, canned	SC	244	1	
& Avocado salad	SMG	318	1	B
Bake, fresh	GHAC	144	1	B
Baked, fresh	FFCB	126	1	B
Barbecued	OC	153	2	B
& Bean salad	CIC	417	1	B
Broccoli shells	KIS	149	1	A
Canapes, hot	JOC	62	2	
& Cannelli beans	SMG	312	1	B
& Capers, tomatoes stuffed w	CIC	38	1	B
Casserole, creamy	BCC	184	1	B
Casserole, quick	JOC	237	1	B
& Cheese spread	EBE	43	1	B
& Chickpea salad	FFCB	435	2	B
Chowder, ten minute	BBA	43	2	B
Company, creamed	BHGN	221	1	B
Curried	BCC	184	1	B
& Dandelion salad	AC	68	1	
Dip	JOC	75	1	
Dip, hot	GHAC	94	1	B
Filling	SC	381	1	
Fish				
Balls	JOC	240	1	B
Croquettes, canned	SC	245	1	
Curry	WC	70	1	B
& Dandelion salad	AC	68	1	
Filling	SC	381	1	
Pies, individual	JOC	239	1	B
Salad	AC	68	1	
Salad	JOC	91	1	B
Sandwich, variations	AC	811	1	
Sauce for cold veal	NYT	455	1	B
Sauce, veal &	AC	334	2	
w Spaghetti, quick	JOC	185	1	B
& Vegetables Italienne, marinated	NYT	39	2	B
Flavor, turkey loaf poached w	FAIC	319	2	C
Grilled, fresh	NYT	261	2	B
Help, stroganoff style	KIS	364	1	B
Kebabs	CFS	219	2	B
Loaf	FFCB	147	1	B
Loaf, canned	SC	244	1	
Mayonnaise	SPGT	85	1	B
Mayonnaise	BB	143	1	
Noodle casserole	GHAC	144	1	B
Noodle casserole	BHGN	220	1	B
Noodle casserole	FFCB	147	1	B
Noodle & mushroom soup casserole	JOC	190	1	B
Olives, lemon & capers, tagliatelle w	CPPC	79	1	A
Pate, molded	GHAC	144	2	B
Patties	BHGN	221	1	B
Patty sandwiches	BCC	322	1	B
Pepper salad, hot	GG	279	1	A
Pie	FFCB	147	1	B
Pie, canned	SC	244	1	
Pies, individual	BHGN	220	1	B
& Potato chip loaf	JOC	239	1	B
& Potato salad	GHAC	279	1	B
& Potato salad	FGCW	136	1	B
Pudding	NYT	262	2	B
Quiche, crustless	BCC	185	1	B
& Rice	FFCB	148	1	B
& Rice, canned	SC	244	1	

RECIPE	BOOK	PAGE	TD	S
Tuna (*cont.*)				
Salad	BCC	263	2	B
Salad	FFCB	438	1	B
Salad	SC	363	1	
Bean &	BCC	269	1	B
Cantaloupe &	BCC	269	2	B
Eggplant &	BBA	142	2	B
Filling	BCC	321	1	B
Macaroni &	BCC	269	2	B
Pasta &	BCC	269	2	B
Tomato &	FAIC	393	1	B
& Salami	CIC	222	2	B
Sandwich casserole w cheese	SC	231	1	
Sauce	FAIC	74	1	B
Sauce	JBC	213	1	A
Sauce	FG	353	1	B
Eggs w	FG	353	1	
For celeriac	VGCB	71	1	B
Shells w	FAIC	160	1	B
Spaghetti w	CIC	102	1	B
Veal w	BCC	215	2	C
Veal w	AC	334	2	
Veal w	JBC	164	2	B
Veal, cold, roast w	FG	359	1	
Veal, cold, sliced w	CIC	276	2	B
Scalloped, w noodles & canned	SC	244	1	
Scalloped w potatoes & canned	SC	244	1	
Shortcakes	BCC	185	1	B
Slices, baked	BCC	324	1	B
Smoked	AC	143		
Souffle	JBC	271	1	B
Souffle	BHGN	202	2	B
Soup, cheesy, quick	BHGN	380	1	B
Soup Martinique	NYTI	121	1	B
& Spaghetti	BCC	184	1	B

RECIPE	BOOK	PAGE	TD	S
& Spinach loaf	MCIC	326	1	B
Spread	FFCB	56	1	B
Steaks, grilled	CF	34	1	B
Steaks, grilled w roasted pepper mayonnaise	CFS	214	2	B
Steaks, sweet & sour, trapani style	MCIC	221	1	B
Steaks w wine, tomatoes & herbs	MAFC	219	2	B
Stuffed tomatoes	BHGN	349	1	B
Stuffing, peppers w	VGCB	204	1	
Stuffing w tomatoes, baked	FFCB	417	2	B
Summer salad	MFC	187	1	B
Tetrazzini, canned	SC	245	1	
& Tomato salad	FAIC	393	1	B
Tomato salad stuffed w	FFCB	437	2	B
w Tomato sauce	JBGF	369	1	B
Tomatoes stuffed w	BHGN	349	1	B
Tomatoes stuffed w capers &	CIC	38	1	B
Tuscan beans & fresh onions	FAIC	102	3	B
Veal patties w anchovies &	MAFC	375	1	B
Vegetable pie	BHGN	221	2	B
Vegetable salad	BBA	148	1	A
& White bean salad	BBA	147	2	B
Tunisian mixed salad	BBA	148	2	B
Turbot en bourride (whitefish)	SP	49	2	C
Turbot, poached	JOC	362	1	
Turkey	JOC	480	3	
A la campagne	JOC	472	2	C
Balls, ground	YGM	74	1	A

TURKEY

RECIPE	BOOK	PAGE	TD	S
Barbecued	OC	140	2	B
Biscuits, old fashioned, creamed	GHAC	163	2	B
Boiled	AC	225	2	
Boning	MAFC	570		
Breast				
Fillets, sauteed w ham, cheese & truffles	CIC	316	3	B
Grilled w ginger rhubarb sauce	CFS	130	2	B
Kale &	VGCB	147	3	B
Roast	MIE	107	2	C
Roast	FFCB	236	1	A
Rolled & stuffed	FAIC	316	2	B
& Broccoli bake	SC	316	1	
Broiled	JOC	466	1	
Broiled	SC	319		
Broiled	JBC	236		
Broth	JOC	146	1	B
Bulgur	MIE	110	2	B
Burgers	JBGF	440	1	B
Carcass soup	JBGF	348	3	B
Carving	GHAC	161		
Carving (photographs)	LT	320		
Carving a	BCC	257		
Carving a (photographs)	NYT	214		
Casserole fricassee	AC	228	2	
Casserole mole	JOC	473	2	
Casserole, vegetables &	JOC	235	2	B
& Chicken, baked in foil	JOC	465	1	
Chowder	JBGF	347	1	B
Confit	FGCW	199	1	B
Cooled	AC	228		
w Cream cheese filling	MAFC	203	1	B
Creamed	JBC	236		B
Crepes	FFCB	296	2	B
Curried w apples & peanuts	GHAC	163	1	B
Curry	JBC	236	1	
Cutlets w marsala	GHAC	162	1	B
Cutlets, sesame	KIS	295	1	B
Defrosting	SC	319		
w Dill sauce, cold	FG	144	2	
Dinner swan song soup	VGCB	232	2	B
Divan	JOC	236	1	B
Divan	BCC	255	1	B
Dressing	JOC	458	1	C
Dumplings	FG	143	2	
Fillets, grilled w cranberry & mustard	CFS	133	2	B
Fillets, supercrunchy	CFS	134	1	B
Flambe, roast	BB	77	2	C
Florentine	VGCB	268	2	B
Florentine	NYT	213	1	B
Frame soup	BHGN	374	2	C
Fricassee	JOC	467	2	C
Fricassee casserole	AC	228	2	
Galantine	JOC	436	3	C
Galantine of	NYT	4	3	C
w Giblet gravy	GHAC	161	1	C
Grilled I	BB	43	1	B
Grilled II	BB	43	1	B
Half boned	MFC2	269		
Hash	JOC	235	1	B
Hash	NYT	216	1	B
Hash, country	GHAC	163	1	B
Hash, variations	AC	227	1	
Hickory garlic scented	CFS	275	3	B

RECIPE	BOOK	PAGE	TD	S
Turkey (*cont.*)				
Loaf	SC	317	1	
Loaf	JBGF	440	2	B
Loaf, cooked	JOC	236	1	B
Loaf, tuna flavor, poached	FAIC	319	2	C
Madras	WC	50	2	B
Maryland	GHAC	162	2	B
Meatballs	JBGF	439	1	B
Meatballs	BCC	259	1	B
w Mole sauce	BB	108	2	C
Mornay, celeriac	VGCB	70	1	B
Mousse	NYT	436	2	B
Mousse	MAFC	560	1	C
Mushrooms gratin of	MAFC	157	1	B
Mushrooms & marsala	FG	144	1	B
Noodles Florentine	NYTI	236	2	C
Parts, grilled	SC	331	2	
Parts, grilled	BB	44	1	
Pasta w cream sauce	FG	145	1	B
Pie	BCC	255	1	B
Pieces grilled	BHGN	31	3	C
w Pine nut rice stuffing, roast	YGM	230	3	C
Pineapple	BCC	258	2	C
Pockets	JBGF	494	1	B
Pot pie	BCC	255	2	B
Preserved	MFC2	315	3	C
Puff sandwiches	BCC	321	1	B
Quenelles	MAFC	189	2	B
Rice	FG	144	2	
& Rice, Basque style	WC	58	1	B
& Rice salad	JBGF	409	2	B
Roast	AC	224	1	
Roast	BCC	256		
Roast	SC	319		
Fennel, stuffed	GG	178	3	C
Foil	SC	319		
w Fruit nut stuffing	MSE	192	3	C
Half	SC	319		
Leftover stuffing	JBC	235		
My own favorite	AC	226	2	
Our favorite way to roast	SP	95	2	C
w Pecan stuffing	GHAC	160	2	C
Plain	JBC	236		
Rolled	BB	78	3	
Stuffed	JBGF	441	2	B
◆	JOC	465	2	C
◆	FFCB	234	2	C
◆	JBC	235		B
w Veal & ham stuffing	BBA	82	3	C
Wild	AC	225	2	
Roasted, spit	SC	331		
Roasting	AC	224		
Roasting	BCC	256		
Roasting in high temperature	NYT	212		
Roasting in low temperature	NYT	212		
Roll	SC	319		
Salad	JBC	251	1	B
Curried in brioche	BBA	148	2	B
Fruited	BCC	265	2	B
Glazed, smoked	BCC	271	2	B
w Pasta	BCC	265	1	B
Smoked	SP	207	1	B
Vegetable	BCC	264	1	B
Salsa mole poblano	FGCW	192	2	C
Salsify hash	VGCB	259	1	B
Sandwich	AC	810	1	
Sandwiches, hot	SC	384	1	B
Scalloped	FFCB	260	1	A
Scallops in balsamic vinegar	CFS	132	2	B

RECIPE	BOOK	PAGE	TD	S
Simmered	FG	142	2	
Smoked	BTSB	30	3	C
On blueberry scones	MSE	58	3	C
Sliced	MSE	293	1	C
& Stilton sandwiches	MSQC	141	1	B
Teriyaki	OC	139	3	C
Soup	SC	395	3	
Soup	FFCB	82	3	B
Soup, Creole	GHAC	105	2	C
Soup, leftover	MIE	78	2	C
Spiced	SC	317	2	
Steak	BB	44	1	A
Steaks grilled w cranberry mustard	CFS	133	2	B
Stew	JOC	467	2	C
Stew, creamed	SC	320		
Stroganoff	SC	317	1	
Stuffed	BB	76	2	C
Stuffed, chart for roasting	SC	319		
Stuffed, chart for roasting in foil	SC	319		
Tetrazzini	JOC	186	2	C
Tetrazzini	JBGF	363	1	B
Tostadas	MIE	109	1	A
Turnovers	NYT	215	2	B
Verde	BBA	100	2	C
Waldorf salad	JBGF	410	1	B
& Yam kebobs	BHGN	307	1	B
Turkish candy	SC	170	1	
Turkish delight	JOC	739	3	B
Turkish eggplant	FGCW	269	2	B
Turkish giblet gravy	GHAC	161	1	C
Turkish gozleme (sauteed zucchini cakes)	GG	398	1	B

RECIPE	BOOK	PAGE	TD	S
Turmeric chicken	NYTI	357	2	B
Turnip	MAFC	485		
Turnip	SC	434	1	
All about	VGCB	324		
Artichokes, braised, w carrots, onions &	MAFC	427	1	B
Baby	MSQC	16	1	A
Baby greens	VGCB	327	1	
Baked	VGCB	327	1	
Boiled	AC	553	1	
Boiled	VGCB	327	1	
Boiled, white	JBC	340	1	B
Braised	AC	553	1	
Braised	FFCB	419	1	B
Braised w butter	MAFC	486	1	B
Carrot dilled, gratin of	VGCB	328	1	B
Cases w two fillings	VGCB	330	1	B
Casserole	MAFC	488	1	B
Casserole	NYT	408	1	B
& Cauliflower puree	GG	105	1	B
& Cheese	BCC	368	1	B
Chicken & chickpeas	VGCB	333	1	B
Chowder, mixed	GG	387	1	B
Cooked	JOC	309	1	B
Cream	AC	553	1	
Creamed	FFCB	418	1	B
Cups, carrots in	AC	504	1	
Cups, peas in	AC	537	1	
Cups, stuffed	JOC	309	1	B
Custard	CW	156	2	B
Dauphinoise	MSQC	137	1	B
Duck, braised	VGCB	332	2	B
Duck casserole, roast	MAFC	279	1	B
& Duck legs	MFC	89	3	A
Duck, squash &	VGCB	282	2	B
Farmhouse	GG	387	1	B

RECIPE	BOOK	PAGE	TD	S
Turnip (*cont.*)				
Finishing touches for steamed or boiled	VGCB	327	1	
Freezing	BHGN	141		
Fresh young white, sauteed in butter	MFC2	407	1	B
Glazed	MAFC	488	1	B
Grated	CF	108	1	B
Grated white	VGCB	328	1	B
Greens, cooking	AC	521		
Greens, hot pepper & cornmeal dumplings	CW	129	1	B
Honey peppered	GG	390	1	B
Lamb (leg of) w	NYT	122		B
Lemon parsleyed	BHGN	406	1	B
Mashed	AC	553	1	
Mushrooms	AC	553	1	
Old fashioned scalloped	VGCB	329	1	B
Ovals, glazed	VGCB	326	1	
Paprikash	GG	392	1	B
Parsley	MFC	179	1	B
Parsleyed	MAFC	487	1	B
& Potatoes puree	MAFC	487	1	B
& Potatoes, pureed	JBGF	532	1	B
Preparing	GG	385		
Puff, whipped	BHGN	406	1	B
Puree	GG	391	1	B
Puree, pear &	CW	132	1	B
Puree w rice, herbs & garlic	MFC2	405	1	B
Puree, white pear &	GF	81	1	C
Pureed, yellow	NYT	408	1	
& Rice puree w herbs & garlic	MFC2	405	1	B
Roasted meat or fowl	FFCB	419	1	B
& Rutabaga salad, tart	VGCB	331	1	B
Rutabaga & shinbone soup	VGCB	331	2	B
Rutabagas & kohlrabi, preparing	BCC	367		
Sausages & rape	FAIC	353	2	B
Savarin, gruyere sauce for	GG	386	1	B
Sicilian style	GG	392	1	B
Soup	VGCB	331	1	B
Soup	NYT	74	1	B
Green	MFC2	18	1	B
Green peas &	CBSS	362	1	B
Potato &	JBGF	321	1	B
White	CBSS	360	1	B
Steamed	VGCB	327	1	
Steamed, white	NYT	407	1	
Stew	CBSS	359	1	B
Stew, beef &	GG	393	2	B
Treat, peppery	JBGF	531	1	B
Whipped	FFCB	418	1	B
Yellow	AC	554		
& Yellow puree, rutabagas	MFC2	406	1	B
Turnovers	JOC	55		
Turnovers	SC	81	3	
Turnovers	FFBB	534	3	C
Apple	AC	615	1	
Apple wine	FFBB	156	2	B
Apricot	FFBB	156	2	B
Cherry	FFBB	156	2	B
Cocktail, piroshki	BBA	16	2	C
Cranberry nut	JBGF	607	1	C
Filled w meat	JOC	224	3	B
Jam	SC	352	1	
Sweet	JOC	608	2	B
Turos delkli (cheese buns)	NYTI	350	2	B

RECIPE	BOOK	PAGE	TD	S
Turtle candies, easy	BCC	119	2	C
Turtle soup	PPLK	212	3	C
Au sherry	CBSS	219	3	B
Cream of	NYTI	124	1	B
Green	JOC	156	3	B
Mock	SC	397	2	
Mock	JOC	156	3	C
Mock, quick	SC	397	2	
Turtles preparing	JOC	380		
Tuscan country bread	FAIC	32	2	B
Tuscan dark bread	FAIC	37	2	B
Tuscan whole wheat bread	FAIC	38	2	B
Tutti frutti	FFCB	708	2	C
Brandied I	NYT	506	3	B
Brandied II	NYT	507	2	C
Cake	JOC	630	2	B
Cockaigne	JOC	780	2	C
Creams	SC	173	1	
Louisiana	SC	56	1	
Parfait	JOC	720	2	B
Twenty-four hour salad	BCC	296	2	B
Twists	FFBB	536	3	C
Twists	FFCB	474	2	B
Two crust pies	SC	341		
Two egg cake, high altitude	JOC	649	1	B
Two egg cake, quick	SC	107	1	B
Tyler pie	AC	629	1	

U

RECIPE	BOOK	PAGE	TD	S
Uccelleti scappati (veal sauce for spaghetti)	NYTI	399	2	B
Unmolding	SC	212		
Unmolding a gelatin salad	BHGN	341		
Unmolding a pate	GF	65		
Unmolding & gelling	JBGF	266		
Upside down cake	JOC	607	1	B
Upside down cake, fruit	AC	655	1	
Uszki (mushroom stuffed dumplings)	VE	56	3	C
Utensils, cooking	JOC	141		

V

RECIPE	BOOK	PAGE	TD	S
Vacherin	MFC	242	3	B
Valentine's devil's food cake	GHAC	128	3	B
Vanilla				
Bavarian cream	NYT	592	2	C
Bean ice cream	BCC	152		
Bean ice cream	NSD	201	1	B
Beans	NSD	29		
Beans, how to infuse into liquids	NSD	29		
Bread	FFBB	455	1	B
Caramels	SC	170	1	
Carrot tart	GG	98	2	B
Chocolate souffle	LM	324	1	
Cream caramels	JOC	732	1	B
Cream filling for Danish pastries	NYT	535	1	
Cream filling, rich	NYTI	290	1	
Cream pie	BHGN	281	2	B
Cream pie I	FFBB	109	2	B
Cream pie II	FFBB	111	2	B
Cream pudding	SC	204	2	
Cupcakes	SC	140	1	C

RECIPE	BOOK	PAGE	TD	S
Crust	FFBB	69	1	B
Icebox dessert, frozen	SC	136	2	B
Sesame	CF	95	1	C
Yogurt, frozen	BTSB	66	2	B
Venison roast, haunch of	BB	80	2	
Variety meat patties	JOC	451	2	B
Veal (see also blanquette de veau, escalope de veau, osso bucco)				
Veal (an early American way of doing scallops)	AC	347		
Veal (wiener schnitzel)	AC	341		
Almonds	NYTI	485	2	C
& Anchovies w cheese (bundles)	CIC	267	1	B
Baked w green peppers	FFCB	182	1	B
Baked w sour cream, cubed	JOC	421	2	B
Balls w tarragon tomato sauce	NYTI	400	1	B
Barbecued	CW	92	2	B
Beef cold fillet of, w mustard sauce	GF	26	2	C
Birds	FFCB	179	2	B
Birds	JOC	420	3	
Alouettes sans tetes	AC	343	1	
Boston Cooking School	AC	344	1	
California	AC	344	1	
w Chicken livers	NYT	166	1	B
w Dill	JBC	175	2	B
w Ham	JBC	174	2	B

RECIPE	BOOK	PAGE	TD	S
Italian	NYT	166	1	B
Salsicciana	NYTI	395	2	B
& Sausage	JBC	174	2	B
Stuffed	NYTI	194	2	B
Thoroughly Western	AC	345	1	
Blanquette de veau	AC	339	2	
Blanquette dill	NYTI	196	2	B
Blanquette of	JBC	173	2	B
Blanquette of	NYT	164	2	B
Blanquette of	FFCB	179	2	B
Bon appetit	NYTI	196	2	B
Bordelaise	NYTI	188	2	B
Braised leg of	FFCB	176	2	B
Braised w ravioli filling	NYTI	417	1	C
Braised w vegetables	WC	93	2	B
Breast				
Anchovy stuffed	NYTI	190	2	B
Braised stuffed	AC	336	2	
Breaded w lemon caper garnish	SMG	202	1	B
Broiled stuffed	CIC	254	2	B
Buying	MFC2	215		
Cold	JBC	169	2	B
w Endive stuffing	VGCB	118	2	B
Mushroom stuffed	GHAC	208	2	B
Plum glazed	GHAC	218	2	B
Roast	MCIC	284	1	B
Roast stuffed	SC	285	2	
Rolled	NYT	161	2	B
Scandinavian style	CFS	279	3	B
Spiced	NYT	13	2	C
w Spinach stuffing	NYT	161	2	B
Stuffed	NYT	163	2	B
Stuffed	JBC	168	2	B
Stuffed braised hot or cold	MFC2	216	2	B

RECIPE	BOOK	PAGE	TD	S
w Sherry lemon marmalade	SP	102	1	B
Stuffed	BB	37	1	B
Stuffed aux pistaches	NYTI	190	2	B
Stuffed, Italian style	JBC	171	2	B
Cold sliced w tuna sauce	CIC	276	2	B
Cordon bleu	NYTI	536	1	B
Cordon bleu	BHGN	240	1	B
Cordon bleu	AC	342	1	
w Cream, minced	AC	343	1	
w Cream sauce	SMG	218	1	B
Creamed	JOC	235	2	B
Creamed, leftover	JOC	229	1	B
Croquettes	JOC	219	3	
Cubes, spaghettini w	NYTI	430	1	B
Curry	SC	287	2	
Cutlet	JOC	403	1	
Cutlets	SC	285	1	
Cutlets	MAFC	369		
Breaded	AC	341	1	
◆	FFCB	177	1	B
◆	JBC	166	1	B
◆	JOC	404	1	A
Breaded holstein	JBC	166	1	B
Breaded, Milan style	CIC	270	1	B
Breaded, Palermo style	MCIC	269	1	B
Breaded w parmesan cheese	JBC	166	1	B
California	GHAC	210	1	B
w Cream sauce	AC	341		
From Ouchy	NYTI	535	1	B
Grilled	SC	329	1	
Ground w bread crumbs & cream	SMG	200	1	B
w Ham & cheese, stuffed	GHAC	210	1	B
Italian, stuffed	NYT	160	1	A
Milanese	AC	341		
Miss Jessie Duncan mock birds	AC	343		
w Noodles, Mexican	SC	286	1	
Parmigiana	AC	342	1	
Potted	SC	286	1	
Provencale	NYTI	192	1	B
Sauteed	FFCB	177	1	A
Stuffed w ham & cheese	GHAC	210	1	B
w Wine	FFCB	178	1	A
Cuts, chart	SC	283		
Cuts for roasting	MAFC	351		
Cuts for stewing	MFC2	209		
Cuts of, chart	JOC	392		
Cuts of (drawings)	FFCB	174		
Drawing	JBC	164		
En daube	AC	337	3	
Fricassee	SC	286	2	
Fried w peas & pappardelle	CPPC	38	1	B
Goulash	NYTI	346	2	B
Goulash, Viennese	NYT	164	2	B
Gratineed w onions & mushrooms	MAFC	355	3	C
Grillades, deep south	NYTI	559	2	B
Grilled w sauce pizzaiola	YGM	66	1	B
& Ham stuffing, turkey roast w	BBA	82	3	C
Heart, broiled	OC	129	1	A
Hearts & peas, sauteed	VGCB	199	1	B
Herbs, scaloppine of	SMG	222	1	B
Hungarian	NYTI	347	2	B

RECIPE	BOOK	PAGE	TD	S
Veal (*cont.*)				
& Kidney casserole	JOC	445	1	B
Kidney	MAFC	416		
Baked	JOC	444	1	
Bordelaise	NYT	169	1	B
Broiled	JBC	176	1	B
Broiled	BB	39	1	
Broiled	AC	362	1	
Deviled	AC	362	1	
Flambe	NYT	169	1	B
Flamed w brandy cream mushroom sauce	MAFC	418	1	B
& Leeks w vinegar sauce	MFC	159	3	B
w Red wine sauce & marrow	MAFC	419	1	B
Saute w wine	AC	364	1	
w Sherry sauce	AC	364	1	
w White wine	NYT	170	1	B
Knuckles braised (ossi buchi)	AC	338	2	
Knuckles, stewed	AC	339	3	
Lamb, sweetbreads w basil sauce	GF	185	3	B
Leg of roast	JBC	163	2	B
Leg of roast	NYT	151	2	B
Leg of roast w anchovies	JBC	163	2	B
w Lemons & capers, roast	SPGT	72	2	B
& Lentil pilaf	WC	103	1	B
Liver	PPLK	114	2	B
Liver, grilled, Florentine style	OC	129	1	B
Liver loaf to be eaten cold	AC	354	2	
Loaf	MAFC	375	1	B
◆	AC	350	2	
◆	FFCB	180	1	B
◆	JOC	432	2	C
◆	NYT	168	1	B
Boiled eggs	AC	352	2	
Cooked	JOC	236	1	B
Ham	SC	298	1	
Jellied	SC	371	2	
Jellied	AC	351	2	
Lemon	AC	351	2	
Loin	LM	232	2	
Braised, stuffed w vegetables	BBA	61	3	C
Double-larded w ham	AC	334	2	
Kidney-stuffed	AC	335	2	
Of roast, w sweetbread mousse	GF	38	3	C
Scallops stuffed w foie gras & truffles	MFC2	223	3	B
Stuffed w orange sauce	MFC	148	3	B
Marengo	AC	340	2	
Marengo	NYTI	197	2	B
Medallions meaux w mustard sauce	MFC	146	1	B
Medallions w onion marmalade	MFC	147	2	B
Medallions w port wine sauce	MFC	146	2	B
Menagere, roast	NYTI	189	2	B
Minced, w cream & mushrooms	FFCB	182	1	B
Mold, steamed	JOC	210	2	B
Mousse, jellied	JOC	97	2	C
Mushroom stuffed w breast of	GHAC	208	2	B
Mushroom stuffed w pork &	NYTI	374	1	C

RECIPE	BOOK	PAGE	TD	S
w Mushrooms & cream	SMG	216	1	B
& Olives on skewers	OC	108	2	B
& Onion stew, pearly	SP	188	2	C
Or beef cutlets, deep fried	FAIC	281	2	B
Oreganata	NYTI	396	1	B
Oscar	BCC	216	2	B
Oven roasted	FFCB	174	1	B
& Oyster crepes	PPLK	123	3	B
Oysters & artichoke over pasta	PPLK	126	3	B
Oysters & sweetbreads pastry	AC	357	2	
Paillard of	AC	348	1	
Pain de veau	MAFC	375	1	B
Paneed w czarina sauce	PPLK	117	2	B
Paneed w fettuccini	PPLK	115	2	B
Papillote	JOC	404	2	
Paprika	NYT	160	1	B
Paprika	FFCB	178	1	B
Paprika & wine	SC	286	1	
Paprikash	WC	106	1	B
Parmesan	EBE	68	2	B
Parmesan	KIS	285	1	A
Parmigiana	GHAC	210	1	B
Parmigiana	JOC	404	1	
Parmigiana	JBC	170	1	B
Pasta salad w pesto dressing	BBA	149	2	B
Pastry, sweetbreads, oysters &	AC	357	2	
Pate, ham, pork &	MAFC	566	3	C
Pate w pork liver	MAFC	568	3	C
Patties	JOC	428	2	C
Patties	NYTI	493	1	C
Patties	BHGN	240	1	B
w Cream herb sauce	MAFC	373	1	B
w Mushrooms	MAFC	374	1	B
w Tomatoes, onions & herbs	MAFC	372	1	B
w Tuna & anchovies	MAFC	375	1	B
Paupiettes	JOC	420	3	
Paupiettes de veau	NYTI	194	2	B
& Pepper steak, braised	BB	36	1	A
Peppers	NYT	160	1	B
Peppers Romano	WC	97	1	B
Piccata	BCC	225	1	B
Piccata	NYTI	396	1	B
Piccata	MSQC	208	1	B
Piccatta "sting"	KIS	288	1	B
Pie	AC	326		
Pie, English	FFCB	180	2	B
Pork & mushrooms	SMG	206	1	B
Pork pate	FG	180	3	B
Pork pie	JOC	420	1	B
Pork pie, tourtiere	AC	426	1	
Pork, sausages, truffles & foie gras	MFC2	295	3	
Pot roast	JOC	420	1	
Pot roast of savory	NYT	152	2	C
Pot roast, sherried	BHGN	240	2	B
Pot roasted	FFCB	176	2	B
Pressed	FFCB	181	2	B
Pudding of chicken breast & prosciutto	FAIC	375	2	B
Quenelles	MAFC	189	2	B
Ragout, chestnut	GHAC	211	2	B
Ragout crepes w sage	SPGT	71	2	B
Ravioli filling braised	NYTI	417	1	C
& Red pepper loaf	CW	33	2	B

RECIPE	BOOK	PAGE	TD	S
Veal (*cont.*)				
& Rice cooked, curried	JOC	229	2	B
w Ripe olives	NYT	165	2	B
Roast	AC	332		
Roast	CF	108	2	B
A la Francaise	NYTI	189	2	B
Barded	CFS	267	2	B
Basic sauce for	AC	333		
Farci	JOC	402	3	
& Frankfurters	NYTI	394	2	B
Of pan	CIC	252	1	B
Of sliced & stuffed	MFC2	219	3	C
& Pork, Bavarian	NYTI	311	2	B
Rosemary	NYT	153	2	B
Self basting (photographs)	OC	44		
Stuffed	JOC	402	3	
Stuffed & baked in pastry crust	MFC2	223	3	
Swiss	BHGN	240	2	B
Roasted w ham & cheese	MAFC	357	3	C
Roasting, chart	SC	285		
Roasting, timetable	BCC	215		
Roll	SP	106	3	C
Roll Sicilian	AC	346	2	
Rollatine of, w egg filling	SMG	220	1	B
Rolled	LT	256	1	
Rolls w anchovies	NYT	165	1	B
Rolls, stuffed	MCIC	268	1	B
Rolls, stuffed w apples	BBA	101	2	B
Rolls w tomato sauce	CIC	265	1	B
Rosemary	KIS	291	1	B
Roulade, Lithuanian	AC	345	2	
Round roast, spicy	GHAC	208	2	B
Rump w sour cream	NYT	152	2	B
Salad	AC	71	1	
Salad	JBC	251	1	B
Salsify ragout	VGCB	259	2	B
Sausage	MFC2	290	3	C
A cloak	OC	109	1	B
To cook & serve w potatoes	MFC2	292	3	C
& Pork w truffles & foie gras	MFC2	295	3	
Skewered w sage & white wine	MCIC	276	1	B
Saute	JBC	172	1	B
Saute	BCC	216	1	B
Saute de veau	MAFC	359		
Saute w green pepper	JBC	173	1	B
Saute w mushrooms	NYTI	197	1	B
Sauteed w spinach	LM	40	3	B
Scallopini	BB	96	1	B
Scallopini	JOC	403	1	
Scallopini w tomatoes	JOC	403	1	A
Scallops	MAFC	364		
Scallops	JOC	404	1	
A la provencale	NYT	159	1	B
Breaded	NYT	156	2	B
Breaded	NYTI	7	1	B
Chasseur	NYTI	193	1	B
w Cheese	NYTI	535	1	B
w Cream	JBC	166	1	B
w Ham	JOC	404	1	B
w Lemon	AC	347	1	
w Mustard cream sauce	SP	103	1	B
Sauteed w brown tarragon sauce	MAFC	367	1	B
Sauteed w mushrooms & cream	MAFC	366	1	B

RECIPE	BOOK	PAGE	TD	S
Sauteed w mushrooms & tomatoes	MAFC	368	1	B
Viennese	JBC	166	1	B
Scaloppine	SC	286	1	
Scaloppine	JBC	165	1	A
Alla marsala	JBC	165	1	A
Alla marsala	MSQC	68	1	B
w Asparagus in foil	MCIC	265	2	B
Breaded	LT	253	1	
w Cheese	NYT	158	1	B
w Crumbs & cheese	JBC	165	1	A
w Lemon	NYTI	396	1	B
Marsala	FFCB	178	1	A
Marsala I	NYTI	397	1	B
Marsala II	NYTI	397	1	B
w Marsala cream	MCIC	260	1	B
w Mozzarella	MCIC	264	1	B
w Mushrooms	NYTI	398	1	B
w Mushrooms	NYT	158	1	A
w Mushrooms	JBC	165	1	A
Parmesan	NYTI	398	1	B
w Prosciutto	NYT	158	1	A
Sauteed w anchovies & capers	MCIC	262	1	B
Sauteed w lemon sauce	CIC	262	1	B
Sauteed w marsala	CIC	261	1	B
w Tarragon	JBC	165	1	B
w Tomatoes	CIC	164	1	B
Schnitzel & kidneys	NYT	159	1	B
Shanks				
Braised	BCC	216	2	B
Braised	NYTI	192	2	B
Braised	MCIC	273	1	B
Braised, Milan style	CIC	256	2	B
Braised, Trieste style	CIC	259	1	B
Braised w wine, tomatoes, lemon & orange	MFC2	213	2	B
Greek style	NYTI	331	2	B
w Prosciutto & peas	NYTI	401	2	B
Shoulder (of)				
Braised	JBC	167	2	B
Braised w aspic	JBC	168	2	B
Braised, glazed w prunes	JBC	167	2	B
Braised, Nicoise	JBC	168	2	B
Braised w olives	JBC	167	2	B
Braised w white wine	MCIC	282	1	B
w Chicken liver stuffing	NYT	163	2	B
Jelly stuffed	AC	336	2	
Roast	SP	102	2	B
Stuffed	AC	335	2	
Stuffed	NYT	162	2	C
Stuffed	JBC	168	1	B
Snow peas & water chestnuts	WC	94	2	B
Spanish style w almond sauce	WC	109	1	B
& Spinach roll	MCIC	280	2	B
& Spinach, sauteed	LM	40	3	B
Steaks	MAFC	371		
& Noodles, Mexican	JOC	420	1	B
Sauteed w paprika	SMG	209	1	B
Stuffed w onions	NYTI	72	2	B
w Wine sauce	BB	36	1	A
Steamed between two plates	MCIC	218	1	B

RECIPE	BOOK	PAGE	TD	S
Veal (*cont.*)				
Stew (see also Blanquette de veau)	MAFC	359		
◆	JOC	419	2	B
◆	WC	106	1	B
◆	MFC	145	2	B
w Arugula & asparagus	SPGT	35	2	B
Baked	NYTI	71	2	B
w Carrots, onions, potatoes, & peas	MFC2	212	2	B
Elaborate	JOC	419	2	B
w Onions & mushrooms	MAFC	362	2	B
w Red wine	JOC	419	2	B
w Sage & white wine	CIC	273	1	B
w Sour cream	NYT	165	2	B
w Tomatoes & mushrooms, brown	MAFC	360	2	B
w Tomatoes, mushrooms & cream	MFC2	210	2	B
w Tomatoes & peas	CIC	274	1	B
Stir fry noodles	WC	109	1	B
Stock	FFCB	82	3	C
Stock	JOC	490	2	B
Stock	MAFC	109	2	C
Stock, brown	MFC	66	2	B
Stock, jellied	JOC	96	2	B
Stock, mixed	OC	167	2	B
Stroganoff	SC	304	1	
Stuffed kohlrabi	GG	218	2	B
Stuffed "little bundles"	FAIC	331	1	B
Stuffed w sweet red peppers	CW	56	1	B
Stuffed w zucchini	WC	104	2	B
Stuffing for ravioli	NYTI	417	1	B
Swiss style	NYTI	537	1	B
Tartare	GF	176	1	C
Terrine	JOC	435	3	
Tidbits w mushrooms braised herb-flavored	MCIC	277	1	B
Timbales	JOC	208	2	B
Tongue	MFC2	242	2	B
Tongue	BTSB	20	3	B
Tongue, boiled	FAIC	269		
w Tuna fish sauce	AC	334	2	
w Tuna fish sauce, cold	NYT	455	1	B
w Tuna sauce	AC	334	2	
w Tuna sauce	JBC	164	2	B
w Tuna sauce	BCC	215	2	C
w Tuna sauce, cold roast	FG	359	1	
w Water chestnuts	MIE	143	2	B
w Water chestnuts	EBE	67	2	B
White fricassee of	AC	338	2	
Veau aux amandes (veal w almonds)	NYTI	485	2	C
Veau moutarde cote de	BBA	60	2	B
Veau normande escalopes de	BBA	60	1	B
Veau ragout de	MFC2	209		
Veau tour de	BBA	62	3	B
Vegetable				
A la Grecque	JOC	255		
A la Grecque	WC	14	1	B
A la Grecque	JBC	242		
A la Grecque, marinated	VE	156	1	
All about	FFCB	355		
All about	JBC	282		
Almond medley	MC	137	1	B
Antipasto, raw	BHGN	336	2	C

VEGETABLE

RECIPE	BOOK	PAGE	TD	S
Aromatic	FFCB	59	1	B
Assorted	SMG	33	1	B
Au gratin	NYT	387	1	B
Au gratin	BCC	332	1	
Baked, a mold	FAIC	426	2	B
Basket, filling	MIE	20		
& Bean salad w rice or pasta	JBGF	402	1	B
Bean soup	FFCB	94	1	C
Beef, chinoiserie	BBA	52	2	A
Beef salad	BCC	272	2	B
Beef soup	BCC	306	1	B
Beef soup, quick & easy	MIE	72	2	C
Beef soup, southern style	SC	397	2	C
Beet soup	GHAC	102	1	C
Blanching for crudites	MSE	68		
Blended	SMG	235	1	B
Bouquet	GHAC	255	1	B
Broth	JOC	148	1	B
Campfire	JOC	253		
Canned, low acid	FFCB	721	3	
Canned, using	AC	558		
Canning	BHGN	135		
Casserole, potluck	BHGN	406	1	C
Casserole, summer	BB	135	1	B
Charcoal broiled	CFS	252	3	B
Charcoal broiled	CIC	400	1	B
& Cheese chowder w beer	CBSS	363	1	B
& Cheese pie	MIE	64	1	B
& Cheese pie	JBGF	398	2	B
w Cheese sauce	BCC	332	1	
Chowder	MC	16	2	B
Chowder	JOC	151	2	B
Chowder	CBSS	364	1	B
Chowed, Chinese	FG	314	1	B
Cocktails	SC	47	1	

RECIPE	BOOK	PAGE	TD	S
Cooking, chart	BHGN	385		
& Cream cheese	SC	373	1	
Croquettes	CF	91	1	C
Curry	JBGF	396	2	B
Curry	VE	260	1	B
Curry tofu	YGM	90	1	A
Decorating w	GHAC	230		
Deep fried	AC	555		
Dill	GHAC	254	1	B
Dilled	BCC	7	2	B
Flowers making (photographs)	LM	65		
Flowers making (photographs)	LT	22		
Fondues, all about	JOC	254		
Freezing	BHGN	127		
Frittata	BCC	162	1	B
Frittata	MSE	295	2	B
Fritters, pureed	JOC	222	1	A
Frozen, cooking	JOC	253		
& Fruits, chart	BHGN	420		
Gelatin salad, molded	JOC	99	2	B
Glazed	GF	70	1	C
Grilled	OC	96	2	B
Grilled, frozen	SC	334	1	
Grilled, mixed w aioli	GRIL	72	2	B
Grilling	GR	58		
& Hard cooked egg casserole	JOC	202	2	B
Herb seasoned	BHGN	43	1	B
High altitude, cooking	JOC	253		
Hors d'oeuvres	CPMC	106	1	C
Important for stock soups, stews	CBSS	34		
Irish	SC	427	1	
Juice aspic, canned	JOC	101	2	B
Julienning	FGCW	257		
Kabobs	GHAC	225	2	B

RECIPE	BOOK	PAGE	TD	S
Vegetable (*cont.*)				
Kebabs, Italian-seasoned	BHGN	43	1	B
Lemon buttered	GHAC	254	1	C
Macedoine Russian salad	AC	42	1	
Marinated	MC	58	1	B
Marinated	CW	57	2	B
Marinated garden	GHAC	276	2	C
Melange, roasted	GHAC	254	1	B
Mirepoix of	FG	243	1	B
Mixed baked	MCIC	394	1	B
Mixed, buttered	SMG	231	1	B
Mixed sauteed	FG	198	1	B
Mixed steamed	FG	264	1	
Mixtures	MAFC	484	1	B
Mousseline	PPLK	263	3	B
Mozzarella baked melange of	SMG	223	1	B
w Mustard dressing, cold	FG	195	1	B
w Mustard vinaigrette	MSE	98	1	C
North Beach	FGCW	258	1	B
Nutrients dictionary	JBGF	133		
Oil roasted, summer	SP	168	1	B
Omelet	JB	56	1	
Omelet, French	BHGN	200	1	A
Panning	JOC	252		
Pate	SPGT	33	3	C
Pie, Russian	VE	158	2	B
Platter	JBGF	290	1	
Platter, three star	WC	29	1	B
Preparing for cooking	JOC	250		
Puree, white	CPMC	205	1	B
Pureed	GF	81	2	C
Purees	GF	191	1	C
Purees, making	GHAC	255		
Ragout fall	CPMC	140	1	B
Raw dip	EBE	40	1	B
Red, white, green	KIS	186	1	A
Reheating	JOC	254		
Relish	BHGN	145	3	
& Rice stuffing	GHAC	147		
Ring, basic	SC	411	1	
Ring, jellied	FFCB	446	2	B
Salad	LT	55	1	B
24-hour	BHGN	331	3	C
Armenian	EBE	133	3	B
Basic	VGCB	342	1	B
Buffet	AC	49	1	
French	VE	109	1	B
Frozen	SC	369	2	
Holiday	VE	112	3	C
Marinated	VE	110	3	B
Marinated, Italian	SP	205	3	B
Mixed	BCC	284	2	B
Mixed, cooked	CIC	416	1	B
Moroccan	BBA	148	2	B
Raw	MC	41	1	B
Winter	SP	163	1	B
Sandwiches, grilled, variations	MC	86	1	B
Sauce blender	JOC	312	1	B
Sauce for ravioli	FGCW	152	1	B
Sauce spring	FAIC	62	1	B
Sauces for	GHAC	265		
Saute, fresh	MC	148	2	B
Saute, Italian	FG	191	1	B
Saute of	SMG	227	1	B
Sauteed	SMG	57	1	B
Scalloped	BCC	332	1	
Seasoning, chart	BHGN	378		
Sherbet	VGCB	343	2	B
Slices, baked	BCC	324	1	B
Souffle	AC	555		
Souffle	JOC	205	2	B
Souffle, basic	SC	411	1	
Soup	CIC	66	2	B

RECIPE	BOOK	PAGE	TD	S
Vegetable (*cont.*)				
Terrine	VGCB	338	2	
Toppers	BHGN	388		
Toss, Oriental	BHGN	331	1	B
Toss, winter	BCC	280	1	B
Vinaigrette sauce	JBC	242		
Vinaigrettes	GF	31	1	C
& Walnut pate	MC	90	1	B
Wok top stuffing mix	WC	37	1	B
Vegetarian eggrolls	MC	170	3	B
Vegetarian loaf	SC	185	1	
Veloute sauce	NYT	444	1	
◆	BCC	328	1	B
◆	VE	83	1	
◆	FG	227	1	B
◆	MAFC	57	1	B
◆	AC	458	1	
◆	JOC	324	1	B
◆	FFCB	266	1	B
Veloute sauce, chicken w	NYTI	214	2	B
Veloute sauce, enriched	VE	83	1	
Veloute sauce, thickened	JOC	324	1	B
Velvet	JOC	334	1	A
Velvet cake	FFCB	510	1	B
Velvet chocolate	NYT	631	2	C
Velvet coffee	NYT	631	2	C
Velvet custard pie	NYT	530	1	B
Velvet fruit	NYT	631	2	C
Velvet nut	NYT	631	2	C
Velvet royal egg yolk	NYT	631	2	C
Velvet spice cake	JOC	628	2	B
Venetian torte	SC	138	1	B
Venetian verze sofegae (smothered cabbage)	GG	80	2	B
Venison				
Basting liquid for spitted haunch of	AC	237	2	
Chili	AC	239		
Chops	BB	51	1	
Chops, marinated	BHGN	270	3	B
Chops, pan broiled	BB	51	1	
Chops w sour cream	BB	51	1	
Dried	AC	239		
Goulash	NYT	181	2	B
Hamburger	JOC	455	2	
Hamburgers	AC	236		
Hams	AC	239		
Jelly	FFCB	702	2	C
Leg of, marinated	FFCB	226	3	C
Leg of, spitted boned or haunch of	AC	236	2	
Marinade	JOC	337	3	B
Meat loaf	JOC	455	2	
Mock	AC	240	3	
Other uses for	AC	239		
Pie	AC	235		
Pot roast	BHGN	270	2	B
Pot roasted	AC	239	2	
Preparing	JOC	454		
Roast	NYTI	314	2	C
Roast, haunch of	NYT	181	2	C
Roast, haunch of	AC	237	2	
Roast, mock	BB	66	2	
Saddle of, roast	BB	79	2	
Saddle of, roast	AC	237	2	
Saddle of, roast, young	AC	238	2	
Sauce for	AC	457	1	
w Sauerbraten	BCC	260	3	C
Sausage	AC	239		
Steak	BB	50	1	
Steak	JOC	455	3	B
Broiled	AC	235		
Broiled	FFCB	226	2	A
w Chestnut sauce	FFCB	226	2	B
Marinated	BB	50	1	
& Pepper	BB	50	1	

RECIPE	BOOK	PAGE	TD	S
St. Hubert	NYT	182	3	B
w Wine sauce	GHAC	214	1	B
Stew	GHAC	214	2	B
Tenderloin, broiled	AC	238		
Vericheesey casserole	MC	108	1	B
Vermicelli	KIS	227	1	A
Vermicelli	KIS	235	1	A
Carrie Lee's	YGM	225	1	C
Chinese	KIS	121	1	A
Chinese	YGM	41	1	A
w Fresh tomato sauce	FFCB	332	1	B
Italian	KIS	121	1	A
Pesto tomatoes stuffed w	MSE	286	2	C
w Spinach	BCC	61	1	B
& Vegetable soup	MSE	114	1	C
Vermont biscuits	GHAC	363	1	B
Vermouth				
Carrots	FGCW	261	1	B
Cassis	BB	169	1	A
Chicken tomatoes & shallots &	FGCW	173	1	A
Court bouillon	JBC	69	1	
Lamb shanks barbecued w	OC	113	2	B
Pork	OC	123	2	B
Rabbit in	FGCW	232	2	B
Salmon fillet poached in	KIS	146	1	A
Sauce, Japanese	FGCW	359	1	
Tomatoes & onions	YGM	41	1	A
Zucchini	KIS	124	1	A
Zucchini	YGM	149	1	A
Vichyssoise	BHGN	379	2	B
◆	FFCB	91	1	B
◆	VGCB	159	1	B
◆	JBC	277	3	
◆	CBSS	337	1	B
◆	SC	402	1	
◆	JOC	159	1	B

RECIPE	BOOK	PAGE	TD	S
◆	GHAC	99	2	B
◆	MAFC	39	1	B
◆	SPGT	54	3	C
◆	MC	33	2	B
◆	JBGF	329	2	B
◆	MSE	116	1	B
A la Ritz	NYT	83	2	C
Broccoli	GG	59	2	C
Clam	BBA	44	2	C
Mushroom	MSE	284	2	C
Vicksburg cheese	JOC	67	1	
Vienna pastry	JOC	592	3	B
Vienna rolls	JOC	568	3	C
Vienna rolls	SC	74	2	
Vienna steaks	FFCB	180	1	A
Vienna tarts	SC	351	1	
Vienna torte	SC	133	1	
Vienna torte	EBE	158	2	B
Viennese pastry w cream cheese	AC	636	1	
Vietnamese fish sauce	CFS	85	1	A
Vinaigrette	BBA	131	1	A
◆	GRIL	72	1	B
◆	GF	245	1	B
◆	OC	162	1	A
Avocado w warm tomato & basil	MSQC	49	1	B
Balsamic	SP	211	1	B
Basic, variations	FFCB	450	1	B
Basic, variations	MIE	246	1	B
Basil walnut	SP	232	1	B
Beans	AC	597	1	
Blueberry	SP	147	1	B
Citrus	BHGN	351	1	B
Classic cold, asparagus w	GG	26	1	B
Creamy	JBGF	553	1	B
Creamy mustard	MSQC	121	1	B
Creme	MAFC	95	1	A
Dressing	BHGN	351	1	B

RECIPE	BOOK	PAGE	TD	S
Vinaigrette (*cont.*)				
Dressing	SC	374	1	
Dressing	FGCW	377	1	
Dressing for celeriac	VGCB	72	1	B
Fancy	VE	97	1	
Favorite	SP	147	1	B
For carrot & mandarin orange salad	MSQC	213	1	B
For fennel salad w red onions & tomatoes	MSQC	53	1	A
For fruit salads	VE	98	1	
For lima bean & radicchio salad	MSQC	153	1	B
For Nicoise salad a la Middlefield	MSQC	116	1	B
For seafood salad	MSQC	60	1	B
For tomato & baby string beans	MSQC	93	1	B
For tomato, red onion & thyme salad	MSQC	85	1	B
For warm potatoes on lettuce	MSQC	192	1	B
Fresh tomato	MFC	101	1	C
Green peppercorn	SP	230	1	B
Herbs, capers & onion	MAFC	95	1	A
Honey mustard for chicory salad	MSQC	160	1	B
Hot pepper	CW	129	2	
Jerusalem artichokes	AC	470	1	
Lemon	SP	202	1	B
Lemony	GHAC	210	1	
Light, for Boston lettuce salad	MSQC	29	1	A
Light, for lettuce salad	MSQC	104	1	A
Little Joe's	FGCW	378	1	B
Melon, red & green salad w	GG	188	1	B
Mustard	CF	59	1	B
Mustard	MFC	101	1	B
Orange	SPGT	156	1	B
Pesto	FGCW	130	1	B
Pig's hocks	AC	423		
Raspberry	MIE	244	1	A
Raspberry	SP	230	1	B
Raspberry, for watercress salad w pears & blue cheese	MSQC	136	1	B
Sauce	NYT	455	1	B
◆	SMG	189	1	A
◆	JOC	311	1	A
◆	JBC	256		
◆	MAFC	94	1	A
◆	AC	78		
Sauce w herbs	SMG	159	1	A
Sauce, simple	GG	117	1	A
Sauerkraut	AC	501	1	
Shallot & tarragon	BBA	149	1	B
Sharp	VE	98	1	
Sherry	SP	231	1	C
Simple	VE	97	1	
Strong	CW	153	1	A
Strong	CF	51	1	B
Tomato	SPGT	35	1	B
Tomato & basil	MSQC	49	1	B
Walnut oil	SP	232	1	A
White wine	FGCW	128	1	B
Vinegar				
Balsamic	SP	211		
Basil	BTSB	189	1	C
Bean soup	CBSS	253	3	B
Beet	SC	437	3	
Burnet	JOC	496	3	

RECIPE	BOOK	PAGE	TD	S
Celery	SC	437	3	
Chili	BTSB	189	1	C
Chili	JOC	496	1	
Chive	BTSB	188	1	C
Cider	SC	437	3	
Different kinds of	JOC	495		
Dill	BTSB	189	1	C
Dill	SC	437	3	
Garlic	SC	373	3	
◆	BTSB	188	1	C
◆	JOC	496	3	
◆	SC	437	3	
Health	SC	437	1	
Herb	JOC	496	1	
Herb flavored	FGCW	380	1	
Herb, quick	JOC	496	1	
Herbed	BCC	299	1	B
Hot pepper	PPLK	273	1	B
Interesting uses for	SP	346		
Mint	BTSB	189	1	C
Mint	SC	437	3	
Pie	NYT	530	1	B
Pie	FFBB	102	1	B
Raspberry	AC	770	1	
◆	FGCW	379	3	B
◆	BCC	299	1	B
◆	MIE	244	3	C
Red raspberry	JOC	496	3	
Red wine	BTSB	185	3	C
Sauce for chicken sauteed w wild mushrooms	MFC	83	2	B
Sauce, pork wine &	FGCW	213	2	B
Shallot	BTSB	188	1	C
Spiced	BBA	163	3	C
Spiced	JOC	496	3	
Strawberry	BCC	299	1	B
Taffy	AC	838	2	
Tarragon	SC	437	3	

RECIPE	BOOK	PAGE	TD	S
Tarragon	BTSB	187	1	C
Tarragon	JOC	496	3	
Wine, making your own	FGCW	376		
Violets candied	AC	837	2	
Violets crystallized	BTSB	261	3	
Virgin Island	MSE	158	1	A
Vitello tonnato (braised veal)	BBA	61	3	B
◆	NYT	167	2	B
◆	NYTI	400	2	C
◆	FFCB	181	2	B
◆	JBC	164	2	B
◆	GF	142	2	C
Vitello tonnato, quick	FFCB	182	1	B
Vitello tonnato (w tuna fish sauce)	AC	334	2	
Vodka bottle, iced, making (photographs)	LT	84		
Vodka, lemon flavored	BTSB	219	1	B
Vodka martini	SC	61	1	
Vol au vent (pastry)	JOC	596	2	A
Vol au vent	SC	343	3	
Vol au vent	NYT	537	2	C
A l'ancienne	LT	414	2	
A la moderne	LT	416	2	
Cover, making	MFC2	131		
Large	MFC2	126	3	B
Large patty shells	AC	639	1	
Making	MFC2	123		
Patty shells	MFC2	123		
Puff pastry for	MFC2	118	3	
Vollkornbrot (wheat bread)	CBB	111	3	C
Vortlimpa (beer bread)	CBB	142	2	C

W

RECIPE	BOOK	PAGE	TD	S
Wafer				
Almond lacy, curved	MFC2	475	1	C
Caraway & potato	SC	406	1	
Charleston benne	FFCB	558	1	C
Cheese	MAFC	197	1	C
Cheese	FFCB	66	1	C
Cheese refrigerator	JOC	174	1	C
Crumb crust, chocolate	GHAC	321		
Crumb crust, vanilla	GHAC	321		
Crust, vanilla	BHGN	290	1	B
Curled	SC	162	2	
Drop butter	JOC	655	1	C
English, rolled	FFCB	557	2	C
Ginger	SC	154	1	
Ginger, thin	FFBB	252	1	C
Gluten	SC	406	1	
Hazelnut	JOC	669	1	C
Jubilee	JOC	660	1	C
Lacy, ice cream &	MFC2	475	1	C
Lemon	BTSB	241	1	C
Lemon, old fashioned, jumbo	MHGD	324	1	C
Mint	BCC	120	2	C
Oatmeal, crisp	MHGD	304	1	C
Oatmeal, flourless	JOC	658	1	C
Oatmeal, glazed	JOC	658	1	C
Pecan	JOC	669	1	C
Peppermint cream	JOC	729	1	B
Potato caraway	SC	406	1	
Puffed	SC	406	1	
Rolled	SC	161	1	

RECIPE	BOOK	PAGE	TD	S
Sesame	EBE	25	1	C
Sesame seed	FFBB	211	1	C
Sesame vanilla	CF	95	1	C
Shells, chocolate	SC	344	2	
Shrewsbury	SC	162	1	
Swedish	SC	101	1	C
Vanilla	FFBB	213	1	C
Vanilla	BTSB	241	1	C
Vanilla icebox dessert, frozen	SC	136	2	B
Waffle	BCC	30	1	A
◆	BHGN	88	1	B
◆	AC	798	1	
◆	BTSB	123	1	A
◆	FFCB	499	1	B
◆	JOC	216	1	B
Bacon	JBC	23	1	
Bacon & corn meal	JOC	217	1	B
Belgian	AC	798	1	
Blueberry	BCC	30	1	A
Buttermilk	AC	798	1	
Buttermilk	JOC	217	1	B
Buttermilk, Johnny Appleseed a la mode	GHAC	303	1	
Buttermilk pecan	GHAC	371		
Cauliflower & cheese	GG	111	1	B
Cheese	SC	97	1	B
Cheese	JOC	217	1	B
Cheese & bacon	BCC	30	1	A
Chocolate	JOC	218	1	B
Chocolate	SC	97	1	B
Coconut	JOC	217	1	B
Cornmeal	AC	799	1	
Cornmeal	FFCB	500	1	B
Cornmeal	SC	97	1	C
Dessert	JOC	702	1	B
English walnut	SC	97	1	

RECIPE	BOOK	PAGE	TD	S
French toast	JOC	218	1	B
Fruit	JOC	217	1	B
Gingerbread	SC	98	1	B
Golden yam	JOC	217	1	B
Making	JOC	216		
Maple dessert	NSD	242	1	B
Mix	BTSB	121	1	A
Nut	JOC	217	1	B
Pecan	SC	97	1	
Plain	SC	97	1	B
Raisin	JOC	217	1	B
Recipe, basic	NYT	488	1	B
Rich cream	AC	798	1	
Sour cream	AC	798	1	
◆	JBC	23	1	
◆	JOC	217	1	B
◆	SC	97	1	
Soybean	SC	97	1	
Special	FFCB	500	1	B
Sponge cake	SC	97	1	
Sweet	JBC	23	1	
Sweet milk	JBC	23	1	
Whipped cream	SC	97	1	B
Whole wheat	BCC	30	1	A
Whole wheat nut	NYT	488	1	B
Waldorf salad	BCC	297	1	B
◆	VGCB	78	1	B
◆	JOC	92	1	B
◆	SC	366	1	
◆	GRIL	98	1	B
◆	FFCB	441	2	B
◆	GHAC	283	1	B
◆	BHGN	342	2	C
Blue moon	MC	56	1	B
California	MC	56	1	B
Danish	MC	57	1	B
Deluxe	MC	57	1	B
Pears in	BCC	297	1	B
Supreme	BCC	297	1	B
Walnut				
Almond puffs	MFC2	473	1	C
Apple salad, autumn	SP	219	1	B
Balls	FFCB	693	2	A
Barley	FFCB	311	1	B
Bars, meringue	FFCB	567	1	C
Berry salad	BBA	140	1	B
Bleu broccoli w	GG	61	1	B
Bonbons, date	SC	177	1	
Bread	MFC	207	3	C
Bread, black	CBB	654	3	C
Bread, Portuguese sweet	MHGD	268	1	C
Bread, pumpkin	CBB	412	1	C
Burger, lentil	MC	106	2	B
Cake	NYT	572	2	B
Cake	MFC2	490	1	
Cake	MCIC	427	1	B
Apple chunky	SP	271	1	C
w Apricot filling & glazed fondant	MFC2	492	1	
Chocolate	BCC	68	1	C
Prune	BCC	73	1	C
Rum prune	FFBB	370	2	C
Torte date	SC	127	1	B
Candied	NSD	355	2	B
Caramel ice cream	MFC2	423	3	C
Caramel loaf cake, black	FFBB	324	1	C
Cauliflower	AC	506	1	
Cheddar balls w bechamel, baked	VE	199	1	C
& Cheese souffle	VE	180	1	B
& Chicken w	BHGN	299	1	B
Chocolate filling	GHAC	344		
Cinnamon buns	GHAC	362	2	C
Clusters, chocolate	FFBB	203	2	C
Coating for fish fillets	GHAC	142	1	B
Coconut bars, black	SC	164	1	

RECIPE	BOOK	PAGE	TD	S
Walnut (*cont.*)				
Cookies	CW	57	1	B
Cookies, black	SP	258	2	C
Cookies, black	FFBB	202	2	C
Crackers	FFBB	593	1	C
& Cream cheese pastry	NSD	131	1	C
Cream pie	FFBB	116	2	B
Creams	SC	372	1	
Crescents	SC	82	2	
Crunch topping for sweet potato pie	GHAC	318	2	C
Date bonbons	SC	177	1	
Dip feta	MC	90	1	B
Dressing	BBA	144	1	A
Eggplant, caviar, cold filling w	MFC2	353	1	B
Fig triangles	CF	75	1	C
Filling	SC	150	1	
Filling, chocolate	GHAC	344		
Filling for coffee cake	SC	83	1	
Filling, toasted	JOC	648	1	A
Fougasse	CPMC	231	3	C
Fudge frosting, black	NYT	575	1	B
Glaze, lamb loin chops w	BHGN	267	1	B
Green sauce w	FAIC	58	2	B
Hearth bread	BBA	179	2	B
Ice cream, caramel	MFC2	423	3	C
Kisses, date	SC	163	1	
Layer cake, date	SC	112	1	B
Marinade	GRIL	36	1	A
Mocha cake	FFCB	509	2	B
Mushroom stuffed w cheese &	SP	12	2	B
Paste, duck liver, green beans &	CPPC	112	2	B
Pastry crust	GHAC	321		
Pate de campagne	SP	26	3	C
Penuche easy	BHGN	115	2	B
Pie, maple	MC	200	1	B
Pie, oatmeal, creamed	FFBB	140	1	B
& Pigeon salad	MFC	185	2	B
Pizza, anchovies, onion confit &	CPPC	153	3	B
& Port cheese	BBA	23	2	B
Roll	SC	123	1	B
w Roquefort butter	KIS	313	1	B
Rotelle bacon	MSQC	185	1	B
Salad				
Barley &	GHAC	275	2	B
Endive &	BBA	143	1	B
Fennel &	BBA	143	2	B
Lentil &	SP	160	3	B
Mushroom &	CW	37	1	B
Spinach, apple &	KIS	275	1	A
Sauce	FAIC	61	1	B
Chicken w	NYTI	553	2	B
Cranberry, currant &	MSE	188	1	C
Dessert	BTSB	161	1	B
For pasta	GHAC	265		
Sauteed	GG	268	1	B
Sherry	FFCB	689	1	B
Souffle	SC	195	1	
Spirit balls	AC	711	1	
Sticks	SC	167	1	
Tart, caramel	NSD	154	3	B
Tart from St. Paul de Vence	MHGD	44	3	C
Tart, prune	FFBB	174	2	B
Tart w whipped cream	CW	49	2	B
Torte	SC	133	1	B
Torte, chocolate	JOC	639	2	B
Torte, chocolate	SC	127	1	B
Torte, date	SC	127	1	B

RECIPE	BOOK	PAGE	TD	S
Tossed salad	BCC	280	1	B
Wafers, chocolate	FFCB	554	1	C
Wheat bread	CBB	117	2	C
& White bean salad	CF	87	1	B
Zucchini &	AC	546	1	
War bread	CBB	239	2	C
War cake	FFBB	321	1	C
Washington pie	FFBB	299	2	B
Washington pie	AC	657	1	
Wasps' nests (Christmas cookie)	FFCB	558	2	C
Wassail (drink—apple cider)	BCC	21	1	C
Wassail	JOC	51		
Wassail bowl	BBA	27	2	B
Water bath boiling	NYT	494	2	
Water bath processing	BHGN	123		
Water bread	FFCB	466	2	B
Water chestnut salad, endive &	CF	119	1	B
Water chestnuts	JOC	520	1	
Water chestnuts wrapped in bacon	KIS	310	1	C
Water for cooking, all about	JOC	493		
Water lily salad	SC	362	1	
Water rolls	FFCB	466	2	B
Watercress				
& Avocado ring	NYT	432	2	B
Biscuits	NYT	478	1	C
Butter	FFCB	57	1	B
& Cauliflower puree cream	MAFC	460	1	B
Cream cheese	SC	38	1	
& Cream cheese spread, nut	SC	380	1	
Dressing	JOC	312	1	B
& Endive salad	MSE	168	1	C
& Endive salad	SMG	293	1	B
& Goat cheese scramble	GG	198	1	A
& Lentil soup	CF	142	1	B
Mushroom crepes	GG	197	1	C
& Mushrooms w mustard dressing	KIS	118	1	A
Omelet	JBC	57	1	
Orange slices & avocado salad	FFCB	430	1	B
Pineapple snow	GG	199	1	B
Pork	NYT	140	1	B
Puree, pea &	CF	39	1	B
Raita	VE	261	1	B
& Roasted onion puree	CF	115	2	B
Salad (variations)	VGCB	247	1	B
Butter lettuce &	GRIL	87	1	B
Chinese style	JBC	247	1	B
Endive &	NYT	418	1	B
Julienned pears, blue cheese &	MSQC	136	1	B
Red green	JBGF	548	1	B
Sandwiches	GF	44	1	C
Sandwiches	FFCB	58	1	B
Sauce	VGCB	254	1	B
Sauce	JOC	316	1	B
Sauce for frogs' legs mousseline	MFC	118	3	B
Sauteed	MSQC	165	1	A
Soup	SC	402	1	
◆	MAFC	38	1	B
◆	MSE	123	1	C
◆	MFC	69	1	B
Chilled	GHAC	99	2	B
Clear	JOC	148	1	B

RECIPE	BOOK	PAGE	TD	S
Watercress Soup (*cont.*)				
Cold	MAFC	39	1	B
Cream of	MSE	223	2	A
◆	SP	46	2	B
◆	MAFC	41	1	B
◆	JOC	160	1	B
◆	NYTI	128	1	B
◆	FFCB	87	1	B
Cauliflower &	MFC2	13	1	B
Fish ball &	CBSS	208	3	B
Potato, basil &	SPGT	143	2	B
& Tomato, cold	JBGF	330	2	B
Zucchini &	SP	45	2	B
Spring onion soup	CBSS	369	1	B
Stir fried	CF	55	1	B
Watermelon	MSE	157	1	B
Carving (photographs)	LT	37		
Cocktail	SC	44	1	
Fruit bowl	BB	161	1	
Glaze	AC	441		
Ice	FGCW	398	3	B
Iced	MSQC	109	1	B
Mousse	BCC	147	2	B
Pickle	FFCB	716	2	B
Pickle ginger	FFCB	716	2	B
Pickles	NYT	503	2	B
Preserves	SC	441	2	
Rind, pickled	JOC	785	3	C
Rind, pickled, sweet	SC	459	3	
Rind pickles	AC	822	2	
Supreme	BB	161	2	
Supreme	BCC	128	1	C
Tipsy	AC	760	1	
Waterzooie (thick chicken soup)	NYTI	22	1	B
Wattles, sauce of chicken livers, crests &	FAIC	75	1	B

RECIPE	BOOK	PAGE	TD	S
Wax beans	AC	478	1	
Braised w onions lettuce & cream	MAFC	448	1	B
Frozen	MAFC	449	1	B
Frozen	AC	478	1	
Salad	SC	359	1	
Sauteed, spinach &	GG	347	2	B
Sweet & sour	AC	479	1	
Wedding bread	CBB	616	1	B
Wedding cake	MSE	276	2	C
Wedding cake	SC	116	3	
Wedding cake	JOC	623	3	
All about	FFBB	384		
Apricot almond	SPGT	116	3	C
Mexican	EBE	176	1	C
Weeds, edible	AC	559		
Weights & measurements	JBC	xiv		
Weights & measures	CBSS	416		
Weiner schnitzel	JBC	166	1	B
Weinschaum	JOC	686	1	B
Weinschaum sauce	JOC	710	1	B
Welsh cakes	FFBB	270	2	C
Welsh rabbit	BCC	169	1	B
◆	FFCB	351	1	B
◆	AC	118	1	
◆	BHGN	204	1	B
◆	GHAC	115	1	B
I	NYT	317	1	B
II	NYT	317	1	B
Bread	FFBB	470	2	B
Classic	VE	213	1	A
Welsh Rarebit	SC	233	1	
◆	FFCB	351	1	B
◆	JBC	29	1	B
◆	JOC	242	1	B
Welshman's ramos fizz	BBA	27	1	A
Western chrysanthemum bowl	BBA	31	2	B

RECIPE	BOOK	PAGE	TD	S
Whole Grain (*cont.*)				
Bread cockaigne	JOC	559	2	C
Bread plus	JOC	559	2	C
Bread sticks	JOC	570	1	C
Refrigerator rolls	JOC	569	1	C
Rolls	JOC	566	3	C
Whole wheat				
Banana bread	MHGD	262	1	B
Batter bread, sesame millet	FFBB	469	2	B
Bread	BHGN	61	2	B
◆	VE	32	2	B
◆	NYT	469	2	C
◆	SC	69	2	C
◆	FFCB	465	2	C
A good	AC	783	2	
Batter	CBB	130	1	C
Buttermilk	CBB	103	2	C
Entire	FFBB	456	1	C
Honey	BCC	46	3	C
Honey lemon	CBB	100	3	C
Italian	MCIC	50	3	B
Quick	FFCB	485	1	B
Sourdough	CBB	283	3	C
Sourdough, California	CBB	292	3	C
Sweet, quick	JOC	576	1	B
Tuscan	FAIC	38	2	B
Caper bread	FFBB	456	2	C
Carrot pitas	JBGF	578	3	C
Cinnamon buns	NYT	475	2	C
Cinnamon & nutmeg cookies	MHGD	320	1	C
Cookies	BHGN	167	1	C
Gingerbread from New Orleans	MHGD	280	1	C
Gugelhupf	CBB	109	3	C
Health bread	SC	70	2	C
Herb bread	CBB	439	2	C
Orange bread	CBB	133	1	B
Pudding steamed	SC	191	2	
Raisin cookies	JBGF	610	1	C
Rolls, brown	FFBB	496	2	C
Rolls, quick	NYT	474	2	C
Soy rolls	FFBB	497	2	C
Walnut cake	MHGD	96	2	C
Yogurt date-nut gingerbread	MHGD	279	1	C
Wholesome health bread	FFBB	458	2	C
Wiener backendl (chicken dish)	NYTI	8	2	C
Wiener schnitzel (breaded veal cutlet, see also veal chop)				
◆	JOC	404	1	A
◆	SC	285	1	
◆	AC	341		
◆	NYTI	536	2	B
Wiener schnitzel a la Luchow	MIE	142	1	B
Wild rice	SP	345		
Chicken souffle	GHAC	116	2	B
w Green onions & mushrooms	GRIL	95	1	B
Soup	BCC	309	1	B
Stuffing	MSE	167	3	A
Stuffing, rock cornish game hens w	FFCB	253	3	B
Stuffing, rock cornish hens w	GHAC	159	2	B
Wilted dandelion salad	AC	39	1	
Wilted lettuce	AC	38	1	
Wind cake	AC	683	1	
Windtorte, Spanische	NYTI	14	3	C

RECIPE	BOOK	PAGE	TD	S
Wine				
Basting sauce	BHGN	32	1	B
Blackberry	SC	438	3	
Bowl May	NYT	650	3	C
Butter sauce, white	GRIL	38	1	A
Celery in	SC	418	1	
Chianti, peaches in	FAIC	496	2	B
Chianti, strawberries in	FAIC	496	2	B
Concord grape, large quantity	SC	437	3	
Cooking w	MAFC	31		
Currant	SC	438	3	
Custard	FGCW	392	1	B
Custard	JOC	686	1	B
Dandelion	SC	438	3	
Dressing	SC	378	1	
Eggs, poached	JOC	196	1	B
Elderberry	SC	438	3	
Food, matching	FGCW	403		
Gelatin	JOC	696	2	B
Gelatin	FGCW	373	1	B
Glazed ham	OC	124	2	B
Grape	SC	437	3	
Grape, dry	SC	437	3	
Grapefruit	SC	438	3	
Ham baked	JBC	207		
Hard sauce	FFCB	641	1	B
Jellies	FGCW	372	3	
Jelly	AC	735	2	
Jelly	FFCB	621	2	B
Jelly	SC	202	2	
Jelly glaze	GHAC	164		
Leeks in	GG	247	1	B
Log cheese	BHGN	13	1	B
Marinade (see also marinade, wine)				
Marinade, red	GRIL	34	1	B
Marinade, red pepper	CFS	287	1	A

RECIPE	BOOK	PAGE	TD	S
Merchant's sauce	JBC	262	1	
Mince meat	SC	346	2	
Mulled	NYT	650	1	C
Mulled	SC	63	1	B
Mulled	MSE	217	1	C
Mulled, quantity	JOC	51		
& Mushroom sauce	BHGN	358	1	B
Mushrooms & onions in	JOC	282	1	B
Mushrooms & onions in	SC	422	1	
Mushrooms stuffed	JBC	316	1	
Mutton leg, marinated	MAFC	341	3	C
Oranges, chilled & sliced	NYT	620	2	B
Peaches	BCC	127	1	B
Pears poached in, w basil	YGM	214	1	C
Pears w red	AC	766	1	
Pork chops w	SC	294	1	
Pork w vinegar sauce	FGCW	213	2	B
Pudding	FGCW	390	1	
Punch, cranberry	JBGF	288	1	C
Punch, sparkling	SC	57	1	
Punch, white	BHGN	48	2	
Quail	NYT	178	2	B
Rabbit	NYTI	206	2	B
Raisin	SC	438	3	
Red beet w port	SC	438	3	
Red butter for steak	NYT	458	1	A
Red, oranges in	MSQC	33	1	B
Rhubarb	SC	438	3	
Sauce	BHGN	238	1	B
Basic	SC	217	1	
Fish fillets poached w	JBC	69	1	
Flank steak w	SC	271	2	
For meat or game	SC	391	1	

Y

RECIPE	BOOK	PAGE	TD	S
Yorkshire pudding muffin tins	JBC	137	1	
Yorkshire pudding, rib roast	BHGN	233	3	C

Z

RECIPE	BOOK	PAGE	TD	S
Zaartar bread	FG	365	2	C
Zabaglione (cake)	FGCW	392	1	B
◆	NYT	603	1	B
◆	JOC	686	2	B
◆	CIC	444	1	B
◆	SP	274	1	B
◆	VE	266	2	B
◆	MIE	315	1	B
◆	KIS	330	1	B
Bombe al	NYTI	446	2	B
Cream w peaches, poached w pistachios	GF	143	2	B
Dessert, chocolate	NYTI	445	2	B
Freddo	MHGD	366	2	B
w Grand Marnier	MSQC	69	1	B
Orange	BBA	212	1	B
Sauce, red pepper, basil	CFS	314	1	A
Semifredo	YGM	180	2	C
Zabaione (pastry-filling)	FAIC	433	1	A
Zabaione whipped cream	FAIC	435		
Zampino beans, Bretonne	NYTI	392	2	C
Zampone cotechino, boiled	FAIC	269		
Zarda (Indian rice pudding)	NYT	590	2	C
Zeppelin (bread)	CBB	73	3	C
Zeppole di San Giuseppe (fried cream puffs)	NYTI	443	3	C
Zest, cooking w	SP	215		
Zesting citrus fruits	NSD	30		
Zinfandel & pear tart	NSD	98	2	B
Zinfandel pears, figs, poached in cassis	CPMC	92	2	B
Zinfandel sauce	GRIL	34	1	C
Zinfandel sauce, lamb leg of, butterflied w	GRIL	67	2	B
Ziti, hearty home style w meat sauce	GHAC	261	2	B
Ziti w marinara sauce, sausage & cheese	NYTI	431	1	C
Zombie (drink)	JOC	46	1	A
Zuccanoes (stuffed zucchini)	MC	120	1	B
Zucchini	SC	434	1	
A l'orange	EBE	122	1	B
A la Grecque	NYT	425	1	B
A la Nancy	BBA	137	2	C
A skillet	NYT	411	1	B
Apples	KIS	292	1	B
Armenian style	NYT	408	2	B
Artichoke hearts, oven fried	GHAC	88	1	B
Au bon gout	NYT	409	1	B
Au gratin	NYTI	254	1	B
Bake, Italian	MIE	237	1	B
Baked	BBA	137	1	B
Baked, w garlic, parsley & bechamel	MFC2	367	1	B

RECIPE	BOOK	PAGE	TD	S
Zucchini (*cont.*)				
Baked, tomatoes &	SMG	109	1	B
& Basil sauce, fusilli, creamy	CIC	106	1	B
Basil soup	CBSS	370	2	B
Basil & tomatoes	MFC	179	1	B
Beef	WC	92	1	B
Blanching	MFC2	364		
Blossoms, fried	CIC	399	2	B
Boats, baked & stuffed	CIC	395	1	B
Boiled	JBC	333	1	B
Boiled	FAIC	425		
Bread	JBGF	594	1	B
◆	SP	250	2	B
◆	MSE	298	2	B
◆	FFBB	553	2	C
◆	BCC	36	2	C
◆	SC	71	1	C
◆	VGCB	281	1	B
Bread, Lynn's spicy	VGCB	281	1	C
Broiled	BCC	361	1	B
Bundles	YGM	143	1	B
& Cabbage in skillet	AC	494	2	
Cake, chocolate	FFBB	345	1	C
Cakes, sauteed	GG	398	1	B
Carrots	FGCW	257	1	B
Carrots w fresh mint	SMG	29	1	B
Casserole	MFC	180	2	B
Casserole, eggplant &	SC	420	1	
Cheese casserole, Marley's	JBGF	399	1	B
w Cherry tomatoes & garlic	SMG	215	1	B
Chicken stuffed w	GG	405	2	A
Chilled, green	BBA	111	2	A
Cookies	BCC	99	1	C
Crusted pizza	MC	150	1	B
Dilled	MIE	236	1	B
Dilled	BCC	362	1	B
Eggs baked	VE	165	2	B
& Feta pancakes	MC	146	1	B
Flan	NYTI	434	1	B
Florentine	AC	555	1	
Flowers filled w shrimp mousse	MFC	27	3	B
Flowers, fried	FAIC	425	1	B
Flowers & rice salad	GF	140	1	C
French fried	BB	133		
French fried	JBC	334	1	
Fresh, rosemary	FG	194	1	B
Fried	FAIC	426		
Fried	PPLK	34	1	A
w Artichoke hearts	GHAC	88	1	B
Deep	JOC	303	1	
Fettuccine	MCIC	194	3	B
Flour & water batter	CIC	392	1	B
w Vinegar	CIC	393	1	B
Frittata	JBGF	485	1	B
Frittata	KIS	192	1	A
Frittata	JBGF	485	1	B
Fritters	FGCW	93	2	B
Fromage	GG	400	1	B
& Fusilli w basil sauce	CIC	106	1	B
Garlic grated & sauteed in olive oil	MFC2	370	1	B
Garlic sauteed in olive oil	MFC2	365	1	B
Garlic & tomato, sliced	CIC	394	1	B
& Garlic w tomatoes & basil	MFC2	368	1	B
Garlic zapped	CFS	251	1	B
Grated	MSQC	209	1	B

ZUCCHINI

RECIPE	BOOK	PAGE	TD	S
Grated & sauteed w butter & shallots	MFC2	369	1	B
Grated & sauteed w olive oil & garlic	MFC2	370	1	B
Grated & simmered in cream	MFC2	370	1	B
Gratin of rice w onions & cheese	MFC2	371	1	B
Gratineed w cheese sauce	MFC2	367	1	B
Grilled	GRIL	93	1	B
Halves w parsnip puree	VGCB	189	1	
Herbs & garlic, sauteed	AC	546	1	
Hoecake	GG	402	1	B
Italian style	WC	31	1	B
Julienne of	MSE	223	1	A
Lamb balls	WC	110	2	B
Lamb noisettes, eggplant &	MFC	144	2	B
Lasagne	MC	125	1	B
◆	BBA	111	2	B
◆	SC	434	2	
◆	JBGF	400	1	B
Lebanese	FG	370	1	B
Lemon salad	GG	400	2	B
& Linguini, baked	VGCB	280	1	C
Loaf from Seattle	MHGD	255	1	B
Mexican	KIS	205	1	A
Molded custard, onions & cheese	MFC2	372	2	B
Muffin gems, Eleanor Tobin's mother's	GG	403	1	C
Muffins w basil	CBB	418	1	C
& Mushroom casserole	NYT	410	1	B
Nut loaf	BHGN	78	1	B
& Oatmeal muffins	GHAC	368	1	C

RECIPE	BOOK	PAGE	TD	S
w Oil & lemon	SMG	59	1	B
Omelet	SC	226	1	B
Onions	SC	435	1	
Pancakes	GG	406	1	A
Pancakes	YGM	171	1	B
Pancakes	BBA	137	1	B
Parcels	OC	96	1	B
Parmesan	BBA	137	1	B
Parmesan	MC	125	1	B
Parmesan bread	JBGF	593	1	B
Pasta	VGCB	279	1	B
Peeling, salting & blanching	MFC2	363		
Pepper skillet	BCC	362	1	B
Peppers w lamb stuffing &	VGCB	204	1	
Peppers & tomatoes	VGCB	277	1	B
Pickles	GG	402	2	B
Pickles, Evelyn Higginbotham's	VGCB	282	1	B
Pickles, sliced	AC	825	3	
Pieces, sauteed & baked w cheese	MFC2	366	1	B
Pilaf	FG	197	1	B
& Pineapple salad	BCC	289	2	B
Pizza w zucchini crust	JBGF	481	2	B
Pizzas	BBA	17	1	
Potato, eggplant & whole garlic	MSQC	144	1	B
Potato & tomato salad	FFCB	433	1	B
Pound cake	GG	407	2	C
Puff paste	LM	136	1	B
Puree	MC	24	1	B
Quiche	VE	154	2	B
Rice	SC	435	1	
Rice filling	GHAC	246	1	B
Ring	FFCB	411	1	B

RECIPE	BOOK	PAGE	TD	S
Zucchini (*cont.*)				
Risotto	CIC	191	2	B
Rosemary stuffed	NYTI	404	1	B
Rotini	KIS	163	1	B
Salad	LM	154	1	B
Salad	CIC	415	1	B
Bowl	BHGN	331	1	B
Carrot &	FGCW	134	1	
Marinated	BHGN	335	1	B
Oriental	MIE	274	1	B
w Pepper, cold	VGCB	205	1	B
Warm	GG	399	1	B
Sauce	BHGN	355	1	B
Saute of grated, w chopped spinach	MFC2	370	1	B
Saute & salad, red pepper &	VGCB	205	1	B
Sauteed	BB	133		
Sauteed	JBC	334	1	B
Sauteed	FFCB	411	1	B
Butter, lemon & parsley	MFC2	364	1	B
Cheese	JBC	334	1	B
Fennel	YGM	75	1	A
Garlic	JBC	334	1	B
Olive oil, garlic & parsley	MFC2	365	1	B
Onion	JBC	334	1	B
Onions	MCIC	405	1	B
Oregano	MCIC	407	1	B
Tomato	JBC	334	1	B
Scallops & artichoke hearts, skewered	GRIL	71	2	B
Simmered in cream & tarragon	MFC2	366	1	B
Soup	BCC	310	1	B
& Brown rice	VGCB	278	1	B
Chicken &	GG	398	2	B
Chilled & dilled	MIE	83	3	B
Cream of	MFC2	18	1	B
Mexican	JBGF	350	1	B
Spice cake	BCC	74	1	C
Spiced	YGM	83	1	A
Spread	BBA	23	1	B
Squash blossoms & goat cheese	GG	404	2	B
Stuffed	FFCB	304	2	B
Stuffed	NYT	410	2	B
w Almonds & cheese	MFC2	374	1	B
Baby	SPGT	163	2	B
w Corn & cheese	VGCB	276	1	B
w Meat & cheese	CIC	397	1	B
w Meat & rice	JBGF	471	2	B
w Rice & peppers	MFC2	376	1	B
w Seafood & seafood cream sauce	PPLK	69	3	B
Tomato	FGCW	264	1	B
Turkish style	MC	131	1	B
w Summer herbs	SMG	147	1	B
w Summer herbs	SMG	97	1	B
To grate & salt	MFC2	368		
Tomato-cheese	EBE	121	1	B
Tomato & cheese pie	VGCB	280	2	B
w Tomato & herbs, gratin of	MCIC	404	1	B
Tomato kabobs	OC	96	1	A
Tomato & potato tian	MSQC	129	1	B
& Tomato salad	NYTI	434	1	C
Tomatoes, peppers, garlic & basil	MFC2	368	1	B
Tousled	GG	401	1	B
Veal stuffed	WC	104	2	B
w Vermouth	YGM	149	1	A
w Vermouth	KIS	124	1	A

RECIPE	BOOK	PAGE	TD	S
Walnuts	AC	546	1	
& Watercress soup	SP	45	2	B
Zuccotto (nut & chocolate filled dessert)	CIC	438	2	B
Zucotte (braised garlicky winter squash)	GG	335	1	B
Zuger kirschtorte (cherry-brandy dessert)	MHGD	55	3	C
Zupa szczafu (Polish sorrel soup)	GG	187	1	B
Zuppa Inglese	MCIC	424	2	B
◆	NYTI	441	3	C
◆	NYT	572	3	B
◆	FAIC	453		
Zweiback	SC	73	2	
◆	SC	343	2	
◆	JOC	587	1	
◆	BTSB	236	3	C
Crust, cheesecake w	SC	347	2	B
Crusts	JOC	593	1	A
Torte	SC	134	1	B
Torte, chocolate	SC	134	1	B